PEARSON
myspanishlab ¡Hola!

Part of the award-winning MyLanguageLabs suite of online learning and assessment systems for basic language courses, MySpanishLab brings together—in one convenient, easily navigable site—a wide array of language-learning tools and resources, including an interactive version of the *¡Arriba!* student text, an online Student Activities Manual, and all materials from the audio and video programs. Chapter Practice Tests, tutorials, and English grammar Readiness Checks personalize instruction to meet the unique needs of individual students. Instructors can use the system to make assignments, set grading parameters, listen to student-created audio recordings, and provide feedback on student work. MySpanihLab can be packaged with the text at a substantial savings. For more information, visit us online at www.mylanguaelabs.com/books.html.

A GUIDE TO *¡ARRIBA!* ICONS

✓	**Readiness Check for MSpanishLab**	This icon, located in each chapter opener, reminds students to take the Readiness Check in MySpanishLab to test their understanding of the English grammar related to the Spanish grammar concepts in the chapter.
¡Hola!	**MySpnishLab**	This icon indicates that additional resources for pronunciation and culture are available for students in MySpanishLab.
🔊	**Text Audio Program**	This icon indicates that recorded material to accompany *¡Arriba!* is available in MySpanishLab, on audio CD, or on the Companion Website.
👥	**Pair Acivity**	This icon indicates that the activity is designed to be done by students working in pairs.
👥	**Group Activity**	This icon indicates that the activity is designed to be done by students working in small groups or as a whole class.
👥	**Information Gap Activity**	This icon indicates that the activity is designed to be done in pairs, with each student having different information. The information for Student A is included in the chapter; Student B's information is found in Appendix 1, pp. A-1–A-23.
🌐	**Web Activity**	This icon indicates that the activity involves use of the Internet.
🎬	**Video**	This icon indicates that a video episode is available for the *¡Pura vida!* video series that accompanies the *¡Arriba!* text. The video is available on DVD and in MySpanishLab.
📖	**Student Activities Manual**	This icon indicates that there are practice activities available in the *¡Arriba!* Student Activities Manual. The activities may be found either in the printed version of the manual or in the interactive version available through MySpanishLab. Activity numbers are indicated in the text for ease of reference.
🌐	**Interactive Globe**	This icon indicates that additional cultural resources in the form of videos, web links, interactive maps, and more, relating to a particular country, are organized on an interactive globe in MySpanishLab.
Media Share	**MediaShare**	This icon, presented with all *¿Cuánto saben?* boxes, refers to the video-posting feature available on MySpanishLab.

D0124144

Dedicado a
Mabel J. Cameron
(1914–2004)

Y a Manuel Eduardo
Zayas-Bazán Recio
(1912–1991)

"Y aunque la vida murió,
nos dejó harto
consuelo su memoria"
—JORGE MANRIQUE

Every fall, millions of monarch butterflies rise from their summer homes in North America and begin a thousand-mile migration to the warm and welcoming habitats of Mexico and Latin America. It's an amazing journey! Their trip is also an apt metaphor for what you will experience as a student of Spanish: as you ascend in language proficiency, you will cross borders to gain a butterfly's-eye view of the people, the history, the arts, and the ways of living that define the fascinating cultures of the 21 Spanish-speaking countries around the world.

¡ARRIBA!

Brief Edition

¡ARRIBA!

Comunicación y cultura

SIXTH EDITION

Eduardo Zayas-Bazán

Emeritus, East Tennessee State University

Susan M. Bacon

Emerita, University of Cincinnati

Holly J. Nibert

Western Michigan University

Prentice Hall

BOSTON   COLUMBUS   INDIANAPOLIS   NEW YORK   SAN FRANCISCO   UPPER SADDLE RIVER
AMSTERDAM   CAPE TOWN   DUBAI   LONDON   MADRID   MILAN   MUNICH   PARIS   MONTRÉAL   TORONTO
DELHI   MEXICO CITY   SÃO PAOLO   SYDNEY   HONG KONG   SEOUL   SINGAPORE   TAIPEI   TOKYO

Executive Editor, Elementary Spanish: Julia Caballero
Editorial Assistant: Samantha Pritchard
Executive Marketing Manager: Kris Ellis-Levy
Senior Marketing Manager: Denise Miller
SenioMarketing Coordinator: Bill Bliss
Development Editor: Celia Meana
Development Editor for Assessment: Melissa Marolla Brown
Senior Managing Editor for Product Development:
   Mary Rottino
Associate Managing Editor (Production): Janice Stangel
Senior Production Project Manager: Nancy Stevenson
Executive Editor, MyLanguageLabs: Bob Hemmer
Senior Media Editor: Samantha Alducin
Media/Supplements Editor: Meriel Martínez

Associate Design Director: Leslie Osher
Art Director: Miguel Ortiz
Text & Cover Designer: Anne DeMarinis
Senior Art Director: Pat Smythe
Art Director: Miguel Ortiz
Senior Manufacturing & Operations Manager: Nick Sklitsis
Operations Specialist: Cathleen Petersen / Brian Mackey
Full-Service Project Management: Melissa Sacco,
   PreMediaGlobal
Composition: Courier/Kendallville
Printer/Binder: Lehigh - Phoenix Color
Cover Printer: Lehigh - Phoenix Color
Publisher: Phil Miller

This book was set in Minion 10/12.

Credits and acknowledgments borrowed from other sources and reproduced, with permission, in this textbook appear on appropriate page within text (or on pages A-79–A-80).

Library of Congress Cataloging-in-Publication Data
Zayas-Bazán, Eduardo.
  Árriba! : comunicación y cultura / Eduardo Zayas-Bazán, Susan M. Bacon, Holly J. Nibert. — 6th ed.
    p. cm.
  Includes bibliographical references and index.
  ISBN-13: 978-0-205-74037-6 (alk. paper : student ed.)
  ISBN-10: 0-205-74037-5 (alk. paper : student ed.)
  1. Spanish language—Textbooks for foreign speakers—English.   I. Bacon, Susan M.   II. Nibert, Holly J.   III. Title.
  PC4112.Z38 2010
  468.2'421—dc22

                                                                                       201004409

10 9 8 7 6 5 4 3 2 1

Prentice Hall
is an imprint of

Student Edition, ISBN-10: 0-205-74037-5
Student Edition, ISBN-13: 978-0-205-74037-6
Brief Edition, ISBN-10: 0-205-78315-5
Brief Edition, ISBN-13: 978-0-205-78315-1
Annotated Instructor's Edition, ISBN-10: 0-205-82753-5
Annotated Instructor's Edition, ISBN-13: 978-0-205-82753-4

www.pearsonhighered.com

Brief Contents

STRUCTURES	CULTURE	READING AND WRITING

Preface

¡Arriba! brings Spanish to life!

We were very pleased by the enthusiastic response to the changes we made in the fifth edition of *¡Arriba!,* and our aim has been to make the sixth edition an even more complete and flexible program for first-year Spanish courses, one that instructors with varying teaching styles can adopt with confidence. With help from a core panel of reviewers, we have made many important refinements in the student text. But we have also extensively revised the other components of the *¡Arriba!* program, with the goal of creating a completely integrated whole that will allow students to have a successful and rewarding learning experience.

Since it was first published in 1993, *¡Arriba! Comunicación y cultura* has been used successfully by thousands of instructors and hundreds of thousands of students throughout North America. Originally conceived to address the need for an elementary Spanish text that went beyond grammar drills to develop cultural insight and communication skills, it has come to be known as a **highly flexible program**—one that can be used effectively in a wide range of academic settings by instructors who teach the course in different ways and use technology to varying degrees. Adopters have consistently praised *¡Arriba!* for its clarity and for providing materials that are both motivating and easy to use in the classroom. We believe that they will find those qualities reflected in the sixth edition as well.

New to This Edition

Drawing on the success of previous editions, the sixth edition of *¡Arriba!* has been carefully crafted to introduce another generation of students to Spanish language and culture. Like its predecessors, the new edition has been designed as an eclectic and flexible text that is clear, easy to use, and motivating to students—and as a text that reflects the diversity (of gender, ethnicity, age, and lifestyle) in today's society. But while the goals remain the same, many refinements and additions have been made. The comprehensive array of supplemental materials has also been carefully reviewed and revised, and several new features have been added to the program. Specific changes include the following:

- **Shorter dialogs and new visuals aid and motivate vocabulary learning.** The *¡Así lo decimos!* sections now feature two to three shorter dialogs, each accompanied by new line drawings, replacing the longer dialogs and readings of the previous edition. Dividing the content into smaller chunks and providing mulitple contexts makes the presentation more manageable. All new dialogs reflect authentic use of language and preview chapter vocabulary and grammar structures. Audio recordings of all the dialogs and vocabulary items in this section are available in the text audio program.

- New **margin boxes offer new opportunities for cross-cultural learning.**
  — **Regional variations** in the Spanish-speaking world are presented in *Variaciones* boxes and appear in each vocabulary section. They offer alternate words and expressions without adding more words to the active vocabulary list.
  — **Cultural contrasts and practical facts** of interest about the Spanish-speaking world are presented in *Cultura en vivo* boxes throughout the chapter. They seamlessly integrate culture and ask students to make comparisons

> **Variaciones**
> Names for technology also vary: *laptop* is **la (computadora) portátil** in Latin America and **el (ordenador) portátil** in Spain. Cell phone is generally **el (teléfono) celular** in Latin America and **el (teléfono) móvil** in Spain.

with their own experiences. Podcasts relating to the cultural content will also be available in MySpanishLab.

— **The Spanish-speaking population of the United States and Canada** is represented in *Presencia hispana* boxes where cultural, historical, and/or political facts of interest help to bring Hispanic culture to the forefront while making the cultural learning experience personal and relevant.

- **New** two-page cultural spread gives students a personal and authentic glimpse into the cultures of the Hispanic world. *Perfiles* is a **new** two-page spread at the end of *Primera parte* that replaces *Comparaciones* from the previous edition. The spread is divided into two sections, *Mi experiencia* and *Mi música.*

¡Hola!
Cultura en vivo

Students in Mexico, as in many parts of the world, begin their specializations very early in their university careers. The curriculum is usually fixed and the number of courses students must take varies with the *facultad*. During their final semesters students have more choice, but still mostly within their majors. In your opinion, what are advantages and disadvantages of this type of curriculum?

Presencia hispana

Mexican Americans are U.S. residents who trace their ancestry to Mexico. They are variously known as *chicanos*, *xicanos*, *mexicanos*, or Mex-Americans, although *chicano* is the preferred identification for many. In the U.S. there are currently 25 million legal residents of Mexican heritage, and an estimated 6 to 7 million undocumented immigrants. Mexico allows its citizens to maintain dual citizenship with the U.S. How does this law benefit Mexican Americans?

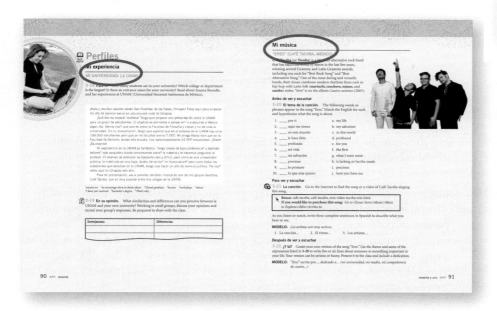

— Written in the **first person**, *Mi experiencia* is a personal account of a young person's experience in the culture and country of focus. Young people share their perspectives in the form of postings on blogs, message boards, and so on, to report culture in a context that is relevant to students.

— All-new music selections chosen from the country/region of focus are featured in *Mi música.* Replacing *Ritmos* from the previous edition, the song selections reflect the musical preferences of the person featured in *Mi experiencia*. Students are directed to search online to view videos or listen to the song selection on their own. All songs are available for purchase online in a specially created *¡Arriba!* playlist.

- **New** Section-ending self-checks now include situations that give students the opportunity to demonstrate their understanding of the concepts presented in each section. The communicative objectives of each chapter are collected in new *¿Cuánto saben?* boxes at the end of each *parte* and assist students in determining how well they have mastered the material. Instructors may also choose to use them to measure student success as part of the Student Learning Outcomes. Boxes have been expanded to include role plays with cues in *Para empezar* to help students get started. Check boxes remain for students to check off as they accomplish each communicative objective. Students can use the MediaShare feature available in MySpanishLab to post videos of their role-plays for the class.

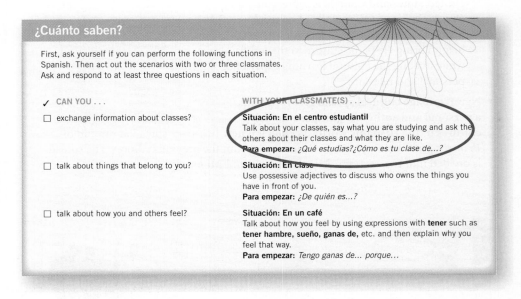

¿Cuánto saben?

First, ask yourself if you can perform the following functions in Spanish. Then act out the scenarios with two or three classmates. Ask and respond to at least three questions in each situation.

✓ CAN YOU . . .	WITH YOUR CLASSMATE(S) . . .
☐ exchange information about classes?	**Situación: En el centro estudiantil** Talk about your classes, say what you are studying and ask the others about their classes and what they are like. **Para empezar:** *¿Qué estudias?¿Cómo es tu clase de…?*
☐ talk about things that belong to you?	**Situación: En clase** Use possessive adjectives to discuss who owns the things you have in front of you. **Para empezar:** *¿De quién es…?*
☐ talk about how you and others feel?	**Situación: En un café** Talk about how you feel by using expressions with **tener** such as **tener hambre, sueño, ganas de,** etc. and then explain why you feel that way. **Para empezar:** *Tengo ganas de… porque…*

- **Many activities now include multiple steps that allow students to move smoothly from individual to pair work.** These *Pasos* provide better sequencing while at the same time break down the task into smaller steps.

- New **visually engaging, two-page cultural spreads pique students' interest with additional cultural information about the country/region of focus.** The *Panoramas* spread in the *Nuestro mundo* section of each chapter now includes a map with a **new** Fact Box with information pertinent not only to the country/region but also to the chapter theme. Students may view the *Vistas culturales* video and other resources using the *Panoramas* Interactive Globe in MySpanishLab. A **new** Web-based activity, *Proyecto,* with one or two comprehension activities, rounds out the section.

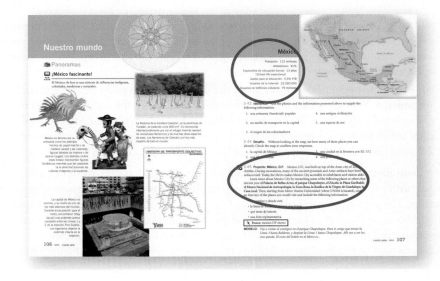

- **Eight new readings reflect current events and create balance in the text between cultural and literary readings.** The new readings, found in the *Páginas* sections, include "Cuando era puertorriqueña (fragmento)" by Esmeralda Santiago, "En solidaridad" by Francisco Jiménez, and "La azucena del bosque" (a Guaraní legend).

- **Changes to the scope and sequence and appendices create a better balance of grammatical topics across chapters.** Specific changes include the following:
  — In *Capítulo 4*, the present tense of *poner, salir,* and *traer* has been moved to *Segunda parte* to balance better the grammatical load.
  — Coverage of the subjunctive with impersonal expressions is now presented within their semantic group. For example, with verbs of volition we include *es necesario, es importante,* and so on, and with doubt and denial, *es increíble, es dudoso,* etc.
  — Formal commands have been moved to *Capítulo 10* from *Capítulo 11* to place them physically and conceptually closer to the subjunctive.
  — Informal commands are now presented in *Capítulo 11*. In addition, the subjunctive and the indicative with adverbial clauses has been moved to *Primera parte* while the subjunctive with indefinite and nonexistent antecedents can now be found in *Capítulo 11,* moved from *Capítulo 15*.
  — *Nosotros* commands now appear in *Capítulo 14,* moved from *Capítulo 10* for a better balance of grammar topics in later chapters.

- **New *Expansión gramatical*** (Appendix 2) includes the grammar points that were previously incorporated in *Capítulos 10–15*. In this way, we lighten the grammar load and are able to include more language input to reinforce and expand students' lexicon and cultural understanding. Grammar topics include:
  — Indirect commands
  — The present perfect subjunctive
  — The future perfect and the conditional perfect
  — Pluperfect subjunctive and the conditional perfect
  — The passive voice

- **New orthographic changes, recently instituted by the Spanish Royal Academy, are now included.** In addition to eliminating the accent from the adverb *solo* and the demonstrative pronouns, changes to the alphabet and new spelling rules have been added. Teacher annotations explaining the changes accompany each new feature.

- **New annotations in the Annotated Instructor's Edition provide a wealth of additional suggestions to help instructors get the most out of each chapter.** The new annotations were added to provide more support to instructors, to facilitate different teaching styles, to assist in measuring Student Learning Outcomes, and to provide clear direction for lesson planning. A new annotation in the chapter opener lists all sections and activities corresponding to each of The Five C's. All these annotations enhance activities in the text by offering ideas for pre-activity warm-ups and tips on implementation, as well as suggestions for wrap-up and expansion. The new annotations likewise include optional activities made available for extra practice or as alternatives to activities in the text. These activities are clearly labeled to help instructors know when best to use them, time permitting. They can be easily downloaded from the Instructors Resource Center (IRC). In addition, various notes are included that suggest ways an instructor can deepen student understanding of certain structures in the target language. Finally, numerous new annotations provide additional cultural information which the instructor may choose to share with the class.

Organization and Pedagogy

Like its predecessors, the sixth edition of *¡Arriba!* consists of 15 thematically organized chapters. The first 12 chapters present essential communicative functions and structures, along with basic cultural information about the countries that make up the Hispanic world. The last 3 chapters present more advanced structures together with thematically focused cultural material. Besides the full edition, a brief version of the text, consisting of the first 12 chapters only, is also available. We also offer a loose-leaf, 3-hole-punched version that offers an upfront savings to your students.

All chapters have the same basic organizational structure, with content presented in three major sections. The language material that forms the core of each chapter is divided into two distinct instructional units, *Primera parte* and *Segunda parte*. The third, entitled *Nuestro mundo*, is a synthesizing section that presents cultural information along with activities designed to develop students' reading and writing skills. A two-page spread at the beginning of each chapter serves as an advanced organizer and presents the chapter's communicative objectives.

The *Primera* and *Segunda partes* are largely parallel in their organizational structure. They include the following sections:

- *¡Así lo decimos!* presents new vocabulary related to the chapter theme. This section begins with *¡Así es la vida!* which are lively conversations that set the stage for the communicative functions and culture to be presented more formally later in the chapter. All new drawings are used extensively to provide visual context for vocabulary learning and practice. Words are listed in practical, functional groups to facilitate student retention, and audio recordings and flashcards available on **MySpanishLab** provide additional reinforcement. This section also offers a wide variety of practice activities, ranging from more guided to more open-ended activities, among them an audio activity that builds on the language sample introduced in *¡Así es la vida!*

- *¡Así lo hacemos!* presents grammar structures related to the chapter's communicative objectives. We made the explanations clear and concise with short, bulleted points followed immediately by examples. Wherever possible, we have supplemented grammar concepts with helpful and (we hope) entertaining illustrations. **Study Tips** at the end of certain grammar explanations assist students with structures that non-native speakers of Spanish often find difficult, and additional structures are elaborated further in the *Expansión* boxes, also located in this section. A wide variety of practice activities is provided for each grammatical topic, moving from form-focused to meaning-focused to more open-ended communicative activities. In addition, **MySpanishLab** provides students with animated tutorials explaining Spanish grammar topics as well as the English grammar topics students should have a clear understanding of to successfully approach the grammar in each chapter. The lab also features extra practice activities, practice tests, and oral practice activities. Readiness Check icons in each chapter opener remind students to visit MySpanishLab to complete a pre-test that will help determine whether they are ready to understand the chapter's grammar lessons.

- The *¿Cuánto saben?* boxes at the end of each part serve as a form of self-assessment. They are designed to remind students of the communicative objectives for the chapter and assist them in determining how well they have mastered the material. Students can post their examples using the Mediashare feature in **MySpanishLab**. Situations in *¿Cuánto saben?* boxes can also be used by instructors to assess Student Learning Outcomes and determine whether students can perform the communicative objectives. By performing these situations and using the target vocabulary and structures presented in the chapter, students will demonstrate to what extent they can fluently produce appropriate lexicon and desired language forms. Suggested rubics for assessing students can be found in the Instructor's Resource Manual.

- *Letras y sonidos* boxes offer a brief presentation of an important pronunciation topic. The purpose of these boxes is to help students improve their listening and speaking skills. All presentations have been recorded and are available for students in **MySpanishLab** with additional support provided in the Pronunciation Guide in **MySpanishLab.** Practice activities are available in the **Student Activities Manual (SAM)**.

- *Perfiles* (in the *Primera parte* only) presents information regarding the Spanish-speaking world while focusing on authentic culture and personalized experiences, then asks students to compare what they have learned with aspects of their own culture. In *Mi experiencia*, the *Para ti* questions invite students to reflect on their experiences within their own culture, while the *En tu opinión* activities encourage them to discuss topics further in small groups. *Mi música* offers students a more current sampling of music from across the Spanish-speaking world. Search terms are provided to students to access videos, audio, and lyrics of each song selection. All songs have been collected into a special *¡Arriba!* playlist and are available for purchase online.

- *Observaciones* (in the *Segunda parte* only) offers a comprehensive and engaging set of activities based on the corresponding episode of the video filmed specifically to accompany *¡Arriba!* This sitcom-like video, *¡Pura vida!,* features the interactions of five young adults who have all found their way to a residence in Costa Rica. The pre-viewing, viewing, and post-viewing activities in the text are designed to help students follow the story that unfolds in each episode.

The *Nuestro mundo* section of each chapter includes the following elements:

- *Panoramas* is a visually and textually panoramic presentation of the Hispanic country or region that is the focus of the chapter. The material is supported by activities that encourage students to discuss the regions and topics, do additional research on the Internet, and make comparisons between the targeted country's culture and their own. A new Fact Box provides additional information relevant to the country/region of focus and to the chapter theme. These boxes are designed specifically to reflect the topic of the chapter and will vary throughout the text to provide a broad understanding of the Spanish-speaking world.

- *Páginas* focuses on the development of reading skills. The readings include excerpts from magazine and newspaper articles, a fable, poems, short stories, plays, and novel excerpts. All are authentic or semi-authentic texts written by Hispanic writers from various parts of the Spanish-speaking world, including the United States. All of the readings are accompanied by pre- and post-reading activities.

- *Taller* provides guided writing activities that incorporate the vocabulary, structures, and themes covered elsewhere in the chapter. Writing assignments are varied, ranging from personal and business correspondence to fables. Each assignment is presented in a process-oriented manner, encouraging students to follow a carefully planned series of steps that includes both self-monitoring and peer editing.

Each chapter concludes with a comprehensive, clearly organized list of all active vocabulary words introduced in the chapter. This section also includes grammatical references for quicker access to information.

Program Components

Student Resources

AUDIO CDS FOR THE TEXT
The recordings on this CD set correspond to the listening comprehension activities in the textbook as well as the *¡Así es la vida!* dialogs and the *Letras y sonidos* pronunciation sections. These recordings are also available within MySpanishLab and the Companion Website.

STUDENT ACTIVITIES MANUAL

The *¡Arriba!* **Student Activities Manual,** available both in print and within **MySpanishLab,** includes a vast number of practice activities, many of which are audio- or video-based, for each chapter of the text. It also contains speaking activities that are recordable in MySpanishLab. The activities are integrated and organized to mirror the corresponding textbook chapter. Each chapter of the manual includes a *Letras y sonidos* section, a *Perfiles* section, two *¿Cuánto saben?* sections, comprehensive activities on the *Observaciones* video segments, and a *Nuestro mundo* section.

ANSWER KEY FOR THE STUDENT ACTIVITIES MANUAL

The **Answer Key** contains answers to all activities in the **Student Activities Manual.**

AUDIO CDS FOR THE STUDENT ACTIVITIES MANUAL

The recordings on this CD set correspond to the listening comprehension activities in the *¡Arriba!* **Student Activities Manual.** These recordings are also available within MySpanishLab and the Companion Website.

SUPPLEMENTARY ACTIVITIES

This *¡Arriba!* supplement provides additional activities that can be used in class or assigned for out-of-class work. Integrating highly motivational activities such as games, crossword puzzles, fill-in-the-blank activities, and paired activities, it is a rich resource for a variety of teaching situations.

QUICK GUIDE TO SPANISH GRAMMAR

This brief supplement (with laminated pages to ensure durability) provides students with a handy reference source on the key points of Spanish grammar. It is available at a special discount in value packs with the *¡Arriba!* student text.

¡PURA VIDA! VIDEO

¡Pura vida! is an original story-line video filmed specifically to accompany *¡Arriba!* Over the course of its 15 episodes, students follow the interactions of five principal characters who find themselves living together in a youth hostel in San José, Costa Rica. Students are able to see how the vocabulary and grammar structures presented in the textbook are used in realistic situations while gaining a deeper understanding of Hispanic culture. The sitcom-like format allows instructors to show or assign segments for some chapters without having to do so for others. Pre-viewing, viewing, and post-viewing activities are found in the *Observaciones* sections of the textbook and the **Student Activities Manual.** The video is available for student purchase on DVD, but is also available within **MySpanishLab,** with and without captions. In addition, the video is available to instructors on DVD.

Meet The Cast!
Here are the main characters of *¡Pura vida!* whom you will get to know as you watch the video:

   Silvia

| Doña Maria | Felipe | Hermés | Silvia | Patricio | Marcela |

VISTAS CULTURALES VIDEO

The Telly™ award-winning *Vistas culturales* video provides students with a rich and dynamic way to expand, enhance, and contextualize the cultural materials they study in the *Panoramas* section of the textbook. The 18 ten-minute vignettes include footage from every Spanish-speaking country. Each of the accompanying narrations, which employ vocabulary and grammar designed for first-year language learners, was written by a native of the featured country or region. The video is available for student purchase on DVD, but both it and the accompanying Video Guide are within **MySpanishLab,** with and without captions. In addition, the video is available to instructors on DVD.

- **Vistas Culturales Video Guide** The video guide includes useful vocabulary and pre-, during-, and post-viewing activities designed to guide students as they view each country segment.

ENTREVISTAS VIDEO

The *Entrevistas* video consists of guided but authentic interviews with native Spanish speakers on topics related to each chapter's theme. Participants employ target grammatical structures and vocabulary while providing broader cultural perspectives on chapter themes. The video is available for student purchase on DVD and is also available within **MySpanishLab** through links on a new interactive globe. In addition, the video is available to instructors on DVD.

Instructor Resources

ANNOTATED INSTRUCTOR'S EDITION (AIE)

The *¡Arriba!* AIE now has a **new** format, with slightly larger pages, to allow inclusion of a great deal of helpful new material. Icons are placed at appropriate points throughout each chapter to indicate related resources available in other components of the *¡Arriba!* program (see chart on page i for the icon key). The number of marginal instructor annotations has been greatly increased. The annotations fall into several categories:

- **The Five C's:** Lists all the sections and activities in the chapter that correspond to each of The Standards for Foreign Language Learning.
- **Student learning outcomes:** Suggestions for using *¿Cuánto saben?* boxes to measure student learning outcomes.
- **General introduction of . . . :** Contextualizes or provides an overview of an entire chapter or *parte.*
- **Note on . . . :** Additional information on cultural references (such as well-known people, artwork, music, etc.), grammatical functions, or vocabulary usage, beyond what is provided in the student text.
- **Presentation tip for . . . :** Suggestions for presenting new material to students, whether it is vocabulary, grammar, or culture.
- **Comprehension check for . . . :** Brief Q & A activities to confirm comprehension during instructor presentation of material.
- **Warm-up for . . . :** Suggestions for activating students' prior knowledge or helping set up an activity before carrying it out.
- **Expansion of . . . :** Ideas for lengthening or adding to an activity, such as by asking additional questions or by applying the information to students' lives.
- **Optional activity before/after . . . :** Independent activities separate but related to those in the student text that offer instructors further options for classroom practice with students. These are also available for download from the Instructor Resource Center (IRC).
- **Wrap-up:** Suggestions for concluding an activity effectively, such as by drawing a conclusion based on the students' responses or by sampling or reviewing student responses.
- **Audioscript for . . . :** The written script of what is heard on the accompanying audio program.

INSTRUCTOR'S RESOURCE MANUAL (IRM)

The *¡Arriba!* **IRM** is a comprehensive resource, available for download within MySpanishLab and on our Instructor Resource Center, that instructors can use for a variety of purposes. Contents include:

- An introduction that discusses the philosophy behind the *¡Arriba!* program, a guide to using the text's features, and a guide to other program components.

- Pointers for new instructors, including lesson planning, classroom management, warm-ups, error correction, first day of class, quizzes/tests, and other teaching resources.

- An explanation of the North American educational system, written (in Spanish) for instructors who may be unfamiliar with it.

- Sample syllabi showing how the *¡Arriba!* program can be used in traditional and hybrid classroom settings and at different paces.

- Full lesson plans for all chapters.

- The audioscript for the **Student Activities Manual** audio program.

- A guide to rubrics with samples for writing and oral assessments.

- Optional Activities, provided in Word, are available for download to use in class as described in the Annotated Instructor's Edition in the marginal teacher notes.

- The videoscripts for all three *¡Arriba!* videos (*¡Pura vida!, Vistas culturales,* and *Entrevistas*), as well as suggested activities for the *Entrevistas* video. (Activities for *¡Pura vida!* and *Vistas culturales* are available in other components of the program.)

POWERPOINT PRESENTATIONS

This new set of **PowerPoint Presentations** includes visual materials from the textbook, together with dynamic presentations on each grammar point covered in the text.

TESTING PROGRAM

The *¡Arriba!* **Testing Program**, now fully online, has been revised to mirror the content of the textbook in this edition, and has been carefully edited to ensure close coordination with the main text and **Student Activities Manual.** In addition to finished, ready-to-use tests for each chapter, it contains over 500 testing modules from which instructors can draw to create customized tests. The assessment goal, content area, and response type are identified for each module. Available within **MySpanishLab** is a user-friendly test-generating program known as **MyTest** that allows instructors to select, arrange, and customize testing modules to meet the needs of their courses. Once created, tests can be printed on paper or administered online.

AUDIO ON CD FOR THE TESTING PROGRAM

This CD contains the recordings to accompany the listening comprehension activities in the *¡Arriba!* **Testing Program.** These recordings are also available within MySpanishLab.

Online Resources

MYSPANISHLAB

MySpanishLab is a widely adopted, nationally hosted online learning system designed specifically for students in college-level language courses. It brings together—in one convenient, easily navigable site—a wide array of language-learning tools and resources, including an interactive version of the *¡Arriba!* **Student Activities Manual,** an interactive version of the *¡Arriba!* student text, and all materials from the *¡Arriba!* audio and video programs. Readiness checks, practice tests, and tutorials personalize instruction to meet the unique needs of individual students. Students can also post videos using the MediaShare feature, listen to podcasts, and view other resources using the *Panoramas* Interactive Globe. Instructors can use the system to make assignments, set grading parameters, provide feedback on student work, add new content, access instructor resources, and hold online office hours. Instructor access is provided at no charge. Students can purchase access codes online or at their local bookstore. For more information, including case studies that illustrate how **MySpanishLab** saves time and improves results, visit www.mylanguagelabs.com.

COMPANION WEBSITE

The open-access **Companion Website** features access to the recordings found on the Audio CDs to Accompany the Text and the Audio CDs to Accompany the Student Activities Manual as well as information about the music playlist.

Acknowledgments

The sixth edition of *¡Arriba!* is the result of careful planning between ourselves and our publisher and ongoing collaboration with students and you—our colleagues—who have been using the first, second, third, fourth, and fifth editions. We look forward to continuing this dialog and sincerely appreciate your input. We owe special thanks to the many members of the Spanish teaching community whose comments and suggestions helped shape the pages of every chapter. We gratefully acknowledge and thank in particular our reviewers for this sixth edition:

Frances Alpren, *Vanderbilt University*
Luz María Álvarez, *Johnson County Community College*
Stephanie M. Álvarez, *University of Texas - Pan American*
Stacy Amling, *Des Moines Area Community College, Boone Campus*
Debra Andrist, *Sam Houston State University*
José Badillo, *Metropolitan Community College in Omaha, Nebraska*
Sonia Barrios Tinoco, *Seattle University*
Marie Blair, *University of Nebraska-Lincoln*
Miryan Boles, *Texas Southern University*
Lillie Busby, *Sam Houston State University*
Alicia T. Casals, *Texas Southern University*
Christine Coleman Núñez, *Kutztown University of Pennsylvania*
Lina L. Cofresí, *North Carolina Central University*
David Cruz de Jesus, *Baruch College, CUNY*
David D. Dahnke, *Lone Star College - North Harris*
John B. Davis, *Indiana University, South Bend*
Keri Dutkiewicz, *Davenport University*
Margaret Eomurian, *Houston Community College*
Timothy J. Erskine, *Western Michigan University*
Marisela Fleites-Lear, *Green River Community College*

Ana M. Hnat, *Houston Community College*
Silvia Huntsman, *Sam Houston State University*
Qiu Y. Jiménez, *Bakersfield College*
Sheila Jones, *Sam Houston State University*
Lunden MacDonald, *Metropolitan State College of Denver*
Carlos Martínez, *New York University*
Joseph McClanahan, *Creighton University*
Ryan J. Minier, *Western Michigan University*
Norma A. Mouton, *Sam Houston State University*
Catherine Ortiz, *University of Texas at Arlington*
Christine R. Payne, *Sam Houston State University*
Sue Pechter, *Nortwestern University*
Edith S. Pequeño, *Blinn College*
Nilsa O. Pérez-Cabrera, *Blinn College*
Kay E. Raymond, *Sam Houston State University*
Ray S. Rentería, *Sam Houston State University*
Victor E. Slesinger, *Palm Beach State College*
John P. Sullivan, *Prairie View A&M University*
Hilde M. Votaw, *University of Oklahoma*
Michael Vrooman, *Grand Valley State University*
Mary H. West, *Des Moines Area Community College, Ankeny Campus*
Olivia Yáñez, *College of Lake County*

We are grateful to the many who granted permission to use photos and literary selections (see Text and Photo Credits).

We wish to express our gratitude and appreciation to the many people at Prentice Hall who contributed their ideas, tireless efforts, and publishing experience to the sixth edition of *¡Arriba!* We are especially grateful for the guidance of Celia Meana, development editor, for all of her work, suggestions, attention to detail, and dedication to the text. Her support and spirit helped us to achieve the final product. We would also like to thank the contributors who assisted us in the preparation of the sixth edition: Catherine Hebert and John B. Davis for co-authoring the **Testing Program,** Christine Coleman Núñez for her work on the **Instructor's Resource Manual,** and Evelyn F. Brod and Teresa Roig-Torres for authoring the **Supplementary Activities.** We also wish to express our gratitude to Marie Blair and Nilsa Pérez-Cabrera for all of their hard work and great attention to detail as page proof reviewers. We are very grateful to other colleagues and friends at Pearson Education/Prentice Hall: Meriel Martínez, Media Editor, for helping us produce the audio programs and Companion Website; Melissa Marolla Brown, Development Editor for Assessment, for the diligent coordination among the text, **Student Activities Manual,** and **Testing Program**; Samantha Alducin, for helping us produce such a great video. We are very grateful to our **My SpanishLab** team, Bob Hemmer, Samantha Alducin, and Mary Reynolds, for the creation of the *¡Arriba!* **MySpanishLab** course. Thanks to Katie Corasaniti, Editorial Coordinator, and Samantha Pritchard, Editorial Assistant, for attending to many administrative details.

We are very grateful to our marketing team, Kris Ellis-Levy, Denise Miller, and Bill Bliss, for their creativity and efforts in coordinating all marketing and promotion for this edition. Thanks, too, to our production team, Mary Rottino, Janice Stangel, and Nancy Stevenson, who guided *¡Arriba!* through the many stages of production; to our partners at PreMedia Global, especially Melissa Sacco, for her careful and professional editing and production services. We also thank our art manager, Gail Cocker, and illustrator, Andrew Lange, for the amazing creativity and beautiful illustrations. Special thanks to Leslie Osher, Miguel Ortiz, and Anne DeMarinis for the gorgeous interior and cover designs. Finally, we would like to express our sincere thanks to Phil Miller, Publisher, and Julia Caballero, Executive Editor, for their guidance and support through every aspect of this new edition.

Finally, our love and deepest appreciation to our families: Lourdes, Cindy, Eddy, and Lindsey, Elena, Ed, Lauren, and Will; Wayne, Alexis, Sandro, Ignacio and Isla; Camille, Chris, Eleanor, Teresa and Toby; and Pete, Valayda and Jesse, Roger and Britt, Dave, Nancy, Wesley, and Megan, Leisa and David, and Tammy.

Eduardo Zayas-Bazán
Susan M. Bacon
Holly J. Nibert

¡ARRIBA!

1

Hola, ¿qué tal?

Readiness Check

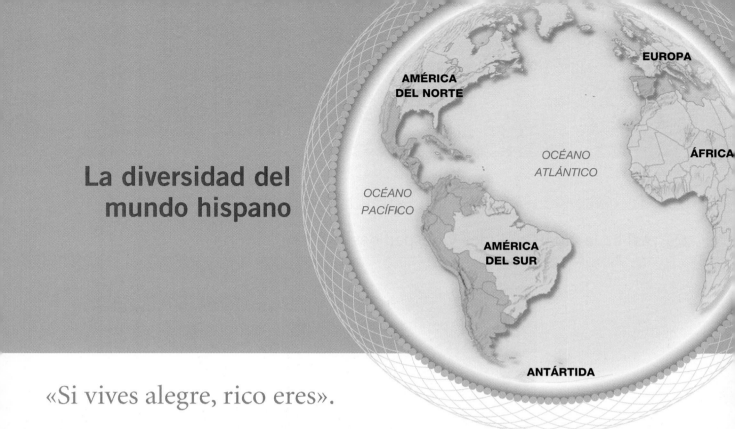

La diversidad del mundo hispano

EUROPA

AMÉRICA DEL NORTE

ÁFRICA

OCÉANO ATLÁNTICO

OCÉANO PACÍFICO

AMÉRICA DEL SUR

ANTÁRTIDA

«Si vives alegre, rico eres».

Refrán: If your life is happy, you are rich. (Your wealth lies in your happiness.)

El descubrimiento de América por Cristóbal Colón.
Salvador Dalí, 1958.

Historia de México desde la conquista hasta el futuro.
Diego Rivera, 1930.

¡Así lo decimos!¹ VOCABULARIO

📖 ¡Así es la vida!² Saludos y despedidas
01-01

En la universidad los estudiantes y los profesores conversan.³

JORGE:	Hola, María Luisa. ¿Cómo estás?
MARÍA LUISA:	Muy bien, Jorge. ¿Y tú? ¿Qué tal?
JORGE:	¿Yo? ¡Fenomenal!

PROFESORA LÓPEZ:	Hola, buenas tardes. ¿Cómo se llama usted?
ROBERTO:	Me llamo Roberto Gómez.
PROFESORA LÓPEZ:	Mucho gusto. Soy la profesora López.
ROBERTO:	Encantado.

LUPITA:	Hasta luego, Juan.
JUAN:	¡Nos vemos!

¹That's how we say it!
²That's life
³**Estudiante**, **profesor**, and **conversan** are cognates, words that are similar in English and Spanish. Do you recognize other cognates in the dialogs?

Vocabulario Saludos y despedidas

Variaciones

Numerous greetings and farewells are used in the Spanish-speaking world and variations are common. The expression **¿Qué onda?** (*What's up?*) is popular in Mexico. A brief **Buenas** for *good afternoon/evening* is typical in Spain. Speakers from many Latin American countries commonly use the expression **¡Chau!** (also spelled **¡Chao!**) to say *Good-bye!*

Saludos · Greetings

Buenos días. *Good morning.*
Buenas noches. *Good evening.*
Buenas tardes. *Good afternoon.*
¿Cómo está usted? *How are you?* (formal)
¿Cómo estás? *How are you?* (informal)
Hola. *Hello, Hi.*
¿Qué pasa? *What's happening?*
      What's up? (informal)
¿Qué tal? *What's up?* (informal)

Respuestas · Responses

De nada. *You're welcome.*
¿De verdad? *Really?*
Encantado/a. *Pleased to meet you.*
Gracias. *Thank you.*
Igualmente. *Likewise.*
Lo siento. *I'm sorry.*
Más o menos. *So-so.* (lit. *More or less.*)
Mucho gusto. *Nice to meet you.*
(Muy) Bien. *(Very) Well.*
(Muy) Mal. *(Very) Bad.*
Todo bien. *All's well.*

Despedidas · Farewells

Adiós. *Good-bye.*
Hasta luego. *See you later.*
Hasta mañana. *See you tomorrow.*
Hasta pronto. *See you soon.*
Nos vemos. *See you.*

Presentaciones · Introductions

¿Cómo se llama usted? *What's your name?* (formal)
¿Cómo te llamas? *What's your name?* (informal)
Me llamo... *My name is . . .* (lit. *I call myself . . .*)
Mi nombre es... *My name is . . .*
Soy... *I am . . .*

Títulos · Titles

el señor (Sr.) *Mr.*
la señora (Sra.) *Mrs., Ms.*
la señorita (Srta.) *Miss*

Sustantivos · Nouns

la clase *class*
el estudiante *student (male)*
la estudiante *student (female)*
el profesor *professor (male)*
la profesora *professor (female)*
la tarea *homework*
la universidad *university*

la profesora

el estudiante

Otras palabras y expresiones · Other words and expressions

¿Cómo se escribe...? *How do you spell . . . ?*
con *with*
mi/mis *my*
o *or*
tu/tus *your* (informal)
y *and*

Letras y sonidos

Spanish Vowels

In Spanish, each of the five letters **a, e, i, o, u** corresponds to one and only one vowel *sound*. In English, these same five letters correspond to many different vowel sounds, which tend to be long and glided. For example, the letter *a* creates five different vowel sounds in the following words: f*a*ther, c*a*t, *a*pproach, bl*a*me, *a*we.

What vowel sound in English corresponds to each of the letters **a, e, i, o, u** in Spanish?

- The letter **a** is pronounced like the *a* in f*a*ther, but is shorter.

  | más | pasa | nada | mañana | encantada |

- The letter **e** is pronounced like the *e* in th*ey*, but is shorter with no final glide.

  | es | tres | mesa | deporte | interesante |

- The letter **i** is pronounced like the *i* in mach*i*ne, but is shorter.[1]

  | mi | niño | libro | tímido | inteligente |

- The letter **o** is pronounced like the *o* in al*o*ne, but is shorter with no final glide.

  | o | hola | color | exótico | nosotros |

- The letter **u** is pronounced like the *u* in fl*u*te, but is shorter.

  | tú | azul | lunes | gusto | música |

APLICACIÓN

1-1 ¿Qué tal? If you heard the statements or questions on the left, how would you respond? Choose from the list of options on the right.

MODELO: Adiós.

  Hasta luego.

1. _____ Soy el doctor Gómez.
2. _____ Gracias.
3. _____ ¿Cómo se llama usted?
4. _____ Mucho gusto.
5. _____ ¿Cómo estás?
6. _____ Buenas tardes, Tomás.
7. _____ Adiós.
8. _____ Estoy muy mal.

a. Me llamo Pedro Guillén.
b. Buenos días, doctor.
c. Buenas tardes, profesora.
d. Hasta mañana.
e. ¿De verdad? Lo siento.
f. De nada.
g. Igualmente.
h. Estoy muy mal.

1-2 ¿Quiénes son? (Who are they?) Listen to the short conversations and write the number of each conversation next to the corresponding situation below.

_____ two friends saying good-bye

_____ a teacher and student introducing themselves

_____ a young person greeting an older person

_____ two friends greeting each other

_____ two students introducing themselves

---

[1]Be careful to avoid the *i* sound in s*i*t in the following words, since this sound does not exist in Spanish: **inteligente, interesante, introvertido, impaciente, tímido, simpático, misterioso.**

1-3 ¡Hola! The following people are meeting for the first time. What would they say to each other?

MODELO:

el profesor Solar,
Ester Muñoz

PROFESOR SOLAR: *Buenas tardes. Soy el profesor Solar.*
ESTER: *Buenas tardes, profesor Solar. Soy Ester Muñoz.*
PROFESOR SOLAR: *Mucho gusto.*
ESTER: *Igualmente.*

la Sra. Aldo,
la Sra. García

Patricia, Marcos

Eduardo, Manuel

1-4 Saludos. Read about different ways to greet someone in Spanish-speaking countries.

Paso 1 Before you begin to read, think about how you greet people you're meeting for the first time. How do you greet relatives? Friends? Does the age of the person you are greeting make a difference? When do people embrace, hug, or kiss each other on the cheek in the U.S. and Canada?

> Many Spanish speakers use nonverbal signs when interacting with each other. These signs will vary, depending on the social situation and on the relationship between the speakers. In general, people who meet each other for the first time shake hands (**dar la mano**) both when greeting and when saying good-bye to each other. Relatives and friends, however, are usually more physically expressive. Men who know each other well often greet each other with an **abrazo** (*hug*) and pats on the back. Women tend to greet each other and their male friends with one (Latin America) or two (Spain) light kisses on the cheeks.

 Paso 2 Introduce yourself to five of your classmates. Shake hands or kiss lightly on the cheek as you ask them their names and how they are doing. Then say good-bye.

1-5A ¿Cómo está usted? (*When you see the icon of two people with a line between them, one of you will assume the **A** role in the text; the other, the **B** role in **Appendix 1** for **B Activities**.*) Assume the role of instructor; your partner is your student. Act out the following conversation in which you greet each other and ask how things are. Use the information provided to complete your end of the conversation. **Estudiante B,** please see **Appendix 1,** page A-1 for your part.

MODELO: ESTUDIANTE A: *Buenos días…*
ESTUDIANTE B: *Hola…*

Estudiante A:

> - It's morning. You greet the student, introduce yourself, and ask his/her name.
> - Respond that you feel great today. Ask how he/she is feeling.
> - Say that you are surprised and that you are sorry.
> - Respond to the student.

¡Hola!
Cultura en vivo

The comfortable physical distance between Hispanics when holding a conversation is much closer than in many other cultures. Anglo-Americans tend to feel comfortable when they maintain at least arm's distance from the person to whom they are talking. As a test, stand at arm's distance from a classmate, then take one step closer. How do you feel at each distance?

¡Así lo hacemos!¹ ESTRUCTURAS

  1. The Spanish alphabet[2]

The Spanish alphabet contains twenty-seven letters, including one that does not appear in the English alphabet: **ñ**[3].

Letra (*Letter*)	Nombre (*Name*)	Ejemplos (*Examples*)	Pronunciación (*Pronunciation*)
a	a	Ana	
b	be	Bárbara	The letters **b** and **v** are pronounced exactly alike, as a **b**.
c	ce	Carlos, Cuba, Cecilia	In all varieties of Spanish, the letter **c** before **a**, **o**, or **u** sounds like English *k*. In Latin America, the letter **c** before **e** or **i** is pronounced like English *s*. In most of Spain, **c** before **e** and **i**, and the letter **z**, are pronounced like the English *th* in *thanks*.
d	de	Dios, Pedro	
e	e	Ernesto	
f	efe	Fernando	
g	ge	gato, gusto, gitano	The letter **g** before **a**, **o**, or **u** is pronounced like the English *g* in *gate*. Before **e** or **i**, the letter **g** is pronounced the same as Spanish **j** (or a hard English *h*).
h	hache	Hernán, hola, hotel	The letter **h** is always silent.
i	i	Inés	
j	jota	José	The letter **j** is like a hard English *h* sound.
k	ka	kilómetro, karate	The letter **k** is not common and usually appears only in words borrowed from other languages.
l	ele	Luis	
m	eme	María	
n	ene	Nora, nachos	
ñ	eñe	niño	The **ñ** sounds like *ny* as in *canyon*.
o	o	Óscar	
p	pe	Pepe	
q	cu	Quique, química	
r	ere	Laura, Rosa	At the beginning of a word, **r** is always pronounced like a trilled **rr**.
s	ese	Sara	
t	te	Tomás	
u	u	usted, Úrsula	
v	uve	Venus, vamos	The letters **b** and **v** are pronounced exactly alike, as a **b**.
w	doble uve	Washington, windsurf	The letter **w** is not common and usually appears only in words borrowed from other languages.
x	equis	excelente, México	Usually like *ks,* but also occasionally like Spanish **j**.
y	ye (i griega)	soy, Yolanda, maya	The letter **y** is a semivowel at the end of a syllable, as in English *toy,* or is a consonant at the beginning of a syllable, as in English *yard*.
z	zeta	Zorro, lápiz	In Latin America, the letter **z** is pronounced like English *s*. In most of Spain, it sounds like the English *th* in *thanks*.

---

¹That's how we do it!
²In 2010, the *Real Academia Española* revised the Spanish alphabet, eliminating *ch, ll* and changing the names of some letters. The *ch* and *ll* sequences still exist: Chile (pronounced as in English), llama (pronounced like [yama]).
³The letter **ñ** follows the **n** in the dictionary.

APLICACIÓN

1-6 ¿Qué vocal falta? Complete the names of these famous **hispanos** with the missing vowels. **¡Ojo!** (Watch out!): When a letter carries an accent, say **con acento** after saying the name of the letter: **eme - a - ere - i con acento - a (María).**

MODELO: _____ v _____   M _____ nd _____ s   (actriz)
        e, a, e, e (Eva Mendes)

1. J _____ nn _____ fer   L _____ p _____ z   (actriz y cantante)
2. C _____ mer _____ n   D _____ _____ z   (actriz)
3. R _____ f _____ el   N _____ d _____ l   (tenista)
4. J _____ ss_____ c_____   _____ lb _____   (actriz)
5. P _____ bl _____   P _____ c _____ ss __   (pintor)

¿Cómo se escribe "cigüeña" (*stork*)?

1-7 ¿Qué consonante falta? What consonants are missing from the names of these countries in the Spanish-speaking world?

MODELO: Mé ___ i ___ o
        x (equis), c (ce)

1. Ar _____ enti _____ a   6. El Sa _____ _____ ado _____
2. Bo _____ i _____ ia   7. Re _____ ública Do _____ ini _____ ana
3. _____ erú   8. Co _____ _____ a _____ ica
4. E _____ ua _____ or   9. Para _____ ua _____
5. Ve _____ e _____ ue _____ a   10. Espa _____ a

1-8 ¿Quién soy yo? (*Who am I?*) With your partner, take turns dictating your full names to each other. Then check to see whether your spelling is correct.

1-9A Otra vez, por favor (*please*). Take turns spelling out the words in parentheses to your partner while he/she writes them down. Be sure to first say in what category they belong. If you need to hear the spelling again, ask your partner to repeat by saying **Repite, por favor. Estudiante B,** please see **Appendix 1,** page A-1.

MODELO: cosa (*thing*) (quesadilla)
        ESTUDIANTE A: *Es una cosa, cu - u - e - ese - a - de - i - ele - ele - a*
        ESTUDIANTE B: (After writing down the word) *¿Es una quesadilla?*
        ESTUDIANTE A: *Correcto.*

Estudiante A:

I say and spell . . .	I write . . .
1. persona famosa (George López)	1. persona famosa: _____
2. ciudad (Lima)	2. ciudad (*city*): _____
3. cosa (banana)	3. cosa: _____
4. ciudad (Albuquerque)	4. ciudad: _____

2. The numbers *0–100*

Numbers in Spanish are expressed as follows:

0–9	10–19	20–29	30–39
cero	diez	veinte	treinta
uno	once	veintiuno	treinta y uno
dos	doce	veintidós	treinta y dos
tres	trece	veintitrés	treinta y tres
cuatro	catorce	veinticuatro	treinta y cuatro
cinco	quince	veinticinco	treinta y cinco
seis	dieciséis	veintiséis	treinta y seis
siete	diecisiete	veintisiete	treinta y siete
ocho	dieciocho	veintiocho	treinta y ocho
nueve	diecinueve	veintinueve	treinta y nueve

40–49:	cuarenta, cuarenta y uno, cuarenta y dos, cuarenta y tres...
50–59:	cincuenta, cincuenta y uno, cincuenta y dos, cincuenta y tres...
60–69:	sesenta, sesenta y uno, sesenta y dos, sesenta y tres...
70–79:	setenta, setenta y uno, setenta y dos, setenta y tres...
80–89:	ochenta, ochenta y uno, ochenta y dos, ochenta y tres...
90–99:	noventa, noventa y uno, noventa y dos, noventa y tres...
100–109:	cien, ciento uno, ciento dos, ciento tres...

- **Uno** becomes **un** before a masculine singular noun and **una** before a feminine singular noun.

un libro	*one book*	**una mesa**	*one table*
un profesor	*one professor (male)*	**una profesora**	*one professor (female)*

- In compound numbers, -**uno** becomes -**ún** before a masculine noun and -**una** before a feminine noun.

veintiún libros	*twenty-one books*
veintiuna profesoras	*twenty-one female professors*

- The numbers **dieciséis** through **diecinueve** (16–19) and **veintiuno** through **veintinueve** (21–29) are generally written as one word. The condensed spelling is not used after 30.

- **Cien** is used when it precedes a noun or when counting the number 100 in sequence.

cien estudiantes	*one hundred students*
noventa y ocho, noventa y nueve, **cien**	*ninety-eight, ninety-nine, one hundred*

- **Ciento** is used in compound numbers from 101 to 199.

ciento uno	*one hundred and one*
ciento cuarenta y cinco	*one hundred and forty-five*
ciento diez	*one hundred and ten*
ciento noventa y nueve	*one hundred and ninety-nine*

The ancient Maya developed a precise base-20 counting system that included zero (shell), one (dot), and five (bar). Can you see the number 18?

APLICACIÓN

1-10 ¿Qué número falta?   Figure out the patterns of numbers below and complete them with the logical numbers in Spanish.

MODELO: uno, _____tres_____, cinco, _____siete_____, nueve, _____once_____

1. dos, _____, seis, ocho, _____, doce, _____

2. _____, _____, cinco, siete, _____, once

3. uno, cinco, nueve, _____, diecisiete, veintiuno, _____

4. cinco, diez, _____, veinte, veinticinco, _____, _____

5. treinta, cuarenta, _____, _____, setenta, _____, _____

6. once, veintidós, _____, cuarenta y cuatro, cincuenta y cinco _____, setenta y siete, _____

7. veintiuno, veintitrés, veinticinco, _____, veintinueve, _____

8. noventa, ochenta, _____, sesenta, cincuenta, _____, _____

¿Cuál es tu número favorito?

1-11 Te toca a ti (*It's your turn*).   Challenge a classmate with an original sequence of numbers. See the previous activity for models.

1-12 ¿Cuál (*What*) es tu número de teléfono?   In preparation for getting together to work on future projects, exchange phone numbers with three or four other classmates. Notice that telephone numbers in Spanish can be stated in groups of two digits rather than in single digits.

MODELO: E1: *¿Cuál es tu número de teléfono?*
E2: *(301) 555-2240: tres, cero, uno, cinco, cincuenta y cinco, veintidós, cuarenta*

En Guatemala, ¿qué número marcas para llamar al extranjero (*internationally*)?

1-13 ¿Qué se hace en Madrid (*What do people do . . .*)? On what page of the tourist guide can you find information about what to do in Madrid?

En Madrid

La **Semana Santa** en Madrid ofrece un buen número de procesiones.

El 30 se corre la famosa **Mapoma** (Maratón Popular de Madrid).

El 23 se celebra el **Día del Libro**. Se ofrece una gran variedad de libros por todo el centro de la ciudad.

Atención: Noten que los museos tienen horas especiales durante la Semana Santa.

Bienvenida a los participantes del Congreso de Inmunología Humana que tiene lugar en el Hotel Principado.

El teléfono turístico: 902 202 202.

La línea turística proporciona amplia información sobre hoteles, restaurantes, camping, hostales, etc., las mejores ofertas para viajar, dónde y cómo reservar.

010 Teléfono del consumidor.

Toda la información cultural y de servicios del Ayuntamiento de Madrid.

MARZO - 2010

Ballet	.13	Fiestas	.20
Conciertos	.12	Miscelánea	.23
Congresos	.18	Música	.20
Datos útiles	.26	Niños	.22
Deportes	.14	Ópera	.14
Exposiciones	.4	Paseo del arte	.31
Ferias	.14	Puntos de interés	.27

EDITA Patronato Municipal de Turismo Mayor, 69, 28013
Madrid. Tel. 91 588 29 00
El p.m.t. no se responsabiliza de los cambios de última hora.

MODELO: _20_ música
en la página veinte

1. _____ puntos de interés
2. _____ datos útiles
3. _____ congresos
4. _____ niños
5. _____ conciertos

6. _____ ballet
7. _____ paseo del arte
8. _____ deportes
9. _____ fiestas
10. _____ ópera

01-17 to 01-22

3. The days of the week, the months, and the seasons

Los días de la semana (*Days of the week*)

- The days of the week in Spanish are written in lower-case and are all masculine.

- Calendars usually begin the week with Monday, not Sunday.

septiembre						
lunes	martes	miércoles	jueves	viernes	sábado	domingo
1	2	3	4	5	6	7

- The definite article is not used after **es** when telling what day of the week it is.
  Hoy **es jueves.**   *Today is Thursday.*

- *On Monday . . . , on Tuesday . . . ,* etc., is expressed by using the definite article **el.**
  El examen es **el lunes.**   *The exam is on Monday.*

- In the plural, the days of the week express the idea of doing something regularly.
  Voy al gimnasio **los sábados.**   *I go to the gym on Saturdays.*

- Days that end in **-s** have the same form in the singular and the plural. **El lunes** becomes **los lunes** in the plural.
  La clase de filosofía es **los lunes,**   *Philosophy class is on Mondays,*
  los miércoles y **los viernes.**   *Wednesdays, and Fridays.*

Los meses del año (*Months of the year*)

- Months are written in lower-case in Spanish.

enero							
L	M	M	J	V	S	D
						1
2	3	4	5	6	7	8
9	10	11	12	13	14	15
16	17	18	19	20	21	22
23	24	25	26	27	28	29
30	31					

febrero						
L	M	M	J	V	S	D
			1	2	3	4	5
6	7	8	9	10	11	12
13	14	15	16	17	18	19
20	21	22	23	24	25	26
27	28					

marzo						
L	M	M	J	V	S	D
		1	2	3	4	5
6	7	8	9	10	11	12
13	14	15	16	17	18	19
20	21	22	23	24	25	26
27	28	29	30	31		

abril						
L	M	M	J	V	S	D
					1	2
3	4	5	6	7	8	9
10	11	12	13	14	15	16
17	18	19	20	21	22	23
24	25	26	27	28	29	30

mayo						
L	M	M	J	V	S	D
1	2	3	4	5	6	7
8	9	10	11	12	13	14
15	16	17	18	19	20	21
22	23	24	25	26	27	28
29	30	31				

junio						
L	M	M	J	V	S	D
				1	2	3	4
5	6	7	8	9	10	11
12	13	14	15	16	17	18
19	20	21	22	23	24	25
26	27	28	29	30		

julio						
L	M	M	J	V	S	D
					1	2
3	4	5	6	7	8	9
10	11	12	13	14	15	16
17	18	19	20	21	22	23
24	25	26	27	28	29	30
31						

agosto						
L	M	M	J	V	S	D
					1	2	3	4	5	6
7	8	9	10	11	12	13
14	15	16	17	18	19	20
21	22	23	24	25	26	27
28	29	30	31			

septiembre						
L	M	M	J	V	S	D
					1	2	3
4	5	6	7	8	9	10
11	12	13	14	15	16	17
18	19	20	21	22	23	24
25	26	27	28	29	30	

octubre						
L	M	M	J	V	S	D
						1
2	3	4	5	6	7	8
9	10	11	12	13	14	15
16	17	18	19	20	21	22
23	24	25	26	27	28	29
30	31					

noviembre						
L	M	M	J	V	S	D
			1	2	3	4	5
6	7	8	9	10	11	12
13	14	15	16	17	18	19
20	21	22	23	24	25	26
27	28	29	30			

diciembre						
L	M	M	J	V	S	D
				1	2	3
4	5	6	7	8	9	10
11	12	13	14	15	16	17
18	19	20	21	22	23	24
25	26	27	28	29	30	31

Mi cumpleaños es en **noviembre.**   *My birthday is in November.*
Hay veintiocho días en **febrero.**   *There are twenty-eight days in February.*

- To ask the date say:

  ¿Cuál es la fecha?
  ¿Qué fecha es? }   *What's today's date?*

  To answer say:

  Hoy es (el) dos de febrero.[1]   *Today is February 2nd.*

- Use cardinal numbers with dates (**el cuatro, el once**), except for the first day of the month which is **el primero.**

  el cinco de mayo.   *May 5th.*
  el primero de enero.   *January 1st.*

Las estaciones del año (*Seasons of the year*)

- The seasons in Spanish are not capitalized.

el invierno

la primavera

el verano

el otoño

- The definite article is used to talk about the seasons but is omitted to say what season it is.

  ¿Cómo es **la primavera** aquí?   *What is spring like here?*
  Es **verano** ahora en Argentina.   *It's summer now in Argentina.*

---

[1]Spanish speakers will often omit **el** before the number when referring to today's date.

APLICACIÓN

1-14 Fiestas importantes en el mundo hispano. Match the holidays to the dates they are celebrated in the Spanish-speaking world.

MODELO: El día de la Independencia de México es en el otoño.
El 16 de septiembre es el día de la Independencia de México.

1. _____ En EE. UU. es una fiesta para celebrar la cultura mexicana.

2. _____ El día de la Raza (o el día de Cristóbal Colón) es en el otoño.

3. _____ La fiesta de la Virgen de Guadalupe es en el invierno.

4. _____ El día festivo (*holiday*) para los trabajadores es en la primavera.

5. _____ En Costa Rica, el día de la Madre es en el verano.

6. _____ En Pamplona, España, se celebran los sanfermines[1] por nueve días en el verano.

a. el 12 de diciembre
b. del 6 al 14 de julio
c. el 5 de mayo
d. el 15 de agosto
e. el 12 de octubre
f. el primero de mayo

Ernest Hemmingway conmemoró las fiestas de San Fermín en *The Sun Also Rises*.

Presencia hispana

Cinco de Mayo marks the victory of Mexican forces under General Ignacio Zaragoza over the French at the Battle of Puebla on May 5, 1862. Although the Mexican army suffered defeats soon afterward, the *Batalla de Puebla* came to symbolize Mexican unity and patriotism. Today, it has been highly commercialized and is celebrated more actively in the U.S. than in Mexico, which instead celebrates its independence from Spain on September 16, 1810. Do you celebrate **Cinco de mayo**?

1-15 Fechas importantes en EE. UU. y Canadá. Tell the dates of the following celebrations.

MODELO:

 el diecisiete de marzo

1.

2.

3.

4.

---

[1] **Los sanfermines** is a masculine one-word plural noun referring to the festivities that honor Saint Fermin (**San Fermín**) in Spain.

1-16 Las estaciones del año. Remember that the seasons in the northern and southern hemispheres are inverted. Write the season in which each month falls in the northern hemisphere. Then do the same with the southern hemisphere (*el Cono Sur*).

	Hemisferio Norte	Cono Sur
1. agosto	_____	_____
2. julio	_____	_____
3. diciembre	_____	_____
4. marzo	_____	_____
5. octubre	_____	_____
6. septiembre	_____	_____

Es junio y Miguel esquía en Bariloche, Argentina.

1-17A Los días, los meses y las estaciones. Take turns asking each other questions to fill in the missing days, dates, and months on each of your grids. **Estudiante B**, please see **Appendix 1**, page A-2.

MODELO: ESTUDIANTE A: (You need) *¿Un mes de otoño?*
ESTUDIANTE B: (You have) *octubre*

Estudiante A:

You need . . .	My partner gives me . . .	Your partner needs . . .
1. el día de la Independencia		el 14 de febrero
2. un día con nueve letras		enero
3. un mes con treinta días		mayo
4. un día que no hay (*there are no*) clases		febrero
5. un mes de verano		el lunes

1-18 ¿Cuándo es tu cumpleaños? In groups of six or seven students, take turns reporting your birthdays. Have one person fill in the dates for each month reported. Present your findings to the class using the following questions as a guide.

MODELO: *Mi cumpleaños es el 17 de enero.*

1. ¿Cuál (*Which*) es el mes más común?

2. ¿Cuál es el mes menos común?

3. ¿Hay (*Are there*) dos personas con el mismo día de cumpleaños?

Los cumpleaños de los estudiantes									
enero	17								
febrero									
marzo									
abril									
mayo									
junio									
julio									
agosto									
septiembre									
octubre									
noviembre									
diciembre									

¿Cuánto saben?

01-23 to 01-27

First, ask yourself whether you can perform the following functions in Spanish. Then act out the scenarios with two or three classmates. Ask and respond to at least three questions in each situation.

✓ CAN YOU . . .

☐ meet and greet others?

☐ spell your name?

☐ perform simple math problems in Spanish?

☐ talk about the calendar and dates?

WITH YOUR CLASSMATE(S) . . .

Situación: En clase
This is your first day of class. Take turns introducing yourself as a professor or student and ask others their names.
Para empezar (*Getting started*): ¿Cómo te llamas?
¿Cómo se llama usted?

Situación: En el centro de estudiantes internacionales
You and your partner are welcoming students to a reception for international students and need to write everyone's name on name tags. Take turns asking their names and how to spell them.
Para empezar: ¿Cómo te llamas? ¿Cómo se escribe...?

Situación: Planes para una fiesta
Challenge each other to calculate how many soft drinks (*refrescos*) and pizzas you need if you invite 5, 10, or another number of friends.
Para empezar: Con cinco amigos, necesitamos diez refrescos y... pizzas. Con... amigos, necesitamos...

Situación: En un café
Share within the group your favorite holidays. Which ones do you have in common?
Para empezar: ¿Cuál es tu día festivo favorito?
El día festivo favorito de muchos (many) es...

📖 Perfiles

01-28
to 01-29

Mi experiencia

SOY BILINGÜE

1-19 Para ti (*For you*).   Do you have friends or family members who speak more than one language? Did they grow up speaking two languages, learn a second language in school, or live in a place where English was not the primary language? What are the economic, political, and social advantages to being bilingual and bicultural in today's world? Read the excerpt from Oscar Ponce Torres's blog below about growing up bilingual.

¡Hola! ¿Qué pasa? My name is Óscar Ponce Torres and I live in New York City. My family is originally from Puerto Rico; my parents moved to New York when I was just a kid. Growing up, I spoke Spanish at home and learned English in school, like most of my friends in the neighborhood. I'm very proud of my Puerto Rican heritage and of being both bicultural and bilingual. Currently, I study international business at New York University, and in the future I hope to work with a company with locations here and abroad. I know that being able to speak two languages offers many professional and social opportunities, but for me, speaking Spanish and English with family and friends is what I know; it's my experience. And when we get together, there's always music playing in the background, including the latest by the group Aventura. Listen to the song "Mi corazoncito" for a sense of what it sounds like to live in a bilingual world.

Presencia hispana

Because the Spanish settled much of the North American continent before other nationalities, when states came into the Union, many of the inhabitants were descendents of the first settlers who arrived with Spanish explorers. Can you name the states that were originally territory dominated by Spain?

1-20 En su opinión.   With a partner, explore your experiences and ideas about bilingualism by discussing the following questions.

1. What are your reasons for studying Spanish?

2. Do you plan to use Spanish in a particular career or in another facet of your life? How so?

3. Have you studied or do you speak other languages besides English and Spanish? What about your friends and family?

4. Do you think it is important to know more than one language? Why or why not?

5. What other people in the media or public eye can you name that are bilingual? How has it helped them?

Mi música

"MI CORAZONCITO" (AVENTURA, EE. UU.)

The group Aventura formed in the Bronx in 1994. Their musical style is **bachata,** whose themes are often romantic with tales of heartbreak. Aventura has a particular **bachata** style combining the traditional sound with hip-hop, R & B, and reggaeton, as well as using both English and Spanish lyrics. The members of Aventura are "Romeo" Santos, Lenny Santos, Max Santos, and Henry Santos Jeter.

Antes de ver y escuchar (*Pre-viewing and -listening*)

1-21 Estilos musicales. With what American or Latin rap artists are you familiar? Which ones have been honored with a Grammy? Have you ever heard a **bachata**? Of the following musical styles, which ones do you prefer and why?

country   metálica   pop   R & B   rap   rock

1-22 Mi corazoncito. The title of the song means "my little heart" and is typical of a **bachata** rhythm and theme. Here are some of the words you will hear in the song. Guess their meanings and write down their equivalents in English before listening to the song. If necessary, consult a Spanish-English dictionary.

1. amor _____
2. imaginación _____
3. hombre _____
4. bohemio loco _____
5. poeta _____
6. negro _____

Para ver y escuchar (*Viewing and listening*)

1-23 La canción. Connect with the Internet to find a site on which Aventura performs this piece. You may also want to search for the lyrics (*letra*). In what way is this song considered a **bachata**? How does it compare to country music in the U.S.?

> **Busca**[1]: mi corazoncito aventura video; mi corazoncito aventura letra
>
> **If you would like to purchase this song:** *Go to iTunes Store>Music>More to Explore>iMix>Arriba 6e*

Después de ver y escuchar (*Post-viewing and -listening*)

1-24 Descripciones. You are a true aficionado/a of **bachata** music. Indicate in the spaces below with an "X" which statements you believe to be true of "Mi corazoncito." Most descriptions use a cognate.

_____ Es interesante.   _____ Es misteriosa.   _____ Es romántica.

_____ Es fascinante.   _____ Es divertida (*fun*).   _____ Es exótica.

1-25 Investigación. Research information about the lead singer of Aventura and complete this biographical information about him: **nombre completo, lugar de nacimiento, el título de una canción** *hit*.

> **Busca:** romeo santos aventura

---

[1]Note that accents, *tildes* and capital letters are not required for Internet searches.

Segunda parte

¡Así lo decimos! VOCABULARIO

 ¡Así es la vida! En la clase de geografía

01-01
to 01-30

¿Qué pasa hoy en la clase de la profesora García?

Paulina

Miguel

Ramón

PROFESORA GARCÍA:	Buenos días. Saquen la tarea para hoy. Miguel, lee el número uno, por favor.
MIGUEL:	Perdone, profesora, no tengo la tarea.
PROFESORA GARCÍA:	¿Paulina?
PAULINA:	Un momento, profesora. Necesito mi portátil.
PROFESORA GARCÍA:	¿Ramón?
RAMÓN:	Perdone, profesora. Repita, por favor.
PROFESORA GARCÍA:	Pero, ¡qué barbaridad! ¡Qué estudiantes!

01-31 to 01-37

🔊 **Vocabulario** En la clase

Variaciones

A few words for colors vary in the Spanish-speaking world. **Color café** may be expressed as **pardo** or **marrón**. **Rosado** may be **color rosa,** and **morado** may be **púrpura** or **color violeta.** Also, **anaranjado** may be simply **naranja.**

Variaciones

Names for technology also vary: *laptop* is **la (computadora) portátil** in Latin America and **el (ordenador) portátil** in Spain. Cell phone is generally **el (teléfono) celular** in Latin America and **el (teléfono) móvil** in Spain.

¿De qué color es? | What color is it ?

amarillo/a	*yellow*
anaranjado/a	*orange*
azul	*blue*
blanco/a	*white*
color café	*brown*
gris	*gray*
morado/a	*purple*
negro/a	*black*
rojo/a	*red*
rosado/a	*pink*
verde	*green*

Objetos en la clase | Objects in the classroom

el bolígrafo	*pen*
la calculadora	*calculator*
la computadora (portátil)	*computer (laptop)*
el cuaderno	*notebook*
el diccionario	*dictionary*
el lápiz	*pencil*
el libro	*book*
el mapa	*map*
el marcador	*marker*
la mesa	*table*
la mochila	*backpack*
el papel	*paper*
la pizarra (blanca)	*chalkboard (whiteboard)*
la puerta	*door*
el reloj	*clock, watch*
la silla	*chair*
el teléfono celular/móvil	*cell phone*
la tiza	*chalk*

Otros sustantivos | Other nouns

el hombre	*man*
la mujer	*woman*

Adjetivos | Adjectives

barato/a	*cheap, inexpensive*
caro/a	*expensive*
claro/a	*light (color)*
grande	*big*
oscuro/a	*dark (color)*
pequeño/a	*small*

Adverbio | Adverb

aquí	*here*

Verbos | Verbs

hay	*there is/are*
necesitar	*to need*
ser	*to be*
tengo (tener)	*I have (to have)*

Otras expresiones | Other expressions

¡Qué barbaridad!	*What nonsense!*
¡Qué estudiantes!	*What students!*

el cuaderno verde

la computadora portátil

Expresiones para los estudiantes | Expressions for students

No comprendo. *I don't understand.*
No sé. *I don't know.*
Repita[1], por favor. *Repeat, please.*

✳ Expresiones para la clase[2] | Expressions for the class

Abre (Abran) el libro. *Open your book(s).*
Cierra (Cierren) el libro. *Close your book(s).*
Contesta (Contesten) en español. *Answer in Spanish.*
Escribe (Escriban) en la pizarra. *Write on the board.*
Escucha. (Escuchen.) *Listen.*
Estudia. (Estudien.) *Study.*
Lee (Lean) el diálogo. *Read the dialog.*
Repite. (Repitan.) *Repeat.*
Saca (Saquen) la tarea. *Take out your homework.*
Ve (Vayan) a la pizarra. *Go to the board.*

---

[1]**Repita** is a formal command, appropriate to use with your professor.
[2]These commands are for one student. Commands for the whole class are given in parentheses.

APLICACIÓN

1-26 ¿Qué hay en la clase?   Take inventory of your classroom. Indicate how many of each item there are.

MODELO: ___20___ estudiantes
              Hay veinte estudiantes.

_____ pizarra(s)   _____ cuaderno(s)

_____ bolígrafo(s)   _____ silla(s)

_____ mesa(s)   _____ reloj(es)

_____ mapa(s)   _____ libro(s) de español

1-27 ¿Cuál es tu color favorito?   What determines color preferences among different people? The following activity presents a possible factor.

Paso 1   Find out which colors are most popular in your class. Ask the person next to you what his/her favorite color is. That person will ask the next, and so forth until everyone has responded. One person will tally the results for the class by sex (men vs. women).

Paso 2   Now read the following article from *Vanidades*, a popular magazine throughout Latin America, based on a survey of men and women and their color preferences. Skim the reading. Don't try to understand every word. Read for general meaning to answer the questions below.

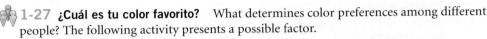

Ellos, ellas y los colores

En un hospital de París se desarrolló un estudio en el que se les pidió a pacientes adultos, hombres y mujeres, que pintaran acuarelas con sus colores favoritos. En los resultados se observó que el 85% de los hombres prefirió usar los tonos verdes y los azules, mientras que la mayoría de las mujeres escogió los rojos y los amarillos, mostrando así —una vez más— las marcadas diferencias que en cuanto a preferencias de colores existen entre los dos sexos.

Vanidades, 34 (20), p. 16.

1. Where did the study take place?

2. Who were the subjects interviewed?

3. What percentage of men is mentioned?

4. What colors are mentioned?

5. Now compare your class with the subjects in the article by responding **Sí** or **No** to these statements:

   "Los hombres del estudio son como (*like*) los hombres (*men*) de la clase".
   "Las mujeres del estudio son como las mujeres (*women*) de la clase".

🔊 **1-28 ¿Qué haces cuando…? (What do you do when . . . ?)** Listen to a Spanish teacher make various requests in the classroom, and write the number of each request next to what you would do.

_____ I answer in Spanish.   _____ I close the book.

_____ I open my book.   _____ I listen to the music.

_____ I read the dialog.   _____ I repeat the month.

_____ I write the sentence.   _____ I go to the board.

1-29A ¡Escucha bien! Take turns telling each other in Spanish what to do using the cues in English and acting out the commands. **Estudiante B,** please see **Appendix 1,** page A-2.

MODELO: (Open your book.)

ESTUDIANTE A: *Abre el libro.*

ESTUDIANTE B: (opens his/her book)

ESTUDIANTE A: *Correcto.*

Estudiante A:

> You say in Spanish:
>
> 1. (Go to the door.)
> 2. (Repeat your name.)
> 3. (Write the date.)

1-30A Un pedido (order) por teléfono. You are a student departmental worker. Below is a list of items you need for your department. Call the bookstore and give the clerk your supply order. Mark the items your clerk can supply as he/she may have a lesser quantity. When you finish, compare your lists. **Estudiante B,** please see **Appendix 1,** page A-2.

MODELO: ESTUDIANTE A: *Necesitamos cinco calculadoras. ¿Hay cinco calculadoras?*

ESTUDIANTE B: *Sí, tengo diez. / No, solamente (only) hay cuatro.*

Estudiante A:

_____ 1 reloj	_____ 14 cuadernos	_____ 20 diccionarios
_____ 10 sillas	_____ 80 bolígrafos	_____ 75 cajas (*boxes*) de tiza
_____ 5 mapas	_____ 90 lápices	_____ 100 cajas de papel
_____ 33 libros	_____ 11 mesas	

1-31 Veo algo… (I see something . . .) Describe an object to see whether your classmate can guess what it is. Use colors and adjectives from **¡Así lo decimos!**

MODELO: E1: *Veo algo verde y grande.*

E2: *¿Es la pizarra?*

¡Así lo hacemos! ESTRUCTURAS

4. Subject pronouns and the present tense of *ser*

01-38 to 01-40

In Spanish, subject pronouns refer to people (*I, you, he,* etc.).[1]

Subject pronouns			
SINGULAR		**PLURAL**	
yo	*I*	**nosotros/nosotras**[3]	*we*
tú	*you* (inf.)[2]	**vosotros/vosotras**[3]	*you* (inf., Spain)
usted (Ud.)	*you* (for.)[2]	**ustedes (Uds.)**	*you* (for.)
él, ella	*he, she*	**ellos, ellas**[3]	*they* (m./f.)

Just like the verb *to be* in English, the verb **ser** in Spanish has irregular forms. You have already used several of them. Here are all of the forms of the present indicative, along with the subject pronouns.

ser (*to be*)						
	SINGULAR			**PLURAL**		
yo	**soy**	*I am*	nosotros/as	**somos**	*we are*	
tú	**eres**	*you are* (inf.)	vosotros/as	**sois**	*you are* (inf.)	
usted (Ud.)	**es**	*you are* (for.)	ustedes (Uds.)	**son**	*you are* (for.)	
él/ella	**es**	*he/she is*	ellos/ellas	**son**	*they are*	

- Because the verb form indicates the subject of a sentence, subject pronouns are usually omitted unless they are needed for clarification or emphasis.

  ¿Eres de Puerto Rico?   *Are you from Puerto Rico?*
  Sí, soy de Puerto Rico.   *Yes, I'm from Puerto Rico.*
  Yo no, pero **ellos** son de Puerto Rico.   *I'm not, but they're from Puerto Rico.*

- There are four ways to express *you*: **tú, usted, vosotros/as,** and **ustedes. Tú** and **usted** are the singular forms. **Tú** is used in informal situations, that is, to address friends, family members, and pets. **Usted** denotes formality or respect and is used to address someone with whom you are not well acquainted or a person in a position of authority (a supervisor, teacher, or older person).[4]

- **Vosotros/as** and **ustedes** are the plural counterparts of **tú** and **usted,** respectively, but in all of Latin America, **ustedes** is used for both the informal and formal plural *you*. **Vosotros/as** is used in Spain to address more than one person in an informal context (a group of friends or children).[5]

- Although **tú** is the most commonly used subject pronoun in Spanish to express informal *you* in the singular, many speakers, like those in Argentina, Uruguay, and Chile, use **vos**.

---

[1]Subject pronouns are not generally used for inanimate objects or animals (except when referring to pets).
[2]Abbreviations: inf. (informal); for. (formal).
[3]**Nosotros, vosotros, ellos:** masculine, or masculine and feminine group; **nosotras, vosotras, ellas:** all feminine group.
[4]In the families of some Hispanic countries, children use **usted** and **ustedes** to address their parents as a sign of respect.
[5]**¡Arriba!** uses **ustedes** as the plural of **tú,** except where cultural context would require otherwise.

- The pronouns **usted** and **ustedes** are commonly abbreviated as **Ud.** and **Uds.** or **Vd.** and **Vds.**

- The verb **ser** is used to express origin, occupation, or inherent qualities.

¿De dónde **eres**?	*Where are you from?*
Soy de Toronto.	*I am from Toronto.*
¿Cómo **es** la profesora?	*What is the teacher like?*
Es muy paciente.	*She is very patient.*

APLICACIÓN

1-32 Dos artistas importantes. Learn more about the two artists whose artwork is featured in the chapter opener.

Paso 1 Read the description below and underline the forms of **ser.**

Salvador Dalí y Diego Rivera son dos de los artistas más famosos del mundo. Sus pinturas son admiradas por expertos y por estudiantes de arte. Los dos artistas son del siglo XX, pero sus experiencias y sus estilos son muy diferentes. Salvador Dalí es español. Es de Figueras, un pueblo cerca de Barcelona. Su esposa, Gala, también es famosa. Dalí es famoso no sólo por su arte surrealista, sino también por su apariencia extravagante. *El descubrimiento de América por Cristóbal Colón* conmemora el famoso viaje de Colón en 1492. La muerte de Dalí es en 1989 a la edad de ochenta y cuatro años.

Diego Rivera es mexicano. Es de Guanajuato, una ciudad colonial al norte de la Ciudad de México. El año de su nacimiento es 1886 y el año de su muerte es 1957. Rivera es famoso por sus murales que describen (*depict*) la historia de México, especialmente la conquista de México por los españoles. *Historia de México desde la conquista hasta el futuro* es un mural muy grande. Su estilo es realista. La esposa de Diego Rivera es Frida Kahlo, una artista mexicana muy famosa también.

Paso 2   Now answer in Spanish, based on the reading in **Paso 1** about Salvador Dalí and Diego Rivera.

1. Where is Dalí from? Where is Rivera from?

2. What do Rivera and Dalí have in common?

3. How do they differ?

4. Have you ever seen a painting or mural by either of these artists?

5. Both artists had wives who also were well known in their own right. Who are they?

1-33 En la clase de arte moderno.   Complete María Antonia's description of her art class using the correct form of **ser** in each blank.

Hay veinte estudiantes en la clase de arte moderno. Nosotros (1) _____ estudiantes de arte en la Universidad de Granada. La profesora de la clase (2) _____ la señora Martínez. Ella (3) _____ de Colombia y (4) _____ pintora. Las clases (5) _____ muy buenas, pero los exámenes (6)_____ difíciles. Los artistas españoles (7) _____ muy interesantes y los latinoamericanos (8) _____ excelentes. Los estudiantes (9) _____ inteligentes y yo (10) _____ muy feliz (*happy*) en la clase.

1-34 Ramón y Rosario.   Two students meet in the student union before class.

Paso 1   Fill in the blanks in the following conversation with the correct forms of the verb **ser**.

RAMÓN: Hola, yo (1) _____ Ramón Larrea Arias.

ROSARIO: Encantada, Ramón. (2) _____ Rosario Vélez Cuadra.

RAMÓN: ¿De dónde (3)_____?

ROSARIO: (4) _____ de Puerto Rico, ¿y tú?

RAMÓN: (5) _____ de Panamá, pero mis padres (*parents*) (6) _____ de Colombia.

ROSARIO: ¿Cómo (7) _____ tu clase de inglés?

RAMÓN: Mi clase (8) _____ muy interesante y mis compañeros de clase (9) _____ muy simpáticos (*nice*).

ROSARIO: ¿Cómo (10) _____ la profesora?

RAMÓN: (11) _____ muy inteligente. Ella (12) _____ de Canadá.

ROSARIO: ¡Ay, lo siento! Tengo clase ahora. Hasta luego, Ramón.

RAMÓN: Nos vemos, Rosario.

Paso 2   Now create a similar dialog to exchange information about yourselves or a personality you create.

5. Nouns and articles

Words that identify persons, places, or objects are *nouns*.
Spanish nouns—even those denoting nonliving things—are
either masculine or feminine in gender.

El género de los sustantivos (*The gender of nouns*)

The definite article (*the*) must agree with the noun.

	Masculine		Feminine	
Singular	el muchacho	*the boy*	la muchacha	*the girl*
	el libro	*the book*	la mesa	*the table*
	el hombre	*the man*	la mujer	*the woman*

There are many clues that will help you identify the gender of a noun.

- Most nouns ending in **-o** or those denoting male persons are masculine: **el libro, el hombre.** Most nouns ending in **-a** or those denoting female persons are feminine: **la mesa, la mujer.** Some common exceptions are: **el día** and **el mapa,** which are masculine.

- Many person nouns have corresponding masculine **-o** and feminine **-a** forms.

  el amigo / la amiga   *male/female friend*
  el niño / la niña   *boy/girl*

- Most masculine person nouns ending in a consonant simply add **-a** to form the feminine.

  el profesor / la profesora   *male/female professor*
  el señor / la señora   *Mr./Mrs.*

- Certain person nouns use the same form for masculine and feminine, but the article used indicates the gender.

  el artista / la artista   *male/female artist*
  el estudiante / la estudiante *male/female student*
  el poeta / la poeta   *male/female poet*

- Nouns ending in **-e** or a consonant can be masculine or feminine. The article indicates what the gender of the noun is.

  la clase   *class*
  el lápiz   *pencil*

- Most nouns ending in **-ad** and **-ión** are feminine.

  la universidad   *university*
  la nación   *nation*

- Most nouns ending in **-ma** are masculine.

  el problema   *problem*
  el drama   *drama*
  el enigma   *enigma*

Los artículos definidos (*Definite articles*)

In Spanish, there are four forms of the definite article (*the* in English):

	Masculine	Feminine
Singular	el	la
Plural	los	las

- Use the definite article with titles when talking about someone (even yourself), but not when addressing someone directly.

El profesor Gómez es interesante.	*Professor Gómez is interesting.*
Soy **el** profesor Gómez.	*I'm Professor Gómez.*
¡Buenos días, profesor Gómez!	*Good morning, Professor Gómez!*

El plural de los sustantivos (*Plural forms of nouns*)

Masculine		Feminine	
los muchachos	*the boys*	**las muchachas**	*the girls*
los libros	*the books*	**las mesas**	*the tables*
los hombres	*the men*	**las mujeres**	*the women*

- Nouns that end in a vowel form the plural by adding -**s**.

  el libro → los libros   **la mesa → las mesas**   **la clase → las clases**

- Nouns that end in a consonant add -**es**.

  la mujer → las mujeres   **la universidad → las universidades**

- Nouns that end in a -**z** change the **z** to **c** in the plural.

  el lápiz → los lápices   **la actriz** (*actress*) **→ las actrices**

- When the last syllable of a word that ends in a consonant has an accent mark, the accent is no longer needed in the plural.

  la lección → las lecciones   **la conversación → las conversaciones**

Los artículos indefinidos (*Indefinite articles*)

In Spanish, there are four forms of the indefinite article (*a/an* in English):

	Masculine		Feminine	
Singular	**un** bolígrafo	*a pen*	**una** silla	*a chair*
Plural	**unos** bolígrafos	*some pens*	**unas** sillas	*some chairs*

- Indefinite articles (*a, an, some*) also agree with the noun they modify. **Un** and **una** are equivalent to *a* or *an*. **Unos** and **unas** are equivalent to *some* (or *a few*).

- In Spanish, the indefinite article is omitted when telling someone's profession, unless you qualify the person (good, bad, hardworking, etc.).

Lorena es profesora de matemáticas.	*Lorena is a mathematics professor.*
Lorena es **una** buena profesora.	*Lorena is a good professor.*

APLICACIÓN

1-35 ¿Masculino o femenino?   Say whether the following nouns are masculine (M) or feminine (F). Then provide the definite article.

MODELO: _____ libro
_M: el_ libro

1. _____ universidad
2. _____ mesa
3. _____ muchacho
4. _____ mujer
5. _____ problema
6. _____ lápiz
7. _____ silla
8. _____ poema

1-36 ¿Qué necesita?   Say what the following people or places need. Use the indefinite article and the items below.

bolígrafos	cuaderno	lápices	mesa	puerta
calculadora	diccionario	libros	microscopio	reloj
computadora	estudiantes	mapas	papeles	sillas

MODELO: ¿Qué necesita un profesor de informática (_computer science_)?
Necesita una computadora...

¿Qué necesita...

1. un profesor de historia?
2. un científico (_scientist_)?
3. una profesora de biología?
4. un matemático?
5. una profesora de ingeniería (_engineering_)?
6. un estudiante?

1-37 ¿Qué hay?   Describe where the following items can be found using the correct definite and indefinite articles.

MODELO: _Hay una profesora en la clase._

Ô Y EN

¿Qué hay?	**¿Dónde? (Where?)**
cuaderno(s)	silla(s)
estudiante(s)	clase
puerta	mesa(s)
teléfono(s) celular(es)	pizarra
computadora portátil	mochila
mochilas	
ejemplos de gramática	
diccionarios	

1-38 ¿Qué hay en tu mochila?   Ask each other what you have in your backpacks.

MODELO: E1: _¿Hay un lápiz en tu mochila?_
E2: _Sí, hay un lápiz. (No, no hay un lápiz.)_

📖 6. Adjective forms, position, and agreement

01-45
to 01-50

- Descriptive adjectives, such as those denoting size, color, and shape, describe and give additional information about objects and people.

una clase **grande**	*a big class*
un cuaderno **rosado**	*a pink notebook*

- Here are some adjectives to help you talk about yourself and others.

aburrido/a	*boring*	**perezoso/a**	*lazy*
bueno/a	*good*	**simpático/a**	*nice, amusing*
malo/a	*bad*	**trabajador/a**	*hardworking*

- This list of adjectives is made up of cognates, words that are similar in Spanish and English. Can you guess their meanings?

exótico/a	**introvertido/a**
extrovertido/a	**misterioso/a**
fascinante	**optimista**
ideal	**paciente**
idealista	**pesimista**
impaciente	**realista**
inteligente	**romántico/a**
interesante	**tímido/a**

- Descriptive adjectives agree in gender and number with the nouns they modify; they generally follow the nouns.

el profesor **bueno**	*the good professor*
la señora **simpática**	*the nice lady*
los bolígrafos **rojos**	*the red pens*

- The adjectives **bueno** and **malo** may be placed before or after nouns. When placed before a masculine singular noun, the final **-o** is dropped.

un **buen** estudiante	*a good student*
un **mal** cantante	*a bad singer*

- Adjectives ending in **-e** or a consonant have the same masculine and feminine forms.

un libro **grande**	*a big book*
una clase **grande**	*a big class*
un carro **azul**	*a blue car*
una silla **azul**	*a blue chair*

- For adjectives of nationality that end in a consonant, and adjectives that end in **-dor,** add **-a** to form the feminine.

el profesor **español**	*the Spanish professor*
la estudiante **española**	*the Spanish student*
un libro **francés**[1]	*a French book*
una mujer **francesa**	*a French woman*
un hombre **trabajador**	*a hardworking man*
una profesora **trabajadora**	*a hardworking professor*

- The adjective **grande** changes to **gran** before a singular noun to mean *great*.

una universidad **grande**	*a big university*
una **gran** universidad	*a great university*

---

[1]If the masculine has an accented final syllable, the accent is dropped in the feminine and the plural forms.

APLICACIÓN

1-39 Parejas. Choose logical adjectives below and write them in the blanks to modify the nouns that follow. Pay close attention to the gender and number of the nouns.

anaranjadas	caros	extrovertidas	morado	rosada	simpática	tímido	trabajadores

1. las sillas _anaranjadas_
2. el bolígrafo _morado_
3. los relojes _caros_
4. la mochila _rosada_

5. la estudiante _simpática_
6. el muchacho _tímido_
7. los profesores _trabajadores_
8. las amigas _extrovertidas_

1-40 ¿De qué color? Look at the following items in your classroom and state what color each is.

MODELO: la pizarra
La pizarra es negra.

1. el mapa _azul_
2. los lápices _verde_
3. el libro de español _verde_
4. los cuadernos _negro_

5. las sillas _amarillo_
6. la puerta _café_
7. los papeles del profesor / de la profesora _es floral y blanco_
8. la mochila de... (John, etc.) _negro_

1-41 Palifruta. Answer these questions based on the ad at the right.

1. ¿De qué color es el palifruta de limón?
2. ¿De qué color es el palifruta de grosella (*currant*)?
3. ¿Son saludables (*healthy*) los palifrutas? ¿Por qué?

Más fresco que la fruta
PALIFRUTA
100% x 100% Natural
Grosella
Limón
SIN CONSERVANTES
SIN COLORANTES
SIN SABORES ARTIFICIALES
PARA LLEVAR : 24 unidades en 2 sabores
DE VENTA EXCLUSIVA EN TIENDAS
Heladerías Zanzíbar®

1-42 ¿Cómo es? ¿Cómo son? Combine nouns and adjectives to make logical sentences in Spanish. Remember to use the correct forms of **ser** and make articles, nouns, and adjectives agree in gender and number.

MODELO: los estudiantes
Los estudiantes son buenos.

el libro de español		fascinante
los profesores		interesante
las sillas		simpático
la clase		inteligente
mis amigos y yo		bueno/malo
la pizarra	(no) ser	norteamericano/español/...
yo		rojo/anaranjado/amarillo/negro/...
el bolígrafo		barato/caro
la universidad		grande/pequeño
mis clases		trabajador

1-43 Una encuesta. Take a survey of class members to find out what they consider to be the ideal qualities of the following people, places, and things. Respond with your own opinions as well.

MODELO: E1: *¿Cómo es la clase ideal?*
E2: *La clase ideal es pequeña.*
E1: *La clase ideal es interesante.*

1. ¿Cómo es el/la profesor/a ideal?

2. ¿Cómo son los amigos/as ideales?

3. ¿Cómo es el libro ideal?

4. ¿Cómo es la universidad ideal?

5. ¿Cómo son los carros (*cars*) ideales?

6. ¿Cómo son los restaurantes ideales?

Media Share
01-51
to 01-54

¿Cuánto saben?

First, ask yourself whether you can perform the following functions in Spanish. Then act out the scenarios with two or three classmates. Ask and respond to at least three questions in each situation.

✓ CAN YOU . . .	WITH YOUR CLASSMATE(S) . . .
☐ describe your classroom?	**Situación: En la universidad** You each have a different Spanish class. Describe them to each other including the professors, students, and classroom objects. Include descriptive adjectives with colors when appropriate. **Para empezar (*Getting started*):** *¿Cómo es tu clase de español? ¿Cómo son…?*
☐ respond to classroom instructions?	**Situación: En la clase de español** Take turns using classroom expressions to tell the group what to do. They will either perform the function, ask the person to repeat it, or say that they do not understand or don't know. **Para empezar:** *Abre…*
☐ talk about yourself and others?	**Situación: Yo soy…** You and your classmates are running for office in your university's student government. Introduce yourselves, say where you are from and describe the kind of people you are. **Para empezar:** *Me llamo/Soy… Soy de… y soy…*
☐ identify colors and talk about your favorite color?	**Situación: En clase** Ask your partner about his/her favorite color. Then challenge each other to identify the color of different objects around you as one of you points them out. What color is most prevalent? **Para empezar:** *¿Cuál es tu color favorito? ¿De qué color es esto (this)? El… es el color más común.*

Observaciones

¡Pura vida! EPISODIO 1

¡Pura vida! is an ongoing series that takes place in Costa Rica.

Antes de ver el video

1-44 ¿Cómo es Costa Rica? Costa Rica, known for its natural beauty and national efforts to maintain a varied ecosystem, is a tropical country with several climatic zones and four mountain ranges with seven active volcanoes. Earth tremors and small quakes shake the country from time to time. Read about San José, its capital, and answer the questions that follow in English.

> San José, la capital de Costa Rica, está situada[1] en el valle central del país[2], a una elevación de 3.795 pies de altura, con los volcanes Poás, Irazú y Barba al norte y la Sierra de Talamanca al sur. La ciudad tiene una población de 350.000 habitantes; la temperatura promedio[3] oscila entre 19 y 22 grados centígrados.
>
> En el centro de San José los turistas pueden ver[4] el Teatro Nacional, con su arquitectura barroca y neoclásica. Es el edificio[5] más notable de la ciudad. Otros lugares[6] de interés son el Museo del Oro Precolombino, el Museo de Jade, el Museo Nacional y el Museo de Arte Moderno. El suburbio de Escazú tiene excelentes restaurantes y una animada[7] vida nocturna.

[1]*located* [2]*country* [3]*average* [4]*see* [5]*building* [6]*places* [7]*lively*

1. Where is the capital of Costa Rica located?
2. What volcanoes are to the north of San José?
3. What is San José's average temperature?
4. What is the most remarkable building in San José?
5. Where can you find excellent restaurants and lively nightlife?

El Museo de Arte Moderno en San José

A ver el video

 1-45 Los personajes. Watch the first episode of **¡Pura vida!** and watch for the ways the characters greet each other. Take note of what seems to cause cultural confusion. Then, identify the characters using the brief descriptions below.

DM: Doña María

H: Hermés

F: Felipe

1. _____ Es fotógrafo.
2. _____ Tiene una camioneta (*van*).
3. _____ Compra (*buys*) fruta.
4. _____ Va al trabajo (*work*).

Después de ver el video

 1-46 La ciudad de San José. Connect with the Internet to search for photographs of the city of San José. Write three adjectives to describe the city.

> **Busca:** san jose costa rica

MODELO: La ciudad es…

Nuestro mundo

 Panoramas

 La diversidad del mundo hispano

01-58

Throughout *¡Arriba!* we encourage you to discover the diversity of Hispanic cultures across five continents. Use these images and your inference skills to understand the text. Look for words that are similar to English words (cognates) to help you derive their meaning. How does the Spanish colonization of the Americas differ from that of the English?

Tikal, Guatemala

A partir del siglo XVI, los exploradores españoles sacaron oro (*gold*) y plata (*silver*) de las Américas. Guardaban (*They kept*) las riquezas en la Torre de Oro en Sevilla.

La Torre de Oro, Sevilla, España

En el Nuevo Mundo, los españoles encontraron civilizaciones avanzadas como las de los incas, los aztecas y los mayas. Encontraron también paisajes extraordinarios.

Hace siglos (*For many centuries*) que se usan barcos de juncos (*reeds*) en el lago Titicaca.

Parque Nacional Torres del Paine, Chile

Lago Titicaca, Perú

La diversidad del mundo hispano

Número de hispanohablantes

en el mundo:	417 milliones
en EE.UU.:	45 millones (15%)
en Canadá:	800.000 (25%)
Estatus del español:	2° en el mundo (después del mandarín)
El español es lengua oficial en:	21 países

1-47 **Identifica.** Use the information in the photo captions and the Fact Box to identify the following.

1. the number of countries where Spanish is an official language

2. what was kept in the Torre de Oro de Sevilla

3. motives for the exploration of the Americas

4. important pre-Columbian cultures in the Americas in the sixteenth century

5. an adjective in Spanish to describe the Parque Nacional Torres del Paine, Chile

6. the number of Spanish speakers in the world

7. the percentage of the U.S. population that speaks Spanish

1-48 **Desafío.** Without looking at the map, work together to see how many Spanish-speaking countries you can name. After checking your answers, compare your results with those of other groups in the class.

1-49 **Proyecto: El Viejo Mundo y el Nuevo Mundo.** The cultural and physical diversity of the Hispanic world offers a wealth of opportunities for travel. Choose from **Barcelona, Cartagena de Indias, la Patagonia, Machu Picchu, Sevilla, Tikal,** or another place that interests you, to investigate more about its characteristics. Use the Modelo to write a summary of what you find; include the information that follows.

- su nombre y dónde está (*where it's located*)
- algún sitio histórico o de belleza (*beauty*) natural interesante
- cómo es
- una foto representativa

> ✎ **Busca:** barcelona, cartagena de indias, patagonia, machu picchu, sevilla, tikal

MODELO: *El sitio arqueológico de Copán está en Honduras. Es un sitio muy importante de la antigua civilización maya. Es importante ver las pirámides y las estelas de Copán. La foto es de Waxakajuun Ub'aah K'awiil.*

Para empezar: *[Nombre] está en... Es un sitio muy [adjetivo]. Tiene (it has)... Es importante ver (see)... La foto es de...*

Páginas

Versos sencillos, "XXXIX" (José Martí, Cuba)

The readings in *Páginas* come from the Spanish-speaking world and were written for native Spanish speakers. Remember that you do not have to comprehend every word in order to understand the passage and glean essential information. The related activities will help you develop reading comprehension strategies.

José Martí (1853–1895) was a prolific writer, intellectual, and patriot. Besides being known for his struggle to gain Cuba's independence from Spain, he is famous for his poetry, some of which has been popularized through song ("Guantanamera"). This selection comes from a series of short poems entitled *Versos sencillos* and discusses how the poet treats both his friends and his enemies.

ANTES DE LEER (*PRE-READING*)

1-50 Los cognados. Spanish and English share many cognates, words or expressions that are identical or similar in two languages— for example, **profesor**/professor and **universidad**/university. When you read Spanish, cognates will help you understand the text. Skim the poem and list the cognates you see. Then for each cognate, guess the meaning of the phrase in which it appears.

A LEER (*READING*)

1-51 El poema. First read the poem silently. Then, when you feel confident of its meaning, read it aloud.

XXXIX

Cultivo una rosa blanca,	
En julio como en enero,	
Para el amigo sincero	
Que me da° su mano° franca.	*gives/hand*
Y para el cruel que me arranca°	*yanks out*
El corazón° con que vivo,	*heart*
Cardo° ni ortiga° cultivo:	*thistle/nettle, a prickly plant*
Cultivo una rosa blanca.	

DESPUÉS DE LEER (*POST-READING*)

1-52 **¿Comprendiste? (*Did you understand?*)** Which of the following seem to describe the poet from what he writes?

1. Es blanco.

2. Es optimista.

3. Tiene amigos.

4. Tiene enemigos.

5. Es generoso.

6. Su mes favorito es julio.

1-53 **Los símbolos.** We often use colors as symbols for other things. Work with a classmate to match these colors with what you believe they could symbolize. What else do they symbolize for you?

1. _____ el rojo   a. la pureza (*purity*), la paz (*peace*)

2. _____ el amarillo   b. el misterio

3. _____ el blanco   c. la juventud (*youth*)

4. _____ el verde   d. la pasión

5. _____ el negro   e. la cobardía (*cowardice*)

1-54 **Guantanamera.** The song based on *Versos sencillos* has been performed and recorded countless times. Connect with the Internet to search for a version of the song. Write a short paragraph to answer the questions that follow.

> **Busca:** guantanamera video

- ¿Cómo se llama el/la cantante o el grupo?

- ¿De dónde es/son?

- ¿Cómo es/son?

- ¿Cómo es la canción?

1-55 **Tu "Guantanamera".** This song was written in the 1920's and popularized on a local Cuban radio program where the host closed each show by commenting in song on a current (often controversial) news event. The verse structure with eight syllables lent itself to fresh content any time the singer wished to improvise. Work together to compose a verse in English for "Guantanamera," and then share yours with the rest of the class.

MODELO: *I have an app for directions*
                  and one for restaurants around
                  I have an app for directions
                  and one for restaurants around
                  but when it comes to learning Spanish
                  I find that no good apps abound. . .
                  Guantanamera, guajira guantanamera...

📖 Taller

01-60

1-56 Una carta de presentación. When you write a letter of introduction, you want to tell something about your physical and personal characteristics and something about your life. In this first introduction, think of information you would share with a potential roommate. Follow the steps below to write five sentences in Spanish to include with a housing application.

> Santa Clara, CA
> 25 de septiembre de 2011
>
> ¡Hola!
>
> Me llamo Susanita. Soy extrovertida y simpática. Tengo clases muy interesantes. Mi profesora de español es la señora Carro. Es muy inteligente y trabajadora. Mi cumpleaños es el 10 de abril. Mi color favorito es el amarillo. . .
>
> ¡Hasta pronto!
>
> *Susanita*

ANTES DE ESCRIBIR (*PRE-WRITING*)

- Write a list of adjectives that describe you.
- Write a list of adjectives that describe your classes and your professors.

A ESCRIBIR (*WRITING*)

- Introduce yourself.
- Using adjectives from your list, describe what you are like. Use the connector **y** (*and*) to connect thoughts.
- Describe your classes and your professors.
- Say what your favorite color is (**Mi color favorito es el...**).
- Add any other personal detail about yourself (your birthday, favorite day of the week, etc.).

DESPUÉS DE ESCRIBIR (*POST-WRITING*)

- **Revisar** (*Review*)
  - ☐ Go back and make sure all of your adjectives agree with the nouns they modify.
  - ☐ Check your use of the verb **ser.**
- **Intercambiar** (*Exchange*)
  Exchange your letter with a classmate's. Then make suggestions and corrections, and add a comment about the letter.
- **Entregar** (*Turn in*)
  Rewrite your letter, incorporating your classmate's suggestions. Then turn in the letter to your instructor.

🔊 Vocabulario

Primera parte

Saludos Greetings

Buenos días. *Good morning.*
Buenas noches. *Good evening.*
Buenas tardes. *Good afternoon.*
¿Cómo está usted? *How are you? (for.)*
¿Cómo estás? *How are you? (inf.)*
Hola. *Hello, Hi.*
¿Qué pasa? *What's happening? What's up? (inf.)*
¿Qué tal? *How are you? What's up? (inf.)*

Presentaciones Introductions

¿Cómo se llama usted? *What's your name? (for.)*
¿Cómo te llamas? *What's your name? (inf.)*
Me llamo… *My name is … (lit. I call myself…)*
Mi nombre es… *My name is …*
Soy… *I am …*

Respuestas Responses

De nada. *You're welcome.*
¿De verdad? *Really?*
Encantado/a. *Nice to meet you.*
Gracias. *Thank you.*
Igualmente. *Likewise.*
Lo siento. *I'm sorry.*
Más o menos. *So-so (lit. More or less.)*
Mucho gusto. *Nice to meet you*
(Muy) Bien. *(Very) Good*
(Muy) Mal. *(Very) Bad*
Todo bien. *All's well*

Despedidas Farewells

Adiós. *Good-bye.*
Hasta luego. *See you later.*
Hasta mañana. *See you tomorrow.*
Hasta pronto. *See you soon.*
Nos vemos. *See you.*

Títulos Titles

el señor (Sr.) *Mr.*
la señora (Sra.) *Mrs., Ms.*
la señorita (Srta.) *Miss*

Sustantivos Nouns

la clase *class*
el estudiante *student (male)*
la estudiante *student (female)*
el profesor *professor (male)*
la profesora *professor (female)*
la tarea *homework*
la universidad *university*

Otras palabras y expresiones Other words and expressions

¿Cómo se escribe…? *How do you spell . . .?*
con *with*
mi/mis *my*
o *or*
tu/tus *your (inf.)*
y *and*

Segunda parte

En la clase In the classroom

el bolígrafo *pen*
la calculadora *calculator*
la computadora (portátil) *computer (laptop)*
el cuaderno *notebook*
el diccionario *dictionary*
el lápiz *pencil*
el libro *book*
el mapa *map*
el marcador *marker*
la mesa *table*
la mochila *backpack*
el papel *paper*
la pizarra (blanca) *chalkboard (white board)*
la puerta *door*
el reloj *clock, watch*
la silla *chair*
el teléfono celular/móvil *cell phone*
la tiza *chalk*

Otros sustantivos Other nouns

el hombre *man*
la mujer *woman*

Adjetivos Adjectives

barato/a *cheap, inexpensive*
caro/a *expensive*
claro/a *light (color)*
grande *big*
oscuro/a *dark (color)*
pequeño/a *small*

Los colores Colors

amarillo/a *yellow*
anaranjado/a *orange*
azul *blue*
blanco/a *white*
color café *brown*
gris *gray*
morado/a *purple*
negro/a *black*
rojo/a *red*
rosado/a *pink*
verde *green*

Adverbio Adverb

aquí *here*

Verbos Verbs

hay *there is/are*
necesitar *to need*
ser *to be*
tengo (tener) *I have (to have)*

Otras expresiones Other expressions

¡Qué barbaridad! *What nonsense!*
¡Qué estudiantes! *What students!*

Numbers 0–100 *See page 10.*
Expressions for students and the class *See page 21.*
The days of the week *See page 13.*
Subject pronouns *See page 24.*
The months and the seasons *See page 13–14.*
Descriptive adjectives *See page 30.*

2

¿De dónde eres?

Readiness Check

Descubre España

«Dime con quien andas
y te diré quien eres».

Refrán: You can judge a man by the company he keeps.

Pablo Picasso, pintor prolífico, nació en Málaga. Esta es una de sus obras más famosas.

Con sus tres grandes victorias en 2010 (Roland Garros, Wimbledon y el US Open), Rafael Nadal se ha convertido en el número uno del mundo en tenis por segunda vez en tres años. Es el mejor tenista en la historia de España.

¡Así lo decimos! VOCABULARIO

¡Así es la vida! ¿Quiénes son?

El Café Hemisferio es un lugar muy popular entre los estudiantes de la Universidad Complutense de Madrid.

PACO: ¿Quién es la muchacha morena, la que tiene la computadora portátil?

CHEMA: Es Isabel, una estudiante de Sevilla. Y la otra muchacha, con el suéter negro, es Clara.

ISABEL: ¿Quién es el chico joven con la mochila?

CLARA: Es Carlos. Y la mujer que está con él es la profesora Vargas. Es venezolana y muy buena profesora de filosofía.

ÁNGELES: ¡Pero, hombre! ¿De quién recibes tantos correos electrónicos?

RAMÓN: ¡Es que tengo muchos amigos!

Vocabulario Las descripciones y las nacionalidades

Variaciones

In the Spanish-speaking world, many terms are used to describe an attractive physical appearance. In Spain, **guapo/a** is used frequently to describe both males and females. In Mexico, **linda** is typical to refer to a female. The terms **bonita** and **hermosa** are used in many countries, but again, only for a female. In addition to **guapo**, a man is usually **atractivo, apuesto, buen tipo,** or **bien parecido.**

Adjetivos descriptivos Descriptive adjectives

activo/a   *active*
alto/a   *tall*
bajo/a   *short*
bonito/a   *pretty, cute*
delgado/a   *slender*
entusiasta   *enthusiastic*
feo/a   *ugly*
flaco/a   *skinny*
gordo/a   *fat*
guapo/a   *good-looking*
joven   *young*
moreno/a   *dark (skin, hair)*
nuevo/a   *new*
pobre   *poor*
rico/a   *rich*
rubio/a   *blond (fair)*
viejo/a   *old*

La mujer es joven, bonita y rica.

Algunas nacionalidades[1] Some nationalities

argentino/a   *Argentine*
canadiense   *Canadian*
chileno/a   *Chilean*
colombiano/a   *Colombian*
cubano/a   *Cuban*
dominicano/a   *Dominican*
ecuatoriano/a   *Ecuadorian*
español/a   *Spanish*
mexicano/a   *Mexican*
norteamericano/a (estadounidense)   *American*
panameño/a   *Panamanian*
peruano/a   *Peruvian*
puertorriqueño/a   *Puerto Rican*
salvadoreño/a   *Salvadoran*
venezolano/a   *Venezuelan*

El muchacho colombiano es entusiasta.

El muchacho es alto y la muchacha es baja.

Los lugares Places

la capital   *capital city*
la ciudad   *city*
el país   *country*

Las personas People

el/la amigo/a   *friend*
el/la muchacho/a   *boy/girl*
los padres   *parents*

Adverbios Adverbs

ahora (mismo)   *(right) now*
también   *also*
tarde   *late*
temprano   *early*

Conjunciones Conjunctions

pero   *but*
porque   *because*

---

[1]Adjectives of nationality are not capitalized in Spanish.

Cultura en vivo

In Spain, students often frequent a **bar estudiantil** where they can have a coffee or other refreshment between classes. The bar may be on or off campus or in a student residence, **colegio mayor.** How does this compare with your university?

APLICACIÓN

2-1 ¿Quién eres tú? Listen to José and his friends talk about themselves. Based on the information in **¡Así es la vida!,** write the number of each monologue next to the corresponding name.

_____ Carlos _____ Isabel _____ Paco _____ Ramón _____ la profesora Vargas

2-2 La Feria del Caballo. Complete the conversation between two people who meet at the *Feria del Caballo* in southern Spain. Use words and expressions from the following list.

~~amiga~~	aquí	capital	~~cómo~~
~~argentino~~	~~eres~~	~~española~~	me llamo

JUAN: ¡Hola! Soy Juan Luis Ruiz. ¿(1) _____ te llamas?

MARISOL: (2) _____ Marisol. ¿De dónde (3) _____, Juan?

JUAN: Soy (4) _____.

MARISOL: ¡Ah! Mi (5) _____ Ana es de Mendoza, en el oeste de Argentina.

JUAN: Yo soy de Buenos Aires, la (6) _____. ¿Y tú, Marisol? ¿De dónde eres?

MARISOL: Ay, yo soy (7) _____. Soy de (8) _____, de Jerez de la Frontera.

La gente baila en la calle durante la Feria del Caballo en Jerez de la Frontera, España.

2-3 ¿Cómo son?   Take turns describing the people, places, and things listed below using words from the list and see if you agree with each other. Say **Sí, es cierto** to indicate that you agree. If you don't, offer your own opinion. Be sure that adjectives agree with the nouns they modify.

dominicano/a	moreno/a	bonito/a
norteamericano/a	la capital	un país
una ciudad	pequeño/a	colombiano/a
peruano/a	delgado/a	grande
español/a	puertorriqueño/a	joven
rico/a	mexicano/a	rubio/a
chileno/a	viejo/a	

MODELO: Madrid
　　　　　　E1: *Madrid es una ciudad pequeña.*
　　　　　　E2: *No es cierto. Es grande.*

México	Isabel Allende	Bolivia
Buenos Aires	Manny Ramírez	Penélope Cruz
Lima	Los Ángeles	Madrid

2-4 ¿Cuál es su (*his/her*) nacionalidad?   Give the names of the countries where the following people are from and their nationalities.

MODELO: Felipe de Borbón / España
　　　　　　E1: *¿De dónde es Felipe de Borbón?*
　　　　　　E2: *Es de España. Es español.*

1. Shakira / Colombia
2. Penélope Cruz y Pedro Almodóvar / España
3. José Martí / Cuba
4. Mariano Rivera / Panamá
5. Salma Hayek / México
6. Pedro Martínez / República Dominicana
7. Yo…
8. Nosotros…

Pedro Almodóvar, director, con Penélope Cruz, actriz

Shakira, cantautora y roquera

Pedro Martínez, beisbolista

Presencia hispana

Many immigrants from the Basque region of Spain settled in the western regions of North America beginning as early as 1840. Then, during World War II, the U.S. government recruited Basque workers to help alleviate labor shortages. There are people of Basque heritage in every state, but nowhere is there a greater Basque presence than in Idaho, where many important community and political leaders are of Basque descent. Both **eusquera** and **español** are official languages of the Basque region of Spain. What ethnic groups predominate in your area? Do any preserve their heritage language?

2-5 Yo soy…   With a partner, take turns introducing yourselves, saying where you are from and what you are like.

MODELO: *Hola, soy _____. Soy de_____. Soy_____ y_____. No soy_____.*

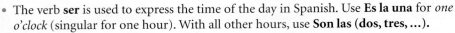

1. Telling time

02-07
to 02-10

¿Qué hora es?

- The verb **ser** is used to express the time of the day in Spanish. Use **Es la una** for *one o'clock* (singular for one hour). With all other hours, use **Son las (dos, tres, …).**

  Es la una.   *It's one o'clock.*
  Son las dos de la tarde.   *It's two o'clock in the afternoon.*

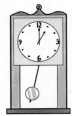

- To express minutes *past* or *after* an hour, use **y.**

  Son las tres **y** veinte.   *It's twenty past three. (It's three twenty.)*

- To express minutes before an hour (*to* or *till*) use **menos.**[1]

  Son las siete menos   *It's ten to (till) seven.*
    diez.

- The terms **cuarto** and **media** are equivalent to the English expressions *quarter* (fifteen minutes) and *half* (thirty minutes). The numbers **quince** and **treinta** are interchangeable with **cuarto** and **media.**

  Son las cinco menos **cuarto**   *It's a quarter to five. (It's four*
    (quince).   *forty-five.)*
  Son las cuatro y **media (treinta).** *It's half past four. (It's four thirty.)*

- For *noon* and *midnight*, use **(el) mediodía** and **(la) medianoche. El** and **la** may be used when saying that something occurs *at noon* or *at midnight*.

  Es **mediodía.**   *It's noon (midday).*
  Mi amigo llega a **(la) medianoche.** *My friend arrives at midnight.*

---

[1]This is how time is traditionally told. It is now common to use **y** for :01 to :59. **7:50 = Son las siete y cincuenta.**

- To ask at what time an event takes place, use **¿A qué hora...?** To answer, use **a la/las** + *time*.

¿A qué hora es la clase?	*(At) What time is the class?*
Es **a las** ocho y media.	*It is at half past eight.*

- The expressions **de la mañana, de la tarde,** or **de la noche** are used when telling specific times. **En punto** means *on the dot* or *sharp*.

La fiesta es a las ocho **de la noche**.	*The party is at eight o'clock in the evening.*
El partido de fútbol es a las nueve **en punto**.	*The soccer game is at nine sharp.*

- The expressions **por la mañana, por la tarde,** and **por la noche** are used as a general reference to *in the morning, in the afternoon,* and *in the evening*.

No tengo clases **por la mañana**.	*I don't have classes in the morning.*

- In many Spanish-speaking countries, the 24-hour clock is used for schedules and official timekeeping. The zero hour is equivalent to midnight, and 12:00 is noon. The p.m. hours are 13:00–24:00. To convert from the 24-hour clock, subtract 12 hours from hours 13:00 and above.

  21:00 = **las nueve de la noche**

  16:30 = **las cuatro y media de la tarde**

Study tips – Learning to tell time in Spanish

1. To become proficient in telling time in Spanish, you'll need to make sure you have learned Spanish numbers well. Practice counting by fives to thirty: **cinco, diez, quince, veinte, veinticinco, treinta.**
2. Think about and say aloud times that are important to you: **Tengo clases a las nueve, a las diez..., Hay una fiesta a las...,** etc.
3. Every time you look at your watch, say the time in Spanish.

APLICACIÓN

2-6 La vida diaria de Rafael Nadal. Refer back to page 41 to see a photo of Rafael Nadal, the famous Spanish tennis player. Read about Nadal's schedule then answer the questions that follow in Spanish.

> Rafael Nadal, el famoso tenista español, tiene un día muy activo. A las siete de la mañana, está en la cancha de tenis. Practica con su instructor hasta[1] las diez de la mañana. A las once y media, está en casa con su familia. A la una y cuarto de la tarde, está en un restaurante. A las cinco, está en la Casa del Café en el centro. A las nueve de la noche, está otra vez en casa con su familia. Ahora, son las once y media y Rafael ve[2] la televisión. Mañana es otro[3] día.

[1]*until* [2]*is watching* [3]*another*

1. ¿A qué hora está en un restaurante?

2. ¿Dónde está a las cinco?

3. ¿A qué hora está en casa con su familia?

4. ¿Qué hora es ahora?

5. Y tú, ¿dónde estás a las siete y media de la mañana?

2-7 Mi día.   What is a typical day for you? How does your schedule compare to those of your classmates?

Paso 1   First complete these statements as they relate to you.

MODELO: Estoy en la universidad *a las ocho de la mañana*.

1. Me levanto (*get up*) _____.
2. Trabajo (*I work*) _____.
3. Estudio _____.
4. Estoy en clase _____.
5. Estoy en casa _____.
6. Estoy en la cafetería de la universidad _____.

Paso 2   Now compare your responses with those of a classmate.

MODELO: *Yo estoy en la universidad a las ocho de la mañana. ¿Y tú?*

2-8 ¿Qué hora es?   Look at the clocks and say whether the following statements are **cierto** or **falso.** Correct any false statements.

MODELO:

Son las dos y cuarto de la tarde.
Falso, son las dos y media de la tarde.

1. Son las dos y cuarto de la noche.

2. Son las siete menos cuarto de la mañana.

3. Son las ocho menos veinte de la noche.

4. Son las cuatro menos cuarto de la mañana.

5. Son las doce menos diez de la noche.

6. Es medianoche.

2-9A **¿A qué hora?**   Complete your calendar by asking your partner when the events with missing times take place. To ask your partner to repeat something, remember to say: **Repite, por favor. Estudiante B,** please see **Appendix 1,** page A-3.

MODELO: la clase de inglés (9:30)
> ESTUDIANTE A: *¿A qué hora es la clase de inglés?*
> ESTUDIANTE B: *Es a las nueve y media de la mañana.*

Estudiante A:

Hora	Actividad
08:00	la clase de historia
_____	la clase de arte
11:45	la clase de español
_____	la conferencia[1]
14:55	la reunión
_____	el examen
17:40	el partido de fútbol
_____	el programa "Ídolo americano" en la televisión
21:15	la fiesta
_____	el programa de noticias en la televisión

[1]*lecture*

 2-10   Investigación. El AVE.   *El AVE (Tren de Alta Velocidad)* is Spain's popular high-speed train. Connect to the Internet and search for links to the *AVE* web page, where you will find information about schedules and train service from Madrid to Barcelona, Málaga, and Sevilla. Select the destination city and route most interesting to you and provide the following information.

> **Busca:** renfe horarios y precios; renfe ave

- un destino desde Madrid
- número de tren
- hora de salida (*departure*)
- hora de llegada (*arrival*)
- días y fechas que no tiene servicio
- precio para clase turista
- 2 prestaciones (*services*) en clase turista
- precio total en dólares

 ¡Hola!

Cultura en vivo

Many believe that punctuality is more relaxed in the Hispanic world. It is true that in social contexts, guests often arrive later than the appointed time for a party. However, in most countries, trains and buses adhere to strict schedules and leave and arrive on time. In business and academic contexts, practices vary, but it is becoming more common for meetings and classes to begin on time. When is punctuality important for you, and when is it acceptable to be late?

2. Formation of *yes/no* questions and negation

La formación de preguntas *sí/no*

- In Spanish, a *yes/no* question uses rising intonation. There are three ways to form a *yes/no* question, depending on the intent of the speaker. Note that an inverted question mark (¿) is used at the beginning of the question, and the standard question mark (?) closes the question.

- To request new information, invert the order of the subject (S) and verb (V) found in a declarative sentence.

    Declarative (S + V):

    Picasso es de Málaga.   *Picasso is from Málaga.*

    Request new information: (V + S):

    ¿Es Picasso de Málaga?   *Is Picasso from Málaga?*

- To express disbelief about information already given, maintain the declarative order (S + V), but with rising intonation (called an *echo* question).

    ¿Picasso es de Málaga?   *Picasso is from Málaga?*

- To confirm information already given or supposed, simply add a tag word or phrase, such as **¿no?** or **¿verdad?** with rising intonation to the end of the statement.

    Rafael Nadal es de Mallorca, ¿no?
    Penélope Cruz es de Madrid, ¿verdad?

Negación

- To make a sentence negative, simply place **no** before the verb.

    Juan **no** es de Portugal.   *Juan is not from Portugal.*

    Nosotros **no** somos de España.   *We're not from Spain.*

- When answering a question in the negative, the word **no** followed by a comma also precedes the verb phrase.

    ¿Son los cantantes Thalia y   *Are the singers Thalia*
    José José de España?   *and José José from Spain?*
    No, no son de España.   *No, they're not from Spain.*

50 ●●● cincuenta

APLICACIÓN

2-11 ¿Es verdad? Take turns asking and answering *yes/no* questions. Comment on the truthfulness of each other's responses. Include one original question.

MODELO: E1: *¿Eres norteamericano/a?*
E2: *No, no soy norteamericano/a.*
E1: *¿De verdad?*
E2: *Sí, de verdad. Soy de Francia.*

1. ¿Eres canadiense?

2. ¿Son profesores tus padres?

3. Tus amigos son trabajadores, ¿no?

4. ¿Eres de San Francisco?

5. Tu familia es rica, ¿verdad?

6. ¿Son pobres los profesores?

7. Eres bajo/a, ¿no?

8. ¿…?

2-12 ¿Verdad? Ask each other questions based on the following statements by inverting the subject and the verb, or using a tag question. Respond to your partner's questions in a truthful manner.

MODELO: La novela *Don Quijote* es famosa.
E1: *¿Es famosa la novela* Don Quijote? *(La novela* Don Quijote *es famosa, ¿verdad?)*
E2: *Sí, la novela* Don Quijote *es famosa.*

1. La actriz Eva Mendes es baja y fea.

2. Pedro Almodóvar es director de cine.

3. Pablo Picasso es pintor.

4. El flamenco es un baile español.

5. Los tenistas españoles son perezosos.

6. Édgar Rentería es jugador de béisbol.

7. Penélope Cruz y Javier Bardem son poetas.

8. Alberto Contador es un ciclista famoso.

Alberto Contador, ganador del Tour de Francia 2010

3. Interrogative words

02-17
to 02-22

¿Quién eres tú?

- Interrogative words are often used at the beginning of a sentence to form questions. Here is a list of the most frequently used interrogative words:

Palabras interrogativas		Ejemplos	
¿Cómo...?	How . . . ? What . . . ?	**¿Cómo** estás? **¿Cómo** eres?	How are you? What are you like?
¿Cuál(es)...?	Which (one/ones) . . . ?	**¿Cuál** es tu libro?	Which one is your book?
¿Cuándo...?	When . . . ?	**¿Cuándo** es tu clase de español?	When is your Spanish class?
¿Cuánto/a(s)?	How much (many) . . . ?	**¿Cuántos** estudiantes hay?	How many students are there?
¿Dónde...?	Where . . . ?	**¿Dónde** hay una silla?	Where is there a chair?
¿De dónde...?	From where . . . ?	**¿De dónde** es Almodóvar?	Where is Almodóvar from?
¿Adónde...?	(To) Where . . . ?	**¿Adónde** vas?	Where are you going?
¿Por qué...?	Why . . . ?	**¿Por qué** no hay clase hoy?	Why is there no class today?
¿Qué...?	What . . . ?	**¿Qué** estudias?	What are you studying?
¿Quién(es)...?	Who . . . ?	**¿Quién** es ella?	Who is she?
¿De quién(es)...?	Whose . . . ?	**¿De quién** es el bolígrafo?	Whose is the pen?

- When you ask a question using an interrogative word, your intonation usually will fall.

  ¿Cómo se llama el profesor?   *What is the professor's name?*

- Both **qué** and **cuál** may be translated as *what* or *which*, but they are not interchangeable. Generally, **qué** is used to request a definition or explanation. It can also be followed by a noun to mean *which*. **Cuál** implies a choice or selection and generally is not followed by a noun. Use the plural **cuáles** when that choice includes more than one person or thing.

¿Qué tienes?	*What do you have?*
¿Qué es esto?	*What is this?*
¿Qué clase tienes ahora?	*Which (What) class do you have now?*
¿Cuál prefieres?	*Which (one) do you prefer?*
¿Cuál es la fecha de hoy?	*What is today's date?*
¿Cuáles son los meses del año?	*What are the months of the year?*

52 ●●● cincuenta y dos

APLICACIÓN

2-13 Los sanfermines. People from around the world flock to Pamplona for *San Fermín*, one of Spain's most famous festivals.

Paso 1 First read the description of this festival; then match the questions and their responses that follow.

La fiesta de San Fermín en España es muy famosa. Siempre es en Pamplona, en el norte de España. El primer día es el 6 de julio y el último día es el 14 de julio. Durante nueve días sueltan[1] los toros que corren[2] por las calles. Los jóvenes corren delante[3] de los toros. Es muy peligroso, pero también muy emocionante.[4] El novelista norteamericano Ernest Hemingway, famoso por *The Sun Also Rises,* describió muy bien la fiesta de los sanfermines.

[1]*turn loose* [2]*run* [3]*in front* [4]*exciting*

1. _____ ¿Dónde es la fiesta?
2. _____ ¿Cuándo es el primer día de la fiesta?
3. _____ ¿Cuál es el último día de la fiesta?
4. _____ ¿Quiénes corren por las calles?
5. _____ ¿Cómo es la fiesta?
6. _____ ¿Quién es el autor norteamericano que se asocia con esta fiesta?

a. Ernest Hemingway
b. emocionante
c. el 6 de julio
d. en Pamplona, España
e. los toros y los jóvenes
f. el 14 de julio

Paso 2 Now use interrogative words to complete the following conversation between two people who meet in Pamplona and are planning to run with the bulls.

JESÚS: Hola, (1) ¿ _____ te llamas?

CARMEN: Me llamo Carmen Domínguez. ¿Y tú?

JESÚS: Soy Jesús Sánchez, soy de Salamanca. Y tú, (2) ¿ _____ eres?

CARMEN: Soy de Bilbao. (3) ¿ _____ estás aquí en Pamplona?

JESÚS: Pero chica, ¡estoy aquí para correr con los toros en las fiestas! Es mi primera visita a Pamplona.

CARMEN: Pues, yo participo casi todos los años. (4) ¿ _____ haces[1] en Salamanca?

JESÚS: Soy estudiante de literatura inglesa. Me gusta mucho Hemingway y estoy aquí para vivir los sanfermines como en la novela.

CARMEN: ¡Genial! (5) ¿ _____ estudias?

JESÚS: En la Universidad de Salamanca… Ay, estoy un poco nervioso. ¿(6) _____ son los toros? ¿Son muy grandes?

CARMEN: ¡Imagínate! Son grandes y rápidos, pero es una experiencia muy emocionante.

JESÚS: Y ¿_____ empezamos[2] a correr?

CARMEN: ¡Ahora! ¡Vamos! ¡Ya están aquí los toros!

JESÚS: ¡Ay, Dios mío!

[1]*do you do* [2]*begin*

¡Hola!
Cultura en vivo

Many of the residents of Pamplona leave the city during *los sanfermines* as more than 200,000 tourists descend on the town for that week. These inexperienced runners often take risks that cause unnecessary injuries. What kind of event or festival would make you want to leave town for a few days?

2-14 Rafael Nadal. Read the description about Rafael Nadal, and then answer the questions below.

Rafael Nadal Perera es uno de los tenistas más famosos del mundo. Es originalmente de la isla de Mallorca, España, donde nace el 3 de junio de 1986. En 2002, a los quince años, gana en Mallorca el primer torneo importante. Es uno de los tenistas más jóvenes en alcanzar[1] el puesto[2] número dos del mundo. En 2008 gana treinta y dos torneos, incluyendo los *ATP Master Series* de Monte Carlo, Roma, Montreal, Madrid y Wimbledon y llega a ser número uno del mundo en tenis. Sus fanáticos están convencidos de que Rafa permanecerá[3] en ese puesto por muchos años.

[1]*reach*   [2]*position*   [3]*will remain*

1. ¿De dónde es Rafael Nadal?

2. ¿Cuándo nace?

3. ¿Qué gana a los quince años?

4. ¿Cuántos torneos gana en 2008?

5. ¿De qué están convencidos sus fanáticos?

2-15 ¿Qué? o ¿Cuál? Complete the questions with **qué** or **cuál(es)** depending on the context. Then answer the questions.

MODELO: ¿*Cuál* es la fecha de hoy?
        Es 2 de octubre.

1. ¿ _____ hora es?

2. ¿ _____ es tu clase favorita?

3. ¿ _____ es tu cuaderno?

4. ¿ _____ día es hoy?

5. ¿A _____ hora es la clase de español?

6. ¿ _____ es la fecha de tu cumpleaños?

7. ¿ _____ son tus libros en la mesa?

8. ¿ _____ hay en tu mochila?

 2-16A ¿Quién eres? ¿Cómo eres? Ask questions to learn about your partner's new identity.

Paso 1 Assume the identity of one of the people outlined below and read through the information. **Estudiante B,** please see **Appendix 1,** page A-3.

Estudiante A:

♂	♀
Ramón Santos Gómez	Luisa Pérez Fernández
Universidad Autónoma Nacional	Universidad Complutense de Madrid
España	Colombia
biología	sociología
el profesor Sánchez	la profesora Alvarado
fantástico	muy interesante
50 estudiantes en la clase	25 estudiantes en la clase
alto y delgado	baja y bonita

Paso 2 Ask each other about yourselves to find out what you have in common. Use interrogatives such as **qué, dónde, cómo, cuántos/as,** and **cuál** in the following prompts to help you form your questions. **Estudiante B,** please see **Appendix 1,** page A-3.

MODELO: ESTUDIANTE A: *¿Dónde estudias?*
ESTUDIANTE B: *Estudio en la Universidad Nacional. ¿Y tú? ¿Dónde estudias?*
ESTUDIANTE A: *Estudio…*

Estudiante A:

1. ¿_____ te llamas?
2. ¿_____ estudias?
3. ¿De _____ eres?
4. ¿_____ eres?

5. ¿_____ es tu clase de…?
6. ¿_____ es el profesor de…?
7. ¿_____ es tu clase favorita?
8. ¿_____ estudiantes hay en la clase?

2-17 Profesor/a… Ask your professor several questions. He/she will respond truthfully to some, but not all of the questions. See if you can guess which answers are true and react with **¡Es cierto!** or **¡No es verdad!**

MODELO: ESTUDIANTE: *Profesor/a, ¿de dónde es usted?*
PROFESOR/A: *Soy de Bolivia.*
ESTUDIANTE: *¿De verdad?*
PROFESOR/A: *Sí, es cierto, de la ciudad de La Paz.*

¿Cuánto saben?

02-23
to 02-27

First, ask yourself if you can perform the following functions in Spanish. Then act out the scenarios with two or three classmates. Ask and respond to at least three questions in each situation.

✓ CAN YOU . . .

☐ describe yourself, other people, and things?

☐ ask and respond to simple questions?

☐ ask for and tell time?

WITH YOUR CLASSMATE(S) . . .

Situación: Gente bonita
You're looking at a magazine with popular personalities. Take turns describing the people you see and agree or disagree with each other according to your opinion. Use descriptive adjectives such as **alto/a, guapo/a, joven,** etc.
Para empezar: *Para mí, Penélope Cruz es…*

Situación: En un café
You meet each other for the first time when you share a table in the coffee shop. Ask each other questions to find out what you have in common. Use interrogatives such as **cómo, dónde, qué, cuál,** etc.
Para empezar: *Hola, ¿cómo te llamas? ¿Cuál es tu…?*

Situación: En grupo
You've formed a small group to work on a joint project. Ask each other what time your classes are to see when it is convenient to meet outside of class. Include **de la mañana, de la tarde,** and **de la noche** as needed.
Para empezar: *¿A qué hora…? ¿Cuándo…?¿Tienes clase a …?*

📖 Perfiles

02-28 to 02-29

Mi experiencia

NOMBRES, APELLIDOS Y APODOS (*NICKNAMES*)

2-18 Para ti. How does a name reflect a person's heritage? When do women in the U.S. and Canada keep their maiden names after marriage? Are there instances when married women use both their maiden and their married names? If you are a woman, do you plan to keep your maiden name if you marry? Why or why not? Do you have a nickname? Read about Gladys's experiences in Spain learning about names and think about what your complete name would be if you followed the same custom.

¡Saludos de Gladys García Sandoval! ¡Escribo desde Salamanca, España! This is my first year abroad studying film at the Universidad de Salamanca, and I'm writing this blog to keep my friends up-to-date with my experiences.

This week the department is doing a film series of one of my favorite actors, Penélope Cruz Sánchez, although you probably know her best as Penélope Cruz. People's names here fascinate me: people use both their paternal surnames (**el apellido paterno**) and their maternal surnames (**el apellido materno**), so in Penélope's case, you can guess that her father's last name is **Cruz** and her mother's **Sánchez**. Recently married, she still keeps **Cruz** as her surname. I think there are advantages to these naming practices; for example, if a woman gets married (or divorced, for that matter), her name never changes, as she keeps her paternal surname throughout her life. This way too, her children will keep her family name alive. It's curious though, that some people are known by their **apellido materno,** as is the case with president José Rodriguez **Zapatero** and the famous actor **Javier** Ángel Encinas **Bardem.** I think the popular media may be responsible for this usage, or perhaps these are personal choices. What is important for me is that with this custom, a person's name becomes his/her identification for life and reflects family pride. Of course many people here also use **apodos.** In magazines I see that Penélope's friends call her **Pe,** but other nicknames can be hard to figure out. For example, everyone calls my friend, **Chema,** which is a popular nickname in Spain for José María, his real name.

One of my favorite Spanish musicians is Alejandro Sánchez Pizarro, better known as Alejandro Sanz. He's so handsome! I'm hoping to meet him while I'm here! Ha, ha! Have you heard his song with Alicia Keys? You really need to listen to their song, "Looking for Paradise." ¡Es genial!

👥 **2-19 En su opinión.** Take turns asking and answering the following questions.

1. ¿Cuál es el apellido paterno del Presidente del Gobierno de España? ¿Cuál es el apellido materno de Penélope?

2. ¿Cuál es la nacionalidad de todas estas personas famosas? ¿Cuáles son sus apodos?

3. ¿Cuál es tu apellido materno? ¿Y tu apellido paterno?

4. ¿Tienes apodo? ¿Tienes algún amigo con un apodo raro o extraño? ¿Por qué tiene ese apodo?

Mi música

"LOOKING FOR PARADISE" (ALEJANDRO SANZ, ESPAÑA; ALICIA KEYS, EE. UU.)

Throughout his life and professional career, Alejandro Sanz has worked to broaden his musical style while never venturing far from his strengths. By the end of the nineties, he'd expanded his fan base from Spain to the world, collaborating with fellow Latin superstars, most memorably Shakira in her massive Grammy-winning hit "La Tortura." In "Looking for Paradise" from *Paraíso Express*, Sanz collaborates with Alicia Keys in a bilingual love song.

Antes de ver escuchar

2-20 La letra. Complete the table below with the correct definite and indefinite articles for the words found in the lyrics of "Looking for Paradise." Guess what each means, and then use a bilingual dictionary and the glossary at the back of the textbook to find out the meanings of the words.

Palabra	Artículo definido	Artículo indefinido	Significado en inglés
paraíso			
mundo			
momento			
sentimiento			
vida			
música			
camino			

Para ver y escuchar

 2-21 La canción. This song relates a search for someone. Connect to the Internet to search for a video or recording of Sanz and Keys performing this piece. You may also want to search for the lyrics (*letra*).

> **Busca:** looking for paradise sanz video; looking for paradise sanz letra
>
> **If you would like to purchase this song:** *Go to iTunes Store>Music> More to Explore>iMix>Arriba 6e*

As you listen or watch, write down your answers to the following questions.

1. ¿Cuál es el título de la canción?
2. ¿Qué instrumentos escuchas en la canción? (el piano, el sintetizador, la guitarra, el violín…)
3. ¿Cómo es el ritmo de la canción? (lento, rápido, melancólico…)
4. ¿Cómo es la canción en tu opinión? ¿Te gusta? ¿Por qué?

Después de ver y escuchar

 2-22 Comprensión. Practice asking and answering the questions in 2-21 with a partner.

2-23 Descripciones. Use the photo of Alejandro Sanz and Alicia Keys and adjectives from **¡Así lo decimos!** to describe each artist in Spanish.

MODELO: *Alejandro Sanz es...   Alicia Keys es...*

Due 10-3 whole pg

¡Así lo decimos! VOCABULARIO

 ¡Así es la vida! ¿Qué pasa?

02-30

En la Facultad de Lenguas en la Universidad Complutense de Madrid, Celia busca un tutor.

SECRETARIA:	Hola, buenas tardes.
CELIA:	Buenas tardes. Soy estudiante de intercambio[1] de Canadá y…
SECRETARIA:	Muy bien. ¿Y…?
CELIA:	Necesito ayuda. Estudio lenguas y…
SECRETARIA:	Ya sé. Mañana tiene examen y necesita tutor. ¿Su nombre y número de teléfono…?

[1]*exchange*

SECRETARIA:	Hola, Rogelio. ¿Qué pasa?
ROGELIO:	Bueno, busco trabajo como tutor de lenguas.
SECRETARIA:	¡Qué suerte! Aquí tienes el nombre y número de teléfono de una chica que tiene examen mañana.
ROGELIO:	Perfecto. Hablo con ella ahora mismo. ¡Gracias!

Vocabulario ¿Qué haces? ¿Qué te gusta hacer?

02-31
to 02-34

Otras nacionalidades (País) | Other nationalities (Country)

alemán¹, alemana (Alemania) *German (Germany)*
brasileño/a (Brasil) *Brazilian (Brazil)*
chino/a (China) *Chinese (China)*
coreano/a (Corea) *Korean (Korea)*
francés, francesa (Francia) *French (France)*
inglés, inglesa (Inglaterra) *English (England)*
italiano/a (Italia) *Italian (Italy)*
japonés, japonesa (Japón) *Japanese (Japan)*
portugués, portuguesa (Portugal) *Portuguese (Portugal)*
ruso/a (Rusia) *Russian (Russia)*

Me gusta
leer un libro.

Variaciones

In Mexico, the verb **platicar** is used commonly in place of **hablar** to express *to talk or to have a conversation.* **Hablar,** in contrast, usually means *to call (by phone)* in Mexico, whereas in other countries, **llamar** is the verb typically used.

¿Qué haces? | What do you do?

abrir *to open*
asistir a *to attend*
aprender *to learn*
ayudar *to help*
bailar *to dance*
beber *to drink*
buscar *to look (for)*
comer *to eat*
comprar *to buy*
comprender *to understand*
creer *to believe*
deber (+ *infinitive*) *to owe (to ought to do something)*
decidir *to decide*
desear *to wish*
enseñar *to teach*
escribir *to write*
escuchar *to listen*
estudiar *to study*
hablar *to speak, talk*
leer *to read*
llegar *to arrive*
mirar *to look at*
practicar (un deporte) *to practice, to play (a sport)*
preparar *to prepare*
recibir *to receive*
tomar *to drink, to take*
trabajar *to work*
vender *to sell*
ver *to see, to watch*
viajar *to travel*
vivir *to live*

Me gusta ver la
televisión.

Me gusta hablar
por teléfono.

Adjetivos | Adjectives

difícil *difficult*
fácil *easy*

 ¿Te gusta
tomar café?

Otras palabras y expresiones | Other words and expressions

las lenguas *languages*
¿Qué te gusta hacer? *What do you like to do?*
Me gusta² (+ *infinitive*) *I like (+ infinitive)*
Te gusta (+ *infinitive*) *You (inf.) like (+ infinitive)*
¡Qué suerte! *How lucky!*

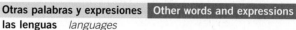

¹In Spanish, the masculine singular form of the nationality will often correspond to the language spoken in the country.
²You will learn more about *gustar* and similar verbs in *Capítulo 6.*

Letras y sonidos

More on vowels in Spanish

In addition to the vowel sounds for **i** and **u** (**li-bro, lu-nes**), these letters also may represent *glides,* which are brief, weak sounds that combine with a vowel to form a single syllable. The letter **y** also represents a glide in some words.

a-diós	sie-te	vein-te	soy	hay
nue-vo	gua-po	Eu-ro-pa	es-tu-diáis	U-ru-guay

The letters **i** and **u** are not always glides when next to other vowels in Spanish, however. When they are vowels and not glides, a written accent mark is used.

dí-a	rí-o	pa-ís	Ra-úl

APLICACIÓN

2-24 ¿Quién es? Refer to **¡Así es la vida!** on page 58 and identify the speaker of each statement below.

C: Celia   **R:** Rogelio   **S:** la secretaria

1. _____ Busco trabajo.
2. _____ Necesito tutor.
3. _____ Tengo examen mañana.
4. _____ Trabajo en una oficina.

5. _____ Soy estudiante de intercambio.
6. _____ Mi clase es difícil.
7. _____ Soy un poco impaciente.
8. _____ Hablamos más de una lengua.

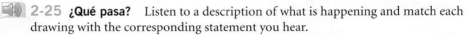

2-25 ¿Qué pasa? Listen to a description of what is happening and match each drawing with the corresponding statement you hear.

_____ _____ _____ _____ _____ _____

2-26A ¿De dónde eres? Take turns identifying the country your partner is from based on the language he/she tells you he/she speaks. Remember that in Spanish, the masculine form of the nationality corresponds to the language spoken there. **Estudiante B,** please see **Appendix 1,** page A-4.

MODELO: ESTUDIANTE A: *Hablo italiano.*
ESTUDIANTE B: *¿Eres de Italia?*
ESTUDIANTE A: *Sí, es verdad.*

Estudiante A:

Hablo...	Mi compañero/a es de...
1. inglés	Alemania
2. coreano	Japón
3. ruso	China
4. portugués	España

2-27 ¿Qué te gusta hacer? Tell a classmate three activities that you like and three that you don't like to do. Do you have any interests in common?

MODELO: *Me gusta practicar fútbol, pero no me gusta leer novelas.*

(No) Me gusta...

hablar con mi familia

comer chocolate *Me gusta*

No me gusta comprar por Internet

No me gusta escribir poesía

practicar los verbos

trabajar por la noche *Me gusta*

llegar temprano a clase

vivir en la residencia

viajar

escuchar música

tomar café

aprender lenguas

preparar comida mexicana

ver la televisión

leer novelas

beber agua mineral

asistir a conciertos

bailar en el Carnaval

2-28 ¿Debo o no? There are some things you ought to do and others you ought not do.

Paso 1 First, check off the things which, in your opinion, you should and shouldn't do from the following list.

Debo...	No debo...	
☑	☐	aprender los verbos en español
☐	☑	bailar hip-hop
☐	☑	beber café descafeinado
☐	☐	comer en casa
☑	☐	ayudar a los amigos
☑	☐	vivir en España
☐	☑	escribir un mensaje de texto en clase
☐	☑	estudiar francés
☑	☐	escuchar música clásica
☑	☐	leer novelas románticas
☐	☑	vender mi carro
☑	☐	comprar una bicicleta

 Paso 2 Now compare your lists with those of a partner to see what you have in common and how you differ.

MODELO: E1: *Debo asistir a la clase de español.*
E2: *Yo también debo asistir a la clase de español.*

El Carnaval es popular en muchos países hispanos. Este es un desfile (*parade*) por las calles de Tenerife, España.

¡Hola!
Cultura en vivo

The celebration of *Carnaval* was originally a pagan ritual. It was outlawed in Spain during the Franco dictatorship, but has seen a revival since his death in 1975. In Latin America, the most famous *Carnaval* is in Rio de Janeiro; however, it is celebrated widely throughout the continent, each place adapting it to the local culture. Which U.S. city is famous for its celebration of *Carnaval*?

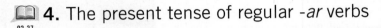

¡Así lo hacemos! ESTRUCTURAS

📖 4. The present tense of regular *-ar* verbs

02-37
to 02-39

¿Qué estudias?

Estudio matemáticas.

Spanish verbs are classified into three groups according to their infinitive ending (**-ar, -er,** or **-ir**). Each of the three groups uses different endings to produce verb forms (conjugations) in the various tenses.

- The present tense endings of **-ar** verbs are as follows.

hablar (*to speak*)		
yo	habl + o	→ habl**o**
tú	habl + as	→ habl**as**
Ud.	habl + a	→ habl**a**
él/ella	habl + a	→ habl**a**
nosotros/as	habl + amos	→ habl**amos**
vosotros/as	habl + áis	→ habl**áis**
Uds.	habl + an	→ habl**an**
ellos/as	habl + an	→ habl**an**

- The following verbs are regular **-ar** verbs that are conjugated like **hablar**.

ayudar	*to help*	**estudiar**	*to study*
bailar	*to dance*	**llegar**	*to arrive*
buscar	*to look for*	**mirar**	*to look at*
comprar	*to buy*	**preparar**	*to prepare*
desear	*to wish*	**tomar**	*to take, to drink*
enseñar	*to teach*	**trabajar**	*to work*
escuchar	*to listen*	**viajar**	*to travel*

- The Spanish present indicative tense has several equivalents in English. In addition to the simple present, it can express ongoing actions and even the future tense. Note the following examples.

Estudio ingeniería. { *I study engineering.*
I am studying engineering.

Practicamos golf mañana. *We will play golf tomorrow.*

Study tips – Learning regular verb conjugations

1. The first step is being able to recognize the infinitive stem: the part of the verb before the ending.

Infinitive			Stem
hablar	habl**ar**	→	habl
estudiar	estudi**ar**	→	estudi
trabajar	trabaj**ar**	→	trabaj

2. Practice conjugating several **-ar** verbs in writing first. Identify the stem, then write the various verb forms by adding the present tense endings listed.

3. Next practice **-ar** verb conjugations orally. Create two sets of index cards. Write a subject pronoun on each card for one set. For the other, write a regular **-ar** verb. Select one card from each set and conjugate the verb with the selected pronoun.

4. Think about how each verb action relates to your own experience by putting verbs into a meaningful context. For example, **Estudio matemáticas. Juan estudia ingeniería.**

APLICACIÓN

2-29 Preguntas y respuestas. With a classmate, take turns matching the following questions with logical responses.

1. ___E___ ¿Qué compras en la librería?
2. ___D___ ¿Quién enseña literatura española?
3. ___B___ ¿Qué necesitas para la clase de matemáticas?
4. ___A___ ¿Con quiénes estudias?
5. ___H___ ¿Qué instrumento musical practicas?
6. ___C___ ¿Quién prepara la comida en tu casa?
7. ___G___ ¿Dónde trabajas?
8. ___F___ ¿Cuándo y dónde escuchas música?

a. con mis amigos de la residencia
b. una calculadora
c. mi padre (*father*)
d. la profesora Rodríguez
e. libros y lápices
f. por la noche en mi dormitorio
g. en una oficina
h. el trombón

2-30 ¿Qué hacen? What is everyone doing today?

Paso 1 Match each drawing with an activity listed below, then create a sentence based on the information you have.

MODELO: practicar tenis
Eugenia practica tenis.

Eugenia

a. **Jacinto**

b. **Arturo**

c. **Víctor / Catalina**

d. **Leonor**

e. **Luis / Memo**

f. **Sonia**

g. **Ramona**

h. **Alma / Lili**

1. ___C___ bailar en una fiesta
2. ___B___ buscar trabajo
3. ___H___ estudiar en la biblioteca
4. ___G___ preparar una pizza
5. ___F___ hablar por teléfono
6. ___E___ viajar a España
7. ___A___ escuchar música
8. ___D___ trabajar en el laboratorio

Paso 2 Now use the drawings in **Paso 1** to ask a classmate whether he/she does these activities and when.

MODELO: E1: *¿Y tú? Practicas tenis como* (like) *Eugenia?*
E2: *Sí, practico tenis.*
E1: *¿Cuándo?*
E2: *Todos los días. ¿Y tú?*

5. The present tense of regular *-er* and *-ir* verbs

02-40 to 02-44

- You have just learned the present tense forms of regular **-ar** verbs. The following chart includes the forms for regular **-er** and **-ir** verbs.

¿Viven Uds. en la capital?

No, vivimos en la costa.

	comer (*to eat*)	vivir (*to live*)
yo	como	vivo
tú	comes	vives
Ud.	come	vive
él/ella	come	vive
nosotros/as	comemos	vivimos
vosotros/as	coméis	vivís
Uds.	comen	viven
ellos/as	comen	viven

- The present tense endings of **-er** and **-ir** verbs are identical except for the **nosotros** and **vosotros** forms.

- The following verbs are regular **-er** and **-ir** verbs.

-er		**-ir**	
aprender (**a** + *infinitive*)	*to learn (to do something)*	**abrir**	*to open*
beber	*to drink*	**asistir a**	*to attend*
comprender	*to understand*	**decidir**	*to decide*
creer	*to believe*	**escribir**	*to write*
deber (+ *infinitive*)	*to owe (ought to do something)*	**recibir**	*to receive*
leer	*to read*		
vender	*to sell*		

- **Ver** (*to see, to watch*) is an **-er** verb with an irregular **yo** form. Also note that the **vosotros/as** form has no accent because it is only one syllable.

ver (*to see, to look at*)			
yo	**veo**	nosotros/as	**vemos**
tú	**ves**	vosotros/as	**veis**
Ud.	**ve**	Uds.	**ven**
él/ella	**ve**	ellos/as	**ven**

APLICACIÓN

2-31 Cecilia Álvarez. Cecilia is a student at a Spanish university.

Paso 1 Read about Cecilia and her plans. Underline all **-er** and **-ir** verbs and identify the infinitive of each one. **OJO** (*watch out!*): Some verbs are neither.

MODELO: Todos los días escribe un email a sus padres. (*escribir*)

Hola, soy Cecilia Álvarez y vivo en Madrid, España. Asisto a la Universidad Complutense donde estudio relaciones internacionales. Creo que es importante aprender otras lenguas y comprender otras culturas, por eso también estudio francés e inglés. Asisto a clase los lunes, miércoles y viernes. Los viernes después de las clases, mis amigos y yo vamos[1] a un bar cerca de la universidad donde tomamos una caña y unas tapas y decidimos qué hacer[2] por la noche. Normalmente vamos a la discoteca Danzoo y allí vemos a todos los amigos. Después de bailar toda la noche, tomamos chocolate y churros en un café que abre a las 6:00 de la mañana. ¿Y el resto del fin de semana? ¡Vivimos en la biblioteca!

Chocolate y churros, ¡qué ricos!

[1]*go* [2]*to do*

Paso 2   Now answer questions based on what you have just read.

1. ¿Dónde vive Cecilia?

2. ¿Por qué estudia otras lenguas?

3. ¿Qué hace (*does she do*) los lunes, miércoles y viernes?

4. ¿Adónde va después de clase?

5. ¿A quiénes ven en la discoteca

6. ¿Qué come Cecilia por la mañana con sus amigos?

2-32 Unas actividades típicas.   Complete the following sentences logically by conjugating the verb in parentheses and adding a logical ending.

MODELO: Mis compañeros y yo (asistir a)…
asistimos a la clase de español los lunes, miércoles y viernes.

1. Mi familia y yo (vivir)…

2. En clase los profesores (escribir)…

3. Normalmente tú (recibir)…

4. En el mercado, el comerciante (vender)…

5. En el café, tú y yo (beber)…

6. Antes de (*Before*) entrar en clase, la profesora (abrir)…

7. Yo siempre (leer)…

8. En casa, mis amigos (ver)…

2-33 ¿Cuándo? ¿A qué hora?   How do you compare your routines?

Paso 1   Take turns asking each other when or at what time you do the following activities. Be sure to conjugate the verbs in your questions and responses.

MODELO: ¿cuándo / **ver** / la televisión?
E1: *¿Cuándo ves la televisión?*
E2: *Veo la televisión los sábados.*

1. ¿cuándo / **vender** / los libros?

2. ¿a qué hora / **asistir** / a clase?

3. ¿cuándo / **escribir** / correos electrónicos?

4. ¿a qué hora / **deber /** trabajar?

5. ¿a qué hora / **beber/** café?

6. ¿a qué hora / **ver** / las noticias (*news*)?

Paso 2   Now summarize what you have in common and how you differ.

MODELO: *Nosotros vemos la televisión los sábados. Él/ella también ve la televisión los viernes pero yo no.*

Presencia hispana

Spanish cuisine has become increasingly popular in the U.S. Go to any large city to find a **tapas** bar where you can sample some of the popular delicacies found in Spanish bars, such as **chorizo** (*sausage*), **pinchos de tortilla** (*slices of Spanish omelet*), and **calamares** (*squid*), to name a few. You can eat **tapas** any time, usually accompanied by a glass of wine or a **caña,** a small beer. How do **tapas** compare with the snacks that you usually have?

2-34 ¿Qué pasa?   Take turns using the verbs listed below to describe the scene in the photograph: include what there is, who the people are, what they are like, what they are doing, and what they are not doing. Use your imagination.

abrir	caminar	escuchar	hablar	mirar	ver
asistir a	escribir	vender	leer	ser	vivir

MODELO: (ver) *Veo un reloj...*

2-35A Entrevistas.   Ask each other questions to share the information below. Be sure to respond using complete sentences and logical information. **Estudiante B,** please see **Appendix 1,** page A-4.

MODELO: ESTUDIANTE A: *¿A qué hora llegas a clase?*
ESTUDIANTE B: (1:30 p.m.) *Llego a la una y media de la tarde.*

Estudiante A:

Mis preguntas	Mis respuestas
1. ¿Cuándo estudias?	• sí, es muy interesante
2. ¿Qué lenguas hablas bien?	• programas de *reality*
3. ¿Lees el periódico?	• pizza
4. ¿Asistes a clase los martes?	• música popular o de *rap*
5. ¿Qué deporte practicas?	• en casa o en la biblioteca

2-36 ¿Y tú?   Write a short paragraph in which you discuss your activities using verbs that end in **-ar, -er,** and **-ir** (refer back to **¡Así lo decimos!** for a list). Connect your thoughts by using the expressions **pero, y,** and **también.**

MODELO: *Estudio dos lenguas: inglés y español. También estudio ciencias y administración de empresas. Trabajo en la cafetería. Me gusta escribir poesía y asistir a conciertos de música rock.*

6. The present tense of *tener*

- The Spanish verb **tener** (*to have*) is irregular. As in English, **tener** is used to show possession.

  Tengo tres clases y un laboratorio.   *I have three classes and a lab.*

  ¿Tienes un bolígrafo?   *Do you have a pen?*

tener (*to have*)			
yo	**tengo**	nosotros/as	**tenemos**
tú	**tienes**	vosotros/as	**tenéis**
Ud.	**tiene**	Uds.	**tienen**
él/ella	**tiene**	ellos/as	**tienen**

- **Tener que** + *infinitive* is used to express obligation (*to have to*).

  Mañana **tengo que** asistir a clase.   *Tomorrow I have to attend class.*

  ¿Tienes que leer una biografía de Picasso?   *Do you have to read a biography about Picasso?*

APLICACIÓN

2-37 Mis obligaciones. There's often not enough time in the day to do all you have to.

Paso 1 First, check off the activities you need to do tomorrow.

Tengo que...

- ☐ asistir a clase.
- ☐ llegar temprano a clase.
- ☒ estudiar la lección.
- ☒ comprar comida.
- ☐ escribir una composición.
- ☐ ver una película.
- ☐ practicar un deporte.
- ☐ escuchar música.
- ☒ ayudar a un/a amigo/a.

Paso 2 Refer back to your responses above to compare what you each have to do and not do tomorrow. Which of you has more obligations?

MODELO: E1: *¿Qué tienes que hacer mañana?*

            E2: *Mañana tengo que practicar tenis y hablar con el profesor. No tengo que estudiar. ¿Y tú?*

            E1: *Pues, creo que tengo más obligaciones...*

2-38 ¿Qué tienen en común?   Write eight sentences in Spanish, saying what various people have in common. Use the verbs **ser** and **tener,** as well as other verbs from the chapter.

MODELO: *Christina Aguilera y Shakira son bonitas. Tienen muchos amigos. Trabajan mucho.*

Christina Aguilera	El príncipe Felipe de España	Shakira
Alberto Contador	Eva Méndez	Penélope Cruz
Paz Vega	Enrique Iglesias	Eva Longoria Parker
Yo	Bono	Peyton Manning
Bill Gates	Tú	Pitbull
Venus Williams	Rafael Nadal	Benjamin Bratt

2-39A ¿Tienes?   Take turns asking each other if you have the items on your list. If your partner has the item you want, you make a pair. The first person who has five pairs of items wins. **Estudiante B**, please see **Appendix 1**, page A-4.

MODELO: ☐ un libro de historia
ESTUDIANTE A: *¿Tienes un libro de historia?*
ESTUDIANTE B: *Sí, tengo. (No, no tengo libro de historia, pero tengo un libro de física.)*

Estudiante A:

☐ un libro de español   ☐ una novela de Hemingway
☐ una pintura de Picasso   ☐ un reloj grande
☐ un examen fácil   ☐ un buen amigo
☐ una mesa roja   ☐ un/a profesor/a inteligente
☐ un lápiz azul   ☐ un libro nuevo
☐ una mochila negra   ☐ un cuaderno viejo

02-48
to 02-52

¿Cuánto saben?

First, ask yourself if you can perform the following functions in Spanish. Then act out the scenarios with two or three classmates. Ask and respond to at least three questions in each situation.

✓ CAN YOU . . .

☐ talk about what you do and what you like to do?

☐ talk about what you have, and what you have to do or should do?

WITH YOUR CLASSMATE(S) . . .

Situación: En un café
You've just been introduced to each other. Discuss what you do on a daily basis and what you like to do to find out what you have in common. Use a variety of **-ar, -er, -ir** verbs, and **(no) me gusta** with infinitives.
Para empezar: *Me gusta estudiar... También yo...*

Situación: En una fiesta
Which of you is busier? Take turns comparing your busy lives, each trying to outdo the other in order to get some sympathy. Be sure to use **tener que** and **deber,** and appropriate responses, such as **Lo siento** and **¿De verdad?**
Para empezar: *Tengo que preparar... Debo estudiar...*

Observaciones

¡Pura vida! EPISODIO 2

Antes de ver el video

2-40 Silvia es española. Read the following information about Spain, and then decide whether the statements that follow are **cierto (C)** or **falso (F).** Correct any false statements.

> España es el tercer país más grande de Europa después de Rusia y Francia. Por su diversidad y su mezcla[1] de gentes y tradiciones, España es un país muy diferente al resto de Europa. Los grupos que han influido[2] en la historia del país son: los iberos, los celtas, los griegos, los romanos, los árabes y los judíos.
>
> Ahora, España está dividida en 17 comunidades autónomas y dos ciudades autónomas. Aunque hay diferencias entre las comunidades, todas comparten[3] muchas tradiciones y costumbres, como el horario.
>
> En España el horario es muy diferente al de EE. UU. y Canadá. Por ejemplo, en los restaurantes se sirve el almuerzo[4] entre las 13:00 y las 15:30 horas. La cena[5] se sirve de las 20:30 a las 23:00 horas. En los bares y restaurantes se comen *tapas,* los deliciosos aperitivos españoles, todo el día.

Se comen las tapas a cualquier hora del día.

[1]*mixture*   [2]*have influenced*   [3]*share*   [4]*lunch*   [5]*dinner*

1. _____ España es más grande que Francia.

2. _____ Las diferentes comunidades comparten muchas de las tradiciones.

3. _____ En España se sirve el almuerzo al mediodía.

4. _____ Las tapas se sirven en el desayuno.

A ver el video

2-41 Los otros (*other*) personajes. Watch the second episode of **¡Pura vida!** and listen to the characters describe each other. Then, write a description for Silvia, Patricio, and Marcela, using correct forms of logical adjectives from the following list.

alegre	colombiano	cubano	español
guapo	inteligente	moreno	simpático

Silvia

Patricio

Marcela

Después de ver el video

2-42 ¿Cuál es tu opinión? Choose two of these countries and state why you would visit them.

Argentina   Colombia   Costa Rica   Cuba   España   México

MODELO: *Visito_____ porque es _____ y _____.*

Nuestro mundo

Panoramas

Descubre España

Millones de turistas visitan España todos los años para experimentar sus bellas vistas, su rica historia, su innovador presente y su fabulosa comida.

La Alhambra de Granada construida por los árabes, siglo XIV

El acueducto de Segovia construido por los romanos, siglo I–II

Mariscos del mar Cantábrico

Las altas montañas de Sierra Nevada, Andalucía

El encantador pueblo de Calella de Palafrugell, Costa Brava, Cataluña

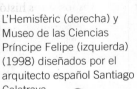

L'Hemisfèric (derecha) y Museo de las Ciencias Príncipe Felipe (izquierda) (1998) diseñados por el arquitecto español Santiago Calatrava

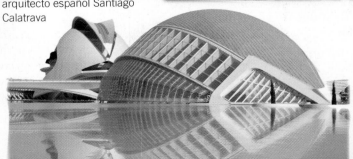

España

Población: 40,5 millones

Lengua nacional: castellano (español)

Lenguas regionales: gallego, eusquera (vasco), aranés, catalán, valenciano

Turistas cada año: 60 millones

Estudiantes universitarios: 1,5 millones

Edad mínima para beber alcohol: 16 años

Edad mínima para conducir[1]: 18 años

_____

[1]*drive*

2-43 Identifica. Use the information in the photos and Fact box to identify the following.

1. unas montañas altas _____

2. el nombre de un arquitecto español famoso _____

3. una construcción romana _____

4. una construcción árabe _____

5. el número de turistas que visitan España cada año _____

6. dónde está la Costa Brava _____

2-44 Desafío. Locate these places using the map of Spain above.

1. la capital de España
2. donde está situada la Alhambra
3. donde está situado el acueducto de Segovia
4. la Costa Brava
5. el Mar Cantábrico
6. las Islas Canarias

 2-45 Proyecto: España. Spain attracts 60 million tourists every year, making it one of the most attractive destinations in the world. About 35% of all tourists visit Madrid, Barcelona, Andalucía, and/or Valencia. Choose one of these destinations, or another that interests you, and connect to the Internet to investigate more about sites that attract people to Spain. Use the Modelo to write a summary of what you find; include the following information:

- su nombre y dónde está (*where it is*)
- su población
- cómo es
- unos sitios históricos importantes
- un producto importante
- una foto representativa

 Busca: Spain tourism

MODELO: *La ciudad de Segovia está a media hora en tren de Madrid, y el tren cuesta solo diez euros. Tiene 55.000 habitantes. Es una bella ciudad con monumentos romanos y árabes. Entre los tesoros arquitectónicos figuran el acueducto romano del siglo I y el Alcázar (un castillo árabe) del siglo XI. Los turistas también visitan la Catedral de Segovia del siglo XVI. En Segovia la cerámica y los productos de cuero* (leather) *son muy populares.*

Cinemundo entrevista a Pedro Almodóvar

Pedro Almodóvar is one of Spain's most celebrated movie directors. Almodóvar's success derives from his own keen observations of film techniques and of life in general. His films and their actors have earned numerous awards, including an Oscar for Best Foreign Language Film for *Todo sobre mi madre*. Here Pedro Almodóvar (**PA**) responds to an interview by a reporter for the film magazine, *Cinemundo* (**CM**).

ANTES DE LEER

2-46 Conocimiento previo. It often helps to refer to background knowledge to help understand a reading. What are some of the question words you would expect to see in an interview? What kinds of questions would you expect to be asked by someone interviewing a movie director?

A LEER

2-47 Busca las palabras interrogativas. Skim through the interview and underline interrogatives in the text. Do the types of questions coincide with your conjecture about the content of the interview?

Cinemundo entrevista a Pedro Almodóvar

CM: Señor Almodóvar, muchas gracias por concederme[1] esta entrevista. Para empezar, ¿cuál es su nombre completo?

PA: Me llamo Pedro Almodóvar Caballero, pero no uso mi apellido materno. Creo que es más fácil así.

CM: Es verdad, especialmente porque usted es tan conocido[2]. Y entre los amigos, ¿tiene apodo?

PA: No, por Dios. No me gustan los apodos, soy simplemente Pedro para todos. Sólo[3] en mi pueblo me llaman Pedrito, y bueno, sólo a ellos se lo permito.

CM: ¿Y de dónde es usted originalmente?

PA: Soy manchego[4], de Calzada de Calatrava, un pequeño pueblo de La Mancha. Estudié en la ciudad de Cáceres. A la edad de dieciséis años fui solo[5] a Madrid. Fue difícil vivir sin mi familia, pero poco a poco aprendí a vivir en una ciudad nueva.

CM: Usted tiene mucho éxito con sus películas. ¿Cuál de ellas prefiere?

PA: Estoy muy orgulloso de todas mis películas, pero la que más me gusta es *Los abrazos rotos* en la que aparece Penélope Cruz. Ella es una actriz extraordinaria y sin duda, merece otro Óscar más. En la película, ella vive dos vidas y tiene dos apariencias y personalidades muy diferentes. En la primera vida tiene el pelo castaño[6] y es muy seria. En su otra vida, es rubia, despreocupada[7] y escandalosa[8]. Como en muchas de mis películas, hay humor, pero también hay un mensaje[9] social.

CM: ¿Es verdad que sus películas son autobiográficas?

PA: Bueno, todas tienen algo autobiográfico, pero aún más que eso[10], presento tabúes sociales. Quiero que las personas que vean mis películas cuestionen sus creencias[11] y la moralidad social.

CM: ¿Cuál va a ser su próxima película?

PA: Primero voy a ir de vacaciones a las Islas Canarias y tomar algún tiempo para recuperar mi creatividad. Luego, vamos a ver…

CM: Muchísimas gracias, señor Almodóvar, y ¡muy buena suerte!

PA: ¡Igualmente!

---

[1]*grant me* [2]*well known* [3]*Only* [4]*native of La Mancha* [5]*by myself* [6]*brown hair* [7]*carefree* [8]*outrageous* [9]*message*
[10]*even more than that* [11]*beliefs*

DESPUÉS DE LEER

2-48 Haz las preguntas. Complete the questions with the most appropriate interrogative words. Then answer the questions.

1. ¿ —————— se llama la revista?

2. ¿ Con —————— es la entrevista?

3. ¿ De —————— es?

4. ¿ En —————— ciudad estudia?

5. ¿ —————— es su película favorita?

6. ¿ —————— va de vacaciones ahora?

2-49 ¿Qué opinas tú? Indicate your response to each of the following statements to express your opinions.

1. Voy mucho al cine.	**Sí**	**No**	
2. Prefiero ver videos en casa.	**Sí**	**No**	
3. Me gustan las películas internacionales.	**Sí**	**No**	**No sé** (*I don't know*)
4. Me gustan las películas de Almodóvar.	**Sí**	**No**	**No sé**
5. En mi opinión, Penélope Cruz es una excelente actriz.	**Sí**	**No**	**No sé**

 2-50 Penélope Cruz. This talented actress has performed in several Almodóvar films. Connect with the Internet to see images of her; then write a short paragraph describing her.

Busca: penelope cruz foto bio

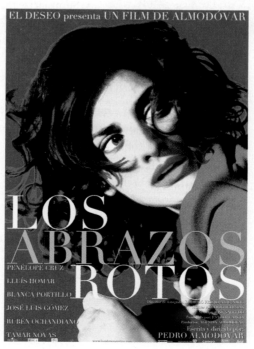

2-51 Una entrevista y un sumario. Summarize information from an interview for an article in *¡Aló!*, a Spanish magazine that depicts the lives of the rich and famous.

ANTES DE ESCRIBIR

- Write questions you'd like to ask a famous Spaniard, such as Fernando Alonso, Penélope Cruz, Javier Bardem, José Rodríguez Zapatero, Picasso, Santiago Calatrava, Rafael Nadal, Alejandro Amenábar, or Alejandro Sanz. Use the following interrogatives:

  ¿Cómo...?

  ¿Dónde...?

  ¿Qué...?

  ¿Cuándo...?

  ¿Por qué...?

  ¿Cuál(es)...?

  ¿Quién(es)...?

  ¿De dónde...?

- Write at least one question using the verb **tener**.
- **Entrevista.** Interview a classmate who will role-play as a famous Spaniard, then write up the responses.

A ESCRIBIR

- Summarize the information for your article. Use connecting words such as **y, pero** (*but*), and **por eso** (*therefore*).
- Write at least six sentences about your famous person.

DESPUÉS DE ESCRIBIR

- **Revisar.** Review your summary to assure the following:
  - ☐ agreement of nouns, articles, and adjectives
  - ☐ agreement of subjects and verbs
  - ☐ correct spelling, including accents
- **Intercambiar**
  Exchange your summary with a classmate's; make suggestions and corrections.
- **Entregar**
  Rewrite your summary, incorporating your classmate's suggestions. Then turn in the summary to your instructor.

🔊 Vocabulario

Primera parte

Adjetivos de nacionalidad   Adjectives of nationality

argentino/a   *Argentine*
canadiense   *Canadian*
chileno/a   *Chilean*
colombiano/a   *Colombian*
cubano/a   *Cuban*
dominicano/a   *Dominican*
ecuatoriano/a   *Ecuadorian*
español/a   *Spanish*
mexicano/a   *Mexican*
norteamericano/a (estadounidense)   *American*
panameño/a   *Panamanian*
peruano/a   *Peruvian*
puertorriqueño/a   *Puerto Rican*
salvadoreño/a   *Salvadorian*
venezolano/a   *Venezuelan*

Adjetivos descriptivos   Descriptive adjectives

activo/a   *active*
alto/a   *tall*
bajo/a   *short*
bonito/a   *pretty, cute*
delgado/a   *slender*
entusiasta   *enthusiastic*
feo/a   *ugly*
flaco/a   *skinny*
gordo/a   *fat*
guapo/a   *good-looking*
joven   *young*
moreno/a   *dark (skin, hair)*
nuevo/a   *new*
pobre   *poor*
rico/a   *rich*
rubio/a   *blond (fair)*
viejo/a   *old*

Lugares   Places

la capital   *capital city*
la ciudad   *city*
el país   *country*

Las personas   People

el/la amigo/a   *friend*
el/la muchacho/a   *boy/girl*
los padres   *parents*

Adverbios   Adverbs

ahora (mismo)   *(right) now*
también   *also*
tarde   *late*
temprano   *early*

Conjunciones   Conjunctions

pero   *but*
porque   *because*

Segunda parte

Verbos   Verbs

abrir   *to open*
asistir a   *to attend*
aprender   *to learn*
ayudar   *to help*
bailar   *to dance*
beber   *to drink*
buscar   *to look for*
comer   *to eat*
comprar   *to buy*
comprender   *to understand*
creer   *to believe*
deber (+ *infinitive*)   *to owe (to ought to do something)*
decidir   *to decide*
desear   *to wish*
enseñar   *to teach*
escribir   *to write*
escuchar   *to listen*
estudiar   *to study*
hablar   *to speak*
leer   *to read*
llegar   *to arrive*
mirar   *to look at*
practicar (un deporte)   *to practice, to play (a sport)*
preparar   *to prepare*
recibir   *to receive*
tener   *to have*
tomar   *to drink, to take*
trabajar   *to work*
vender   *to sell*
ver   *to see, to watch*
viajar   *to travel*
vivir   *to live*

Adjetivos   Adjectives

difícil   *difficult*
fácil   *easy*

Otras nacionalidades (País)   Other nationalities (Country)

alemán, alemana (Alemania)   *German (Germany)*
brasileño/a (Brasil)   *Brazilian (Brazil)*
chino/a (China)   *Chinese (China)*
coreano/a (Corea)   *Korean (Korea)*
francés, francesa (Francia)   *French (France)*
inglés, inglesa (Inglaterra)   *English (England)*
italiano/a (Italia)   *Italian (Italy)*
japonés, japonesa (Japón)   *Japanese (Japan)*
portugués, portuguesa (Portugal)   *Portuguese (Portugal)*
ruso/a (Rusia)   *Russian (Russia)*

Otras palabras y expresiones   Other words and expressions

las lenguas   *languages*
¿Qué te gusta hacer?   *What do you (inf.) like to do?*
Me gusta (+ *infinitive*)   *I like (+ infinitive)*
Te gusta (+ *infinitive*)   *You (inf.) like (+ infinitive)*
¡Qué suerte!   *How lucky!*

Telling time   *See page 46.*   **Interrogative words**   *See page 52.*

3
¿Qué estudias?

Readiness Check

¡México fascinante!

ESTADOS UNIDOS

OCÉANO ÁRTICO

CANADÁ

OCÉANO PACÍFICO

ESTADOS UNIDOS

OCÉANO ATLÁNTICO

MÉXICO

Golfo de México

«La educación no es para enseñar qué pensar, sino a pensar».

Refrán: "Education serves not to teach *what* to think, but rather *to think*."

Frida Kahlo pintó muchos autorretratos (*self-portraits*) y cuadros menos personales, como *Viva la vida*. Hoy en día se le considera una de las mejores (*best*) pintoras del mundo hispano. Fue la esposa del gran muralista mexicano Diego Rivera.

Los mariachis son los más genuinos exponentes de la música mexicana. Son populares en los restaurantes, los bailes, las fiestas y las bodas.

¡Así lo decimos! VOCABULARIO

 ¡Así es la vida! La vida universitaria

03-01

UNIVERSIDAD NACIONAL AUTÓNOMA DE MÉXICO		
CLASES		CRÉDITOS
0101	HISTORIA ECONÓMICA	6
0102	ECONOMÍA POLÍTICA	6
0201	TEORÍA ECONÓMICA	6
0202	MATEMÁTICAS	6
0301	INVESTIGACIÓN	6

Un horario complicado.

MARCELA: Oye, Pedro, ¿qué materias tienes este semestre?

PEDRO: A ver, tengo siete en total: historia económica, economía política, teoría económica, investigación, matemáticas...

MARCELA: ¡Estás loco! ¡Todas son muy difíciles! Yo solamente tengo cuatro clases este semestre.

PEDRO: Sí tienes razón, pero mis clases son todas obligatorias para la carrera de economía.

Ana tiene prisa mientras Beatriz escribe un correo electrónico.

ANA: ¿Tienes hambre? Yo sí. ¿Vamos a comer algo?

BEATRIZ: Ahora mismo no. Tengo que escribir otro correo electrónico más y después comemos.

ANA: ¡Escribe más rápido! Ya es la una y tenemos que comer antes de la clase de geología a las dos.

Hola, José. ¿Vamos a tomar un café después de clase?

Vocabulario Las materias académicas y la vida estudiantil

03-02 to 03-06

Variaciones
In Spain, **la administración de empresas** is more commonly **las empresariales**.

Las materias | (Academic) Subjects

la administración de empresas   *business administration*
la arquitectura   *architecture*
el arte   *art*
la biología   *biology*
el cálculo   *calculus*
las ciencias políticas   *political science*
las ciencias sociales   *social sciences*
las comunicaciones   *communications*
la contabilidad   *accounting*
el derecho   *law*
el diseño   *design*
la educación física   *physical education*
la economía   *economics*
la estadística   *statistics*
la filosofía   *philosophy*
las finanzas   *finance*
la física   *physics*
la geografía   *geography*
la geología   *geology*
la historia   *history*
la informática / la computación   *computer science*
la ingeniería (eléctrica)   *(electrical) engineering*
las matemáticas   *mathematics*
la medicina   *medicine*
la pedagogía   *teaching, education*
la química   *chemistry*
la veterinaria   *veterinary science*

La chica estudia informática.

Sustantivos | Nouns

la carrera   *career, field*
el/la chico/a   *boy/girl*
el correo electrónico   *e-mail*
el dinero   *money*
el horario (de clases)   *(class) schedule*
el semestre   *semester*
el trimestre   *trimester*
el videojuego   *video game*

el correo electrónico

Variaciones
In Mexico and other Latin American countries, the noun **chico/a** is used as an adjective synonymous with **pequeño/a** or *small*, for example, **un país chico** (or even **chiquito, chiquitito**). The term **chavo/a** is a common alternative for *boy/girl* in Mexico.

Adjetivos | Adjectives

complicado/a   *complicated*
exigente   *challenging, demanding*
obligatorio/a   *obligatory, required*

el chico con un videojuego

Adverbios | Adverbs

antes (de)   *before*
bastante   *quite, fairly*
después (de)   *after*
solamente   *only*

APLICACIÓN

3-1 Y tú, ¿qué estudias? Talk about what you study.

Paso 1 First, check off the subjects you have this term.

MODELO: *Estudio...*
☑ biología, ☑ cálculo, ☑ español y ☑ química.

☐ administración de empresas
☐ alemán
☐ álgebra
☐ antropología
☐ árabe
☐ arte
☐ biología
☐ cálculo
☐ ciencias políticas

☐ ciencias sociales
☐ comunicaciones
☐ coreano
☐ chino
☐ derecho
☐ educación física
☑ español
☐ filosofía y letras
☐ física

☐ francés
☐ geografía
☐ geología
☐ historia
☐ informática
☐ ingeniería
☑ inglés
☐ japonés
☐ literatura

☑ matemáticas   *Comp*
☐ medicina
☐ música
☐ pedagogía
☐ portugués
☐ psicología
☐ química
☐ ruso
☐ sociología

Paso 2 Now, compare your list with that of another student.

MODELO: E1: *Estudio biología, cálculo, español y química. Todas mis materias son difíciles. Y tú, ¿qué estudias?*
E2: *Estudio biología, español, historia y sociología. Tengo clase todos los días.*

3-2 Materias en El Tec. El Instituto Tecnológico de Estudios Superiores de Monterrey (ITESM), popularly known as El Tec, has campuses all over Mexico, each with a particular academic strength.

Paso 1 Here is a schedule of classes for students in international business at El Tec. Choose three courses that interest you and create a possible schedule in the grid below.

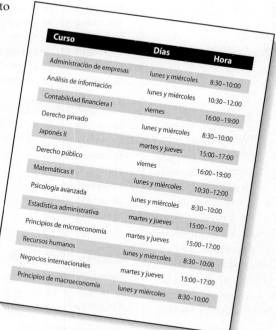

Curso	Días	Hora
Administración de empresas	lunes y miércoles	8:30–10:00
Análisis de información	lunes y miércoles	10:30–12:00
Contabilidad financiera I	viernes	16:00–19:00
Derecho privado	lunes y miércoles	8:30–10:00
Japonés II	martes y jueves	15:00–17:00
Derecho público	viernes	16:00–19:00
Matemáticas II	lunes y miércoles	10:30–12:00
Psicología avanzada	lunes y miércoles	8:30–10:00
Estadística administrativa	martes y jueves	15:00–17:00
Principios de microeconomía	martes y jueves	15:00–17:00
Recursos humanos	lunes y miércoles	8:30–10:00
Negocios internacionales	martes y jueves	15:00–17:00
Principios de macroeconomía	lunes y miércoles	8:30–10:00

Cursos	Días	Horas
1.		
2.		
3.		

Paso 2   Share your schedule with a classmate and answer the questions that follow based on your conversations.

MODELO: E1: *¿Qué estudias este semestre?*
E2: *Administración de empresas.*
E1: *¿Cuándo?*
E2: *Los lunes y los miércoles a las ocho y media.*

1. ¿Quién tiene el horario más conveniente? ¿Por qué?

2. ¿Quién tiene el horario más difícil? ¿Por qué?

3. ¿Quién tiene el horario más interesante? ¿Por qué?

 3-3 El horario de Alberto y Carmen.   Listen to Alberto and Carmen talk about their schedules. Then select the name of the person described in each statement.

1. Estudia matemáticas.	Alberto	Carmen
2. Estudia química.	Alberto	Carmen
3. Tiene examen hoy.	Alberto	Carmen
4. Tiene que hablar con el profesor.	Alberto	Carmen
5. Trabaja esta noche.	Alberto	Carmen
6. Va a una fiesta esta noche.	Alberto	Carmen
7. Tiene una clase difícil.	Alberto	Carmen
8. Tiene un profesor exigente (*demanding*).	Alberto	Carmen

3-4 ¿Cuántas?   In groups of three or four students, make a chart similar to the one below to decide on a time when you are all free to meet outside of class to work on a group project. Take turns asking the following questions so that all members share their schedules.

1. ¿Qué estudias este semestre (trimestre)?

2. ¿A qué hora es la clase de ...? ¿Qué días de la semana?

3. ¿Cuándo trabajas?

	lunes	martes	miércoles	jueves	viernes	sábado	domingo
9:00	*Sara: cálculo*		*Sara: cálculo*		*Sara: cálculo*	*Sara: trabajo*	
10:00	*Todos: español*	*Todos: español*	*Todos: español*	*Todos: español*			
11:00							
¿...?							

Students in Mexico, as in many parts of the world, begin their specializations very early in their university careers. The curriculum is usually fixed and the number of courses students must take varies with the *facultad.* During their final semesters students have more choice, but still mostly within their majors. In your opinion, what are advantages and disadvantages of this type of curriculum?

¡Así lo hacemos! ESTRUCTURAS

03-07 to 3-10

1. The numbers *101 – 3.000.000*

Quinientos, seiscientos, setecientos, ochocientos, novecientos, ¡mil!

Numbers greater than 100 are expressed as follows:

101	ciento uno/a	800	ochocientos/as
200	doscientos/as	900	novecientos/as
300	trescientos/as	1.000	mil
400	cuatrocientos/as	4.000	cuatro mil
500	quinientos/as	100.000	cien mil
600	seiscientos/as	1.000.000	un millón (de)
700	setecientos/as	3.000.000	tres millones

- **Ciento** is used in compound numbers between 100 and 200.
  ciento diez, **ciento** treinta y cuatro, etcétera

- When 200 to 900 modify nouns, they agree in gender with them.
  doscient**as** universidades   quinient**os** libros
  seiscient**as** veintiuna alumnas   cuatrocient**os** cincuenta y un profesores

- **Mil** is never used with **un** and is never used in the plural for counting.
  mil, dos **mil**, tres **mil**, etcétera

- In Spanish, the year is always expressed in thousands.
  mil novecientos noventa y dos   *nineteen ninety-two (1992)*
  dos mil once   *two thousand eleven/twenty eleven (2011)*

- The plural of **millón** is **millones**, and when followed immediately by a noun, both take the preposition **de**.
  un millón **de** pesos
  dos millones **de** dólares
  dos millones trescientas mil personas

- In Spain and in most of Latin America, thousands are marked by a period and decimals by a comma.

Spain/Latin America	United States/Canada
$1.000	$1,000
$2,50	$2.50
$10.450,35	$10,450.35
2.341.500	2,341,500

APLICACIÓN

3-5 ¿Qué número es?   Write the numerals that are represented below.

MODELO: doscientos cuarenta y nueve
               249

1. quinientos noventa y dos   _____
2. diez mil setecientos once   _____
3. un millón seiscientos treinta y tres mil doscientos nueve   _____
4. novecientos mil ciento veintiuno   _____
5. dos millones ochocientos mil ochocientos ochenta y ocho   _____
6. ciento cuarenta y cinco   _____

3-6 ¿En qué año? When did these events take place?

Paso 1 Write out each year, and then match it with an historical event.

MODELO: 1776

mil setecientos setenta y seis; la independencia de Estados Unidos

1. _____ 1492   a. los Juegos Olímpicos en Londres
2. _____ 2012   b. la Guerra Civil española
3. _____ 2000   c. la Gran Depresión
4. _____ 1929   d. el nuevo milenio
5. _____ 1810   e. la conquista de México por Hernán Cortés
6. _____ 1936   f. la Guerra de Independencia de México
7. _____ 1521   g. la llegada (*arrival*) de Cristóbal Colón a Santo Domingo
8. _____ 2010   h. la Copa Mundial de Fútbol en Sudáfrica

Paso 2 Now, write out two other important years and have classmates say what other events took place.

 3-7A **Inventario en el almacén (*warehouse*).** You and your classmate are stock workers compiling end-of-year inventory figures. Each of you is missing data. Take turns asking each other questions to fill in the missing parts on each of your grids. **¡Ojo!** (*Watch out!*) Watch for agreement. Then check all your figures by calling out each item and quantity. **Estudiante B**, see **Appendix 1**, page A-5.

MODELO: ESTUDIANTE A: (You need) *¿Cuántas mesas tienes?*
         ESTUDIANTE B: (You have) *Tengo setecientas cuarenta y siete mesas.*

Estudiante A:

_____ escritorios	525 calculadoras
816 pizarras	_____ computadoras
111.000 cuadernos	1.526 diccionarios
_____ mapas	2.400 libros de texto
110 sillas	_____ bolígrafos
11.399 lápices	600.450 CD

 3-8 La lotería del Tec de Monterrey. The Tec has a yearly lottery in which they give away houses, furniture, cars, and shopping sprees. You have just won the million **peso** (about $69,000) shopping spree. Together with a partner, decide how you will spend your prize money without going over budget.

MODELO: E1: *Compramos dos escritorios ejecutivos por treinta mil pesos.*
         E2: *No, mejor compramos uno ejecutivo y uno pequeño por diecisiete mil pesos.*

Presupuesto (*Budget*) $1.000.000 (PESOS)

escritorio ejecutivo	$15.000	reloj Rolex	$645.000
bicicleta	$1.290	carro híbrido	$387.000
silla de plástico	$250	sillón de cuero (*leather*)	$3.000
computadora portátil	$15.000	iPhone	$2.500
televisor plasma	$10.000	televisor pequeño	$1.500
mesa pequeña	$1.800	reproductor Blu-Ray	$2.500
carro alemán	$640.000	miscelánea	¿...?

Presencia hispana

Mexican Americans are U.S. residents who trace their ancestry to Mexico. They are variously known as *chicanos, xicanos, mexicanos,* or Mex-Americans, although *chicano* is the preferred identification for many. In the U.S. there are currently 25 million legal residents of Mexican heritage, and an estimated 6 to 7 million undocumented immigrants. Mexico allows its citizens to maintain dual citizenship with the U.S. How does this law benefit Mexican Americans?

📖 2. Possessive adjectives

- You have already used **mi(s)** and **tu(s)** to express possession. Here are all the forms of possessive adjectives in Spanish.

Subject pronoun	With singular nouns	With plural nouns	
yo	**mi**	**mis**	*my*
tú	**tu**	**tus**	*your (inf.)*
Ud.	**su**	**sus**	*your (form.)*
él/ella	**su**	**sus**	*his, her*
nosotros/as	**nuestro/a**	**nuestros/as**	*our*
vosotros/as	**vuestro/a**	**vuestros/as**	*your (inf.)*
Uds.	**su**	**sus**	*your (form.)*
ellos/as	**su**	**sus**	*their*

- In Spanish, two factors determine the form of a possessive adjective: the possessor and the entity or thing possessed. Possessive adjectives agree in number with the nouns they modify, not the possessor. Note that **nuestro/a** and **vuestro/a** are the only possessive adjectives that show both gender and number agreement.

mi libro	*my book*	**mis** libros	*my books*
nuestra universidad	*our university*	**nuestras** universidades	*our universities*

- Possessive adjectives are always placed before the nouns they modify.

  Tus clases son grandes.   *Your classes are big.*
  Nuestros amigos llegan a las ocho.   *Our friends arrive at eight o'clock.*

- In Spanish, the construction **de** + *noun* can also be used to indicate possession. It is equivalent to the English *apostrophe s*.

  La música de Tacvba es bonita.   *Tacvba's music is pretty.*
  La hermana de Marcela estudia derecho.   *Marcela's sister studies law.*

- When the preposition **de** is followed by the definite article **el**, it contracts to **del**: **de** + **el** = **del**.[1]

  Los exámenes del profesor son difíciles.   *The professor's exams are difficult.*
  No es mi cuaderno, es de él.   *It's not my notebook, it's his.*

EXPANSIÓN More on structure and usage
Su and *sus*

The possessive adjectives **su** and **sus** can have different meanings (*your, his, her, their*). The context in which they are used indicates who the possessor is.

María y José leen **su** libro.   *María and José read their book.*
Ramón habla con **sus** amigos.   *Ramón speaks with his friends.*

When the identity of the possessor in the third person is not clear, the construction **de** + *noun* or **de** + *pronoun* can be used for clarification.

¿**De quién** es el libro?   *Whose book is it?*
Es **su** libro. Es el libro **de Paco.**   *It's his book. It's Paco's book.*
¿Son **sus** amigas?   *Are they her friends?*
Sí, son las amigas **de ella.**   *Yes, they're her friends.*

---

[1]The preposition **de** does not contract with the subject pronoun **él**.

APLICACIÓN

3-9 Pedro. Pedro is a student at a university in Monterrey, Mexico.

Paso 1 Read about Pedro and underline all of the possessive adjectives.

Soy Pedro, estudiante del Tec de Monterrey. Mi carrera es ingeniería eléctrica.
Tengo clases por la mañana y trabajo por la tarde. Vivo en un apartamento cerca
de la universidad, pero voy a mi casa los fines de semana. Mi familia vive en
Guanajuato. Mis clases más difíciles son informática y estadística. El profesor
de estadística tiene su doctorado de una universidad norteamericana. Este año
voy a ser estudiante de intercambio[1] en Canadá, donde voy a estudiar francés,
también. Mi novia[2] es de Quebec. Voy a conocer[3] a su familia y a sus amigos.

[1]*exchange student* [2]*girlfriend* [3]*meet*

Paso 2 Now write as many questions as you can about him to ask a classmate.

MODELO: E1: *¿Cuándo son sus clases?*
            E2: *Sus clases son por la mañana.*

3-10 ¿De quién/es es/son? Combine elements from each column to say to whom or
what the following things belong.

MODELO: *La clase de ingeniería eléctrica es del profesor joven. Es su clase.*

la clase de ingeniería eléctrica	el departamento de ingeniería
el reloj de plástico	los profesores de química
las sillas	*el profesor joven*
los diccionarios	el estudiante de geografía
el libro de arte	mi amigo
la mochila vieja	la niña pequeña
los bolígrafos rojos	la universidad
el horario de clases	el banco (*bank*)
los mapas	la profesora de diseño
el dinero	la cafetería
el correo electrónico	la estudiante de arte
las clases difíciles	la biblioteca (*library*)

3-11 Un campus excepcional. Think about your own university campus.

Paso 1 Complete the sentences with appropriate possessive adjectives and mark whether each statement is true for you or your campus. Then add two or three statements of your own.

	Cierto	Falso
MODELO: *Yo tengo cinco materias. Todas <u>mis</u> materias son interesantes.*	☑	☐
1. Nosotros tenemos un gimnasio impresionante. _____ gimnasio es nuevo y conveniente.	☐	☐
2. La librería vende muchos libros, y _____ precios son buenos.	☐	☐
3. Yo tengo un apartamento en el campus. _____ apartamento es grande y moderno.	☐	☐
4. Tú tienes una computadora portátil. _____ computadora es nueva y rápida.	☐	☐
5. Elena y Carmen tienen buenos horarios de clase. Todas _____ clases son después de las 10:00 de la mañana.	☐	☐
6. La profesora de geología tiene doscientos estudiantes en una de _____ clases. Todos _____ estudiantes son inteligentes y trabajadores.	☐	☐

Paso 2 Now, compare your opinions with a classmate. Do you agree?

MODELO: E1: *Yo tengo cinco materias. Todas <u>mis</u> materias son interesantes.*
E2: *Yo también. (Yo tengo cuatro materias. Todas mis materias son interesantes también.)*

3-12 ¿Cómo es? Take turns telling each other what the following things and people are like. Be sure to ask at least two follow-up questions to find out more about each topic.

MODELO: clase
E1: *¿Cómo es tu clase de inglés?*
E2: *Mi clase es buena.*
E1: *¿Sí? ¿Por qué?*
E2: *Porque el profesor es muy interesante.*
E1: *¿Sí? ¿Quién es?*
E2: *Es el Profesor Anderson.*

1. amigos	3. ciudad/pueblo (*town*)	5. profesor/a de...	7. trabajo
2. apartamento	4. universidad	6. familia	8. horario

3-13 Una universidad excepcional. In groups of three, write a description of your university using the features below and others that occur to you. Then read your description aloud to see which group has the most detailed description. Be sure that all adjectives agree with the nouns they modify.

la universidad	el programa de estudios	los equipos deportivos
los salones de clase	los estudiantes	los profesores
la cafetería	el horario de clases	los exámenes
las computadoras	los clubes sociales	la librería (*bookstore*)
el campus	los amigos	las clases de lenguas

MODELO: *Nuestra universidad es pequeña pero bonita. Tiene...*

03-15
to 03-17

3. Other expressions with *tener*

- You have used **tener** to show possession and to say you *have to* (*do something*).

  Tengo muchos amigos. *I have many friends.*

  Tienes que asistir a clase. *You have to attend class.*

- There are other common expressions that use **tener** where English uses the verb *to be*. Note that many of these refer to things we might feel (hunger, thirst, cold, etc.)

  ¿**Tienes** hambre? *Are you hungry?*

  No, pero **tengo** frío. *No, but I'm cold.*

  Tenemos prisa. *We're in a hurry.*

  Tienen ganas de visitar *They feel like visiting (are*
  México. *eager to visit) Mexico.*

¡Maribel tiene miedo!

| tener calor | tener frío | tener hambre | tener sed | tener miedo | tener sueño |

tener cuidado tener prisa tener razón tener ganas (de)

- Use the verb **tener** to express age.

  tener... años *to be . . . years old*

  ¿Cuántos años tienes? *How old are you?*

¿Cúantos años tienes?

Tengo cinco.

APLICACIÓN

3-14 En un concierto de Café Tacvba. Silvia and Patricio are going to a Café Tacvba concert.

Paso 1 First, read the conversation between Silvia and Patricio before the concert. Underline all of the expressions that use **tener.**

PATRICIO: El concierto es en media hora, ¿quieres algo?

SILVIA: Sí, una limonada porque tengo mucho calor y mucha sed.

PATRICIO: Tengo ganas de tomar un café fuerte porque tengo un poco de sueño. Con siete materias, siempre tengo que estudiar hasta muy tarde.

SILVIA: Como tenemos prisa, ¿por qué no vamos al bar de la esquina ahora y también comemos un sándwich?

PATRICIO: Tienes razón, tengo hambre. Vamos al bar ahora mismo.

Paso 2 Now answer the questions using expressions with **tener.**

1. ¿Por qué quiere una limonada Silvia?
2. ¿De qué tiene ganas Patricio y por qué?
3. ¿Por qué tiene sueño Patricio?
4. ¿Por qué crees que tienen prisa Silvia y Patricio?
5. ¿Qué van a hacer (*do*) antes del concierto? ¿Por qué?

3-15 ¿Y tú…? Match these statements to say when you feel the following and expand the context to explain. If none of the choices are appropriate, supply a new one. More than one answer is possible in some cases.

MODELO: *Tengo ganas de visitar… México porque allí hablan español.*

1. _____Tengo frío…
2. _____Tengo calor…
3. _____Tengo ganas de comer…
4. _____Tengo sed…
5. _____Tengo prisa…
6. _____Tengo cuidado…
7. _____Tengo sueño…
8. _____Tengo miedo…

a. en el desierto…
b. en el verano…
c. en un examen…
d. a las dos de la mañana…
e. en el invierno…
f. en una película (*movie*) de horror…
g. en un buen restaurante…
h. cuando tengo que llegar a tiempo (*on time*)…

3-16 ¿Cuántos años tienen? You may be familiar with these famous Mexicans. Take turns saying how old they are.

MODELO: Felipe Calderón, presidente de México (1962)
Tiene... años.

1. Carlos Fuentes, autor (1928)
2. Carlos Slim, empresario y uno de los hombres más ricos del mundo (1940)
3. Alfonso Cuarón, director de cine, *Y tu mamá también* (1961)
4. Carlos Santana, músico (1947)
5. Salma Hayek, actriz (1966)
6. Carlos Contreras, deportista de NASCAR (1970)
7. Laura Esquivel, novelista, *Como agua para chocolate* (1950)
8. Alejandro González Iñárritu, director de cine, *Amores perros* (1963)

¿Cuántos años tiene el presidente Felipe Calderón?

3-17 Investigación. Research the group Café Tacvba and write a paragraph about them in which you answer the questions that follow.

> **Busca:** cafe tacvba, cafe tacuba

- ¿Cuáles son sus nombres completos y sus apodos (*nicknames*)?
- ¿De dónde son?
- ¿Cuántos años tienen?
- ¿Cómo es su música?
- ¿Dónde va a ser su próximo concierto?
- ¿Vas a asistir? (*Sí, voy ... / No, no voy ...*)

03-18 to 03-22

¿Cuánto saben?

First, ask yourself if you can perform the following functions in Spanish. Then act out the scenarios with two or three classmates. Ask and respond to at least three questions in each situation.

✓ CAN YOU ...

☐ exchange information about classes?

☐ talk about things that belong to you?

☐ talk about how you and others feel?

WITH YOUR CLASSMATE(S) ...

Situación: En el centro estudiantil
Talk about your classes, say what you are studying and ask the others about their classes and what they are like.
Para empezar: *¿Qué estudias?¿Cómo es tu clase de...?*

Situación: En clase
Use possessive adjectives to discuss who owns the things you have in front of you.
Para empezar: *¿De quién es...?*

Situación: En un café
Talk about how you feel by using expressions with **tener** such as **tener hambre, sueño, ganas de,** etc. and then explain why you feel that way.
Para empezar: *Tengo ganas de... porque...*

📖 Perfiles

Mi experiencia

MI UNIVERSIDAD: LA UNAM

3-18 Para ti. How many students are in your university? Which college or department is the largest? Is there an entrance exam for your university? Read about Susana Buendía and her experiences at UNAM (Universidad Nacional Autónoma de México).

¡Hola y muchos saludos desde San Cristóbal de las Casas, Chiapas! Estoy aquí para empezar mi año de servicio social en una escuela rural de Chiapas.

¡Qué día me espera[1] mañana! Tengo que preparar una presentación sobre la UNAM para un grupo de estudiantes. El objetivo es animarles a pensar en[2] ir a estudiar a México algún día. Menos mal[3] que solo es sobre la Facultad de Filosofía y Letras y no de toda la universidad. En mi presentación, tengo que explicar que en el sistema de la UNAM hay unos 168.000 estudiantes pero que en mi facultad somos 7.000. Mi amiga Marta dice que en la Facultad de Derecho, donde ella estudia, hay aproximadamente 23.000 estudiantes. ¡Órale! ¡Es enorme!

Mi experiencia en la UNAM es fantástica. Tengo clases de tipo conferencia[4] y también talleres[5] más pequeños donde conversamos sobre[6] la materia y le hacemos preguntas al profesor. El examen de admisión es bastante caro y difícil, pero como es una universidad pública, la matrícula es muy baja. Acabo de recibir[7] mi licenciatura[8] pero como todos los estudiantes que estudian en la UNAM, tengo que hacer un año de servicio público. Por eso[9] estoy aquí en Chiapas este año.

Para mi presentación, voy a ponerles también música de uno de mis grupos favoritos, Café Tacvba, que es muy popular entre mis amigos en la UNAM.

[1]*awaits me*   [2]*to encourage them to think about*   [3]*Thank goodness*   [4]*lecture*   [5]*workshops*   [6]*about*
[7]*I have just received*   [8]*bachelor's degree*   [9]*That's why*

3-19 En su opinión. What similarities and differences can you perceive between la UNAM and your own university? Working in small groups, discuss your opinions and record your group's responses. Be prepared to share with the class.

Semejanzas:	Diferencias:

Mi música

"ERES" (CAFÉ TACVBA, MÉXICO)

Café Tacvba (or Tacuba) is a Mexican alternative rock band that has taken the world by storm in the last few years, winning several Grammy and Latin Grammy awards, including one each for "Best Rock Song" and "Best Alternative Song." One of the most daring and versatile bands, their music combines modern rhythms from rock to hip-hop with Latin folk (**mariachi, ranchero, tejano,** and **samba**) styles. "Eres" is on the album *Cuatro caminos* (2003).

Antes de ver y escuchar

3-20 El tema de la canción. The following words or phrases appear in the song "Eres." Match the English for each and hypothesize what the song is about.

1. _____ por ti
2. _____ aquí me tienes
3. _____ en este mundo
4. _____ le hace falta
5. _____ profundo
6. _____ mi vida
7. _____ mi salvación
8. _____ preciosa
9. _____ lo primero
10. _____ lo que más quiero

a. my life
b. my salvation
c. in this world
d. profound
e. for you
f. the first
g. what I want most
h. is lacking or he/she needs
i. precious
j. here you have me

Para ver y escuchar

 3-21 La canción. Go to the Internet to find the song or a video of Café Tacvba singing this song.

> **Busca:** cafe tacvba, cafe tacuba, eres video tacvba eres letra
>
> **If you would like to purchase this song:** *Go to iTunes Store>Music>More to Explore>iMix>Arriba 6e*

As you listen or watch, write three complete sentences in Spanish to describe what you hear or see.

MODELO: *Los artistas son muy activos.*

1. La canción...   2. El ritmo...   3. Los artistas...

Después de ver y escuchar

3-22 ¿Y tú? Create your own version of the song "Eres." Use the theme and some of the expressions listed in **3-20** to write five or six lines about someone or something important in your life. Your version can be serious or funny. Present it to the class and include a dedication.

MODELO: *"Eres" escrito por..., dedicada a... (mi universidad, mi madre, mi compañero/a de cuarto...)*

Segunda parte

¡Así lo decimos! VOCABULARIO

 ¡Así es la vida! ¿Dónde está la librería?

El campus de la Universidad Nacional Autónoma de México (UNAM) es enorme y tiene muchos edificios. Los estudiantes nuevos en la universidad buscan diferentes lugares en el mapa.

MARCELA: Pedro, tengo que ir a la librería para comprar un diccionario. ¿Dónde está?

PEDRO: Mira el mapa. Está enfrente de la Facultad de Medicina. ¿Vamos juntos ahora?

BETO: Oye, Tomás, ¿sabes dónde está la biblioteca?

TOMÁS: Pues mira, está cerquita[1], al lado de la librería.

ROSA: ¿Y la cancha de tenis?

TOMÁS: Está detrás del estadio. Vamos, te acompaño.

---

[1]cerquita = *cerca*. In Mexico it is common to use diminutives, in this case meaning "really close."

Vocabulario Los edificios de la universidad

Variaciones

In Spain, **la cancha de tenis** is more commonly **la pista de tenis**. In Argentina and Chile, the noun **cancha** is used in numerous expressions outside of sport, such as **¡Abran cancha!** (*Make way!*) and **sentirse en su cancha** (*to be in one's element*).

Los edificios	**Buildings**
el auditorio	*auditorium*
la biblioteca	*library*
la cafetería	*cafeteria*
la cancha de tenis	*tennis court*
el centro estudiantil	*student union*
el estadio	*stadium*
la Facultad de Arte	*School of Art*
la Facultad de Ciencias	*School of Science*
la Facultad de Derecho	*School of Law*
la Facultad de Filosofía y Letras	*School of Humanities*
la Facultad de Ingeniería	*School of Engineering*
la Facultad de Medicina	*School of Medicine*
la Facultad de Pedagogía	*School of Education*
el gimnasio	*gymnasium*
el laboratorio (de lenguas / de computadoras)	*(language/computer) laboratory*
la librería	*bookstore*
el museo	*museum*
el observatorio	*observatory*
la rectoría	*president's office*
el teatro	*theater*

en el museo

¿Dónde está?	**Where is it?**
al lado (de)	*beside, next to*
a la derecha (de)	*to the right (of)*
a la izquierda (de)	*to the left (of)*
cerca (de)	*nearby (close to)*
delante (de)	*in front (of)*
detrás (de)	*behind*
enfrente (de)	*facing, across (from)*
entre	*between*
lejos (de)	*far (from)*

en el teatro

Adverbios	**Adverbs**
casi	*almost*
siempre	*always*
solo	*only*

Otras palabros y expresiones	**Other words and expressions**
mira	*look*
pues	*well*
Te acompaño	*I'll go with you*
Vamos	*Let's go*

en la biblioteca

Verbos	**Verbs**
estar	*to be*
hacer	*to do, to make*
ir (a)	*to go*

el observatorio

Letras y sonidos

Syllabification

In Spanish, a syllable is a unit of timing for rhythm. Every syllable contains one vowel, which may be accompanied by glides and/or consonants.[1] Consonants combine with vowels to form syllables as follows.

- A single consonant (including **ch, ll, rr**) attaches to the following vowel.

  se-ño-ri-ta   **mu-cha-cho**   **bo-ca-di-llo**   **pi-za-rra**

- Two consonants attach to the following vowel when they consist of a strong consonant (**p, b, t, d, c, g, f**) followed by **r** or **l**.

  a-brir   **pro-ble-ma**   **no-so-tros**   **bo-lí-gra-fo**

  When two consonants do not form this combination, they are separated.

  tar-de   **de-por-te**   **blan-co**   **es-tu-dian-te**

- With combinations of three consonants that include **p, b, t, d, c, g, f** plus **r** or **l**, in positions two and three, the last two consonants attach to the following vowel.

  com-pli-ca-do   **hom-bre**   **es-cri-to-rio**   **in-glés**

  Without this sequence of sounds, only the last consonant attaches to the following vowel.

  pers-pec-ti-va   **ins-ta-lar**   **cons-tan-te**   **sols-ti-cio**

- With four consonants, the last two always attach to the following vowel.

  ins-truc-tor   **abs-trac-to**

APLICACIÓN

3-23 **¿Dónde está…?**   Give the location of the following buildings using the maps on page 92. What do you associate with these places?

MODELO: _____ la cancha de tenis

Está cerca del estadio. En la cancha de tenis los estudiantes practican tenis. Es un deporte rápido y difícil.

Lugares

1. __D__ la librería
2. __C__ la biblioteca
3. __F__ la cafetería
4. __A__ el gimnasio
5. __B__ el teatro
6. __E__ el estadio

Direcciones

a. Está al lado del estadio.
b. No está en el mapa.
c. Está al lado de la librería.
d. Está enfrente de la Facultad de Medicina.
e. Está a la izquierda del gimnasio.
f. Está detrás de la biblioteca.

3-24 **Nuestra universidad.**   Work together with a partner to write five sentences about where buildings are located on your campus, some true and others false. Then find a new partner and take turns reading your sentences, answering whether they are true or false and correcting false ones. Be prepared to share some of your sentences with the class.

MODELO: E1: *La biblioteca está lejos del laboratorio de lenguas.*
E2: *¡No es cierto! La biblioteca está muy cerca del laboratorio de lenguas.*

[1]Syllables with glides are discussed in *Capítulo 2.*

3-25 En la cola (*Standing in line*). Listen to a description of people standing in line. Place the number of the description in front of the name of each person.

_____ Marcela

_____ Mercedes

_____ Pepe

_____ Adrián

_____ Paula

Marcela   Pepe   Paula   Mercedes   Adrián

3-26 ¿Dónde están? ¿Cómo son? Where or who are the people in the following drawings? Include a few additional ideas about each.

MODELO:

El profesor Romero está en un laboratorio de... *la Facultad de Ciencias. Enseña química. Es viejo.*

1.

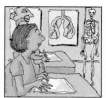

Lisa está en una clase de...

2.

Ana y Germán están en...

3.

Catalina y Jacobo compran libros en...

3-27A Las materias, la hora, el lugar. Take turns asking and answering questions in order to complete the missing information on your class schedules. **Estudiante B,** see **Appendix 1,** page A-5.

MODELO: ESTUDIANTE A: *¿A qué hora es la clase de...?*
ESTUDIANTE B: *¿Qué clase es a la/s...?*
ESTUDIANTE A: *¿Dónde es la clase de...?*
ESTUDIANTE B: *¿Quién es el/la profesor/a de...?*

Estudiante A:

Hora	Clase	Lugar	Profesor/a
	cálculo		María Gómez García
9:00	diseño	Facultad de Arte	
	biología		Julia Gómez Salazar
12:00		Facultad de Letras	Juan Ramón Jiménez
	física		Carlos Santos Pérez

¡Así lo hacemos! ESTRUCTURAS

03-34 to 03-39 **4.** The present tense of *ir* and *hacer*

¡Hola, Susana! ¿Adónde vas?

Voy a hacer mi tarea en la biblioteca.

- The Spanish verbs **ir** and **hacer** are irregular.

ir (*to go*)			
SINGULAR		PLURAL	
yo	**voy**	nosotros/as	**vamos**
tú	**vas**	vosotros/as	**vais**
Ud.	**va**	Uds.	**van**
él/ella	**va**	ellos/as	**van**

hacer (*to do; to make*)			
SINGULAR		PLURAL	
yo	**hago**	nosotros/as	**hacemos**
tú	**haces**	vosotros/as	**hacéis**
Ud.	**hace**	Uds.	**hacen**
él/ella	**hace**	ellos/as	**hacen**

- **Hacer** is only irregular in the first-person singular: **hago**.

   Hago la tarea por las noches.   *I do homework at night.*

- **Ir** is generally followed by the preposition **a**. When the definite article **el** follows the preposition **a**, they contract to **al: a** + **el** = **al**.

   Luis y Ernesto van **al**   *Luis and Ernesto are going*
      centro estudiantil.   *to the student center.*

- The construction **ir a** + *infinitive* is used in Spanish to express future action. It is equivalent to the English construction *to be going to* + *infinitive*.

   ¿Qué **vas a hacer** esta noche?   *What are you going to do tonight?*
   Voy a estudiar en la biblioteca.   *I'm going to study in the library.*

- When you are asked a question using **hacer**, you usually respond with another verb.

   Ricardo, ¿qué **haces** aquí?   *Ricardo, what are you doing here?*
   Busco un libro para mi clase.   *I'm looking for a book for my class.*

- **Hacer** is also used in idiomatic expressions such as: **hacer un viaje** (*to take a trip*) and **hacer preguntas** (*to ask questions*).

   Tengo que **hacer una pregunta.**   *I have to ask a question.*
   Susana va a **hacer un viaje**   *Susana is going to take a trip*
      a San Miguel.   *to San Miguel.*

APLICACIÓN

3-28 Gael García Bernal.
This Mexican film star
(*Amores perros, Y tu mamá
también, Babel, Diarios de
motocicleta*) is considered
one of Mexico's finest actors,
and has been recognized by
People en español as one of the
25 most beautiful people in
the world.

Paso 1 First, read the
newspaper article from *La
Opinión* about what he is
going to do next; underline all
forms of the verb **ir a** +
infinitive.

 Paso 2 Now, using the
expressions given below, prepare questions based on the previous article. Then take turns
asking and answering questions with a partner.

Un hijo para Gael

En una entrevista con *People en español*, Gael García
Bernal informa que ahora con la llegada de su primer
hijo va a dedicar los próximos meses a su familia,
especialmente a su novia, la actriz Dolores Fonzi, y al
pequeño, Lázaro. Los tres van a pasar un tiempo juntos
en Guadalajara cerca de la familia de él. Sus padres van
a ayudar a cuidar al niño. En ese tiempo, Gael también
va a preparar su próximo papel[1] con el director
Alfonso Cuarón. Es la segunda vez que los dos van a
trabajar juntos. Entre las estrellas de la película, se
incluyen además Javier Bardem y Salma Hayek.
Según los rumores, van a filmar la película en
México. Seguro que va a ser otro éxito[2] más para el
joven actor.

[1]*role* [2]*success*

MODELO: E1: *¿Con quiénes va a pasar unos meses?*
E2: *Con su novia y su hijo. ¿Dónde…?*

1. ¿Dónde…?   3. ¿Qué…?   5. ¿Por qué…?
2. ¿Cuándo…?   4. ¿Quiénes…?   6. ¿Cómo…?

3-29 ¿Qué hacen? Guess what the following people are doing according to where
they are. Complete each sentence with the correct form of **hacer** and an appropriate
completion from the list below.

| amigos | la comida | ejercicios | la lección | la tarea | el trabajo |

MODELO: sándwiches
En la cafetería, la señora *hace sándwiches*.

1. En la biblioteca, yo _____.   4. En la oficina, los secretarios _____.
2. En clase, nosotros _____.   5. En el restaurante, el chef _____.
3. En el gimnasio, tú _____.   6. En una fiesta, todos nosotros _____.

3-30 Planes para un partido. In groups of three, make plans to attend a soccer game
at a rival university. Use the following questions to guide you.

MODELO: ¿Adónde van?
Vamos a Indiana University para asistir al partido de fútbol.

1. ¿Con quiénes van?   5. ¿Qué van a hacer?
2. ¿Adónde van?   6. ¿Qué no van a hacer?
3. ¿Por cuánto tiempo van?   7. ¿Qué van a comprar?
4. ¿A qué hora van?   8. ¿Cuándo van a regresar (*return*)?

5. The present tense of *estar*

The English verb *to be* has two equivalents in Spanish, **ser** and **estar**. You have already learned the verb **ser** in **Capítulo 1,** and you have used some forms of **estar** to say how you feel, to ask how someone else feels, and to say where things and places are. The chart shows the present tense forms of **estar**.

estar (*to be*)			
SINGULAR		**PLURAL**	
yo	**estoy**	nosotros/as	**estamos**
tú	**estás**	vosotros/as	**estáis**
Ud.	**está**	Uds.	**están**
él/ella	**está**	ellos/as	**están**

- **Estar** is used to indicate the location of specific objects, people, and places.

  Ana Rosa y Carmen **están** en la cafetería.   *Ana Rosa and Carmen are in the cafeteria.*
  La cafetería **está** en el centro estudiantil.   *The cafeteria is in the student center.*

- **Estar** is also used to express a condition or state, such as how someone is feeling.

  ¡Hola, Luis! ¿Cómo **estás**?   *Hi, Luis! How are you?*
  Hola, Sara. **Estoy** cansado. Elena **está**   *Hi, Sara. I'm tired. Elena is sick.*
  enferma.

- Adjectives that describe physical, mental, and emotional conditions are used with **estar**.

aburrido/a	*bored*	**enojado/a**	*angry*
cansado/a	*tired*	**nervioso/a**	*nervous*
casado/a (con)	*married (to)*	**ocupado/a**	*busy*
contento/a	*happy*	**preocupado/a**	*worried*
enamorado/a (de)	*in love (with)*	**triste**	*sad*
enfermo/a	*sick*		

Samuel y Eva **están** casados.   *Samuel and Eva are married.*
Ramón **está** divorciado.   *Ramón is divorced.*
Alicia **está** enamorada del novio de Úrsula.   *Alicia is in love with Ursula's boyfriend.*

APLICACIÓN

3-31 Frida y Diego. Frida Kahlo lived her final years in her family home, La Casa Azul, with her husband, muralist Diego Rivera. After her death, the house was converted into a museum.

Paso 1 First, read the description of the Frida Kahlo museum housed in La Casa Azul. Underline the forms of **estar**.

La Casa Azul, Museo Frida Kahlo está en la colonia[1] de Coyoacán, un barrio bonito que está cerca de la UNAM. La casa está pintada de azul, el color favorito de Frida. El museo reúne una colección extensa de fotografías, libros y otros objetos personales de Frida y Diego que representan diferentes aspectos de su vida personal y artística. En una foto vemos a Frida que está en su estudio donde pinta uno de sus cuadros famosos. Los colores de las frutas y de los animales son muy vívidos. En otra foto Frida y Diego están juntos. Frida es muy delgada y baja. Diego, en cambio, es muy alto y gordo. Ellos están muy contentos y es fácil ver que están muy enamorados. En muchas fotos, Frida está con personajes importantes como Leon Trotsky y André Breton. El museo está abierto[2] de martes a domingo de 10 a 6 de la tarde.

[1]*neighborhood* [2]*open*

Paso 2 Now, answer the questions based on what you read above.

1. ¿Dónde está la casa de Frida y Diego?

2. ¿De qué color está pintada la casa?

3. ¿Qué hace Frida en una de las fotos?

4. ¿Con quién está en otra foto?

5. ¿Cómo están Frida y Diego cuando están juntos? ¿Por qué?

La Casa Azul

3-32 Planes para una visita al Museo Frida Kahlo. Complete the telephone conversation between two friends planning to visit the Frida Kahlo Museum with the correct forms of the verb **estar**.

JULIA: ¿Bueno?

CELIA: Julia, habla Celia. ¿Cómo (1) **estás** (tú)?

JULIA: Muy bien, ¿y tú?

CELIA: Yo (2) **estoy** bastante ocupada y estoy atrasada (*late*). ¡Oye!, ¿dónde (3) **estás** (tú) ahora?

JULIA: (4) **Estoy** en mi oficina.

CELIA: Pero, ¿no te acuerdas (*you remember*) que hoy vamos al Museo Frida Kahlo con Carlos y Juan?

JULIA: ¡Es verdad! ¿Qué hora es? ¿Dónde (5) **están** Carlos y Juan?

CELIA: Ellos ya (*already*) (6) **están** en Coyoacán.

JULIA: Ay, van a (7) **estar** preocupados, ¿no?

CELIA: No creo, pero me imagino que (8) **están** aburridos de esperar (*waiting*). ¡Tenemos que (9) **estar** allí ya!

JULIA: Salgo inmediatamente.

CELIA: (10) **Está** bien. Nos vemos en quince minutos.

3-33 En la cafetería. Challenge each other to identify people in the drawing by saying how they feel and why. Use **estar** with adjectives and expressions with **tener**.

cansado/a	enamorado/a
contento/a	enfermo/a
enojado/a	ocupado/a
nervioso/a	preocupado/a

MODELO: E1: *Está enfermo. Tiene mucho frío y necesita ir a casa.*
E2: *Es Pedro. Es verdad; tiene que ir a casa.*

3-34 ¿Cómo estás? Imagine that you are in the following situations. Say how you feel using the verb **estar** and an appropriate adjective from the list, and explain why.

aburrido/a	contento/a	enojado/a	nervioso/a	enfermo/a
cansado/a	enamorado/a de	ocupado/a	triste	preocupado/a

MODELO: en una fiesta
Estoy contento/a porque estoy con mis amigos.

1. a la medianoche
2. en clase
3. después de un examen
4. cuando hay mucho trabajo
5. en el hospital
6. con una persona especial
7. con Gael García Bernal
8. en una ciudad grande
9. en el gimnasio
10. lejos de la familia

3-35 Lo siento, no está aquí. Imagine that you are trying to avoid talking to someone on the telephone. Take turns inventing excuses for each other when the person calls. Here are some possibilities.

Lugares		**Razones**	
biblioteca	museo	enfermo/a	partido
hospital	restaurante	examen	clase de arte
estadio	centro estudiantil	proyecto importante	reunión con amigos

MODELO: E1: *Hola, ¿está Carlos?*
E2: *Lo siento, Carlos está en el gimnasio. Está con su novia.*
E1: *¿De verdad? ¡Yo estoy en el gimnasio y ellos no están aquí!*

3-36A ¿Dónde estoy? Take turns acting out your situations while your partner tries to guess where you are on campus. **Estudiante B**, see **Appendix 1,** page A-5. Then challenge other members of the class to guess where you are by acting out what you are doing.

MODELO: ESTUDIANTE A: (act out reading a book) *¿Dónde estoy?*
ESTUDIANTE B: *Estás en la biblioteca.*

Estudiante A:

1. (eating in the cafeteria)
2. (playing baseball in the stadium)
3. (listening to *¡Arriba!* dialogs in the language lab)
4. (buying books in the bookstore)
5. ¿...?

6. Summary of uses of *ser* and *estar*

In general, *ser* is used to express "traits." More specifically, it is used . . .

- with the preposition **de** to indicate origin and possession, and to tell what material something is made of.

Salma y Gael son de México.	*Salma and Gael are from Mexico.*
Las pinturas son de Diego.	*The paintings are Diego's.*
El bolígrafo es de plata.	*The pen is (made of) silver.*

Bob es de California.

- with adjectives to express characteristics of the subject, such as size, color, shape, religion, and nationality.

Tomás es alto y delgado.	*Tomás is tall and thin.*
Los jóvenes son católicos.	*The young men are Catholic.*
Somos mexicanos.	*We are Mexican.*

- with the subject of a sentence when followed by a noun or noun phrase that restates the subject.

Mi hermana es artista.	*My sister is an artist.*
Leo y Ligia son mis padres.	*Leo and Ligia are my parents.*

- to express dates, days of the week, months, and seasons of the year.

Es primavera.	*It's spring.*
Es (el) 10 de octubre.	*It's October 10th.*

- to express time.

Son las cinco de la tarde.	*It's five o'clock in the afternoon.*
Es la una de la mañana.	*It's one in the morning.*

- with the preposition **para** to tell for whom or for what something is intended or to express a deadline.

¿Para quién es la calculadora?	*For whom is the calculator?*
La composición es para el viernes.	*The composition is for (is due) Friday.*

- with impersonal expressions.

Es importante ir al laboratorio.	*It's important to go to the laboratory.*
Es fascinante estudiar la cultura hispana.	*It's fascinating to study Hispanic culture.*

- to indicate where and when events take place.

La fiesta es en mi casa.	*The party is at my house.*
El concierto es a las ocho.	*The concert is at eight.*

In general, *estar* is used to express "states." More specifically, it is used . . .

- to indicate the location of persons and objects.

La librería está cerca.	*The bookstore is nearby.*
Guadalajara está en México.	*Guadalajara is in Mexico.*

El museo está allí a la derecha.

- with adjectives to describe the state or condition of the subject.

Las chicas están contentas.	*The girls are happy.*
Pedro está enfermo.	*Pedro is sick.*

- with descriptive adjectives (or adjectives normally used with **ser**) to indicate that something is exceptional or unusual. This structure is often used this way when complimenting someone and in English is sometimes expressed with *look*.

  Carlitos, tienes ocho años; ¡estás muy grande!

  Señora Rubiales, usted está muy elegante esta noche.

  Carlitos, you're eight years old; you are (look) so big!

  Mrs. Rubiales, you are (look) especially elegant tonight.

Changes in meaning with *ser* and *estar*

- Some adjectives have different meanings depending on whether they are used with **ser** or **estar.**

Adjective	With *ser* (traits)	With *estar* (states)
aburrido/a	to be boring	to be bored
bonito/a	to be pretty	to look pretty
feo/a	to be ugly	to look ugly
guapo/a	to be handsome	to look handsome
listo/a	to be clever	to be ready
malo/a	to be bad, evil	to be ill
rico/a	to be rich	to taste good (food)
verde	to be green (color)	to be green (not ripe)
vivo/a	to be smart, cunning	to be alive

- Remember to use **hay** to say *there is/are.* It's frequently used with **mucho, poco,** or a number.

  Esta noche **hay** una fiesta en mi casa.

  Hay más de 44.000.000 de hispanos que viven en EE. UU.

  Hay muchos jóvenes en la discoteca.

  There's a party at my house tonight.

  There are more than 44,000,000 Hispanics living in the U.S.

  There are many young people at the disco.

APLICACIÓN

3-37 La familia Montesinos.   The Montesinos family lives in Mexico's second largest city, known also as the birthplace of the *mariachi.*

Paso 1   First, read the description of the Montesinos family and underline all the forms of **ser** and **estar**. Identify why they are used in each example.

MODELO: Los señores Montesinos <u>son</u> mexicanos. (*trait: nationality*)

La familia Montesinos

La familia Montesinos es una familia mexicana que vive en Guadalajara. Guadalajara está cerca de la costa pacífica de México. Guillermo, el papá, es muy trabajador. Olga Marta, la mamá, es de la Ciudad de México ý es muy simpática. Ellos tienen tres hijos: Billy, Martita y Érica. Billy es muy responsable. Está casado con María Josefa y ahora ellos están en Alemania donde Billy estudia ingeniería. Martita es muy inteligente. Ahora está en la capital donde visita a sus abuelos. Érica es muy alta y delgada y además, es muy trabajadora como su papá. Ella está en la biblioteca porque tiene que hacer su tarea. Esta noche la familia está muy contenta porque va a tener una fiesta para el aniversario de Guillermo y Olga Marta. Es importante invitar a toda la familia y a todos los amigos.

Paso 2 Now answer the following questions based on what you have read about the Montesinos family.

1. ¿De dónde es la familia?

2. ¿Dónde está la ciudad?

3. ¿Cómo es el papá?

4. ¿Cuántos hijos tienen?

5. ¿Quién está casada con Billy?

6. ¿Dónde viven los abuelos?

7. ¿Cómo es Érica?

8. ¿Por qué invitan a toda la familia esta noche?

En febrero la familia Montesinos visita el refugio de las monarcas en Michoacán donde cada año llegan millones de mariposas.

3-38 En la casa de mi hermandad (*sorority*). Ana belongs to a sorority in her university.

Paso 1 First, complete Ana's description of her sorority and what is happening tonight using the correct forms of **ser** or **estar,** or the verb **hay.**

Mi hermandad (1) _____ grande, (2) _____ treinta y cuatro hermanas. La casa (3) _____ un poco pequeña. (4) _____ en la avenida Florida que (5) _____ en el centro de la ciudad y muy cerca de la universidad. Esta noche (6) _____ una fiesta en nuestra casa. La fiesta para reclutar (*recruit*) nuevas hermanas (7) _____ a las ocho de la noche. Las nuevas hermanas siempre llegan temprano y ahora (8) _____ en la sala con Claudia, la presidenta de la hermandad. Ella (9) _____ muy social. (10) _____ también muy inteligente. La profesora Pérez, nuestra consejera, (11) _____ simpática. Ella (12) _____ psicóloga. Todas las hermanas (13) _____ en el patio con la profesora Pérez. Rosa, mi compañera de cuarto no, porque (14) _____ enferma. Rosa (15) _____ en cama (*bed*). (16) _____ las ocho y quince de la noche y (17) _____ muchas chicas en mi casa. Hay dos futuras hermanas muy interesantes. Carlota (18) _____ una joven alta y atlética; Sara (19) _____ la joven baja y rubia. (20) _____ argentinas, de Buenos Aires. ¡Bienvenidas, amigas! (21) _____ música, refrescos y comida. ¡Todo (22) _____ para celebrar esta importante ocasión!

Paso 2 Now write a short paragraph about someone you know. Include the following information:

¿Quién es?

¿Dónde está en este momento?

¿De dónde es?

¿Qué hace ahora?

¿Cómo es?

¿Qué va a hacer en el futuro?

¿Por qué?

Cultura en vivo

La lucha libre (*wrestling*) is a popular spectator sport in Mexico. One of the most famous wrestlers was *El Santo,* who became a folk hero and a symbol of justice for the common man through his appearances in comic books and movies. The anniversary of his death in 1984 is still commemorated by pilgrimages from all over Mexico to his mausoleum in Mexico City. Can you name a personality in the U.S. with a similar following since his or her death?

3-39A **¿Quién es?**   Take turns describing the following people using **ser, estar,** and **tener** and guessing who the person is. **Estudiante B**, see **Appendix 1,** page A-6.

MODELO: ESTUDIANTE A: *Es una mujer. Tiene treinta años. Es muy inteligente. Está aquí en la clase con nosotros...*

ESTUDIANTE B: *¡Es la profesora!*

Estudiante A:

1. Óscar de la Hoya (*champion boxer*)
2. LeBron James (*professional basketball player*)
3. Hulk Hogan (*professional wrestler*)
4. ¿...?

03-51 to 03-55

¿Cuánto saben?

First, ask yourself if you can perform the following functions in Spanish. Then act out the scenarios with two or three classmates. Ask and respond to at least three questions in each situation.

✓ CAN YOU . . .	WITH YOUR CLASSMATE(S) . . .
☐ describe yourself and others?	**Situación: En una fiesta** Introduce yourself and talk about yourself using the verb **ser** to say where you are from, your profession, what you are like, and the verb **estar** to say how you feel with adjectives such as **cansado/a, enojado/a, ocupado/a,** etc. and where places are located. Ask questions to find out about the other person, as well. **Para empezar:** *Hola, yo soy... y soy de...*
☐ make plans to do something with someone?	**Situación: En la biblioteca** Ask and answer questions about where you are going later and what you are going to do. Make plans to do something tonight. **Para empezar:** *¿Qué haces?*
☐ ask for and give simple directions?	**Situación: Estudiantes nuevos** Ask for and give directions to several places on campus. Use adverbs such as **cerca de, enfrente de,** etc. to say where things are. **Para empezar:** *¿Dónde está...?*

Observelations

03-56
to 03-58

¡Pura vida! EPISODIO 3

Antes de ver el video

3-40 Nuestra Tierra. Patricio and Silvia decide to meet at *Nuestra Tierra*, a restaurant in San José. Read the following review; then judge whether the statements that follow are **cierto (C)** o **falso (F)**.

> ¡Qué lugar más divertido! Este restaurante ofrece "cocina local típica" y tiene una atmósfera atractiva para complementar la comida. A primera vista es un lugar rústico, sin embargo, hay un señor que toca la guitarra y meseros que sirven la comida de una manera cordial. Como decoración hay cebollas[1] que cuelgan del techo[2], y cestas de legumbres[3] frescas.
>
> En este restaurante se puede comer bien y barato, y tomar la famosa cerveza *Imperial*. Sirven platos típicos costarricenses y es un gran lugar para empezar la noche. Está abierto[4] 24 horas todos los días y está ubicado en la Calle 15 con la Avenida 2, de San José.

[1]onions   [2]hanging from the ceiling   [3]vegetables   [4]open

1. ____ *Nuestra Tierra* es un restaurante de comida típica salvadoreña.
2. ____ Los meseros son bastante impacientes.
3. ____ Es un lugar muy elegante.
4. ____ Se sirve la cerveza *Imperial*.
5. ____ Está cerrado (*closed*) los lunes.

A ver el video

3-41 Los otros personajes. Watch the third episode of ¡**Pura vida!** where you will hear Silvia use the word **manzana** and Patricio will correct her using the word **cuadra.** Can you guess what the words mean? Then complete the following sentences by matching the phrases below.

| Silvia | Patricio | Hermés |

1. ____ Silvia está cerca de...
2. ____ El restaurante está...
3. ____ Patricio desea estudiar...
4. ____ Es necesario tomar un examen...
5. ____ Patricio solicita...
6. ____ Uno de los requisitos para Patricio es ser...

a. en una universidad norteamericana.
b. bastante lejos.
c. una beca *Fulbright*.
d. la Avenida Central.
e. colombiano.
f. de inglés.

Después de ver el video

3-42 Cómo llegar a *Nuestra Tierra*. Connect with the Internet to search for a map of downtown San José. Find the *Avenida Central* and see if you can find the corner where *Nuestra Tierra* is located. How many blocks would you have to walk?

> ↘ **Busca:** mapa centro san jose costa rica

Nuestro mundo

📖 ¡México fascinante!

03-59
to 03-60

El México de hoy es una síntesis de influencias indígenas, coloniales, modernas y naturales.

México es famoso por su artesanía como los alebrijes hechos de papel maché o de madera (*wood*) y las calaveras, figuras talladas de madera o de azúcar (*sugar*). Los alebrijes (sobre estas líneas) representan figuras fantásticas mientras que las calaveras (a la derecha) fusionan las culturas indígenas y la española.

La Reserva de la biosfera Celestún, en la península de Yucatán, se extiende unos 600 km^2. Es reconocida internacionalmente por ser el refugio invernal (*winter*) de numerosos flamencos y de muchas otras especies de aves. Los flamencos de Celestún son los más rosados de todo el mundo.

SISTEMA DE TRANSPORTE COLECTIVO
Red del Metro

La capital de México es enorme, y su metro es uno de los más extensos del mundo. Durante la excavación para el metro, encontraron (*they found*) una pirámide azteca completa entre las Líneas 1 y 2 de la estación Pino Suárez. Los ingenieros dejaron la pirámide intacta en la estación.

México

Población: 112 millones

Alfabetismo: 91%

Expectativa de educación formal[1]: 13 años

Gastos para la educación: 5,5% PIB

Usuarios de la Internet: 23,3 millones

Usuarios de teléfonos celulares: 79 millones

---

[1] School life expectancy

3-43 Identifica. Use the photos and the information presented above to supply the following information.

1. una artesanía (*handcraft*) popular
2. un medio de transporte en la capital
3. el origen de los colonizadores
4. una antigua civilización
5. una especie de ave

3-44 Desafío. Without looking at the map, see how many of these places you can identify. Check the map to confirm your responses.

1. la capital de México
2. una playa famosa
3. una ciudad en la frontera con EE. UU.
4. una península

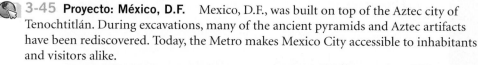 **3-45 Proyecto: México, D.F.** Mexico, D.F., was built on top of the Aztec city of Tenochtitlán. During excavations, many of the ancient pyramids and Aztec artifacts have been rediscovered. Today, the Metro makes Mexico City accessible to inhabitants and visitors alike.

Learn more about Mexico City by researching some of the following places or others that interest you: **el Palacio de Bellas Artes, el parque Chapultepec, el Zócalo, la Plaza Garibaldi, el Museo Nacional de Antropología, la Zona Rosa, la Basílica de la Virgen de Guadalupe, la Casa Azul.** Then, starting from Metro Station Universidad (where UNAM is located), create an itinerary of the places you would visit and include the following information:

- su nombre y dónde está
- la línea de Metro que tienes que tomar
- qué tiene de interés
- una foto representativa

> **Busca:** mexico DF metro

MODELO: *Voy a visitar el zoológico en el parque Chapultepec. Para ir, tengo que tomar la Línea 3 hasta Balderas, y después la Línea 1 hasta Chapultepec. Allí voy a ver los osos panda. El costo del boleto en el Metro es...*

El Museo de Antropología de México

ANTES DE LEER

3-46 **Una hipótesis.** Use the text format, title, and other visual clues along with background knowledge to get an idea of what the text is about. As you read, test your hypothesis to see if your initial guesses were correct. Sometimes, you will have to revise your hypothesis as you read.

3-47 **Formular una hipótesis.** Answer these questions before reading to formulate a hypothesis about its content.

1. ¿Dónde?
2. ¿Quiénes?
3. ¿Cuándo?

A LEER

3-48 **El museo.** Read the following text to discover more about this world-famous museum.

Visite el Museo Nacional de
ANTROPOLOGÍA
de México

El Museo Nacional de Antropología del Distrito Federal de México fue inaugurado en 1964 para albergar[1] lo más representativo de los avances de la época en la investigación antropológica sobre el mundo prehispánico y sus descendientes, los pueblos indígenas de México.

La Sala de los mayas en el museo contiene una importante colección de piezas[2] de las ancestrales comunidades mayas, que nos permiten apreciar diferentes etapas[3] y escenarios de su historia y su visión del mundo. En la sala hay testimonios de la vida diaria[4], de sus costumbres y tradiciones en torno a[5] la guerra[6], al comercio y a su pensamiento[7] religioso con prácticas rituales.

Los mayas desarrollaron una brillante cultura, construyendo grandes centros cívico-ceremoniales con pirámides y bellas obras[8] de arte.

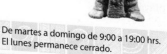

De martes a domingo de 9:00 a 19:00 hrs. El lunes permanece cerrado.

ADMISIÓN:

$51.00 M.N., de martes a sábado

Exentos de pago de 9:00 a 17:00 hrs:

- Niños menores de 13 años
- Estudiantes y profesores con credencial vigente[9]
- Adultos mayores de 60 años
- Jubilados[10], pensionados y discapacitados[11]
- Pasantes[12] e investigadores[13] que cuenten con el permiso del INAH (Instituto Nacional de Antropología e Historia)
- Todos los visitantes están exentos de pago los domingos de 9:00 a 17:00 hrs.

[1]house [2]pieces, items [3]stages [4]daily [5]pertaining to [6]war [7]thought [8]works [9]in force, in effect [10]retired persons
[11]disabled [12]Teachers [13]researchers

DESPUÉS DE LEER

3-49 ¿Comprendiste?   Complete each statement logically.

1. El museo está en...
   a. Teotihuacán.
   b. México, D.F.
   c. Cancún.

2. La colección maya incluye...
   a. figuras de guerreros.
   b. pinturas de los años 1950.
   c. animales prehistóricos.

3. La colección refleja...
   a. la vida religiosa.
   b. las fiestas del pueblo.
   c. el uso de animales domésticos.

4. Si no quieres pagar (*pay*), lo visitas el...
   a. sábado.
   b. domingo.
   c. lunes

5. Los martes no paga(n)...
   a. nadie (*no one*).
   b. las mujeres.
   c. los adultos mayores de sesenta años.

 3-50 El Museo Nacional de Antropología.   Connect with the Internet to visit this renowned museum in Mexico City. Look for the information that follows.

> **Busca:** museo nacional antropologia mexico

1. tres salas permanentes

2. una exposición temporal

3. una pieza interesante

 3-51 En mi opinión.   Compare your opinions with a classmate's by responding to the following statements using one of the expressions from the list.

| Sí, seguramente... | Sí, probablemente... | No... |

1. Tengo ganas de visitar México algún día.

2. Voy a visitar el Museo Nacional de Antropología.

3. Voy a visitar las pirámides.

4. Me gusta la arqueología.

5. Me gusta el arte.

Los mayas y los aztecas conmemoraban la muerte de sus enemigos con tallados (*carvings*) de sus víctimas.

📖 Taller

03-62
to 03-63

3-52 Un correo electrónico a un/a amigo/a. How would you describe your college experience to a Spanish-speaking friend or student in an e-mail?

A:	rmejias@lenguaspearson.mx
DE:	sbuendia@arribamail.com
ASUNTO:	Mi universidad

Hola, Raquel:
Hoy es 14 de octubre y estoy aquí en la biblioteca del Tec...
Espero recibir tu respuesta pronto.
Un abrazo de...

ANTES DE ESCRIBIR

- Respond to these questions before writing an e-mail to a friend about your student experience.

¿Cuál es la fecha de hoy?	¿Cómo son los profesores?
¿Dónde estás?	¿Dónde haces tu tarea?
¿Te gusta la universidad?	¿Dónde comes?
¿Qué estudias este semestre (trimestre/año)?	¿Adónde vas por la noche?
¿A qué hora son tus clases?	¿Qué vas a hacer mañana?
¿Recibes buenas notas (*grades*)?	¿...?

A ESCRIBIR

- Use the e-mail format above, beginning with **A, DE, ASUNTO**, and a greeting.

- Incorporate your answers to the previous questions in the e-mail. Connect your ideas with words such as **y, pero,** and **porque**.

- Ask your addressee for a reply to your e-mail.

- Close the e-mail with a farewell: **Un abrazo de**...

DESPUÉS DE ESCRIBIR

- **Revisar.** Review the following elements of your e-mail:
  - ☐ use of **ir, hacer,** and other **-er** and **-ir** verbs
  - ☐ use of **ser** and **estar**
  - ☐ agreement of subjects and verbs
  - ☐ agreement of nouns and adjectives
  - ☐ correct spelling, including accents

- **Intercambiar**
  Exchange your e-mail with a classmate's; make grammatical corrections and content suggestions. Then, respond to the e-mail.

- **Entregar**
  Rewrite your original e-mail, incorporating your classmate's suggestions. Then, turn in your revised e-mail and the response from your classmate to your instructor.

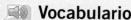

Vocabulario

Las materias (Academic) Subjects

la administración de empresas *business administration*
la arquitectura *architecture*
el arte *art*
la biología *biology*
el cálculo *calculus*
las ciencias políticas *political science*
las ciencias sociales *social science*
las comunicaciones *communications*
la contabilidad *accounting*
el derecho *law*
el diseño *design*
la educación física *physical education*
la economía *economics*
la estadística *statistics*
la filosofía *philosophy*
las finanzas *finance*
la física *physics*
la geografía *geography*
la geología *geology*
la historia *history*
la informática / la computación *computer science*
la ingeniería (eléctrica) *(electrical) engineering*
las matemáticas *mathematics*
la medicina *medicine*
la pedagogía *teaching, education*
la química *chemistry*
la veterinaria *veterinary science*

Sustantivos Nouns

la carrera *career, field*
el/la chico/a *boy/girl*
el correo electrónico *e-mail*
el dinero *money*
el horario (de clases) *(class) schedule*
el semestre *semester*
el trimestre *trimestre*
el videojuego *video game*

Adjetivos Adjectives

complicado/a *complicated*
exigente *challenging; demanding*
obligatorio/a *obligatory; required*

Adverbios Adverbs

antes (de) *before*
bastante *quite; fairly*
después (de) *after*
solamente *only*

Otras expresiones con tener Other expressions with *tener*

tener... años *to be . . . years old*
tener calor *to be warm, hot*
tener cuidado *to be careful*
tener frío *to be cold*
tener ganas (de) *to feel like*
tener hambre *to be hungry*
tener miedo *to be afraid*
tener prisa *to be in a hurry*
tener razón *to be right*
tener sed *to be thirsty*
tener sueño *to be sleepy*

Los edificios Buildings

el auditorio *auditorium*
la biblioteca *library*
la cafetería *cafeteria*
la cancha de tenis *tennis court*
el centro estudiantil *student union*
el estadio *stadium*
la Facultad de Arte *School of Art*
la Facultad de Ciencias *School of Science*
la Facultad de Derecho *School of Law*
la Facultad de Filosofía y Letras *School of Humanities*
la Facultad de Ingeniería *School of Engineering*
la Facultad de Medicina *School of Medicine*
la Facultad de Pedagogía *School of Education*
el gimnasio *gymnasium*
el laboratorio (de lenguas / de computadoras) *(language/computer) laboratory*
la librería *bookstore*
el museo *museum*
el observatorio *observatory*
la rectoría *president's office*
el teatro *theater*

¿Dónde está...? Where is . . .?

al lado (de) *beside, next to*
a la derecha (de) *to the right (of)*
a la izquierda (de) *to the left (of)*
cerca (de) *nearby (close to)*
delante (de) *in front (of)*
detrás (de) *behind*
enfrente (de) *facing, across (from)*
entre *between*
lejos (de) *far (from)*

Adverbios Adverbs

casi *almost*
siempre *always*
solo *only*

Otras palabras y expressions Other words and expressions

mira *look*
pues *well*
Te acompaño *I'll go with you*
Vamos *Let's go*

Verbos Verbs

estar *to be*
hacer *to do; to make*
ir *to go*

Expressions with *todo/a/os/as* See page 80.
Expressions with *hacer* See page 96.
The Numbers *101–3.000.000* See page 82.
Adjectives with *estar* See page 98.
Possessive adjectives See page 84.

4

¿Cómo es tu familia?

Readiness
Check

América Central I: Guatemala, El Salvador, Honduras

«Al hombre mayor, dale honor».

Refrán: Respect your elders.

Rigoberta Menchú recibió el Premio Nobel por su lucha por los derechos humanos de los indígenas de Guatemala.

Tikal, Guatemala, es uno de los sitios más importantes de la civilización maya.

¡Así lo decimos! VOCABULARIO

 ¡Así es la vida! Una tamalada

 Las mujeres de la familia Suárez preparan tamales para la fiesta de cumpleaños del abuelo.

CLARA: Suegra, ¿qué servimos con los tamales?

CHELA: Suegra, ¿qué piensas que prefiere tomar el abuelo?

ANITA: Tía Chela, tenemos refrescos, ¿no?

 Los hombres de la familia Suárez esperan la comida.

JOAQUÍN: Feliz cumpleaños, papá.

EL ABUELO
(DON RAMÓN): Gracias, hijo. ¡Qué deliciosos van a estar los tamales de tu mamá!

TOMÁS: ¡Salud!

TOMASITO: Papi, ¿cuándo vamos a almorzar? ¡Tengo hambre!

Vocabulario Miembros de la familia

04-02 to
04-06

04-02 to
04-06

Variaciones

In Mexico, **padre** is used as an adjective to mean *awesome*, as in **¡Qué padre!**, **Está muy padre**, or **¡Padrísimo!** The term **madre** is used in a lot of Mexican slang, so much so that it often is avoided in favor of **mamá** when speaking about someone's mother.

Variaciones

In Spain, the terms **tío/tía** have a colloquial meaning roughly equivalent to American English *guy/gal, dude, buddy.*

Miembros de la familia	Family members
el/la abuelo/a	*grandfather/grandmother*
el/la cuñado/a	*brother-in-law/sister-in-law*
el/la esposo/a	*husband/wife*
el/la hermanastro/a	*stepbrother/stepsister*
el/la hermano/a	*brother/sister*
el/la hijo/a	*son/daughter*
la madrastra	*stepmother*
la madre	*mother*
el/la nieto/a	*grandson/granddaughter*
el/la novio/a	*boyfriend/girlfriend, groom/bride*
la nuera	*daughter-in-law*
el padrastro	*stepfather*
el padre	*father*
el/la perro/a	*dog*
el/la primo/a	*cousin*
el/la sobrino/a	*nephew/niece*
el/la suegro/a	*father-in-law/mother-in-law*
el/la tío/a	*uncle/aunt*
el yerno	*son-in-law*

mi abuela
Marina: 65 años

mi abuelo
Ramón: 70 años

mi madre
Clara: 30 años

mi padre
Tomás: 35 años

mi tío
Joaquín: 45 años

mi tía
Chela: 45 años

mi hermana
Anita: 10 años

yo (Tomasito): 6 años

mi primo
Beto: 8 años

Verbos	Verbs
almorzar (ue)	*to have lunch*
costar (ue)	*to cost*
dormir (ue)	*to sleep*
empezar (ie)	*to begin*
encontrar (ue)	*to find*
entender (ie)	*to understand*
ganar	*to earn*
jugar a (ue)	*to play*
pasar	*to spend (time)*
pensar (ie) en	*to think (about)*
pensar (ie) (+*infinitive*)	*to plan (to do something)*
pedir (i)	*to ask for, to request*
perder (ie)	*to lose*
poder (ue)	*to be able, can*
preferir (ie)	*to prefer*
querer (ie)	*to want, to love*
recordar (ue)	*to remember*
repetir (i)	*to repeat, to have a second helping*
servir (i)	*to serve*
soñar (ue) (con)	*to dream (about)*
venir (ie)	*to come*
volver (ue)	*to return*

Adjetivos	Adjectives
casado/a	*married*
divorciado/a	*divorced*
mayor	*older*
menor	*younger*
soltero/a	*single, unmarried*
unido/a	*close, close-knit*

Otras palabras y expresiones útiles

algún día	*someday*
la comida	*food*
conmigo	*with me*
contigo	*with you*
el refresco	*soft drink*

APLICACIÓN

4-1 ¿Quién es quién? Look at Tomasito's family tree on the previous page and explain the relationships between the members.

MODELO: Tomasito y Anita.

Son hermanos. Anita es la hermana de Tomasito y él es el hermano de ella.

1. don Ramón y doña Marina
2. Chela y Beto
3. Chela y don Ramón
4. Anita y Beto
5. Beto y Tomás
6. don Ramón y Anita
7. Joaquín y Clara
8. Tomás y don Ramón y doña Marina

4-2 La boda (*wedding*) de Clara y Tomás. Answer the following questions based on the invitation to the wedding of Clara Sosa Sánchez and Tomás Suárez Ferrero.

1. ¿Quiénes son los novios?

2. ¿Cómo se llama el padre de la novia?[1]

3. ¿Cómo se llama la madre de la novia?

4. ¿Quiénes son los futuros suegros de Clara?

5. ¿Dónde es la ceremonia? ¿Y la recepción?

6. ¿En qué fecha y a qué hora es la ceremonia?

José Sosa Beléndez
Elena Sánchez de Sosa
y
Ramón Suárez Buenahora
Marina Ferrero de Suárez
tienen el honor de invitarle
al matrimonio de sus hijos
Clara y Tomás
el viernes veintisiete de mayo
de dos mil once
a las tres de la tarde
Misa Nupcial en
Iglesia San Jorge
San Salvador, El Salvador
Recepción y cena
Salón Real, Hotel Princesa

---

[1]See **Perfiles: Nombres, apellidos y apodos** in **Capítulo 2** for information on Hispanic last names.

🔊 **4-3 Entre familia.** Learn about Clara's family before she married Tomás.

Paso 1 Listen as Clara describes her family and complete her family tree by writing the names of the three generations of family members that live at home.

Clara

Paso 2 Take another look at the family tree you completed in **Paso 1** and give the relationships for each of these people.

MODELO: *Clara es la hija de José Luis…*(etc.)

👥 **4-4 Tu árbol genealógico.** Draw a family tree, based on your own family, in which some of the members are real and some are fictitious. Take turns describing your family and deciding if each is telling the truth about family members.

MODELO: E1: *Mi abuelo se llama don Juan. Es moreno, muy guapo y bastante rico. Es muy popular entre las mujeres.*
E2: *No es verdad. No te creo. / ¿De verdad? Cuéntame más.* (Tell me more.)

👥 **4-5 ¿Cómo es tu familia?** With a classmate, take turns asking and answering questions about your families.

MODELO: E1: *¿Viven tus abuelos con tu familia?*
E2: *Sí, viven con nosotros. ¿Y tus abuelos?*
E1: *No, mis abuelos no viven con nosotros.*

1. ¿Viven tus abuelos con tu familia?

2. ¿Dónde vive tu familia?

3. ¿Cuántos hermanos o hermanas tienes?

4. ¿Trabajan o estudian tus hermanos?

5. ¿Cuántos primos tienes?

6. ¿Viven cerca tus primos?

7. ¿…?

¡Así lo hacemos! ESTRUCTURAS

04-07 to 04-12

1. The present tense of stem-changing verbs: *e → ie, e → i, o → ue*

¿Quiere un sándwich de pollo?

No señor, prefiero una hamburguesa.

You have already learned how to form the present tense of regular **-ar**, **-er**, and **-ir** verbs and a few irregular verbs. The following verbs require a change in the stem vowel[1] of the present forms, except in **nosotros/as** and **vosotros/as**. There are three main stem changes: **e** to **ie**; **e** to **i**; **o** to **ue**. There is one verb, **jugar**, that has a **u** to **ue** stem change.

El cambio e → ie

- In this stem-changing pattern, the **e** of the stem changes to **ie** in all forms except **nosotros/as** and **vosotros/as**.

querer (*to want, to love*)			
yo	qu**ie**ro	nosotros/as	queremos
tú	qu**ie**res	vosotros/as	queréis
Ud.	qu**ie**re	Uds.	qu**ie**ren
él/ella	qu**ie**re	ellos/as	qu**ie**ren

- The following are some common **e → ie** verbs.

empezar	*to begin*
entender	*to understand*
pensar (en)	*to think (about)*
pensar (+ *infinitive*)	*to plan (to do something)*
perder	*to lose*
preferir	*to prefer*

Te **quiero,** cariño.	*I love you, dear.*
Siempre **pensamos en** nuestro abuelo.	*We always think about our grandfather.*
Pienso ver una película esta noche.	*I plan to see a movie tonight.*
¿A qué hora **empieza** la función?	*At what time does the show start?*

- Like **tener,** the verb **venir** (*to come*) has an additional irregularity in **yo.**

tener			
yo	**tengo**	nosotros/as	tenemos
tú	t**ie**nes	vosotros/as	tenéis
Ud.	t**ie**ne	Uds.	t**ie**nen
él/ella	t**ie**ne	ellos/as	t**ie**nen

venir			
yo	**vengo**	nosotros/as	venimos
tú	v**ie**nes	vosotros/as	venís
Ud.	v**ie**ne	Uds.	v**ie**nen
él/ella	v**ie**ne	ellos/as	v**ie**nen

Tengo que pasar por mi novia a las ocho.	*I have to stop by for my girlfriend at eight.*
Si Ester y Rubén **vienen** el viernes, yo **vengo** también.	*If Ester and Rubén come Friday, I'll come too.*

---

[1] In these forms the stem contains the stressed syllable.

El cambio e → i

- Another stem-changing pattern changes the stressed **e** of the stem to **i** in all forms except **nosotros/as** and **vosotros/as.**

¡Repito! ¡No estoy enojada contigo!

pedir (*to ask for, to request*)			
yo	pido	nosotros/as	pedimos
tú	pides	vosotros/as	pedís
Ud.	pide	Uds.	piden
él/ella	pide	ellos/as	piden

- All **e → i** stem-changing verbs have the **-ir** ending. The following are some other common **e → i** verbs.

repetir	*to repeat, to have a second helping*
servir	*to serve*

La instructora **repite** las instrucciones solo una vez.	*The instructor repeats the instructions only one time.*
¿**Servimos** la sopa primero?	*Do we serve the soup first?*

El cambio o → ue

- Another category of stem-changing verbs is one in which the **o** changes to **ue.** As with **e → ie** and **e → i,** there is no stem change in the **nosotros/as** and **vosotros/as** forms.

Ella siempre sueña que está en la playa.

volver (*to return, to come back*)			
yo	v**ue**lvo	nosotros/as	volvemos
tú	v**ue**lves	vosotros/as	volvéis
Ud.	v**ue**lve	Uds.	v**ue**lven
él/ella	v**ue**lve	ellos/as	v**ue**lven

- Other commonly used **o → ue** stem-changing verbs include the following:

almorzar	*to have lunch*
costar[1]	*to cost*
dormir	*to sleep*
encontrar	*to find*
jugar[2] **a**	*to play*
poder	*to be able, can*
recordar	*to remember*
soñar (con)	*to dream (about)*

Mañana **juego** al tenis con mi tía.	*Tomorrow I'm playing tennis with my aunt.*
Almorzamos con mis abuelos todos los domingos.	*We have lunch with my grandparents every Sunday.*
¿**Sueñas con** ser rico algún día?	*Do you dream about being rich someday?*
No **recuerdo** a mi tía muy bien.	*I don't remember my aunt very well.*

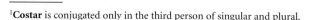

[1]**Costar** is conjugated only in the third person of singular and plural.
[2]**Jugar** follows the same pattern as **o → ue** verbs, but the change is **u → ue.**

APLICACIÓN

Presencia hispana

Many immigrants from Central America have been reluctant to become involved in politics because in their home countries it was dangerous to organize politically. Newly arrived immigrants are not always welcomed by established Hispanic communities. When you think about Hispanics in the U.S. and Canada, do you distinguish between nationalities?

4-6 Una entrevista con Rigoberta Menchú. Rigoberta Menchú won the Nobel Peace Prize in 1992 for her work with the indigenous peoples of Guatemala.

Paso 1 Read the interview with her and underline all of the stem-changing verbs.

REPORTERA: Señora Menchú, usted es famosa por su trabajo con los indígenas de Guatemala. También tiene un Premio Nobel por sus esfuerzos[1]. ¿Qué piensa hacer ahora?

RIGOBERTA: Pienso trabajar por los derechos humanos[2] para las personas oprimidas[3] del mundo.

REPORTERA: ¿Viene a Washington este año?

RIGOBERTA: No, este año no pienso ir porque estoy en Nueva York. Sirvo en un comité de las Naciones Unidas.

REPORTERA: Veo que usted no pierde la oportunidad de continuar su trabajo y el Premio Nobel de la Paz confirma su dedicación. Por cierto, ¿cómo recuerda la ceremonia de los Premios Nobel?

RIGOBERTA: Pues, recuerdo muy bien la ceremonia, pero no puedo recordar los nombres de toda la gente[4]. Algún día voy a volver a Estocolmo para visitar los museos y pasar más tiempo con la gente.

REPORTERA: ¿Con qué sueña usted?

RIGOBERTA: Sueño con un mundo mejor y pido paz para todos.

REPORTERA: Encuentro admirable su generosidad. Gracias.

---

[1]*efforts* [2]*human rights* [3]*oppressed* [4]*people*

Paso 2 Answer the following questions based on the interview.

1. ¿Por qué es famosa Rigoberta Menchú?

2. ¿Qué piensa hacer este año?

3. ¿Qué hace en Nueva York?

4. ¿Qué no recuerda bien de su tiempo en Estocolmo?

5. ¿Por qué quiere volver a Estocolmo?

6. ¿Con qué sueña ahora?

7. ¿Para quiénes pide paz?

4-7 Ana María y Antonio hacen planes. Antonio has invited his friend, Ana María, to visit him in Ciudad de Guatemala. Complete her explanation with the correct forms of logical verbs from the list. (You may use some verbs more than once.)

costar	jugar	perder	poder
entender	pensar	preferir	querer

Antonio y yo (1) _Pensamos_ hacer planes para el viernes. Nosotros
(2) _Podemos_ ir al cine. Antonio (3) _quiere_ ver una película nueva
de El Salvador que se llama *Sobreviviendo Guazapa*[1]. Yo (4) _entiendo_ las películas
francesas, pero Antonio no (5) _entiende_ francés. Su madre (6) _Piensa_
que debemos jugar al tenis. Antonio (7) _puede_ jugar al tenis, pero yo no
(8) _juego_ muy bien. A Antonio le gusta jugar conmigo porque yo siempre
(9) _pierdo_. También hay un concierto de música hondureña el viernes, pero los
boletos (*tickets*) (10) _cuestan_ mucho. ¡Es mejor pasar el viernes en casa con la
familia!

4-8 Desafío: Entre familia. Using the verbs listed below, race to write as many meaningful sentences in Spanish as you can. Each sentence must have a different subject, verb, and complement, and must include family members. The first person who believes he/she has six correct sentences calls out *¡TENGO!* The rest of the group will judge if your sentences are correct.

MODELO: *(Yo) Almuerzo con mis primos en la universidad.* (correcto)

costar	jugar (a)	poder	recordar
dormir	pedir	preferir	soñar (con)
empezar	pensar	querer	volver (a)

---

[1]See *Páginas* for a review of this movie

Cultura en vivo

Tamales are a favorite food throughout Central America and Mexico. They are made with corn mass stuffed with a **relleno** (*filling*) of chicken or pork, then wrapped in corn husks or plantain leaves and steamed. In some countries, **tamales** are usually reserved for Christmas and other special occasions when friends and family get together for a **tamalada**, a **tamal**-making party. The **tamalada** is a special time for everyone to share news and events while they work. What food traditions bring your family together?

4-9 En casa. Every household is different.

Paso 1 First write complete sentences as they are true for your household. Be sure to conjugate the verbs to agree with their subjects.

MODELO: En casa nosotros (**servir**)... (refrescos; café; agua; cerveza...) con la cena (*dinner*).
En casa, servimos refrescos con la cena.

En casa...

1. Yo (**almorzar**)... (solo/a; con mi novio/a; con mi familia; con mis amigos/as...).

2. Durante la cena, mi familia (**preferir**)... (ver la televisión; hablar de política; escuchar la radio; hablar de fútbol...).

3. Nosotros (**dormir**) la siesta... (después de la cena; todos los días; por una hora; cuando tenemos sueño...).

4. Mis (amigos/hermanos) (no) (**poder**)... (comer conmigo; ver la televisión conmigo; estudiar conmigo; trabajar conmigo...).

5. Mañana nosotros (**pensar**) preparar comida ... (mexicana; italiana; francesa; americana...).

6. Cuando hay una comida especial, mis (padres; hermanos; amigos) (**volver**)... (tarde; temprano; a tiempo).

7. Hoy, yo (no) (**querer**)... (preparar la cena; jugar al tenis; ir a la biblioteca...).

8. Esta noche, mis amigos (**soñar**) con... (ir a un concierto; tener una fiesta; jugar a...).

Paso 2 Now compare your households to see what you have in common.

MODELO: E1: *En mi casa, servimos refrescos con la cena. ¿Y en tu casa?*
E2: *Bueno, en mi casa servimos agua o café.*

En mi casa servimos tamales en Navidad.

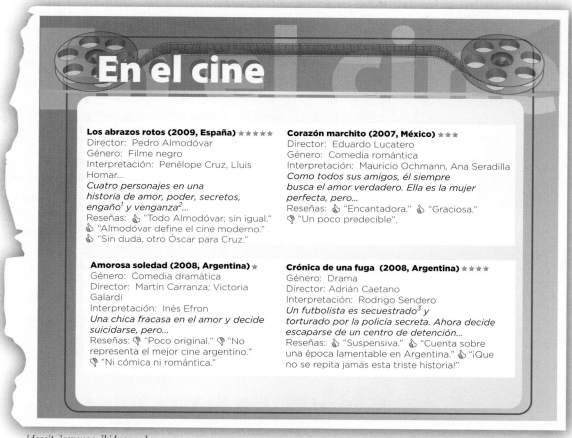

4-10 Festival de cine. Take a look at the announcement below to see what movies will be shown during the Latino film festival. Then in groups, discuss which movies you prefer to see and why. Which is the most popular among your group? Use the different types of movies listed to help in your discussion.

En el cine

Los abrazos rotos (2009, España) ★★★★★
Director: Pedro Almodóvar
Género: Filme negro
Interpretación: Penélope Cruz, Lluis Homar...
Cuatro personajes en una historia de amor, poder, secretos, engaño[1] y venganza[2]...
Reseñas: 👍 "Todo Almodóvar; sin igual." 👍 "Almodóvar define el cine moderno." 👍 "Sin duda, otro Óscar para Cruz."

Corazón marchito (2007, México) ★★★
Director: Eduardo Lucatero
Género: Comedia romántica
Interpretación: Mauricio Ochmann, Ana Seradilla
Como todos sus amigos, él siempre busca el amor verdadero. Ella es la mujer perfecta, pero...
Reseñas: 👍 "Encantadora." 👍 "Graciosa." 👎 "Un poco predecible".

Amorosa soledad (2008, Argentina) ★
Género: Comedia dramática
Director: Martín Carranza; Victoria Galardi
Interpretación: Inés Efron
Una chica fracasa en el amor y decide suicidarse, pero...
Reseñas: 👎 "Poco original." 👎 "No representa el mejor cine argentino." 👎 "Ni cómica ni romántica."

Crónica de una fuga (2008, Argentina) ★★★★
Género: Drama
Director: Adrián Caetano
Interpretación: Rodrigo Sendero
Un futbolista es secuestrado[3] y torturado por la policía secreta. Ahora decide escaparse de un centro de detención...
Reseñas: 👍 "Suspensiva." 👍 "Cuenta sobre una época lamentable en Argentina." 👍 "¡Que no se repita jamás esta triste historia!"

[1]*deceit* [2]*revenge* [3]*kidnapped*

películas...	de acción
	sentimentales
	de 3D
	de misterio
	trágicas
	humorísticas
	del director español Almodóvar
	de suspenso
	mexicanas/argentinas/españolas...

MODELO: *Quiero ver* Corazón marchito *porque prefiero las comedias sentimentales.*

📖 2. Direct objects, the personal *a*, and direct object pronouns

¿Quieres invitar a Jorge?

¡Sí, vamos a invitarlo!

Los complementos directos

- A direct object is the noun that generally follows and receives the action of the verb. The direct object is identified by asking *whom* or *what* about the verb. Note that the direct object can either be an inanimate object (**un carro**) or a person (**su amigo Luis**).

  Pablo va a comprar **un carro.**   *Pablo is going to buy a car.*
  Anita llama **a su amigo Luis.**   *Anita calls her friend Luis.*

La *a* personal

- When the direct object is a definite person or persons, an **a** precedes the noun in Spanish. This is known as the personal **a.** However, the personal **a** is usually omitted after the verb **tener.**

  Quiero mucho **a** mi papá.   *I love my father a lot.*
  Julia y Ricardo tienen un hijo.   *Julia and Ricardo have a son.*

- The personal **a** is not used with a direct object that is an unspecified or indefinite person.

  Ana quiere un novio inteligente.   *Ana wants an intelligent boyfriend.*

- The preposition **a** followed by the definite article **el** contracts to form **al.**

  Alicia visita **al** médico.   *Alicia visits the doctor.*

- When the interrogative **quién(es)** requests information about the direct object, the personal **a** precedes it.

  ¿A quién llama Elisa?   *Whom is Elisa calling?*

- The personal **a** is required before every specific human direct object in a series.

  Visito **a** Emilio y **a** Lola.   *I visit Emilio and Lola.*

Los pronombres de complemento directo

A direct object noun is often replaced by a direct object pronoun. The chart below shows the forms of the direct object pronouns.

Te quiero mucho.

	Singular		**Plural**
me	*me*	**nos**	*us* / we
te	*you* (inf.)	**os**	*you* (inf.)
lo/la	*you* (for.) (masc./fem.)	**los/las**	*you* (for.) (masc./fem.)
lo/la	*him/her, it* (masc./fem.)	**los/las**	*them* (masc./fem.)

- Direct object pronouns are generally placed directly before the conjugated verb. If the sentence is negative, the direct object pronoun goes between **no** and the verb.

  ¿Me buscas?   *Are you looking for me?*
  No, no **te** busco.   *No, I'm not looking for you.*

- Third-person direct object pronouns agree in gender and number with the nouns they replace.

  Quiero **el dinero.** → **Lo** quiero.

  Necesitamos **los cuadernos.** → **Los** necesitamos.

  Llamo **a Mirta.** → **La** llamo.

  Buscamos **a las chicas.** → **Las** buscamos.

- Direct object pronouns are commonly used in conversation when the object is established or known. When the conversation alternates between first and second persons (*me, us, you*), remember to make the proper transitions.

Hijo, ¿cuándo **nos** llamas?	*Son, when will you call us?*
Los llamo esta noche, padre.	*I'll call you tonight, father.*
Querida, ¿**me** quieres de verdad?	*Dear, do you really love me?*
Sí, **te** quiero con todo el corazón.	*Yes, I love you with all my heart.*

- In constructions that use the infinitive, direct object pronouns may either precede the conjugated verb or be attached to the infinitive.

  Adolfo va a llamar **a Ana.**   *Adolfo is going to call Ana.*

  Adolfo va a llamar**la.**
  Adolfo **la** va a llamar.   *Adolfo is going to call her.*

- In negative sentences, the direct object pronoun is placed between **no** and the conjugated verb, or is attached to the infinitive.

  Adolfo no **la** va a llamar.
  Adolfo no va a llamar**la.**   *Adolfo is not going to call her.*

APLICACIÓN

4-11 Una visita al Museo Popol Vuh.   This museum houses an impressive collection of art and artifacts.

Paso 1   Read about the museum and underline all direct objects.

El Museo Popol Vuh reúne una de las mejores colecciones de arte prehispánico y colonial de Guatemala. La colección incluye obras maestras[1] del arte maya elaboradas en cerámica, piedra[2] y otros materiales. Además, posee un importante conjunto[3] de obras de platería[4] e imaginería[5] colonial.

El museo está en el Campus Central de la Universidad Francisco Marroquín, en Ciudad de Guatemala. Este museo ofrece una oportunidad única para apreciar la historia y cultura de Guatemala. Si visitas esta ciudad, tienes que visitar el museo y apreciar sus artefactos mayas.

Dirección: Avenida La Reforma, 8-60, Zona 9, 6° piso.

Horario: de lunes a sábado de 9:00 a 16:30 hrs.

---

[1]*masterpieces*   [2]*stone*   [3]*group*   [4]*silver*   [5]*statuary*

Paso 2 ¿Cómo es el museo?   Now answer questions based on what you have read above.

1. ¿Dónde está el museo?

2. ¿Por qué es importante?

3. ¿A qué hora lo abren de lunes a sábado? ¿Y los domingos?

4-12 En la Universidad Francisco Marroquín. Juan Antonio is a student at the Universidad Francisco Marroquín in Ciudad de Guatemala. Read the conversation between him and Ana María; underline the direct objects and write the personal **a** (or **al**) wherever necessary.

ANA MARÍA: Oye, Juan Antonio. ¿(1) _A_ quién ves todos los días?

JUAN ANTONIO: Yo siempre veo (2) _A_ Tomás en la universidad. Tomamos (3) _____ café todas las tardes.

ANA MARÍA: ¿Ven (4) _____ muchos amigos allí?

JUAN ANTONIO: Sí, claro. Siempre vemos (5) _A_ Mercedes y (6) _A_ Gustavo. A veces (*Sometimes*) sus compañeros de cuarto toman (7) _____ un refresco con nosotros también.

ANA MARÍA: ¿Son interesantes sus compañeros de cuarto?

JUAN ANTONIO: Tomás y Gustavo tienen (8) _____ un compañero de cuarto muy simpático y la compañera de cuarto de Mercedes es muy sociable. Esta noche todos, menos Gustavo, vamos a ver (9) _____ una película muy buena. Gustavo no puede ir porque tiene que visitar (10) _al_ padre de su novia.

ANA MARÍA: ¿Invitas (11) _a_ mi amigo Héctor también?

JUAN ANTONIO: ¡Claro que sí!

4-13 Servicio en una escuela rural hondureña. Students from several universities in the U.S., Mexico, and Canada often perform service in rural Honduras. Complete the exchanges between Ester and the director of this school in Concepción. First underline the direct object in each question and then answer the questions using a direct object pronoun.

MODELO: DIRECTOR: ¿Tienes la cámara para sacar fotos de los niños?
ESTER: *Sí, la tengo.*

Los estudiantes en Concepción posan para la cámara.

DIRECTOR: ¿Tienes las medicinas para los niños?
ESTER: 1. Sí, las tengo.

DIRECTOR: ¿Quieres ver la biblioteca de la escuela?
ESTER: 2. Sí, la quiereo

DIRECTOR: ¿Tienes tu cuaderno para escribir tus observaciones?
ESTER: 3. Sí, lo tengo.

DIRECTOR: ¿Ves a los niños que vienen a saludarte?
ESTER: 4. Sí, los veo

DIRECTOR: ¿Deseas visitar la clínica ahora?
ESTER: 5. Sí, la desea

DIRECTOR: ¿Quieres visitar el mercado de artesanías de los estudiantes?
ESTER: 6. Sí, lo quireo visitar

4-14A Una entrevista para *Prensa Libre*. *Prensa Libre* is an independent newspaper in Guatemala. You are reporters who are preparing to interview the **Presidente de la República**. Ask and respond logically to each other's questions, being careful to use correct object pronouns and verb forms. **Estudiante B,** please see **Appendix 1,** page A-6.

MODELO: Estudiante A: *¿Tienes tu cámara?*
Estudiante B: *Sí, la tengo.*

Estudiante A

Mis preguntas	Mis respuestas a las preguntas de mi compañero/a
1. ¿Tienes la dirección de la casa del presidente?	_____ Claro, quiere verlo.
2. ¿El presidente tiene la lista de preguntas?	_____ No lo toca bien, pero le gusta la música.
3. ¿Necesitamos fotografías de la familia?	_____ Sí, pero no lo juega muy bien.
4. ¿El presidente habla inglés?	_____ Sí, lo recibe en el palacio presidencial.
5. ¿Escucha música clásica?	_____ No, no tiene tiempo para leerla.
6. ¿El presidente y su familia van a visitar El Salvador en mayo?	_____ Si, voy a llamarlo ahora.

4-15 En tu familia. Ask each other who does the following activities in your family. Be careful to conjugate the verbs in boldface and use the correct object pronouns in your responses.

MODELO: siempre **leer** novelas románticas
E1: *En tu familia, ¿quién siempre <u>lee</u> novelas románticas?*
E2: *Mi hermana siempre <u>las</u> lee.*

1. **ver** mucho la televisión
2. **llamarte** por teléfono constantemente
3. siempre **buscar** su celular
4. siempre **necesitar** dinero

5. **querer** ver videos de acción
6. **estudiar** muchas lenguas extranjeras
7. **preferir** música *rock*
8. **pedir** café en un restaurante

¿Cuánto saben?

Media Share

04-20 to 04-25

With two or three classmates, act out the following scenarios. Ask and respond to at least four questions in each situation.

✓ CAN YOU . . .

☐ talk about your family?

☐ express desires and preferences?

☐ plan activities?

WITH YOUR CLASSMATE(S) . . .

Situación: En el centro estudiantil
Ask about each other's families, what they do, and what they're like.
Para empezar: *¿Cómo es tu...? ¿Qué hace tu...?*

Situación: Por teléfono
Call a friend on the phone to make plans to do something tomorrow. Use stem-changing verbs like **preferir, querer, costar, jugar, perder, poder,** etc.
Para empezar: *¿Aló...? Habla... ¿Quieres ver una película o prefieres...?*

Situación: Una fiesta
Make plans for a party. Discuss several options, stating what you are going to serve and do for the party. Ask and respond to questions using direct objects and direct object pronouns, **lo, la, los, las.**
Para empezar: *¿Vamos a servir tamales o pizza? ¡Tamales y pizza! Vamos a comprarlos en la pizzería hondureña...*

📖 Perfiles

04-26 to 04-27

Mi experiencia

LA FAMILIA HISPANA ¿TÍPICA?

4-16 Para ti.   Which family members do you consider to be part of your immediate family? How many of them live at home? Would any of your family members ever consider moving away for economic reasons? Do you know any non-traditional couples? Read the following response from a young Honduran woman to a posting on Pregunta.com asking about the typical Hispanic family. Do you think there is such a thing as a typical Hispanic family?

Chicacuriosa **pregunta**: ¿Hay una familia típica hispana?
Mejor respuesta:
Maríahondureña **responde:**

Desde mi punto de vista, hay tanta variedad que es imposible generalizar el concepto de "familia hispana". Además,[1] con la globalización, la movilidad y los cambios culturales durante los últimos[2] años, el término "familia" es muy dinámico. Primero, tenemos que considerar la migración, especialmente en los países centroamericanos por razones económicas y políticas. En mi país, Honduras, es común que los padres y los hijos mayores dejen[3] a sus familias y busquen trabajo para luego mandarles[4] dinero. Las mujeres, como mi mamá y yo, tenemos que trabajar para mantener a los niños más pequeños. Sin embargo, tenemos el apoyo[5] familiar de mis tíos y de mis abuelos para mantener la unidad familiar. Segundo, con el aumento[6] del nivel de educación de la mujer, el índice de natalidad[7] ha bajado[8] de más de cuatro hijos por mujer a solo tres. Así que la idea del núcleo familiar con madre, padre e hijos no es universal y es imposible decir que hay un solo modelo.

   Un cantautor popular hondureño que habla de este tema de la globalización es Guillermo Anderson. Me gustan mucho sus canciones porque combina el humor con la realidad.

[1]*In addition*   [2]*recent*   [3]*leave behind*   [4]*send them*   [5]*support*   [6]*increase*   [7]*birthrate*   [8]*has decreased*

4-17 En su opinión.   Take turns reacting to each of the following statements.

MODELO: Me gusta vivir en casa con mis padres.
            Estoy de acuerdo (I agree). / *No estoy de acuerdo.*

1. Para mí, el núcleo familiar consiste en los padres, los hijos, los abuelos y toda la familia política (*in-laws*).

2. Me gusta vivir cerca de mi familia.

3. Tengo una buena relación con mis primos.

4. Los recién casados (*newlyweds*) deben vivir lejos de los suegros.

5. Es importante que la mujer sea económicamente independiente.

6. Creo que es natural permitir el matrimonio entre parejas homosexuales.

Mi música

"EL ENCARGUITO" (GUILLERMO ANDERSON, HONDURAS)

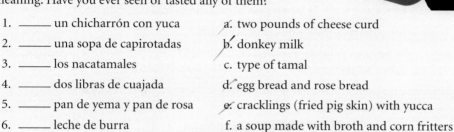

Guillermo Anderson was born in the port town of La Ceiba, where all Caribbean cultures of Honduras are in evidence: descendants of Mayans and other indigenous people, the **garífuna** slaves from West Africa, European settlers, and **mestizos.** His music reflects all of these ethnic groups.

"El encarguito" is a humorous piece about **un encarguito** (*care package*) that a person sends to a family member abroad.

Antes de ver y escuchar

4-18 Comida hondureña. Use context and cognates to match some of the foods mentioned in the song with their English meaning. Have you ever seen or tasted any of them?

1. _____ un chicharrón con yuca
2. _____ una sopa de capirotadas
3. _____ los nacatamales
4. _____ dos libras de cuajada
5. _____ pan de yema y pan de rosa
6. _____ leche de burra

a. two pounds of cheese curd
b. donkey milk
c. type of tamal
d. egg bread and rose bread
e. cracklings (fried pig skin) with yucca
f. a soup made with broth and corn fritters with eggs and cheese

Para ver y escuchar

 4-19 La canción. Connect with the Internet to search for a link to Guillermo Anderson performing this song. He expresses concerns about getting his **encarguito** safely through customs (*la aduana*). Which of the following likely represents his dilemma?

> **Busca:** guillermo anderson video encarguito; guillermo anderson letra encarguito
>
> **If you would like to purchase this song:** *Go to iTunes Store>Music>More to Explore>iMix>Arriba 6e*

1. _____ El encarguito es demasiado (*too*) grande.
2. _____ No se permite entrar con comida ni bebidas (*drinks*) en otro país.
3. _____ La persona que lleva el encarguito lo va a comer en el viaje.
4. _____ La persona que recibe el encarguito ha cambiado de casa (*changed address*).

Después de ver y escuchar

 4-20 Investigación: La garífuna. In the 17th century, several slave ships destined for Central America sank in storms, but some of the slaves were rescued by the indigenous Caribs who quickly assimilated them into their culture. The West Africans contributed instruments and rhythms to Latin music. Search the Internet for an example of **garífuna** music, and then write a paragraph describing the music, performers and your impressions. Use at least five different verbs from **Capítulo 4, Primera parte.**

> **Busca:** musica garifuna video

 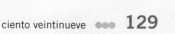

Segunda parte

¡Así lo decimos! VOCABULARIO

¡Así es la vida! Una invitación

Raúl invita a Laura a ver una película.

RAÚL: Laura, soy Raúl. Te llamo para ver si quieres ir al cine esta noche.

LAURA: Me gustaría... ¿Sabes qué película ponen?

RAÚL: Sí, hay una película nueva en el Rialto de El Salvador. No sé si la conoces. Se llama *Sobreviviendo Guazapa*. Es a las siete. ¿Vamos?

LAURA: Un momento, me llama mi madre. Te llamo en unos minutos.

Pasan unos minutos y Laura llama a Raúl.

LAURA: Hola Raúl, lo siento, pero no puedo salir esta noche. ¿Qué tal si vamos mañana?

RAÚL: Sí, claro. Nos vemos mañana.

Vocabulario Lugares de ocio

04–29 to
04–33

Variaciones
Although **entrada**
(from **entrar,** *to enter*)
is understood in most
countries, in Mexico
and areas of South
America **boleto** is more
common and generally
refers to occupying
a seat.

Variaciones
In Spain you'll hear **peli**
for **película.** Also, the
adjective phrase **de
película** colloquially
means *fantastic, dream,*
as in **una casa
de película**
(*a dream house*).

Variaciones
When you answer the
phone in many
Spanish-speaking
countries, you'll use
¿Aló?. However, in
Mexico, you're more
likely to use **¿Bueno?,**
and in Spain, **¿Diga?** or
¿Dígame?.

El ocio | Leisure time

el café (al aire libre) *(outdoor) cafe*
el centro *downtown*
el cine *movie theater*
el concierto *concert*
la entrada *admission ticket*
la función *show*
la orquesta *orchestra*
el parque *park*
el partido *game*
la película *movie*

Verbos | Verbs

conocer *to know (someone), to be
familiar with (something)*
invitar *to invite*
pasear *to take a walk*
poner *to put, to place*
poner una película *to show a movie*
saber *to know something*
saber + infinitive *to know how to do something*
salir *to leave, to go out*
tocar *to play (an instrument, music)*
traer *to bring*

Para hacer una invitación | Extending invitations

¿Qué tal si...? *How about . . . ?*
¿Quieres ir a...? *Do you want to go to . . . ?*
¿Te gustaría (+ infinitive)...? *Would you like
(+ infinitive) . . . ?*
¿Vamos a...? *Should we go . . . ?*

Para aceptar una invitación | Accepting invitations

De acuerdo. *Fine with me, Okay.*
Me encantaría. *I would love to.*
Paso por ti. *I'll come by for you, I'll pick you up.*
Sí, claro. *Yes, of course.*

Para rechazar una invitación | Rejecting invitations

Estoy muy ocupado/a. *I'm very busy.*
Gracias, pero no puedo... *Thanks, but I can't . . .*
Lo siento, tengo que... *I'm sorry, I have to . . .*

Toman un refresco en un café al aire libre.

Escuchan la música clásica que toca
la orquesta.

Piensan asistir
a una función.

ciento treinta y uno ●●● **131**

Letras y sonidos

Word stress and written accent marks in Spanish

Most words in Spanish (for example, all nouns, verbs, adjectives, and adverbs) carry word stress, where one syllable in the word is given special emphasis. In Spanish, word stress always falls on one of the last three syllables of the word: **tra-ba-ja-<u>dor</u>, in-te-li-<u>gen</u>-te, sim-<u>pá</u>-ti-co.** In some cases, word stress is indicated in writing with an accent mark, or **acento (ortográfico),** according to the following rules:

- Usually, words ending in a consonant (except **n** or **s**) are stressed on the *last syllable.*

  a-<u>brir</u>   ins-truc-<u>tor</u>   es-pa-<u>ñol</u>   re-<u>loj</u>   us-<u>ted</u>   ac-<u>triz</u>

  Exceptions to this rule require a written accent mark.

  <u>Víc</u>-tor   <u>ú</u>-til   di-<u>fí</u>-cil   <u>fút</u>-bol   <u>lá</u>-piz   <u>sánd</u>-wich

- Usually, words ending in a vowel or the consonant **n** or **s** are stressed on the *second to last syllable.*

  bo-<u>ni</u>-ta   tra-<u>ba</u>-jo   tra-<u>ba</u>-jan   <u>jo</u>-ven   tra-<u>ba</u>-jas   no-<u>so</u>-tros

  Exceptions to this rule require a written accent mark.

  es-<u>tá</u>   a-<u>quí</u>   es-<u>tán</u>   lec-<u>ción</u>   es-<u>tás</u>   in-<u>glés</u>

- Words with stress on the *third to last syllable* always require a written accent mark.

  <u>nú</u>-me-ro   <u>mú</u>-si-ca   bo-<u>lí</u>-gra-fo   <u>jó</u>-ve-nes   <u>miér</u>-co-les

- Some words are identical in spelling but different in emphasis and meaning. In such cases, words with emphasis are marked with a written accent to differentiate them from the versions without emphasis, which have a different meaning.

  él = *he*   **tú** = *you*   **mí** = *(to) me*   **¿Qué?** = *What?*   **¿Có-mo?** = *How?*

  el = *the*   **tu** = *your*   **mi** = *my*   **que** = *that*   **co-mo** = *how, as, like*

- A written accent mark also is used with an **i** or **u** to indicate hiatus (that is, when one of these letters, adjacent to another vowel, represents a separate syllable).

  <u>dí</u>-a   <u>grú</u>-a   pa-<u>ís</u>   Ra-<u>úl</u>

APLICACIÓN

4-21 Una invitación. State whether each statement is **cierto** or **falso** or **no se sabe** (*no information*) based on the conversation between Laura and Raúl in **¡Así es la vida!** Correct any false statements.

1. _____ Raúl invita a Laura al cine.

2. _____ Raúl sabe qué película ponen.

3. _____ La película es a las siete y media.

4. _____ Laura pasa por la casa de Raúl.

4-22 Otras actividades. Complete this paragraph about Raúl and Laura's day together with logical words or expressions from **¡Así lo decimos!**

Raúl y Laura van al (1) _____ para ver una película. Llegan unos minutos antes para comprar (3) _____. Después de la película, caminan por (2) _____ y toman refrescos en un café (4) _____. La música que toca la (5) _____ es maravillosa. El día siguiente, Laura invita a Raúl a ir a un (6) _____ de béisbol.

Una Cordial Invitación

Te invito a…

🔊 **4-23 Marilú invita a José.** Listen as Marilú and José talk on the telephone. Then complete each statement based on their conversation.

1. Marilú invita a José a _____.

   a. comer   b. bailar   c. pasear por el parque

2. José acepta la invitación para _____.

   a. esta noche   b. mañana   c. las tres de la tarde

3. Los chicos también van a ver _____.

   a. un partido   b. una película   c. un programa de televisión

4. Es evidente que los chicos son _____.

   a. hermanos   b. amigos   c. novios

5. Marilú y José no tienen que estudiar porque _____.

   a. mañana no hay clases   b. su clase es fácil   c. no hay tarea para mañana

🍦 **4-24 Ahora tú.** Take turns inviting each other to do something together. Ask what day, where, what time, and so on. The model will give you some ideas of questions you can ask in your conversation.

MODELO: E1: *Oye, ... ¿Quieres ir . . . ?*
E2: *No sé. (¿Cuándo? / ¿Dónde? / ¿A qué hora? / ¿Por qué? / ¿Con quiénes?)*
E1: *. . .*

4-25A ¡Estoy aburrido/a! Tell a classmate that you are bored so that he/she will invite you to do something. Reject at least three of the invitations, making excuses. Accept one or more that seem the most interesting. **Estudiante B,** please see **Appendix 1,** page A-6.

MODELO: ESTUDIANTE A: *Estoy aburrido/a.*
ESTUDIANTE B: *¿Quieres ir a bailar?*
ESTUDIANTE A: *Me encantaría. ¡Vamos! / Gracias, pero no puedo. No tengo dinero.*

Estudiante A:

Algunas excusas:		
estar cansado/a	no tener carro	no tener dinero
no tener ganas	no tener tiempo	tener mucho trabajo

🗣 **4-26 El fin de semana.** In groups of three or four, make plans for this weekend. Use the questions below as a guide for your conversation. Then, prepare a summary for the class.

¿Adónde quieren ir?	¿Qué necesitan?	¿Con quiénes van?
¿Qué quieren hacer?	¿Qué día?	¿Quién paga?
¿Cómo es?	¿A qué hora empieza?	¿A qué hora vuelven a casa?

MODELO: *Vamos a un partido de fútbol el sábado a la una de la tarde. Después vamos a pasear por el centro y ver a nuestros amigos. Los invitamos a tomar un refresco en el Café Luna. Luego, volvemos a casa en autobús. Llegamos a casa a las siete y media.*

¡Hola!
Cultura en vivo ✳

In Spanish-speaking countries, it is common for one person to pay for each round of drinks or a meal rather than for each person to pay for his or her own. Additionally, it is normal for a person who is celebrating a birthday to invite everyone else rather than be invited. Do you invite or get invited on your birthday?

¡Así lo hacemos! ESTRUCTURAS

04-36 to 04-39

3. Demonstrative adjectives and pronouns

Adjetivos demostrativos

Demonstrative adjectives point out people and objects and the relative position and distance between the speaker and the object or person modified. The chart below shows the forms of demonstrative adjectives in Spanish.

	Singular	Plural		Related adverbs
masculine	este	estos	*this/these (close to me)*	**aquí** (*here*)
feminine	esta	estas		
masculine	ese	esos	*that/those (close to you)*	**allí** (*there*)
feminine	esa	esas		
masculine	aquel	aquellos	*that/those (over there,*	**allá** (*over there*)
feminine	aquella	aquellas	*away from both of us)*	

Este chico es muy guapo.

Sí, pero aquel es muy rico.

- Demonstrative adjectives are usually placed before a modified noun and agree with them in number and gender.

  ¿De quién son **esos** refrescos? *To whom do those soft drinks belong?*

- Note that the **ese/esos** and **aquel/aquellos** forms, as well as their feminine counterparts, are equivalent to the English *that/those*. In normal, day-to-day usage, these forms are interchangeable, but the **aquel** forms are preferred to point out objects and people that are relatively farther away than others.

  ¿Cuánto cuestan **esas** rosas   *How much are those roses and those*
  y **aquellas** violetas?   *violets (further away, over there).*

- Demonstrative adjectives are usually repeated before each noun in a series.

  Esta película y **estos** actores   *This movie and these actors are*
  son mis favoritos.   *my favorites.*

Pronombres demostrativos

- When you omit the noun, the adjective becomes a pronoun (this one, those ones, etc.) and maintains the same form as the adjective.

  ¿Ves a **ese** hombre alto?   *Do you see that tall man?*
  ¿Cuál? ¿**Ese** o **aquel**?   *Which one? That one (closer) or*
      that one (farther away)?

- The neuter forms **esto, eso,** and **aquello** do not have plural forms. They are used to point out ideas, actions, or concepts, or to refer to unspecified objects or things.

  Aquello no me gusta.   *I don't like that.*
  No comprendo **eso**.   *I don't understand that.*
  Esto está mal.   *This is wrong.*

- These forms are also used to ask for a definition of something.

  ¿Qué es **esto /eso**?   *What's this/that?*
  Es un teatro.   *It's a theater.*

APLICACIÓN

4-27 Información: San Salvador. Laura is visiting San Salvador for the first time and is gathering information about what she should do during her stay.

Paso 1 Read the conversation between Laura and a Tourist Information agent who explains some of the most popular points of interest. Underline the demonstrative adjectives and pronouns.

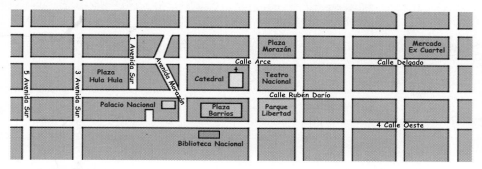

AGENTE: Este es un mapa del centro de la ciudad y algunos puntos de interés.

LAURA: Ah, verdad. ¿Qué es esto enfrente de la Plaza Barrios?

AGENTE: Bueno, hay tres edificios enfrente de la Plaza. Ese, cerca de usted, es la Biblioteca Nacional, donde mucha gente hace investigación sobre la historia de El Salvador. Este, cerca de mí, es el Palacio Nacional.

LAURA: ¿Y aquella iglesia?

AGENTE: Aquella es la Catedral. Usted debe visitarla.

LAURA: ¿Y el mercado?

AGENTE: Es aquel edificio en la Calle Delgado. Si quiere, puede ir en taxi o caminar unas cuadras. En ruta, puede comprar entradas para un concierto en aquel edificio, el Teatro Nacional.

LAURA: ¡Mil gracias por toda esta información!

Paso 2 Using the information about San Salvador from **Paso 1**, discuss with your partner what places you would like to visit. Use the drawing above to ask and respond to questions about the city.

MODELO: E1: *¿Quieres visitar esta catedral?*
E2: *No, prefiero visitar aquel parque.*

4-28 ¿Qué es esto? Take turns asking each other to identify at least three classroom objects.

MODELO: E1: (point to table close to both of you) *¿Qué es esto?*
E2: *Es una mesa. ¿Y aquello (away from both of you)?*
E1: *Es...*

4-29 Mi familia. Bring in a photo of your family or make a drawing of an imaginary family. Hold up your photo/drawing for the others to see and take turns asking and telling about family members.

MODELO: E1: *¿Quién es esa señora?*
E2: *Esta es mi madre. Es alta y delgada. Tiene... años.*
E3: *¿Cómo se llama aquel señor?*

Presencia hispana

El Salvador has a population of 6 million people. It is estimated that due to political, social, and economic strife, some 2 million have emigrated to the U.S. or Canada. This means that hundred of thousands of families left behind in El Salvador have been affected as well. Many fear that the massive migration has led to the deterioration of those families and contributed to the country's wide-spread delinquency. How can families maintain cohesion when members are forced to be separated?

4. The present tense of *poner*, *salir*, and *traer*

¿Traes la comida ahora?

Sí, la pongo en la mesa en un momento.

You have already learned some Spanish verbs that are irregular only in the **yo** form of the present indicative tense (**hacer → hago; ver → veo**). With these verbs, all other forms follow the regular conjugation patterns.

	poner (*to put, to place*)	salir (*to leave, to go out*)	traer (*to bring*)
yo	**pongo**	**salgo**	**traigo**
tú	pones	sales	traes
Ud.	pone	sale	trae
él/ella	pone	sale	trae
nosotros/as	ponemos	salimos	traemos
vosotros/as	ponéis	salís	traéis
Uds.	ponen	salen	traen
ellos/as	ponen	salen	traen

Si **traes** tu libro, te ayudo. — *If you bring your book, I'll help you.*
Siempre **salgo** a las ocho. — *I always go out at eight.*

EXPANSIÓN

More on *salir*

Each of the following expressions with **salir** has its own meaning.

salir de: *to leave a place, to leave on a trip*
   Salgo **de** casa a las siete. — *I leave home at seven.*

salir para: *to leave for (a place), to depart*
   Mañana **salen para** Tegucigalpa. — *Tomorrow they leave for Tegucigalpa.*

salir con: *to go out with, to date*
   Diana **sale con** Lorenzo. — *Diana goes out with Lorenzo.*

salir a (+ infinitive): *to go out (to do something)*
   Salen a cenar los sábados. — *They go out to have dinner on Saturdays.*

APLICACIÓN

4-30 Un correo electrónico de mamá. Clara's parents like to stay in touch.

Paso 1 Read the e-mail and underline the forms of **poner**, **salir**, and **traer**.

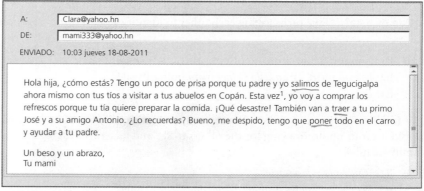

A: Clara@yahoo.hn
DE: mami333@yahoo.hn
ENVIADO: 10:03 jueves 18-08-2011

Hola hija, ¿cómo estás? Tengo un poco de prisa porque tu padre y yo salimos de Tegucigalpa ahora mismo con tus tíos a visitar a tus abuelos en Copán. Esta vez[1], yo voy a comprar los refrescos porque tu tía quiere preparar la comida. ¡Qué desastre! También van a traer a tu primo José y a su amigo Antonio. ¿Lo recuerdas? Bueno, me despido, tengo que poner todo en el carro y ayudar a tu padre.

Un beso y un abrazo,
Tu mami

[1]*This time*

Paso 2   Now, answer the following questions based on the e-mail.

1. ¿Dónde viven los padres de Clara? ¿Dónde viven sus abuelos?

2. ¿Qué hacen los padres de Clara hoy?

3. ¿Quién compra los refrescos?

4. ¿Qué hacen a las diez de la mañana?

5. ¿Quién prepara la comida?

6. ¿Quiénes más van con los padres de Clara?

Si estás en Copán, debes visitar las ruinas mayas.

4-31 **Tomás y Clara van a San Salvador.**   Complete the following paragraph about a business trip Clara is taking with her husband using the correct forms of logical verbs from the list below. **¡Ojo!** (**Watch out!**) You will have to use the infinitive form for one of them.

poner	salir	traer	ver

Esta tarde mi esposo Tomás y yo (1) _____ para la capital de El Salvador. Antes de (2) _____, (yo) (3) _____ la guía turística en mi maleta[1]. Después, (4) _____ las noticias en la televisión para escuchar el pronóstico meteorológico para la capital. En mi oficina, mi secretaria me (5) _____ el itinerario con la información del hotel y las fechas. Ella (6) _____ todos mis papeles en el maletín[2]. Ahora todo está en orden para salir. Mi esposo y yo vamos al aeropuerto dos horas antes del vuelo[3]. Desafortunadamente, cuando quiero pagar al taxista, veo que no (7) _____ dinero. Afortunadamente, mi esposo tiene dinero, y yo después, (8) _____ a buscar un cajero automático[4].

_____

[1]*suitcase*   [2]*briefcase*   [3]*flight*   [4]*ATM*

4-32 **En una fiesta familiar.**   You and your partner are getting ready for a family gathering, which you both will attend tonight. Separately, write four questions about who is responsible for what tasks in preparation for the party. Use a different subject, verb, and complement in each question. Then ask each other your questions, being careful to respond with an appropriate subject.

MODELO: E1: *¿Quién pone las flores en la mesa?*
E2: *Mi padre las pone.*

Acción necesaria:	Persona(s) responsable(s):
comprar los nachos	los invitados (*guests*)
hacer los sándwiches	tú
poner la comida en la mesa	mi hermana ,
preparar los refrescos	todos nosotros
salir a buscar más sillas	mis tíos
traer la música	los padres
invitar al novio de Ana	mi primo

4-33 ¿Con quién sale…? Have fun imagining who is dating whom these days. Take turns asking each other about following people, and add other names you want to spoof. Then ask for additional information, such as where they are going, what time they are leaving, and why they are going.

tú	Manny Ramírez	el presidente de Guatemala
John Leguizamo	Alexis Bledel	Wilmer Valderrama
Jamie-Lynn Sigler	ustedes	su esposo/a
nosotros	Rigoberta Menchú	el ministro de cultura de Colombia
Batman	Mario López	la esposa del presidente de El Salvador

MODELO: Shakira

E1: *¿Con quién sale Shakira ahora?*

E2: *Sale con Antonio de la Rúa.*

E1: *¿Adónde van?*

E2: *Van a Colombia.*

E1: *¿A qué hora salen? ¿Por qué van?*

E2: *Salen a la medianoche. Van porque quieren visitar a los padres de ella.*

4-34 Planes. Take turns finding out about each other's plans for the weekend.

MODELO: ¿A qué hora **salir** (tú) para…?

E1: *¿A qué hora sales para la casa de tu familia?*

E2: *Salgo para su casa a las diez de la mañana.*

1. ¿Adónde **salir** (tú) …?
2. ¿Con quiénes **ir** (tú) a…?
3. ¿Quién **hacer**…?
4. ¿Dónde **poner** (tú)…?
5. ¿Quién **traer**…?
6. ¿Qué **ver**(tú)…?

4-35 ¿Quiénes? Walk around the classroom and ask your classmates questions using the information in the chart below. Make sure you ask each person a different question. Then write their response in the box.

MODELO: **poner** tus libros en la mochila

E1: *Becky, ¿pones tus libros en la mochila?*

E2: *Sí, los pongo en la mochila. (No, no los pongo.)*

YOU WRITE: *Becky (no) pone sus libros en la mochila.*

poner tomate en su hamburguesa	**traer** su libro a clase	**salir** tarde para sus clases
_____	_____	_____
salir los sábados con los amigos	**ver** a su familia este fin de semana	**ver** películas españolas
_____	_____	_____
traer dinero hoy	**poner** azúcar en su café	**traer** su teléfono celular
_____	_____	_____
ver el fútbol en la televisión	**salir** para su casa este fin de semana	**poner** chocolate en su leche (*milk*)
_____	_____	_____

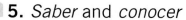

5. *Saber* and *conocer*

04-43 to
04-46

Although the verbs **saber** and **conocer** can both mean *to know*, they are not interchangeable. Note that both verbs have irregular **yo** forms while all other forms follow the regular conjugation patterns.

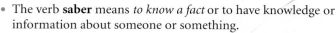

	saber (*to know*)	conocer (*to know*)
yo	**sé**	conozco
tú	**sabes**	conoces
Ud.	**sabe**	conoce
él/ella	**sabe**	conoce
nosotros/as	**sabemos**	conocemos
vosotros/as	**sabéis**	conocéis
Uds.	**saben**	conocen
ellos/as	**saben**	conocen

¡Ellos saben bailar muy bien!

María, conoces a Pablo, ¿verdad?

- The verb **saber** means *to know a fact* or to have knowledge or information about someone or something.

¿**Sabes** dónde está el cine?	*Do you know where the movie theater is?*
No **sé.**	*I don't know.*

- With an infinitive, the verb **saber** means *to know how to do something.*

La tía Berta **sabe** bailar tango.	*Aunt Berta knows how to dance the tango.*

- **Saber** may be followed with an interrogative word or **si** (*if*).

¿**Sabes dónde** es la fiesta?	*Do you know where the party is?*
No **sé si** mis padres quieren salir esta noche.	*I don't know if my parents want to go out tonight.*

- **Conocer** means *to be acquainted* or *to be familiar* with a person, place, or thing.

Tina **conoce** a mis abuelos.	*Tina knows (is acquainted with) my grandparents.*
Conozco San Salvador.	*I know (am acquainted with) San Salvador.*

- Use the personal **a** with **conocer** to express that *you know a specific person.*

La profesora **conoce a** mis tíos.	*The professor knows my aunt and uncle.*

Study tips for *saber* and *conocer*

saber

- knowing a fact or information
- knowing a skill (how to do something)
- may be followed by an infinitive or interrogative word or **si**

conocer

- knowing people
- knowing a place
- *never* followed by an infinitive or **si**

APLICACIÓN

4-36 Una chica extraordinaria. Julia Catalina Flores has an extraordinary talent for a girl her age.

Paso 1 First read the article about Julia and answer the questions based on the reading.

Julia Catalina Flores: la charanguista más joven de El Progreso

Julia Catalina Flores Ramírez sabe tocar la guitarra y desde la edad de 6 años toca en la banda de su papá. (Foto por Suyapa Carias)

¿Conoces a Julia? Pues si la ves en el grupo de su padre, vas a saber que es una chica extraordinaria. Aunque es pequeña y tímida, es una experta tocando el *charango*, un instrumento hondureño similar a la guitarra. Ella dice que conoce su charango como a un miembro de su familia.

Julia vive en el pueblo de El Progreso en el norte de Honduras donde todos la conocen. Cuando las personas la escuchan tocar, están maravilladas por su talento. Ella dice que le gusta tocar con su familia y hacer feliz a la gente. Ya sabe tocar más de 200 canciones. Si la quieres escuchar, el grupo cobra unos 25 lempiras por canción. Pero tienes que viajar a Honduras, porque ella es muy joven para salir de viaje como música profesional.

1. ¿Dónde vive Julia?

2. ¿Cómo es?

3. ¿Qué sabe hacer?

4. ¿Cuántas canciones sabe?

5. ¿La puedes escuchar en tu ciudad?

6. ¿Quieres conocerla algún día? ¿Por qué?

¡*Hola!*

Cultura en vivo

Instruments used in Salvadoran popular music include marimba, flutes, drums, scrapers, and gourds, as well more recently imported guitars and other instruments. Political chaos tore El Salvador apart in the late twentieth century, and music was often suppressed, especially that with strong indigenous influences. Why is music censored?

Paso 2 Now use the correct forms of **saber** and **conocer** to complete the following conversation between Marcela and Carmiña, who would like to meet Julia.

MODELO: Mi primo _conoce_ a Julia Catalina Flores.

MARCELA: ¿(1) (tú) _____ a Julia también?

CARMIÑA: No, yo no la (2) _____ personalmente pero (3) _____ que es hondureña.

MARCELA: Todos (4) _____ que ella toca muy bien el charango, ese instrumento musical similar a la guitarra.

CARMIÑA: Marcela, ¿(5) _____ si Julia vive en El Progreso?

MARCELA: Sí, vive allí. Su familia es muy famosa. Mi esposo y yo (6) _____ a su tío, pero no (7) _____ dónde viven exactamente.

CARMIÑA: Quiero invitarlos a una fiesta, pero no (8) _____ si pueden ir. ¿(9) (tú) _____ si tienen planes este fin de semana?

MARCELA: Seguramente su tío lo (10) _____; voy a llamarlo ahora. (11) (yo) _____ que tengo su número de teléfono en casa.

CARMIÑA: ¿(12) _____ (tú) cuántos años tiene Julia ahora?

MARCELA: (Yo) No (13) _____ exactamente, pero (14) _____ que es muy joven.

4-37A Entrevista. Read the following profile about the person you will be role-playing. Answer your partner's questions based on the information you have. Then interview your partner using the questions below to find out about him/her. Write down his/her answers. **Estudiante B,** please see **Appendix 1,** page A-7.

MODELO: ESTUDIANTE A: *¿Conoces a alguna* (any) *persona famosa?*
ESTUDIANTE B: *Sí, conozco a Ricky Martin. Soy amigo/a de él.*

Estudiante A:

> Soy intérprete personal del presidente de Honduras.
>
> Juego muy bien al tenis.
>
> Voy mucho a El Salvador y a Honduras y muy poco a EE. UU.
>
> El músico Guillermo Anderson es un buen amigo.
>
> Hablo inglés y francés.
>
> Estudio la política y los gobiernos de Centroamérica.

1. ¿Sabes hablar alguna lengua indígena?
2. ¿Conoces las ruinas mayas en Guatemala?
3. ¿Qué instrumento sabes tocar?
4. ¿Sabes jugar bien al béisbol?
5. ¿Conoces a alguna persona famosa de Costa Rica?
6. ¿Qué ciudades centroamericanas conoces?

4-38 Desafío: Un sabelotodo (*know it all*). Write three truthful sentences in Spanish about things you and others know or know how to do, and three about people and places you know. Each sentence must have a different subject and complement. The first person who thinks he/she has three correct sentences with **saber** and three with **conocer** calls out *¡TENGO!* The rest of the group will judge if your sentences are correct.

MODELO: *Mi hermano sabe tocar la guitarra.*
Yo no conozco a Guillermo Anderson. (etc.)

Clara y Tomás no conocen bien la ciudad.

¿Tus amigos saben bailar?

4-39 **¿Quién?** Ask as many classmates as possible questions regarding the topic in each box in the chart below. Write the name of each person on the chart, noting his/her answer (as **sí** or **no**). **¡OJO!** Be sure to use the correct verbs (**sabes/sé** or **conoces/conozco**) and the personal **a** as needed in your questions and responses.

MODELO: la fecha de hoy
E1: *¿Sabes la fecha de hoy?*
E2: *Sí, la sé. Es 15 de noviembre.*
E2: *¿Conoces el restaurante mexicano de esta ciudad?*
E1: *No, no conozco el restaurante mexicano de esta ciudad. (No, no lo conozco.)*

la fecha de mañana	el número de teléfono del/de la profesor/a	si hay un restaurante salvadoreño	una persona hispana
_____	_____	_____	_____
el restaurante español	una persona de Centroamérica	cuándo hay examen	dónde vive el presidente de Guatemala
_____	_____	_____	_____
cantar en español	jugar al béisbol	la capital de Honduras	preparar café
_____	_____	_____	_____
bailar bien	una ciudad interesante	un actor famoso	mi nombre
_____	_____	_____	_____

04-47 to
04-52

¿Cuánto saben?

With two or three classmates, act out the following scenarios.
Ask and respond to at least four questions in each situation.

✓ CAN YOU . . .

☐ extend invitations?

☐ point out people and things to others?

☐ discuss things and people you know?

WITH YOUR CLASSMATE(S) . . .

Situación: Por teléfono
Call a friend and invite him or her to do something with you. Decide between you what you want to do, when, and who else you should invite.
Para empezar: *¿Aló...? ¿Te gustaría...?*

Situación: Actores y músicos
You are at a party with celebrities. Use demonstrative adjectives and pronouns (**este, ese, aquel** and their various forms) to talk about some of the people you see close by, further away, and far away from you. Be sure to use gestures to illustrate the demonstratives.
Para empezar: *Esta fiesta es muy buena, pero no me gusta ese actor. Aquella señorita que está allá es muy bonita...*

Situación: Chismes (Gossip)
Try to one-up each other by saying what and whom you know and what you know how to do, using **conocer** and **saber**.
Para empezar: *Conozco a Peyton Manning...*

📖 Observaciones

¡Pura vida! EPISODIO 4

In this episode you'll learn more about Felipe's family and an upcoming wedding.

Antes de ver el video

4-40 Una boda. In her blog, Marcela tells about a wedding she'll attend in her hometown in Mexico. Read her description and answer the questions that follow in Spanish.

Los mariachis tocan en una boda mexicana.

> Mi primo Tomás se casa con su novia Carolina el mes que viene. En mi pueblo, en el estado de Michoacán, una boda es un evento de tres días o más. Primero, hay fiestas familiares con amigos en las que los novios reciben regalos[1] para su nuevo hogar[2]. La boda es muy solemne; generalmente se celebra en una iglesia con una misa[3]. Después hay una gran fiesta con música de mariachis, baile y grandes cantidades de comida. Se sirven tamales, chiles rellenos y muchas cosas más. ¡Y claro, un pastel[4] grande! Esta fiesta dura hasta la madrugada[5] cuando todos desayunamos juntos. Las bodas en México son eventos de mucha fiesta y felicidad.

[1]gifts [2]home [3]mass [4]cake [5]dawn

1. ¿Dónde vive Marcela?

2. ¿Cuántos días dura una boda en su pueblo?

3. ¿Qué pasa después de la ceremonia en la iglesia?

4. ¿Cuántos días duran las bodas que tú conoces?

A ver el video

🎬 **4-41 Hay una boda.** Watch the fourth episode of **¡Pura vida!** You will hear Felipe and Marcela discuss an upcoming wedding. Complete the statements that follow.

Felipe recibe un traje (*suit*)

Marcela

Felipe

1. La boda es el _____.

2. Claudia es la _hermana_ de Felipe.

3. Marcela tiene una _hermanastra_ la hija de la segunda esposa de su papá.

4. En Madrid, Felipe tiene muchos _primos_.

5. Elvira es la _novia_ de Felipe.

Después de ver el video

🌐 **4-42 Los mariachis.** Connect with the Internet to search for more photos of mariachis and to hear their music. What instruments do you hear?

> 🖱 **Busca:** mariachis foto; mariachis video

_____ la guitarra   _____ el violín   _____ el tambor

_____ la trompeta   _____ el piano   _____ el guitarrón (guitarra grande)

Nuestro mundo

 **Panoramas**

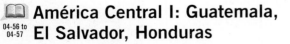 **América Central I: Guatemala, El Salvador, Honduras**

04-56 to
04-57

El paisaje (*landscape*), la economía y el modo de vivir en Guatemala, El Salvador y Honduras presentan contrastes notables. Los tres son países en vías de desarrollo (*developing*). La población, mayormente mestiza, todavía conserva muchas tradiciones de su pasado indígena.

Concepción, Honduras

Es evidente el contraste de la vida en zonas rurales y en las ciudades grandes. Por razones económicas, muchas personas buscan mejores oportunidades en la capital o en el extranjero (*abroad*). Las remesas (envíos monetarios) que mandan representan una significante proporción de la economía de los países centroamericanos.

Centro comercial Miraflores, Ciudad de Guatemala

Estas niñas usan hermosos huipiles tejidos (*woven*) y bordados a mano (*embroidered by hand*) como sus antepasados mayas.

En las zonas remotas, es común usar la antigua manera de moler (*grind*) el maíz.

El Salvador tiene 22 volcanes. Su terreno montañoso dificulta la comunicación entre los pueblos y las ciudades.

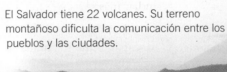

Guatemala, El Salvador, Honduras

	GT	HN	SV
Población:	13 millones	7,6 millones	7 millones
Tasa de natalidad:	3,5 (hijos/mujer)	3,3	3
PIB[1] per cápita:	$5.400	$3.700	$6.400
Remesas:	12% (de la economía)	25%	18%
Otros sectores:	agricultura (69%)	agricultura (80%)	turismo (80%)

4-43 Identifica. Use the photos and the information from the Fact Box to identify or explain the following:

1. un producto agrícola importante en la dieta de Centroamérica

2. la gran civilización que dominaba mucho de Centroamérica en la época precolombina

3. qué es un huipil

4. la importancia de remesas (*monetary remittances*) en la economía de estos países

5. dónde viven los ricos en estos países

4-44 Desafío. Use the map above to identify these characteristics and places.

1. las capitales de estos tres países
2. el país que tiene frontera con México
3. el país más grande de los tres
4. los países con costa en el mar Caribe

 4-45 Proyecto: Guatemala, El Salvador, Honduras. Choose from the following places or themes: **Copán, el Petén, Guillermo Anderson, la topografía y el clima, Chichicastenango, el ecoturismo en El Salvador** or another that interests you and research more about the cultures of these countries. Write a summary of what you find; include the information that follows.

- su nombre y dónde está
- por qué es importante
- cómo es
- si quieres visitarlo o verlo algún día y por qué
- si piensas estudiar más sobre este tema
- una foto representativa

> **Busca:** [*nombre del lugar*]; ecotourism el salvador; guillermo anderson; topography [*nombre del lugar*]; etc.

MODELO: *La cultura maya es evidente en el sitio arqueológico de El Petén…*

---

[1] **PIB:** *Producto Interno Bruto* (GDP: Gross Domestic Product) is the market value of all final goods and services made within the borders of a country in a year. This figure is often positively correlated with standard of living.

 **Páginas**

04-58

Sobreviviendo Guazapa, Cinenuevo

From 1980–1992 in El Salvador, the right-wing military forces and the left-wing guerilla coalition FMLN engaged in a bloody civil war. The most infamous assassination was that of Archbishop Óscar Romero while he was celebrating mass in 1980. Much has been written about the culprits and victims of the war. *Sobreviviendo Guazapa* is the first feature-length film written and produced in El Salvador with a full cast of Salvadoran, primarily novice actors.

ANTES DE LEER

4-46 Pistas extratextuales (*Extra-textual clues*). The publication in which you find an article often gives away its content. The following selection comes from a web site called Cinenuevo. Think about these clues before you read the selection.

1. ¿Quiénes crees que visitan la página web Cinenuevo?
2. En tu opinión, ¿cuáles de estas películas **no** aparecen en Cinenuevo?

   las clásicas   las de Hollywood   las independientes   las premiadas (*award-winning*)

A LEER

4-47 Las secciones. As you read the review, identify the headings you see. What other headings would you expect?

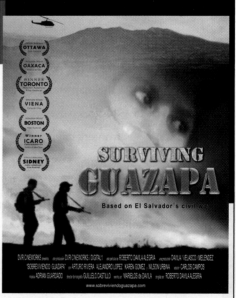

GÉNERO: Aventura/Drama
DIRECTOR/PRODUCTOR: Roberto Dávila
DURACIÓN: 1 hora, 53 minutos
AUDIO: Español, Digital Surround

Sinopsis

Dos combatientes enemigos entre sí[1], atrapados en el caos de los ataques al volcán de Guazapa, se unen para salvar sus vidas. En el camino se encuentran con una niña perdida[2] y deciden ayudarla a volver con su familia. A partir de ese momento, enfrentan juntos múltiples pruebas de sobrevivencia[3].

Sobre la película

Es la primera película salvadoreña de ficción sobre la guerra civil realizada por salvadoreños. El inicio del rodaje[4], se vio retrasado por los huracanes *Wilma*, *Stan* y *Katrina*. Para el *casting* hubo convocatoria abierta a través de periódicos locales. Varios de los actores seleccionados no tenían experiencia, pero se destacaron[5] en la prueba.

Actores y extras recibieron entrenamiento militar previo al rodaje. Hubo dos accidentes durante el rodaje en que resultaron lastimados[6] los actores principales. La realización de la película tomó tres años.

Premios

Sobreviviendo Guazapa ha sido Selección Oficial en más de seis festivales internacionales de cine, galardonada con un Premio Especial en el Festival de Cine Hispano de Toronto, honrada como Premio deApertura del Festival de Cine de Viena, Austria y ganadora de Premio a Mejor Actor en el Festival Ícaro.

Según el crítico Héctor Ismael Sermeño (*Trazos culturales*): Su gran logro[7] es ver la guerra a la distancia, sin pasiones personales, ideologías partidarias o sentimentales… Dávila no quiere reflejar la historia, la utiliza como marco[8] para contar su argumento y lo hace con dignidad.

[1]*themselves* [2]*lost* [3]*survival* [4]*filming* [5]*they stood out* [6]*injured* [7]*achievement* [8]*framework*

DESPUÉS DE LEER

4-48 ¿Comprendiste?   Respond briefly in Spanish to the following questions according to what you have read.

1. ¿Cuánto tiempo duró (*lasted*) la realización de la película?

2. ¿Por qué hubo (*were there*) demoras?

3. ¿Qué entrenamiento recibieron (*received*) los actores?

4. ¿Qué premios tiene?

5. ¿Qué opinión tiene de la película el crítico Héctor Ismael Sermeño?

4-49   En su opinión.   Work together to express your opinions about these issues. Use the following statements in your discussion.

Estoy de acuerdo.	No opino.	No estoy de acuerdo.

1. En la guerra (*war*), son las familias las que sufren más.
2. No hay "guerra justa".
3. Los políticos verdaderamente no entienden el costo de una guerra.
4. Las mujeres deben participar con los hombres en la defensa de la patria.

El arzobispo Óscar Romero denunció la violencia militar de los años 70 en El Salvador. Este monumento a la Memoria y la Verdad en el parque Cuscatlán, San Salvador conmemora su vida y obras.

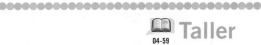

4-50 Una invitación. In this activity, you will write a short e-mail, similar to the one below, to invite a friend to spend the weekend with you.

A:	Pilardelagloria@fusion.com
DE:	Maluisa1992@ecorreo.hn
ASUNTO:	fin de semana en La Ceiba
ENVIADO:	30-5-2011, 21:00

¡Querida Pilar!
¿Qué tal? Aquí estamos toda la familia en La Ceiba, Honduras, para pasar dos semanas de vacaciones. Conoces a mi amigo, Pancho, ¿verdad? Pues, el 7 de junio es su cumpleaños y queremos invitarte a pasar el fin de semana con nosotros aquí en la costa…

ANTES DE ESCRIBIR

- Provide the information you plan to include in your invitation using the following list as a guide. Make a list based on the following information.

dónde estás ahora	¿Con quiénes?	¿Por cuánto tiempo?
la invitación	¿Cuándo?	cosas que necesita traer
algunas actividades	¿Por qué?	¿más información?

A ESCRIBIR

- **Saludo.** Use the e-mail format of the sample invitation above, including the headers and greeting. Choose from the following greetings: **Mi querido/a amigo/a** (*My dear friend*), **Queridísima familia** (*Dearest family*), **Querido/a...** (*Dear . . .*)

- **El mensaje.** Incorporate the information you listed above. Use words such as **y**, **pero**, and **porque** to link your ideas.

- **Respuesta.** Ask for a reply to your letter: **Responde pronto**.

- **Despedida.** Close the letter with a farewell. Choose from: **Un abrazo** (*A hug*), **Un beso** (*A kiss*), **Afectuosamente** (*Affectionately*), **Con cariño** (*With affection*), **Saludos de** (*Best wishes from*)

DESPUÉS DE ESCRIBIR

- **Revisar.** Review the following elements in your letter:
  - ☐ use of stem-changing verbs **poner, salir,** and **traer**
  - ☐ use of **saber** and **conocer** and the personal **a**
  - ☐ use of direct objects and direct object pronouns
  - ☐ use of demonstratives (**este, ese, aquel,** etc.)
  - ☐ correct spelling, including accents

- **Intercambiar**
  Exchange your invitation with a classmate's; make grammatical corrections and content suggestions. Then respond to the invitation.

- **Entregar**
  Rewrite your original invitation, incorporating your classmate's suggestions. Then turn in your original invitation and the response from your classmate to your instructor.

 # Vocabulario

Primera parte

Miembros de la familia   Family members

el/la abuelo/a   *grandfather/grandmother*
el/la cuñado/a   *brother-in-law/sister-in-law*
el/la esposo/a   *husband/wife*
el/la hermanastro/a   *stepbrother/stepsister*
el/la hermano/a   *brother/sister*
el/la hijo/a   *son/daughter*
la madrastra   *stepmother*
la madre   *mother*
el/la nieto/a   *grandson/granddaughter*
el/la novio/a   *boyfriend/girlfriend, groom/bride*
la nuera   *daughter-in-law*
el padrastro   *stepfather*
el padre   *father*
el/la perro/a   *dog*
el/la primo/a   *cousin*
el/la sobrino/a   *nephew/niece*
el/la suegro/a   *father-in-law/mother-in-law*
el/la tío/a   *uncle/aunt*
el yerno   *son-in-law*

Verbos   Verbs

almorzar (ue)   *to have lunch*
costar (ue)   *to cost*
dormir (ue)   *to sleep*
empezar (ie)   *to begin*
encontrar (ue)   *to find*
entender (ie)   *to understand*
ganar   *to earn*
jugar a (ue)   *to play*
pasar   *to spend (time)*
pensar (ie) (en)   *to think (about)*
pensar (ie) (+infinitive)   *to plan (to do something)*
pedir (i)   *to ask for, to request*
perder (ie)   *to lose*
poder (ue)   *to be able, can*
preferir (ie)   *to prefer*
querer (ie)   *to want, love*
recordar (ue)   *to remember*
repetir (i)   *to repeat, to have a second helping*
servir (i)   *to serve*
soñar (ue) (con)   *to dream (about)*
venir (ie)   *to come*
volver (ue)   *to return*

Adjetivos   Adjectives

casado/a   *married*
divorciado/a   *divorced*
mayor   *older*
menor   *younger*
soltero/a   *single, unmarried*
unido/a   *close, close-knit*

Otras palabras y expresiones útiles

algún día   *someday*
la comida   *food*
conmigo   *with me*
contigo   *with you*
el refresco   *soft drink*

Segunda parte

El ocio   Leisure time

el café (al aire libre)   *(outdoor) café*
el centro   *downtown*
el cine   *movie theater*
el concierto   *concert*
la entrada   *admission ticket*
la función   *show*
la orquesta   *orchestra*
el parque   *park*
el partido   *game*
la película   *movie*

Verbos   Verbs

conocer   *to know (someone), to be familiar with (something)*
invitar   *to invite*
pasear   *to take a walk*
poner   *to put, to place*
poner una película   *to show a movie*
saber   *to know something*
saber + infinitive   *to know how to do something*
salir   *to leave, to go out*
tocar   *to play (an instrument, music)*
traer   *to bring*

Hacer una invitación   Extending invitations

¿Qué tal si…?   *How about . . . ?*
¿Quieres ir a…?   *Do you want to go to . . . ?*
¿Te gustaría (+ inf.)…?   *Would you like (+ inf.) . . . ?*
¿Vamos a…?   *Should we go . . . ?*

Para aceptar una invitación   Accepting invitations

De acuerdo.   *Fine with me, Okay.*
Me encantaría.   *I would love to.*
Paso por ti.   *I'll come by for you, I'll pick you up.*
Sí, claro.   *Yes, of course.*

Para rechazar una invitación   Rejecting invitations

Estoy muy ocupado/a.   *I'm very busy.*
Gracias, pero no puedo…   *Thanks, but I can't . . .*
Lo siento, tengo que…   *I'm sorry, I have to . . .*

Direct object pronouns   *See page 124.*   **Demonstrative adjectives and pronouns**   *See page 134.*

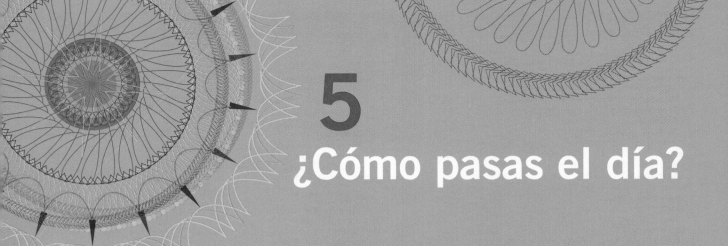

5

¿Cómo pasas el día?

Readiness
Check

América Central II: Costa Rica, Nicaragua, Panamá

«Un lugar para cada cosa y cada cosa en su lugar».

Refrán: A place for everything and everything in its place.

Los sensacionales paisajes y la increíble diversidad de flora y fauna atraen a muchos visitantes a Costa Rica, Nicaragua y Panamá todos los años.

Las molas tienen su origen en las islas de San Blas, Panamá, pero son populares por toda Centroamérica. Estos hermosos textiles representan la flora y la fauna de la región.

¡Así lo decimos! VOCABULARIO

¡Así es la vida! El arreglo personal

 Fabián tiene cita con Rosario a las nueve de la mañana. Ahora son las nueve y quince.

FABIÁN:	¿Sí?
ROSARIO:	¡Hola, Fabián!
FABIÁN:	¿Sí? ¿Quién es?
ROSARIO:	¡Yo! ¡Rosario! Estoy aquí en el Café Solo. ¿Dónde estás tú?
FABIÁN:	¡Ay! En la cama. Llego en cinco minutos. Solo tengo que levantarme, ducharme, afeitarme, peinarme, vestirme...
ROSARIO:	¡Fabián! ¡Eres un caso!

 Rosario toma su desayuno y piensa...

ROSARIO:	A veces este Fabián me pone furiosa. Nunca se despierta a tiempo. Bueno, también es un buen amigo y siempre nos divertimos juntos.

Vocabulario Las actividades diarias

Ramón se afeita con una navaja.

Actividades diarias Daily activities

acostarse (ue) *to go to bed*
afeitarse *to shave*
bañarse *to take a bath*
cepillarse (los dientes) *to brush (your teeth)*
despertarse (ie) *to wake up*
dormirse (ue, u) *to fall asleep*
ducharse *to take a shower*
lavarse (la cara) *to wash (your face)*
levantarse *to get up, to stand up*
maquillarse *to put on makeup*
peinarse (el pelo) *to comb (your hair)*
quitarse (la camisa) *to take off (your shirt)*
secarse *to dry oneself*
sentarse (ie) *to sit down*
vestirse (i, i) *to get dressed*

Variaciones

Levantarse can mean *to get up (in the morning)* or *to stand up (from a sitting position)*. In parts of Latin America, however, to stand up is often expressed with **pararse**.

Algunas partes del cuerpo Some parts of the body

la cara *face*
los dientes *teeth*
la mano *hand*
la nariz *nose*
el ojo *eye*
el pelo *hair*

María se maquilla después de bañarse.

Algunas emociones Some emotions

ponerse contento/a *to become happy*
    furioso/a *angry*
    molesto/a *annoyed*
sentirse (ie, i) *to feel*

Artículos de uso personal Personal care items

el brillo de labios *lip gloss*
el champú *shampoo*
la crema (de afeitar) *(shaving) cream*
el jabón *soap*
el maquillaje *makeup*
la máquina de afeitar *electric razor*
la navaja de afeitar *razor*
el peine *comb*
el secador *hair dryer*

José se cepilla los dientes.

Nieves se duerme en la biblioteca.

APLICACIÓN

5-1 Rosario está molesta. Contesta las preguntas basadas en la conversación entre Rosario y Fabián.

1. ¿Dónde está Rosario?

2. ¿Dónde está Fabián?

3. ¿Por qué está molesta Rosario?

4. ¿Qué tiene que hacer Fabián?

5. ¿Cuánto tiempo dice Fabián que necesita para llegar al café?

6. ¿Crees que Rosario va a ponerse furiosa al llegar Fabián al café?

7. ¿Cuánto tiempo necesitas normalmente para arreglarte (*get ready*) por la mañana?

5-2 ¿Qué tienen que hacer? Identifica qué tienen que hacer estas personas cada día. Añade (*Add*) más información sobre cada dibujo (*drawing*).

MODELO: *Pancho tiene que acostarse temprano porque mañana tiene que ir a la escuela.*

Pancho

1.

Juanito

2.

Maribel

3.

Alonso

4.

Tomás

5.

Carlos

6.

Sara

7.

doña María

8.

tía Luisa

5-3 ¿Qué asocian con...? Formen dos equipos (*teams*) para ver cuántas palabras o expresiones pueden asociar con las siguientes actividades.

MODELO: afeitarse
la cara, la crema de afeitar, la navaja,...

1. bañarse
2. mirarse
3. secarse
4. peinarse

5. despertarse
6. cepillarse
7. sentarse
8. levantarse

9. ponerse impaciente
10. ponerse nervioso/a
11. maquillarse
12. sentirse cansado/a

5-4 **El arreglo personal.** Hay una gran variedad de productos de maquillaje y arreglo personal.

Paso 1 Conéctate a la Internet y busca un producto de arreglo personal. Descríbelo e incluye cuánto cuesta. ¿Es para hombres o para mujeres? ¿Es un producto bueno en tu opinión? ¿Quieres comprarlo? ¿Por qué?

> **Busca:** productos belleza; maquillaje; secadores pelo; jabones; maquinas afeitar

MODELO: *Toja Sensible es una crema de afeitar para hombres. La compro porque...*

Paso 2 Ahora diseña un anuncio para vender un producto original. Usa el modelo.

> **!** **¿Quieres una cara joven y bella?**
>
> ¡Necesitas usar CremaBella todos los días!
> Fórmula original de los antiguos mayas.
> La diferencia en solo 8 días.
> ¡Resultados garantizados!
>
> La puedes comprar en www.cremabella.com
> Oferta especial por Internet: 3 meses por solo $19,95 al mes.

5-5 **Los señores Rodríguez.** Escucha la descripción de la rutina diaria de la familia Rodríguez. Indica a quién(es) se refiere cada oración a continuación: al Sr. Rodríguez, a la Sra. Rodríguez o a los dos.

La actividad	El señor	La señora	Los dos
1. Debe levantarse temprano todos los días.	_____	_____	_____
2. Trabaja en una oficina.	_____	_____	_____
3. Le gusta bañarse por la mañana.	_____	_____	_____
4. Tiene que afeitarse.	_____	_____	_____
5. Toma café en el desayuno.	_____	_____	_____
6. Almuerza con otras personas.	_____	_____	_____
7. Hace ejercicio después de comer.	_____	_____	_____
8. Prepara la cena.	_____	_____	_____

5-6A **Compras para su clóset del baño.** Tienen que equipar el clóset de su baño y no quieren gastar (*spend*) mucho dinero. Tú tienes una lista de productos; tu compañero/a tiene el volante (*flier*) con los productos en venta. Decidan qué productos van a comprar. ¿Cuánto gastan en total? **Estudiante B,** por favor ve al **Apéndice 1,** página A-7.

MODELO: ESTUDIANTE A: *Necesitamos... ¿Cuánto cuesta(n)?*
ESTUDIANTE B: *Está(n) en venta esta semana por... / Lo siento, no está(n) en venta esta semana.*
ESTUDIANTE A: *Bien, vamos a comprar... por... en total. / Entonces, necesitamos...*

Estudiante A:

> **Lista de compras:**
>
> ☐ 2 cepillos de dientes ☐ jabón de mano ☐ 2 peines de plástico
> ☐ champú para rubios ☐ brillo de labios ☐ secador eléctrico
> ☐ crema para afeitar ☐ 2 navajas de afeitar ☐ loción

¡Así lo hacemos! ESTRUCTURAS

1. Reflexive constructions: Pronouns and verbs

Isabel **se peina.**
Isabel combs her hair.

A reflexive construction is one in which the subject is both the performer and the receiver of the action expressed by the verb.

• The drawing on the left depicts a reflexive action (Isabel is combing her own hair); the drawing on the right depicts a nonreflexive action (Isabel is combing her sister's hair).

Isabel **peina** a su hermana.
Isabel combs her sister's hair.

Los pronombres reflexivos

• Reflexive constructions require the reflexive pronouns.

Subject pronoun	Reflexive pronoun	Verb (lavarse)
yo	**me** (*myself*)	**lavo**
tú	**te** (*yourself*)	**lavas**
Ud.	**se** (*yourself*)	**lava**
él/ella	**se** (*himself, herself*)	**lava**
nosotros/as	**nos** (*ourselves*)	**lavamos**
vosotros/as	**os** (*yourselves*)	**laváis**
Uds.	**se** (*yourselves*)	**lavan**
ellos/as	**se** (*themselves*)	**lavan**

• Reflexive pronouns have the same forms as direct object pronouns, except for the third-person singular and plural. The reflexive pronoun of the third-person singular and plural is **se.**

Paco **se** baña.	*Paco bathes.*
Los niños **se** levantan temprano.	*The children get up early.*

• As with object pronouns, reflexive pronouns are placed immediately before the conjugated verbs. In Spanish the definite article, not the possessive adjective, is used to refer to parts of the body and articles of clothing.

Me lavo **las** manos.	*I wash my hands.*
Pedro se pone **el** sombrero.	*Pedro puts on his hat.*

• With infinitives, reflexive pronouns are either attached to the infinitives or placed in front of the conjugated verbs.

Sofía, ¿vas a maquillar**te** ahora?
Sofía, ¿**te** vas a maquillar ahora? } *Sofía, are you going to put on your makeup now?*

• In English, reflexive pronouns are frequently omitted, but in Spanish, reflexive pronouns are required in all reflexive constructions.

Pepe **se afeita** antes de acostarse.	*Pepe shaves before going to bed.*
Marina siempre **se baña** a las ocho.	*Marina always bathes at eight.*

Los verbos reflexivos

- Verbs that describe personal care and daily habits carry a reflexive pronoun if the same person performs and receives the action.

Me voy a acostar temprano.	*I'm going to bed early.*
Mis hermanos se despiertan tarde todas las mañanas.	*My brothers wake up late every morning.*

- Such verbs can also be used nonreflexively when someone other than the subject receives the action.

Elena **acuesta** a su hija menor.	*Elena puts her youngest daughter to bed.*
¿**Despiertas** a tu compañero de cuarto?	*Do you wake up your roommate?*

- In Spanish, verbs that express feelings, moods, and conditions are often used with reflexive pronouns. A reflexive pronoun is usually not required in English. Instead, verbs such as *to get* or *to become* or other nonreflexive verbs are used.

alegrarse (de)	*to become happy*
divertirse (ie, i)	*to have fun*
enamorarse (de)	*to fall in love (with)*
enfermarse	*to become sick*
enojarse (con)	*to get angry*
olvidarse (de)	*to forget*

Me alegro de ganar.	*I am happy to win.*
Siempre **nos divertimos** en la fiesta.	*We always have fun at the party.*
Luis **va a enamorarse de** Ana.	*Luis is going to fall in love with Ana.*
Jorge **se enoja** si pierde.	*Jorge gets angry if he loses.*
Me olvido de todo cuando la veo.	*I forget everything when I see her.*

- Some verbs have different meanings when used with reflexive pronouns.

Nonreflexive		Reflexive	
acostar (ue)	*to put to bed*	**acostarse (ue)**	*to go to bed*
dormir (ue, u)	*to sleep*	**dormirse (ue, u)**	*to fall asleep*
encontrar	*to find*	**encontrarse (con)**	*to meet up with someone*
enfermar	*to make sick*	**enfermarse**	*to become sick*
ir	*to go*	**irse**	*to go away, to leave*
levantar	*to lift*	**levantarse**	*to get up*
llamar	*to call*	**llamarse**	*to be called (as when giving your name)*
poner	*to put, to set*	**ponerse**	*to put on (clothing), to become*
quitar	*to remove*	**quitarse**	*to take off (clothing)*
vestir (i, i)	*to dress*	**vestirse (i, i)**	*to get dressed*

Las construcciones recíprocas

- The plural reflexive pronouns **nos, os,** and **se** may be used with verbs that take direct objects to express reciprocal actions. The verbs can be reflexive or nonreflexive verbs, and these actions are conveyed in English with *each other* or *one another.*

Nos queremos mucho.	*We love each other a lot.*
Los novios **se ven** todos los días.	*The sweethearts see one another every day.*

¡Ay! Parece que se quieren mucho.

APLICACIÓN

5-7 Mariano Rivera, un panameño en Nueva York. Mariano Rivera es uno de los beisbolistas más destacados (*prominent*) de los Yankees.

Paso 1 Lee sobre la vida de Mariano Rivera y subraya (*underline*) los verbos reflexivos. Indica cuál es el sujeto (*subject*) de cada verbo.

MODELO: Los beisbolistas <u>se alegran</u> cuando ganan un partido. (sujeto: los beisbolistas)

Mariano Rivera

Mariano Rivera es un jugador de los Yankees de Nueva York y lleva años en Manhattan. Su vida es muy activa. Tiene que levantarse temprano porque tiene que practicar béisbol todos los días para estar en buenas condiciones físicas. Después de practicar, se sienta en su club para ver la televisión. Por la tarde, se divierte con sus amigos en un café y se pone muy contento cuando tocan música latina, especialmente la de sus compatriotas Los Rabanes. Por la noche, después de hacer ejercicio en un gimnasio, se baña y se acuesta temprano, pues al día siguiente se despierta a las seis de la mañana porque tienen un partido en Boston esa noche. Seguramente todos van a divertirse mucho después de ganar el partido.

Paso 2 Ahora, prepara cuatro preguntas para hacerle a otro miembro de la clase y contesta las de él/ella.

MODELO: E1: *¿Dónde vive Mariano Rivera?*
E2: *Vive en Nueva York.*

5-8 ¿En qué orden lo haces? Pon (*put*) estas actividades en orden lógico según (*according to*) tu rutina diaria. Después, compara tu orden con el de un/a compañero/a. ¿Son similares o diferentes?

_____ me duermo   _____ me peino

_____ me lavo   _____ me cepillo los dientes

_____ me afeito   _____ me despierto

_____ me acuesto   _____ me lavo la cara

5-9 **Parejas famosas.** Describe la relación que tienen las siguientes personas.

Algunas parejas

Peter Griffin y Brian Griffin (*Family Guy*)

Will Schuester y Sue Sylvester (*Glee*)

Hugo Chávez y Evo Morales

los republicanos y los demócratas

los perros (*dogs*) y los gatos (*cats*)

Marc Anthony y Jennifer López

Tú y yo

¿...?

Algunas relaciones

quererse

llamarse

escribirse

verse

(**no**) admirarse

detestarse

adorarse

tolerarse

Los guacamayos se quieren mucho.

MODELO: Romeo y Julieta

Romeo y Julieta se quieren mucho.

5-10 **Nuestras rutinas.** ¿Tienes mucho en común con tu compañero/a de clase?

Paso 1 Primero, indica si haces las siguientes actividades e incluye cuándo y cómo.

> despertarse antes de las siete de la mañana
>
> ducharse por la noche o por la mañana
>
> maquillarse todos los días
>
> acostarse temprano o tarde los fines de semana
>
> divertirse en una fiesta
>
> afeitarse con navaja o con máquina de afeitar

MODELO: *Siempre me despierto antes de las siete de la mañana.*

Paso 2 Ahora, pregúntale a tu compañero/a si hace estas mismas cosas (*same things*). Incluye dos preguntas originales. Después, describan qué tienen ustedes en común: **Mi compañero/a y yo nos ....**

MODELO: E1: *Siempre me despierto antes de las siete de la mañana. Y tú, ¿cuándo te despiertas?*

E2: *Normalmente, me despierto antes de las siete también. / No me despierto antes de las siete. Me despierto a las ocho.*

5-11 **Las emociones y las reacciones.** Túrnense para hacerse preguntas sobre cómo se sienten en las siguientes situaciones.

MODELO: llegas tarde a clase
E1: *¿Qué pasa cuando llegas tarde a clase?*
E2: *Me pongo nervioso/a.*

- sacas una "A" en un examen
- conoces a una persona importante
- pierdes tu libro de texto
- ves un programa violento en la televisión
- estás en una clase aburrida
- ves el "Daily Show" o el "Colbert Report" en *Comedy Central*
- te olvidas de la tarea
- el/la profesor/a llega tarde para un examen

5-12 **Una relación especial.** Túrnense para hacerse preguntas sobre relaciones especiales que tienen con algunas personas. Puede ser con un/a novio/a, un/a amigo/a o un familiar.

MODELO: E1: *¿Se conocen bien?*
E2: *Sí, nos conocemos bastante bien.*

1. ¿Con qué frecuencia se ven?
2. ¿Dónde se encuentran generalmente?
3. ¿Cuántas veces al día se llaman por teléfono?
4. ¿Qué se dicen cuando se ven?
5. ¿Se quieren mucho?
6. ¿Cuándo se mandan (*send*) textos por teléfono?
7. ¿Se entienden bien?
8. ¿Se respetan mucho?

5-13 **Rétense (*Challenge each other*).** Formen dos equipos y un miembro de la clase hace de árbitro (*referee*). Cada equipo tiene que escribir cinco preguntas para el otro equipo usando verbos reflexivos. Una persona diferente del equipo contesta para su equipo y el árbitro decide si contesta bien. Al final, el equipo que tiene el mayor número de respuestas correctas gana.

MODELO: EQUIPO 1: *¿Cúando te enojas?*
EQUIPO 2: *Me enojo cuando no tengo razón.*
ÁRBITRO: *¡Correcto! / Lo siento, no es correcto.*

2. Comparisons of equality and inequality

Comparaciones de igualdad

- To compare things that are equal, English uses *as ... as*. In Spanish, you make comparisons of equality with adjectives and adverbs by using the following construction.

> **tan** + *adjective/adverb* + **como**

Joaquín es **tan** amable **como** Roberto.	*Joaquín is as nice as Roberto.*
María no habla **tan** despacio **como** su hermana.	*María doesn't speak as slowly as her sister.*

- Make comparisons of equality with nouns by using the following construction. Note that **tanto** is an adjective and agrees in gender and number with the noun or pronoun it modifies.

> **tanto/a(s)** + *noun* + **como**   — *equal*

Marta tiene **tantos** amigos **como** ustedes.	*Marta has as many friends as you.*
Tú tienes **tanta** paciencia **como** Eugenio.	*You have as much patience as Eugenio.*

- Make comparisons of equality with verbs by using the following construction.

> *verb* + **tanto como**

Mis hermanos se enamoran **tanto como** tú.	*My brothers fall in love as much as you.*

Comparaciones de desigualdad

- A comparison of inequality expresses *more than* or *less than*. Use this construction with adjectives, adverbs, or nouns.

> **más/menos** + *adjective/adverb/noun* + **que**

adjective

Mercedes es **menos** responsable **que** Claudio.	*Mercedes is less responsible than Claudio.*

adverb

Yo me visto **más** rápidamente **que** tú.	*I get dressed faster than you.*

noun

Esta casa tiene **menos** cuartos **que** la otra.	*This house has fewer rooms than the other.*

- Make comparisons of inequality with verbs using the following construction:

$$verb + \textbf{más/menos} + \textbf{que}$$

Estudio **más que** tú.   *I study more than you (do).*

- With numerical expressions, use **de** instead of **que.**

  Tengo **más de** cinco buenos amigos. *I have more than five good friends.*

Resumen (*Summary*) de las comparaciones de igualdad y de desigualdad

Equal comparisons	
nouns:	**tanto/a(s)** + *noun* + **como** + *noun* or *pronoun*
adjectives/adverbs:	**tan** + *adj./adv.* + **como** + *noun* or *pronoun*
verbs:	*verb* + **tanto como** + *noun* or *pronoun*
Unequal comparisons	
adjs./advs./nouns:	**más/menos** + *adj./adv./noun* + **que** + *noun* or *pronoun*
verbs:	*verb* + **más/menos** + **que** + *noun* or *pronoun*
with numbers:	**más/menos** + **de** + *number*

Los adjetivos comparativos irregulares

Some Spanish adjectives have both regular and irregular comparative forms. The irregular forms do not require *más/menos*:

Adjective	Regular form	Irregular form	
bueno/a	más bueno/a	mejor	*better*
malo/a	más malo/a	peor	*worse*
viejo/a	más viejo/a	mayor	*older*
joven	más joven	menor	*younger*

[handwritten: When referring to better or worse]

- The irregular forms **mejor** and **peor** are more commonly used than the regular forms.

Esta casa es **mejor** que esa.	*This house is better than that one.*
Rafael es **peor** que Luis.	*Rafael is worse than Luis.*
Me siento **mejor** hoy.	*I feel better today.*
Dormimos **peor** cuando hace calor.	*We sleep poorly when it is hot.*

- **Mayor, menor,** and **más joven** are commonly used with people; **más viejo** may be used with inanimate objects.

[handwritten: When referring to older or younger]

Manuel es **menor** que Berta y yo soy **mayor** que Manuel.	*Manuel is younger than Berta and I am older than Manuel.*
San José, Costa Rica, es **más vieja** que Managua, Nicaragua.	*San José, Costa Rica, is older than Managua, Nicaragua.*

APLICACIÓN

5-14 Dos chismosas (*gossips*). Estás en una fiesta cuando escuchas una conversación entre dos personas chismosas.

Paso 1 Subraya (*Underline*) las comparaciones de igualdad y de desigualdad en la conversación.

MODELO: La blusa de doña Carmen es <u>más fea que</u> la de doña Luisa.

CARLOTA: Creo que el champú que usa Elena es peor que el que uso yo.

ÁNGELA: Es verdad que su pelo no es tan bonito como el tuyo[1].

CARLOTA: ¿Crees que ella es tan rica como dice?

ÁNGELA: No, pero creo que es más rica que nosotras. Sin embargo, es menos rica que su esposo.

CARLOTA: Pero su esposo no tiene tantos carros como tú.

ÁNGELA: Es cierto, pero mis carros son menos grandes y elegantes que los carros de su esposo.

CARLOTA: ¿Y quién crees que es mayor? ¿Tú o Elena?

ÁNGELA: ¡Qué barbaridad! Yo soy mucho más joven que ella. Ella tiene más de cincuenta años. Yo tengo menos de cuarenta.

CARLOTA: Bueno, estoy aburrida. Vamos a casa. No me gusta la comida aquí. En casa la comida es mejor que la comida que hacen aquí.

ÁNGELA: Tienes razón. ¡Esta comida es peor que la comida nuestra! ¡Vamos!

CARLOTA: Perdón, Elena, pero estamos muy cansadas y tenemos que levantarnos más temprano que de costumbre[2] mañana. Gracias, su fiesta es perfecta. ¡La comida está deliciosa!

[1]*yours* [2]*usual*

Paso 2 Ahora, túrnense para hacer y contestar preguntas sobre la conversación y añadir (*add*) más detalles.

MODELO: E1: *¿Cómo es el champú que usa Elena?*
E2: *Es peor que el champú que usa Carlota.*
E1: *¿Por qué?*
E2: *Porque no es tan caro. Elena compra el champú en Econo Mart.*

5-15 Los Grammy. Ustedes son reporteros/as para la ceremonia de los Grammy en Hollywood y ven llegar a las estrellas (*stars*). Cada uno/a debe hacer por lo menos cinco comparaciones según los datos publicados sobre estas personas. Añadan otros detalles basados en sus fotos.

Enrique Iglesias

Fecha de nacimiento: 1975
Estatura: 1,91 m
Número de premios Grammy: 2
Número de álbumes vendidos: 4 millones

Paulina Rubio

Fecha de nacimiento: 1971
Estatura: 1,63 m
Número de premios Grammy: 0
Número de álbumes vendidos: 25 millones

Rubén Blades

Fecha de nacimiento: 1948
Estatura: 1,80 m
Número de premios Grammy: 8
Número de álbumes vendidos: 75 millones

Gloria Estefan

Fecha de nacimiento: 1957
Estatura: 1,58 m
Número de premios Grammy: 6
Número de álbumes vendidos: 16 millones

Juanes

Fecha de nacimiento: 1972
Estatura: 1,72 m
Número de premios Grammy: 18
Número de álbumes vendidos: 12 millones

Christina Aguilera

Fecha de nacimiento: 1980
Estatura: 1,56 m
Número de premios Grammy: 5
Número de álbumes vendidos: 20 millones

MODELO: *Enrique Iglesias es más guapo que Rubén Blades.*

5-16 Sus preferencias. En grupos de tres, hablen de sus preferencias sobre los siguientes temas y por qué prefieren uno más que otro. Antes de empezar, preparen sus preferencias y opiniones. Usen comparaciones para expresar sus opiniones.

> las escuelas privadas *vs.* las escuelas públicas
> una casa *vs.* un apartamento
> vivir en la ciudad *vs.* vivir en las afueras
> los programas de cable *vs.* los de NBC, CBS o ABC
> los correos electrónicos *vs.* los mensajes de texto
> las películas de acción *vs.* las sentimentales

MODELO: E1: *Yo creo que las escuelas públicas son más baratas que las escuelas privadas.*
E2: *Sí, pero las clases en las escuelas privadas son más pequeñas.*
E3: *Pues yo prefiero las escuelas públicas porque tienen más deportes.*

¡Hola! **Cultura en vivo**

In contrast with people in the U.S. and Canada, people in Latin America tend to prefer living in the city where they have easy access to public transportation, schools, and shopping. Instead of inner-city slums, the poor areas of a city are in the outskirts. Do you see trends changing in your city or town? Why or why not?

Media Share

05-21 to 05-26

¿Cuánto saben?

Primero, pregúntate si puedes llevar a cabo (*carry out*) las siguientes funciones comunicativas en español. Después, júntate con dos o tres compañeros/as de clase para presentar las situaciones. Hagan y respondan a por lo menos cuatro preguntas en cada situación.

✓ CAN YOU . . .

☐ describe your daily routine and habits?

☐ express needs related to personal care?

☐ express emotional states?

☐ compare objects and people?

WITH YOUR CLASSMATE(S) . . .

Situación: Un apartamento
Entrevista a otro/a estudiante para ver si son compatibles como compañeros/as de apartamento. Usen verbos reflexivos como **levantarse, acostarse, y dormirse** para describir sus rutinas diarias y hábitos. Al final, decidan si son o no son compatibles.
Para empezar: *Me gusta levantarme... Siempre me despierto...*

Situación: Un producto nuevo
Son un/a vendedor/a y un/a cliente interesado/a en una línea nueva de productos para el arreglo personal. Uno/a presenta los productos (**maquillaje, un secador, una máquina de afeitar,** etc.) y explica por qué son una buena compra. El/La otro/a estudiante hace preguntas sobre los productos.
Para empezar: *Usted debe comprar esta máquina de afeitar. Cuesta solo cien dólares y es super cómoda...*

Situación: Confesiones
Conversen sobre cómo reaccionan en diferentes situaciones. Usen verbos como **sentirse, alegrarse y ponerse.**
Para empezar: *Siempre me pongo nervioso cuando la profesora me hace una pregunta en clase. ¿Y tú?...*

Situación: En una fiesta
Conversen sobre las personas que observan en una fiesta y sus acciones. Usen comparaciones de adjetivos, adverbios y sustantivos.
Para empezar: *En esta fiesta hay tantos chicos como chicas. Creo que Ramón baila mejor que Luis, pero Luis es mucho más guapo...*

📖 Perfiles

Mi experiencia

ECO VOLUNTARIADO EN COSTA RICA

5-17 Para ti. ¿Hay parques nacionales en tu país que se dedican a conservar especies en peligro de extinción? ¿En qué lugares es popular hacer ecoturismo o eco voluntariado? Para ti, ¿qué diferencias hay entre el turismo y el ecoturismo? ¿Te interesa la naturaleza? ¿Por qué? Lee la entrada de Ramón Vázquez en un foro sobre el eco voluntariado.

Foro   Eco voluntariado en Tortuguero
29-sep-2011

¡Hola! Acabo de tener otra experiencia súper emocionante aquí en Tortuguero, Costa Rica, uno de los parques nacionales más importantes del mundo para la protección de las tortugas marinas. Soy de Panamá pero cada año viajo hasta Tortuguero como voluntario para ayudar en la protección de esta especie de tortugas que está en peligro de extinción. Todos los años las tortugas llegan aquí entre julio y septiembre para poner sus huevos[1]. Participo con mis amigos en los programas de criadero[2] dirigidos por un grupo de naturalistas. Durante las masivas arribadas (así es como se llama la llegada de las tortugas a la playa), voluntarios como yo desenterramos[3] los huevos y los llevamos a un lugar seguro hasta que nacen las crías[4]. De esta manera aseguramos que un gran número de crías sobrevivan[5]. Después, recogemos las crías en cubetas[6] y vamos hasta la orilla del mar donde, con mucho cuidado, las depositamos. ¡Tienes que ver cómo corren las pequeñas tortugas hacia el mar! Repito esta experiencia todos los años aunque[7] es un viaje de más de setecientos kilómetros en carro desde Panamá, pero como voy con amigos y escuchamos música de nuestros grupos favoritos (Los Rabanes por ejemplo), el viaje es más entretenido. Acampamos por el camino y hasta[8] a veces dormimos en la playa. ¿Te animas[9]?

Ramon Vázquez
Panamá

[1]*lay their eggs*   [2]*hatchery*   [3]*dig up*   [4]*hatchlings*   [5]*survive*   [6]*buckets*   [7]*even though*   [8]*even*   [9]*Are you game*

5-18 En su opinión. Túrnense para expresar y anotar sus opiniones. ¿En qué puntos están de acuerdo?

1. Cuando voy de vacaciones, me levanto temprano.   Sí   No
2. Me gusta el ecoturismo.   Sí   No
3. Es bueno proteger las especies en peligro de extinción.   Sí   No
4. Me gustaría hacer eco voluntariado algún día.   Sí   No
5. No es importante ducharme todos los días cuando estoy de vacaciones.   Sí   No
6. Prefiero la ciudad al campo como destino cuando viajo.   Sí   No

5-19 Una visita a Tortuguero. Conéctate a la Internet para ver imágenes o videos de Tortuguero y usa comparaciones para escribir tres observaciones en forma de *blog* sobre el lugar.

> 🖱 **Busca:** video tortuguero

MODELO: *La playa es más bonita que las playas de California.*

Mi música

"EVERYBODY" (LOS RABANES, PANAMÁ)

Los Rabanes es un grupo panameño ganador de un Grammy Latino. Originalmente tocaba en bares y clubes, pero rápidamente se conoció su música por todo el mundo. Hoy se le considera el grupo más popular de Panamá. Sus canciones mezclan letras (*lyrics*) en español y en inglés, pero muchas veces las palabras que usan en inglés son irónicas o sarcásticas. Su música combina reggaetón y rock. Los miembros son Emilio Regueira Pérez (voz y guitarra), Christian Torres (voz, bajo y guitarra) y Javier Saavedra (percusión).

Antes de ver y escuchar

5-20 Comparaciones. Usando comparaciones de igualdad y de desigualdad, escribe oraciones en español para comparar estas cosas o conceptos.

MODELO: bailar / cantar (fácil)
Es más fácil bailar bien que cantar bien.

1. tocar guitarra / cantar (interesante)
2. ir en carro / ir en autobús (rápido)
3. las vacaciones en la playa / las vacaciones en el campo (divertido)
4. bailar en una fiesta / observar a la gente en una fiesta (agradable)
5. escuchar música / ver un video musical (aburrido)

Para ver y escuchar

 5-21 La canción. Conéctate a la Internet para buscar un video de "Everybody" de Los Rabanes cantando esta canción. Escribe una descripción de los cantantes y las acciones en la canción. ¿Cómo son físicamente? ¿Cuántos años tienen? ¿Cómo es la canción? ¿Cómo es el ritmo? ¿Qué hacen los cantantes en el video? ¿Se divierten?

> **Busca:** everybody rabanes video; everybody rabanes letra
>
> **Si te interesa comprar la canción:** *Go to iTunes Store>Music>More to Explore>iMix>Arriba 6e*

Después de ver y escuchar

 5-22 ¿Cómo se comparan? Escribe un mínimo de cinco comparaciones iguales y/o desiguales que se te ocurran (*that occur to you*) al ver el video. Puedes incluir algunos de estos temas.

- la música
- el baile
- los músicos
- las personas que bailan
- el medio de transporte
- los animales

MODELO: *En el video hay tantas mujeres como hombres...*

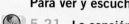

Segunda parte

¡Así lo decimos! VOCABULARIO

¡Así es la vida! Vamos a limpiar

05-29

Vera quiere invitar a algunos amigos esta noche para una fiesta en el apartamento donde vive con sus tres amigos. Desgraciadamente, la casa está muy desordenada.

Ahora Vera está enojada y les escribe una nota a sus compañeros.

ENRIQUE— Debes vaciar el lavaplatos y sacar la basura.

ROGELIO— Tienes que recoger la ropa del piso y pasar la aspiradora en la sala.

ESTELA— Necesitas lavar el piso de la cocina y poner la mesa.

Yo voy a comprar los refrescos y vuelvo a las seis.

— Vera

Vocabulario Los quehaceres domésticos

05-30
to 05-35

Aparatos domésticos | Household appliamces

la aspiradora	*vacuum cleaner*
la lavadora	*washing machine*
el lavaplatos	*dishwasher*
la plancha	*iron*
la secadora	*clothes dryer*

Tomás va a recoger la ropa del piso.

Muebles y accesorios | Furniture and accessories

la cama	*bed*
la cómoda	*dresser*
el cuadro	*painting*
el estante	*bookcase*
la lámpara	*lamp*
la mesa de noche	*nightstand*
el sillón	*armchair, overstuffed chair*
el sofá	*sofa, couch*

Teresa pone la mesa.

Las partes de una casa | Parts of a house

el baño	*bathroom*
la casa	*house, home*
la cocina	*kitchen*
el comedor	*dining room*
el cuarto	*room, bedroom*
el dormitorio	*bedroom*
el garaje	*garage*
el jardín	*garden*
el pasillo	*hallway*
el patio	*patio, backyard*
el piso	*floor*
la sala	*living room*
la terraza	*terrace*

Variaciones
Depending on where you are, **piso** can mean *floor,* or *story (of a building).* You will hear **piso** for *floor (of a room)* in Latin America, but in Spain **suelo** for *floor,* and **piso** for *apartment.* How then do you find an apartment in other countries? Use **departamento** in Mexico and Argentina, and **apartamento** in Colombia and other places.

Los quehaceres domésticos | Household chores

hacer la cama	*to make the bed*
lavar (el piso/los platos)	*to wash (the floor / the dishes)*
limpiar/ordenar la casa	*to clean / to straighten up the house*
llenar/vaciar el lavaplatos	*to fill / to empty the dishwasher*
pasar la aspiradora	*to vacuum*
poner/quitar la mesa	*to set / to clear the table*
recoger la ropa (del piso / de la secadora)	*to pick up / to collect clothes (from the floor / from the dryer)*
sacar la basura	*to take out the garbage*

Salva tiene que pasar la aspiradora.

05-36
to 05-37

Letras y sonidos

The consonant *h* and the sequence *ch* in Spanish

In Spanish, the letter **h** is silent. In other words, it is a letter for which there is no corresponding sound.

ho-la   **ha**-cer   **hom**-bre   **her**-mo-sa   que-**ha**-ce-res

In the sequence **ch**, however, the letters **c** and **h** combine to create one single sound **ch**, which is pronounced the same as in English *church*.

mu-**cho**   no-**che**   plan-**cha**   cu-**chi**-lla   mu-**cha**-**cho**

APLICACIÓN

5-23 En el apartamento de Vera.   Completa las siguientes frases lógicamente según las instrucciones de Vera en **¡Así es la vida!**

MODELO: Estela tiene que lavar... *el piso de la cocina.*

1. __E__ Vera se pone...
2. __F__ Limpian la casa antes de...
3. __A__ Enrique necesita vaciar...
4. __C__ Enrique tiene que sacar...
5. __H__ Es necesario pasar...
6. __D__ Rogelio necesita recoger la ropa...
7. _____ Estela tiene que poner...
8. _____ Vera escribe una lista de...

a. el lavaplatos.
b. los quehaceres.
c. la basura.
d. del piso.
e. la mesa.
f. la fiesta.
g. enojada.
h. la aspiradora.

5-24 ¡Emparejar!   ¿Dónde encuentras las siguientes cosas? Empareja (*Match*) la letra del lugar con el objeto lógico y di (*say*) dónde está.

MODELO: el carro
             El carro está en el garaje.

1. __E__ la bicicleta
2. __C__ el sofá
3. __D__ la ropa
4. __F__ la cama
5. __B__ el lavaplatos
6. __A__ la mesa y las sillas

a. el comedor
b. la cocina
c. la sala
d. la cómoda
e. el garaje
f. el dormitorio

5-25 ¿Quién lo hace en tu casa?   Túrnense para decir quién hace estos quehaceres en su casa y decidan cuál de ustedes es más trabajador/a.

MODELO: lavar los platos
             E1: *Mi hermano los lava.*
             E2: *Pues, en mi casa yo los lavo. Creo que soy más trabajador que tú.*

1. pasar la aspiradora
2. hacer las compras
3. vaciar el lavaplatos
4. poner la mesa
5. sacar la basura
6. hacer las camas
7. lavar la ropa
8. ordenar la casa
9. limpiar el baño

5-26 ¡Todo lo que necesita para la casa! Escucha el siguiente anuncio de radio sobre los productos para la casa. Escribe el nombre y el precio de cada producto debajo del dibujo correspondiente.

MODELO: *Una silla: $19*

1.

la aspiradora

_____

2. *la lavadora y la secadora*

_____

3. *la mesa de noche*

_____

¡Hola!
Cultura en vivo

Because electricity is a comparatively expensive commodity, electrical appliances are not as common in many Latin American homes as in the U.S. and Canada. However, middle-class homes are more likely to have hired help to assist with daily chores. Would you prefer to have the latest electrical appliances, or hired help to assist you with your chores?

4.

el sofa

_____

5.

_____

6.

el lavaplatos

_____

5-27A En la agencia de bienes raíces (*real estate*). Buscas una casa o apartamento en Panamá para ti y algunos compañeros. A continuación tienes información para contestar a las preguntas del/de la agente de bienes raíces. **Estudiante B,** por favor ve al **Apéndice 1,** página A-8.

MODELO: ESTUDIANTE A: *Busco una casa o un apartamento.*
ESTUDIANTE B: *¿Para cuántas personas?*
ESTUDIANTE A: *Para cinco, y las mujeres quieren…*

Estudiante A:

- hay cinco personas: dos hombres y tres mujeres
- las mujeres quieren habitaciones privadas
- todos quieren estar cerca de la playa
- quieren una cocina grande y un patio
- tienen un perro

- la casa debe tener un garaje para un carro y cuatro bicicletas
- debe tener por lo menos dos baños, uno con ducha
- quieren estar cerca de la línea de autobús
- pueden pagar entre $1.000 y $1.200 al mes, luz y gas incluidos

5-28 El plan (*floor plan*) de mi casa. Dibuja (*Draw*) el plan de tu casa o apartamento (real o imaginario) en una hoja. Incluye los cuartos, los pasillos y los muebles. Descríbeselo a tu compañero/a para que él/ella lo reproduzca en su papel. Comparen los resultados. ¿Se comunican bien? Ahora escucha y dibuja la descripción de tu compañero/a.

MODELO: *Mi apartamento es pequeño. Tiene…*

EXPANSIÓN
Preposiciones de lugar
To describe the location of a person or an object, use the following prepositions:

arriba de *above*
contra *against*
debajo de *under, below*
dentro de *within, inside of*
sobre *on*

¡Así lo hacemos! ESTRUCTURAS

📖 3. The superlative

¡Yo soy la más alta!

¡Yo soy la más pequeña!

¡Yo soy la más inteligente!

05-38 to 05-40

- A superlative statement expresses the highest or lowest degree of a quality: for example, the most, the greatest, the least, or the worst. To express the superlative in Spanish, the definite article is used with **más** or **menos.** Note that the preposition **de** is the equivalent of *in* or *of* after a superlative.

> *definite article* + **más** or **menos** + *adjective* + **de**

Antonio es **el más alto de** mis hermanos.   *Antonio is the tallest of my brothers.*

Este jabón es **el menos caro de** todos.   *This soap is the least expensive of all.*

- When a noun is used with the superlative, the definite article precedes the noun in Spanish.

Mi brillo de labios es **el brillo de labios más** caro que venden aquí.   *My lip gloss is the most expensive lip gloss they sell here.*

La casa de Carlos es **la** casa **más** popular **del** barrio.   *Carlos's house is the most popular house in the neighborhood.*

- Adjectives and adverbs that have irregular forms in the comparative use the same irregular forms in the superlative.

Juan es **el mejor de** mis amigos.   *Juan is the best of my friends.*

La tía Isabel es **la mayor de** mis tías.   *Aunt Isabel is the oldest of my aunts.*

APLICACIÓN

5-29 El Canal de Panamá. La nación de Panamá controla el canal desde el 31 de diciembre de 1999.

Más de 14.000 barcos pasan por el canal cada año.

Paso 1 Lee el párrafo siguiente y subraya los superlativos.

El Canal de Panamá no es el más largo, ni el más ancho[1], ni el más profundo[2], ni el más antiguo del mundo. Pero sí es el único que conecta dos océanos: el Atlántico y el Pacífico, y aún hoy es la vía de agua navegable más importante del mundo. Al principio, enfermedades como la malaria, la fiebre[3] amarilla y el cólera causaron los problemas más graves de la construcción del canal. De todos, primero los franceses y después los norteamericanos, George Goethals fue el ingeniero que tuvo más éxito[4] en terminar el proyecto. Cuando completó el canal en 1914, era[5] el peor momento de esa época: el comienzo de la Primera Guerra Mundial. Hoy en día, el canal todavía es una de las obras de ingeniería más impactantes del mundo.

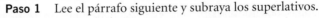

[1]*widest*   [2]*deepest*   [3]*fever*   [4]*success*   [5]*it was*

Paso 2   Contesta las siguientes preguntas sobre el artículo para después escribir un breve resumen (*brief summary*) de la importancia que tiene el Canal de Panamá.

1. ¿Qué conecta el canal?

2. ¿Por qué es importante?

3. ¿En qué año se completó?

4. ¿Cuáles eran (*were*) los problemas más graves al principio?

5. ¿Cuál fue el ingeniero que tuvo (*had*) más éxito?

6. ¿Qué otro evento importante también comenzó en 1914?

5-30 Otros superlativos de Centroamérica.   Busca en el mapa de Centroamérica en **Nuestro mundo** (página 179) el nombre de estos lugares superlativos.

MODELO: el país de Centroamérica más montañoso
   Honduras es el país más montañoso de Centroamérica.

1. el país más grande de Centroamérica

2. el lago más grande de Nicaragua

3. el país más pequeño de Centroamérica

4. el país más estrecho (*narrow*)

5-31 Entre todos.   Usen diferentes formas del superlativo y comparativo para comparar las personas, cosas o lugares en cada serie. Usen los verbos, los adjetivos y los sustantivos de la lista. Después, expresen su opinión sobre los diferentes aspectos o características de cada uno.

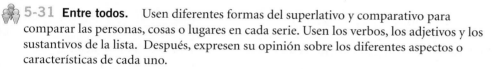

Verbos	Adjetivos		Sustantivos
actuar	caro/a – económico/a	grande – pequeño/a	actor/actriz
cantar	delicioso/a	lujoso/a (*luxurious*)	deporte
costar	divertido/a	mejor – peor	persona
maquillarse	emocionante	mayor – menor	
ser	generoso/a – tacaño/a	rápido/a	
vestirse	gordo/a – delgado/a	ridículo/a	

MODELO: Bill Gates – Carlos Slim – Elizabeth Taylor
   E1: *Creo que Bill Gates es más rico que Elizabeth Taylor.*
   E2: *Y Carlos Slim es el más rico de los tres.*
   E3: *Pero Elizabeth Taylor es la más elegante de los tres...*

1. Queen Latifah – Oprah – Whitney Houston

2. Penélope Cruz – Daisy Fuentes – Mariah Carey

3. Enrique Iglesias – Juanes – Los Rabanes

4. los carros japoneses – los carros alemanes – los carros norteamericanos

5. la comida mexicana – la comida italiana – la comida francesa

6. el béisbol – el fútbol – el básquetbol

7. la ciudad de Miami – la ciudad de Chicago – la ciudad de San Francisco

Presencia hispana

Waves of immigration from Central American countries to the U.S. and Canada have been largely due to political upheaval in the home countries of immigrants, with the notable exceptions of those from Costa Rica and Panama. Costa Rican immigrants are often university-educated scholars who come for research opportunities not available at home. In the U.S. and Canada, they do not typically form **barrios** to the extent other immigrants do. In addition to political stability, what other factors would encourage a person to stay in his or her home country?

📖 4. The present progressive

05-41
to 05-43

Están llamándose por teléfono.

- The present progressive tense describes an action that is in progress at the time the statement is made. It is formed using the present indicative of **estar** as an auxiliary verb and the present participle (the **-ando/-iendo** form) of the main verb. The present participle is invariable regardless of the subject. It never changes its ending. Only **estar** is conjugated when using the present progressive forms.

Present progressive of *hablar*			
yo	estoy hablando	nosotros/as	estamos hablando
tú	estás hablando	vosotros/as	estáis hablando
Ud.	está hablando	Uds.	están hablando
él/ella	está hablando	ellos/as	están hablando

- To form the present participle of regular **-ar** verbs, add **-ando** to the verb stem:

> hablar + -ando → **hablando**

Los niños **están bailando** en la sala.   *The children are dancing in the living room.*

- To form the present participle of **-er** and **-ir** verbs, add **-iendo** to the verb stem:

> comer + -iendo → **comiendo**   escribir + -iendo → **escribiendo**

Los niños **están bebiendo** leche.   *The children are drinking milk.*
Estoy escribiendo la composición.   *I'm writing the composition.*

- **Leer** has an irregular present participle. The **i** from **-iendo** changes to **y.**

> leer + iendo → **leyendo**

- **-Ir** verbs with a stem change will also have a change in the participle. This change will be indicated when you first encounter the infinitive.

dormir (ue, u)	*to sleep*	→	**durmiendo**	*sleeping*
pedir (i, i)	*to ask for*	→	**pidiendo**	*asking for*
servir (i, i)	*to serve*	→	**sirviendo**	*serving*

- Reflexive pronouns and object pronouns can either precede **estar** or be attached to the participle. Add an accent when the pronoun is attached to the participle.

Carlos está vistiéndo**se**.
Carlos **se** está vistiendo.   } *Carlos is getting dressed.*

Estamos mirándo**te**.
Te estamos mirando.   } *We're looking at you.*

APLICACIÓN

5-32 ¿Qué estamos haciendo? Empareja el lugar donde estamos con la actividad más lógica que estamos haciendo.

MODELO: Estamos en el laboratorio de ciencias.
Estamos estudiando para un examen de biología.

1. _____ Estamos en un café.
2. _A_ Estamos en el sofá.
3. _H_ Estamos en el parque.
4. _____ Estamos en un concierto.
5. _____ Estamos en clase.
6. _____ Estamos en un partido.
7. _____ Estamos en la biblioteca.
8. _____ Estamos en casa a las dos de la mañana.

a. Estamos viendo la televisión.
b. Estamos escuchando música.
c. Estamos escribiendo apuntes en un cuaderno.
d. Estamos jugando al tenis.
e. Estamos leyendo un libro.
f. Estamos tomando un refresco.
g. Estamos durmiendo.
h. Estamos haciendo un pícnic.

5-33 ¡Imagínate! Escribe dónde te imaginas que están estas personas y lo que están haciendo ahora. Puedes usar las actividades de la lista.

asistir	dormir	jugar	pasar
cantar	escribir	lavarse	ponerse
cepillarse	hablar	limpiar	preparar
despertarse	hacer	maquillarse	vestirse

MODELO: el presidente de México
El presidente de México está en Washington. Está visitando al presidente de Estados Unidos.

Personajes

1. Peyton Manning y Brett Favre
2. Joaquín Phoenix
3. Derek Jeter
4. Eva Longoria Parker y Tony Parker
5. Pedro Almodóvar
6. Mariano Rivera
7. Ricky Martin y Shakira
8. el vicepresidente de EE. UU.

5-34 Lo siento, no está disponible (*available*). Ustedes son recepcionistas en un hotel de cinco estrellas en Ciudad de Panamá. Túrnense para inventar excusas para explicar por qué algunos de los huéspedes (*guests*) importantes no pueden atender las llamadas.

MODELO: E1: *Buenos días. ¿Me permite hablar con el presidente Obama?*
E2: *Lo siento; el señor Obama no está disponible ahora. Está hablando con el presidente de Panamá.*

Algunos de los huéspedes importantes

Mariah Carey y Paulina Rubio
Venus y Serena Williams
la chef Rachael Ray

Michelle Obama
Eminem y Kanye West
Roselyn Sánchez
(*Without a Trace*)

Kobe Bryant
Stephen Colbert
Homer y Marge Simpson

EXPANSIÓN

When making excuses, there are several fillers you can use to stall for time and come up with a reasonable response:

este... *uhh...*
bueno... *well...*
el problema es que... *the problem is that...*
lo siento, pero... *I'm sorry, but...*

5-35A **¿Qué estoy haciendo?**   Mientras (*While*) actúas una de las siguientes situaciones, tu compañero/a trata de adivinar (*guess*) lo que estás haciendo. Túrnense para actuar y adivinar. **Estudiante B,** por favor ve al **Apéndice 1,** página A-9.

MODELO: afeitarse

ESTUDIANTE A: (act out shaving)

¿Qué estoy haciendo?

ESTUDIANTE B: *Estás afeitándote.*

Estudiante A:

1. cepillarse los dientes
2. maquillarse
3. bañarse
4. sacar la basura
5. acostarse
6. ponerse nervioso/a

Estoy afeitándome.

Media Share

05-44 to 05-48

¿Cuánto saben?

Primero, pregúntate si puedes llevar a cabo (*carry out*) las siguientes funciones comunicativas en español. Después, júntate (*get together*) con dos o tres compañeros/as de clase para presentar las situaciones. Hagan y respondan a por lo menos cuatro preguntas en cada situación.

✓ CAN YOU . . .

☐ talk about what you do around the house?

☐ describe people or things using superlatives?

☐ describe what is happening at the moment?

WITH YOUR CLASSMATE(S) . . .

Situación: En casa
Decidan entre ustedes quién se encarga de (*is responsible for*) los quehaceres de la casa.
Para empezar: *Paco tiene que...*

Situación: Alquilo apartamento
Uno/a de ustedes quiere alquilar (*to rent*) su apartamento. Túrnense para describirlo y hacer preguntas sobre dónde está el apartamento, sus habitaciones y los muebles. Usen comparaciones y superlativos en su descripción.
Para empezar: *Mi apartamento es más grande que otros en el barrio y también es el más económico...*

Situación: Por teléfono
Observen a sus compañeros/as de clase y explíquense lo que están haciendo en este momento.
Para empezar: *Ana está escribiendo en su portátil...*

Observaciones

05-49 to 05-51

¡Pura vida! EPISODIO 5

En este episodio hay conflicto entre Hermés y Marcela.

Antes de ver el video

5-36 Los quehaceres de la casa. En muchas familias de clase media es común tener ayuda de alguien (*someone*) en la casa. Lee la situación de la familia de Silvia y contesta brevemente las siguientes preguntas en español.

Una casa de apartamentos en Madrid.

> Vivimos en Madrid. Como[1] mi padre y mi madre trabajan fuera[2] de casa, tenemos una señora que nos ayuda con los quehaceres. Se llama Ana y viene todos los lunes, miércoles y viernes. Pasa tres o cuatro horas lavando la ropa, ordenando la casa, lavando los platos y limpiando los pisos. Algunas veces, también va al mercado y hace las compras para la cena, pero mi mamá siempre prepara la comida. Con frecuencia tenemos visita[3] los viernes por la noche: mis abuelos y mis tíos o algunos amigos de la oficina de mis padres. En esas ocasiones, Ana prepara algo especial, como una paella o una torta. Gracias a la ayuda de Ana, el día siguiente solo tenemos que vaciar el lavaplatos.

[1]*Since* [2]*outside* [3]*guests*

1. ¿Dónde vive la familia de Silvia?

2. ¿Por qué necesitan a una señora que les ayuda a mantener la casa?

3. ¿Cuáles son los quehaceres de Ana?

4. ¿Quién normalmente prepara la cena?

5. Si hay visita el viernes, ¿qué tiene que hacer la familia los sábados?

A ver el video

5-37 Hay conflicto en casa. Mira el quinto episodio de **¡Pura vida!** para identificar el conflicto entre Marcela y Hermés. Luego, empareja (*pair*) las frases para formar oraciones lógicas.

Marcela

Marcela y Hermés

La lista de quehaceres

1. _____ Hermés trabaja...
2. _____ A Marcela le molestan...
3. _____ Hermés dice que siempre...
4. _____ Marcela dice que ella siempre...
5. _____ Según Silvia, cada uno...

a. los papeles que están en el piso.
b. saca la basura.
c. plancha su ropa y hace su cama.
d. lavando platos en un restaurante.
e. limpia el baño.

Después de ver el video

5-38 Servicio de limpieza. Conéctate a la Internet para buscar un servicio de limpieza. Escoge uno que te guste y anota los servicios y el costo, si se incluye.

Busca: servicio domestico; servicio limpieza domestica

Nuestro mundo

Panoramas

América Central II:
Costa Rica, Nicaragua, Panamá

05-52 to 05-53

Los primeros habitantes de estas regiones llegaron (*arrived*) hace más de 30.000 años. Los españoles llegaron hace poco más de 500.

Según una leyenda salvadoreña, durante la colonia española una erupción de este volcán facilitó el triunfo de los campesinos sobre los ricos terratenientes (*landowners*) españoles.

En 2014, Panamá celebra el centenario de la construcción del Canal e inaugura una gran expansión del mismo. La nueva vía (*lane*) va a acomodar las súper naves que antes eran demasiado grandes para navegar el Canal.

La gran variedad de flora y fauna en las selvas centroamericanas se ve representada tanto en artefactos precolombinos como en artesanías indígenas.

Costa Rica, Nicaragua, Panamá

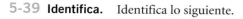

	Costa Rica	Nicaragua	Panamá
Población:	4 millones	6 millones	3 millones
Población urbana:	63%	57%	73%
Servicio militar:	No tiene fuerzas militares.	Voluntario	No tiene fuerzas militares.
Propiedad de viviendas[1]:	75 %	79%	78%
PIB per cápita:	$11.600	$2.900	$11.600

[1]Home ownership

5-39 Identifica. Identifica lo siguiente.

1. el país con la mayor población en las ciudades
2. el país con el menor PIB por persona
3. el tema (*theme*) de muchas de las artesanías
4. lo que va a pasar en el año 2014
5. un fenómeno natural relacionado con una leyenda (*legend*)
6. los países sin fuerzas militares

5-40 Desafío. Usa el mapa para identificar estos lugares y sus características.

1. las capitales de estos tres países
2. sus costas
3. el país más grande de los tres
4. el país con frontera con Honduras
5. la ruta del Canal (del norte al sur o del oeste al este)

5-41 Proyecto: América Central: Costa Rica, Nicaragua, Panamá. Estos tres países contribuyen mucho a la economía, la política y la cultura de la región. Escoge uno de los siguientes lugares, personas o temas, u otro que te interese, para investigar: **el Canal de Panamá, el ecoturismo, Óscar Arias, los indios Kuna, el fútbol en Costa Rica, una casa o apartamento en Costa Rica/Nicaragua/Panamá.** Usa el Modelo para escribir un resumen en el que incluyas lo siguiente:

- su nombre y dónde está
- por qué es importante o interesante
- cómo es
- si quieres visitarlo o verlo algún día y por qué
- si piensas estudiar más sobre este tema
- una foto representativa

> **Busca:** canal panama; oscar arias; kuna, etc.

MODELO: *El país de Costa Rica es muy popular entre muchos estadounidenses y canadienses para invertir (invest) en una segunda casa y eventualmente vivir allí....*

📖 Páginas

05-54

Playa Cacao

ANTES DE LEER

5-42 Lo que ya sabes. Lo que (*What*) ya sabes es importante para entender lo que lees. Por ejemplo, en la construcción de una casa, los materiales dependen del clima y de otros factores como el gusto (*taste*) de la persona, su situación económica, etc. Antes de leer la descripción de la casa que aparece a continuación, piensa en tus preferencias para comprar una casa.

Para mí, la casa debe...

1. _____ tener muchos dormitorios
2. _____ respetar el medio ambiente (*environment*)
3. _____ estar cerca de buenas escuelas
4. _____ estar en un barrio seguro (*safe*)
5. _____ tener una cocina bien equipada
6. _____ costar más (menos) de $150.000
7. _____ otros requisitos (*requirements*)...

A LEER

5-43 Esta casa. Mientras lees la descripción de esta casa, compárala con tu casa ideal. ¿Qué tiene la casa que te gusta? ¿Qué tiene la casa que no te gusta?

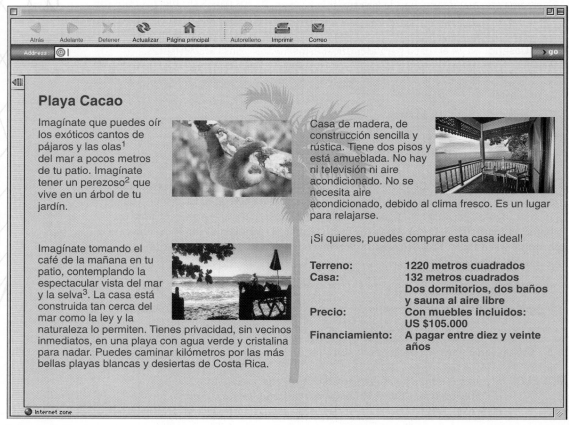

Playa Cacao

Imagínate que puedes oír los exóticos cantos de pájaros y las olas[1] del mar a pocos metros de tu patio. Imagínate tener un perezoso[2] que vive en un árbol de tu jardín.

Imagínate tomando el café de la mañana en tu patio, contemplando la espectacular vista del mar y la selva[3]. La casa está construida tan cerca del mar como la ley y la naturaleza lo permiten. Tienes privacidad, sin vecinos inmediatos, en una playa con agua verde y cristalina para nadar. Puedes caminar kilómetros por las más bellas playas blancas y desiertas de Costa Rica.

Casa de madera, de construcción sencilla y rústica. Tiene dos pisos y está amueblada. No hay ni televisión ni aire acondicionado. No se necesita aire acondicionado, debido al clima fresco. Es un lugar para relajarse.

¡Si quieres, puedes comprar esta casa ideal!

Terreno:	1220 metros cuadrados
Casa:	132 metros cuadrados
	Dos dormitorios, dos baños y sauna al aire libre
Precio:	Con muebles incluidos: US $105.000
Financiamiento:	A pagar entre diez y veinte años

[1]*waves* [2]*sloth* [3]*jungle*

DESPUÉS DE LEER

5-44 ¿Comprendiste? Resume (*Summarize*) las características de la casa que aparece en la página web.

1. dónde está   _____

2. número de dormitorios   _____

3. accesorios incluidos   _____

4. número de pisos   _____

5. número de baños   _____

6. ¿A/C?   _____

7. precio (*price*)   _____

8. ¿vista (*view*)?   _____

5-45 ¿Compras esta casa? Hablen sobre si piensan comprar o no esta casa y por qué.

MODELO: E1: *Compro esta casa porque...*

E2: *Pues, yo no la compro porque...*

5-46 Comprar casa. Conéctate a la Internet y busca una casa o un apartamento que se vende en Costa Rica, Panamá o Nicaragua. Escribe la información de la casa o apartamento en la lista a continuación.

> **Busca:** comprar casa costa rica, etc.

Dónde está: _____

El número de dormitorios: _____

Los metros cuadrados (o pies cuadrados): _____

El número de baños: _____

¿Tiene algo especial? _____

El precio: _____

¿Es una buena casa para tu familia? Explica por qué sí o por qué no. _____

Compro esta casa porque tiene un patio muy bonito.

Taller

05-55

5-47 Un anuncio de venta. En esta actividad vas a diseñar (*design*) un anuncio o página web para vender una casa como la que aparece en **Páginas**.

ANTES DE ESCRIBIR

- Comienza con una lista para dar más información sobre tu casa o condominio.
  - ☐ su ubicación (ciudad, país, cerca de...)
  - ☐ los metros cuadrados
  - ☐ los dormitorios y su descripción
  - ☐ los accesorios incluidos
  - ☐ los accesorios extras: patio, piscina (*pool*), vista, cancha de tenis, etcétera
  - ☐ las actividades que uno puede hacer en la casa o en la comunidad
  - ☐ el precio
  - ☐ las fotos o dibujos para ilustrar la casa o condominio

A ESCRIBIR

- **Descripción.** Ahora escribe dos párrafos para describir la casa. Recuerda, deseas venderla.

DESPUÉS DE ESCRIBIR

- **Revisar.** Revisa la descripción para verificar los siguientes puntos:
  - ☐ el uso correcto de los verbos reflexivos
  - ☐ el uso de comparativos y superlativos
  - ☐ el uso del presente progresivo
  - ☐ la ortografía, incluidos los acentos
- **Intercambiar**
  Intercambia tu anuncio con el de un/a compañero/a y comenten sobre el diseño de cada anuncio y si es efectivo.
- **Entregar**
  Revisa tu anuncio e incorpora las sugerencias de tu compañero/a. Después, dale el anuncio y las respuestas de tu compañero/a a tu profesor/a.

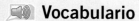

Vocabulario

Primera parte

Las actividades diarias **Daily activities**

acostarse (ue) *to go to bed*
afeitarse *to shave*
bañarse *to bathe*
cepillarse *to brush*
despertarse (ie) *to wake up*
dormirse (ue, u) *to fall asleep*
ducharse *to take a shower*
lavarse *to wash*
levantarse *to get up, to stand up*
maquillarse *to apply makeup*
peinarse *to comb*
quitarse (la camisa) *to take off (your shirt)*
secarse *to dry oneself*
sentarse (ie) *to sit down*
vestirse (i, i) *to get dressed*

Algunas emociones **Some emotions**

ponerse contento/a *to become happy*
furioso/a *angry*
molesto/a *annoyed*
sentirse (ie, i) *to feel*

Algunas partes del cuerpo **Some parts of the body**

la cara *face*
los dientes *teeth*
la mano *hand*
la nariz *nose*
el ojo *eye*
el pelo *hair*

Artículos de uso personal **Personal care items**

el brillo de labios *lip gloss*
el champú *shampoo*
la crema (de afeitar) *(shaving) cream*
el jabón *soap*
el maquillaje *makeup*
la máquina de afeitar *electric razor*
la navaja de afeitar *razor*
el peine *comb*
el secador *hair dryer*

Segunda parte

Los accesorios y los muebles **Furniture and accessories**

los aparatos domésticos *household appliances*
la aspiradora *vacuum cleaner*
la cama *bed*
la cómoda *dresser*
el cuadro *painting*
el estante *bookcase*
la lámpara *lamp*
la lavadora *washing machine*
el lavaplatos *dishwasher*
la mesa de noche *nightstand*
la plancha *iron*
la secadora *clothes dryer*
el sillón *armchair, overstuffed chair*
el sofá *sofa, couch*

Los quehaceres domésticos **Household chores**

hacer la cama *to make the bed*
lavar (los platos / el piso) *to wash (the dishes / the floor)*
limpiar/ordenar la casa *to clean / straighten up the house*
llenar el lavaplatos *to load the dishwasher*
pasar la aspiradora *to vacuum*
poner la mesa *to set the table*
quitar la mesa *to clear the table*
recoger la ropa (del piso / de la secadora) *to pick up / collect clothes (from the floor / dryer)*
sacar la basura *to take out the garbage*
vaciar el lavaplatos *to empty the dishwasher*

Las partes de una casa **Parts of a house**

el baño *bathroom*
la casa *house, home*
la cocina *kitchen*
el comedor *dining room*
el cuarto *room, bedroom*
el dormitorio *bedroom*
el garaje *garage*
el jardín *garden*
el pasillo *hallway*
el patio *patio, backyard*
el piso *floor*
la sala *living room*
la terraza *terrace*

Reflexive pronouns *See page 156.*
Comparisons of equality and inequality *See pages 161–162.*

Verbs that express feelings, moods, and conditions *See page 157.*
Prepositions of place *See page 171.*

Expressions with the noun *vez* *See page 160.*
The superlative *See page 172.*

6

¡Buen provecho!

Readiness
Check

Chile: un país de contrastes

«Disfruta, come y bebe que la vida es breve».

Refrán: Enjoy, eat, and drink, for life is short.

La larga costa de Chile abunda en pescado y otras delicias del mar.

El pintor chileno Claudio Bravo pintó *Contra Luz*, una naturaleza muerta (*still life*).

Primera parte

¡Así lo decimos! VOCABULARIO

 ¡Así es la vida! ¡Buen provecho!

 El Café del Mar es un restaurante popular en Viña del Mar, Chile.

MANOLO: Mesero, la cuenta, por favor.

MESERO: Enseguida, señor.

JORGE: Oye Manolo, ¿cuánto dejamos de propina?

ELÍAS: ¿Qué te apetece, querida?

ESME: A ver... un bistec, una ensalada, el pastel de limón y una copa de vino tinto.

MATILDE: ¡No me gustan los mariscos!

GRACIELA: Pero Matilde, ¡son la especialidad de la casa!

Vocabulario Las comidas y las bebidas

06-02
to 06-09

Variaciones
Names for foods vary
considerably in the
Spanish-speaking
world. In Spain, **la
banana** is **el plátano, la
papa** is **la patata,** and **el
jugo** is **el zumo.**

Variaciones
Un sándwich in Mexico
is on sliced white bread;
most prefer **una torta**
on a hard roll. In Spain,
un bocadillo made on
a fresh baguette
is popular.

Variaciones
In Spain, **el/la
mesero/a** is **el/la
camarero/a.**

Las comidas   Meals

el almuerzo   *lunch*
la cena   *dinner*
el desayuno   *breakfast*
la merienda   *afternoon snack*

Las proteínas y las carnes   Proteins and meats

el bistec   *steak*
el bocadillo / el sándwich   *sandwich*
los camarones   *shrimp*
el huevo   *egg*
el jamón   *ham*
los mariscos   *shellfish*
el pescado   *fish*
el pollo   *chicken*
el queso   *cheese*
la sopa   *soup*

Las frutas, las verduras...   Fruits, vegetables . . .

el ajo   *garlic*
el arroz   *rice*
la banana   *banana*
la cebolla   *onion*
la fresa   *strawberry*
los frijoles   *beans, legumes*
las judías verdes   *green beans, string beans*
la lechuga   *lettuce*
el maíz   *corn*
la manzana   *apple*
la naranja   *orange*
el pan   *bread*
la papa   *potato*
el tomate   *tomato*
las uvas   *grapes*
la zanahoria   *carrot*

Los condimentos   Condiments

el aceite (de oliva)   *(olive) oil*
el azúcar   *sugar*
la mantequilla   *butter*
la sal y la pimienta   *salt and pepper*
el vinagre   *vinegar*

Las bebidas   Beverages

el agua (mineral)   *(mineral) water*
la cerveza   *beer*
el jugo   *juice*
la leche   *milk*
el té   *tea*
el vino (tinto, blanco)   *(red, white) wine*

Le encanta la ensalada de
lechuga y tomate.

Los postres   Desserts

el flan   *custard dessert*
las galletas   *cookies*
el helado (de vainilla)   *(vanilla) ice cream*
el pastel (de manzana)   *(apple) pie*
la torta   *cake*
el yogur   *yogurt*

En un restaurante   In a restaurant

la cuenta   *bill*
la especialidad de la casa   *house specialty*
el menú   *menu*
el/la mesero/a   *waiter/waitress*
la propina   *tip*

Expresiones   Expressions

¡Buen provecho!   *Enjoy!*
¿Desea(n) algo de tomar/comer?   *Would you
like something to drink/eat?*
Enseguida.   *Right away.*
¿Qué te apetece (comer)?   *What do you feel
like (eating)?*

Adjetivos   Adjectives

caliente   *hot*
picante   *hot (spicy)*

Verbos   Verbs

cenar   *to have dinner*
dar   *to give*
decir (i, i)   *to say*
dejar   *to leave (behind)*
desayunar   *to have breakfast*

APLICACIÓN

6-1 En el restaurante. Indica a quién se refiere lo siguiente en el restaurante en ¡Así es la vida!

1: Manolo   **2:** Esme   **3:** Jorge   **4:** Matilde   **5:** Graciela

1. __4__ Detesta los mariscos.
2. __1__ Pide la cuenta.
3. __2__ Tiene mucha hambre.
4. __2__ Pide una comida grande.
5. _____ Está un poco molesto/a.
6. __3__ Está un poco preocupado/a.

6-2 ¿Qué es? Empareja la comida con su descripción.

MODELO: Es verde. Forma parte de una ensalada.
   la lechuga

1. __c__ Es una fruta amarilla.
2. __f__ Se comen con el arroz.
3. __a__ Es una carne rosada.
4. __h__ Es un postre con muchas calorías.
5. __e__ Es una bebida con cafeína.
6. __b__ Es rojo y se usa en la salsa picante.
7. __g__ Es un postre frío hecho con crema, huevos y azúcar.
8. __d__ Se comen y también se usan para hacer vino.

a. el jamón
b. el tomate
c. la banana
d. las uvas
e. el té
f. los frijoles negros
g. el helado
h. la torta de chocolate

6-3 ¡Buen provecho! Indica en la cuenta a la derecha la comida y la bebida que piden Marta y Arturo en el *Café El Náufrago* con **A** (Arturo) o **M** (Marta).

6-4 Ahora tú. Primero seleccionen un restaurante que conocen y luego túrnense para preguntarse qué piden para cada comida.

MODELO: la cena

   E1: *¿Qué pides para la cena en Don Pancho?*
   E2: *Pido una ensalada de pollo.*
   E1: *¿Es todo?...*

1. la cena
2. el desayuno
3. la merienda
4. el almuerzo / la comida

PESCADOS Y MARISCOS

Café El Náufrago

Avenida Allende 489 • Tel. 311-1539 • Valparaíso

FECHA __/__/__   MESERO/A _____   MESA ___

	TOTAL
VINO ——— TINTO ——— BLANCO	
REFRESCO ——— AGUA MINERAL ——— CERVEZA	
JUGO DE MANZANA ——— DE NARANJA	
DE TORONJA ———	
CAMARONES ———	
ATÚN ———	
FILETE DE PESCADO ———	
CALAMARES ———	
SALMÓN ———	
BOCADILLO DE CHORIZO ———	
ENSALADA MIXTA ———	
PAPAS FRITAS ——— TOMATE Y CEBOLLA	
PAN ——— PAPA AL HORNO	
HELADO DE LIMÓN ——— DE CHOCOLATE	
FLAN ———	
ENSALADA DE FRUTAS ———	
CAFÉ ——— TÉ	
CUENTA TOTAL	
(IVA Y SERVICIO INCLUIDOS)	

6-5 Las rutinas. En grupos de tres, descubran cuántas personas comparten (*share*) estas costumbres (*customs*) e indiquen los resultados.

MODELO: **desayunar** todos los días
E1: *¿Desayunas todos los días? Yo, sí.*
E2: *No, solo cuando tengo tiempo.*
E3: *Sí, siempre desayuno.*

Preferencias	Número de personas en su grupo que dicen sí
desayunar todos los días	_____
cenar a las diez de la noche	_____
ser vegetariano/a	_____
comer más pescado que carne	_____
tomar café con la comida	_____
ser alérgico/a a los mariscos	_____
almorzar en la universidad	_____
preferir la leche a los refrescos	_____

¿Eres vegetariano/a?

6-6 ¿Qué compramos para la cena? Decidan qué van a comprar para la cena en cada una de estas situaciones. Mencionen por lo menos tres alimentos para cada situación.

MODELO: Tienen invitados en casa y les gusta preparar platos tradicionales.
Vamos a comprar un pollo grande, papas, lechuga y tomates para hacer una ensalada. Para el postre…

1. Uno/a de Uds. es vegetariano/a.
2. Uno/a de Uds. está a dieta.
3. Uno/a de Uds. está entrenándose (*training*) para un maratón.
4. Uds. están muy ocupados/as y no tienen mucho tiempo.

6-7 Tu pirámide. En 2005 se introdujo una nueva pirámide de la alimentación.

Paso 1 Conéctate a la Internet para hacer un análisis de los alimentos que necesitas.

> **Busca:** plan mipiramide

Completa el siguiente cuadro según los resultados.

Edad:	
Sexo:	
Número de calorías diarias:	
Cantidad de productos lácteos:	
Cantidad de aceites:	
Cantidad de carnes y otras proteínas:	
Límite diario de grasas sólidas y azúcares:	

Paso 2 Ahora compara tu cuadro con el de otra persona en la clase.

MODELO: E1: *Según la pirámide, debo tomar tres tazas de productos lácteos. Creo que tomo más de tres, porque tomo leche con todas las comidas y me gusta mucho el yogur. ¿Y tú?*
E2: *Pues, yo debo tomar…*

Presencia hispana

According to the U.S. Department of Agriculture (USDA), Hispanic-American families have a tremendous influence on food production in the U.S. First, they are more likely than other families to prepare their food at home. Second, they usually shop for fresh fruits and vegetables. However, because of the diversity of Hispanic cultures, their cuisine cannot be generalized. It ranges from bland to spicy, and may include corn tortillas, rice, or potatoes. What Hispanic foods can you find in your neighborhood supermarket?

¡Así lo hacemos! ESTRUCTURAS

1. Indirect objects, indirect object pronouns, and the verbs *decir* and *dar*

06-10
to 06-16

¿Me puede mostrar los modelos más económicos?

Los pronombres de complementos indirectos

An indirect object indicates to or for whom an action is carried out. In Spanish the indirect object pronoun is also used to indicate from whom something is bought, borrowed, or taken away.

Indirect object pronouns			
Singular		**Plural**	
me	*(to) me*	nos	*(to) us*
te	*(to) you*	os	*(to) you* (fam. Sp.)
le	*(to) you* (for.)	les	*(to) you*
le	*(to) him, her*	les	*(to) them*

- The indirect object pronouns are identical to the direct object pronouns, except for the third-person singular and plural forms.

- Indirect object pronouns agree only in number with the noun to which they refer. There is no gender agreement.

    Le lavo los platos.　　　　　　　*I'll wash the dishes for her.*
    ¿**Me** preparas arroz para la cena?　*Will you prepare rice for dinner for me?*

- Indirect object pronouns usually precede the conjugated verb.

    Te compramos el almuerzo.　　　*We'll buy you lunch.*

- In negative sentences the indirect object pronoun is placed between **no** and the conjugated verb.

    No **les** recomiendo ese restaurante.　*I won't recommend that restaurant to them.*

- In constructions with an infinitive, the indirect object pronouns may either precede the conjugated verb or be attached to the infinitive.

    El mesero **nos** va a traer la cuenta. ⎫
    El mesero va a traer**nos** la cuenta. ⎬ *The waiter is going to bring us the check.*

- Since **le** or **les** can have different meanings, you can add a prepositional phrase (**a él, a ella, a Ud., a ellos, a ellas, a Uds.**) for clarification.

    Le preparamos la comida.　　　　*We prepare him / her / you (s.) the meal.*
    Le preparamos la cena **a ella**.　　*We prepare **her** dinner.*
    Les traigo un refresco.　　　　　*I bring them / you (pl.) a drink.*
    Les traigo un refresco **a Uds.**　　*I bring **you** (pl.) a drink.*

- The prepositional phrase can also be used for emphasis. In the following examples, the phrases **a mí, a ti** and **a nosotros** are not required grammatically, but the indirect object pronouns **me, te** and **nos** *are* required. Note that the pronouns that follow prepositions are the same as subject pronouns with the exception of **yo** and **tú**. These are replaced by **mí** and **ti**.

    Te invito a un café **a ti,** no a ellos.　*I'll invite **you** for coffee, not them.*
    ¡Juan **nos** va a hacer un pastel　　*Juan is going to make a special cake for **us**!*
    　especial **a nosotros!**
    ¡Mi novio **me** preparó una cena　　*My boyfriend prepared **me** a delicious dinner!*
    　deliciosa **a mí!**

- The familiar plural form, **os** (**vosotros**), is used in Spain.

Decir y dar

The irregular verbs **decir** and **dar** often take indirect object pronouns.

- **Decir** is an e → i stem-changing verb with an irregular first-person singular form (like **tener** and **venir**).

decir (*to say*)			
yo	d**i**go	nosotros/as	decimos
tú	d**i**ces	vosotros/as	decís
Ud.	d**i**ce	Uds.	d**i**cen
él/ella	d**i**ce	ellos/as	d**i**cen

- **Dar** has an irregular first-person singular form like **ser** and **estar**.

dar (*to give*)			
yo	d**oy**	nosotros/as	damos
tú	das	vosotros/as	dais
Ud.	da	Uds.	dan
él/ella	da	ellos/as	dan

Todos los días le **decimos** "buenos días" a la profesora.	*Every day, we say "hello" to the professor.*
Todos los días ella nos **da** una prueba.	*Every day, she gives us a quiz.*

APLICACIÓN

6-8 Sebastián Piñera, presidente de la República de Chile. Antes de las elecciones, Sebastián Piñera pronunció (*he gave, delivered*) un discurso en el que hizo (*he made*) muchas promesas. La revista en línea *NuevaPolítica.com* publica un resumen de su plataforma.

Paso 1 Lee el resumen y subraya los pronombres de objeto indirecto.

En un discurso esta semana, el candidato a la presidencia Sebastián Piñera nos promete que Chile va a continuar y aumentar los programas sociales de su predecesora Michelle Bachelet. "Primero, yo les digo a los chilenos fuerte y claro: en nuestro gobierno vamos a fortalecer[1] y ampliar[2] la red social para proteger no solamente a los más humildes, sino también a nuestra clase media". Además, nos afirma que va a "fortalecer el trabajo, la educación y la familia". Va a crearles a los chilenos un millón de trabajos para erradicar el desempleo, una de las más importantes causas de la pobreza. Nos dice que va a llevarles a los jóvenes pobres más oportunidades para hacer deporte. Y va a crearles más oportunidades de educación y trabajo a los discapacitados[3]. Finalmente, Sebastián Piñera va a darles a sus ministros la responsabilidad de proponer nuevas leyes para el bienestar de la nación. Nos explica el candidato, "Ustedes me dicen que quieren trabajar conmigo. Les prometo que voy a mejorar la economía, el sistema de seguro social y además, voy a trabajar para mejorar el sistema de educación. Les aseguro[4] que el gobierno va a respetar a todos los chilenos, hombres y mujeres. Hoy, le prometo a Chile que vamos a continuar nuestro desarrollo[5] económico, político y social para el bien de todos".

Sebastián Piñera, electo presidente de Chile en 2010.

---

[1]*strengthen* [2]*expand* [3]*disabled* [4]*assure* [5]*development*

Paso 2 Ahora, escribe una lista de por lo menos cinco promesas que el candidato Piñera les hace a los chilenos. ¿Cuál de esas promesas te parece la más importante y por qué?

MODELO: *Les promete a los chilenos que va a continuar los programas de su predecesora.*

6-9 Ahora tú. Te vas a Chile por un año. Contesta las siguientes preguntas sobre lo que va a pasar.

MODELO: ¿Cuándo vas a darnos tu nueva dirección?
Voy a darles mi nueva dirección ahora.

1. ¿Quién te compra el boleto (*ticket*) de avión?
2. ¿Quién te explica el sistema universitario chileno?
3. ¿A quién le vendes tu bicicleta o tu carro antes de salir del país?
4. ¿Quién te recoge la correspondencia en la oficina postal?
5. ¿A quiénes les mandas (*send*) fotos?
6. ¿A quiénes les escribes sobre tus experiencias?

6-10 En tu familia. Conversen sobre quiénes toman la responsabilidad de los siguientes quehaceres de la famila.

MODELO: prepararte una sopa cuando estás enfermo/a
Mi padre me prepara una sopa cuando estoy enfermo/a.

1. lavarte la ropa
2. enseñarte a cocinar
3. darle de comer a la mascota (*pet*)
4. prepararte un pastel en tu cumpleaños
5. hacerte la cama
6. limpiarles el baño a los padres

6-11 Algo especial. En grupos de tres o cuatro, hablen de lo que ustedes dan o dicen en las siguientes situaciones.

MODELO: a tu hermana en su cumpleaños
Le digo: "Feliz cumpleaños" y le doy un beso.

1. a tu madre el Día de las Madres
2. a tu padre el Día de los Padres
3. a tu esposo/a o novio/a el día de su aniversario
4. a tu profesor/a al final del curso

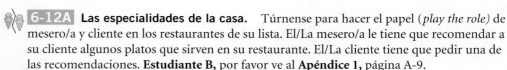 **6-12A Las especialidades de la casa.** Túrnense para hacer el papel (*play the role*) de mesero/a y cliente en los restaurantes de su lista. El/La mesero/a le tiene que recomendar a su cliente algunos platos que sirven en su restaurante. El/La cliente tiene que pedir una de las recomendaciones. **Estudiante B,** por favor ve al **Apéndice 1,** página A-9.

MODELO: ESTUDIANTE A: *Por favor, ¿qué me recomienda Ud. aquí en Casa Roma?*
ESTUDIANTE B: *Nuestra especialidad es la comida italiana. Le recomiendo la pasta con mariscos o la pizza Margarita.*
ESTUDIANTE A: *¿Me trae por favor la pizza Margarita?*
ESTUDIANTE B: *¡Enseguida!*

Estudiante A:

Restaurantes que visito:	Restaurantes donde trabajo y sus especialidades:
El Unicornio	**El Rincón Argentino:** todo tipo de carnes: bistec, carne asada, hamburguesas
Café del Diablo	**Cafetería Universo:** especializado en sándwiches y ensaladas: sándwiches de jamón, queso, pavo, pescado; ensaladas de pollo y de verduras
Cocina Cándida	**Casa Miguel:** comida mexicana: quesadillas con pollo, mariscos o jamón; arroz con pollo

¡Hola!
Cultura en vivo

In many places, the cost of service is included in, or added to the check in a restaurant. Oftentimes, there will be a note at the bottom of the check that states **Servicio incluido.** Although you are not obligated to leave an additional tip, many patrons leave a few coins, especially if they are regular customers. When in doubt, ask the waiter if service is included.

2. *Gustar* and similar verbs

The verb **gustar** is used to express preferences, likes, and dislikes. **Gustar** literally means *to be pleasing,* and the verb is used with an indirect object pronoun.

Me gusta desayunar todos los días. *I like to eat breakfast everyday.*
(Eating breakfast is pleasing to me.)

Los restaurantes caros no **le gustan**. *He doesn't like expensive restaurants. (Expensive restaurants are not pleasing to him.)*

- The subject of the verb **gustar** is whatever is pleasing to someone. Because we generally use **gustar** to indicate that something (singular) or some things (plural) are pleasing, **gustar** is most often conjugated in the third-person singular or third-person plural forms, **gusta** and **gustan.** The indirect object pronoun indicates who is being pleased.

Nos gusta la torta de chocolate. *We like chocolate cake.*
No me gustan los frijoles. *I don't like beans.*

- To express the idea that one likes to do something, **gustar** is followed by an infinitive. In such cases the third-person singular of **gustar** is used, even when you use more than one infinitive.

Me gusta preparar la cena *I like to prepare dinner and*
y lavar los platos. *wash the dishes.*

- Some other verbs like **gustar** are listed below. Note that the equivalent expressions in English are not direct translations.

aburrir	*to bore, to tire*
apetecer	*to feel like (to appeal to)*
encantar	*to like very much, to be extremely pleasing*
fascinar	*to fascinate, to be attractive*
interesar	*to interest, to be in someone's interest*
molestar	*to be a bother, to annoy*
parecer	*to seem*
quedar	*to be left (over), to remain*

Me molestan las cocinas sucias. *Dirty kitchens annoy me.*
Este vino **nos parece** caro. *This wine seems expensive to us.*

- Remember, you can use a prepositional phrase beginning with **a** to emphasize, clarify, or contrast the indirect object pronoun.

A mí me encanta la cocina, *I love the kitchen, but you don't.*
pero **a ti** no.

A José le encantan los camarones, *José loves shrimp, and you?*
¿y **a Uds.**?

¿Te gusta mi coche?

Sí, me gusta mucho.

06-17
to 06-23

APLICACIÓN

6-13 A los pingüinos…   La Patagonia es una enorme región al extremo sur de Sudamérica situada en Argentina y Chile. Allí vive una variedad de vida marina, incluyendo lobos marinos (*sea lions*) y pingüinos.

Paso 1   Lee el párrafo siguiente sobre los pingüinos de la Patagonia chilena y subraya los verbos como **gustar** (V), sus sujetos (S) y sus complementos indirectos (I).

MODELO: *A mí <u>me</u> <u>interesan</u> <u>los animales marinos</u>.*
                     I   V   S

A muchas personas les fascinan los pingüinos que habitan en las costas del sur de Chile. Son casi como pequeños seres humanos en la manera en que cuidan a sus crías[1]. A los pingüinos también les gusta observar a la gente y no le tienen miedo. Para comer, les encantan los calamares y otros mariscos que pescan del mar. Los pingüinos son protegidos estrictamente por los parques nacionales de Chile y está prohibido darles comida. A mí me parecen animales preciosos, pero no me interesa tener uno como mascota[2]. Prefiero verlos libres.

---

[1]*young*   [2]*pet*

Paso 2   Ahora, contesta las preguntas, basándote en la lectura en **Paso 1.**

1. ¿Dónde viven los pingüinos?
2. ¿Qué les gusta hacer?
3. ¿Qué les encanta comer?
4. ¿Por qué nos fascinan?
5. ¿A ti te interesa tener uno como mascota?

6-14 Me interesa(n). Me gusta(n). Me molesta(n).   Todos tenemos nuestras preferencias. ¿Cuáles compartes (*share*) con tus compañeros/as de clase?

Paso 1   Completa el cuadro con cosas y actividades que te interesan, te gustan o te molestan. Puedes usar las siguientes frases.

preparar comida complicada	tomar vino con la cena	los restaurantes de especialidad… (india, mexicana, china…)
limpiar la cocina	las galletas	la comida vegetariana (picante, rápida…)
el café sin azúcar	conocer Chile	los restaurantes elegantes y caros
los vinos chilenos	salir a comer	trabajar como mesero/a

MODELO:

interesar	gustar	molestar
Me interesan las matemáticas.	*Me gusta la comida picante.*	*Me molestan los restaurantes sucios.*

Paso 2   Ahora, levántense y pregúntenles a por lo menos tres otros estudiantes qué les interesa, gusta, molesta. ¿Qué tienen en común?

MODELO: E1: *¿Qué te interesa?*
                     E2: *Me interesa viajar. También me gusta…*

6-15 Una postal de la Patagonia. Usa los pronombres de complemento indirecto y los verbos correspondientes de la lista para completar la carta.

| apetecer | encantar | fascinar | gustar | interesar | parecer | quedar |

Querida Isabel:

Te escribo desde Chile para contarte sobre mi viaje a la Patagonia. Es una región bellísima con montañas y costas, y una gran variedad de animales. Nuestro guía Antonio conoce bien la flora y la fauna de esta región. A mí (1) _____ las plantas y los animales, pero a Carlos y Ana (2) _____ los lobos marinos[1] que llegan aquí para cuidar a sus crías[2]. A muchas personas (3) _____ observarlos durante este tiempo. Todos los días (4) (a mí) _____ salir temprano para ver los pájaros que viven en la costa. Desafortunadamente, solo (5) (a nosotros) _____ un día más aquí.

En fin, Isabel, me encanta estar aquí. Y a ti, (6) ¿ _____ venir un día para ver los lobos marinos? (7) (A mí) ¡ _____ una idea excelente!

Un abrazo,
Eduardo

_____

[1]*sea lions* [2]*young*

Los lobos marinos están protegidos en toda la costa de Chile.

6-16 Su opinión. Conversen sobre sus opiniones acerca de las comidas.

MODELO: las cafeterías estudiantiles

E1: *¿Te gustan las cafeterías estudiantiles?*
E2: *¡Sí, me encantan porque son económicas! Y las sopas que sirven, ¡qué ricas!*

1. los platos picantes
2. los mariscos
3. las frutas tropicales
4. los postres
5. la comida rápida
6. los productos orgánicos

¿Cuánto saben?

06-24 to 06-29

Primero, pregúntate si puedes llevar a cabo (*carry out*) las siguientes funciones comunicativas en español. Después, júntate con dos o tres compañeros/as de clase para presentar las situaciones. Hagan y respondan a por lo menos cuatro preguntas en cada situación.

✓ CAN YOU . . .

☐ discuss food, eating preferences, and ordering meals?

☐ talk about things and express to whom or for whom?

☐ express likes and dislikes?

WITH YOUR CLASSMATE(S) . . .

Situación: En un restaurante
Dos de Uds. son clientes y otro/a es el/la mesero/a. Van a preguntar y responder sobre las especialidades de la casa y pedir comida y bebida. Usen el vocabulario y las expresiones en **¡Así lo decimos!**
Para empezar: *Buenas tardes, ¿desean algo de tomar?*

Situación: Un/a amigo/a enfermo/a
Uno/a de sus amigos está enfermo/a y no puede asistir a clase. Túrnese para decir qué van a hacer para él/ella.
Para empezar: *Le voy a preparar una sopa de pollo...*

Situación: Después de la clase
Van a hablar de sus opiniones sobre la universidad, los equipos de fútbol, etc., y otros temas de interés mutuo. Usen verbos como **gustar, interesar, molestar** y **parecer**.
Para empezar: *A mí me gusta(n)... ¿Y a ti?*

📖 Perfiles

06-30
to 06-31

Mi experiencia

TREN DE LA RUTA DEL VINO

6-17 Para ti. Cuando vas a celebrar una comida especial, ¿vas siempre a un restaurante? ¿Comes en un lugar especial, como en un barco o un tren? ¿Conoces algún restaurante de degustación? ¿Cuáles son las ventajas (*advantages*) y las desventajas (*disadvantages*) de un menú de degustación (*tasting menu*)? A continuación, tienes un anuncio de la página web de la oficina de turismo de Chile sobre una "excursión culinaria". Mientras lees la descripción, piensa en las razones por las que te gustaría (*would like*) acompañar a Felipe, o no.

Tren de la ruta del vino

Temporada: Disponible todo el año

Duración: 1 día

Tarifas: Adultos: **USD 144,00;** jubilados: **125,00;** menores de 12 años: **85,00**

¡Acompáñenme por la ruta del vino a bordo de un tren histórico!

Bienvenidos, me llamo Felipe y soy su guía en este recorrido por el hermoso Valle de Colchagua, la famosa región de los vinos chilenos. Descubran conmigo el fascinante mundo del vino, su elaboración y sus técnicas de degustación[1] en el mismo lugar donde se produce. Durante nuestro recorrido, desde San Fernando hasta Santa Cruz, pueden probar los mejores vinos y comida de la región. Para completar su experiencia a bordo, les ofrecemos música de los artistas chilenos más conocidos, como Alberto Plaza y Myriam Hernández. ¿Les apetece acompañarme? ¡Espero que sí! A la derecha tienen el itinerario.

10:30 hrs. Salida del Tren del Vino rumbo a Santa Cruz. Degustación a bordo de vinos del Valle de Colchagua; tabla individual de pescados, quesos, panes artesanales y frutos secos.

12:00 hrs. Llegada a la Estación de Trenes de Paniahue, Santa Cruz. Baile folklórico nacional, "Pié de cueca".

13:00 hrs. Almuerzo en la viña[2] "Paraíso del Valle", visita a sus instalaciones y degustación de vinos.

17:00 hrs. Visita a "Viñedos Emilia", sus instalaciones y degustación de vinos.

18:30 hrs. Salida de buses rumbo a Santiago.

[1]*tasting* [2]*vineyard*

6-18 En su opinión. Comparen este tipo de experiencia culinaria con otra que hayan tenido (*you have had*) o que les gustaría (*would like*) tener. ¿Qué aspectos son similares? ¿Cuáles son distintos? ¿Te gustaría ir en el "tren de la ruta del vino"? ¿Por qué?

Mi música

"AHORA" (ALBERTO PLAZA, CHILE)

Al chileno Alberto Plaza se le considera uno de los cantautores contemporáneos más originales de Latinoamérica. Estudió tres carreras universitarias (ingeniería, economía y publicidad), pero no terminó ninguna, pues su amor por la música era más fuerte. Hasta ahora, ha dado más de mil conciertos y ha vendido más de un millón de discos. En esta canción le revela sus pensamientos a su exnovia.

Antes de ver y escuchar

6-19 Adiós. Imagínate que tu pareja termina su relación amorosa contigo. Piensa qué le dices y qué le das antes de que se vaya (*before he/she leaves*).

MODELO: *Le digo que es una buena persona...*

Para ver y escuchar

 6-20 La canción. Conéctate a la Internet para buscar un video de Alberto Plaza en el que (*in which*) le canta esta canción a su ex novia.

> **Busca:** video ahora alberto plaza; letra ahora alberto plaza
>
> **Si te interesa comprar la canción:** *Go to iTunes Store > Music>More to Explore>iMix>Arriba 6e*

¿Cuál de las siguientes declaraciones es la más probable y por qué?

1. _____ Él la ama pero ella se casa con otro.
2. _____ Ella lo ama a él, pero él ya no la ama a ella.
3. _____ Ella vuelve, pero sólo en los sueños de él.
4. _____ Él se va a buscarla.

Después de ver y escuchar

 6-21 Investigación. Myriam Hernández es otra cantante chilena contemporánea. Haz una investigación en la Internet para encontrar un video de ella. Primero describe el video. Luego compara su estilo de cantar con el de Alberto Plaza. ¿Prefieres uno al otro? Explica.

> **Busca:** myriam hernandez video

Segunda parte

¡Así lo decimos! VOCABULARIO

¡Así es la vida! "Platos fáciles en veinte minutos o menos"

06-32

Ayer Enrique les preparó un plato sabroso a sus amigos.

MAMÁ:	¡Aló, hijo! ¿Cómo te va? ¿Recibiste el mensaje de texto que te mandé ayer?
ENRIQUE:	Sí, mamá. Disculpa. No te llamé. Invité a algunos amigos para ver el partido de fútbol en la tele.
MAMÁ:	¿Ah sí? ¿Qué les preparaste?
ENRIQUE:	¡Algo fácil! Guacamole con nachos.
MAMÁ:	Y… ¿cómo sabes tú hacer guacamole?
ENRIQUE:	Encontré la receta en el sitio web: "Platos fáciles en veinte minutos o menos". Sólo tiene cinco ingredientes: un aguacate maduro, un limón, ajo, cilantro picado y sal. Se mezcla todo en un tazón de cristal. Es todo.
MAMÁ:	Ay, hijo. ¡Ya no me necesitas para nada!

🔊 **Vocabulario** En la cocina

06-33
to 06-37

Fríe los huevos
en la sartén.

Variaciones

In Spain, **el refrigerador** is more commonly called **el frigorífico** or **la nevera,** and **la cocina** is used instead of **la estufa,** since **la estufa** refers to a portable space heater.

En la cocina | **In the kitchen**

la cafetera   *coffee maker*
la cazuela   *stewpot, casserole dish, saucepan*
la estufa   *stove*
el microondas   *microwave*
el refrigerador   *refrigerator*
la sartén   *skillet*
el tazón (de cristal)   *(glass) bowl*
la tostadora   *toaster*

En la mesa | **On the table**

la cuchara   *spoon*
el cuchillo   *knife*
el plato   *plate*
la servilleta   *napkin*
la taza   *cup*
el tenedor   *fork*
el vaso   *glass*

Le echa
pimienta
a la ensalada.

Actividades en la cocina | **Kitchen activities**

calentar (ie)   *to heat*
cocinar   *to cook*
cortar   *to cut*
echar   *to add, throw in*
freír (i, i)[1]   *to fry*
guardar   *to save, to keep, to put away*
hornear   *to bake, to roast*
mezclar   *to mix*
pelar   *to peel*
picar   *to chop*
tostar (ue)   *to toast*

En la receta | **In the recipe**

asado/a   *roasted*
la cucharada   *tablespoon*
la cucharadita   *teaspoon*
frito/a   *fried*
al horno   *baked*
a la parrilla   *grilled*
la pizca   *pinch (of salt, pepper, etc.)*

Mezcla los
ingredientes
en el tazón.

Expresiones útiles | **Useful expressions**

¡Qué rico!   *How delicious!*
¡Qué sabroso!   *How delicious!*
¡Qué asco!   *How revolting!*
¡Qué ridículo!   *How ridiculous!*

Pica la cebolla.

---

[1]frío, fríes, fríe, freímos, freís, fríen; freí, freíste, frió, freímos, freísteis, frieron

Letras y sonidos

The sequences *s, z, ce, ci* in Spanish

Generally in Spanish, the letters **s** and **z,** as well as **c** before the vowels **e** and **i,** all correspond to the same sound: the *s* sound in English *sip.*

<u>s</u>al   de-<u>s</u>a-yu-no   a-<u>z</u>ú-car   <u>ce</u>-na   ha-<u>cer</u>   de-<u>cir</u>

In most parts of Spain, only the letter **s** sounds like the *s* in English *sip.* The letter **z,** as well as **ce** and **ci,** are pronounced like the *th* sound in English *thanks.* Keep these differences in mind as you refine your listening skills. Follow the pronunciation that is consistent with the variety of Spanish that you want to speak, Latin American or Peninsular.

APLICACIÓN

6-22 ¿Qué necesitas para...? Indica un utensilio o aparato que necesitas para hacer lo siguiente.

MODELO: congelar el helado
el congelador

1. _____ mezclar la sopa   a. la sartén
2. _____ freír las papas   b. la cafetera
3. _____ pelar la manzana   c. la cuchara
4. _____ medir (*measure*) el azúcar   d. el tazón
5. _____ mezclar los huevos   e. el microondas
6. _____ preparar el café   f. la taza
7. _____ calentar la pizza   g. el cuchillo

6-23 ¿Qué hacen? Describe lo que hacen las personas en cada dibujo con expresiones de **¡Así lo decimos!**

MODELO:

Mario
Mario hornea el pollo.

1.

Lola

2.

El señor Barroso

3.

Dolores

4.

Diego

5.

Estela

6.

Pilar

¡Hola!

Cultura en vivo

Bread is a staple in many cultures. In Hispanic cultures, it also figures in many expressions: "*Las penas* (sorrows) *con pan son menos*", or when something or someone is really good, "*tan bueno como el pan*", or "*Contigo pan y cebolla*", meaning that with you (my love) we can make do with only bread and onions. The term *compañero/a* derives from *con+pan+ero,* a person with whom you would share bread. What is the English equivalent of *compañero*?

6-24 En la cocina con el chef Emilio. Escucha la preparación del flan, un postre muy popular en todo el mundo hispano. Indica los ingredientes, los utensilios y las acciones que el chef Emilio utiliza para preparar esta receta.

Ingredientes	Utensilios	Acciones
_____ agua	_____ estufa	_____ echar
_____ azúcar	_____ cucharada	_____ calentar
_____ huevos	_____ licuadora (*blender*)	_____ cortar
_____ jugo de limón	_____ molde	_____ guardar
_____ leche condensada	_____ sartén	_____ hornear
_____ leche evaporada	_____ tazón	_____ mezclar
_____ vainilla	_____ taza	_____ servir

El flan es un postre popular.

 6-25 En mi cocina. Túrnense para hacerse estas preguntas sobre sus rutinas y preferencias. ¿Qué tienen en común?

1. ¿Cómo prefieres el pescado? ¿Al horno, a la parrilla o frito?

2. ¿Cómo prefieres el pollo? ¿Asado, a la parrilla o frito?

3. ¿Qué comida hay en tu refrigerador en estos momentos?

4. ¿Qué le echas usualmente a la ensalada?

5. ¿Qué comidas preparas en el microondas?

6. ¿Qué frutas pelas antes de comerlas?

 6-26A El arroz con pollo. El arroz con pollo es un plato muy conocido en todo el mundo hispano. **Estudiante A** tiene la receta y **Estudiante B** tiene algunos ingredientes y utensilios en su cocina. Escriban una lista de los ingredientes que necesitan comprar y los utensilios que necesitan pedir prestados (*borrow*) para preparar este plato. **Estudiante B,** por favor ve al **Apéndice 1,** página A-10.

MODELO: ESTUDIANTE A: *Necesitamos una taza de arroz.*
ESTUDIANTE B: *No tenemos suficiente arroz. Tenemos que comprarlo.*
ESTUDIANTE A: (Escribe en la lista) *arroz.*

Estudiante A:

Arroz con pollo

Ingredientes

aceite de oliva
un pollo grande
media taza de jugo de limón
dos dientes de ajo
una cebolla grande
un pimiento verde
sal
una taza de arroz

Utensilios

una cuchara grande
un cuchillo grande que corta bien
una sartén
un tazón de cristal

Para comprar: **Para pedir prestado (*borrow*):**
arroz

3. The preterit of regular verbs

06-39
to 06-44

So far you have learned to use verbs in the present indicative tense. In this chapter you will learn about the preterit, one of two simple past tenses in Spanish. In **Capítulo 8,** you will be introduced to the imperfect, which is also used to refer to events in the past.

¿Comieron bien?

Preterit of regular -ar, -er, and -ir verbs			
	-ar	**-er**	**-ir**
	tomar	**comer**	**vivir**
yo	tom**é**	com**í**	viv**í**
tú	tom**aste**	com**iste**	viv**iste**
Ud.	tom**ó**	com**ió**	viv**ió**
él/ella	tom**ó**	com**ió**	viv**ió**
nosotros/as	tom**amos**	com**imos**	viv**imos**
vosotros/as	tom**asteis**	com**isteis**	viv**isteis**
Uds.	tom**aron**	com**ieron**	viv**ieron**
ellos/as	tom**aron**	com**ieron**	viv**ieron**

- The preterit tense is used to report actions completed at a given point in the past and to narrate past events.

Preparé sopa de mariscos para la cena.	*I prepared seafood soup for dinner.*
Ayer **comimos** en la cafetería de la universidad.	*Yesterday we ate at the university cafeteria.*

- The preterit forms for **nosotros** of **-ar** and **-ir** verbs are identical to the corresponding present tense forms. The situation or context of the sentence will clarify the meaning. Here are some expressions that are used to talk about the past.

anoche	*last night*
anteayer	*the day before yesterday*
ayer	*yesterday*
el año (lunes, martes, etcétera) pasado	*last year (Monday, Tuesday, etc.)*
el mes pasado	*last month*
la semana pasada	*last week*

Siempre **hablamos** de recetas de cocina.	*We always talk about cooking recipes.*
La semana pasada **hablamos** de tu receta de pollo.	*Last week we talked about your chicken recipe.*
Vivimos aquí ahora.	*We live here now.*
Vivimos allí el año pasado.	*We lived there last year.*

- Always use an accent mark in the final vowel for the first- and third-person singular forms of regular verbs, unless the verb is only one syllable.

Compré aceite de oliva.	*I bought olive oil.*
Ana Luisa no **comió** el postre.	*Ana Luisa didn't eat the dessert.*
Vi una receta interesante en ese libro.	*I saw an interesting recipe in that book.*

Los verbos que terminan en *-car*, *-gar* y *-zar*

- Verbs that end in **-car**, **-gar**, and **-zar** have the following spelling changes in the first-person singular of the preterit. All other forms of these verbs are conjugated regularly.

c → qu	buscar	yo	bus**qué**
g → gu	llegar	yo	lle**gué**
z → c	almorzar	yo	almor**cé**

Bus**qué** la receta en la Internet. *I looked for the recipe on the Internet.*
Lle**gué** muy contento ayer. *I arrived very happy yesterday.*
Almor**cé** poco hoy. *I had little for lunch today.*

- In addition to verbs such as **jugar (a)**, **empezar**, and **practicar** you have already learned, the following verbs also follow this pattern.

explicar	*to explain*
pagar	*to pay*
tocar	*to touch, to play a musical instrument*

APLICACIÓN

6-27 Una tortilla española. La tortilla española es muy fácil de preparar. Camila la prepara con frecuencia para sus invitados (*guests*).

Paso 1 Lee el párrafo en el que Camila explica la preparación de la tortilla española y subraya los verbos en el pretérito.

Me levanté temprano y salí para el mercado donde compré seis huevos, dos cebollas y dos papas. Una vez en casa, lavé bien las papas y las pelé. Luego, corté las papas y las cebollas en pedazos muy pequeños. Eché un poco de aceite de oliva en una sartén. Lo calenté y cociné las papas y las cebollas. Batí seis huevos en un tazón. Les eché un poco de sal a los huevos y luego los eché a la sartén. Mezclé todos los ingredientes con la espátula. Le di la vuelta[1] a la tortilla a los cinco minutos y la cociné tres minutos más. Preparé un plato con un poco de perejil[2] y les serví la tortilla a mis invitados.

---

[1]*turned*   [2]*parsley*

Paso 2 Ahora, contesta las preguntas basadas en la actividad anterior.

1. ¿Cuándo salió Camila para el mercado?
2. ¿Cuáles son los ingredientes de la tortilla española?
3. ¿Qué cocinó primero?
4. ¿Cuántos huevos usó?
5. ¿Por cuánto tiempo cocinó la tortilla?
6. ¿Quiénes la comieron?

6-28 Un a cena inolvidable.   Usa el pretérito de los verbos de la lista para completar el párrafo.

buscar	encontrar	invitar	llegar •	salir
comer	gustar	llamar	pagar	tomar

El sábado pasado encontré un restaurante que me (1) _____ mucho. Nosotros (2) _____ el nombre del restaurante en la guía telefónica. Yo (3) _____ para hacer una reservación. Nosotros salimos a las siete de la noche y (4) _____ al restaurante a las siete y media. La comida estuvo (*was*) muy buena. Yo comí un bistec y mis amigos (5) _____ arroz con pollo. Todos nosotros (6) _____ agua mineral y, después, café. A la hora de pagar, abrí mi bolsa y (7) _____ mi tarjeta de crédito, pero no la encontré. ¡Qué vergüenza! Menos mal que mis amigos generosos (8) _____ por mí. (9) _____ del restaurante a las dos de la mañana. El sábado siguiente, yo (10) _____ a todos a cenar a mi casa.

6-29 *Afrodita:* una novela de Isabel Allende.   Esta es una novela de cuentos, recetas y otros afrodisíacos.

Paso 1   Lee la siguiente entrevista con esta famosa escritora chilena sobre su novela.

ENTREVISTADOR:	Isabel, ¿por qué escribiste *Afrodita*?
ISABEL:	Bueno, como indica el título completo, *Afrodita: Cuentos, recetas y otros afrodisíacos*, es un libro sobre la comida, pero no sus aspectos nutritivos sino los que se asocian con el amor. Lo escribí en 1996 después de pasar más de un año de luto[1] por la muerte de mi hija, Paula. Por fin encontré la inspiración para escribir y decidí escribir una novela de humor.
ENTREVISTADOR:	¿Y por qué decidiste escribir sobre la comida?
ISABEL:	Soy amante de la comida, especialmente la chilena, pero también escribí anécdotas personales relacionadas con la preparación de la comida. Y siempre incluí la receta.
ENTREVISTADOR:	¿Son ciertas todas las cosas que cuentas en esta novela? ¿Ocurrieron de verdad?
ISABEL:	Bueno, mi padrastro dice que soy una mentirosa, y es verdad que exagero, pero estos son mis recuerdos de cosas que realmente ocurrieron. Yo solamente añadí algunos detalles[2] para hacerlas más interesantes. También investigué el interés por la comida a través de los siglos, por ejemplo en la época de Napoleón y Josefina.
ENTREVISTADOR:	¿Cuál es tu obra favorita?
ISABEL:	La verdad, es *Paula*. Es una memoria que escribí basada en las entradas en mi diario durante la enfermedad y después de la muerte de mi hija, Paula. Fue una experiencia muy difícil para mí, pero también la más satisfactoria porque recordé los momentos más importantes de la vida de mi familia.

----

[1]*mourning*   [2]*details*

Paso 2   Ahora, contesta las preguntas según la información de la entrevista.

1. ¿Cuándo escribió *Afrodita*?

2. ¿Por qué la escribió?

3. ¿Piensa Isabel que escribe la verdad?

4. ¿Qué investigó para escribir *Afrodita*?

5. ¿Cuál es el tema de *Paula*? ¿Crees que es una historia fantástica como sus otros cuentos? Explica.

6-30 Te creo; no te creo.   Escribe tres oraciones ciertas y tres oraciones falsas. Luego reta (*challenge*) a un/a compañero/a para decidir si lo que dices es cierto o falso.

beber	comer	conocer (a)	llevar	salir con	visitar
besar (a)	comprar	llegar	pagar	trabajar (en)	vivir

MODELO: E1: *Una vez conocí a Isabel Allende.*
E2: *¿Cuándo?*
E1: *En 2010.*
E2: *Te creo. / No te creo.*

6-31 Este fin de semana.   Usa verbos de la lista para escribir cinco oraciones contando lo que hiciste (*you did*) durante el fin de semana. Después, cuéntaselo a tu compañero/a, quien te va a hacer más preguntas.

cocinar	comprar	estudiar	llamar	preparar	trabajar
comer	escribir	leer	mirar	salir	ver

MODELO: E1: *Estudié el sábado todo el día.*
E2: *¿Qué hiciste el sábado por la noche?*
E1: *Salí con…*

6-32A Charadas.   Túrnense para representar estas y otras acciones en el pasado para ver si su compañero/a puede adivinar la acción. **Estudiante B,** por favor ve al **Apéndice 1,** página A-10.

MODELO: Estudiante A: (Act out: *Corté el pan.*)
Estudiante B: *Cortaste el pan.*

Estudiante A:

Comí un chile picante.	Comí un sándwich.
Preparé un jugo de naranja.	Le eché sal y pimienta a la sopa.
Pelé una zanahoria.	¿...?

4. Verbs with irregular forms in the preterit (I)

¿Qué plato pidió?

Prefirió el arroz con pollo.

El pretérito de los verbos con cambio radical, e → i, o → u

Stem-changing -**ir** verbs in the present also have stem changes in the preterit. The changes are **e → i** and **o → u** and occur only in the third-person singular and plural.

	pedir (*to ask for*)	dormir (*to sleep*)
yo	pedí	dormí
tú	pediste	dormiste
Ud.	pidió	durmió
él/ella	pidió	durmió
nosotros/as	pedimos	dormimos
vosotros/as	pedisteis	dormisteis
Uds.	pidieron	durmieron
ellos/as	pidieron	durmieron

These verbs follow the same pattern:

pedir (i, i)	*to ask for*	
preferir (ie, i)	*to prefer*	
repetir (i, i)	*to repeat*	
seguir (i, i)	*to follow, to continue*	
sentir (ie, i)	*to feel, to be sorry for*	
servir (i, i)	*to serve*	

La mesera **repitió** las especialidades del día. *The waitress repeated today's specials.*

Los chicos **durmieron** diez horas anoche. *The kids slept ten hours last night.*

Verbos que cambian la *i* en *y* en la tercera persona del singular y del plural

Verbs that end in -**er** and -**ir** preceded by a vowel (for example, **creer, leer,** and **oír**) change the **i → y** in the third-person singular and plural. All forms of these verbs are accented in all persons except the third-person plural.

	creer (*to believe*)	oír (*to hear*)
yo	creí	oí
tú	creíste	oíste
Ud.	**creyó**	**oyó**
él/ella	**creyó**	**oyó**
nosotros/as	creímos	oímos
vosotros/as	creísteis	oísteis
Uds.	**creyeron**	**oyeron**
ellos/as	**creyeron**	**oyeron**

Mamá no te **creyó** esta mañana. *Mother didn't believe you this morning.*

Leyeron la receta con cuidado. *They read the recipe carefully.*

¿**Oíste** que hay un restaurante chileno en Chicago? *Did you hear that there is a Chilean restaurant in Chicago?*

APLICACIÓN

6-33 Jumbo. *Jumbo* es un hipermercado enorme en Santiago de Chile.

Paso 1 Lee sobre las compras que hicieron (*did*) Rosario, la chef del restaurante Cocina Porteña, y su ayudante la semana pasada en *Jumbo*. Luego, completa las oraciones que siguen.

La semana pasada mi ayudante y yo decidimos hacer las compras en el nuevo *Jumbo* que abrieron recientemente en el Unicentro de Santiago. Cuando llegamos allí, encontramos una sección grande de frutas y verduras, otras de carnes y pescado y finalmente toda clase de bebidas. Compramos comida y también artículos para la cocina. ¡Qué tentación! Compré una cazuela grande y mi ayudante compró una sartén de hierro. Después comimos una merienda en el restaurante que tienen en el súper. Mi ayudante pidió pastel de limón y yo pedí pastel de manzana. La mesera nos sirvió café con el pastel. Mi ayudante compró un libro de recetas españolas y las leímos en el restaurante. Cuando regresamos a nuestro estudio, me senté a la mesa a leer, pero me dormí enseguida.

1. En Jumbo, Rosario y su ayudante _____ muchas cosas.
2. Rosario y su ayudante _____ una sección de frutas y verduras.
3. El ayudante _____ una sartén.
4. Los dos _____ pastel y _____ café.
5. Los dos _____ el libro de recetas.
6. Rosario _____ a la mesa y _____ a leer, pero _____ enseguida.

Paso 2 Ahora contesta las preguntas sobre tu última visita a un hipermercado.

1. ¿A qué hora saliste para el hipermercado?
2. ¿Qué viste?
3. ¿Qué encontraste?
4. ¿Qué compraste?
5. ¿A qué hora volviste a casa?

6-34 Ayer, en el bar estudiantil. Combina elementos de cada columna y forma oraciones para explicar lo que pasó en el bar estudiantil ayer.

MODELO: *Mis amigos pidieron leche para su café.*

1. nosotros	oír...
2. los profesores	preferir...
3. nuestros amigos	pedir...
4. yo	leer...
5. la mesera	repetir...
6. tú	sentir...

Presencia hispana

Of the popular soft drinks in the Spanish-speaking world, you will see Coca-Cola most often, followed closely by Pepsi. However the appearance and formula may not be the same as in the U.S. Go to a Latin American grocery store, and you will often see these and other beverages sold in glass bottles rather than in cans. The Latin American versions are made with sugar, rather than high fructose corn syrup, producing a less sweet beverage than the U.S. formula. Recently, however, there has been a movement to switch back to using sugar in U.S. beverage production. Why do you think this is?

6-35 Verdadero o falso. Túrnense para contar anécdotas personales que pueden ser verdaderas o falsas. Usen expresiones útiles de **¡Así lo decimos!** en sus respuestas.

MODELO: E1: *Una vez pedí camarones con helado.*

E2: *¡Qué ridículo! No te creo. No los pediste.*

Una vez....

1. (servir)...

2. (oír)...

3. (pedir)...

4. (preferir)...

5. (leer)...

Una vez comí
un bocadillo más
grande que yo.

 6-36A ¿Qué pasó? Túrnense para preguntarse qué pasó en las siguientes situaciones. **Estudiante B,** por favor ve al **Apéndice 1,** página A-11.

MODELO: en la fiesta familiar

ESTUDIANTE A: *¿Qué pasó en la fiesta familiar?*

ESTUDIANTE B: *Mi mamá sirvió nuestra comida favorita.*

Estudiante A:

Situaciones	Algunas actividades
1. en la cafetería estudiantil	• pedir tomates y cebollas para la sopa
2. en una película que viste	• no ver el cuadro de Picasso
3. en clase ayer	• acostarse tarde

Media Share

06-49
to 06-54

¿Cuánto saben?

Primero, pregúntate si puedes llevar a cabo (*carry out*) las siguientes funciones comunicativas en español. Después, júntate con dos o tres compañeros/as de clase para presentar las situaciones. Hagan y respondan a por lo menos cuatro preguntas en cada situación.

✓ CAN YOU . . .

☐ discuss foods, cooking, and recipes?

☐ talk about events in the past?

WITH YOUR CLASSMATE(S) . . .

Situación: En la cocina
Están preparando una receta sencilla en casa. Conversen sobre los ingredientes y los utensilios que necesitan.
Para empezar: *¿Qué preparamos? ¿Tenemos...?*

Situación: En una fiesta
Conversen sobre lo que pasó y qué hicieron (*did*) ayer en una fiesta. Usen una variedad de verbos en el pretérito.
Para empezar: *Ayer en la fiesta de Daniel, bailé con...*

Observaciones

¡Pura vida! EPISODIO 6

En este episodio hay una sorpresa (*surprise*) en la comida.

Antes de ver el video

6-37 Las empanadas. Cada país tiene sus especialidades culinarias; en Argentina, entre otras, son las empanadas. Lee la receta siguiente y haz una lista de los ingredientes.

> En Argentina, la empanada es una de las entradas[1] más populares en un restaurante, en un pícnic o como merienda. Se prepara con masa de harina[2] rellena de una mezcla de carne, huevos, aceitunas[3], cebollas y pasas[4]. Se sirve con una salsa que se llama chimichurri. La chimichurri es una mezcla de aceite de oliva, jugo de limón, perejil[5], ajo, cebolleta[6], orégano y una pizca de sal y pimienta.

[1]*appetizers* [2]*flour* [3]*olives* [4]*raisins* [5]*parsley* [6]*shallots*

A ver el video

6-38 Hay una sorpresa en la comida. Mira el sexto episodio de ¡Pura vida! para identificar la sorpresa que hay en la comida. Luego, completa las oraciones siguientes con palabras lógicas según el video.

El pícnic

La comida

¡Felipe se quedó sin propina!

| un postre | serpiente | unos tacos de pollo | una tortilla de patatas |

1. Silvia preparó _____, un plato español.

2. Marcela compró _____ en un restaurante mexicano.

3. Hermés preparó _____: arroz con leche de coco.

4. Las empanadas de Felipe llevan un ingrediente sorpresa: carne de _____.

Después de ver el video

6-39 Los otros platos. Conéctate a la Internet para buscar recetas para los otros platos del pícnic. Escoge una que te guste e indica los ingredientes que ya tienes en casa y los que tienes que comprar para poder preparar el plato.

> ↘ **Busca:** tacos de pollo; tortilla de patatas; empanada criolla; arroz con leche de coco; salsa chimichurri; salsa de tomate mexicana

Nuestro mundo

 Panoramas

06-58 to 06-59

Chile: un país de contrastes

Por su larga costa, la industria pesquera es sumamente importante en Chile. Chile produce una gran variedad de pescados y mariscos que no solo se consume en Chile, sino que también se exporta a todo el mundo.

El clima templado del valle central es ideal para el cultivo de frutas y verduras, muchas de las cuales se exportan a EE. UU. y a Canadá durante el invierno norteamericano. El vino chileno es uno de los más apreciados del mundo.

Los muchos parques nacionales, como Torres del Paine en el sur del país, protegen los maravillosos paisajes de Chile y atraen a miles de turistas cada año para hacer alpinismo y acampar.

Chile

Población: 17 millones
Festival importante: Fiesta de la Vendimia[1], marzo
Costas: 6.500 km
Productos de exportación: $50 billones/año: cobre[2]
frutas, pescado, papel y pulpa[3],
productos químicos, vino
PIB per cápita: $15.000

---

[1]*grape harvest*   [2]*copper*   [3]*wood pulp*

6-40 Identifica.   Identifica lo siguiente.

1. productos chilenos que se consumen en Norteamérica
2. una zona natural y turística de Chile
3. la extensión de su costa
4. los países en su frontera

6-41 Desafío.   Usa el mapa para identificar estos lugares y sus características.

1. ¿Cuál es su capital?
2. ¿Qué océano está al oeste del país?
3. ¿Qué país está al este?
4. ¿Cómo es el clima en Punta Arenas?

 6-42 Proyecto: Chile.   Después de dieciséis años de dictadura militar, Chile retornó a un gobierno democrático en 1989. Hoy en día, tiene un gobierno estable y una economía variada y fuerte. Escoge un lugar, una persona o un tema como **la gastronomía chilena, la viticultura chilena, la minería chilena, Sebastián Piñera, un restaurante chileno, un músico famoso chileno,** u otro que te interese para investigar más sobre Chile. Usa el Modelo para escribir un resumen en el que incluyas lo siguiente:

- su nombre y dónde está
- por qué es importante o interesante
- cómo es
- si quieres conocerlo/la algún día y por qué
- si piensas estudiar más sobre este tema
- una foto representativa

> **Busca:** gastronomia chilena; viticultura chilena; mineria chilena; sebastian pinera restaurante chileno; musico famoso chileno

MODELO: *Chile tiene muchos restaurantes informales que se especializan en platos típicos de la región y que siempre tienen una buena selección de vinos chilenos. Es muy popular también comer al aire libre, como en este restaurante en Viña del Mar. En este restaurante, que se llama Vista del Mar, se sirven pescados, mariscos, carnes y vegetales frescos. Para el postre, hay fruta o flan. Y para beber, limonada, agua mineral o vino, café o té. El precio de una comida aquí es de ocho a diez dólares.*

¿Eres un gastrosexual? ¿Conoces a uno?

ANTES DE LEER

6-43 ¿Por qué lees? Cuando lees un artículo en una revista ¿qué es lo que te atrae la atención? ¿Es el nombre de la revista? ¿El título del artículo? ¿La foto? ¿El formato? A continuación tienes un artículo en una revista conocida. Explica lo que esperas del artículo antes de leerlo.

A LEER

6-44 Puntos importantes. Ahora anota cuatro características de un gastrosexual.

GASTRÓNOMO MODERNO	**¿Eres un gastrosexual? ¿Conoces a uno?**

Gastrosexual:

- *Sustantivo*. Una persona que se apasiona por la comida y el placer[1] que se deriva de ella. Típicamente es un hombre que usa su talento culinario para impresionar a sus amigos, especialmente a su pareja[2].
- *Adjetivo*. Apasionado por la comida, su preparación y su consumo. Fascinado por la apariencia física de la comida y por su combinación de sabores.

Una investigación reciente sobre este fenómeno revela lo siguiente:

1. El tiempo que los hombres dedican a cocinar y a limpiar la cocina ha subido de cinco minutos al día en 1961 a 27 minutos en el 2009.
2. La cocina ya no es exclusivamente territorio femenino.
3. Hay todo tipo de gastrosexuales: hombres y mujeres, pero tienden a ser…
   - hombres
   - de 25 a 44 años de edad
   - de movilidad social ascendente
   - conocedores de la cocina internacional
4. Las razones de este fenómeno son…
   - Hay un aumento del número de hombres solteros; esto los obliga a cocinar.

- El 70% de las mujeres trabajan fuera de la casa. Ellas insisten en que su pareja las ayude con los quehaceres.
- Los hombres prefieren la cocina y la oportunidad de mostrar su creatividad a otros quehaceres.
- Es una forma de auto-actualización.
- Es un pasatiempo, no un deber.
- Es una manera de seducir a la pareja.
- Hay muchos *chefs* célebres masculinos. Estos cocineros famosos les sirven como modelos a los hombres.

5. Al gastrosexual le encanta viajar, especialmente para probar[3] platos nuevos y para obtener ingredientes y utensilios auténticos.

¿Eres un gastrosexual? ¿Conoces a uno?

[1]*pleasure* [2]*partner* [3]*to taste*

DESPUÉS DE LEER

6-45 Más información. Contesta estas preguntas sobre el artículo.

1. ¿Cuántos minutos pasan los hombres en la cocina hoy en día?
2. ¿Hay mujeres gastrosexuales?
3. ¿Hay un aumento o descenso en el número de hombres solteros hoy en día?
4. ¿Qué porcentaje de mujeres trabajan fuera de la casa ahora?
5. ¿Por qué prefieren los hombres la cocina más que otros quehaceres de la casa?
6. ¿Quiénes les sirven como modelos a los hombres gastrosexuales?
7. ¿Por qué le gusta viajar al gastrosexual?

6-46 En tu experiencia. ¿Eres un gastrosexual? ¿Conoces a uno/a? Describe una persona que sea como la descripción en el artículo.

MODELO: *Conozco a una persona que es gastrosexual. ¡Soy yo! Me gusta…*

6-47 Un sondeo (poll). ¿Cuáles son sus opiniones sobre la cocina?

Paso 1 Responde al sondeo siguiente.

1. _____ Soy hombre   _____ Soy mujer

2. Generalmente, dedico… minutos al día a cocinar y limpiar la cocina.

   _____ 30 minutos o más   _____ menos de 15 minutos

   _____ 15 a 30 minutos   _____ no cocino ni limpio

3. Prefiero cocinar…

   _____ con mis amigos   _____ solo/a

   _____ con una persona especial _____ No cocino.

4. En la cocina…

   _____ me gusta experimentar   _____ tengo recetas favoritas
   con los ingredientes
                                   _____ uso exclusivamente el microondas
   _____ sigo una receta

5. Para mí, cocinar es…

   _____ una oportunidad para   _____ necesario, pero no muy divertido
   ser creativo/a
                                   _____ una pérdida (waste) de tiempo
   _____ un pasatiempo divertido

6. Me gusta mucho la comida…

   _____ internacional   _____ rápida

   _____ sencilla, pero orgánica   _____ cualquiera (any) cuando tengo
                                   hambre

 Paso 2 Ahora comparen sus opiniones. ¿Hay una diferencia entre los hombres y las mujeres de esta clase?

📖 Taller

06-61
to 06-62

6-48 **Una reseña (*review*) virtual de un restaurante.** Puedes encontrar reseñas de restaurantes en el periódico, en una revista culinaria o en la Internet. La reseña te ayuda a decidir si te interesa visitar el restaurante. Escribe una reseña para ayudar a otros a encontrar un restaurante bueno por la Internet.

ANTES DE ESCRIBIR

- Piensa en el nombre de un restaurante, dónde se encuentra y por qué lo recomiendas.
- Contesta las siguientes preguntas para organizar tus ideas:
  - ☐ ¿Cuántas estrellas tiene (de ✷: muy económico e informal a ✷✷✷: muy caro y elegante)?
  - ☐ ¿Dónde está?
  - ☐ ¿Tiene una cocina (*cuisine*) especial?
  - ☐ ¿Cuáles son sus especialidades?
  - ☐ ¿Cómo es su ambiente (formal, informal)?
  - ☐ ¿Tiene música?
  - ☐ ¿Cómo es el servicio?
  - ☐ ¿Qué comiste cuando lo visitaste?
  - ☐ ¿Qué te gustó o no te gustó?
  - ☐ ¿Cuánto costó?
  - ☐ ¿Aceptan reservaciones?
  - ☐ ¿Cuál es tu recomendación?

A ESCRIBIR

- Organiza tus respuestas en un párrafo.

MODELO: *El café Joe's es un lugar informal; no tiene ninguna estrella…*

DESPUÉS DE ESCRIBIR

- **Revisar.** Revisa tu reseña para verificar los siguientes puntos:
  - ☐ el uso del pretérito
  - ☐ la concordancia de adjetivos y sustantivos
  - ☐ alguna frase superlativa (es el restaurante más/menos… de…)
  - ☐ la ortografía (*spelling*)
- **Intercambiar**
  Intercambia tu reseña con la de un/a compañero/a. Mientras leen las reseñas, hagan comentarios y sugerencias sobre el contenido, la estructura y la gramática.
- **Entregar**
  Pon tu reseña en limpio (*make a clean copy*), incorporando las sugerencias de tu compañero/a. Después, entrégasela a tu profesor/a.

🔊 Vocabulario

Las comidas Meals

el almuerzo *lunch*
la cena *dinner*
el desayuno *breakfast*
la merienda *afternoon snack*

Las comidas y las bebidas Foods and beverages

el aceite (de oliva) *(olive) oil*
el agua (mineral) *(mineral) water*
el ajo *garlic*
el arroz *rice*
el azúcar *sugar*
la banana *banana*
el bistec *steak*
el bocadillo / el sándwich *sandwich*
los camarones *shrimp*
la carne *meat*
la cebolla *onion*
la cerveza *beer*
el flan *custard dessert*
la fresa *strawberry*
los frijoles *beans, legumes*
las frutas *fruits*
las galletas *cookies*
el helado (de vainilla) *(vanilla) ice cream*
el huevo *egg*
el jamón *ham*
las judías verdes *green beans, string beans*
el jugo *juice*
la leche *milk*
la lechuga *lettuce*
el maíz *corn*
la mantequilla *butter*
la manzana *apple*
los mariscos *shellfish*
la naranja *orange*
el pan *bread*
la papa *potato*
el pastel (de manzana) *(apple) pie*
el pescado *fish*
el pollo *chicken*
el postre *dessert*
el queso *cheese*
la sal y la pimienta *salt and pepper*
la sopa *soup*
el té *tea*
el tomate *tomato*
la torta *cake*
las uvas *grapes*
las verduras *vegetables*
el vinagre *vinegar*
el vino (tinto, blanco) *(red, white) wine*
el yogur *yogurt*
la zanahoria *carrot*

En un restaurante In a restaurant

la cuenta *bill*
la especialidad de la casa *house specialty*
el menú *menu*
el/la mesero/a *waiter/waitress*
la propina *tip*

Adjetivos Adjectives

caliente *hot*
picante *hot (spicy)*

Verbos Verbs

cenar *to have dinner*
dar *to give*
decir (i, i) *to say*
dejar *to leave (behind)*
desayunar *to have breakfast*

En la cocina In the kitchen

la cafetera *coffee maker*
la cazuela *stewpot, casserole dish, saucepan*
la estufa *stove*
el microondas *microwave*
el refrigerador *refrigerator*
la sartén *skillet, frying pan*
el tazón (de cristal) *(glass) bowl*
la tostadora *toaster*

En la mesa On the table

la cuchara *spoon*
el cuchillo *knife*
el plato *plate*
la servilleta *napkin*
la taza *cup*
el tenedor *fork*
el vaso *glass*

Verbos Verbs

calentar (ie) *to heat*
cocinar *to cook*
cortar *to cut*
echar *to add, throw in*
freír (i, i) *to fry*
guardar *to save, to keep, to put away*
hornear *to bake, to roast*
mezclar *to mix*
pelar *to peel*
picar *to chop*
tostar (ue) *to toast*

En la receta In the recipe

asado/a *roasted*
la cucharada *tablespoon*
la cucharadita *teaspoon*
frito/a *fried*
al horno *baked*
a la parrilla *grilled*
la pizca *pinch (of salt, pepper, etc.)*

Expresiones Expressions

¡Qué rico! *How delicious!*
¡Qué sabroso! *How delicious!*
¡Qué asco! *How revolting!*
¡Qué ridículo! *How ridiculous!*

Expressions in a restaurant *See page 187.*
Adverbial expressions in the past *See page 202.*
Indirect object pronouns *See page 190.*
Verbs with a spelling change (-gué, -qué) in the preterit *See page 203.*
***Gustar* and similar verbs** *See page 193.*

7
¡A divertirnos!

OBJETIVOS COMUNICATIVOS

- Talking about activities you like to do in your free time
- Making plans to do something
- Talking about some activities in the past
- Talking about indefinite people and things, and people and things that do not exist

- Talking about different sports
- Reporting more past events and activities
- Taking shortcuts in conversation to avoid repetition

Readiness
Check

Las islas hispánicas del Caribe: Cuba, Puerto Rico y República Dominicana

«Vive duro y a lo loco que la vida dura muy poco».

Refrán: Enjoy yourself; it's later than you think.

Al dominicano Ramón Oviedo se le considera uno de los pintores expresionistas más importantes del siglo XXI. Esta obra se titula *Juan, no le hagas cosquillas a Pedro* (Juan, don't tickle Pedro).

El dominicano Juan Luis Guerra es uno de los músicos latinos más famosos del mundo.

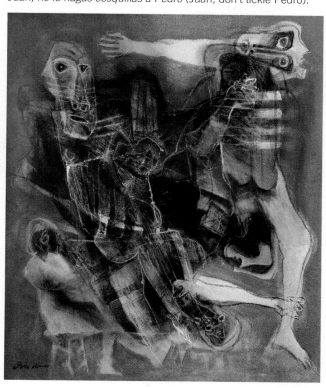

¡Así lo decimos! VOCABULARIO

¡Así es la vida! El fin de semana

¿Te divertiste este fin de semana?

MANUEL: ¿Qué hiciste este fin de semana?

LUISA: Fui a la playa Luquillo[1] con algunos amigos. ¿Y tú?

MANUEL: Mi novia y yo dimos un paseo por el Viejo San Juan.

PEDRO: Fuimos a ver la última película de Benicio del Toro. ¡Fue fabulosa!

TERESA: ¿De verdad? ¿La vieron en el Multiplex?

FELIPE: Estuve enfermo todo el fin de semana en casa. ¡Fue horrible!

VERÓNICA: ¡Qué mala suerte! ¿Fuiste al médico? No es contagioso, ¿verdad?

---

[1]Luquillo es una de las playas más lindas de Puerto Rico.

Vocabulario El tiempo libre

07-02
to 07-08

Variaciones
Although **el traje de baño** is widely used and understood, **el bañador** is common in Spain and **la trusa** in Cuba.

Variaciones
Los lentes de sol are also **los anteojos de sol** in the Americas and **las gafas de sol** in Spain.

Variaciones
Many Spanish speakers in the Caribbean use **¡Chévere!** to express excitement over an invitation or event. In Argentina and Uruguay, you'll hear **¡Bárbaro!** and in Mexico, **¡Qué padre!**

En la playa At the beach

la bolsa	*bag*
la heladera	*cooler*
el hielo	*ice*
los lentes de natación	*swim goggles*
los lentes de sol	*sunglasses*
la sombrilla	*umbrella*
la toalla	*towel*
el traje de baño	*swimsuit*

Los pasatiempos Pastimes

dar un paseo	*to go out, to take a walk*
hacer un pícnic	*to have a picnic*
ir a una discoteca	*to go to a club*
leer una novela	*to read a novel*
un periódico	*a newspaper*
una revista	*a magazine*
nadar en el mar	*to swim in the ocean*
una piscina	*a swimming pool*
pasarlo bien	*to have a good time*
volar (ue) un papalote	*to fly a kite*

¿Qué tiempo hace? What is the weather like?

está nublado	*it's cloudy*
hace...	*it's . . .*
buen/mal tiempo	*good/bad weather*
(mucho) calor	*(very) hot*
(mucho) fresco	*(very) cool*
(mucho) frío	*(very) cold*
(mucha) humedad	*(very) humid*
(mucho) sol	*(very) sunny*
(mucho) viento	*(very) windy*
hay...	*there's . . .*
(mucha) contaminación	*(a lot of) pollution/smog*
(mucha) humedad	*(a lot of) humidity*
(muchos) chubascos	*(many) showers*
llover (ue)	*to rain*
nevar (ie)	*to snow*

Opiniones y sugerencias Opinions and suggestions

Es un día perfecto para...	*It's a perfect day for . . .*
¡Oye!	*Listen!*
¿Qué tal si...?	*What if . . . ?*

Reacciones Reactions

¡Estupendo!	*Terrific!*
¡Fabuloso!	*Fabulous! Great!*
¡Fantástico!	*Fantastic!*
¡Magnífico!	*Great! Wonderful!*
Me da igual.	*It's all the same to me.*
No te preocupes.	*Don't worry.*
¡Qué mala suerte!	*What bad luck!*

Teresita llevó sus lentes de sol y un sombrero grande.

Dorotea llevó una bolsa grande a la playa.

Se sentaron en las sillas bajo una sombrilla.

APLICACIÓN

7-1 ¿Qué hacer? Algunos amigos están haciendo planes para el fin de semana. Completa las oraciones con la expresión adecuada de la lista.

MODELO: No quiero quemarme (*get burned*) en el sol. ¿Hay <u>sombrillas</u> en la playa?

1. ¡Oye! ¿Te apetece bailar y escuchar música? ¿Vamos a _____?
2. Hace buen tiempo. ¿Por qué no vamos al parque, llevamos sándwiches y hacemos _____?
3. Hoy hace sol. Vamos a dar _____ por el parque.
4. Los refrescos están en _____.
5. El sábado va a hacer mucho calor. ¿Qué tal si vamos a nadar en _____?
6. El domingo hay un partido de básquetbol. ¿Lo vemos en _____?
7. ¡Qué feo! Hace muy mal tiempo: está nublado y hay _____.
8. Si hace mal tiempo, es un día perfecto para leer _____ tranquilamente en casa.

a. un paseo
b. el mar
c. una revista
d. una discoteca
e. la televisión
f. un pícnic
g. contaminación
h. la heladera

7-2 ¿Dónde…? Mira este mapa meteorológico e identifica el lugar donde se encuentra el tiempo indicado.

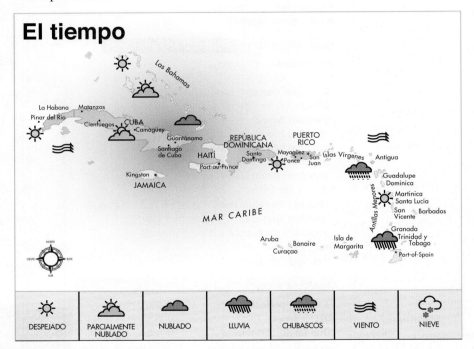

MODELO: Hay chubascos.
          Hay chubascos en las Islas Vírgenes.

1. Está nublado.
2. Está lloviendo.
3. Hace viento.
4. Hace mucho sol.
5. Está nevando.

7-3 El pronóstico (forecast) del tiempo. Escucha el pronóstico del tiempo que se da en la radio para esta semana. Luego, completa la siguiente información.

Ciudad: _____

Siglas (*call letters*) de la emisora de radio: _____

Fecha: _____

Estación del año: _____

Tiempo de ayer: _____

Pronóstico para hoy: _____

Pronóstico para mañana: _____

Una actividad que puedes hacer mañana: _____

7-4 ¿Qué te gusta hacer cuando…? Túrnense para contestar las siguientes preguntas. Usen las actividades de la lista en sus respuestas.

Algunas actividades

dar un paseo / una fiesta	ir a un partido / a un concierto
dormir una siesta	leer una novela / el periódico en el patio
esquiar en la nieve / en el agua	nadar en la piscina / en el mar
hacer un pícnic	tomar el sol (*sunbathe*) / un refresco con hielo
divertirme con los amigos	ver una película / la televisión
volar un papalote	ir al centro comerical / a un buen restaurante

MODELO: E1: *¿Qué te gusta hacer cuando nieva?*
              E2: *Me gusta esquiar.*

¿Qué te gusta hacer cuando…

1. hace calor, pero no tienes aire acondicionado?
2. llueve?
3. hace frío en la playa?
4. hace viento?
5. hace mucho sol?
6. hace buen tiempo, pero estás enfermo/a?

7-5 Un clima ideal. Escribe cinco oraciones completas para describir un lugar que para ti tiene un clima ideal y donde puedes hacer actividades que te gustan. Luego, descríbeselo al resto de la clase. Entre todos, escojan (*choose*) el lugar favorito.

MODELO: *Para mí,… tiene un clima ideal porque…*

7-6A Una invitación al concierto de Jennifer López (J.Lo) y Marc Anthony. Invita a tu compañero/a a ir contigo a este concierto. Usa la información del cartel a la derecha para contestar las preguntas de tu compañero/a. **Estudiante B,** por favor ve al **Apéndice 1,** página A-11.

MODELO: ESTUDIANTE A: *¿Quieres ir a un concierto de J.Lo y Marc Anthony?*
            ESTUDIANTE B: *¡Estupendo! ¿A qué hora empieza?*

Estudiante A:

Presencia hispana

New York City is a popular living destination for many Puerto Ricans, Cubans, and Dominicans, among other nationalities. **Neoyorquinos** maintain their traditions even while assimilating to life in the **Gran Manzana.** Sonia Sotomayor, the U.S. Supreme Court justice appointed by President Obama, is a **neoyorquina** of Puerto Rican heritage, as are Jennifer López and Marc Anthony. Can you name any others?

¡J.Lo y Marc Anthony en concierto!

¡Sus mejores éxitos!

San Juan, Puerto Rico
Entrada $200 - $150 - $80 (Estudiantes)

Sábado, 8:00 PM
Estadio Roberto Clemente

¡Así lo hacemos! ESTRUCTURAS

1. Irregular verbs in the preterit (II)

07-09
to 07-13

- The verbs **ser, ir, estar, tener, dar,** and **ver** all have irregular forms in the preterit.

Irregular preterit forms					
	ser/ir	**estar**	**tener**	**dar**	**ver**
yo	fui	estuve	tuve	di	vi
tú	fuiste	estuviste	tuviste	diste	viste
Ud.	fue	estuvo	tuvo	dio	vio
él/ella	fue	estuvo	tuvo	dio	vio
nosotros/as	fuimos	estuvimos	tuvimos	dimos	vimos
vosotros/as	fuisteis	estuvisteis	tuvisteis	disteis	visteis
Uds.	fueron	estuvieron	tuvieron	dieron	vieron
ellos/as	fueron	estuvieron	tuvieron	dieron	vieron

- The verbs **ser** and **ir** have the same forms in the preterit. The context of the sentence or the situation will clarify the meaning.

  ¿Sabes?, nuestros abuelos también **fueron** jóvenes.   *You know, our grandparents were also young.*

  Fuimos a dar un paseo al centro.   *We went downtown for a walk.*

- Note that **estar** and **tener** have the same irregularities in the preterit.

  Gloria **estuvo** en la feria internacional.   *Gloria was at the international fair.*

  Gloria **tuvo** que irse temprano.   *Gloria had to leave early.*

- **Dar** and **ver** use the same endings as regular **-er** and **-ir** verbs. However, the first and third persons have only one syllable and do not require an accent mark.

  Víctor me **dio** una película excelente.   *Víctor gave me an excellent movie.*

  Los **vi** entrar al teatro.   *I saw them enter the theater.*

- The preterit form of **hay** (from the verb **haber**) is **hubo** for both singular and plural.

  Ayer **hubo** un partido de fútbol en el estadio.   *Yesterday there was a soccer game in the stadium.*

  Hubo más de 50.000 espectadores.   *There were more than 50,000 spectators.*

APLICACIÓN

7-7 Una fiesta en Santo Domingo.   Empareja cada pregunta con la respuesta más lógica.

1. _____ ¿Dónde fue la fiesta?
2. _____ ¿Quiénes estuvieron?
3. _____ ¿Tuviste que salir temprano?
4. _____ ¿Quién fue con Graciela?
5. _____ ¿Vieron a alguna celebridad?
6. _____ ¿Le diste algo al anfitrión (*host*)?

a. Todos nuestros amigos.
b. Sí, una botella de vino.
c. Sí, vimos a Juan Luis Guerra.
d. No, no salí hasta las dos.
e. Su novio, Carlos.
f. En casa de Ramón y Silvia.

7-8 Un concierto de Juan Luis Guerra.   Ayer por la noche fuiste con varios amigos a un concierto de Juan Luis Guerra en Santo Domingo.

Paso 1   Completa el párrafo con la forma correcta del pretérito del verbo entre paréntesis.

Ayer (1) _____ (haber) un concierto de Juan Luis Guerra, el famoso cantante dominicano. Mis amigos y yo (2) _____ (llegar) al estadio a las siete. En la puerta, un agente nos (3) _____ (pedir) las entradas y nosotros le (4) _____ (dar) las cuatro entradas. (5) _____ (Ir) hasta los asientos, pero (6) _____ (tener) mala suerte. Yo (7) _____ (tener) que sentarme detrás de un chico super alto y mis amigos (8) _____ (tener) que sentarse detrás de unos altavoces (*speakers*) enormes. La verdad es que yo no (9) _____ (ver) mucho. Pero sí (10) _____ (oír) bien la música y (11) _____ (sentir) la emoción de un concierto en vivo. (12) _____ (Ser) una experiencia estupenda y todos nosotros lo (13) _____ (pasar) muy bien.

Juan Luis Guerra y su banda 4.40 han ganado varios Premios Grammy y Grammy Latinos.

  Paso 2   Conéctate a la Internet para ver el sitio oficial de Juan Luis Guerra. Allí puedes ver videos de sus canciones. Contesta las preguntas a continuación sobre uno de ellos.

Busca[1]: pagina fan oficial juan luis guerra

1. ¿Dónde fue? ¿En un concierto? ¿Otro lugar?
2. ¿Cuántas personas cantaron?
3. ¿Cómo fue la música?
4. ¿Qué más viste?

---

[1]Note that accents, tildes, and capital letters are not required for Internet searches.

7-9A **Una fiesta sorpresa.** En el foro de un amigo hay entradas (*entries*) sobre una fiesta sorpresa que hubo. Cada uno/a de ustedes tiene parte de la información sobre la fiesta. Háganse preguntas para saber qué pasó en la fiesta. **Estudiante B,** por favor ve al **Apéndice 1,** página A-11.

Estudiante A:

La información que necesito:	**La información que tengo:**
1. ¿Para quién fue la fiesta?	Buscar
2. ¿Cómo reaccionó ella?	
3. ¿Qué le dieron?	**Juan Tiburón**
4. ¿Quién tuvo que salir temprano?	La fiesta que di

La información que tengo (contenido):

Juan Tiburón

La fiesta que di

Amigos presentes: Carlos y su novia; Ramón y su hermano; yo; Luisita
Amigos que faltaron: Inés–estuvo enferma, Rafa–tuvo que estudiar
Comida que serví: nachos, guacamole, pastel de cumpleaños, helado
Bebidas: refrescos, cerveza, mojitos
…

7-10 ¿Quién…? En grupos de cuatro, túrnense para hacerse preguntas sobre lo que hicieron la semana pasada. Escriban el nombre de la persona que hizo la actividad en su caja correspondiente.

¿Quién...?

dar un paseo	estar enfermo/a	llegar tarde a clase
darle flores a tu mamá	ir a un partido	tener problemas con el carro
empezar un trabajo importante	ir a una discoteca	tener que trabajar mucho
estar en clase	jugar al tenis	ver una película

MODELO: jugar al béisbol

E1: *Carlos, ¿jugaste al béisbol la semana pasada?*
E2: *Sí, jugué al béisbol el lunes. (No, no jugué al béisbol.)*
E3: *Y tú, Juana, ¿Fuiste a almorzar con tus padres el sábado?*
E4: *No, fui a almorzar con mis padres el domingo.*

2. Indefinite and negative expressions

- In Spanish, verbs are affirmative unless they are made negative through the use of **no** or a negative expression. Following is a list of common negative expressions and their affirmative equivalents.

Afirmativo		Negativo	
algo	something, anything	**nada**	nothing, not anything
alguien	someone, anyone	**nadie**	nobody, no one
algún, alguno/a(s)	any, some	**ningún, ninguno/a(s)**	none, not any
alguna(s) vez (-ces)	sometime(s)	**ninguna vez**	never
siempre	always	**nunca, jamás,**	
también	also, too	**tampoco**	neither, not either
o... o	either . . . or	**ni... ni**	neither . . . nor

- There can be more than one negative expression (a double or triple negative) in a single sentence in Spanish. When **no** is used in a sentence, a second negative (**nada, nadie, ningún**) can either immediately follow the verb or be placed at the end of the sentence.

  No fuimos **nunca** a la playa con Lourdes. — *We never went to the beach with Lourdes.*

  No le dimos los sándwiches a **nadie.** — *We did not give the sandwiches to anyone.*

- When the negative expression precedes the verb, **no** is omitted.

  Nunca fuimos a la playa con Lourdes. — *We never went to the beach with Lourdes.*

  A **nadie** le dimos los sándwiches. — *We didn't give the sandwiches to anyone.*

- The expressions **nadie** and **alguien** refer only to persons and require the personal **a** when they appear as direct objects of the verb.

  No vi **a nadie** en el agua. — *I didn't see anyone in the water.*

  ¿Viste **a alguien** especial anoche en la discoteca? — *Did you see someone special last night at the club?*

- The adjectives **alguno** and **ninguno** drop the **-o** before a masculine singular noun in the same way the number **uno** shortens to **un.** Note the use of a written accent when the **-o** is dropped.

  Ningún amigo vino al partido. — *No friend came to the game.*

  ¿Te gusta **algún** tipo de refresco? — *Do you like any type of refreshment?*

- **Ninguno/a** is almost always used in the singular, not the plural form. The exception would be when used with inherent plural nouns such as things that come in pairs.

  ¿Quedan **algunas** entradas? — *Are there any tickets left?*

  No, no me queda **ninguna** entrada. — *No, there aren't any tickets left.*

  ¿Encontraste mis lentes? — *Did you find my glasses?*

  No, no encontré **ningunos** lentes. — *No, I didn't find any glasses.*

- Once a sentence is negative, all other indefinite words are also negative.

  Lucía **no** conoce a **nadie** en la fiesta **tampoco.** — *Lucía doesn't know anybody at the party either.*

  No voy a traer **ni** refrescos **ni** sándwiches para **nadie.** — *I am bringing neither refreshments nor sandwiches for anyone.*

APLICACIÓN

7-11 Una entrevista con Willy Chirino. Willy Chirino nació en Cuba y vino a EE. UU. a la edad de trece años con la llamada Operación Pedro Pan. Tiene unos veinte álbumes, varios de oro y platino, y recibió un Premio Grammy por Mejor Álbum Salsa/Merengue. Hoy se le considera uno de los salseros más destacados (*outstanding*) del mundo.

Paso 1 Primero, lee la entrevista con Willy Chirino y subraya todas las expresiones indefinidas y negativas.

Willy Chirino

ENTREVISTADORA:	Willy, es un honor conocerte y poder hablar contigo. ¿Deseas algo de beber? ¿Una botella de agua? ¿Algún refresco?
WILLY:	No, gracias. No quiero nada por ahora.
ENTREVISTADORA:	Bueno. Tienes siempre tanta energía. ¿No te cansas[1] nunca?
WILLY:	Pues, sí. Algunas veces cuando viajo mucho. Pero mi esposa, Lisette, siempre me acompaña, y eso ayuda.
ENTREVISTADORA:	Eres famoso por ser salsero y merenguero. Bailas, cantas… ¿Sabes cantar en algún idioma además del español y del inglés?
WILLY:	No, no canto en ningún otro idioma, pero algún día pienso grabar[2] algunas canciones en portugués. Soy amante de la música brasileña.
ENTREVISTADORA:	Tu esposa es cantante, también, ¿verdad?
WILLY:	Sí, es una excelente cantante y compositora. Siempre está a mi lado.
ENTREVISTADORA:	¿Das conciertos en Cuba?
WILLY:	No, nunca. Pero espero volver algún día.

---

[1]*get tired*   [2]*to record*

Paso 2 Ahora contesta las preguntas que siguen, basándote en la entrevista.

1. ¿Qué toma Willy en la entrevista?
2. ¿Cuándo se cansa?
3. ¿Cuándo está solo en sus viajes?
4. ¿En qué idiomas canta? ¿Canta en algún otro idioma?
5. ¿Qué hace su esposa?
6. ¿Cuándo espera volver a Cuba?

Paso 3   Willy Chirino, sitio oficial. Conéctate a la Internet para escuchar alguna canción de Willy Chirino y ver fotos y videos de él. Busca información adicional sobre él y escribe un párrafo en que incluyas esta información.

Busca: willy chirino sitio oficial

1. ¿En qué ciudad y en qué año nació?
2. ¿Cuál es el propósito de su fundación?
3. Escucha una selección de su música o ve uno de sus videos. ¿Cómo es?
4. ¿Quieres escuchar más? ¿Por qué?

7-12 Sus pasatiempos. Muchas personas tienen algún pasatiempo que hace la vida más agradable.

 Paso 1 Túrnense para preguntarse sobre sus gustos. Usen las expresiones **siempre, algunas veces, casi nunca** y **nunca,** y añadan más información personal. Háganse por lo menos una pregunta original.

Algunas actividades

dar paseos en el invierno	ver películas extranjeras (*foreign*)
ir a un partido los sábados	hacer un pícnic en el verano
ir a una discoteca con los amigos	ir a conciertos de música rock
salir con los amigos los viernes	¿...?

MODELO: ver películas de ciencia ficción

E1: *¿Ves películas de ciencia ficción?*

E2: *¡Siempre! Soy muy aficionado/a a las películas de ciencia ficción. El otro día, vi Avatar...*

Paso 2 Resume (*Summarize*) la información de las actividades en el **Paso 1**. Incluye las opiniones de tu compañero/a y las tuyas (*yours*), también. ¿Son muy diferentes?

MODELO: *Mi amigo José casi nunca ve películas de ciencia ficción, pero yo las veo algunas veces.*

¿Cuánto saben?

07-19 to 07-23

Primero, pregúntate si puedes llevar a cabo las siguientes funciones comunicativas en español. Después, júntate con dos o tres compañeros/as de clase para presentar las situaciones. Hagan y respondan a por lo menos cuatro preguntas en cada situación.

✓ CAN YOU . . .

☐ talk about activities you like to do in your free time?

☐ make plans to do something?

☐ talk about some activities in the past?

☐ talk about indefinite people and things, and people and things that do not exist?

WITH YOUR CLASSMATE(S) . . .

Situación: Con sus amigos
Conversen sobre actividades que les gusta hacer en su tiempo libre. Hablen de si las hacen adentro o afuera y por qué.
Para empezar: *¿Qué prefieres hacer los viernes por la noche?*

Situación: Planes para salir este fin de semana
Uno/a de Uds. tiene boletos para un evento especial. Hagan planes para ir juntos. Incluyan información sobre el evento, dónde, cuándo, y lo que van a hacer después.
Para empezar: *Tengo boletos para un concierto de Lady Gaga. ¿Qué tal si...?*

Situación: Por teléfono
Uno/a llama a su mejor amigo/a para hablar sobre lo que hicieron el fin de semana pasado. Usen verbos como **dar, estar, ir** y **haber** en el pretérito.
Para empezar: *¿Qué hiciste este fin de semana?*

Situación: Solos en casa
Conversen sobre lo que hacen en casa cuando no hay nadie. Usen expresiones negativas como **nadie** y **nunca** y afirmativas como **alguien** y **siempre**.
Para empezar: *¿Qué haces cuando estás solo/a en casa?¿Algo especial?*

📖 Perfiles

07-24
to 07-25

Mi experiencia

UNA QUINCEAÑERA

7-13 Para ti. En muchas culturas es común celebrar ciertos cumpleaños de forma especial, por ejemplo el *bar mitzvah* o el *bat mitzvah*, los dulces dieciséis, o los veintiún años. ¿Celebraste alguno de estos eventos? ¿Cómo fue? A continuación, Graciela te explica cómo fue su fiesta de quince años.

> Hola, soy Graciela Sandoval y vivo en San Juan, Puerto Rico. Quiero contarles sobre el día de mi fiesta de quinceañera, el día que recuerdo con más emoción. Pasó ya hace tres años, pero ninguna joven jamás olvida su fiesta de quince años, no solo porque marca la transición de niña a mujer de una manera muy tradicional, sino también porque es una oportunidad de divertirse con la familia y los amigos en un ambiente súper elegante.
> La celebración empezó con una misa[1]. Entré en la iglesia con mi vestido de princesa, acompañada de mi amigo David, mi pareja, y siete damas de honor con sus acompañantes. Después de la misa, dejé mi ramo de flores en el altar de la Virgen María. La celebración continuó con una gran fiesta en el hotel La Concha en la playa donde hubo un enorme banquete y un pastel igual de grande. Después de la cena bailamos de todo: merengue, pop, salsa, y por supuesto, todo lo último[2] de Ricky Martin, ¿cómo no? Mis padres me dieron una fiesta inolvidable y sé que gastaron mucho dinero. Por eso, algunas familias ahora ofrecen a sus hijas la oportunidad de escoger entre una fiesta, un carro o un viaje al extranjero. ¡Pero yo no cambio mi experiencia por nada del mundo!

[1]*mass*   [2]*the latest*

👥👥 **7-14 En su opinión.** Comparen la celebración que tuvo Graciela con algunas celebraciones importantes en su familia y entre sus amigos. ¿Qué tienen en común? ¿En qué se diferencian? Incluyan estos puntos de comparación:

- las fiestas grandes y costosas
- los regalos extravagantes
- los aniversarios importantes como los quince, los dieciséis o los veintiún años
- la música y los bailes en una fiesta
- la comida y la bebida
- alguna tradición o costumbre (*custom*) que se observó
- las preparaciones

MODELO: *Graciela celebró su quinceañera, pero yo celebré...*

Mi música

"PÉGATE" (RICKY MARTIN, PUERTO RICO)

Ricky Martin se incorporó al grupo juvenil Menudo a la edad de trece años. Cinco años más tarde lanzó su carrera de actor y solista. Su álbum *Vuelve* vendió más de 6 millones de copias y con él ganó su primer Grammy. En la Universidad de Miami grabó un concierto para *MTV Unplugged* y cerró el programa con "Pégate". En esta canción, Martin expresa sus deseos para un mundo mejor.

Antes de ver y escuchar

7-15 El mensaje. Aquí hay una lista de frases que vas a escuchar en la canción "Pégate". Identifica cuáles llevan un mensaje positivo y cuáles un mensaje negativo.

1. "cosas buenas para mi pueblo"
2. "amor puro"
3. "pa'l (para el) dolor (*pain*) pa'l mal de amores"
4. "dejando atrás los problemas"
5. "esta noche quiero fiesta"
6. "un río de bondad"

Para ver y escuchar

 7-16 La canción. Conéctate a la Internet para buscar una versión de "Pégate". ¿Cómo caracterizas su estilo? ¿Animado? ¿Romántico? ¿Triste? ¿Alegre? ¿Crees que es una buena canción para una fiesta de quinceañera? ¿Para alguna otra celebración? ¿Cuál? Explica.

> **Busca:** pegate video; pegate letra
>
> **Si te interesa comprar la canción:** *Go to iTunes Store>Music>More to Explore> iMix>Arriba 6e*

Después de ver y escuchar

 7-17 Para un mundo mejor. ¿Qué hiciste alguna vez para hacer el mundo mejor? Usa la lista siguiente y otras actividades en el pretérito para escribir un breve párrafo. Después explica tus actividades a un/a compañero/a de clase.

MODELO: *Una vez fui voluntario/a en un hogar para jubilados (retirement home).*

- donar dinero, tiempo, comida...
- reciclar plásticos, papel, botellas...
- ser voluntario/a en un programa para niños, mayores, animales abandonados...
- votar en las elecciones
- ser generoso con mi familia, mis amigos, mi comunidad...
- ir en bicicleta, en autobús, en tren... a...

Segunda parte

¡Así lo decimos! VOCABULARIO

📖 ¡Así es la vida! Actividades deportivas

07-26

🔊 En el centro deportivo los atletas hablan sobre los problemas que tuvieron.

JAVI: ¿Qué le dijiste al árbitro?

RAÚL: Nada importante. Solo que no quise aceptar su decisión.

🔊

VALERIA: ¿Dónde pusiste mis lentes de natación?

GABI: Te los di esta mañana. Están en tu bolsa.

🔊 **SAMUEL:** ¿Trajiste tu raqueta?

NICO: No, no pude encontrarla.

07-27
to 07-32

Vocabulario Los deportes y las actividades deportivas

Términos deportivos   `Sports terms`

el/la aficionado/a   *fan*
el/la árbitro/a   *referee*
el/la campeón/campeona   *champion, winner*
el/la entrenador/a   *coach, trainer*
la temporada   *season*

El equipo   `Team, equipment`

el balón   *(soccer, basket) ball*
el bate   *bat*
el guante   *glove*
la pelota   *baseball*
la raqueta   *racket*

Lola hace gimnasia
deportiva.

Variaciones
El baloncesto is used
in Spain, and in some
parts of Latin America,
instead of **el básquetbol**.

Deportes (actividad)   `Sports (activity)`

el alpinismo (hacer...)   *mountain climbing*
el atletismo (correr)   *track and field*
el básquetbol (jugar al...)   *basketball*
el béisbol (jugar al...)   *baseball*
el ciclismo (montar en bicicleta)   *cycling*
el esquí (esquiar)   *skiing*
el esquí acuático (esquiar en el agua)   *water skiing*
el fútbol (americano) (jugar al...)   *soccer (football)*
la gimnasia deportiva (hacer...)   *gymnastics*
el golf (jugar al...)   *golf*
el hockey (jugar al...)   *hockey*
el jogging (hacer...)   *jogging*
la natación (nadar)   *swimming*
el patinaje (patinar)   *skating*
el surfing (surfear)   *surfing*
el voleibol (jugar al...)   *volleyball*

Lorenzo es
miembro
de un equipo
de béisbol.

Variaciones
Jogging emerged as a
fitness fad in the U.S.
and Canada in the
1970s. In Latin
America, the term
hacer jogging was
adopted, whereas in
Spain, the English noun
foot was made into a
gerund, coining the
expression **hacer
footing**, which is
unique to Spain.

Otras actividades deportivas   `Other sporting activities`

empatar   *to tie (the score)*
ganar   *to win*
hacer ejercicio   *to exercise*
levantar pesas   *to lift weights*

Expresiones   `Expressions`

aunque   *although, even though*
entonces   *then*
por eso   *that's why*

A Ramón le gusta esquiar.

Jorge practica atletismo.

Letras y sonidos

The sequences *ca, co, cu, que, qui,* and *k* in Spanish

The letter **c** before the vowels **a, o,** and **u** sounds like the *c* in English *scan* in all varieties of Spanish. The combinations **que** and **qui** in Spanish, as well as the letter **k**, likewise correspond to the *c* sound in *scan*.

<u>ca</u>-lor   <u>co</u>-mi-da   <u>Cu</u>-ba   <u>que</u>-rer   <u>qui</u>-tar-se   <u>ki</u>-lo

Be careful not to pronounce the **u** in the sequences **que** and **qui** as a glide. For example, the first syllable in Spanish **qui-tar-se** sounds like English *key*, not *queen*.

APLICACIÓN

7-18 Los deportistas. Empareja a los siguientes deportistas con su deporte. ¿Cuál de estos deportistas eres tú?

1. _____ basquetbolista   a. el ciclismo
2. _____ nadador/a   b. el patinaje
3. _____ beisbolista   c. el alpinismo
4. _____ esquiador/a   d. el fútbol
5. _____ ciclista   e. el básquetbol
6. _____ futbolista   f. la natación
7. _____ alpinista   g. el tenis
8. _____ gimnasta   h. el béisbol
9. _____ tenista   i. el esquí
10. _____ patinador/a   j. la gimnasia deportiva

7-19 Tony y Eduardo Pérez (padre e hijo). Tony y Eduardo Pérez forman parte de una familia conocida en el mundo de los deportes.

Paso 1 Lee sobre esta pareja de padre e hijo y subraya todas las expresiones deportivas. Luego contesta las preguntas basadas en la lectura.

Tony y Eduardo Pérez

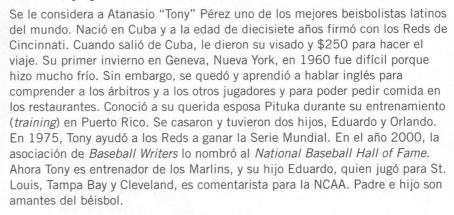

Se le considera a Atanasio "Tony" Pérez uno de los mejores beisbolistas latinos del mundo. Nació en Cuba y a la edad de diecisiete años firmó con los Reds de Cincinnati. Cuando salió de Cuba, le dieron su visado y $250 para hacer el viaje. Su primer invierno en Geneva, Nueva York, en 1960 fue difícil porque hizo mucho frío. Sin embargo, se quedó y aprendió a hablar inglés para comprender a los árbitros y a los otros jugadores y para poder pedir comida en los restaurantes. Conoció a su querida esposa Pituka durante su entrenamiento (*training*) en Puerto Rico. Se casaron y tuvieron dos hijos, Eduardo y Orlando. En 1975, Tony ayudó a los Reds a ganar la Serie Mundial. En el año 2000, la asociación de *Baseball Writers* lo nombró al *National Baseball Hall of Fame*. Ahora Tony es entrenador de los Marlins, y su hijo Eduardo, quien jugó para St. Louis, Tampa Bay y Cleveland, es comentarista para la NCAA. Padre e hijo son amantes del béisbol.

Paso 2   Ahora contesta las preguntas basadas en la lectura.

1. ¿Qué deporte jugó Tony por muchos años?

2. ¿Dónde nació?

3. ¿A qué edad salió de su país?

4. ¿Por qué aprendió a hablar inglés?

5. ¿Qué le pasó en 2000?

6. ¿Qué tienen en común Tony y su hijo, Eduardo?

 7-20 Los deportes.   Escucha a Raquel y a Tomás mientras hablan de sus intereses en los deportes. Indica qué oraciones le corresponden a cada uno. Si una frase no le corresponde a ninguno, marca **ninguno.**

	Raquel	Tomás	Ninguno
juega al béisbol	____	____	____
ve los partidos de fútbol	____	____	____
juega al tenis	____	____	____
monta en bicicleta	____	____	____
practica atletismo	____	____	____
ve el hockey	____	____	____
es campeón/campeona	____	____	____
es entrenador/a	____	____	____
esquía en invierno	____	____	____
ve la natación en los Juegos Olímpicos	____	____	____

7-21A Consejos.   Explíquense cómo se sienten y pidan consejos sobre lo que deben hacer. Pueden aceptar o rechazar (*reject*) los consejos, pero es necesario dar excusas si no los aceptan. **Estudiante B,** por favor ve al **Apéndice 1,** página A-12.

MODELO: ESTUDIANTE A: *Estoy aburrido/a. ¿Qué hago?*
ESTUDIANTE B: *¿Qué tal si das un paseo?*
ESTUDIANTE A: *No quiero. No me gusta salir de noche.*
ESTUDIANTE B: *Bueno, yo voy contigo. ¿Está bien?*
ESTUDIANTE A: *¡Perfecto!*

Estudiante A:

Situaciones y	mis reacciones	Sugerencias para mi compañero/a
Estás enfermo/a.	• ¡Fabuloso!	ir a un partido
Estás cansado/a.	• No me gusta(n)...	jugar al tenis
Necesitas aire fresco.	• ¡Ideal! / ¡Chévere!	dar un paseo
Tienes mucho trabajo.	• ¡Qué buena idea!	jugar al golf
No tienes nada que hacer.	• Me da igual.	trabajar en el jardín
	• ¡Qué mala idea!	leer una novela
	• No quiero porque...	ir a la playa

3. Irregular verbs in the preterit (III)

07-35
to 07-38

Like the verbs presented in **Primera parte,** several other commonly used verbs have irregular stems and special endings in the preterit.

¿Dónde pusiste el balón?

Irregular preterit forms								
	poder	poner	saber	venir	hacer	querer	decir	traer
yo	**pud**e	**pus**e	**sup**e	**vin**e	**hic**e	**quis**e	**dij**e	**traj**e
tú	**pud**iste	**pus**iste	**sup**iste	**vin**iste	**hic**iste	**quis**iste	**dij**iste	**traj**iste
Ud.	**pud**o	**pus**o	**sup**o	**vin**o	**hiz**o	**quis**o	**dij**o	**traj**o
él/ella	**pud**o	**pus**o	**sup**o	**vin**o	**hiz**o	**quis**o	**dij**o	**traj**o
nosotros/as	**pud**imos	**pus**imos	**sup**imos	**vin**imos	**hic**imos	**quis**imos	**dij**imos	**traj**imos
vosotros/as	**pud**isteis	**pus**isteis	**sup**isteis	**vin**isteis	**hic**isteis	**quis**isteis	**dij**isteis	**traj**isteis
Uds.	**pud**ieron	**pus**ieron	**sup**ieron	**vin**ieron	**hic**ieron	**quis**ieron	**dij**eron	**traj**eron
ellos/as	**pud**ieron	**pus**ieron	**sup**ieron	**vin**ieron	**hic**ieron	**quis**ieron	**dij**eron	**traj**eron

- The preterit forms of **poder, poner,** and **saber** have a **u** in the stem.

Pude ir a la piscina.	*I got to go to the pool.*
¿Por qué **pusiste** la toalla allí?	*Why did you put the towel there?*
Supimos quién ganó enseguida.	*We found out (learned about) who won right away.*

- The preterit forms of **venir, hacer,** and **querer** have an **i** in the stem.

¿**Vino** Julio al partido ayer?	*Did Julio come to the game yesterday?*
¿Dónde **hicieron** los uniformes?	*Where did they make the uniforms?*
Quise patear el balón, pero no fue posible.	*I wanted to kick the soccer ball, but it wasn't possible.*

- Whenever the stem of a verb in the preterit ends in **j** as in **decir** and **traer**, the third-person plural ends in **-eron**, not **-ieron.**

Los beisbolistas di**jeron** cosas buenas del entrenador.	*The ballplayers said good things about the trainer.*
Tra**jeron** los esquís al comienzo de la temporada.	*They brought their skis at the beginning of the season.*

Significados especiales en el pretérito

Certain Spanish verbs have different connotations when used in the preterit.

	Present	Preterit
conocer	*to know*	*to meet someone (the beginning of knowing)*
poder	*to be able (have the ability)*	*to manage (to do something)*
no poder	*to not be able (without necessarily trying)*	*to fail (after trying) (to do something)*
(no) querer	*to (not) want*	*to try (to refuse)*
saber	*to know*	*to find out, to learn*

Mario **conoció** a una tenista.	*Mario met a tennis player.*
Supo que su equipo perdió.	*He found out that his team lost.*
No quisimos correr en la lluvia.	*We refused to run in the rain.*

APLICACIÓN

7-22 Una superestrella está en Puerto Rico.
Aquí tienes un artículo publicado en Puerto Rico.

Paso 1   Subraya todos los verbos en el pretérito y escribe sus infinitivos.

Paso 2   Ahora contesta las preguntas, basándote en el artículo.

1. ¿Quién estuvo en Puerto Rico? ¿Por qué es "superestrella"?

2. ¿Qué hizo allí?

3. ¿Cuándo supo su tía que estaba (*he was*) allá?

4. ¿A quiénes más vio?

5. ¿Qué le trajo a la tía?

6. ¿Qué le dijo?

7. ¿Por qué tuvo que irse?

8. ¿Cuál va a ser su próxima película?

LA PRENSA

¡Benicio del Toro vuelve a San Juan!

Hoy, sábado llegó el actor puertorriqueño Benicio del Toro a la capital. Vino a asistir a la fiesta de cumpleaños de su querida tía. Ella no supo de su visita hasta última hora[1]. El actor no quiso revelarle sus planes. Prefirió darle la sorpresa. La primera cosa que hizo al llegar fue ir directamente a su casa en Santurce donde vio a su tía junto con el resto de la familia. Su tía empezó a llorar cuando vio a Benicio. Benicio la abrazó y le dijo, "Tía, ¡feliz cumpleaños!" De regalos, le trajo un bello ramo de flores y un bolso de Carolina Herrera. Según su publicista, Benicio tuvo que volver a Los Ángeles para empezar a trabajar en su nueva película, *Silencio*, con Gael García Bernal.

[1]*last minute*

7-23 Pero ayer... Completa las oraciones, indicando por qué ayer fue diferente. Usa pronombres de complemento directo cuando sea apropiado.

MODELO: Siempre hago ejercicio antes de salir para clase, pero ayer...
Siempre hago ejercicio antes de salir para clase, pero ayer no lo hice.

1. Siempre puedo encontrar a la entrenadora en el gimnasio, pero ayer...

2. Todos los días tenemos noticias deportivas en la radio, pero ayer...

3. Todos los días mis padres quieren asistir a los partidos, pero ayer...

4. Todas las tardes los deportistas hacen ejercicio, pero ayer...

5. Generalmente, los aficionados se ponen contentos, pero ayer...

6. Casi nunca sé quién gana el partido, pero ayer...

7. Por lo general los padres traen refrescos para después del partido, pero ayer...

8. Casi siempre podemos ver el partido en la televisión, pero ayer...

 7-24A Una película excepcional. Ayer saliste al cine con una amiga y lo pasaron muy bien.

Paso 1 Primero conjuga por tu cuenta (*on your own*) los verbos en cada oración en el pretérito y completa las oraciones con información lógica. **Estudiante B,** ve al **Apéndice 1,** página A-12.

MODELO: Ayer (yo) **invitar** a... a ir al cine.
Ayer invité a mi amiga a ir al cine.

Estudiante A:

> Ayer **ver** una película de... en el Cine...
>
> (Yo) **Saber** de la película cuando (yo) **leer** el anuncio en...
>
> Nosotros **ir** a ver la película a la/s...
>
> Nosotros **querer** llegar temprano, pero no **poder** porque **tener** que esperar (*wait for*) por...
>
> Después de la película, mi amiga **decir** "vamos a tomar..."
>
> (Nosotros) **Ir** a...
>
> **Ser** divertido.
>
> Después (nosotros)...

Paso 2 Ahora usa la información que escribiste para contestar las preguntas de tu compañero/a.

4. Double object pronouns

You can take shortcuts in conversation and avoid repetition by using two object pronouns.

Subject pronouns	Indirect object pronouns	Direct object pronouns
yo	me	me
tú	te	te
Ud.	le (*changes to* **se**)	lo/la
él/ella	le (*changes to* **se**)	lo/la
nosotros/as	nos	nos
vosotros/as	os	os
Uds.	les (*changes to* **se**)	los/las
ellos/ellas	les (*changes to* **se**)	los/las

¿Me prestas tu raqueta?

¡Claro! Te la presto.

- When both a direct and an indirect object pronoun are used together in a sentence, they are usually placed before the verb, and the indirect object pronoun precedes the direct object pronoun.

   Julián, ¿**me** traes **la película**?   *Julián, will you bring me the movie?*
   Te la traigo en un momento.   *I'll bring it to you in a moment.*

- The indirect object pronouns **le** (*to you, to her, to him*) and **les** (*to you, to them*) change to **se** when they appear with the direct object pronouns **lo, los, la, las.** Rely on the context of the previous statement to clarify the meaning of **se.**

   ¿Quién **les** trae **el balón**   *Who brings the ball to the players?*
      a los jugadores?
   El entrenador **se lo** trae.   *The coach is bringing it to them.*

- As with single object pronouns, the double object pronouns may be attached to the infinitive or the present participle. In that case, the order of the pronouns is maintained, and an accent mark is added to the stressed vowel of the verb.

   Carlos, ¿puedes **traerme la bolsa**?   *Carlos, can you bring me the bag?*
   Voy a **traértela** enseguida.   *I'll bring it to you right away.*
   Estoy **buscándotela** ahora mismo.   *I am looking for it right now for you.*

Study tips – Using direct and indirect objects together

Here are a few strategies to help you with this structure.

1. Review the use of direct object and direct object pronouns and do the practice activities for reinforcement. See pages 124–125.

2. Also review the use of indirect objects and indirect object pronouns. See pages 190–191.

3. Remember to always combine double object pronouns in the right order: indirect before direct.

4. Become familiar with the sound pronouns make together by repeating out loud phrases such as the following:

me lo da	me las traes
te lo doy	te los traigo
se los da	se las traemos

APLICACIÓN

7-25 Antes de la carrera (*race*). Daniela va a competir en una carrera de ciclismo.

Paso 1 Primero, lee el diálogo entre Daniela y su entrenador, y subraya los pronombres de complemento directo (**D**) e indirecto (**I**). Indica cuál es cuál.

MODELO: *Necesito guantes. ¿A quién <u>se</u> <u>los</u> pido?*
I D

Daniela compite en una
carrera de ciclismo

DANIELA: Sebastián, ¿me pasas la botella de agua, por favor?

ENTRENADOR: En seguida te la doy, Daniela. ¿Dónde te la pongo?

DANIELA: La quiero en mi mochila, gracias Sebastián. Después, ¿me buscas las barras de proteína?

ENTRENADOR: ¿Dónde las busco?

DANIELA: Creo que están en el carro o si no, seguramente mi mamá las tiene. Debes pedírselas a ella. ¿Tienes mis lentes de sol?

ENTRENADOR: Las voy a buscar ahora. ¿Te las traigo?

DANIELA: Sí, y tú también debes ponértelas para verme mejor. Y ahora, ¿me compras un jugo de naranja?

ENTRENADOR: Buena idea, Daniela. Te lo compro ahora mismo. Buena suerte. Te espero en la meta (*finish line*).

Paso 2 Ahora, contesta las preguntas, basándote en el diálogo anterior. Usa pronombres de complemento directo e indirecto en tus respuestas cuando sea necesario.

1. ¿Quién tiene la botella de agua?

2. ¿A quién se la da?

3. ¿Dónde se la pone?

4. ¿Qué más necesita Daniela?

5. ¿Por qué crees que las quiere?

6. ¿Qué desea tomar antes de la carrera?

7. ¿Quién se lo compra?

8. ¿Dónde la espera el entrenador?

7-26 De viaje en República Dominicana. Haz el papel de turista en República Dominicana y responde a las preguntas del guía (*guide*), usando los pronombres de complemento indirecto y directo.

MODELO: GUÍA: ¿Quiere ver el transporte que tomamos mañana?

TÚ: Sí, ¿*me lo* enseña ahora?

1. GUÍA: ¿Quiere ver el restaurante donde vamos a cenar?

   TÚ: —Sí, ¿_____ enseña ahora?

2. GUÍA: ¿Quiere leer el periódico de ayer?

   TÚ: —Sí, ¿_____ trae ahora?

3. GUÍA: ¿Le traigo las guías turísticas?

   TÚ: —No, no es necesario traér_____.

4. GUÍA: ¿Quiere ver el primer hospital del Nuevo Mundo?

   TÚ: —¡Sí! ¿_____ muestra ahora?

5. GUÍA: ¿Les traigo a ustedes los refrescos?

   TÚ: —No, no tenemos sed. No tiene que traér_____.

6. GUÍA: ¿Les enseño el Parque Nacional del Este?

   TÚ: —¡Claro! ¿_____ enseña mañana? Ahora estamos algo cansados.

7. GUÍA: ¿Le doy una propina al mesero?

   TÚ: —Buena idea. Debe dár_____ ahora.

8. GUÍA: ¿Les preparo un cóctel a ustedes?

   TÚ: —No, gracias. No es necesario preparár_____.

7-27A ¿Tienes? Eres entrenador/a y tu asistente va a traerte cosas que necesitas para un partido de béisbol. Pregúntale si tiene las siguientes cosas. Si las tiene, pregúntale si puede traértelas. Si no las tiene, pregúntale si puede buscártelas. Luego, consúltense para hacer una lista de las cosas que tu compañero/a necesita buscar. **Estudiante B,** por favor ve al **Apéndice 1,** página A-13.

MODELO: ESTUDIANTE A: *¿Tienes botellas de agua para los jugadores?*

ESTUDIANTE B: *Sí, tengo botellas de agua. / No, no tengo botellas de agua.*

ESTUDIANTE A: *¿Me las traes? / ¿Me las buscas?*

ESTUDIANTE B: *Sí, te las traigo. / Sí, te las busco.*

Estudiante A:

Necesito:			
1. los guantes	3. el bate de aluminio	5. las pelotas	7. la fruta
2. los sándwiches para el equipo	4. las botellas de agua	6. mis lentes de sol	8. mi cuaderno

¡Hola!

Cultura en vivo

It is much less common for universities in the Spanish-speaking world to have sports teams like those in the U.S. Instead, young people join clubs or simply organize informal games with friends.

7-28 En el campamento de verano. Hagan los papeles de consejero/a (*counselor*) y campistas en un campamento de verano y pídanle varias cosas al/a la consejero/a. El/La consejero/a debe contestar si lo va a hacer o no, usando dos pronombres de complemento directo e indirecto. Pueden usar las sugerencias a continuación.

Acción	Cosas que necesitan	
dar	las toallas	el hielo
pedir	los guantes	la bolsa
preparar	las raquetas	los sándwiches
traer	el chocolate	los esquís

MODELO: E1: *Consejero, nos trae el bate, por favor.*
E2: *¡Claro! Se lo traigo ahora. / Lo siento, no puedo traérselo ahora.*

07-43
to 07-48

¿Cuánto saben?

Primero, pregúntate si puedes llevar a cabo las siguientes funciones comunicativas en español. Después, júntate con dos o tres compañeros/as de clase para presentar las situaciones. Hagan y respondan a por lo menos cuatro preguntas en cada situación.

✓ CAN YOU . . .

☐ talk about different sports?

☐ report more past events and activities?

☐ take shortcuts in conversation to avoid repetition?

WITH YOUR CLASSMATE(S) . . .

Situación: En el estadio
Conversen sobre los deportes que les gusta ver y jugar, y cuándo los hacen. Hablen también sobre los que no les gustan y por qué.
Para empezar: *¿Qué deportes...? ¿Te gusta hacer/jugar al...? ¿Prefieres ... o ...?*

Situación: En una gran reunión familiar
Hablen de personas que conocieron y cosas que supieron en una reunión familiar que tuvieron el año pasado. Usen verbos como **poder, poner, saber, venir, hacer, querer, decir y traer** para hablar sobre esta reunión.
Para empezar: *¿Qué tal tu reunión familiar? ¿Qué hiciste?*

Situación: En el gimnasio
Están haciendo ejercicio en un gimnasio. Pídanse artículos deportivos que necesitan y contesten usando los dos pronombres indirectos y directos.
Para empezar: *¿Me das la pelota? Sí, te la doy.*

Observaciones

¡Pura vida! EPISODIO 7

En este episodio los amigos hablan de los deportes.

Antes de ver el video

7-29 Un evento histórico. En el mundo hispano el fútbol es el juego que más atrae a los fanáticos. Lee la descripción de los últimos minutos de un partido importante y contesta las siguientes preguntas.

> Durban, Sudáfrica — 07-07-2010
>
> España, con la mejor generación de futbolistas de su historia, dio un paso hacia[1] la gloria al ganarle hoy a Alemania 1 a 0 en los semifinales de la Copa Mundial de Sudáfrica-2010. Todo ocurrió gracias a un gol de Carlos Puyol en el minuto 73. El central del Barcelona cabeceó[2] un córner desde la izquierda y así su equipo disputará el domingo el partido final con Holanda. Los holandeses le habían ganado el martes a Uruguay 3 a 2 en un emocionante partido. España fue muy superior a Alemania en todo el partido. Ahora la incógnita final es… ¿España u Holanda?

[1]*toward* [2]*made a head shot*

¿Qué equipo ganó la Copa Mundial del 2010?

1. ¿Dónde fue la competencia?
2. ¿En qué año fue?
3. ¿Qué equipo ganó?
4. ¿Quién hizo un gol?
5. ¿Cuál es la incógnita final?

A ver el video

7-30 Los deportes. Mira el séptimo episodio de **¡Pura vida!** para emparejar los intereses y las características de cada personaje según el video.

| **F:** Felipe | **H:** Hermés | **M:** Marcela | **S:** Silvia |

1. _____ Le encanta surfear.
2. _____ Está triste porque perdió su equipo favorito.
3. _____ Sale mucho al cine, a conciertos, a bailar y más.
4. _____ Prefiere el hockey al fútbol.
5. _____ Su hermana tuvo un novio futbolista.

Marcela

Felipe

Silvia

Después de ver el video

7-31 ESPN Deportes. Conéctate a la Internet para buscar una noticia deportiva que te interese. Escribe un párrafo en que incluyas la información de la lista.

> **Busca:** espn deportes

- el evento
- dónde tuvo lugar
- los personajes
- el resultado

Nuestro mundo

 Panoramas

 Las islas hispánicas del Caribe

07-52
to 07-53

Las aguas cristalinas, el sol, el agua tibia y sus bellas playas atraen miles de turistas a las islas del Caribe.

No es raro ver carros norteamericanos de los años 50 en las calles de La Habana, Cuba. Cayo Hueso (*Key West*), EE. UU. se encuentra a solo 90 millas de Cuba.

San Juan fue fundada en 1521. El Viejo San Juan conserva su encanto colonial.

Los fines de semana es popular ir a El Morro para hacer un pícnic y volar un papalote (o volar chiringa, como dicen en Puerto Rico).

Los españoles construyeron grandes fortalezas para proteger las islas de invasiones de piratas. El Morro rodeó la antigua ciudad de San Juan, Puerto Rico.

Cuba, Puerto Rico y República Dominicana

	Cuba	PR	RD
Población:	11,5 millones	4 millones	10 millones
Las Grandes Ligas (2010):	17	33	77
Medallas olímpicas:	63	4	6
Gobierno:	estado comunista	estado libre asociado a EE. UU.	república democrática

7-32 Identifica. Identifica, describe y/o explica lo siguiente.

1. lo que atrae a muchos turistas a las islas
2. el propósito de El Morro
3. el país con el mayor número de beisbolistas en las Grandes Ligas
4. un pasatiempo popular los domingos en las islas

7-33 Desafío. Consulta el mapa para identificar lo siguiente.

1. el nombre de la isla más grande de las Antillas
2. los dos países que ocupan la isla de La Española
3. la distancia entre Cuba y EE. UU.
4. la isla que ocupó una posición estratégica contra ataques de piratas

 7-34 Proyecto: Las islas hispánicas del Caribe. Estos tres países atraen a turistas de todo el mundo por su templado clima, sus hermosas playas y su rica cultura. Escoge uno de los siguientes temas: **la arquitectura colonial, la comida, un deporte popular, un deportista famoso, Juan Luis Guerra, el merengue** u otro que te interese, para investigar más sobre uno de estos países. Usa el modelo para escribir un resumen en que incluyas lo siguiente:

- su nombre y dónde está
- por qué es importante o interesante
- cómo es
- si quieres visitarlo algún día y por qué
- si piensas estudiar más sobre este tema
- una foto representativa

> **Busca:** merengue; deportes caribe (cuba, puerto rico, republica dominicana); juan luis guerra; arquitectura cuba; comida cuba, etc.

MODELO: *La capital de Puerto Rico fue fundada por los españoles en 1521. El centro histórico de la capital, el Viejo San Juan, tiene muchos edificios del siglo XVI. Hoy en día, San Juan es…*

"Entrevista con Ricky Martin, Embajador de Buena Voluntad de la UNICEF", *Estrella*

Estrella es una revista popular que tiene artículos sobre los personajes más importantes del mundo del espectáculo. En este número resaltan (*feature*) a Ricky Martin después de que fue nombrado Embajador de Buena Voluntad de la UNICEF.

ANTES DE LEER

7-35 ¿Qué sabes?   Antes de leer este artículo, escribe algunos apuntes en español o en inglés sobre lo que sabes de los temas que siguen. Esto te ayuda a anticipar el contenido.

1. la Organización de las Naciones Unidas
2. la UNICEF
3. Ricky Martin

A LEER

7-36 Su causa.   Mientras lees la entrevista, identifica cuál es la causa que apasiona a Ricky Martin y qué hace para cumplir su misión.

REPORTERA:	Ricky, gracias por permitirme esta entrevista. Siempre has abogado por los niños y ahora la UNICEF te ha nombrado Embajador de Buena Voluntad. ¡Felicidades! Este es un gran honor para ti y para Puerto Rico.
R. MARTIN:	Gracias. La verdad, me tomó por sorpresa, pero me siento sumamente orgulloso[1] del honor. Pienso hacer todo lo posible para mejorar la vida de los niños.
REPORTERA:	Según el sitio web de UNICEF, los embajadores son personas con historias personales distintas, pero todos comparten un mismo compromiso[2] para mejorar las vidas de los niños en todo el mundo. ¿Cómo te interesaste en esta causa?
R. MARTIN:	Soy una persona que tiene muchas ventajas[3]. En comparación con muchas personas, mi vida es fácil. Y los niños son las personas que menos pueden defenderse. Tenemos la obligación de abogar[4] por ellos.
REPORTERA:	Como embajador, te cuentas entre personalidades célebres como Whoopie Goldberg, David Beckham y Shakira. ¿Qué haces en concreto para mejorar la condición de los niños necesitados?

[1]*proud*   [2]*commitment*   [3]*advantages*   [4]*advocate*

R. MARTIN: Soy una sola voz entre muchas, pero creo que puedo influir. En 2004 me permitieron dar un discurso ante la Organización de las Naciones Unidas. Les hablé del tremendo problema del tráfico de niños por motivos sexuales. Hay muchas personas que no quieren admitir esta perversidad, pero todos tenemos el deber de enfrentar ese grave problema ahora. Hasta los mismos niños a veces ignoran la ilegalidad y la inmoralidad de su situación. Se calcula que más de 1,2 millones de niños son traficados anualmente para fines de explotación laboral o sexual. ¡Es intolerable!

REPORTERA: También hay una Fundación que lleva tu nombre. ¿Cuáles son las metas[5]?

R. MARTIN: La Fundación Ricky Martin aboga por el bienestar de los niños por todo el mundo en áreas críticas como la justicia social, la educación y la salud. ¿Sabes que cada año más de seis millones de niños menores de cinco años mueren de enfermedades prevenibles? ¡Tenemos que ayudarlos!

REPORTERA: Ricky, estoy segura que nuestros lectores van a querer informarse más. Tienes un sitio en la Internet, ¿verdad?

R. MARTIN: Sí, claro. Es rickymartinfoundation.org. Hay lugar para muchos en nuestra organización.

REPORTERA: Para cerrar esta conversación, Ricky, nuestros lectores quieren saber detalles sobre los nuevos miembros de tu familia.

R. MARTIN: ¡Sí! Soy padre de dos preciosos chiquillos, Matteo y Valentino. Estoy dedicado a criarlos en un mundo mejor.

[5]*goals*

DESPUÉS DE LEER

7-37 ¿Qué aprendiste? Haz una lista de tres o más datos que aprendiste de esta entrevista.

MODELO: *Aprendí que Ricky Martin es puertorriqueño.*

 7-38 La Fundación Ricky Martin. Conéctate al sitio web de la Fundación Ricky Martin para aprender más sobre su misión. Escribe un resumen de uno de sus proyectos.

Busca: fundacion ricky martin

7-39 Una entrada en tu foro electrónico. Cuando escribes tu foro electrónico en la Internet, relatas algo interesante, curioso o significativo que te ha pasado (*has happened to you*) en estos días. Contesta las preguntas a continuación para escribir una entrada.

ANTES DE ESCRIBIR

- Piensa en el apodo que vas a usar en tu foro electrónico. Puedes incluir un icono que te represente también.

- Piensa en lo que hiciste hoy. Escribe una lista de frases para indicar brevemente tus acciones, por ejemplo: **asistir a clase, ver a mis amigos, hablar por teléfono con...**, etc.

- Pon tus acciones en orden cronológico.

A ESCRIBIR

- Comienza tu entrada con una oración para resumir tu día, por ejemplo:

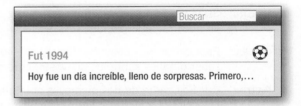

- Escribe sobre cuatro o cinco actividades que hiciste o acontecimientos que ocurrieron.

- Utiliza expresiones de entrada y transición, como **primero, segundo, entonces, después, por eso, aunque,** etc.

- Cierra tu entrada con una oración de despedida.

DESPUÉS DE ESCRIBIR

- **Revisar.** Revisa tu entrada para ver si fluye bien. Luego revisa la mecánica.

  ☐ ¿Incluiste una variedad de vocabulario?

  ☐ ¿Conjugaste bien los verbos en el pretérito?

  ☐ ¿Verificaste la ortografía y la concordancia?

- **Intercambiar**

  Intercambia tu entrada con la de un/a compañero/a. Mientras leen las entradas, hagan comentarios y sugerencias sobre el contenido, la estructura y la gramática.

- **Entregar**

  Pon tu entrada en limpio, incorporando las sugerencias de tu compañero/a. Después, entrégasela a tu profesor/a.

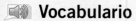

Vocabulario

Primera parte

En la playa   At the beach

la bolsa   bag
la heladera   cooler
el hielo   ice
los lentes de natación   swim goggles
los lentes de sol   sunglasses
la sombrilla   umbrella
la toalla   towel
el traje de baño   swimsuit

Los pasatiempos   Pastimes

dar un paseo   to go out, to take a walk
hacer un pícnic   to have a picnic
ir a una discoteca   to go to a club
leer una novela   a novel
        un periódico   a newspaper
        una revista   a magazine
nadar en el mar   to swim in the ocean
una piscina   a swimming pool
pasarlo bien   to have a good time
volar (ue) un papalote   to fly a kite

¿Qué tiempo hace?   What is the weather like?

está nublado   it's cloudy
hace...   it's . . .
  buen/mal tiempo   good/bad weather
  (mucho) calor   (very) hot
  (mucho) fresco   (very) cool
  (mucho) frío   (very) cold
  (mucha) humedad   (very) humid
  (mucho) sol   (very) sunny
  (mucho) viento   (very) windy
hay...   there's . . .
  (mucha) contaminación   (a lot of) pollution/smog
  (mucha) humedad   (a lot of) humidity
  (muchos) chubascos   there are (many) showers
llover (ue)   to rain
nevar (ie)   to snow

Opiniones y sugerencias   Opinions and suggestions

Es un día perfecto para...   It's a perfect day for . . .
¡Oye!   Listen!
¿Qué tal si...?   What if . . . ?

Reacciones   Reactions

¡Estupendo!   Terrific!
¡Fabuloso!   Fabulous! Great!
¡Fantástico!   Fantastic!
¡Magnífico!   Great! Wonderful!
Me da igual.   It's all the same to me.
No te preocupes.   Don't worry.
¡Qué mala suerte!   What bad luck!

Segunda parte

Los deportes   Sports

el alpinismo   mountain climbing, mountaineering
el atletismo   track and field
el básquetbol   basketball
el béisbol   baseball
el ciclismo   cycling
el esquí   skiing
el esquí acuático   water skiing
el fútbol (americano)   soccer (football)
la gimnasia deportiva   gymnastics
el golf   golf
el hockey   hockey
el jogging   jogging
la natación   swimming
el patinaje   skating
el surfing   surfing
el voleibol   volleyball

Actividades deportivas   Sporting activities

montar en bicicleta   to go bike riding
correr   to run
empatar   to tie (the score)
esquiar (en el agua)   to ski, to water ski
ganar   to win
hacer alpinismo   to mountain climb, to go mountaineering
        ejercicio   to exercise
        jogging   to jog
        gimnasia deportiva   to do gymnastics
jugar al básquetbol   to play basketball
        béisbol   to play baseball
        fútbol (americano)   to play soccer (football)
        golf   to golf
        hockey   to play hockey
        voleibol   to play volleyball
levantar pesas   to lift weights
nadar   to swim
patinar   to skate
surfear   to surf

El equipo   Team, equipment

el balón   (soccer, basket) ball
el bate   bat
el guante   glove
la pelota   baseball
la raqueta   racket

Términos deportivos   Sports terms

el/la aficionado/a   fan
el/la árbitro/a   referee
el/la campeón/campeona   champion, winner
el/la entrenador/a   coach, trainer
la temporada   season

Expresiones   Expressions

aunque   although, even though
entonces   then
por eso   that's why

Indefinite and negative expressions   See page 225.   **Double object pronouns**   See page 237.

8
¿En qué puedo servirle?

OBJETIVOS COMUNICATIVOS

- Talking about clothes and shopping at a department store
- Talking about what used to happen and what you used to do in the past
- Describing a scene in the past

- Shopping for personal care products
- Contrasting what happened in the past with something else that was going on
- Talking about what people say and believe
- Talking about what is done

Readiness
Check

El reino inca:
Perú y Ecuador

«Quien compra ha de tener cien ojos; a quien vende le basta uno solo».

Refrán: The buyer needs a hundred eyes; the seller but one.

Machu Picchu, la misteriosa ciudad de los incas, estuvo "perdida" hasta que la descubrió un arqueólogo en 1910.

"Madre y niño". El ecuatoriano Oswaldo Guayasamín fue uno de los pintores latinoamericanos más importantes del siglo XX. Muchas de sus obras tienen un tema social.

¡Así lo decimos! VOCABULARIO

📖 ¡Así es la vida! De compras
08-01

 En el centro comercial "El Progreso II" en Lima, Perú.
Son las diez de la mañana y empiezan a llegar los clientes.

EL DEPENDIENTE: Estos trajes están en rebaja.

LUIS: ¿Ah sí? Entonces, voy a probarme este traje de lana gris.

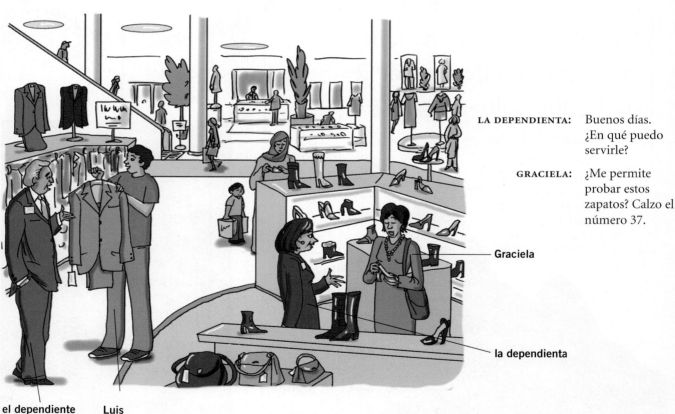

LA DEPENDIENTA: Buenos días. ¿En qué puedo servirle?

GRACIELA: ¿Me permite probar estos zapatos? Calzo el número 37.

Graciela

la dependienta

el dependiente   Luis

Vocabulario Las compras y la ropa

La ropa | Clothes

el abrigo	*coat*
la billetera	*wallet*
la blusa	*blouse*
el bolso	*handbag*
las botas	*boots*
los calcetines	*socks*
la camisa	*shirt*
la camiseta (sin mangas)	*t-shirt (tank top)*
las chanclas	*flip-flops*
la chaqueta	*jacket*
la corbata	*tie*
la (mini)falda	*(mini-)skirt*
la gorra	*baseball cap*
el gorro	*winter hat*
los pantalones (cortos)	*pants (shorts)*
las sandalias	*sandals*
la sudadera (con capucha)	*(hooded) sweatshirt*
el suéter	*sweater*
el traje	*suit*
los vaqueros	*jeans*
el vestido	*dress*
los zapatos (de tacón alto)	*(high-heeled) shoes*

Lugares donde compramos | Places where we shop

el almacén	*department store*
el centro comercial	*shopping center, mall*
el mercado (al aire libre)	*(open-air) market*
la tienda	*store, shop*

En una tienda | At a store

la caja	*register*
el/la cliente	*customer*
el/la dependiente/a	*sales clerk*
el descuento	*discount*
la ganga	*bargain, good deal*
el piso	*floor*
el precio	*price*
el probador	*fitting room*
el recibo	*receipt*
la tarjeta de crédito / débito	*credit / debit card*
la liquidación	*clearance sale*

Telas | Fabrics

el algodón	*cotton*
el cuero	*leather*
la lana	*wool*
la seda	*silk*

Variaciones

La chaqueta is typically a windbreaker. For suit jacket or blazer, use **el saco** in the Americas, or **una americana** in Spain.

Variaciones

Los vaqueros (literally *cowboys*) and **los jeans**, or **los tejanos** (lit. *Texans*) in Spain, **los pantalones de mezclilla** (*of mixed fibers*) in Mexico; **los mecánicos** in Cuba, and **los mahones** in Puerto Rico.

En invierno, ¿llevas gorra o gorro?

¿Están de moda las minifaldas?

Verbos | Verbs

estar en rebaja	*to be on sale*
llevar	*to wear*
pagar (en efectivo)	*to pay (cash)*
probarse (ue)[1]	*to try on*
regatear	*to bargain, haggle over*

Descripciones | Descriptions

de cuadros	*plaid*
de manga corta/larga	*short-/long-sleeved*
de moda	*in style*
de rayas	*striped*

Expresiones para comprar | Shopping expressions

¿En que puedo servirle(s)?	*How can I help you?*
Quiero / Me gustaría...	*I want / would like . . .*
¿Qué tal le queda?	*How does it fit?*
Me queda bien / estrecho/a / grande.	*It fits fine / small / large.*
¿Que número calza?	*What size shoe do you wear?*
¿Qué talla usa?	*What size do you wear?*

[1]In general, **probar** means *to try*. In *Capítulo 6* you learned **probar** in the context of food: *to try* or *to taste* food. In the reflexive construction, **probarse** is used to express *to try something on oneself*, usually referring to clothing.

¿Cuándo llevas camisa y corbata?

APLICACIÓN

8-1 ¿Dónde están? Si ves a estas personas vestidas de la manera descrita (*described*) a continuación, ¿dónde crees que están?

1. _____ El Sr. Domínguez lleva un traje azul oscuro, una camisa blanca y una corbata de seda, y tiene el celular en la mano.

2. _____ Raúl lleva pantalones cortos, una camiseta y unos tenis con calcetines blancos.

3. _____ Maripaz lleva un vestido rosado largo de seda y su amigo lleva un traje formal.

4. _____ Manolito lleva un traje de baño y chanclas.

5. _____ Carmen lleva vaqueros nuevos, un suéter de rayas, pero no lleva zapatos, solo calcetines.

6. _____ El Sr. Cisneros lleva mucha ropa en los brazos y tiene la tarjeta de crédito en la mano.

a. en el probador de un almacén
b. en una fiesta de quinceañera
c. en la playa
d. en las oficinas de un banco
e. en un partido de básquetbol
f. en la caja de una tienda

🔊 **8-2 En el almacén.** Escucha la conversación entre Manuel y la dependienta del almacén Saga Falabella. Primero, indica los productos que Manuel decide comprar; luego, escucha otra vez para escribir el precio de cada artículo. Recuerda que en Perú usan nuevos soles.

	Sí	No	Artículo	Precio
1.	☐	☐	calcetines	_____
2.	☐	☐	camisa	_____
3.	☐	☐	billetera	_____
4.	☐	☐	corbata	_____
5.	☐	☐	pantalones	_____
6.	☐	☐	chaqueta	_____
7.	☐	☐	suéter	_____
8.	☐	☐	traje	_____

Hay una liquidación en la tienda Chic.

8-3A ¿Tienes…?   ¿Qué compró Sara para su viaje a Machu Picchu? Túrnense para completar la información que falta en su recibo. Usen las siguientes preguntas para llenar su recibo: **¿Qué compró por…?; ¿Qué compró de la talla…?; ¿De qué talla es/son…?** Después confirmen las compras que hizo Sara y cuánto gastó. **Estudiante B,** por favor ve al **Apéndice 1**, página A-13.

MODELO: ESTUDIANTE A: *¿Qué compró por veinte nuevos soles?*

ESTUDIANTE B: *Compró una camiseta de algodón. ¿De qué talla es?*

ESTUDIANTE A: *Es de la talla cuarenta.*

ESTUDIANTE B: *Así que compró una camiseta de algodón de la talla cuarenta por veinte nuevos soles.*

Estudiante A:

falabella

DOCUMENTO DE VENTA

OUFDSYEVW9NGOLWI9TOD2OJ

Vendedor	T.T	EmpCent	Operac.	Fecha	Hora	EdPIZN	T
51106219	9	001006	0367886	12/12/2010	19:16	0100000	00

Descripción	Talla	Importe (NUEVOS SOLES)
camiseta de algodón	40	NS 20
blusa de manga corta	36	NS 50
vaqueros	_____	NS 75
suéter de lana	38	_____
chaqueta de cuero		NS 200
_____	39	NS 39
gorra roja	50	_____

TOTAL COMPRA NS

Gracias por su compra.
Visítenos en www.falabella.com

 8-4 ¿Qué llevas cuando?   Pregúntense qué ropa llevan en diferentes ocasiones.

MODELO: E1: *¿Qué llevas cuando tienes examen?*
E2: *Llevo vaqueros y una camiseta.*
E1: *Pues, yo llevo…*

Ocasión

1. asistes a un concierto de música rock
2. te invitan a la casa del jefe/de la jefa de tu departamento
3. visitas Alaska en enero
4. vas a nadar
5. haces una barbacoa en casa para unos amigos
6. juegas al tenis
7. trabajas como mesero/a
8. vas de vacaciones a Machu Picchu

8-5 En la tienda.   En grupos de tres, hagan los papeles de dependiente/a y de clientes en una tienda de ropa elegante. Usen las expresiones de **¡Así lo decimos!** en su conversación y traten de incluir algunas de las siguientes expresiones:

la caja	estar en rebaja	el probador
colores	número que calza	la talla
estilos	me queda / le queda	tarjeta de crédito

MODELO: DEPENDIENTE/A: *Buenas tardes. ¿En qué puedo servirles?*
CLIENTE 1: *Quiero ver…*
CLIENTE 2: *¿Me puede traer…?*

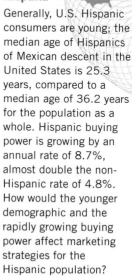

Presencia hispana

Generally, U.S. Hispanic consumers are young; the median age of Hispanics of Mexican descent in the United States is 25.3 years, compared to a median age of 36.2 years for the population as a whole. Hispanic buying power is growing by an annual rate of 8.7%, almost double the non-Hispanic rate of 4.8%. How would the younger demographic and the rapidly growing buying power affect marketing strategies for the Hispanic population?

¡Así lo hacemos! ESTRUCTURAS

1. The imperfect of regular and irregular verbs

08-09
to 08-15

En el pasado, mis padres siempre iban a Falabella y se probaban la ropa. Ahora la compran en la Internet.

El imperfecto de verbos regulares

You have already studied the preterit in **Capítulos 6** and **7.** Here you see the imperfect, another form of the simple past tense in Spanish.

- The imperfect of regular verbs is formed as follows:

	hablar	comer	escribir
yo	habl**aba**	com**ía**	escrib**ía**
tú	habl**abas**	com**ías**	escrib**ías**
Ud.	habl**aba**	com**ía**	escrib**ía**
él/ella	habl**aba**	com**ía**	escrib**ía**
nosotros/as	habl**ábamos**	com**íamos**	escrib**íamos**
vosotros/as	habl**abais**	com**íais**	escrib**íais**
Uds.	habl**aban**	com**ían**	escrib**ían**
ellos/as	habl**aban**	com**ían**	escrib**ían**

- With **-ar** verbs, only the first-person plural form has a written accent mark. The imperfect endings for **-er** and **-ir** verbs are identical, and all forms have a written accent mark.

- The Spanish imperfect has three common English equivalents: the simple past, the past progressive, and the *used to* + infinitive construction.

Rosario **trabajaba** en la tienda.
{ *Rosario worked at the store.*
Rosario was working at the store.
Rosario used to work at the store.

- Use the imperfect to describe repeated, habitual, or continuous actions in the past with no reference to the beginning or ending. Note that the imperfect of **hay** is **había.**

Cuando yo **trabajaba** en el almacén, **recibía** un descuento en todo lo que **compraba.**
When I worked at the department store, I received a discount on everything I bought.

No **había** nadie en el centro comercial ayer.
There was no one in the mall yesterday.

- Use the imperfect to describe an event or action in progress when another event or action takes place (in the preterit) or is occurring (in the imperfect).

Estábamos en la tienda cuando **llegaron** nuestras amigas.
We were in the store when our friends arrived.

Mientras Rosario **compraba** un bolso, Mauricio **miraba** los suéteres.
While Rosario was buying a purse, Mauricio was looking at the sweaters.

- Use the imperfect to describe characteristics or states of being (health, emotions, etc.) in the past when no particular beginning or ending is implied in the statement.

A mi abuela le **gustaba** pasear en bicicleta. **Tenía** mucha energía.
My grandmother liked to go on bike rides. She had a lot of energy.

Ella **estaba** muy contenta en Quito.
She was very happy in Quito.

- The imperfect generally is used with time and age in the past.

¿Qué hora **era** cuando llegaste?
What time was it when you arrived?

Cuando **tenía** diecisiete años, visité Ecuador.
When I was seventeen, I visited Ecuador.

Verbos irregulares en el imperfecto

There are only three verbs that are irregular in the imperfect.

	ir	ser	ver
yo	iba	era	veía
tú	ibas	eras	veías
Ud.	iba	era	veía
él/ella	iba	era	veía
nosotros/as	íbamos	éramos	veíamos
vosotros/as	ibais	erais	veíais
Uds.	iban	eran	veían
ellos/as	iban	eran	veían

- Only the first-person plural forms of **ir** and **ser** have a written accent mark; all forms of **ver** require a written accent.

Cuando yo era joven, veía a mis abuelos todas las semanas. Vivían cerca y yo iba en bicicleta a visitarlos.

APLICACIÓN

8-6 El reino inca. Aquí tienes una descripción de la gran civilización inca, la más importante de Sudamérica, que incluía lo que hoy es Perú y Ecuador.

Paso 1 Subraya los verbos en el imperfecto e identifica el infinitivo.

Cuando los españoles llegaron a Sudamérica, se encontraron con el reino inca, una civilización indígena muy avanzada. El reino inca se extendía desde la región cercana a la línea ecuatorial y a lo largo de la costa del Pacífico, hasta lo que hoy es el norte de Chile. Por el este se extendía a través de los Andes hasta partes de Argentina y Bolivia. Aquel inmenso imperio se llamaba Tahuantinsuyu en quechua, la lengua de los incas. Su nombre quería decir "las cuatro partes", que representaban los cuatro puntos cardinales: norte, sur, este y oeste. En su capital, Cuzco, ahora una ciudad importante de Perú, los incas construyeron edificios de enormes bloques de piedras[1] que se encajaban[2] tan perfectamente que no era posible insertar un cuchillo entre ellas. Aunque la arquitectura de los edificios era de aspecto severo, estos estaban adornados con planchas[3] y ornamentos de oro[4] y plata[5]. Para los incas el oro representaba "las lágrimas[6] del sol" y la plata, "las lágrimas de la luna". En el interior de los templos brillaban esos metales preciosos.

La fortaleza de Sacsahuamán fue construida en el siglo XV para proteger la ciudad de Cuzco.

[1]*stones* [2]*fitted* [3]*sheets* [4]*gold* [5]*silver* [6]*tears*

Paso 2 Ahora contesta las siguientes preguntas, basándote en la lectura.

1. ¿Cómo era el reino inca?

2. ¿Qué países de hoy formaban parte del reino?

3. ¿Qué lengua hablaban?

4. ¿Cuál era su capital?

5. ¿Qué decoraciones usaban en sus edificios?

6. ¿Qué representaba el oro para ellos? ¿Y la plata?

It is a common practice to bargain (*regatear*) with vendors in markets throughout the Spanish-speaking world; however, bargaining is less common in stores and almost unheard of in department stores. The buyer may offer up to a third less than the asking price, and the seller will respond with a higher price. The haggling continues until both parties are satisfied with the price. Bargaining etiquette requires that the buyer be serious about the purchase, not just curious about the price.

8-7 En el mercado de Otavalo. El mercado del pueblo de Otavalo, Ecuador, es famoso por sus artesanías, su comida típica y los turistas que lo visitan.

Paso 1 Usa el imperfecto de los verbos entre paréntesis para completar la entrada que escribió un turista en su diario cuando él y su hermana lo visitaron.

El pueblo de Otavalo está situado a tres horas de Quito. Ese día, (1) _____ (hacer) mucho calor y el cielo (2) _____ (estar) despejado. Nuestro taxista se (3) _____ (llamar) Ramón y (4) _____ (ser) muy simpático. Otavalo (5) _____ (parecer) una ciudad impresionante. (6) _____ (Haber) gente por todas partes vendiendo verduras, pollos, todo tipo de comida, ropa, etcétera. No (7) _____ (poder) creer el espectáculo tan agradable de colores y olores[1]. En uno de los puestos, algunas mujeres (8) _____ (comprar) pulseras[2]; en otro, un hombre (9) _____ (vender) camisas de algodón. Muchas personas (10) _____ (comprar) verduras: cebollas, ajos, etc. En un lugar, algunas personas (11) _____ (preparar) un cochinillo[3] a la parrilla. Por todas partes los clientes y los vendedores (12) _____ (regatear) el precio de sus cosas. Cuando por fin dejamos Otavalo, (13) _____ (ser) las dos de la tarde, la hora del almuerzo. (14) _____ (Estar) exhaustos, pero contentos.

_____

[1]*smells* [2]*bracelets* [3]*young pig*

Se puede comprar de todo en el mercado de Otavalo.

Paso 2 Ahora contesta las siguientes preguntas, basándote en el paso anterior.

1. ¿En qué país está Otavalo?

2. ¿Qué tiempo hacía ese día?

3. ¿Qué se vendía en el mercado?

4. ¿Qué comida había?

5. ¿Cómo se sentían los turistas al final del día?

6. ¿Qué crees que compraron en el mercado?

8-8A ¿Qué pasaba en el almacén ayer? Cada uno/a de ustedes tiene una versión diferente de lo que pasaba ayer en el almacén. Describan lo que ven en su dibujo para encontrar seis diferencias. **Estudiante B,** por favor ve al **Apéndice 1,** página A-14.

MODELO: ESTUDIANTE A: *Una mujer se probaba zapatos.*
ESTUDIANTE B: *Es cierto. Una mujer se probaba zapatos.*

Estudiante A:

8-9 Antes y ahora. ¿Cómo eran las cosas antes y cómo son ahora? Usen las listas de personas y contextos para escribir cinco oraciones. Después compárenlas. ¿Qué aspectos tienen en común?

MODELO: *Antes llevaba pantalones cortos en verano, pero ahora prefiero llevar vaqueros. ¿Y tú?*

Personas:	**Contextos:**
yo	las preferencias en la ropa
mi hermano/a y yo	las compras
mis padres	los pasatiempos
mi mejor amigo/a	los deportes
mis compañeros/as de clase	los hábitos de comer
¿...?	¿...?

8-10 La manera de vestirse. Los niños en esta foto viven cerca de Machu Picchu y se visten de una manera típica de la gente que vive en el altiplano de Perú. En un párrafo, describe la ropa que llevaban ese día. Después usa la imaginación y describe qué hacían antes de tomar esta foto.

MODELO: *Ese día las dos chicas llevaban ...*

En el altiplano de Perú

📖 2. Ordinal numbers

08-16 to 08-18

Puede usar el primer probador.

Ordinal numbers give the order in which things appear or events occur.

primero/a	*first*	**sexto/a**	*sixth*
segundo/a	*second*	**séptimo/a**	*seventh*
tercero/a	*third*	**octavo/a**	*eighth*
cuarto/a	*fourth*	**noveno/a**	*ninth*
quinto/a	*fifth*	**décimo/a**	*tenth*

• Ordinal numbers in Spanish agree in gender and number with the nouns they modify.

    Clarita compró un **segundo** vestido.   *Clarita bought a second dress.*

    Estas son las **primeras** rebajas del año.   *These are the first sales of the year.*

• **Primero** and **tercero** are shortened to **primer** and **tercer** before masculine singular nouns.

    La tienda está en el **tercer** piso.   *The store is on the third floor.*

    Juan es el **primer** dependiente en   *Juan is the first sales clerk*
      vender un abrigo de piel.   *to sell a fur coat.*

• In Spanish, ordinal numbers are rarely used after **décimo.** The cardinal numbers are used instead and follow the noun.

    La liquidación es en el piso **doce.**   *The clearance sale is on the twelfth floor.*

• The opposite of **primero** is **último.**

    Olga fue la **primera** en llegar.   *Olga was the first to arrive. Antonio*
    Antonio fue el **último.**   *was the last.*

APLICACIÓN

8-11A Atención al cliente (*Customer service*).   Cada uno/a de ustedes tiene información del directorio del almacén Saga Falabella. Túrnense para pedir información sobre dónde comprar los siguientes productos o cumplir (*carry out*) algún deber. Añadan más información cuando sea posible. **Estudiante B,** por favor ve al **Apéndice 1,** página A-14.

MODELO: una blusa para tu mamá

ESTUDIANTE A: *Quiero comprar una blusa para mi mamá porque es su cumpleaños.*

ESTUDIANTE B: *La puede buscar en el segundo piso, en Ropa de mujer.*

ESTUDIANTE A: *Muchas gracias.*

Estudiante A:

1. un sándwich y un refresco	4. sandalias de cuero
2. un traje para un evento formal	5. dónde solicitar trabajo
3. una corbata para tu tío	6. una raqueta de tenis

saga falabella.

1.ᵉʳ piso	
2.° piso *Ropa de mujer (trajes, vestidos, ropa informal)*	
3.ᵉʳ piso Ropa infantil (ambos sexos; tallas neonatal a 4)	
4.° piso	
5.° piso Todo para la casa (dormitorio, cocina, sala, comedor)	
6.° piso Muebles para la oficina Equipo electrónico Televisores	
7.° piso	
8.° piso Supermercado	
9.° piso Artículos en liquidación	
10.° piso Cambio de moneda Caja	

8-12 En orden de importancia. Individualmente, pongan los siguientes artículos en orden de importancia en este momento (de primero a décimo). Luego comparen sus resultados.

Mi lista		La lista de mi compañero/a
_____	una corbata de seda	_____
_____	unos zapatos de tacón alto	_____
_____	una camiseta de algodón	_____
_____	unas chanclas	_____
_____	un par de tenis	_____
_____	un traje de rayas	_____
_____	una gorra o un gorro	_____
_____	unos vaqueros	_____
_____	una chaqueta de esquiar	_____
_____	¿...?	_____

MODELO: *Primero, necesito comprar una camisa de manga larga, porque todas mis camisas son viejas. Segundo,... ¿Y tú?*

¿Cuánto saben?

Primero, pregúntate si puedes llevar a cabo (*carry out*) las siguientes funciones comunicativas en español. Después, júntate con dos o tres compañeros/as de clase para presentar las situaciones. Hagan y respondan a por lo menos cuatro preguntas en cada situación.

✓ CAN YOU . . .

☐ talk about clothes and shopping at a department store?

☐ talk about what used to happen and what you used to do in the past?

☐ describe a scene in the past?

WITH YOUR CLASSMATE(S) . . .

Situación: En un almacén
Están en un almacén para hacer algunas compras para una función importante. Expliquen qué quieren comprar, los colores, el estilo, la tela, la talla o el número, etc. Uno/a de ustedes es el/la dependiente/a que también explica en qué piso pueden buscar otros artículos.
Para empezar: *¿En qué puedo servirles?*

Situación: En la casa de un/a amigo/a
Usen el imperfecto para hablar de las cosas que les gustaba hacer cuando eran más jóvenes. Incluyan actividades que siempre hacían y actividades que nunca hacían, y por qué.
Para empezar: *Cuando era joven iba a las tiendas siempre con mi mamá.*

Situación: Las superestrellas
Describan lo que pasaba en tres fotos de una revista de superestrellas. Usen el imperfecto para describir la escena, la gente y su ropa.
Para empezar: *En esta foto...*

📖 Perfiles

08-24 to 08-25

Mi experiencia

DE COMPRAS EN PERÚ

8-13 Para ti. En EE. UU. y Canadá, ¿es típico comprar la comida o la ropa en mercados al aire libre? Explica. ¿Se cierran normalmente las tiendas de tu ciudad a la hora de almorzar? ¿Por qué? A continuación vas a leer una entrada que hizo María Antonia, una chica canadiense, en su primer viaje a Perú. Mientras lees, piensa en las diferencias que existen según tu experiencia.

¡Saludos desde Perú y gracias por leer mi blog! Como esta es mi primera visita a Sudamérica, me impresiona todo lo que veo, especialmente cómo se hacen las compras aquí en comparación con Toronto. Primero, todas las ciudades grandes tienen sus almacenes, pero las horas parecen más cortas, desde las once hasta las ocho. No son muchas horas, ¿verdad? También muchas de las tiendas pequeñas cierran para el almuerzo entre las dos y las cuatro. Por el contrario, hay mercados al aire libre, donde se puede comprar de todo, ropa, comida, artesanías y hasta animales. Pero entre estos dos casos hay también centros comerciales modernos al aire libre como el "Mall Aventura Plaza Trujillo" en Arequipa, el centro comercial más grande del interior del país. Es un lugar de encuentro social donde puedes comprar, pasear o sentarte a ver pasar a la gente. (Aquí me compré el suéter de alpaca que llevo puesto en esta foto). El ambiente[1] es muy agradable: no solo se toca música popular por los audio parlantes[2], sino también hay un escenario donde invitan a músicos a dar conciertos. Así es como conocí la música de Yawar, que aquí es un conjunto muy popular. Seguramente voy a comprar varios discos compactos de ellos antes de volver a mi casa en septiembre.

[1]*atmosphere*   [2]*speakers*

8-14 En su opinión. Conversen sobre los siguientes temas.

- ¿Dónde prefieren comprar? ¿En tiendas especializadas, en almacenes grandes o en tiendas de segunda mano?
- ¿Prefieren los centros comerciales cubiertos (*enclosed*) o los al aire libre? ¿Por qué?
- ¿Con qué frecuencia van a los centros comerciales? Además de comprar, ¿qué más hacen allí?
- Según su experiencia, ¿en qué situaciones se acepta regatear? ¿En la compra de carros, de casas, en un mercado callejero (*fleamarket*), en una tienda de aparatos electrónicos, una tienda de segunda mano...?
- ¿Prefieren tener la opción de regatear o prefieren pagar lo que les pide el vendedor?

Mi música

"COMPAÑERA" (YAWAR, PERÚ)

Este grupo musical, conocido por todo Perú y Bolivia, toma su nombre *Yawar* de una antigua tradición de los incas. El grupo Yawar se conoce por su original mezcla de ritmos andinos y contemporáneos, en los cuales predominan instrumentos como la zampoña (*panpipe*) y la quena (un tipo de flauta).

Antes de ver y escuchar

8-15 "Compañera". A continuación hay algunas palabras y expresiones que vas a escuchar en esta canción. Emparéjalas con sus significados y después adivina (*guess*) el tema de la canción.

1. _____ despedirme   a. soul

2. _____ vida eterna   b. without your kisses

3. _____ una luz que ilumina c. hope

4. _____ alma   d. emotions

5. _____ emociones   e. my pain

6. _____ esperanza   f. a light that shines

7. _____ mi pena   g. say good-bye

8. _____ sin tus besos   h. eternal life

¿Cuál es el tema?

Para ver y escuchar

 8-16 La canción. Conéctate a la Internet para ver un video de "Compañera". ¿Cuáles de estos instrumentos escuchas o ves?

> **Busca:** video yawar companera; letra yawar companera
>
> **Si te interesa comprar la canción:** Go to iTunes Store>Music>More to Explore> iMix>Arriba 6e

_____ el piano   _____ la guitarra   _____ la quena   _____ la zampoña

_____ la batería (*drums*)   _____ la pandereta (*tambourine*)

Después de ver y escuchar

8-17 Una carta de despedida. Escribe una breve carta para explicar por qué tienes que despedirte de tu amor. Incluye por lo menos dos ejemplos con el pretérito y el imperfecto y algunas de las expresiones de la actividad **8-15**.

MODELO: *Cariño:*

Te llamé hoy para decirte que te quiero, pero no estabas en casa. Te quería decir que tengo que irme por un tiempo. Pasé por tu casa pero...

Segunda parte

¡Así lo decimos! VOCABULARIO

📖 ¡Así es la vida! ¿Qué hiciste hoy?

 Victoria no estaba en casa cuando Lucía la llamó por la mañana.

LUCÍA: Oye, Victoria, esta mañana te llamé tres veces al celular, pero no contestaste. ¿Dónde estabas? ¿Qué hiciste hoy?

VICTORIA: Disculpa. Iba a llamarte pero no pude porque tenía que ir de compras. Estaba en el centro comercial y mi celular no tenía buena recepción. Quería comprar una cadena de plata para mi mamá, pero había un montón de gente y estuve en la joyería toda la mañana. Luego fui a la farmacia a comprar unas cosas. Ahora estoy en una perfumería porque necesito jabón y loción. ¿Dónde estás tú?

LUCÍA: En frente de la heladería Veintiún Sabores. ¿Por qué no vienes para acá y tomamos un helado?

🔊 **Vocabulario** Tiendas y productos personales

En la farmacia o perfumería	In the pharmacy or beauty supply shop

el cepillo de dientes   *toothbrush*
la colonia   *cologne*
el desodorante   *deodorant*
la pasta de dientes   *toothpaste*
el perfume   *perfume*
el talco   *talcum powder*

En la joyería	In the jewelry store

el anillo   *ring*
los aretes   *earrings*
la cadena   *chain*
el collar   *necklace*
la pulsera   *bracelet*
el reloj de pulsera   *wristwatch*

Descripciones	Descriptions

de diamantes   *diamond*
de oro   *gold*
de perlas   *pearl*
de plata   *silver*

Más tiendas	More shops

la florería   *flower shop*
la heladería   *ice cream shop*
la papelería   *stationery shop*
la zapatería   *shoe store*

Verbos	Verbs

devolver (ue)   *to return (something)*
gastar   *to spend*
hacer juego (con)   *to match, to go well with*

Variaciones
In Spain, **floristería** is used in place of **florería.**

Variaciones
In Mexico, there are many variations on **heladería.** For example, **una nevería** sells **nieve** (a water-based product like sherbet), and **una paletería** sells **paletas** (water- or cream-based frozen bars on sticks).

Los aretes hacen juego con el collar de perlas.

¿Llevas muchas pulseras?

Se compran flores en una florería.

¿Qué compras en una perfumería?

Letras y sonidos

The sequences *j*, *ge*, *gi*, and *x*

In Spanish, the letter **j**, as well as **g** before the vowels **e** and **i**, all correspond to the same sound, the *h* sound in English *hip:*

jo-ya   tra-je   re-loj   ge-ne-ro-so   gim-na-sio

In some Spanish words, the letter **x** also has the *h* sound:

Mé-xi-co   Xa-vier

In most cases, however, the letter **x** creates two sounds, *k* and *s*, as in English *extra:*

exigente → (e[*k-s*]i-gen-te)   extra → (e[*ks*]-tra)

APLICACIÓN

8-18 Las tiendas especializadas.   Aquí tienes unas tiendas especializadas. Emparéjalas con las cosas que venden.

1. _____ la farmacia
2. _____ la joyería
3. _____ la perfumería
4. _____ la florería
5. _____ la zapatería
6. _____ la librería
7. _____ la papelería
8. _____ la heladería

a. un collar de esmeraldas
b. un helado
c. una novela
d. penicilina
e. rosas
f. invitaciones
g. colonia
h. unas sandalias

¿Qué se puede comprar en esta farmacia?

8-19 ¡Yo también fui de compras!   Lucía también fue de compras ayer. Escucha e indica las tiendas que visitó, los artículos que compró y los que devolvió.

Tiendas	Compró	Devolvió
_____ el almacén	_____ una agenda	_____
_____ la farmacia	_____ una blusa	_____
_____ la joyería	_____ unas sandalias	_____
_____ la papelería	_____ una camisa	_____
_____ la perfumería	_____ talco	_____
_____ la librería	_____ desodorante	_____
_____ el supermercado	_____ un té especial	_____
_____ la zapatería	_____ un frasco de colonia	_____
_____ la tienda pequeña	_____ una torta de queso	_____
_____ la heladería	_____ una falda	_____
_____ la florería	_____ un libro de arte	_____
_____ la panadería (*bakery*)	_____ un reloj	_____

8-20 ¿Hacen juego? Decidan si estos artículos hacen juego. Si no, cámbienlos.

MODELO: un traje de baño y zapatos de cuero
No hacen juego. Es mejor llevar chanclas con un traje de baño.

1. una camisa de cuadros y pantalones de rayas

2. un vestido de seda y botas de cuero

3. un collar de oro y aretes de plata

4. unas sandalias con calcetines

5. unos vaqueros y tenis

6. una gorra y un traje

7. unos vaqueros y aretes de diamantes

8. unos zapatos negros de cuero con calcetines de rayas rojas y blancas

8-21 ¿En qué tiendas compras? Conversen sobre dónde hacen las compras para las siguientes cosas y por qué.

MODELO: *Me gusta comprar helado en la heladería La Crema que está en mi ciudad porque tiene veintiún sabores deliciosos.*

la ropa informal de todos los días

la ropa elegante

las bebidas para una fiesta

un regalo para una persona especial

los productos de higiene personal

la comida

los libros para la universidad

un postre para una cena especial

 8-22 De compras en Lima. Conéctate a la Internet y busca información acerca de una tienda especializada. Escoge (*Choose*) un producto que te interese y contesta las preguntas que siguen.

> **Busca:** donde comprar en lima; donde comprar (perfume, flores, pan, ropa, zapatos, etc.) lima

1. ¿Cuál es el producto?

2. ¿Cómo es?

3. ¿Dónde se vende?

Centro Comercial Largo Mar en Miraflores, Lima, Perú

¡Así lo hacemos! ESTRUCTURAS

3. Preterit versus imperfect

08-34
to 08-40

In Spanish, the use of the preterit and the imperfect reflects the way the speaker views the action or event being expressed in the past. A comparison of their uses follows.

¿Viste las cadenas tan preciosas que llevaba esa chica?

Sí, ¿y viste los aretes? Eran muy bonitos.

The preterit . . .

1. narrates actions or events in the past that the speaker views as completed or finished.

    Victoria y Lucía **hablaron** por teléfono por dos horas.

    Victoria and Lucía talked on the phone for two hours.

2. expresses the beginning or end of a past event or action.

    El zapatero **llegó** a las cinco.

    The shoemaker arrived at five.

    La película **terminó** a las ocho de la noche.

    The movie ended at eight at night.

3. narrates completed events that occurred in a series.

    Carlos **entró** en la farmacia, **vio** a su exnovia y **salió** inmediatamente.

    Carlos entered the pharmacy, saw his ex-girlfriend, and left immediately.

4. expresses changes in mental, physical, and emotional conditions or states in the past.

    Alejandra **se puso** furiosa cuando **vio** el cuarto en desorden.

    Alejandra became furious when she saw the messy room.

    Estuve nerviosa durante la entrevista.

    I was nervous during the interview (but now I'm not).

5. describes weather and scenes as events or within specific time parameters.

    Ayer **fue** un día horrible. **Llovió** e **hizo** mucho viento.

    Yesterday was a horrible day. It rained and was very windy.

The imperfect . . .

1. describes what was happening in the past, usually in relation to another event or at a given time, with no reference to the beginning or end of an action.

    Rosa **hablaba** mientras **miraba** las compras.

    Rosa was talking while she was looking at her purchases.

2. expresses habitual actions or events in the past.

    Pedro **comía** en ese restaurante todos los sábados.

    Pedro used to eat at that restaurant every Saturday.

    Ana **iba** de compras todo el tiempo.

    Ana used to go shopping all the time.

3. expresses time or age in the past.

    Eran las once de la noche.

    It was eleven in the evening.

    Teníamos seis años en el 2000.

    We were six years old in 2000.

4. expresses mental, physical, and emotional conditions or states in the past.

    Alicia **estaba** contenta durante el concierto.

    Alicia was happy during the concert.

    Nos **sentíamos** mal después de comer allí.

    We felt sick after eating there.

5. sets the scene (weather, activities in progress, etc.) for other actions and events that take place.

> **Hacía** muy mal tiempo y **llovía.**   *The weather was bad and it was raining.*
> Yo **leía** en mi cuarto y **esperaba**   *I was reading in my room and waiting*
> la llamada.   *for the call.*

- The preterit and the imperfect are often used together. In the following examples, the imperfect describes what was happening or in progress when another action (in the preterit) interrupted and took place.

> **Conversábamos** con el   *We were talking with the sales clerk when*
> dependiente cuando Lourdes   *Lourdes entered the jewelry store.*
> **entró** en la joyería.
>
> Las chicas **salían** de la tienda   *The girls were leaving the store when Jorge*
> cuando Jorge las **vio.**   *saw them.*

Study Tips — Distinguishing between the preterit and the imperfect

1. Analyze the context in which the verb will be used and decide whether the verb describes the way things were (imperfect) or it tells what happened (preterit).

> **Era** de noche cuando **volvieron** a casa.
> **Era:** describes → *It was nighttime. (Imperfect)*
> **volvieron:** tells what happened → *They returned. (Preterit)*

2. In many instances, both aspects produce a grammatical sentence. Your choice will depend on the message you are communicating.

> Así **fue.**   *That's how it happened.*
> Así **era.**   *That's how it used to be.*
> Ayer **fue** un día   *Yesterday was a horrible day. (This is the*
> horrible.   *point; it's not background information.)*
> **Era** un día horrible.   *It was a horrible day. (This is background*
>   *information for the actions that will be*
>   *narrated.)*

3. Here are some temporal expressions that are frequently (but not always) associated with the imperfect and preterit.

Preterit	**Imperfect**
anoche	a menudo
anteayer	con frecuencia
ayer	de vez en cuando
de repente (*suddenly*)	mientras
esta mañana	frecuentemente
el fin de semana pasado	todos los lunes/martes/...
el mes pasado	todas las semanas
el lunes/martes/... pasado	todos los días/meses
una vez	muchas veces
siempre (*when an end point is obvious*)	siempre (*when an event is repeated with no particular end point*)

APLICACIÓN

8-23 Guayasamín. Este artista se destaca (*stands out*) por su dedicación a los derechos humanos.

Paso 1 Lee la selección sobre el famoso artista ecuatoriano Oswaldo Guayasamín. Después haz una lista con los verbos en el pretérito y otra lista con los verbos en el imperfecto.

Guayasamín en su estudio

Oswaldo Guayasamín nació en Quito el 6 de julio de 1919. De niño, su familia era muy pobre. Se graduó de pintor y escultor en la Escuela de Bellas Artes de Quito. Realizó su primera exposición cuando tenía veintitrés años, en 1942. Durante su vida, recibió muchos premios[1] nacionales y varios internacionales. Tuvo una vida artística muy productiva: hizo cuadros, murales, esculturas y monumentos.

Toda su vida, Guayasamín simpatizó con ideales comunistas y apoyó[2] causas socialistas. Sin embargo, siempre estuvo en contra de todo tipo de violencia. Su obra humanista quiso reflejar la miseria que sufría la mayor parte de la humanidad.

Murió el 10 de marzo de 1999, a los setenta y nueve años, antes de poder terminar la obra que él consideraba su más importante: *La capilla[3] del hombre.*

---

[1]*prizes*   [2]*supported*   [3]*chapel*

Paso 2 Ahora explica por qué se usa el pretérito versus el imperfecto en la biografía de Guayasamín en **Paso 1.**

MODELO: *nació: completed event*

Paso 3 ¿Comprendiste? Contesta las siguientes preguntas basadas en el texto anterior sobre Guayasamín.

1. ¿Dónde y en qué año nació?

2. ¿Cuántos años tenía cuando murió?

3. ¿Con qué causas se identificó durante su vida?

4. ¿Qué honores recibió durante su vida?

5. ¿Qué quiso reflejar Guayasamín en su obra humanista?

6. ¿En qué trabajaba cuando murió?

8-24 Las obras de Guayasamín. Conéctate a la Internet para ver otras obras de Guayasamín. Describe una de sus obras, contestando las preguntas que siguen.

> **Busca:** museo guayasamin

1. ¿Qué tipo de obra es?

2. ¿Qué colores predominan en la obra?

3. ¿Es una imagen triste o alegre? ¿Optimista o pesimista? Explica.

8-25 Una escena en el mercado. Completa el párrafo con la forma correcta del verbo entre paréntesis en el pretérito o el imperfecto, según el contexto.

Cuando llegamos al mercado ese día (1) _____ (había/hubo) mucha actividad: un vendedor de fruta (2) _____ (vendía/vendió) mangos y plátanos. Una artesana (3) _____ (mostraba/mostró) sus tejidos[1] de alpaca. Muchos niños (4) _____ (jugaban/jugaron) en la plaza. De repente, (5) _____ (llegaban/llegaron) algunas nubes muy oscuras y el cielo (6) _____ (se ponía/se puso) muy gris. Luego (7) _____ (empezaba/empezó) a llover y el viento (8) _____ (soplaba/sopló)[2] violentamente. Cuando vino la lluvia, los niños (9) _____ (corrían/corrieron) a sus casas. Los vendedores (10) _____ (cerraron/cerraban) sus puestos[3] y los artesanos (11) _____ (cubrieron/cubrían)[4] sus artículos. La tempestad (12) _____ (duraba/duró) media hora y después, todo (13) _____ (continuaba/continuó) como antes.

————
[1]weavings [2]blew [3]stalls [4]covered

8-26 ¿Cómo era Otavalo? Un amigo te cuenta de su viaje a Otavalo. Combina una frase de la primera columna con una terminación lógica para completar su descripción. Usa el imperfecto del verbo en la primera columna y el pretérito en la segunda columna. Hay más de una combinación posible.

MODELO: **ser** temprano cuando…
Era temprano cuando llegamos a Otavalo.

Lo que pasaba

1. (nosotros/as) **llegar** al mercado cuando…
2. (nosotros/as) **mirar** las camisas de algodón cuando…
3. (nosotros/as) **estar** regateando con la vendedora cuando…
4. (nosotros/as) **pagarle** la camisa cuando…
5. **ser** las doce del día, por eso…
6. **ser** tarde

Lo que ocurrió

• **decidir** almorzar un plato típico
• (ella) **ofrecernos** un precio mucho mejor
• ella **querer** vendernos otra
• **irse** de Otavalo y **regresar** al hotel
• la vendedora **venir** a hablarnos
• **ver** todos los puestos (*stalls*) y las artesanías

8-27 Queríamos… Túrnense para completar las oraciones, indicando lo que querían hacer y lo que hicieron según el contexto. Vean los modelos.

MODELOS: Iba a… esta noche pero…
Iba a ver a mi novio esta noche pero me llamó y me dijo que estaba cansado.
quería… mientras…
Yo quería estudiar mientras escuchaba música.

1. Ayer venía a clase cuando…

2. Una vez el año pasado…

3. Cuando era más joven, frecuentemente…

4. Esta mañana iba a… pero…

5. Muchas veces en el pasado…

6. Ayer tenía ganas de… mientras…

8-28A Artículos encontrados. Ustedes trabajan en la oficina de Artículos encontrados en un almacén. Comparen lo que encontraron con lo que la gente perdió. Cada uno/a tiene parte de la información. **Estudiante B,** por favor ve al **Apéndice 1,** página A-14.

MODELOS: un guante
ESTUDIANTE A: *Encontré un guante.*
ESTUDIANTE B: *¿Era pequeño?*
ESTUDIANTE A: *Sí, era pequeño y de lana.*
ESTUDIANTE B: *Ah, una señora perdió un guante pequeño de cuero. No es de ella.*

Estudiante A:

Encontré:	Alguien perdió:	¿Se encontró?
Modelo: un guante (pequeño; de lana)	• Una señora perdió un guante (pequeño; de cuero)	NO
1. una camisa (azul; talla 40)	• Una chica perdió un bolso (rojo; con una billetera negra)	
2. unas sandalias (amarillas; de tacón alto)	• Una mujer perdió un collar (de oro; largo)	
3. unos vaqueros (de mujer; talla mediana)	• Un chico perdió un zapato (de tenis; número 9; de hombre)	
4. unos calcetines (de algodón; de niño)	• Un joven perdió una camiseta (de algodón; que decía "Ecuador"; roja)	
5. una sudadera (negra; con capucha)	• Una mujer perdió una blusa (blanca; de seda; talla 12)	

📖 4. Impersonal constructions with *se*

Impersonal constructions with **se** are commonly used on signs and in instructions and rules in order to attribute actions to no one in particular.

- Use **se** and the third-person singular of the verb in statements attributed to no one in particular. These are generally followed by an infinitive, a clause introduced by **que,** or an adverb.

  Se prohíbe fumar en el almacén.

  Smoking is prohibited in the department store.

  Se dice que hay una liquidación hoy en la zapatería León.

  They say there is a liquidation sale today in the Leon shoe store.

  Se compra bien en Saga Falabella.

  You (One, They) buy well in Saga Falabella.

¿Qué se prohíbe en el Canal?

- Use the pronoun **se** and the third-person singular or plural form of the verb as a substitute for the passive voice in Spanish to say what is done (see Appendix 2). Notice that the subject of the verb is the object/s that is/are offered, sold, seen, bought, and so on.

  Se ofrecen descuentos en la Internet.

  Discounts are offered on the Internet.

  Se encontró el anillo en el probador.

  The ring was found in the dressing room.

  Se vendían artículos de segunda mano en esta tienda.

  Second-hand articles used to be sold in this store.

APLICACIÓN

8-29 **Un concierto al aire libre.** ¿Te gusta esuchar música al aire libre? Aquí tienes información sobre un concierto de música andina.

Paso 1 Primero, subraya las expresiones con una construcción impersonal con **se**.

Si a usted le apasiona la música andina, lo invitamos este fin de semana a este gran concierto que se conoce como uno de los mejores del mundo y donde se escucha la música más típica de Perú y de Ecuador. Como recuerdo, se venden programas con bellas fotos de los músicos de este espectáculo. La taquilla donde se venden los boletos se abre a las nueve de la mañana y se cierra a las ocho de la noche. Además, se ofrece una gran variedad de precios. Se recibe un descuento si se compran más de cinco boletos. Después del concierto, se puede pasear por los jardines, tomar una copa de champán y conocer a algunos de los músicos.

GRAN CONCIERTO DE
música andina

VENGA Y VEA EL ESPECTÁCULO

sábado, 13 de octubre • 20:00 h
Teatro Municipal

Paso 2 Ahora contesta las siguientes preguntas, basándote en la actividad anterior.

1. ¿Qué se anuncia?

2. ¿Entre qué horas se puede comprar boletos?

3. ¿Cómo son los precios que se ofrecen?

4. ¿Qué tipo de música se oye?

5. ¿Qué más se puede comprar durante el concierto?

6. ¿Qué se hace después del concierto?

8-30 **¿Qué se hace?** Pregúntense si se hacen las siguientes actividades en su universidad o ciudad. Incluyan otros detalles en sus preguntas para poder hablar más sobre estos temas.

MODELO: permitir fumar en esta universidad
¿Se permite fumar en esta universidad? ¿Dónde? ¿Por qué? ¿Cuándo?

- permitir fumar en tu apartamento

- permitir animales domésticos en tu apartamento

- comer bien en tu casa

- poder pasear por la noche en esta ciudad sin tener que preocuparse

- decir que es tradicional o liberal esta ciudad

- dar descuentos a estudiantes en los restaurantes cerca de la universidad

8-31A **Ofertas de esta semana.** Cada uno/a de ustedes tiene parte de un anuncio sobre las ofertas de esta semana en el almacén. Usen una construcción impersonal con **se** en sus preguntas sobre los artículos, los descuentos y los precios para conseguir la información que falta. Empiecen con los artículos que necesitan de su lista.

Estudiante B, por favor ve al **Apéndice 1,** página A-15.

MODELO: cadenas de plata

ESTUDIANTE A: *¿Se venden cadenas de plata?*

ESTUDIANTE B: *Sí, se venden cadenas de plata en el departamento de joyería.*

ESTUDIANTE A: *¿Qué descuentos se dan?*

ESTUDIANTE B: *Se dan descuentos del 25 al 50 por ciento.*

Saga Falabella, Buenos Aires, Argentina

Estudiante A:

Saga Falabella Ofertas Fin de Temporada		
Ofertas por departamento	**Artículos que necesito**	**Descuentos que recibo**
MODELO: *Joyería: Plata y oro: cadenas, aretes... Descuentos del 25% al 50%*	*cadenas de plata*	*del 25% al 50%*
Joyería: Todo menos relojes de pulsera, descuentos del 25% al 50%		
Departamento juvenil:	ropa de niños para el invierno	
Departamento para mujeres chic: Blusas, faldas, vaqueros de diseñador, descuentos del 25%		
Departamento para hombres:	camisas de talla 34 corbatas de seda	
Departamento de calzado: Zapatos tenis, sandalias, calcetines, descuentos del 30% al 50%		
Departamento deportivo:	raquetas de tenis esquís acuáticos	

8-32 Planes para este fin de semana. Hagan planes para hacer algo interesante este fin de semana. Usen una construcción impersonal con **se** para hablar de las posibilidades y hacer sus planes. A continuación tienen algunas expresiones que pueden usar.

se dice que…	se vende(n)…	se necesita(n)…
se cree que…	se abre(n)…	(no) se permite…
se anuncia(n)…	se puede…	¿…?

MODELO: E1: *Se dice que el sábado hay un concierto de Taylor Swift en el estadio de la universidad. ¿Sabes dónde se venden las entradas?*

E2: *Creo que se venden entradas en la Internet o en la taquilla… Se cree que ella…*

08-45
to 08-50

¿Cuánto saben?

Primero, pregúntate si puedes llevar a cabo las siguientes funciones comunicativas en español. Después, júntate con dos o tres compañeros/as de clase para presentar las situaciones. Hagan y respondan a por lo menos cuatro preguntas en cada situación.

✓ CAN YOU . . .

☐ shop for personal care products?

☐ contrast what happened in the past with something else that was going on?

☐ talk about what people say, believe, sell, etc.?

☐ talk about what is done?

WITH YOUR CLASSMATE(S) . . .

Situación: De compras
Uno/a de ustedes necesita comprar varios artículos personales. Explica qué quieres comprar y para quién(es), y decide entre varias opciones. El/la dependiente/a siempre quiere venderles los artículos más caros. Usen el vocabulario y las expresiones de **¡Así lo decimos!**
Para empezar: *Necesito comprar champú y pasta de dientes para mi compañera de cuarto. ¿Tiene alguna rebaja?*

Situación: Un evento importante
Hablen sobre lo que hacían cuando algo importante ocurrió en el pasado, por ejemplo, recibieron alguna noticia importante, anunciaron la muerte de una persona importante o los resultados de una elección política, tuvieron un accidente, etc. Usen expresiones como **anoche, el año pasado, ayer, mientras, de repente,** etc., para describir la acción.
Para empezar: *Ayer veía la televisión cuando de repente anunciaron…*

Situación: Mi tienda favorita
Hablen sobre las mejores tiendas de su ciudad donde pueden comprar los mejores productos por un precio bueno, etc. Usen expresiones como **se dice, se cree,** etc.
Para empezar: *Se dice que este almacén es el más barato de esta ciudad. ¿Estás de acuerdo?*

Situación: Mis productos favoritos
Hablen sobre los mejores productos personales, dónde y por cuánto se venden. Usen expresiones como **se vende, se ofrece, se abre,** etc.
Para empezar: *En mi opinión, el mejor champú se vende en el salón Bello…*

Observaciones

08-51 to 08-54

¡Pura vida! EPISODIO 8

En este episodio Silvia y Marcela van de compras.

Antes de ver el video

8-33 El regateo en los mercados. Lee la explicación de cómo es el regateo en Latinoamérica y contesta las siguientes preguntas.

> En Costa Rica existe la costumbre de regatear el precio de los productos que se venden en los mercados centrales: hamacas[1], sandalias de cuero, platos de cerámica, gorras, joyas, ropa y hasta verduras y comida. El regateo es especialmente intenso en las tiendas de artesanías[2], en las que se venden pequeñas carretas pintadas de colores vivos y otros objetos de madera[3]. Es importante no mostrar mucho interés en el producto que deseas comprar y ofrecer un precio bajo para negociar con el vendedor el precio del producto. El precio final depende de la habilidad de cada cliente.

[1]*hammocks* [2]*crafts* [3]*wood*

En Costa Rica se pintan las carretas (*oxcarts*) de colores vivos.

1. ¿Qué se regatea en Costa Rica?

2. ¿Qué productos se regatean?

3. ¿Qué es importante hacer cuando se regatea?

A ver el video

 8-34 Las compras. Mira el octavo episodio de **¡Pura vida!** para identificar qué compran Silvia y Marcela y para quién lo compran, según el video.

El artículo	¿Lo compra?	¿Para quién?
un arco y una flecha		
unos aretes		
una pieza de madera		
sandalias de cuero		
una blusa		

La vendedora   **De compras**   **Marcela y Silvia**

Después de ver el video

 8-35 Los mercados. Conéctate a la Internet para ver imágenes de mercados en Ecuador y Costa Rica. Escribe un párrafo de por lo menos siete líneas en que describas los productos que veas.

> **Busca:** foto mercado ecuador; foto mercado peru

Panoramas

 ## El reino inca: Perú y Ecuador

08-55
to 08-56

El archipiélago de las Islas Galápagos es famoso por su exquisita variedad de vida marítima y terrestre. Es aquí también donde se encuentra el Centro de Investigación Charles Darwin. Hoy en día, el gobierno ecuatoriano coopera con los movimientos ecológicos para estudiar y proteger las especies únicas, como el galápago (*giant tortoise*), el booby con patas azules (*blue-footed booby*) y la iguana marina.

Según la leyenda, el Padre Sol (que se llamaba Inti Tayta) creó la civilización inca en el lago Titicaca. Los habitantes de esta región conservan sus antiguas tradiciones, incluyendo la construcción y uso de barcos de juncos (*reeds*) del lago.

Una experiencia inolvidable es seguir el Camino Inca por Perú en un viaje de cuatro días. La mejor estación del año para hacer esta excursión es durante la temporada seca: de mayo a octubre. Antes de empezar la excursión, es importante acostumbrarte a la altura de 2.380 m.

Ecuador, tierra de volcanes activos, densas selvas, aguas termales y extravagantes vistas.

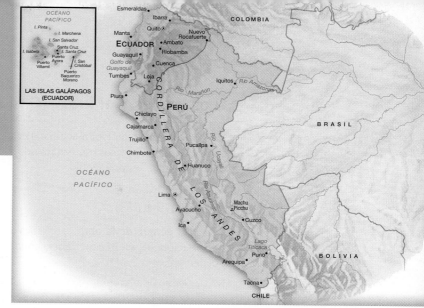

Perú y Ecuador

	Perú	Ecuador
Población:	20,5 millones	14,6 millones
Lenguas:	español, quechua (oficiales); aimara y otras lenguas amazónicas	español (oficial); idiomas amerindios, especialmente quechua
Tarjetas de crédito:	En almacenes y restaurantes grandes; no en mercados ni en restaurantes pequeños.	No en tiendas pequeñas, en mercados, ni en las Islas Galápagos.
Cajeros automáticos[1]:	En todas partes; pero se cobra una comisión del 2% al 3% por uso internacional.	

[1]ATMs

8-36 Identifica. Identifica, describe y/o explica lo siguiente.

1. el científico inglés que hizo investigaciones en las Islas Galápagos
2. un animal protegido en las Islas Galápagos
3. una civilización antigua de América del Sur
4. el dios creador (*creator*) de los incas
5. dónde se encuentra el Camino Inca

8-37 Desafío. Consulta el mapa y la caja para identificar lo siguiente.

1. la capital de Ecuador y la de Perú
2. los países en las fronteras de Perú y de Ecuador
3. dónde se permite usar tarjetas de crédito
4. cuánto se cobra cuando se usa el cajero automático
5. dónde se encuentra el lago Titicaca

 8-38 Proyecto. Escoge uno de los siguientes temas: **música andina, Nazca, Cuzco, Cuenca, Islas Galápagos, la comida** u otro que te interese, para investigar más sobre uno de estos países. Usa el Modelo para escribir un resumen en que incluyas lo siguiente:

- su nombre y dónde se encuentra
- por qué es importante o interesante
- cómo era en el pasado; cómo es ahora
- si quieres visitarlo o verlo algún día y por qué
- si piensas estudiar más sobre este tema
- una foto representativa

> **Busca:** musica andina; nazca; comida peru (ecuador); cuzco; cuenca ecuador

MODELO: *Quito es la capital de Ecuador. Se encuentra a una altura de 2.850 metros y está rodeada de las altas montañas de los Andes...*

**Páginas**

"Los rivales y el juez" (Ciro Alegría, Perú)

Ciro Alegría nació en Huamachuco, Perú, en 1909 y murió en 1967. Vivió muchos años entre los indígenas y sus obras dan vida y validez a sus tradiciones y a su folklore. "Los rivales y el juez" es una fábula.

ANTES DE LEER

8-39 El género de la obra. Si sabes el género (*genre*), puedes anticipar cierta información. Según tu experiencia con las fábulas, ¿cuáles de estas características se pueden aplicar?

_____ Tiene una lección.
_____ Los personajes son dioses.
_____ Es algo que realmente ocurrió.
_____ Los personajes son animales generalmente.

8-40 ¿Quiénes son? Aquí tienes los personajes de esta fábula. Empareja el personaje con su descripción.

El sapo

La cigarra

La garza

1. _____ el sapo   a. pequeña, negra, seis patas

2. _____ la cigarra   b. alta, gris, elegante, pico largo

3. _____ la garza   c. bajo, verde o pardo, cuatro patas, feo

8-41 Para pensar. Piensa en una fábula en inglés y da la información a continuación.

1. el nombre de un escritor de fábulas

2. el nombre en inglés de una fábula famosa

3. el nombre de un personaje ufano (*conceited*)

A LEER

8-42 La historia. Lee la siguiente fábula para saber qué les pasó al sapo, a la cigarra y a la garza.

> ### "Los rivales y el juez°"
>
> Un sapo estaba muy ufano° de su voz y toda la noche se la pasaba cantando:
> toc, toc, toc.
>
> Y una cigarra estaba más ufana de su voz, y se pasaba toda la noche y también todo el día
> cantando: chirr, chirr, chirr.
>
> Una vez se encontraron y el sapo le dijo: "Mi voz es mejor".
>
> Y la cigarra contestó: "La mía es mejor".
>
> Se armó una discusión que no tenía cuándo acabar°.
>
> El sapo decía que él cantaba toda la noche.
>
> La cigarra decía que ella cantaba día y noche.
>
> El sapo decía que su voz se oía a más distancia y la cigarra que su voz se oía siempre.
>
> Se pusieron a cantar alternándose: toc, toc, toc; chirr, chirr, chirr y ninguno se convencía.
>
> Y el sapo dijo: "Por aquí a la orilla° de la laguna, se para° una garza. Vamos
> a que haga de juez".
>
> Y la cigarra dijo: "Vamos". Saltaron y saltaron hasta que vieron a la garza.
>
> Y la cigarra gritó: "Garza, queremos únicamente que nos digas cuál de nosotros dos
> canta mejor".
>
> La garza respondió: "Entonces acérquense° para oírlos bien".
>
> El sapo se puso a cantar, indiferente a todo y mientras tanto la garza se comió a la cigarra.
> Cuando el sapo terminó, dijo la garza: "Ahora seguirá la discusión en mi buche°",
> y también se lo comió. Y la garza, satisfecha de su acción, encogió una pata° y siguió
> mirando tranquilamente el agua.

judge

conceited

had no end

bank/hay

vengan cerca

belly
drew up a leg

DESPUÉS DE LEER

 8-43 ¿Comprendieron? Habla con tu compañero/a de los personajes y la moraleja de la fábula.

1. ¿Quiénes son?

2. ¿Quién canta mejor? ¿Quién es más inteligente?

3. En su opinión, ¿cuál es la moraleja (*moral*)?

4. ¿Conocen otra fábula con una moraleja semejante (*similar*)?

 8-44 Sus animales favoritos. Hablen de los animales que les gustan y de los que no les gustan. Luego expliquen por qué.

8-45 Una fábula. En esta actividad vas a escribir una fábula. Recuerda que los personajes son animales y que debe contener una moraleja explícita o implícita.

MODELO: *En la alta sierra de Perú vivían una alpaca y un cóndor. La alpaca se creía la criatura más bella de todo el mundo. El cóndor también se creía muy, muy bello, aún más bello que la alpaca...*

La alpaca   **El cóndor**

ANTES DE ESCRIBIR

• **Descripción.** Escribe una breve descripción de dos o tres personajes. Incluye sus aspectos físicos y personales.

Algunos animales

la araña	*spider*	**la iguana**	*iguana*
la ardilla	*squirrel*	**el lobo**	*wolf*
el booby con patas azules	*blue-footed booby*	**el loro**	*parrot*
la culebra	*snake*	**el pato**	*duck*
el galápago	*giant tortoise*	**el perro**	*dog*
el gato	*cat*	**el zorro**	*fox*

A ESCRIBIR

• Escribe dos o tres oraciones para describir el lugar. Usa el imperfecto.

• Escribe dos o tres oraciones para explicar el problema o el conflicto entre los personajes. Usa el imperfecto.

• Escribe dos o tres oraciones, describiendo su encuentro (*encounter*) y los resultados. Usa el pretérito.

• Escribe la moraleja (*moral of the story*) para resumir la fábula. La moraleja empieza con esta frase: (*No*) *hay que...*

DESPUÉS DE ESCRIBIR

• **Revisar.** Revisa tu fábula para verificar los siguientes puntos:

☐ el uso del imperfecto (la escena)

☐ el uso del pretérito (los acontecimientos [*events*])

☐ la ortografía y la concordancia

• **Intercambiar.** Intercambia tu fábula con la fábula de otro/a compañero/a para hacer correcciones y sugerencias y para comentar sobre el mensaje (*message*) de la fábula.

• **Entregar.** Pon tu fábula en limpio, incorporando las sugerencias de tu compañero/a. Después, entrégasela a tu profesor/a.

🔊 Vocabulario

La ropa y los accesorios Clothing and accessories

el abrigo *coat*
la billetera *wallet*
la blusa *blouse*
el bolso *bag, purse*
las botas *boots*
los calcetines *socks*
la camisa *shirt*
la camiseta (sin mangas) *t-shirt (tank top)*
las chanclas *flip-flops*
la chaqueta *jacket*
la corbata *tie*
la (mini)falda *(mini-)skirt*
la gorra *cap*
el gorro *winter hat*
los pantalones *pants (shorts)*
las sandalias *sandals*
la sudadera (con capucha) *(hooded) sweatshirt*
el suéter *sweater*
el traje *suit*
los vaqueros *jeans*
el vestido *dress*
los zapatos (de tacón alto) *(high-heeled) shoes*

Lugares donde vamos a comprar Places where we shop

el almacén *department store*
el centro comercial *shopping center, mall*
el mercado (al aire libre) *(open-air) market*
la tienda *store, shop*

En una tienda At a store

la caja *cash register*
el/la dependiente/a *sales clerk*
el descuento *discount*
la ganga *bargain, good deal*
el precio *price*
el probador *fitting room*
el recibo *receipt*
la tarjeta de crédito/débito *credit/debit card*
el/la vendedor/a *vendor, seller*
la liquidación *clearance sale*

Las telas Fabrics

el algodón *cotton*   **la lana** *wool*
el cuero *leather*   **la seda** *silk*

Verbos Verbs

estar en rebaja *to be on sale*
llevar *to wear*
pagar (en efectivo) *to pay (cash)*
probarse (ue) *to try on*
regatear *to bargain, to haggle over*

Descripciones Descriptions

de cuadros *plaid*
de manga corta/larga *short-/long-sleeved*
de moda *in style*
de rayas *striped*

En la joyería At the jewelry store

el anillo *ring*
los aretes *earrings*
la cadena *chain*
el collar *necklace*
la pulsera *bracelet*
el reloj de pulsera *wristwatch*

Descripciones Descriptions

de diamantes *diamond*
de oro *gold*
de perlas *pearl*
de plata *silver*

En la farmacia At the pharmacy

el cepillo de dientes *toothbrush*
la colonia *cologne*
el desodorante *deodorant*
la pasta de dientes *toothpaste*
el perfume *perfume*
el talco *talcum powder*

Las tiendas Shops

la farmacia *pharmacy*
la florería *flower shop*
la heladería *ice cream shop*
la joyería *jewelry store*
la papelería *stationery shop*
la perfumería *beauty supply shop*
la zapatería *shoe store*

Verbos Verbs

devolver (ue) *to return (something)*
gastar *to spend*
hacer juego (con) *to match, to go well with*

Shopping expressions *See page 251.*   **Ordinal numbers** *See page 258.*   **Expressions used with preterit and imperfect** *See page 267.*

9
Vamos de viaje

Readiness
Check

Mar Caribe

VENEZUELA — GUYANA — SURINAM — GUYANA FRANCESA

COLOMBIA

ECUADOR

PERÚ

BRASIL

BOLIVIA

OCÉANO PACÍFICO

PARAGUAY

CHILE

ARGENTINA

OCÉANO ATLÁNTICO

URUGUAY

Los países caribeños de Sudamérica: Venezuela y Colombia

«Allá donde fueres, haz como vieres».

Refrán: When in Rome, do as the Romans do. (lit., *Wherever you go, do as you see.*)

Fernando Botero, pintor y escultor colombiano, es conocido por sus figuras voluptuosas que frecuentemente reflejan un mensaje social o político. La escultura "Hombre a caballo" se encuentra en un parque de Medellín, Colombia, donde Botero nació.

Shakira es ganadora de varios Grammy Latinos. Es mundialmente conocida como cantante y también por sus obras caritativas. En 2006, fundó, con otros artistas famosos, América Latina en Acción Solidaria (ALAS) para combatir la pobreza infantil en Latino América.

Primera parte

¡Así lo decimos! VOCABULARIO

 ¡Así es la vida! De vacaciones

Marisela, Mauricio y Daniel, unos estudiantes universitarios de Caracas, están por abordar un avión para tomarse unas vacaciones en Colombia.

MARISELA: ¡Ay! ¡Toda una semana sin clases! ¡Qué chévere!

MAURICIO: Sí, pero primero tenemos que hacer cola para pasar por el control de seguridad...

DANIEL: ... y quitarnos los zapatos, sacar la portátil de la mochila, ...

MARISELA: ¡Hombre, no es para tanto! ¡Nos vamos de vacaciones!

Mientras esperan...

MARISELA: Oye Daniel, ¿tienes tu tarjeta de embarque a mano?

DANIEL: ¡Claro! Y el itinerario en la maleta. El precio que nos dieron para este viaje, con todo incluido, fue una ganga.

MAURICIO: Es verdad, pasaje de ida y vuelta, hotel en Cartagena, excursión a la isla de San Andrés...

MARISELA: ...¡que tiene una playa fabulosa!

DANIEL: Y todo por solo dos mil doscientos bolívares por persona.

09-02
to 09-08

🔊 **Vocabulario** En el aeropuerto

Variaciones
In Latin America you
purchase **un boleto;**
in Spain, **un billete.**

En la agencia de viajes — At the travel agency
el/la agente de viajes   travel agent
el boleto (electrónico)   (e-)ticket
el folleto   brochure
el pasaje (de ida y vuelta)   (roundtrip) fare, ticket
la reservación / reserva   reservation
el/la viajero/a   traveler

En el aeropuerto — In the airport
la aduana   customs
el avión   plane
el control de seguridad   security checkpoint
el/la inspector/a de aduanas   customs inspector
el pasaporte   passport
la puerta de embarque   boarding gate
la sala de espera   waiting room
el reclamo de equipaje   baggage claim
la tarjeta de embarque   boarding pass
el vuelo   flight

Pasa por el control de seguridad.

En el avión — On the plane
el asiento de pasillo / de ventanilla   aisle seat / window seat
el/la asistente de vuelo   flight attendant
la clase turista   coach class
la demora   delay
la escala   stopover
la llegada   arrival
el/la pasajero/a   passenger
el/la piloto   pilot
la salida   departure

Variaciones
Although **el carro** is
commonly used
throughout the
Americas for *car*,
el auto (from
el automóvil) is
preferred in Argentina
and Chile, la **máquina**
in Cuba, and **el coche** in
Spain (where **el carro**
means *cart, wagon*).

Revisa la hora
de salida.

Verbos — Verbs
abordar   to board
aterrizar   to land
bajarse (de)   to get off (of), to get down (from)
despegar   to take off
esperar   to wait for
facturar el equipaje   to check baggage
hacer cola   to stand in line
hacer la(s) maleta(s)   to pack one's
        suitcase(s)
hacer un crucero   to take a cruise
pasar por (…)   to pass through (. . .)
viajar por barco   to travel by ship
        tren   train
        carro / coche / auto   car
        autobús   bus

Variaciones
For *bus*, **el autobús** is
generally understood
by Spanish speakers,
although the term **el
camión** is more
frequent in Mexico,
especially for a
commuter bus.

Esperan sus maletas en el
reclamo de equipaje.

APLICACIÓN

9-1 En el aeropuerto. Siempre hay mucha actividad en el Aeropuerto Internacional de Maiquetía (Simón Bolívar), Caracas.

Paso 1 Empareja las frases para formar oraciones completas basadas en **¡Así es la vida!**

1. _____ Los tres amigos están esperando en...

2. _____ Antes de abordar el avión, los inspectores de seguridad les revisan...

3. _____ Piensan pasar sus vacaciones en...

4. _____ El paquete que les dieron no costó mucho, fue...

5. _____ Solo pagaron 2.200 bolívares por...

6. _____ Van a estar en Colombia...

a. por una semana.

b. una verdadera ganga.

c. la cola para pasar por el control de seguridad.

d. la isla de San Andrés y la ciudad colonial de Cartagena.

e. la maleta y las bolsas.

f. el pasaje, el hotel y las excursiones.

 Paso 2 Mira el siguiente mapa y traza la ruta entre Caracas, San Andrés y Cartagena de Indias. ¿Cuántos kilómetros hay en total? Después, conéctate a la Internet para localizar los lugares que siguen e indíquenlos en el mapa. Baja (*download*) una foto representativa de un lugar que te interese.

> ↖ **Busca:** isla de margarita, medellin, laguna de guatavita, parque nacional tayrona, salto angel, cueva guacharo

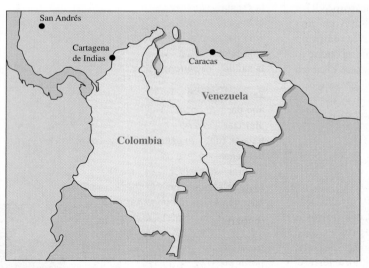

Cartagena de Indias – San Andrés: 827 kms.
Cartagena de Indias – Caracas: 944 kms.

9-2 Planes para un viaje.   Prepara un viaje como el de Marisela y sus amigos. Pon las siguientes actividades en orden lógico para poder hacer el viaje.

Voy a...

___1___ pedir dos semanas de vacaciones

_____ bajarme del avión

_____ abrirle la maleta al aduanero

_____ hacer cola para abordar el avión

_____ hacer la maleta

_____ hablar con un agente de viajes

_____ pedir un taxi para el aeropuerto

_____ darle la tarjeta de embarque al asistente de vuelo

_____ hacer las reservaciones del avión

9-3 En el avión destino a Caracas.   Escribe la palabra o frase que mejor complete cada oración.

MODELO: *Los pasajeros* le piden un refresco al asistente de vuelos.

1. Para las Navidades, tenemos _____ de ida y vuelta de Cleveland a Caracas.

2. Desafortunadamente, no hay vuelos directos. Tenemos que hacer _____ en Miami.

3. Tenemos asientos en _____ porque es más económico que en primera clase.

4. El avión no puede salir a tiempo por la tempestad y los vientos. Hay una _____ de media hora.

5. Si el avión no _____ a tiempo, vamos a perder nuestra conexión en Miami.

6. En Caracas, tenemos que pasar por el control de inmigración y también por la _____ antes de salir del aeropuerto.

9-4 Un vuelo en avión.   Parece que Marisela, Mauricio y Daniel se equivocaron (*made a mistake*) de vuelo. Escucha el anuncio que ellos oyen en el avión. Indica la información correcta del vuelo.

1. aerolínea: a. IBERIA   b. AVENSA   c. LACSA

2. número: a. 895   b. 985   c. 995

3. destino: a. San Juan   b. San José   c. San Andrés

4. comida: a. almuerzo   b. merienda   c. desayuno

5. película: a. cubana   b. venezolana   c. colombiana

6. temperatura: a. 30° C   b. 30° F   c. 32° C

7. hora de llegada: a. 2:30 a.m.   b. 3:30 p.m.   c. 2:30 p.m.

¡Hola!

Cultura en vivo

If you are hungry before boarding your flight in Caracas, you'll find several cafés and restaurants in the airport. A certain menu item is **la arepa,** a staple food that originated in Venezuela and Colombia but is becoming popular in other Latin American countries. It is a flat, unleavened bread made of cornmeal that can be grilled, baked, or fried, then garnished or filled with meat, eggs, vegetables, or cheese. Have you ever tried one or had something similar?

9-5A En el mostrador de AVIANCA. Eres el agente de viajes en el mostrador (*counter*) de la aerolínea AVIANCA (aerolínea colombiana). Primero hazle las preguntas que siguen al viajero / a la viajera y después dale la información que te pide. **Estudiante B,** por favor ve al **Apéndice 1,** página A-16.

MODELO: ESTUDIANTE A: *Buenas tardes. ¿Tiene su tarjeta de embarque?*
ESTUDIANTE B: *No, pero tengo el número de mi reservación.*

Estudiante A:

Preguntas para el/la viajero/a:	Información para darle:
1. el saludo (Buenos/as... ¿En qué puedo servirle?)	• el número del vuelo = AV402
2. el destino (¿Cuál es ...?)	• el número de la puerta de embarque = G26
3. su preferencia para sentarse (¿Dónde prefiere...?)	• la hora de salida = 17:30
4. el número de maletas que facturar (¿Cuántas...?)	• la hora de abordar el avión = 17:00
5. si lleva algún líquido en la maleta (¿Lleva...?)	• comida abordo = cena y refrescos

9-6 Transportes Ejecutivos desde Caracas. A continuación hay un anuncio para viajes en autobús desde Caracas a otras ciudades en Venezuela.

Paso 1 Primero, consulta el mapa de Venezuela en **Nuestro mundo** de este capítulo para escoger una ciudad que te gustaría visitar y explica por qué. Las tarifas están en moneda venezolana, aproximadamente $1 = 4,3 bolívares (Bs.).

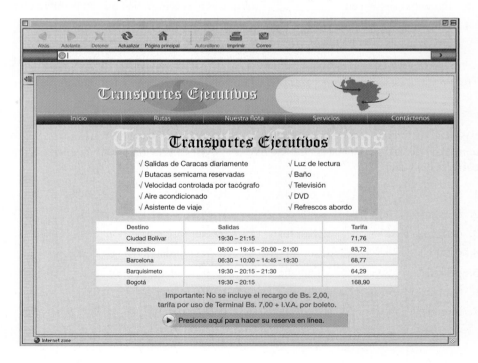

Transportes Ejecutivos

Inicio · Rutas · Nuestra flota · Servicios · Contáctenos

Transportes Ejecutivos

√ Salidas de Caracas diariamente
√ Butacas semicama reservadas
√ Velocidad controlada por tacógrafo
√ Aire acondicionado
√ Asistente de viaje

√ Luz de lectura
√ Baño
√ Televisión
√ DVD
√ Refrescos abordo

Destino	Salidas	Tarifa
Ciudad Bolívar	19:30 – 21:15	71,76
Maracaibo	08:00 – 19:45 – 20:00 – 21:00	83,72
Barcelona	06:30 – 10:00 – 14:45 – 19:30	68,77
Barquisimeto	19:30 – 20:15 – 21:30	64,29
Bogotá	19:30 – 20:15	168,90

Importante: No se incluye el recargo de Bs. 2,00, tarifa por uso de Terminal Bs. 7,00 + I.V.A. por boleto.

▶ Presione aquí para hacer su reserva en línea.

Internet zone

Paso 2 Hablen de sus preferencias sobre los destinos y decidan adónde desean viajar. Comparen el costo de los viajes. ¿Cuáles de las comodidades de estos autobuses les parecen las más atractivas y por qué?

¡Así lo hacemos! ESTRUCTURAS

09-09 to 09-14

1. *Por* or *para*

Although the prepositions **por** and **para** may both be translated as *for* in English, they are not interchangeable. Each word has a distinct use in Spanish, as outlined below.

[Speech bubble: ¿Para qué y por cuánto tiempo vienes a Venezuela?]

[Speech bubble: Vengo para estudiar por un mes.]

[Sign: ADUANA]

Por...

- expresses the time during which an action takes place or its duration (*during, for*).

  | Vamos al aeropuerto **por** la tarde. | *We are going to the airport during the afternoon.* |
  | Pienso estudiar en Caracas **por** un semestre. | *I am planning to study in Caracas for a semester.* |

- expresses *because of, in exchange for,* or *on behalf of.*

Tuve que cancelar el vuelo **por** una emergencia.	*I had to cancel the flight because of an emergency.*
Pagué $250 **por** el boleto.	*I paid $250 for the ticket.*
¿Lo hiciste **por** mí?	*Did you do it for me?*

- expresses the object/goal of an action or a person being sought after (*for*).

  | Venimos **por** usted a las dos. | *We'll come by for you at two.* |
  | Los estudiantes fueron **por** el equipaje. | *The students went for their luggage.* |

- expresses motion (*through, by, along, around*).

  | Pasé **por** la agencia ayer. | *I went by the agency yesterday.* |
  | Las chicas salieron **por** la puerta número 12. | *The girls left through gate number 12.* |

- expresses the means by or manner in which an action is accomplished (*by, for*).

  | ¿Recibiste los pasajes **por** correo electrónico? | *Did you receive the tickets by e-mail?* |
  | Hicimos las reservaciones **por** teléfono. | *We made the reservations by telephone.* |

- is used in many common idiomatic expressions.

por ahora	*for now*
por aquí	*around here*
por Dios	*for heaven's* (lit. *God's*) *sake*
por eso	*that's why*
por ejemplo	*for example*
por favor	*please*
por fin	*finally, at last*
por lo general	*in general*
por supuesto	*of course*
por último	*finally (last item in a statement)*

Para…

- expresses the purpose of an action (*in order to* + infinitive) or of an object (*for*).

Vamos a Colombia **para** conocer el país.	*We're going to Colombia in order to get to know the country.*
La cámara es **para** sacar fotos.	*The camera is for taking pictures.*

- expresses destination (*a place or a recipient*).

Mañana salimos **para** Maracaibo.	*Tomorrow we're leaving for Maracaibo.*
Este pasaje es **para** ti.	*This ticket is for you.*

- expresses work objective.

Ana estudia **para** piloto.	*Ana is studying to be a pilot.*

- expresses time limits or specific deadlines (*by, for*).

Necesito el pasaporte **para** esta tarde.	*I need the passport for this afternoon.*
Pienso estar en Cartagena **para** las tres de la tarde.	*I plan to be in Cartagena by three in the afternoon.*

- expresses in whose opinion.

Para mí siempre es divertido viajar.	*For me, it's always fun to travel.*

Study tips — Distinguishing between *por* and *para*

1. The uses of **por** and **para** have apparent similarities, which sometimes cause confusion. In some cases it may be helpful to link their uses to the questions **¿para qué?** (*for what purpose?*) and **¿por qué?** (*for what reason?*)

—¿**Por qué** viniste?	*Why (For what reason) did you come?*
—Vine porque necesitaba los boletos.	*I came because I needed the tickets.*
—¿**Para qué** viniste?	*For what purpose did you come?*
—Vine **para** pedirte un favor.	*I came (in order) to ask a favor of you.*

2. In many instances the use of either **por** or **para** will be grammatically correct, but the meanings will be different. Compare the following sentences:

Mario viaja **para** Cartagena.	*Mario is traveling to (toward) Cartagena. (destination)*
Mario viaja **por** Cartagena.	*Mario is traveling through (in) (motion) Cartagena.*

3. Remember that after a preposition you use **mí** and **ti** in place of **yo** and **tú.**

Para **mí** es importante viajar. ¿Y para **ti**?	*For me it's important to travel. And for you?*

APLICACIÓN

9-7 Una entrevista con Fernando Botero. Este artista colombiano es uno de los más destacados de este siglo. Es tanto escultor como pintor, y sus obras están en museos y en lugares públicos por todo el mundo.

Paso 1 Lee esta entrevista y subraya las preposiciones **por** y **para**. Después, explica el uso de cada una.

MODELO: ¿<u>Por</u> qué no se quedó en Medellín?
reason or cause

ENTREVISTADORA: Buenas tardes, Sr. Botero. Usted nació en Medellín pero después se fue a vivir a Bogotá. ¿Por qué no se quedó en Medellín?

BOTERO: Me fui por todas las oportunidades que se ofrecían en la capital. Mi primera exposición de pinturas fue en Bogotá cuando tenía veinte años. Después, gané varios premios y decidí ir a Europa. Por supuesto, allí había muchas oportunidades para colaborar con artistas de todo el mundo.

ENTREVISTADORA: ¿Y qué hizo allí?

BOTERO: Primero, viajé por Francia, España e Italia para conocer las grandes obras maestras de los museos europeos. Estudié por varios meses en cada lugar, y luego me fui para México.

ENTREVISTADORA: ¿Y por qué fue a México?

BOTERO: Fui para conocer mejor el arte mexicano, y allí pinté varios cuadros. Luego, salí para Nueva York y en esa ciudad pinté mi *Mona Lisa, 12 años de edad*, que está en el Museo de Arte Moderno.

ENTREVISTADORA: Y, ahora ¿qué hace?

BOTERO: Me interesa el arte colonial y monumental, especialmente la escultura. Vivo en París, Nueva York y Bogotá. Para mí, es una vida llena de satisfacción y por el momento, soy feliz.

Paso 2 Ahora contesta las preguntas siguientes basadas en la entrevista.

1. ¿Cuál es la nacionalidad de Botero?

2. ¿Por qué se fue a vivir a Bogotá?

3. ¿Qué hizo en Europa? ¿Qué oportunidades encontró allí?

4. Después, ¿adónde fue? ¿Por qué?

5. ¿Para qué museo pintó su *Mona Lisa, 12 años de edad*?

6. ¿Qué tipo de arte hace hoy en día?

7. ¿Cómo encuentra su vida ahora?

8. ¿Cuál es tu opinión de su escultura?

El Salto Ángel, Venezuela

9-8 Planes para un viaje al Salto Ángel. Completa cada espacio en blanco con **por** o **para**.

En enero Carmen y yo decidimos hacer un viaje al Salto Ángel en Venezuela. Queríamos ir (1) _____ Semana Santa, que es en la primavera. El día que hicimos los planes, yo pasé (2) _____ Carmen y luego nosotras salimos (3) _____ la agencia de viajes. Carmen y yo caminamos (4) _____ el parque Central, (5) _____ Times Square y, (6) _____ fin, (7) _____ la estación de Grand Central donde encontramos la agencia.

En la agencia le dijimos a la directora que (8) _____ nosotras abril era el mejor mes del año. (9) _____ eso, queríamos hacer el viaje en ese mes. Con la agente hicimos los planes. Íbamos a pescar (10) _____ el río. Íbamos a hacer una excursión (11) _____ el parque nacional. Íbamos a pasar quince días viajando (12) _____ toda la región. ¿Cuánto pagamos (13) _____ un viaje tan bonito? ¡Solo $850! ¡(14) _____ mí era una ganga!

La agente dijo: "Está bien. Estos boletos de avión son (15) _____ ustedes (16) _____ el viaje. Pero deben pasar (17) _____ una librería (18) _____ comprar una guía turística". También teníamos que ir al banco (19) _____ aumentar el límite de nuestra tarjeta de crédito. Y entonces, con todo listo, ¡solo nos quedaba esperar otros tres meses!

9-9 El viaje a un lugar interesante. Ustedes piensan visitar un lugar interesante este verano. Háganse las preguntas a continuación para planear el viaje y después hagan un resumen de sus planes.

1. ¿Para qué hacemos el viaje?
2. ¿Salimos por la mañana o por la tarde?
3. ¿Cuánto dinero vamos a necesitar para el viaje?
4. ¿Por cuánto tiempo vamos?
5. ¿Es necesario cambiar dólares para pagar en ese lugar?

9-10A ¡Planes para las vacaciones de primavera! Hablen sobre los viajes que van a hacer en la primavera, usando las preguntas e información en tu itinerario. Luego, intenta convencer (*convince*) a tu compañero/a para viajar juntos/as. **Estudiante B,** por favor ve al **Apéndice 1,** página A-16.

Estudiante A:

	Mi viaje	El viaje de mi compañero/a
Destino:	*Concepción, Honduras*	
Propósito:	*hacer servicio en una comunidad rural*	
Transporte:	*avión, autobús*	
Ruta:	*Miami, Tegucigalpa*	
Duración del viaje:	*una semana*	
Fecha de llegada:	*el primero de marzo*	

1. ¿Adónde vas?
2. ¿Por qué ruta vas a viajar?
3. ¿Cómo vas a viajar, por tren, por carro, por...?
4. ¿Cuándo es el viaje?
5. ¿Por cuánto tiempo vas?
6. ¿Para qué vas?

Al final, para convencer a tu compañero/a:

7. ¿Por qué no vienes conmigo? Creo que mi viaje va a ser...

Presencia hispana

During the first decade of this century, the number of Venezuelans immigrating to the U.S. grew significantly. Many are middle-class professionals who, fearing the leftist policies of President Hugo Chávez, left Venezuela to settle in Florida and New York. According to the Miami-based newspaper *El Venezolano,* there are some 180,000 Venezuelans living in Florida alone. Don Pan is a chain of Venezuelan bakeries in Florida. What do you imagine is their bread specialty?

09-15
to 09-19

2. Adverbs ending in *-mente*

An adverb modifies a verb, an adjective, or another adverb. In Spanish many adverbs are formed by adding **-mente** to the feminine singular form of adjectives that end in **-o** or **-a.** Adjectives that have only one form simply add **-mente.** Note that the ending **-mente** is equivalent to the English ending *-ly.* Also note that if the adjective requires an accent mark, the accent remains on the adverb.

lento	→	lentamente	rápido	→	rápidamente
alegre	→	alegremente	fácil	→	fácilmente

Teresa canceló el viaje
inmediatamente.

Cartagena de Indias es
particularmente bella.

El piloto habla **especialmente**
bien en inglés.

Teresa canceled the trip
immediately.

Cartagena de Indias is particularly
beautiful.

The pilot speaks especially well in
English.

¡Nos queremos enormemente!

APLICACIÓN

9-11 En el Museo del Oro de Bogotá.   El Museo del Oro fue ampliado en 2008 con un nuevo edificio y con cuatro salas de exposición.

Paso 1   Lee el párrafo sobre una visita al Museo del Oro de Bogotá e identifica los adverbios que terminan en **-mente**. Después, escribe oraciones originales usando cinco de ellos.

Cuando Alina y José vivían en Bogotá, iban frecuentemente al Museo del Oro para ver las diferentes exposiciones que tenían. Para llegar al museo normalmente pasaban por el parque, especialmente cuando hacía buen tiempo. A José siempre le gustaba caminar lentamente, pero Alina tenía más prisa y caminaba rápidamente. En el museo, José se sentaba en los bancos y tranquilamente leía todos los letreros (*signs*) sobre las piezas, pero Alina solamente sacaba fotos de

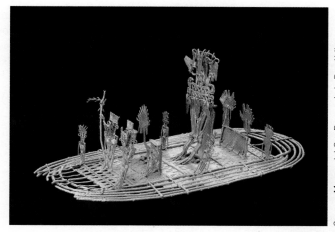

Source: Museo del Oro Banco de la República—Bogotá—Colombia

Según la leyenda, los indios muiscas cubrían (*used to cover*) de oro a su cacique (*chief*).

ellas. Salían puntualmente a la hora que cerraba el museo y generalmente iban a una heladería donde se sentaban a tomar un refresco y a conversar animadamente sobre la visita. Siempre lo pasaban maravillosamente bien. Ahora que viven en Medellín, usualmente visitan el Museo de Botero los domingos.

Paso 2 Contesta ahora las siguientes preguntas sobre el texto que acabas de leer.

1. ¿Cuántas veces iban Alina y José al Museo del Oro?

2. ¿Cómo iban normalmente?

3. ¿Cómo caminaba cada uno?

4. ¿Qué hacía José en el museo? ¿Y Alina?

5. ¿Qué hacían después de visitar el museo?

6. ¿Qué hacen ahora los domingos? ¿Por qué?

 Paso 3   Una visita al Museo.   Conéctate a la Internet y visita el Museo del Oro. Después, identifica qué objeto, en tu opinión, puede corresponder a cada descripción que sigue.

> **Busca:** museo oro, colombia

MODELO: un objeto especialmente bello
> *Los ídolos de los indios muiscas me parecen especialmente bellos.*

1. un objeto enormemente importante

2. un objeto elegantemente diseñado (*designed*)

3. un objeto particularmente original

4. un objeto increíblemente detallado

5. un objeto especialmente impresionante

 9-12A El robo en el museo.   Hubo un robo en un museo en Colombia y ustedes creen que encontraron algunos de los objetos robados. Túrnense para hacerse preguntas y descubrir (*discover*) qué objeto encontró cada uno. Contesten cada pregunta con un adverbio que termina en **-mente. Estudiante B,** por favor ve al **Apéndice 1,** página A-17.

MODELO: Encontré una pintura de Picasso (**enorme**) valiosa.
> ESTUDIANTE A: *¿Qué encontraste?*
> ESTUDIANTE B: *Encontré una pintura de Picasso enormemente valiosa.*

Fernando Botero, "El gato"

Estudiante A:

Preguntas para mi compañero/a	Respuestas para mi compañero
1. ¿Qué encontraste? 2. ¿Cómo es? 3. ¿Quién crees que robó el objeto? 4. ¿Cómo se escapó? 5. ¿Qué hiciste con el objeto?	• Encontré una escultura de Botero (**especial**) voluptuosa. • (**Inmediato**) llamé a la policía. • Me dieron una recompensa (**increíble**) generosa. • La encontré (**fácil**) en el jardín. • Vale (**posible**) más de un millón de dólares.

Complete the dialogue with SER and ES[T]

Mi familia _____ grande, hay qu[e]

casa _____ en la calle Florida. Esta ca[lle]

noche hay una fiesta en mi casa. La fiesta _

_____ de Venezuela, ellos __

_____ alto y guapo. Él _____

simpática. Ella _____ psicóloga. Ahora

ver el partido de fútbol. Mi hermana Laura_

9-13 Desafío (*Challenge*). Formen dos equipos para desafiarse formando adverbios de la lista de adjetivos y usándolos en oraciones lógicas. Cada oración debe tener un mínimo de seis palabras y un verbo diferente.

alegre	cómodo	feliz	maravilloso
amable	cuidadoso	frecuente	particular
animado	difícil	generoso	rápido
ansioso	elegante	lento	raro
brutal	fácil	loco	tranquilo

MODELO: EQUIPO A: frecuente

EQUIPO B: *Viajo frecuentemente a Colombia y Venezuela.*

¿Cuánto saben?

09-20
to 09-24

Primero, pregúntate si puedes llevar a cabo (*carry out*) las siguientes funciones comunicativas en español. Después, júntate con dos o tres compañeros/as de clase para presentar las situaciones. Hagan y respondan a por lo menos cuatro preguntas en cada situación.

✓ CAN YOU . . .

☐ make travel arrangements?

☐ request and give travel-related information?

☐ talk about going to and through places?

☐ describe how and when actions take place?

WITH YOUR CLASSMATE(S) . . .

Situación: En la agencia de viajes
Hagan el papel de agente y viajero/a y pidan/den información sobre viajes. Usen vocabulario y expresiones de **¡Así es la vida!** y traten de (*try to*) hacer/contestar por lo menos cinco preguntas.
Para empezar: *Quiero visitar un lugar especialmente interesante y económico…*

Situación: En el aeropuerto
Hagan el papel de agente y viajero/a y pidan/den información sobre el vuelo (la sala de espera, el reclamo de equipaje, etc.).
Para empezar: *Perdone, ¿me puede decir dónde está… / el número de… / cómo puedo…?*

Situación: Por teléfono con un/a amigo/a
Explíquense qué pasó en el último viaje que hicieron, cómo se prepararon para el viaje, cómo viajaron, por cuánto tiempo fueron, etc. Usen **por** y **para** en sus descripciones.
Para empezar: *Antes de salir, tuve que pasar por la agencia de viajes para reservar el vuelo y…*

Situación: Un viaje inolvidable
Hablen de sus impresiones de un lugar que conocieron. Usen adverbios que terminan en **-mente** para describir qué vieron en ese lugar y qué hicieron allí.
Para empezar: *Vancouver es una ciudad increíblemente bella. Caminamos lentamente por las calles y los parques…*

Perfiles

Mi experiencia

AUYENTEPUY: UN VIAJE DE AVENTURA

9-14 Para ti. ¿Cuáles son algunos de los parques nacionales más importantes de EE. UU. y Canadá? ¿Conoces alguno? ¿Fuiste de camping o hiciste un viaje de aventura? A continuación Felipe te cuenta de una excursión que hizo a Venezuela. ¿Harías (*would you take*) esta excursión también?

¿Qué húbole[1], muchachos? Soy Felipe, de Uruguay. Este verano estoy viajando por Latinoamérica, en mi furgoneta[2], para conocer mejor este tremendo continente. Pienso contarles a todos mis amigos que me siguen por la Internet todas mis aventuras. Primero paré unos días en Venezuela e hice un trekking a Auyentepuy, una montaña en el Parque Nacional Canaima. ¡Qué lugar tan misterioso! Tiene paisajes irregulares, cuevas[3] y ríos que aparecen y desaparecen, rocas y murallas de arenisca[4]. Entiendo bien por qué la llaman la "Montaña del Diablo". El viaje duró diez días y cada noche me quedé en un campamento diferente dentro del parque. Además de trekking, hice kayaking por el río Orinoco. El mejor momento del viaje fue cuando llegué al Salto Ángel y vi las cascadas desde un helicóptero. ¡Qué bárbaro! Bueno, ahora voy hasta Colombia, la tierra de mi "amigo" Juanes, para conocer Villa de Leyva y las cuevas de la región. Cada experiencia y aventura que tengo me hacen recordar la canción de Juanes, "Me enamora", pues para mí, el continente de Latinoamérica es el que me enamora[5]. ¡Hasta la próxima!

[1]*What's up?* (Venezuela)   [2]*van*   [3]*caves*   [4]*walls of sandstone*   [5]*makes me fall in love with it*

9-15 En su opinión. Expliquen si también harían (*would do*) una excursión como la de Felipe y por qué. Después, pongan en orden de preferencia estas actividades y comparen sus gustos.

MODELO: E1: *Sí, me gustaría hacer un viaje como el de Felipe...*
          E2: *No sé. Creo que prefiero...*

_____ bajar una cascada en kayak

_____ hacer un viaje en helicóptero para ver la selva (*jungle*) amazónica

_____ hacer montañismo en los Andes

_____ hacer rafting por un río con fuertes corrientes

_____ hacer windsurf

_____ navegar a vela (*sail*) por alta mar

_____ hacer parapente (*hang-glide*)

_____ hacer salto en bungee

_____ ¿...?

Mi música

"ME ENAMORA" (JUANES, COLOMBIA)

Según el periódico *Los Angeles Times*, Juanes es hoy en día "la figura más importante de la música latina contemporánea". Es ganador de 17 Grammy Latinos y, según la revista *Time*, una de las "cien personas más influyentes del mundo". No solo es el cantante de rock latino con el mayor número de ventas (*sales*), sino también un activista social prominente. En esta canción Juanes se dirige a una persona importante en su vida.

Antes de ver y escuchar

9-16 El por y el para qué. Completa lógicamente cada oración a continuación con **por** o **para** para darte una idea del tema de la canción.

1. El cantante le canta _____ explicarle _____ qué la quiere.

2. La quiere _____ que ella lo hace feliz.

3. _____ él es siempre agradable estar con ella.

4. _____ eso dice que su vida no tiene sentido sin ella.

5. Ella es como el sol _____ él.

6. Sin ella, la vida _____ él es como un remolino de cenizas (*whirlwind of ashes*).

Para ver y escuchar

 9-17 La canción. Conéctate a la Internet para ver un video de "Me enamora". Compara el ritmo de esta canción con otros estilos que conozcas (salsa, pop, rock, etc.). ¿Es más rápido? ¿Más bailable? ¿Más divertido?

 Busca: juanes me enamora video; juanes me enamora letra

Si te interesa comprar la canción: *Go to iTunes Store>Music>More to Explore>iMix>Arriba 6e*

Después de ver y escuchar

 9-18 Las razones. Con un/a compañero/a, identifica cuáles de estas razones se mencionan en la canción. ¿Les parecen válidas? ¿Hay otras más importantes para ustedes?

1. _____ La desea con toda su alma (*soul*).

2. _____ La quiere físicamente.

3. _____ Ella lo quiere a él.

4. _____ Él está perdido sin ella.

5. _____ Él quiere estar con ella para siempre.

Segunda parte

¡Así lo decimos! VOCABULARIO

09-27

📖 ¡Así es la vida! Unos correos electrónicos de Marisela

🔊 Marisela, Mauricio y Daniel lo están pasando de maravilla en Colombia. Ahora Marisela le escribe unos correos electrónicos a su amiga Raquel.

A:	rmejias@ecorreo.com.ve
De:	mchavez@ecorreo.com.ve
Asunto:	¡Saludos desde San Andrés, Colombia!

Hola, Raquel:

Aquí estamos, en la Isla de San Andrés, donde lo estamos pasando súper bien. Nuestro hotel es grande y hermoso, verdaderamente de lujo. Las habitaciones son bien grandes, y la mía tiene jacuzzi y una vista al mar. Todos los días salimos a esquiar y a bucear en las aguas cristalinas del Caribe. Qué bonita la foto, ¿no? Esta tarde vamos a recorrer San Andrés en bicicleta. ¡Te escribo otro vez desde Cartagena!

Besos,
Marisela

A:	rmejias@ecorreo.com.ve
De:	mchavez@ecorreo.com.ve
Asunto:	¡Saludos desde Cartagena, Colombia!

Hola, Raquel:

Ahora en Cartagena nos quedamos en la parte antigua de la ciudad en un hotel colonial con un jardín tropical precioso. Este hotel es más antiguo que el de San Andrés (no hay jacuzzi), pero tenemos una vista impresionante (y hay wifi en el lobby). Aquí te mando una foto digital que saqué de Cartagena. ¡Ojalá que salga bien y la puedas ver!

Besos,
Marisela

Vocabulario Los viajes

En el viaje   On the trip

el adaptador eléctrico   *electrical adapter*
la cámara digital   *digital camera*
la cámara de video   *video camera*
el cargador   *charger*
la gira   *tour*
el/la guía   *tour guide*
la guía turística   *guidebook*
la pila   *battery*
el plano de la ciudad   *city map*
la tarjeta de memoria   *memory card*
la tarjeta postal   *postcard*

la cámara digital

Atracciones turísticas   Tourist attractions

el bosque   *forest*
la catedral   *cathedral*
el centro histórico   *historical center*
la estatua   *statue*
las flores   *flowers*
la isla   *island*
el lago   *lake*
el monumento   *monument*
las montañas   *mountains*
el salto de agua / la catarata   *waterfall*
el volcán   *volcano*

el adaptador eléctrico

En el hotel   At the hotel

el cuarto doble   *double room*
la estadía   *stay*
el/la gerente   *manager*
el hostal   *inn / youth hostel*
el hotel (de lujo)   *(luxury) hotel*
la vista   *view*

las pilas y el cargador

Variaciones
El cuarto doble is **la habitación doble** in Spain. Also, in Spain you will hear **la estancia** in place of **la estadía**.

Actividades típicas de los viajeros   Typical activities for travelers

bucear   *to scuba dive, to swim under water*
comprar recuerdos   *to buy souvenirs*
ir de excursión   *to go on an excursion*
montar a caballo   *to go horseback riding*
     en bicicleta   *bicycle riding*
pasarlo de maravilla   *to have a wonderful time*
pescar   *to fish*
quedarse   *to stay (somewhere)*
recorrer   *to travel around, to tour*
viajar al extranjero   *to travel abroad*

Variaciones
In Mexico and other parts of Latin America, you will also hear **pasarla de maravilla**: **¡La pasé de maravilla en la fiesta!**

el plano de la ciudad

09-32
to 09-33

Letras y sonidos

The letter *g* in sequences other than *ge* and *gi* in Spanish

Remember that in Spanish, the letter **g** before the vowels **e** and **i** sounds like the *h* in English *hip*. In all other sequences, such as **ga**, **go**, and **gu**, the letter **g** creates one of two sounds, depending on the context. After a pause or the letter **n**, the letter **g** sounds like the *g* in English *good*. In all other contexts, the **g** is softer, like the *g* in English *sugar*.

Hard **g**:   ga-lle-ta   gus-to   ten-go   guí-a

Soft **g**:   la-ga-lle-ta   mu-cho-gus-to   ha-go   ham-bur-gue-sa

Note that the letter **u** in the sequences **gue** and **gui** is silent. When two dots (or **diéresis**) are written above the letter **u**, or when **u** is inserted with **ga** and **go**, a glide is created: **bi-lin-güe, pin-güi-no, a-gua, an-ti-guo.**

APLICACIÓN

9-19 Una tarjeta postal desde Venezuela.   Aquí tienes una tarjeta postal de la Isla de Margarita, cerca de la costa de Venezuela. Completa la tarjeta con las siguientes palabras.

excursión	montaña	sol	tarjeta postal
flores	pasamos	tarjeta de memoria	vista

Isla de Margarita

Queridos papás:

Esta es una (1) _____ con foto de la Isla de Margarita desde nuestro hotel. Desde la ventana tenemos una (2) _____ impresionante del mar y de la (3) _____. En el jardín hay unas (4) _____ preciosas. Tuvimos que comprar otra (5) _____ para nuestra cámara porque la original se llenó por completo. Por la tarde, fuimos de (6) _____ a varios lugares. Nadamos y buceamos en el agua azul verdosa del Caribe. Siempre vamos por la mañana para no tomar demasiado (7) _____. En fin, lo (8) _____ de maravilla.

Anita

9-20 Sus gustos.   Túrnense para comparar cómo prefieren pasar sus vacaciones e incluyan una actividad original. ¿Qué tienen en común y cómo se diferencian?

	Me gusta o no...		A mi compañero/a le gusta o no...	
Actividad	**Sí**	**No**	**Sí**	**No**
escalar montañas				
visitar museos				
bucear				
comprar recuerdos				
montar a caballo				
pescar				
nadar en el mar				
ir de excursión				
¿...?				

🔊 9-21 **El viaje de Carlota y Alex.**   Escucha a Carlota según le cuenta a su mamá de su viaje con Alex. Después completa las siguientes oraciones.

1. Regresaron del viaje…

   a. hoy.
   b. ayer.
   c. la semana pasada.

2. Fueron a…

   a. Colombia.
   b. Chile.
   c. Venezuela.

3. Estuvieron allí por…

   a. ocho días.
   b. una semana.
   c. un mes.

4. Una actividad que no hicieron allí fue…

   a. nadar.
   b. montar a caballo.
   c. escalar montañas.

5. Compraron…

   a. pilas.
   b. unas fotos.
   c. unas gafas de sol.

6. Les impresionó especialmente…

   a. el volcán.
   b. el museo de arte.
   c. el salto.

7. Llegaron al lugar…

   a. por las montañas.
   b. a caballo.
   c. en helicóptero.

8. Carlota le dice a su mamá que un día todos van a…

   a. visitar Venezuela.
   b. montar a caballo.
   c. un lugar más económico.

👥 9-22 **¿Cómo reaccionan?**   Túrnense para contar cómo reaccionan o qué hacen cuando les pasa lo siguiente en un viaje.

MODELO: Hay una demora larga en la salida del vuelo.
   E1: *Cuando hay una demora, me pongo impaciente y hablo con el agente.*
   E2: *Pues, yo leo una novela o una revista.*

1. Llego tarde al aeropuerto y pierdo el avión.

2. No hay agua caliente en el baño del hotel.

3. El hotel no tiene mi reservación.

4. Mi equipaje no llega conmigo.

5. No hay vista desde el cuarto del hotel.

6. La cama del hotel es incómoda (*uncomfortable*).

👥 9-23 **Un folleto turístico de Venezuela.**   Lean la información que se incluye en el folleto sobre la cadena de saltos por el río Carrao en Venezuela. Ustedes tienen la oportunidad de viajar a este lugar. Hagan una lista de lo que van a llevar en su viaje y otra lista sobre lo que van a hacer allí.

MODELO: *Vamos a llevar una cámara digital…*

El Río Carrao,
De vuelta al paraíso

Visita el pueblo de Canaima en el río Carrao y vuelve al paraíso. Observa la variedad de flora y fauna, haz deportes acuáticos y visita la cadena de siete saltos. En un tributario del río, experimenta el gozo de tu vida viendo el espectáculo del Salto Ángel, (¡16 veces más alto que las cataratas de Niágara!). ¡Conoce la naturaleza más prístina del mundo!

¡Así lo hacemos! ESTRUCTURAS

📖 3. The Spanish subjunctive: An introduction

Quiero que pase por el Control de Agricultura.

ADUANA

Until now, you have been using verb forms (present, preterit, and imperfect) in the indicative mood. The indicative is used to express real, definite, or factual actions or states of being.

In this chapter you will learn about the subjunctive mood, which is used to express the hypothetical or subjective, such as a speaker's attitudes, wishes, feelings, emotions, or doubts. Unlike the indicative, which states facts, the subjunctive describes reality subjectively.

Es cierto que Luis **va** a Cartagena.   *It's certain that Luis is going to Cartagena.* (Certainty: indicative)

No creo que Luis **vaya** a San Andrés.   *I don't think that Luis is going to San Andrés.* (Uncertainty: subjunctive)

Los verbos regulares del presente de subjuntivo

- The following chart shows the present subjunctive forms of regular verbs. Note that the endings for **-er** and **-ir** are identical.

	hablar	comer	vivir
yo	habl**e**	com**a**	viv**a**
tú	habl**es**	com**as**	viv**as**
Ud.	habl**e**	com**a**	viv**a**
él/ella	habl**e**	com**a**	viv**a**
nosotros/as	habl**emos**	com**amos**	viv**amos**
vosotros/as	habl**éis**	com**áis**	viv**áis**
Uds.	habl**en**	com**an**	viv**an**
ellos/as	habl**en**	com**an**	viv**an**

- Verbs that are irregular in the **yo** form of the present indicative use the same spelling changes for all forms in the present subjunctive. These are not considered irregular in the subjunctive.

Infinitive	Present indicative first-person singular	Present subjunctive
decir	dig**o**	diga, digas, diga,…
hacer	hag**o**	haga, hagas, haga,…
oír	oig**o**	oiga, oigas, oiga,…
poner	pong**o**	ponga, pongas, ponga,…
tener	teng**o**	tenga, tengas, tenga,…
traer	traig**o**	traiga, traigas, traiga,…
venir	veng**o**	venga, vengas, venga,…
ver	ve**o**	vea, veas, vea,…

- The following spelling changes occur in all forms of the present subjunctive with infinitives that end in **-car, -gar,** and **-zar.**

-car:	c → qu	buscar	busque, busques, busque…
-gar:	g → gu	llegar	llegue, llegues, llegue…
-zar:	z → c	empezar	empiece, empieces, empiece…

- The subjunctive forms of **-ar** and **-er** stem-changing verbs have the same pattern of the present indicative.

pensar (ie)	
piense	pensemos
pienses	penséis
piense	piensen
piense	piensen

devolver (ue)	
devuelva	devolvamos
devuelvas	devolváis
devuelva	devuelvan
devuelva	devuelvan

- **-Ir** stem-changing verbs reflect the stem changes of both the present indicative and the preterit. The preterit stem changes occur in the **nosotros/as** and **vosotros/as** forms, where the unstressed **-e-** changes to **-i-**, and the unstressed **-o-** changes to **-u-**. The other persons follow the present-tense pattern.

sentir (ie, i)	
sienta	sintamos
sientas	sintáis
sienta	sientan
sienta	sientan

pedir (i, i)	
pida	pidamos
pidas	pidáis
pida	pidan
pida	pidan

dormir (ue, u)	
duerma	durmamos
duermas	durmáis
duerma	duerman
duerma	duerman

Los verbos irregulares del presente de subjuntivo

- The following verbs are irregular in the present subjunctive. The subjunctive form for **hay** is **haya.**

dar	estar	ir	saber	ser
dé	esté	vaya	sepa	sea
des	estés	vayas	sepas	seas
dé	esté	vaya	sepa	sea
dé	esté	vaya	sepa	sea
demos	estemos	vayamos	sepamos	seamos
deis	estéis	vayáis	sepáis	seáis
den	estén	vayan	sepan	sean
den	estén	vayan	sepan	sean

Espero que llegues pronto.

Usos generales del subjuntivo

- The subjunctive occurs in the dependent clause in a compound sentence and is generally preceded by **que.**

    Queremos **que** viajes al extranjero.

    *We want you to travel abroad. (lit.,
    We want that you travel abroad.)*

- The expression in the main clause determines whether to use the subjunctive or the indicative in the dependent clause. The three most common types of expressions that call for the subjunctive in Spanish are those that express influence, emotion, or doubt or denial. All of these imply uncertainty because the action has yet to occur or is outside of the speaker's experience.

    Insisto en que mi novio visite Cartagena.   *I insist that my boyfriend visit Cartagena.*

    Sientes que nuestra madre no pueda ir.   *You're sorry our mother can't go.*

    Es dudoso que el guía nos lleve a la catedral.   *It's doubtful our guide will take us to the cathedral.*

- If there is no change of subject, the subjunctive is not needed; use the infinitive.

    Queremos viajar al extranjero.   *We want to travel abroad.*

APLICACIÓN

9-24 Botero en el MOMA. Tres obras de Fernando Botero forman parte de la colección permanente del Museo de Arte Moderno en Nueva York.

Paso 1 Lee la conversación entre el agente de Fernando Botero y el encargado (*person in charge*) en el MOMA. Subraya los verbos en el subjuntivo e identifica el infinitivo.

MODELO: Quiero que me <u>traigan</u> un refresco. (*traer*)

Mona Lisa, 12 años de edad

AGENTE: ¡Oye, Ramón! Veo que no hay un salón especial para las obras del Sr. Botero. Insisto en que haya un "Salón Botero".

ENCARGADO: Tienes razón, Ernesto. Voy a hablar con el gerente y decirle que establezca un salón con su nombre.

AGENTE: Perfecto. Y en ese salón, vamos a pedir que traigan sillones cómodos.

ENCARGADO: ¡Buena idea! Espero que pongan flores y refrescos también.

AGENTE: No, refrescos no. Es mejor que los visitantes tomen refrescos en la cafetería.

ENCARGADO: Y es importante que estén presentes un guardia de seguridad y un guía.

AGENTE: Espero que no tengan que pagarles extra.

ENCARGADO: No sé. ¿Quieres que hable con el gerente sobre eso, también?

AGENTE: Sí, y deseo que le dé al artista un contrato especial para esta exposición.

Paso 2 Haz una lista de lo que pide el agente en el **Paso 1.**

MODELO: *un salón especial*

9-25A Desafío (Challenge). Cada uno/a de ustedes tiene una lista de verbos diferentes en el indicativo y el subjuntivo. Dile a tu compañero/a el indicativo del verbo, y él/ella debe darte el presente de subjuntivo de ese verbo. Después muéstrense sus listas de respuestas y ayúdense a corregir las incorrectas. **Estudiante B,** por favor ve al **Apéndice 1,** página A-17.

MODELO: Estudiante A: *Indicativo: tomamos*
Estudiante B: *Subjuntivo: tomemos*
Estudiante A: *Correcto.*

Estudiante A:

Yo digo:	Mi compañero/a debe decir:	Yo marco:	
Indicativo	Subjuntivo	Correcto	Incorrecto
tomamos	*tomemos*	✓	
tengo	tenga		
hablo	hable		
haces	hagas		
pedimos	pidamos		
salen	salgan		
escribe	escriba		
vas	vayas		

9-26 Unos pedidos (*requests*). Imagínense que van de vacaciones a distintos lugares. Túrnense para expresar lo que quieren o no quieren que haga su companero/a durante sus vacaciones. Usen **quiero** o **no quiero** y el subjuntivo.

MODELO: sacar muchas fotos
E1: *Quiero que saques muchas fotos.*
E2: *¡Claro que sí! (No puedo. No tengo cámara.)*

1. visitar los museos

2. conocer gente interesante

3. traerme un recuerdo

4. comprarme una camiseta

5. bucear solo

6. ir de excursion a muchos lugares

7. llamarme todos los días

8. no tomar demasiado (*too much*) sol

Quiero que me compres un recuerdo.

4. The subjunctive to express influence

09-41
to 09-44

- Verbs of influence express the wishes, preferences, suggestions, requests, and implied commands of the speaker. When the verb in the main clause expresses influence, the verb in the dependent clause is expressed in the subjunctive mood. The following are verbs of influence:

aconsejar	to advise	**pedir (i, i)**	to ask
decir	to tell	**permitir**	to permit
desear	to wish, to desire	**prohibir**	to prohibit
insistir (en)	to insist	**querer (ie)**	to want
mandar	to order	**recomendar (ie)**	to recommend
necesitar	to need	**sugerir (ie, i)**	to suggest

- The subject of the verb in the main clause tries to influence the subject of the dependent clause.

  Carmen (querer) + yo (ir):

  Carmen **quiere** que (yo) **vaya** con ella de vacaciones.

  Carmen wants me to go with her on vacation.

  ustedes (necesitar) + yo (llevar):

  ¿**Necesitan** que (yo) los **lleve** al aeropuerto?

  Do you need (for) me to take you to the airport?

  mi novia (desear) + yo (recoger) :

  Mi novia **desea** que (yo) **recoja** las maletas.

  My girlfriend wants me to pick up the luggage.

- Many impersonal expressions also show influence and call for the subjunctive when there is a change of subject.

Es bueno	It's good	**Es mejor**	It's better
Es importante	It's important	**Es necesario**	It's necessary
Es imposible	It's impossible	**Es preciso**	It's essential
Es indispensable	It's crucial	**Es urgente**	It's urgent

  Es imposible que **pasemos** la frontera sin pasaporte.

  It's impossible for us to cross the border without a passport.

  Es indispensable que **compres** un plano de la ciudad.

  It's crucial that you buy a city map.

- When there is no change of subject between the two verbs, use the infinitive.

  Sofía (desear) + Sofía (ir)
  Sofía **desea ir** a pescar.   }   *Sofía wants to go fishing.*

  Es mejor + (conocer)
  Es mejor conocer la ciudad a pie.   }   *It's better to get to know the city on foot.*

- Sentences using verbs such as **aconsejar, decir, pedir, recomendar,** and **sugerir** require an indirect object pronoun. This pronoun refers to the subject of the dependent clause.

  Le aconsejo (a Ud.) que nade más.

  I advise you to swim more. (lit., I advise that you swim more.)

  Nos piden que hagamos más ejercicio.

  They ask us to exercise more. (lit. They ask that we exercise more.)

(¿Necesitan que los lleve a casa?)

- When verbs of communication such as **decir, informar,** and **escribir** are used in the main clause and the subject of the verb is simply reporting information (telling someone something), the indicative is used in the dependent clause. If the verb in the main clause is used in the sense of a command (telling someone to do something), the subjunctive is used.

Information

Julia le **dice** a Juan que **llega** mañana.

El agente nos **informa** que **volvemos** el sábado.

Julia tells Juan that she is arriving tomorrow.
The agent informs us that we're returning on Saturday.

Command

Julia le **dice** a Juan que **llegue** mañana.
El agente nos **informa** que **volvamos** el sábado.

Julia tells Juan to arrive tomorrow.
The agent informs us to return on Saturday.

APLICACIÓN

9-27 Shakira. Shakira, la primera colombiana que ganó un Grammy Latino, es ahora una estrella internacional.

Paso 1 Lee la entrada que hizo Shakira en su diario y completa la lista de lo que estas personas quieren o esperan de ella.

> 18 de septiembre de 2011
>
> Querido diario:
>
> ¡Me encuentro en un momento muy bueno en la vida! Tengo mucha ilusión por todos mis proyectos, pero siempre queda más por hacer. Mis padres quieren que vuelva a Colombia y que pase más tiempo con ellos. Mi agente sugiere que haga más grabaciones, que viaje por Estados Unidos y Canadá, y que vaya a Europa.
> Mis admiradores insisten en que dé más conciertos. Mis amigos colombianos esperan que dedique más tiempo a obras caritativas[1] en Colombia. Mi novio me pide que me case con él y que me convierta en ama de casa. ¿Y yo? ¿Qué quiero yo? Pues, deseo que todo el mundo viva en paz y, especialmente, que disfrute de la música. Ese es mi sueño, pero por ahora, soy feliz.

[1]*charitable*

Lista

1. Su agente:

2. Sus amigos:

3. Sus padres:

4. Ella misma:

5. Sus admiradores:

6. Su novio:

 Paso 2 Conéctate a la Internet para ver más imágenes de Shakira y escuchar su música. ¿Cómo caracterizas su estilo? ¿Animado? ¿Romántico? ¿Melancólico? ¿Alegre?

> **Busca:** shakira

Presencia hispana

Another well-known native of Colombia currently residing in the U.S. is racecar driver Juan Pablo Montoya. Mostly known for his open-wheel racing, he has achieved the rare feat of becoming a crossover race winner on Formula One, ChampCar, IndiCar, GrandAm, and Nascar. Montoya established the Formula Smiles Foundation to help improve sports facilities and infrastructures in Colombia's poor neighborhoods. What other Hispanic personalities living in the U.S. or Canada also work to improve conditions in their home countries?

9-28 En la agencia de viajes. La agente de viajes tiene algunos consejos para sus clientes. Completa sus consejos con el verbo lógico en el subjuntivo de la lista que sigue cada entrada.

MODELO: Sra. Domínguez, ¿prefiere que yo le *mande* su itinerario por correo electrónico? (buscar – mandar – traer)

• Sr. López, es necesario que usted (1) _____ su pasaje con dos semanas de anticipación. Necesito que usted me (2) _____ su número de tarjeta de crédito. (comprar – dar – fumar)

• Juan y Carlos, ustedes saben que ahora las aerolíneas no permiten que los pasajeros (3) _____ en el avión. Si quieren fumar, es mejor que (4) _____ a la sala de fumadores en el aeropuerto antes de abordar. (ir – fumar – llevar)

• Doña María, sugiero que usted (5) _____ las recetas (*prescriptions*) en su bolsa y que (6) _____ copias para poner en la maleta. (hacer – llegar – poner)

• Lupe, es importante que (tú) (7) _____ con dos horas de anticipación antes de tu vuelo. Los agentes de seguridad insisten en que los pasajeros (8) _____ los objetos puntiagudos (*sharp*) en su casa. (comprar – dejar – llegar)

• Sres. Echevarría, les recomiendo que ustedes (9) _____ en el avión porque si no, van a estar muy cansados después de más de siete horas de viaje. Por eso, les sugiero que le (10) _____ café descafeinado al asistente de vuelo. (dormir – ir – pedir)

• Carolina, en países hispanos, vas a escuchar muchos piropos (*compliments*) en la calle. Es importante que no te (11) _____ nerviosa o enojada ni que les (12) _____ porque es parte de la cultura. (pedir – poner – responder)

9-29 El Parque Nacional Tayrona. Este es uno de los parques nacionales más visitados de Colombia. Está en la costa y tiene algunas de las playas y bahías más pintorescas de Colombia. Completa los consejos que te da una agente de viajes con la forma correcta de uno de los verbos siguientes.

ayudar	entrar	pagar	comprar	ir	tener

El Parque Nacional Tayrona

Primero, le aconsejo que (1) _____ listo (*ready*) el pasaporte para poder visitar Colombia. Segundo, le sugiero que (2) _____ una buena guía turística. La puede comprar en cualquier (*any*) librería. Ahora, no se permite que los viajeros (3) _____ al país con frutas u otros comestibles. Una vez en Colombia, le recomiendo que (4) _____ al parque en carro privado y con guía. Es un viaje inolvidable. También, le sugiero que (5) _____ su hotel en el parque aquí en la agencia porque muchas veces cuesta menos desde aquí. Si quiere que le (6) _____ con el viaje, lo hago con mucho gusto.

9-30 ¿Qué esperan tus amigos y tu familia? Tus amigos y tu familia quieren que lo pases bien en tus vacaciones. Combina frases de las dos columnas con **que** para decir lo que desean todos.

MODELO: Mi padre quiere… escribirle una tarjeta postal
Mi padre quiere que yo le escriba una tarjeta postal.

1. Mi madre espera…		pasarlo bien
2. Mi novio/a (esposo/a) desea…		tener mucho dinero
3. Mis amigos me aconsejan…		ir a un país de habla española
4. Mi amigo/a me sugiere…	que	sacar muchas fotos
5. Mi profesor/a de… insiste en…		llevar el pasaporte
6. Mi hermano/a pide…		comprar muchos recuerdos
7. Mi abuelo/a prefiere…		llevar una cámara digital
8. Mis tíos recomiendan…		no hacer deportes extremos

9-31A ¿Qué hacer? Cuando tienen un problema, es normal pedirle consejos a un/a amigo/a. Túrnense para explicarle algún problema a su compañero/a. Él/Ella debe responder de una manera lógica con el subjuntivo. Luego, reaccionen a la recomendación. **Estudiante B,** por favor ve al **Apéndice 1,** página A-17.

MODELO: Te recomiendo que (**estudiar**) mucho.
ESTUDIANTE A: *Tengo un examen de química mañana.*
ESTUDIANTE B: *Te recomiendo que estudies mucho.*
ESTUDIANTE A: *Buena idea. / No tengo tiempo. / No puedo porque…*

Estudiante A:

Mis problemas	Consejos para mi compañero/a
1. Necesito comprar libros para mis clases.	Es mejor que tú (**ir**) solo/a al cine.
2. Hay un crucero de tres días a Cancún, pero nadie quiere ir conmigo.	Te recomiendo que (**limpiar**) la casa antes del fin de semana.
3. Quiero ir de vacaciones, pero no tengo dinero.	Insisto en que (**estudiar**) otro año de español y que luego (**ir**) a estudiar a España o a Latinoamérica.
4. Quiero un trabajo más interesante.	Te pido que (**hablar**) con tu jefe y que le (**pedir**) menos horas de trabajo.

Te recomiendo que hagas un crucero por el Mediterráneo.

9-32 ¿Cuáles son tus deseos?   Escribe cinco deseos que tienes para el futuro. Expresa los deseos con verbos como **querer, desear, preferir, es importante,** etc., usando el subjuntivo cuando haya cambios de sujeto en la oración.

MODELO: *Deseo que mis padres vivan muchos años y que siempre tengamos una buena relación. Espero que mis amigos encuentren un buen trabajo y que ganen mucho dinero. Prefiero viajar después de terminar mis estudios.*

Quiero conocer el mundo y espero que tú me acompañes.

09-45 to 09-49

¿Cuánto saben?

Primero, pregúntate si puedes llevar a cabo las siguientes funciones comunicativas en español. Después, júntate con dos o tres compañeros/as de clase para presentar las situaciones. Hagan y respondan a por lo menos cuatro preguntas en cada situación.

✓ CAN YOU . . .

☐ describe travel and vacation experiences?

☐ try to influence others?

☐ give advice to someone?

WITH YOUR CLASSMATE(S) . . .

Situación: Entre amigos
Cuéntense lo que hicieron en sus últimas vacaciones. Hablen de su hotel, de lo que visitaron, de las excursiones que hicieron, de cómo lo pasaron, si compraron algo, etc.
Para empezar: *El año pasado hice un viaje a…*

Situación: Nuestro próximo viaje
Ustedes no pueden decidir adónde ir en su próximo viaje. Todos tienen opiniones muy fuertes (*strong*). Usen el subjuntivo para convencerse y finalmente, llegar a un acuerdo.
Para empezar: *Quiero ir a… Insisto en que… Es necesario que…*

Situación: Problemas personales
Traten de ayudarse con un problema serio como la falta de dinero, problemas en casa, una clase difícil, un horario imposible, etc. Usen el subjuntivo para darse consejos.
Para empezar: *Te aconsejo que… Es importante que… Insisto en que…*

Observaciones

09-50
to 09-52

¡Pura vida! EPISODIO 9

En este episodio Patricio les sirve de guía a Felipe, a Silvia y a David Ortiz-Smith.

Antes de ver el video

9-33 En peligro de extinción. Lee el siguiente artículo y escribe cinco características del guacamayo.

> El guacamayo es un pájaro de hermoso plumaje. La belleza de sus plumas lo ha puesto en peligro de extinción durante años. Sus colores predominantes, el azul, el rojo y el amarillo, atraen la admiración de todos los que lo ven. Estos bellos pájaros, que pasan la mayor parte del día comiendo y tomando el sol, son los loros[1] más grandes y los más coloridos.
>
> Su hábitat en la América tropical se extiende desde el sur de México hasta Paraguay. Algunas de sus características físicas más sobresalientes, además de su bello plumaje, son su enorme pico[2] largo y curvado, y sus ojos redondos y negros.
>
> En particular, las plumas de los guacamayos eran unos de los objetos más apreciados por las culturas indígenas, ya que las utilizaban para adornar sus vestimentas y accesorios. Incluso, las usaban para comerciar o como regalo de amistad.

[1]*parrots* [2]*beak*

El *Ara macao* habita las selvas desde México hasta Paraguay.

A ver el video

9-34 La excursión. Mira el noveno episodio de **¡Pura vida!** y completa cada oración con la expresión más lógica, según el video.

Patricio

David Ortiz-Smith

Felipe y Silvia

1. _____ es un fenómeno meteorológico que afecta el clima. Ciertos lugares reciben más lluvia; otros reciben menos.

2. El señor David Ortiz-Smith casi pierde el vuelo porque cambiaron _____.

3. Panchito es un _____ joven que duerme en los árboles durante el día.

4. Al final, todos observan _____.

Después de ver el video

 9-35 Un centro de rescate (*rescue*). Conéctate a la Internet para aprender más sobre un centro de rescate en Colombia o en Venezuela. Luego escribe una carta al centro en que expreses tu interés en ser voluntario/a en ese centro.

> **Busca:** centro rescate animales extincion colombia, centro rescate animales extincion venezuela

Nuestro mundo

🔍 **Panoramas**

📖 **Los países caribeños de Sudamérica:**
09-53
to 09-54 **Venezuela y Colombia**

Es posible que conozcas algunas de las obras del escritor colombiano, Gabriel García Márquez, quien ganó el Premio Nobel de Literatura por sus novelas. En EE. UU. se hizo una película de una de sus novelas, *El amor en los tiempos de cólera*.

Aunque el petróleo contribuye al PIB (*GDP*) de Venezuela, todavía hay muchas personas que viven en la miseria en las afueras de la capital, Caracas.

Venezuela atrae a muchos turistas aficionados a los deportes extremos que desean gozar (*enjoy*) de su belleza natural.

Cartagena de Indias fue fundada en 1531. En pocos años su excelente puerto se convirtió en el más importante en el Nuevo Mundo para España. Cartagena llegó a ser una de las ciudades más ricas del Imperio Español.

En Colombia hay vastos depósitos de oro y de piedras preciosas, especialmente de esmeraldas. Estas riquezas figuran en las prendas que llevaban los caciques (*chiefs*) de los indígenas. Los conquistadores españoles sacaron y se llevaron muchas de estas riquezas.

Venezuela y Colombia

	Venezuela	Colombia
Población:	26,8 millones	45,6 millones
Sitios de UNESCO[1]:	3	6
Ingresos del turismo:	$16,8 mil millones	$12,5 mil millones
Clima:	tropical en las costas; más templado en el interior	

[1]Patrimonio de la Humanidad

9-36 Identifica. Identifica, describe o explica lo siguiente.

1. el nombre de un escritor y por qué es famoso
2. por qué Cartagena de Indias era una de las ciudades más importantes de la época colonial
3. el color de una esmeralda
4. un producto importante en la economía de Venezuela
5. los deportes que atraen turistas a Venezuela
6. un metal precioso que se mina en Colombia

9-37 Desafío. Consulta el mapa y la caja para contestar estas preguntas.

1. el país que tiene costas en el Caribe y en el Pacífico
2. la capital de Colombia y la de Venezuela
3. el país que tiene mayores ingresos del turismo
4. el número de sitios en los dos países que forman parte del Patrimonio de la Humanidad de la UNESCO (*World Heritage Sites*)
5. el clima en las zonas interiores de Colombia y Venezuela

 9-38 Proyecto. Estas personas son famosas por sus contribuciones a las artes o por su participación política en su país. Escoge una de las siguientes figuras importantes, u otra que te interese, para investigar más sobre él/ella. Usa el Modelo para escribir un resumen en el que incluyas lo siguiente:

- su nombre y su profesión
- por qué es importante o interesante
- cómo era en el pasado; cómo es ahora
- si quieres conocerlo/la algún día y por qué
- si piensas estudiar más sobre esta persona
- una foto representativa

> **Busca:** shakira; gabriel garcia marquez; juanes; simon bolivar; hugo chavez; juan pablo montoya; antanas mockus; juan manuel santos; alvaro uribe

MODELO: *Dayana Mendoza nació en Caracas en 1986. Sabe varios idiomas y trabaja como modelo. Después de ganar el concurso de Miss Universo en el año 2008, declaró que iba a pasar el año viajando por el mundo para…*

📖 Páginas

09-55

ANTES DE LEER

9-39 Un folleto turístico. De estas actividades, ¿cuáles normalmente encuentras en un folleto turístico? ¿Cuáles son importantes para conocer la cultura de otro lugar?

Normal (N)	Importante (I)
_____ las actividades deportivas	_____ la gastronomía
_____ las fiestas y las ferias	_____ las excursiones
_____ la artesanía	_____ la economía

De estas cosas, ¿cuáles te interesan más a ti? ¿Cuáles son las menos importantes para ti?

A LEER

9-40 Los folletos. Los folletos dan información interesante para que decidas visitar un lugar o país. Las imágenes son para estimularte la imaginación. Pueden ser exóticas, hermosas o simplemente diferentes. Ve las imágenes en el folleto y trata de identificar de qué se trata sin leer el texto.

¡Fiestas Colombianas!

Carnaval (febrero)

Las fiestas de carnaval fueron iniciadas por los españoles y portugueses durante la época de la Colonia, como fiestas de esclavos. El festival más vistoso y colorido es sin duda el de Barranquilla. La palabra "carnaval" proviene de la práctica de poder comer carne antes de empezar la época de Cuaresma[1], porque en esta época los católicos se abstenían de comerla.

Corpus Cristi (mayo–junio)

En ciertas regiones se observa una síntesis de tradiciones indígenas y cristianas.

¡Visite Colombia en cualquier época del año para pasarlo bien!

Semana Santa (marzo–abril)

Las celebraciones de Semana Santa más famosas de Colombia tienen lugar en Popayán y Mompox, donde los colonizadores españoles construyeron muchas iglesias y capillas, todas importantes en los eventos de Semana Santa. Popayán fue fundada en 1536, y la celebración de Semana Santa es tan tradicional como la de Sevilla, España.

Día de la Independencia (20 de julio)

En 1810, el pueblo colombiano, bajo el liderazgo de Simón Bolívar, se liberó de España. Hoy en día se celebra con fuegos artificiales y es un día festivo.

¡Y en cualquier mes del año hay ferias y festivales por todo el país!

[1]Lent

DESPUÉS DE LEER

9-41 Lo normal y lo exótico.   Da tus impresiones sobre la información contenida en el folleto.

1. ¿Cuáles de las imágenes te parecen más exóticas?

2. ¿Cuáles de las imágenes te parecen iguales a celebraciones que ya conoces?

3. ¿Cuáles de las fiestas celebras tú?

4. ¿En qué aspectos son parecidas? ¿En qué aspectos son diferentes?

5. Si algún día visitas Colombia, ¿cuál prefieres conocer?

9-42 En su experiencia.   Las fiestas reflejan la cultura de la gente. Por ejemplo, mucha gente de origen irlandés celebra el día de San Patricio. Hay desfiles, fiestas, comida, bebidas verdes, etc. Escojan una fiesta que se celebre en su ciudad o su pueblo y contesten estas preguntas:

1. ¿Cuál es el origen de la fiesta?

2. ¿Cuándo y cómo se celebra?

3. ¿Participan ustedes en la celebración? ¿Cómo?

4. ¿Es una fiesta que se celebra en el mundo hispano, también?

En Detroit se celebra el Cinco de Mayo.

9-43 Las fiestas y las comidas.   Es común tener comida especial en días festivos. Si te encuentras en Colombia o en Venezuela para la Nochevieja, vas a probar comida muy diferente a la que conoces. Conéctate a la Internet para ver ejemplos de comida típica. Escribe un párrafo, describiendo la comida y sus ingredientes.

> **Busca:** venezuela comida fin ano; colombia comida fin ano

9-44 **Un folleto turístico.** En esta actividad vas a crear un folleto turístico.

MODELO: *¿Por qué conocer Indiana? Por su música, sus deportes, su naturaleza, su arte, su gente…*

ANTES DE ESCRIBIR

- **Ideas.** Piensa en un lugar en el mundo hispano que no conozcas. Haz una lista de lo que quieres saber de este lugar para incluir en el folleto.
- **Investigar.** Busca información e imágenes del lugar en la Internet.

A ESCRIBIR

- Escribe descripciones cortas de las imágenes para el folleto. Incluye puntos interesantes sobre la cultura, la historia, el clima, la comida, fechas importantes, etc.
- Ordena las imágenes y las descripciones en un papel grande.
- Dale un título al folleto.
- Para un modelo, consulta el folleto en la página 314.

DESPUÉS DE ESCRIBIR

- **Revisar.** Revisa tu folleto para verificar los siguientes puntos:
    - ☐ la concordancia de nombres y adjetivos
    - ☐ el uso de **por** y **para**
    - ☐ el uso de adverbios que terminan en **-mente** (**Originalmente el sitio era…**)
    - ☐ el uso del subjuntivo (**Es importante que…; Sugerimos que…; Es necesario que…**)
- **Intercambiar**
  Intercambia tu folleto con el de un/a compañero/a para hacer correcciones y sugerencias y para decidir si quieren visitar el lugar.
- **Entregar**
  Pon el folleto en limpio, incorporando las sugerencias de tu compañero/a. Después, entrégaselo a tu profesor/a.

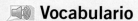
Vocabulario

Primera parte

En la agencia de viajes   At the travel agency

el/la agente de viajes   *travel agent*
el boleto (electrónico)   *(e-)ticket*
el folleto   *brochure*
el pasaje (de ida y vuelta)   *(roundtrip) fare, ticket*
la reservación / reserva   *reservation*
el/la viajero/a   *traveler*

En el aeropuerto At the airport

la aduana   *customs*
el avión   *plane*
el control de seguridad   *security checkpoint*
el/la inspector/a de aduanas   *customs inspector*
el pasaporte   *passport*
la puerta de embarque   *boarding gate*
la sala de espera   *waiting room*
el reclamo de equipaje   *baggage claim*
la tarjeta de embarque   *boarding pass*
el vuelo   *flight*

En el avión   On the plane

el asiento de pasillo / de ventanilla   *aisle seat / window seat*
el/la asistente de vuelo   *flight attendant*
la clase turista   *coach class*
la demora   *delay*
la escala   *stopover*
la llegada   *arrival*
el/la pasajero/a   *passenger*
el/la piloto   *pilot*
la salida   *departure*

Verbos   Verbs

abordar   *to board*
aterrizar   *to land*
bajarse (de)   *to get off (of), to get down (from)*
despegar   *to take off*
esperar   *to wait for*
facturar el equipaje   *to check luggage*
hacer cola   *to stand in line*
hacer la(s) maleta(s)   *to pack the suitcase(s)*
hacer un crucero   *to take a cruise*
pasar por (...)   *to pass through (. . .)*
viajar por barco   *to travel by ship*
tren   *train*
carro / coche / auto   *car*
autobús   *bus*

Segunda parte

En el viaje   On the trip

el adaptador eléctrico   *electrical adapter*
la cámara digital   *digital camera*
la cámara de video   *video camera*
el cargador   *charger*
la gira   *tour*
el/la guía   *guide*
la guía turística   *guidebook*
la pila   *battery*
el plano de la ciudad   *city map*
la tarjeta de memoria   *memory card*
la tarjeta postal   *postcard*

Atracciones turísticas   Tourist attractions

el bosque   *forest*
la catedral   *cathedral*
el centro histórico   *historical center*
la estatua   *statue*
las flores   *flowers*
la isla   *island*
el lago   *lake*
las montañas   *mountains*
el monumento   *monument*
el salto de agua / la catarata   *waterfall*
el volcán   *volcano*

En el hotel   At the hotel

el cuarto doble   *double room*
la estadía   *stay*
el/la gerente   *manager*
el hostal   *inn / youth hostel*
el hotel (de lujo)   *(luxury) hotel*
la vista   *view*

Actividades típicas de los viajeros   Typical activities for travelers

bucear   *to scuba dive, to swim under water*
comprar recuerdos   *to buy souvenirs*
ir de excursión   *to go on an excursion*
montar a caballo   *to go horseback riding*
en bicicleta   *bicycle riding*
pasarlo de maravilla   *to have a wonderful time*
pescar   *to fish*
quedarse   *to stay (somewhere)*
recorrer   *to travel around, to tour*
viajar al extranjero   *to travel abroad*

Expressions with *por* *See page 289.*   **Verbs and expressions of influence** *See page 306.*

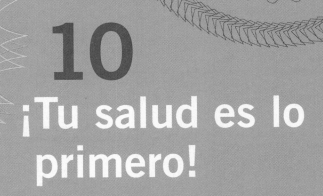

10
¡Tu salud es lo primero!

Readiness
Check

Bolivia y Paraguay: riquezas por descubrir

«Comamos manzanas todo el año y la enfermedad sufrirá un desengaño».

Refrán: Let's eat apples all year long and illness will be deceived. (*An apple a day keeps the doctor away.*)

En Paraguay, *el ñandutí* es una artesanía popular.

Cerca de La Paz, Bolivia, se encuentran los restos de la ciudad de Tihuanaco y su famosa Puerta del Sol, con una imagen del dios creador.

Primera parte

¡Así lo decimos! VOCABULARIO

 ¡Así es la vida! En el consultorio del médico

Muchas personas tienen cita con la doctora Méndez. Mientras esperan, hablan de sus síntomas.

ANABEL: Me torcí la rodilla mientras hacía jogging.

ALFREDO: Y yo, tengo náuseas. ¡Qué mal me siento!

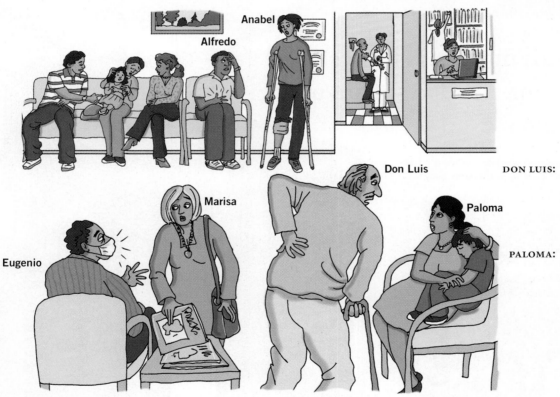

DON LUIS: ¡Ay, cuánto me duele la espalda! No puedo sentarme.

PALOMA: Mi hijo tiene fiebre y no quiere comer nada. No sé si es un simple resfriado o algo más serio.

EUGENIO: Tengo mucha tos y me duele todo el cuerpo. Creo que tengo gripe.

MARISA: Es mejor que se lo diga a la doctora.

Vocabulario Las partes del cuerpo humano

| Las partes del cuerpo humano | Parts of the human body |

la boca	mouth		la muela	molar
el brazo	arm		el oído	ear (inner)
la cabeza	head		la oreja	ear (outer)
el corazón	heart		el pecho	chest
el dedo (del pie)	finger (toe)		el pie	foot
la espalda	back		la pierna	leg
el estómago	stomach		el pulmón	lung
la garganta	throat		la rodilla	knee
la lengua	tongue			

Me duele la garganta.

Variaciones
While most of the Spanish-speaking world says **la gripe**, in Mexico the term used is **la gripa**, with a final **a** instead of **e**.

| Problemas de salud | Health problems |

doler (ue)[1]	to hurt
lastimarse	to hurt oneself
romperse (un hueso)	to break (a bone)
ser alérgico/a a	to be allergic to
tener fiebre (*f.*)	to have a fever
dolor de cabeza (*m.*)	a headache
gripe (*f.*)	a flu
infección (*f.*)	an infection
resfriado (*m.*)	a cold
tos (*f.*)	a cough
náuseas (*f.*)	(to feel) nauseated
torcerse (ue)	to twist
toser	to cough

Variaciones
Lastimarse is more common in the Americas, whereas **hacerse daño** is preferred in Spain.

| Sugerencias y remedios médicos | Medical advice and remedies |

dejar de (fumar)	to quit (smoking)
guardar cama	to stay in bed due to sickness
hacer una cita	to make an appointment
mejorarse	to get better, to get well
respirar	to breathe
seguir (i, i)[2] los consejos del médico	to follow the doctor's advice
tomar la presión	to take blood pressure
la temperatura	temperature

Me duele una muela.

Variaciones
The expression **tomarse la presión** is typical in Latin America; **tomarse la tensión** in Spain.

| Medicinas comunes | Common medicines |

el antiácido	antacid		el calmante	tranquilizer, painkiller
el antibiótico	antibiotic		el jarabe	cough syrup
la aspirina	aspirin		la pastilla	pill, lozenge

| En el consultorio del médico | At the doctor's office |

el diagnóstico	diagnosis		el/la paciente	patient
el dolor	pain, ache		la radiografía	X-ray
la enfermedad	illness		la receta	prescription
el examen físico	checkup		el síntoma	symptom
la inyección	shot		la sala de urgencias	emergency room

Me rompí la pierna.

---

[1] *like* gustar: Me duelen los pies - *My feet hurt.*
[2] sigo, sigues, sigue, seguimos, seguís, siguen; seguí, seguiste, siguió, seguimos, seguisteis, siguieron

APLICACIÓN

10-1 Categorías. Pon una X en la(s) columna(s) que mejor describe(n) la parte del cuerpo y añade una más al final.

Parte del cuerpo	Tienes uno	Tienes dos	Tienes más de dos	Órgano interno
el dedo			X	
el corazón				
la nariz				
el ojo				
el pulmón				
la oreja				
el brazo				
el estómago				
la pierna				
la muela				
¿...?				

10-2 ¿Qué le pasa? Describe lo que les pasa a estas personas y da una posible causa de su(s) problema(s).

MODELO:

Alicia

A Alicia le duele el estómago porque comió dos hamburguesas.

1.

Alberto

2.

Ana María

3.

Samuel y Ricardo

4.
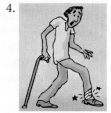

Carlos

5.

Ramiro y Marta

10-3 ¡Qué mal me siento! Escucha a doña Carmen mientras habla por teléfono con su médico; anota sus síntomas, un diagnóstico lógico y el consejo del médico.

Síntoma	Diagnóstico	Consejo
——— tos	——— alergias	——— tomar aspirina
——— fiebre	——— presiones del trabajo	——— descansar
——— dolor de cabeza	——— resfriado	——— comer sopa
——— dolor de estómago	——— gripe	——— comer mejor
——— dolor de garganta	——— úlceras	——— hacer ejercicio
——— dolor en una muela	——— mala dieta	——— tomar antibióticos

 10-4 ¿Cuándo consultas al médico? Pregúntense si consultan al médico en las siguientes situaciones.

MODELO: Te duele la cabeza.
    E1: *¿Consultas al médico si te duele la cabeza?*
    E2: *No. Por lo general tomo dos aspirinas y me siento mejor. ¿Y tú?*

1. Tienes tos.
2. Tienes una fiebre alta.
3. Te duele la espalda.
4. Te rompes un hueso.
5. Necesitas un examen físico para el trabajo.
6. Tienes náuseas.
7. Te duele la garganta.
8. Tienes resfriado.

10-5A Consejos médicos. Habla con tu compañero/a para que te dé consejos sobre los siguientes síntomas. **Estudiante B,** por favor ve al **Apéndice 1,** página A-18.

MODELO: ESTUDIANTE A: *Me duelen los pulmones.*
    ESTUDIANTE B: *Debes dejar de fumar.*

Estudiante A:

Mis síntomas:	Consejos para mi compañero/a:
1. Me duelen las piernas.	• comer carne
2. Creo que tengo fiebre.	• beber un refresco
3. No tengo energía.	• tomar aspirinas
4. No me siento bien.	• descansar mucho y no ir a clase
5. Tengo un resfriado terrible.	• beber mucha cafeína
6. Me duele el estómago.	• tomar jarabe

¿Qué se vende en una farmacia homeopática?

¡Hola!

Cultura en vivo

According to the World Health Organization (WHO), traditional medicine is widely practiced in much of Latin America and is often relied on for primary health care. Herbal medicines are the most lucrative form of traditional medicine, generating billions of dollars in revenue. There are over 2,000 documented indigenous medicinal plants in Bolivia alone. Have you ever taken an herbal remedy?

¡Así lo hacemos! ESTRUCTURAS

 1. Formal commands

Vaya a su casa y guarde cama. Tome estas pastillas por diez días y llámeme si no se siente mejor.

We use commands to give instructions or to ask people to do things. In Spanish, commands have different forms to distinguish between formal (**usted/ustedes**) and informal (**tú/vosotros**) address. Formal commands use subjunctive forms, with the implied meaning that the speaker is trying to influence the listener to do something.

Infinitive	Subjunctive	Formal commands	
		Ud.	**Uds.**
hablar	hable	hable	hablen
comer	coma	coma	coman
escribir	escriba	escriba	escriban
pensar	piense	piense	piensen
pedir	pida	pida	pidan
saber	sepa	sepa	sepan
ir	vaya	vaya	vayan

Cuide su salud. **Coma** comida sana.	*Take care of your health. Eat healthy food.*
Haga una cita con el médico.	*Make an appointment with the doctor.*
Pida una receta para antibióticos.	*Ask for a prescription for antibiotics.*

- Negative commands are formed by placing **no** in front of the command form.

No guarde cama más de dos días.	*Don't stay in bed for more than two days.*
No tosan durante un concierto.	*Don't cough during a concert.*

- Subject pronouns may be used with commands for emphasis or clarification. As a rule, they are placed after the verb.

Tenga **usted** cuidado.	***You** be careful.*
No fumen **ustedes** en el trabajo.	*Don't **you** smoke at work.*

- Object pronouns (direct, indirect) and reflexive pronouns are attached to affirmative commands. With the added syllable, the command then requires a written accent.

¡Váyase de aquí!	*Leave here!*
Tómele la presión, por favor.	*Take her blood pressure, please.*

- Object pronouns and reflexive pronouns precede negative commands.

No se tuerza la rodilla esquiando.	*Don't twist your knee skiing.*
No se lo den a la doctora.	*Don't give it to the doctor.*

APLICACIÓN

10-6 En el consultorio médico. Parece que la doctora Villalba se confunde un poco cuando les da consejos a sus pacientes o le pide algo a su asistente.

Paso 1 Primero, subraya todos los mandatos e identifica los infinitivos.

DOCTORA: Sra. Martínez, usted tiene la gripe porcina[1]. Vaya a su casa y guarde cama. Tome mucha agua y no se bañe por una semana.

DOCTORA: Luisa, por favor llame a la farmacia y dígales que necesitamos una botella grande de aspirinas. Pídales las pastillas grandes, las que no les gustan a los pacientes.

DOCTORA: Sr. Duarte, usted necesita un examen físico completo. Tome esta receta y vaya a un restaurante. Pídale al camarero que le haga el examen.

DOCTORA: Srta. Vera, usted se rompió un dedo. No use la mano durante dos semanas. No cocine ni escriba en la computadora. Tenga cuidado de no lastimarse más.

DOCTORA: Luisa, por favor vaya al departamento de radiografías y busque la de la Srta. Vera. Explíqueles que la necesito ahora mismo. Si dicen que no la tienen, déles una inyección de penicilina.

DOCTORA: Sr. Fernández, usted tiene los pulmones congestionados. Deje de fumar, haga por lo menos una hora de ejercicio diario, y no respire mucho durante dos semanas. Venga a verme en un mes, y por favor, no se mejore.

---

[1]*swine*

Paso 2 Ahora indica cuáles de los consejos son muy lógicos (**L**) y cuáles son ilógicos (**I**) en un consultorio médico.

10-7 El doctor Chiringa. El doctor Chiringa es una persona que siempre les da muchas órdenes a sus pacientes. Completa la conversación que tiene con sus pacientes Roberto y Tomás Cruz, usando mandatos formales.

DR. CHIRINGA: Señores Cruz, ustedes tienen que hacer algo por su salud. No (1) _____ (cenar) tan tarde y no (2) _____ (acostarse) todos los días después de las doce de la noche.

ROBERTO: Sí, doctor, pero es que llegamos del trabajo muy tarde.

DR. CHIRINGA: Entiendo, pero (3) _____ (tener) más cuidado, no (4) _____ (trabajar) tanto. (5) _____ (Llegar) a casa más temprano; (6) _____ (descansar) más y (7) _____ (poner) más atención a su salud.

TOMÁS: Doctor, es que tenemos muchas presiones. Mire usted, por la mañana trabajamos en un restaurante, y después, tenemos otro trabajo en una panadería. Volvemos tarde por la noche, comemos algo rápido y nos acostamos enseguida. Todos los días es igual.

DR. CHIRINGA: Bueno, no (8) _____ (enojarse). (9) _____ (Seguir) estos consejos y, si es posible, (10) _____ (cambiar) de trabajo.

ROBERTO: No es fácil, doctor, siempre estamos buscando otro trabajo mejor.

DR. CHIRINGA: Sí, lo sé. Pero su salud es lo primero.

TOMÁS: ¡De acuerdo, doctor! No (11) _____ (preocuparse). Vamos a seguir sus consejos.

Hispanos en EE. UU.
According to the American Medical Association (AMA), less than 3% of U.S. physicians are Hispanic even though Hispanics make up 16% of the nation's population. To increase the number of minority physicians, the AMA launched the Hispanic Physician Outreach Initiative to discuss strategies for increasing the voice of Hispanic physicians. Why is it important to have Hispanic physicians in Hispanic communities?

10-8 Servicios médicos de urgencias. Ustedes están entrenándose para ser paramédicos. Decidan el orden de importancia de las acciones en cada emergencia y túrnense para darle mandatos a su compañero/a.

MODELO: Un señor no puede respirar: darle oxígeno, darle respiración artificial, llamar a un cardiólogo

E1: *Primero, déle respiración artificial, después llame a un cardiólogo y finalmente déle oxígeno.*

E2: *No, primero llame a un cardiólogo.*

Prepare la ambulancia para una emergencia.

1. Hay un accidente en el centro: avisar al hospital, investigar cuál es el hospital que está más cerca, poner todo el equipo de emergencia en la ambulancia.

2. Un niño tuvo un accidente en su bicicleta: contactar a los padres, llevarlo al hospital, examinarlo para ver si se rompió algún hueso.

3. Hay un escape de gas en una casa de apartamentos: llamar a los bomberos, darles oxígeno a las víctimas, sacar a los residentes del edificio.

4. Un paciente está desorientado: hacerle preguntas, llamar a un familiar, tomarle la presión.

5. Una mujer tiene un tremendo dolor de cabeza: darle un calmante, tomarle la temperatura, preguntarle su nombre.

6. Es necesario preparar el equipo de la ambulancia para empezar un nuevo día: llenar el tanque de gasolina, revisar (*check*) los tanques de oxígeno, reponer (*restock*) las medicinas.

10-9A En la sala de urgencias. Ustedes tienen que decidir qué deben hacer en situaciones urgentes. Un/a estudiante presenta unas situaciones. El otro/la otra responde con instrucciones lógicas de su lista, usando mandatos formales. Túrnense, cambiando de papel. **Estudiante B,** por favor ve al **Apéndice 1,** página A-18.

MODELO: ESTUDIANTE A: *El niño tiene gripe.*
ESTUDIANTE B: *Déle muchos líquidos como jugo o agua.*

Estudiante A:

Situaciones urgentes	Acciones
1. El paciente necesita oxígeno.	• buscarle un calmante
2. A la niña le duele el estómago.	• darle dos aspirinas
3. El bebé está tosiendo mucho.	• darle té con limón
4. La señora tiene una infección en el brazo.	• hacerle una radiografía
5. El Sr. Pérez tiene una fiebre muy alta.	• mandarlo al dentista
6. ¿...?	¿...?

10-10 Consejos sobre la salud. En parejas, escriban en un papel un problema que tienen. Puede ser un problema de salud o de otro tipo. Intercambien papeles con otra pareja y escríbanles seis consejos para remediar su problema. Después, devuélvanse los papeles y escojan el mejor y el peor consejo que recibieron para presentarlos a la clase.

2. The subjunctive to express feelings and emotions

- The subjunctive is used in dependent clauses after verbs and impersonal expressions that express emotions such as hope, fear, surprise, regret, pity, anger, joy, and sorrow.

Temo que tu hija tenga una infección de oído.

Algunos verbos:

alegrarse (de)	*to be glad*
enojar	*to anger*
esperar	*to hope*
estar contento/a (de)	*to be happy*
lamentar	*to regret*
molestar	*to bother*
sentir (ie, i)	*to regret*
sorprender(se)	*to surprise*
temer	*to fear*
tener miedo (de)	*to be afraid*

Algunas expresiones impersonales:

es bueno/malo/mejor	*it's good/bad/better*
es extraño	*it's strange*
es fácil/difícil	*it's easy/difficult*
es fantástico	*it's fantastic*
es lamentable	*it's regrettable*
es una lástima	*it's a shame*
es (i)lógico	*it's (il)logical*
es (im)posible	*it's (im)possible*
es ridículo	*it's ridiculous*
es sorprendente	*it's surprising*

Talisa **lamenta** que su amigo Carlos **esté** enfermo.	*Talisa regrets that her friend Carlos is sick.*
Espero que **hagas** más ejercicio esta semana.	*I hope that you exercise more this week.*
Es fácil que el médico **dé** consejos sobre la salud.	*It's easy for the doctor to give health advice.*

- As with the verbs of influence, verbs that express feelings and emotions require the subjunctive in the dependent clause if the subject is different from that of the main clause. If there is only one subject, the infinitive is generally used in the dependent clause.

Carlos **lamenta estar** enfermo.	*Carlos regrets being sick.*
Esperamos hacer más ejercicio esta semana.	*We hope to exercise more this week.*
Es fácil dar consejos sobre la salud.	*It's easy to give health advice.*

El subjuntivo con Ojalá

- The expression **Ojalá** entered the Spanish language during the Arab occupation of Spain. It comes from an Arabic expression meaning *God (Allah) willing* and is used in Spanish as the equivalent of *I hope that.* **Ojalá** may be used with or without **que** and is followed by the subjunctive.

¡Ojalá (que) nos mantengamos en forma!	*I hope that we stay in shape!*
¡Ojalá (que) visites el spa en Bolivia!	*I hope you visit the spa in Bolivia!*

APLICACIÓN

10-11 Seis consejos para practicar un deporte. Antes de empezar a practicar un deporte, es importante seguir algunos consejos.

Paso 1 Primero, lee los consejos que siguen y subraya todos los mandatos.

---

1. Siga un programa de entrenamiento para estar en forma para su deporte. Comience por caminar o montar en bicicleta durante quince minutos. Gradualmente aumente su entrenamiento con otros ejercicios.

2. Conozca bien y siga las reglas del deporte, especialmente los deportes de contacto. Aprenda de las tácticas de los demás.

3. Use protección apropiada para las rodillas, las manos, los dientes, los ojos y la cabeza. Mantenga la guardia atenta y no tome riesgos[1] innecesarios.

4. Descanse. No se entrene todos los días. Tome días de descanso para evitar lesiones[2].

5. Siempre haga ejercicios de calentamiento para estirar[3] los músculos antes de jugar. Los músculos calientes son menos susceptibles a lastimarse.

6. Nunca juegue si está muy cansado. No ignore el dolor o la fatiga.

---

[1] *risks* [2] *injuries* [3] *stretch*

Paso 2 Ahora usa expresiones de emoción para comentar sobre los consejos para practicar un deporte.

MODELO: *Es sorprendente que algunas personas no sigan un programa de entrenamiento.*

10-12 Un examen médico. Completa la conversación entre el médico y el paciente con la forma correcta del verbo entre paréntesis, usando el indicativo, el subjuntivo o el infinitivo.

PACIENTE: Buenos días, doctor. Me siento muy mal.

MÉDICO: A ver ¿qué le (1) _____ (doler)?

PACIENTE: No me duele nada pero yo (2) _____ (sentirse) mal.

MÉDICO: Bueno, quiero ver cómo está del corazón. Quiero que (3) _____ (quitarse) la camisa y que (4) _____ (respirar) profundamente.

PACIENTE: Espero que no (5) _____ (ser) nada serio.

MÉDICO: No, pero temo que su comida (6) _____ (contener) demasiado colesterol y grasas trans.

PACIENTE: Me sorprende que (7) _____ (decir) eso. Soy vegetariano.

MÉDICO: Mmmm... Me alegro de (8) _____ (saber) eso. ¿Qué come para el desayuno?

PACIENTE: Donuts, galletas y panqueques.

MÉDICO: Ah... ¡Ahora entiendo! Es mejor que (9) _____ (dejar) de comer comida chatarra (*junk*).

10-13 ¡Mejoremos nuestra salud!   ¿Cómo propones cambiar tu vida para mejorar tu salud?

Paso 1   Escribe cinco resoluciones para mejorar la salud que piensas hacer el año que viene.

MODELO: *Espero hacerme un examen físico todos los años.*

 Paso 2   Ahora túrnense para expresar sus resoluciones y reaccionar usando una expresión apropiada para cada resolución.

Ojalá (que)...	Temo que...
Siento que...	Es bueno/malo/mejor que...
Es ridículo que...	Es sorprendente que...
Me alegro de que...	¿...?

MODELO: E1: *Espero hacerme un examen físico todos los años.*
    E2: *Ojalá tengas buenos resultados. Es bueno que consultes al médico.*

10-14 ¿Qué les molesta?   Túrnense para hablar de cosas que les molestan.

MODELO: E1: *Me molesta que la gente fume.*
    E2: *¿Sí? ¿Por qué?*

¿Cuánto saben?

Primero, pregúntate si puedes llevar a cabo las siguientes funciones comunicativas en español. Después, júntate con dos o tres compañeros/as de clase para presentar las situaciones. Hagan y respondan a por lo menos cuatro preguntas en cada situación.

✓ CAN YOU . . .

☐ talk about your health and explain what part of your body hurts?

☐ request that others do something?

☐ express emotions?

WITH YOUR CLASSMATE(S) . . .

Situación: En un consultorio médico
Túrnense para hacer los papeles de médico/a y paciente. Pregúntense y explíquense cuáles son los problemas y los remedios para curarlos. Usen mandatos formales para explicar qué debe hacer el paciente o para darle consejos.
Para empezar: *Doctor, no sé qué me pasa. Me duele...*

Situación: En la sala de urgencias
Hagan los papeles de médicos/as en urgencias que atienden a un paciente que no puede explicar sus problemas. Usen mandatos formales.
Para empezar: *Doctor, deme la radiografía del paciente...*

Situación: Avances médicos
Hablen sobre avances y problemas médicos que conozcan. Usen expresiones de emoción para expresar su opinión.
Para empezar: *Leo en el periódico que hay un nuevo tratamiento para el cáncer. Me alegro de que haya avances... Me sorprende que...*

📖 Perfiles

Mi experiencia

LA MEDICINA TRADICIONAL EN BOLIVIA

10-15 Para ti. ¿Tienes experiencia con la medicina tradicional (la homeopatía, la acupuntura, la medicina naturista)? ¿Qué opinas sobre estas prácticas? ¿Prefieres tomar antibióticos y otras medicinas o buscas otras alternativas? ¿Cuáles funcionan bien para ti? A continuación, lee el blog de Rosario donde nos cuenta de sus experiencias con estas prácticas.

Hola. Soy Rosario Domínguez y soy estudiante de antropología biológica en la Universidad de Toronto. Este año tengo un internado con la Organización Panamericana de la Salud (OPS). Este es mi blog sobre mi año en Bolivia, donde voy a trabajar con la OPS en una comunidad para mejorar la salud de sus habitantes y para aprender sobre la medicina tradicional.

15 de enero

La semana pasada terminamos la orientación y ahora estoy en uno de los pueblos donde voy a hacer mi internado. Allí aprendí que en las zonas más retiradas es muy común que los habitantes tengan más confianza en los médicos tradicionales que en la medicina moderna. Yo creo que es lógico, pues Bolivia tiene una larga tradición con estas prácticas, tanto que el viceministro de Medicina Tradicional e Interculturalidad, Emilio Cusi, es un conocido curandero[1]. ¿Qué curioso, no? Cuando llegué, tenía unos dolores de cabeza terribles a causa de la altura y fui a ver a un médico *kallawaya* quien me preparó mate de coca, un té hecho de las hojas de coca. Aunque[2] al principio tenía mis dudas, poco a poco empecé a sentirme mejor. Nunca se sabe, ¿verdad?

Durante mi internado, vamos a tener un concierto benéfico para recaudar fondos[3] para estas comunidades a la vez que promocionamos el trabajo de la OPS. Entre los artistas, va a tocar Octavia, la banda boliviana más popular de este momento. Sigan mi blog y les cuento más de mis experiencias.

[1]*healer*   [2]*even though*   [3]*raise funds*

 10-16 En su opinión. Como a Rosario, ¿les gustaría investigar más sobre la medicina tradicional? ¿Qué riesgos (*risks*) hay? Hagan una lista de las ventajas y desventajas de cada sugerencia o de cada uno de los siguientes tratamientos. Luego, comparen sus opiniones.

MODELO: una copa de vino diaria para proteger el corazón

E1: *Creo que es una buena idea tomar una copa de vino todos los días para proteger el corazón.*

E2: *No estoy de acuerdo. Las bebidas alcohólicas nunca son saludables y creo que...*

1. la quiropráctica para aliviar el dolor de espalda
2. el té verde para protegerse del cáncer
3. la acupuntura para aliviar el dolor de la rodilla
4. las bebidas "power" para mantenerse fuerte
5. la superfruta *açai* para mantener la buena salud
6. la aspirina para mantener la buena circulación de la sangre (*blood*)

Mi música

"VIAJE" (OCTAVIA, BOLIVIA)

En 1995, Octavia debutó en el MTV Latino, y desde ese momento la banda fue conocida a nivel mundial. Sus discos se han vendido mucho por todas las Américas. Su música recoge la experiencia del boliviano orgulloso de la riqueza de sus raíces étnicas. Sus miembros son Omar (cantante principal) Simón y Vladi (guitarra), Martín (batería) y Jimbo (zampoña).

Antes de ver y escuchar

 10-17 Ir de viaje. ¿Cuáles son algunas de las razones por las que uno/a hace un viaje? ¿Es siempre para llegar a un lugar, o también puede ser para irse de un lugar? Da ejemplos de los dos motivos.

Para ver y escuchar

 10-18 La canción. Conéctate a la Internet para ver un video de Octavia cantando "Viaje". Identifica si el motivo es para llegar a o para irse de un lugar. ¿Qué se descubre al final?

> **Busca:** octavia viaje video; octavia viaje letra
>
> **Si te interesa comprar la canción:** *Go to iTunes Store>Music>More to Explore>iMix>Arriba 6e*

Después de ver y escuchar

10-19 El paisaje. El video de "Viaje" te da una idea del paisaje en zonas remotas de Bolivia. Escribe un párrafo en el que describas lo que ves y cómo imaginas la vida de la gente que vive allí.

MODELO: *Me parece que la zona es muy árida porque…*

10-20 Un concierto para ayudar a la OPS. Imagínense que organizan un concierto para la Organización Panamericana de la Salud (OPS). Trabajen juntos y hagan una lista de las cosas que tienen que hacer o de las preocupaciones que tienen antes del concierto de Octavia.

MODELO: Es necesario que… *le escribamos una invitación al agente de Octavia.*

1. Espero que…
2. Es importante que…
3. Me sorprende que…
4. Me alegro de que…
5. Temo que…

Segunda parte

¡Así lo decimos! VOCABULARIO

¡Así es la vida! ¡Mejora tu salud!

 La doctora Soto Mejía da una clase de nutrición.

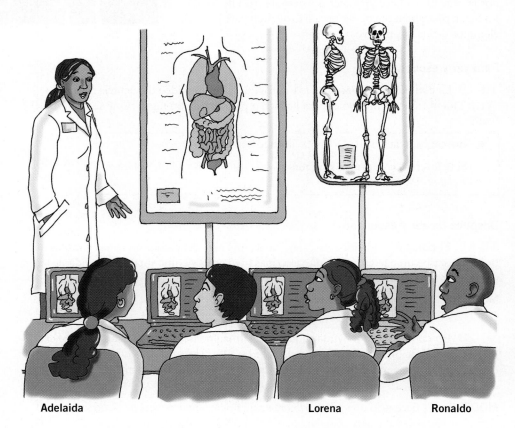

Adelaida	**Lorena**	**Ronaldo**

DRA. SOTO MEJÍA:	¿Cierto o falso? Se puede adelgazar comiendo una dieta de puros carbohidratos.
ADELAIDA:	Cierto, pero enseguida se engorda después.
LORENA:	Cierto, pero el cuerpo necesita proteínas también.
RONALDO:	Depende de si son carbohidratos buenos o malos...
DRA. SOTO MEJÍA:	Me gustan todas sus repuestas, pero dudo que haya una sola respuesta a este dilema.

10-30
to 10-35

Vocabulario Los alimentos

Sigan una dieta rica en... | Follow a diet rich in ...

(los) antioxidantes   *antioxidants*
(el) calcio   *calcium*
(la) fibra   *fiber*
(las) proteínas   *proteins*
(los) carbohidratos complejos   *complex carbohydrates*

En moderación coman alimentos con... | In moderation, eat foods with ...

(los) carbohidratos sencillos   *simple carbohydrates*
(el) colesterol   *cholesterol*
(las) grasas monoinsaturadas (poliinsaturadas)
monounsaturated polyunsaturated fats

Eviten... | Avoid ...

las bebidas alcohólicas   *alcoholic beverages*
la comida chatarra   *junk food*
los dulces   *sweets*
las grasas saturadas (trans)   *saturated (trans) fats*

Las enfermedades y el bienestar | Illnesses and well-being

la diabetes   *diabetes*
los ejercicios aeróbicos   *aerobics*
el estrés   *stress*
el (sobre)peso   *(excess) weight*

Tu línea y tu salud | Your weight and your health

adelgazar   *to lose weight*
bajar de peso   *to lose weight*
cuidar(se)   *to take care (of oneself)*
engordar   *to gain weight*
estar a dieta   *to be on a diet*
guardar la línea   *to stay trim, to watch one's figure*
mantenerse (ie) en forma   *to stay in shape*
padecer (zc) (de)   *to suffer (from)*
ponerse en forma   *to get in shape*
subir de peso   *to gain weight*

Variaciones

La comida chatarra is used mainly in Mexico and Uruguay. **La comida basura** and **las porquerías** are common alternatives in other Spanish-speaking countries. Examples of these foods include **las papas fritas** (in the Americas) and **las patatas fritas** (in Spain) for both *potato chips* and *French fries*.

El médico nos aconseja que evitemos los carbohidratos sencillos.

Es mejor que seleccionemos comidas ricas en proteínas, vitaminas y con poca grasa saturada...

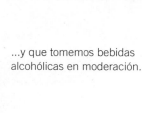

...y que tomemos bebidas alcohólicas en moderación.

Letras y sonidos

The consonants *r* and *rr*

In Spanish, there are two **r** sounds: a flap (or tap) and a trill. A flap involves one quick touch of the tongue behind the upper front teeth. This sound is similar to the English flap made for the letters *tt* in *butter*. A Spanish trill is a rapid series of two or more flaps. English has no trill, but this sound is approximated when imitating a race car revving up its engine.

The trill sound occurs in Spanish in the contexts:

rr:	pe-**rr**o	pi-za-**rr**a	a-bu-**rr**i-do
Word initial:	**R**o-sa	**R**a-món	**r**á-pi-do
After l, n, or **s:**	al-re-de-dor	En-**r**i-que	Is-**r**a-el

In other contexts, the **r** is usually a single flap:

pe-ro   o-pe-**r**ar   es-t**r**és   g**r**a-sa

APLICACIÓN

10-21 Los alimentos. Coloca las comidas a continuación en una categoría apropiada. Hay un ejemplo en cada categoría. Algunas comidas pueden formar parte de más de una categoría.

las bebidas alcohólicas: *el vino*	el calcio: *la leche*	los carbohidratos complejos: *la manzana*	la comida chatarra: *las papas fritas*	el colesterol: *el bistec*
la fibra: *los frijoles*	los carbohidratos sencillos: *el azúcar*	las grasas mono o poliinsaturadas: *el aceite de oliva*	las proteínas: *el pescado*	los antioxidantes: *las fresas*

1. el pollo
2. el flan
3. el helado
4. la hamburguesa
5. los camarones
6. el tequila
7. el yogur
8. los espaguetis
9. la banana
10. los huevos
11. las uvas
12. la cerveza
13. el pan blanco
14. el aceite de maíz
15. la pizza

¿Sigues los consejos de la pirámide alimenticia?

10-22 En la oficina de la doctora Menéndez. Completa los consejos de la Dra. Menéndez con una palabra o expresión del vocabulario de **¡Así lo decimos!** Conjuga los verbos cuando sea necesario.

MODELO: Sra. García, es bueno guardar la línea, es decir, no subir ni bajar mucho de peso.

1. Sra. García, usted tiene mucho ________________ en su vida. Quiero que tome calmantes y que se vaya de vacaciones por una semana.
2. Sra. López, su hijo ________________ de alergias a los productos lácteos. No debe beber leche ni comer helado.
3. Sr. González, para mantenerse en forma, usted debe hacer ________________ como el jogging o el tenis. Pronto va a ________________.
4. Srta. Casals, usted está muy flaca. No debe seguir ________________ tan rígida de solo verduras.
5. Sr. Rojas, usted perdió dos kilos este mes. ¿Cómo ________________?

10-23 Un chequeo para la salud. La diabetes es una enfermedad seria.

Paso 1 Completa el cuestionario sobre la diabetes y decide si tienes riesgo.

CHEQUEO PARA SU SALUD...

Los hispanos son más propensos a sufrir diabetes... ¿por qué correr este riesgo sin necesidad?

En honor a la "Semana de Alerta a la Diabetes", hágase una simple prueba. Este servicio es **gratis** para la comunidad. A continuación tiene unas preguntas, solamente necesita responder SÍ o NO y debe anotar 10 puntos por cada respuesta afirmativa.

Estoy sintiendo los siguientes síntomas con regularidad:	SÍ	NO
Sed excesiva	❑	❑
Orino[1] con frecuencia	❑	❑
Mucho cansancio	❑	❑
Pérdida de peso inexplicable	❑	❑
Vista nublada a veces	❑	❑
Tengo más de 40 años:	❑	❑
Según las tablas de peso, tengo más peso del debido:	❑	❑
Soy mujer y he tenido niños que han pesado más de 9 libras al nacer:	❑	❑
Mi madre/padre es diabético/a:	❑	❑
Mi gemelo/a[2] tiene diabetes:	❑	❑
Mi hermano/a tiene diabetes:	❑	❑

Si su total es de 20 o de más de 20 puntos, le recomendamos que se haga una prueba de diabetes, absolutamente gratis.

LAS PRUEBAS SE EFECTUARÁN:

Martes, 19 de marzo—8:00 am -11:00 am
Vestíbulo del Hospital San Vicente
Calle Reina del Río
Asunción

Las personas que deseen hacerse esta prueba no deben comer dos horas antes del examen.

Contaremos con una dietista que podrá informarle sobre las comidas y contestar cualquier pregunta que pueda tener.

Para más información o si quiere recibir nuestra revista gratis, llame al
5-56-68-50

Hospital San Vicente
Calle Reina del Río, Asunción, Paraguay

[1]*urinate* [2]*twin*

Paso 2 ¿Cómo se puede prevenir (*prevent*) la diabetes? Conéctate a la Internet para ver unos consejos y escribe al menos cuatro cosas que puedes hacer para prevenir la diabetes.

Busca: prevenir diabetes

MODELO: *Es importante hacer ejercicio todos los días.*

Presencia hispana

Some ethnic groups, including up to 80% of Hispanic Americans, develop symptoms of lactose intolerance by the time they reach adulthood. Their ancestors did not eat dairy foods, so their bodies were not prepared to digest dairy, and they passed these genes on from generation to generation. However, this has not stopped the National Dairy Council from marketing to Hispanics. What other ethnic groups have high rates of lactose intolerance?

¡Hola!

10-24A Te recomiendo que… Un/a estudiante presenta los siguientes problemas y el/la otro/a ofrece recomendaciones. Túrnense, cambiando de papel. Pueden usar **te/le/les recomiendo que** más el subjuntivo. **Estudiante B,** por favor ve al **Apéndice 1,** página A-19.

MODELO: ESTUDIANTE A: *Estoy muy flaco/a.*
ESTUDIANTE B: *Te recomiendo que comas tres comidas completas todos los días.*

Estudiante A:

Mis problemas:	Recomendaciones para mi compañero/a:
1. Quiero bajar de peso.	• tomar pastillas para el colesterol
2. Necesito bajar mi nivel de azúcar.	• tomar una bebida llena de vitaminas
3. Fumo más de un paquete de cigarrillos todos los días.	• tomar antiácidos
4. Mi hermano tiene dolor de cabeza.	• tomar antibióticos
5. Mi tío padece de Alzheimer.	• (no) tomar bebidas alcohólicas

10-25 Una encuesta (*poll*) médica. Con frecuencia, la Asociación Americana de Diabetes hace encuestas para educar al público y así, prevenir la diabetes.

Paso 1 Escucha y completa la siguiente encuesta telefónica escogiendo entre las respuestas **a, b** y **c** según tu propia situación.

MODELO: ¿Cuántos cigarrillos fuma usted al día?
a. ni uno   b. de cinco a diez   c. más de un paquete
a. ni uno

1. a. 0 mg	b. 300 mg	c. 600 mg
2. a. muchos	b. algunos	c. ni uno
3. a. mucho	b. un poco	c. nada
4. a. de oliva	b. de maíz	c. de animal
5. a. 80%	b. 50–60%	c. 30%
6. a. menos de una vez	b. dos o tres veces	c. todos los días

 Paso 2 Ahora, compara tus respuestas con las de un/a compañero/a para ver quién tiene más riesgo (*risk*) de volverse diabético/a. ¿Hay algo en tu vida que debes cambiar, según esta encuesta y las respuestas de tu compañero/a?

 10-26 ¿Cómo se comparan? Primero, cada uno/a de ustedes deber evaluar su rutina según la lista de actividades a continuación. Usen expresiones como **casi nunca, dos/tres veces a la semana** o **casi todos los días.** Después, comparen su régimen diario. ¿Qué tienen en común y en qué varían?

MODELO: hacer jogging
E1: *No me gusta hacer jogging. Prefiero caminar y lo hago casi todos los días.*
E2: *Pues prefiero hacer jogging, pero solo tres veces a la semana.*

1. hacer ejercicio
2. comer grasa animal
3. padecer de estrés
4. fumar
5. tomar mucha cafeína
6. tomar bebidas alcohólicas
7. dormir de siete a ocho horas por la noche
8. comer comida chatarra

¡Así lo hacemos! ESTRUCTURAS

10-38 to 10-44

3. The subjunctive to express doubt and denial

- The subjunctive is used in dependent clauses after expressions of doubt, uncertainty, or denial. As with other uses of the subjunctive, these expressions suggest that what is commented on is outside of the speaker's experience.

Dudo que las grasas trans sean buenas para la salud.

dudar	*to doubt*
negar (ie)	*to deny*
no pensar (ie)	*to not think*
no creer	*to not believe*
no estar seguro/a (de)	*to not be sure (of)*
es dudoso	*it's doubtful*
no es cierto	*it's not certain*
es increíble	*it's incredible*
no es verdad	*it's not true*

No es cierto que Camilo **padezca** de artritis.
It's not certain that Camilo suffers from arthritis.

No creo que el médico **sepa** el diagnóstico.
I don't believe that the doctor knows the diagnosis.

No estamos seguros de que el ejercicio **beneficie** la salud.
We're not sure that exercise is beneficial for health.

El médico **niega** que mi padre **tenga** un nivel alto de colesterol.
The doctor denies that my father has a high cholesterol level.

- Use the indicative in the dependent clause when there is no doubt, uncertainty, or disbelief about an action or event. For most expressions of doubt or uncertainty, the indicative will be used for the opposing expression (**dudar** versus **no dudar; no creer** versus **creer; no es cierto** versus **es cierto**).

Es cierto que Camilo **padece** de artritis.
It's certain that Camilo suffers from arthritis.

Creo que el médico **sabe** el diagnóstico.
I believe that the doctor knows the diagnosis.

Estamos seguros de que el ejercicio **beneficia** la salud.
We're sure that exercise is beneficial for health.

El médico **no niega** que mi padre **tiene** un nivel alto de colesterol.
The doctor does not deny that my father has a high cholesterol level.

- When the verb **creer** is used in a question, it can imply doubt in the mind of the speaker, thereby triggering the subjunctive in the dependent clause. If the speaker expresses no opinion or does not anticipate a negative response, the indicative is preferred.

¿Crees que el alcohol **afecte** el corazón?	*Do you believe (think) that alcohol affects the heart? (speaker implies doubt)*
¿Crees que el alcohol **afecta** el corazón?	*Do you believe (think) that alcohol affects the heart? (speaker has no opinion)*

- If there is no change of subject, you can use the infinitive.

Carlos niega **tomar** bebidas alcohólicas.	*Carlos denies drinking alcoholic beverages.*
Es increíble **ver** cuántas calorías tiene una hamburguesa.	*It's unbelieveable seeing how many calories a hamburger has.*

El subjuntivo con *tal vez* y *quizá(s)*

- The expressions **tal vez** and **quizá(s)**, meaning *perhaps* or *maybe,* are followed by the subjunctive when the speaker wishes to convey uncertainty or doubt. Both expressions are used without **que.**

Tal vez funcione no comer tanta grasa.	*Perhaps not eating so much fat will work.*
Quizás el ejercicio me **haga** sentir mejor.	*Maybe exercise will make me feel better.*

Es importante que estudies para ser médico.

Resumen de los usos del subjuntivo

You have now seen that the subjunctive is used in dependent clauses when the main clause expresses influence, emotion, doubt, or denial and (with the exception of **tal vez** and **quizás**) there is a change in subject between the two clauses. All of these uses suggest that the action in the dependent clause is outside of the speaker's experience.

Queremos que te cuides mejor.	*We want you to take better care of yourself.*
Dudas que **haga** ejercicio todos los días.	*You doubt that I exercise every day.*
Es una lástima que la madre de Jorge **esté** enferma.	*It's a shame Jorge's mother is sick.*
Ojalá (que) se mejore.	*I hope that she gets better.*
Tal vez el médico me **dé** antibióticos.	*Perhaps the doctor will give me antibiotics.*

APLICACIÓN

10-27 Sobre Raquel Welch. Raquel (Tejada) Welch es de ascendencia inglesa y boliviana. Aunque nació en 1940, todavía se le considera una de las actrices más bellas del cine norteamericano. En esta conversación, un periodista conversa con Marta Salazar, la ayudante de esta extraordinaria actriz.

Paso 1 Lee la entrevista y subraya los verbos en el subjuntivo. Explica por qué se usa el subjuntivo en cada caso.

PERIODISTA: Buenas tardes, Srta. Salazar. Lamento que Raquel no pueda participar en esta entrevista. Ojalá que se encuentre bien.

AYUDANTE: ¡Claro que sí! Es que tiene un ensayo[1] esta tarde y tiene que memorizar su parte. No creemos que termine a tiempo para estar con nosotros. Pero tal vez usted quiera hacerme a mí algunas preguntas sobre su carrera.

PERIODISTA: ¡Sin duda! Quizás usted pueda hablarme un poco sobre la película favorita de ella.

AYUDANTE: Pues, no creo que ella quiera limitarse a solo una, pero quizás usted conozca *Tortilla Soup*. Sé que a Raquel le gustó mucho porque es una comedia con un mensaje serio, y se divirtió mucho rodándola[2].

PERIODISTA: Ella también actuó en la televisión.

AYUDANTE: Es verdad. Estoy segura de que su papel en *American Family* en PBS es uno de sus favoritos. Es dudoso que se repita tal oportunidad en el futuro, pero ¿quién sabe?

Raquel Welch y Héctor Elizondo en *Tortilla Soup*.

PERIODISTA: ¿Cómo se mantiene ella en tan buena forma?

AYUDANTE: Bueno, seguramente algunas personas niegan que esté en perfecta forma, pero es verdad que va al gimnasio todos los días. Para ella, la buena salud es muy importante. No creo que pierda ni un día de ir al gimnasio.

PERIODISTA: Bueno, Srta. Salazar. Muchas gracias, y tal vez veamos a Raquel Welch en otra película pronto.

AYUDANTE: Gracias a usted. ¡Quizás tenga razón! A ella le gusta que la gente todavía la quiera como actriz.

---

[1]*rehearsal* [2]*filming it*

Paso 2 Vuelve a leer la entrevista sobre Raquel Welch y contesta las siguientes preguntas.

1. ¿Quién es Raquel Welch? ¿Cuál es su ascendencia?

2. ¿Por qué le gustó mucho la película *Tortilla Soup*?

3. ¿Qué oportunidad tuvo en la televisión?

4. ¿Cuántos años tiene ahora?

5. ¿Cómo se mantiene en forma?

6. ¿Conoces algunas de sus películas? ¿Crees que tiene mucho talento?

10-28 En el Spa-Hotel Hacienda La Fortuna. A continuación hay un anuncio para un spa en Bolivia. Contesta las siguientes preguntas, usando expresiones de duda, negación y emoción.

Bienvenidos a Hacienda La Fortuna
Spa-Hotel, Lago Títicaca, Bolívia

La Hacienda La Fortuna le ofrece un servicio único y personal. Nuestro spa-hotel tiene todo lo que pueda desear en un solo lugar con un ambiente de total relajamiento. Cuenta con 23 habitaciones de lujo con vistas espectaculares, así como jacuzzi y piscina con agua de manantiales[1] termales.

PLANES

Adelgazamiento
• sauna, masajes, baños termales, yoga, caminatas • consulta médica • lodo[2] medicinal
• dieta de baja grasa • entrenador personal

Antiestrés
• masajes • baño con esencias botánicas • manicura, pedicura

Tratamiento para enfermedades crónicas
• acupuntura • reflexología • baño con barro[3] • dieta de alta proteína y bajos carbohidratos
• control de peso

Contamos con el ambiente perfecto para que sus vacaciones sean inolvidables y muy saludables. Nuestros paquetes le ofrecen planes de adelgazamiento, antiestrés, tratamiento para las enfermedades crónicas, clases de cocina y todo tipo de actividades para que usted pueda olvidarse del estrés.
La variedad de servicios le deja crear su propia experiencia...

Consulte nuestra página web para ver tarifas y fechas.

[1]*springs* [2]*mud* [3]*earth*

MODELO: ¿Vas a bañarte en las aguas termales?
Tal vez me bañe.

1. ¿Vas por más de una semana?
   Quizás...

2. ¿Vas a seguir los consejos del entrenador?
   Creo que...

3. ¿Vas a hacer alguna excursión?
   Estoy seguro/a de que...

4. ¿Tienes una cita para hacerte la pedicura?
   Es dudoso que...

5. ¿Vas a caminar o hacer otro ejercicio?
   Niego que...

6. ¿Vas a divertirte mucho?
   Ojalá...

10-29 El Centro Naturista.   En esta tienda dentro del Spa-Hotel, puedes comprar todo tipo de productos naturales. Completa el diálogo con la forma correcta del verbo entre paréntesis.

SRA. LÓPEZ: Hola, buenos días. ¿Sabe Ud. dónde están las supervitaminas?

DEPENDIENTE: Sí, señora. Creo que (1) _____ (estar) en el pasillo a la izquierda. Estoy seguro de que (2) _____ (haber) por lo menos 10 botellas.

SRA. LÓPEZ: No creo que (3) _____ (necesitar) tantas. ¿Cree que (4) _____ (estar) frescas?

DEPENDIENTE: Tal vez Ud. (5) _____ (querer) ver la fecha de vencimiento (*expiration date*) antes de comprarlas pero no creo que nosotros (6) _____ (vender) aquí productos vencidos.

SRA. LÓPEZ: Claro. ¿Tiene jabones naturales también? Me gustaría comprar algunos.

DEPENDIENTE: Sí, pero dudo que nosotros (7) _____ (tener) una buena selección en este momento. Pienso que nosotros (8) _____ (ir) a recibir una selección más amplia dentro de unos días. No estoy seguro que (9) _____ (llegar) a tiempo. Si quiere, la puedo llamar si los recibimos pronto.

SRA. LÓPEZ: No es necesario, gracias. Quizás (10) _____ (volver) en unos días.

10-30 Un spa para ti.   Conéctate a la Internet para visitar un spa. Completa las siguientes oraciones, dando tu opinión sobre el lugar.

> **Busca:** aguas termales spa; terapia spa hotel +bolivia; terapia spa hotel +paraguay

MODELO: Creo que... *tienen planes muy interesantes.*

1. Dudo que...
2. Espero que...
3. Es importante que...
4. Estoy seguro/a que...
5. Ojalá que...
6. Prefiero que...

10-31A ¿Qué piensan?   Tu compañero/a tiene una revista con información que puede ser cierta o no. Hazle preguntas sobre la información y dale tu opinión. **Estudiante B,** por favor ve al **Apéndice 1,** página A-19.

MODELO: ESTUDIANTE A: *¿Hay algún consejo para una persona que tiene problemas cardíacos?*
ESTUDIANTE B: *Según la revista, la aspirina es buena para el corazón.*
ESTUDIANTE A: *No creo que sea buena idea tomar mucha aspirina.*
ESTUDIANTE B: *Pues, es cierto que es bueno tomar una por día.*

Estudiante A:

Para preguntar:	Para reaccionar:
1. ¿Qué dice sobre el consumo de bebidas alcohólicas?	• (no) creo
2. ¿Es posible adelgazar mucho en poco tiempo?	• (no) es verdad
3. ¿Hay algún tratamiento tradicional para curar el resfriado común?	• ojalá • (no) estoy seguro/a
4. Mi abuelo se preocupa de ser viejo.	• (no) niego
5. ¿Cómo es posible hacer más ejercicio?	• es lógico • me alegro de
6. Tengo muy mala memoria. ¿Qué hago?	• tal vez • es bueno (malo)

10-32 Sus opiniones sobre la salud. Todos tenemos opiniones sobre lo que se debe hacer para mantenerse con buena salud.

Paso 1 Primero, escribe una lista de 10 afirmaciones que sean importantes para ti. Empieza cada afirmación con una cláusula independiente seguida de una dependiente y el subjuntivo o el indicativo según el contexto. También puedes usar un infinitivo. Trata de variar los usos del subjuntivo (influencia, emoción, duda).

MODELO: *Ojalá que todos sigan mis consejos sobre la salud.*
Primero, creo que es importante seguir una dieta saludable.
Segundo,…

Ojalá que todos participen en un maratón.

Paso 2 Ahora formen un grupo de tres o cuatro personas para compartir sus opiniones y consejos. ¿Cuáles tienen en común y en cuáles varían? ¿Quién tiene el consejo más novedoso (*original*)? ¿Quién tiene el consejo menos razonable?

10-45
to 10-49

¿Cuánto saben?

Primero, pregúntate si puedes llevar a cabo las siguientes funciones comunicativas en español. Después, júntate con dos o tres compañeros/as de clase para presentar las situaciones. Hagan y respondan a por lo menos cuatro preguntas en cada situación.

✓ CAN YOU . . .

☐ talk about how to stay fit?

☐ express your opinions and beliefs about something?

WITH YOUR CLASSMATE(S) . . .

Situación: En un gimnasio
Hagan los papeles de entrenador/a personal y cliente. Háganse preguntas y dense consejos para mantenerse en forma.
Para empezar: *¿Qué hago para sentirme mejor? Es necesario que…*

Situación: En un restaurante
Ustedes están leyendo el menú en un restaurante de comida rápida y opinan sobre la comida y sus ingredientes. Usen expresiones como **Dudo que…, No pienso que…, Creo que…, Es increíble que…,** y otras para expresar su opinión y creencias.
Para empezar: *Aquí todo es comida chatarra… Es increíble que…*

Observaciones

10-50
to 10-53

¡Pura vida! EPISODIO 10

En este episodio doña María y Marcela atienden a Patricio porque no se siente bien.

Antes de ver el video

10-33 ¿Tengo gripe o resfriado? Lee el artículo para ver cómo se diferencian los síntomas del resfriado y de la gripe y después haz una lista de los síntomas de cada uno.

El resfriado y la gripe pueden tener muchos de los mismos síntomas. Pero un resfriado generalmente es leve, mientras que la gripe es mucho más intensa.

Con frecuencia, con un resfriado comienzas sintiéndote cansado, estornudando[1], tosiendo y con la nariz tapada[2]. Si tienes fiebre, es baja, solo uno o dos grados más de lo normal. Es probable que te duelan los músculos y la garganta, y que tengas los ojos llorosos y dolor de cabeza.

La gripe comienza de repente[3] y es más fuerte. Es probable que te sientas débil y cansado, y que tengas fiebre alta, tos seca, la nariz tapada, escalofríos[4], dolores musculares, dolor de cabeza intenso, dolor en los ojos y dolor de garganta. Generalmente, toma más tiempo mejorarse de la gripe que de un resfriado. La mejor manera de evitar la gripe es ponerte una vacuna cada otoño.

[1]*sneezing* [2]*stuffy nose* [3]*suddenly* [4]*chills*

¿Hay una cura para el resfriado común?

A ver el video

10-34 Lo que tiene Patricio. Mira el décimo episodio de **¡Pura vida!** para identificar la enfermedad que tiene Patricio.

Patricio está enfermo.

Doña María y Marcela visitan a Patricio.

Marcela va a la farmacia.

Según los síntomas, es probable que Patricio tenga…

_____ resfriado   _____ diabetes   _____ gripe   _____ gastritis

Después de ver el video

10-35 ¿Qué puedo hacer para sentirme mejor? Conéctate a la Internet y lee algunos consejos para sentirte mejor si tienes un resfriado o una gripe. Escribe por lo menos cinco consejos.

> **Busca:** aliviar gripe; aliviar resfriado

Nuestro mundo

Bolivia y Paraguay: riquezas por descubrir

10-54
to 10-55

El embalse (*dam*) de Itaipú en el río Paraná proporciona toda la electricidad que necesita Paraguay y el 25% de la electricidad que usa Brasil. En 1994, la American Society of Civil Engineers lo nombró una de las "siete maravillas del mundo moderno".

Durante los siglos XVII y XVIII, los jesuitas españoles construyeron una cadena de misiones en Paraguay para educar y cristianizar a los indígenas. La Santísima Trinidad de Paraná es "la más grande y la mejor de todas las misiones". Ahora es parte del Patrimonio de la Humanidad de las Naciones Unidas.

Los hermosos paisajes de Bolivia ocultan la difícil vida de la mayoría de sus ciudadanos.

En Bolivia, el salar de Uyuni es un inmenso lago seco (*dry*) lleno de sal. Además tiene grandes depósitos de litio (*lithium*), un elemento con múltiples usos industriales.

Paraguay ha producido varias estrellas del deporte, como José Luis Félix Chilavert González. En su carrera, el arquero (*goalie*) marcó 62 goles, lo que fue por muchos años un récord.

Bolivia y Paraguay

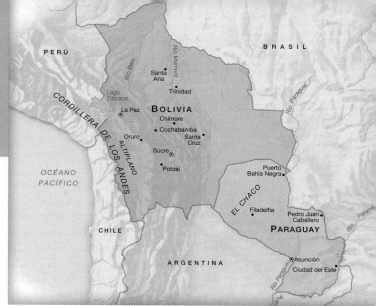

	Bolivia	Paraguay
Población:	9,8 millones	7 millones
Alfabetismo:	87%	94%
Lenguas ficiales:	español, quechua, aimara	español y guaraní
Expectativa de vida:	67 años	76 años
PIB per cápita:	$4.600	$4.100
PIB gastado en la salud:	6,6%	7,6%

10-36 Identifica. Identifica, describe o explica lo siguiente.

1. el deporte que crea fanáticos

2. la importancia del litio

3. el país con terreno montañoso, y la dificultad que esto causa

4. la importancia del embalse de Itaipú

5. el país que tiene una cadena de misiones de los siglos XVII y XVIII

10-37 Desafío. Consulta el mapa y la caja para contestar estas preguntas.

1. el país que gasta más por persona para mantener la salud

2. el país que tiene costa

3. el más poblado

4. el país rico en minerales

5. el país trilingüe

 10-38 Proyecto. Conéctate a la Internet para ver más imágenes de Bolivia y Paraguay. Escribe un párrafo para describir uno de los lugares. Incluye esta información:

- el lugar
- la escena (las montañas, la planicie de los Andes, el agua, etcétera)
- la gente (si la hay)
- el clima
- los recursos naturales y sus productos
- una foto representativa

Busca: imagenes bolivia; imagenes paraguay

MODELO: *Los guaraníes son los indígenas de Paraguay, de partes de Brasil y de Argentina. Tienen su propio idioma, pero muchos son bilingües en español o portugués y guaraní y tienen sus propias tradiciones culturales...*

Páginas

10-56

"La azucena del bosque" (Mito guaraní)

ANTES DE LEER

10-39 Leyendas y mitos. Lee la introducción a continuación e indica si las afirmaciones que la siguen son ciertas o falsas. Corrige las falsas.

Las leyendas y los mitos como tradición oral son populares en todo el mundo hispano. Sirven para transmitir la historia, la cultura y los valores de una generación a la siguiente. Aunque la leyenda se basa en un evento histórico, el mito tiene alguna intervención sobrenatural. Los dos se hacen propiedad de la persona que los cuenta. Por eso, existen muchas versiones de la misma leyenda o del mismo mito, y pueden transformarse a través de los años hasta que haya poca relación entre el mito original y el actual. Lo mismo pasa con leyendas que tal vez tú conozcas, por ejemplo, la de Pocahontas o la de Davy Crockett. A continuación tienes un mito paraguayo que se originó entre los guaraníes antes de la colonización española. Pero es posible que notes alguna semejanza a otras historias que tú conozcas de tu infancia (*childhood*). Este mito explica el origen de una flor común, la azucena del bosque (*forest lily*).

1. Los mitos tienen base histórica.

2. "Pocahontas" es un ejemplo de una leyenda.

3. Las leyendas y los mitos no tienen valor (*value*) cultural.

4. Originalmente las leyendas y los mitos eran literatura escrita.

5. "La azucena del bosque" se originó durante la colonia española.

10-40 Anticipa. Ahora, escribe tres preguntas que quieres contestar en relación a esta historia.

MODELO: *¿Quiénes son los personajes?*

A LEER

10-41 El mito. Ahora lee este mito guaraní. A ver si puedes contestar las preguntas que escribiste en la actividad **10-40**.

Once upon a time there was

ferocious

mixed
skin

he rubbed / sparks

wild pig
lit / he threw / flames
it came off

Había una vez° una hermosa región de la tierra donde solo existían animales. Pasó por allí Tupá, el dios sol, que había creado los animales y los bosques, y decidió crear a los hombres, con suficiente inteligencia para poder gobernar hasta los animales más feroces°. Entonces le pidió a I-Yara, el dueño de las aguas, que trajera un poco de tierra de ese lugar. Tupá amasó° la tierra y le dio forma humana creando dos hombres, uno con la piel° roja llamado Pitá y otro con la piel blanca llamado Morotí.

Estos hombres necesitaban compañeras y Tupá ordenó a I-Yara que, con un poco más de tierra, hiciera a dos mujeres. Y Pitá y Morotí tuvieron muchos hijos con sus mujeres y vivían felices en la selva comiendo de sus frutos.

Pero un día Pitá frotó° dos piedras y salieron unas chispas° y descubrió el fuego. Ese mismo día por casualidad Morotí tuvo que matar un jabalí° que lo atacaba. Al ver que Pitá había encendido° un hermoso fuego, arrojó° el animal muerto a las llamas°. Al poco rato se desprendió° de la carne un olor delicioso y cuando

probaron la carne, les pareció exquisita. Desde ese momento abandonaron la recolección de las frutas y comenzaron a cazar° para comer.

 Con los años fueron perfeccionando sus armas y de esa forma inventaron el arco, la flecha° y la lanza. Debido a que la caza° era cada vez más escasa, empezaron a competir entre ellos y tan grande fue el rencor y el odio° que sintieron entre las dos familias que decidieron separarse.

 Tupá decidió castigarlos° por necios°. El castigo serviría para que no olvidaran que Tupá los había puesto en el mundo para vivir en paz y para amarse los unos a los otros. Provocó entonces una terrible tormenta que duró tres días y tres noches, al cabo de los cuales° salió el sol y por uno de sus rayos bajó a la Tierra I-Yara.

 I-Yara llamó a todas las tribus y las reunió en un claro° del bosque. Allí les habló de esta forma:

 —Tupá, nuestro creador me envía— les dijo a los dos hermanos. —La furia se ha apoderado° de él al conocer la ingratitud de ustedes. Él los creó para que el amor y la paz guiaran sus vidas, pero la codicia° pudo más y se dejaron llevar por la intriga y la envidia. Ustedes son hermanos, hijos de hermanos. Tupá me envía para que hagan la paz entre ustedes.

 —¡Pitá!, ¡Morotí!, ¡Abrácense, Tupá lo manda!

 Arrepentidos y avergonzados° los hermanos se abrazaron y, allí, en presencia de todos, fueron perdiendo sus formas humanas y se fueron fundiendo° hasta convertirse en un solo cuerpo, que se hizo una planta de donde salían ramas° y de las ramas hojas° y flores.

 Y las flores fueron rojas al principio como la piel de Pitá, y con el tiempo perdían su color hasta llegar a ser blancas, como la piel de Morotí. Eran Pitá y Morotí que, convertidos en flores, simbolizaban la unión y la paz entre hermanos.

 Así nació la Azucena del Bosque, que Tupá dejó en la Tierra para recordarles a los hombres que deben vivir en paz.

hunt

arrow
[Debido...caza: *Due to the fact that hunting*]
hatred

punish them / fools

[al...cuales: *at the end of which*]
clearing

has taken hold
greed

ashamed
melting
branches / leaves

DESPUÉS DE LEER

10-42 ¿En qué orden? Pon las oraciones en el orden cronológico de la historia. Luego, termínala.

_____ También creó a dos mujeres y entre ellos tuvieron muchos hijos.

_____ Así descubrieron la delicia de la carne asada.

_____ Uno de ellos era de piel roja; el otro de piel blanca.

_____ Había un hermoso lugar lleno de animales y flores.

_____ Un día, uno de los hombres descubrió el fuego y el otro mató un jabalí.

_____ Tupá se puso enojado al ver su envidia.

_____ El dios sol decidió crear un par de hombres para dominar la naturaleza.

_____ Pero dentro de poco empezaron a discutir porque cada día había menos caza.

A ver si ahora puedes terminar la historia…

10-43 Los valores. Las leyendas y los mitos transmiten los valores de una sociedad. ¿Cuáles de estos valores figuran en esta historia? Explica por qué.

 1. la paz 2. el amor fraternal 3. la rivalidad

10-44 Entrevista. Divídanse en dos grupos. Un grupo representa a Tupá y el otro representa a los dos hermanos. Preparen preguntas para entrevistar al otro grupo, y luego entrevístense.

MODELO: GRUPO 1: *Tupá, ¿Por qué decidió crear dos hombres en vez de uno?*
    GRUPO 2: *Porque…*

Taller

10-57

10-45 Un artículo sobre la salud. En revistas populares para hombres o mujeres es común encontrar artículos que dan consejos sobre la salud. En este taller vas a escribir un artículo al estilo de una de estas revistas.

MODELO:

Consulta Médica

04 abril, 2012

Los tratamientos naturales

La manzanilla

La flor de manzanilla tiene muchos usos en el tratamiento de enfermedades. Tiene un efecto calmante general, alivia el dolor y previene las infecciones. Se usa para aliviar síntomas en personas que tienen baja tolerancia al dolor o que están nerviosas....

ANTES DE ESCRIBIR

- **Ideas.** Piensa en un problema o en una condición que quieres tratar, por ejemplo, la falta de ejercicio, el sobrepeso, los efectos del sol en la piel (*skin*), etcétera.

A ESCRIBIR

- **El problema.** Escribe un párrafo en el que expliques el problema. Indica a cuánta gente afecta y por qué es importante hacer algo para solucionarlo.

- **Estrategias.** Haz una lista de tres a cinco estrategias o consejos que ayuden al lector/a la lectora a seguir tus consejos.

- **Conclusión.** Concluye el artículo de una manera positiva, explicando cómo el lector/la lectora va a sentirse mejor si sigue tus consejos.

- **Ilustrar.** Agrega alguna foto o algún dibujo que ilustre el problema.

DESPUÉS DE ESCRIBIR

- **Revisar.** Revisa tu artículo para verificar los siguientes puntos.
  - ☐ los diferentes usos del subjuntivo
  - ☐ la ortografía y la concordancia

- **Intercambiar**
  Intercambia tu artículo con el de un/a compañero/a para hacer correcciones y sugerencias, y para comentar sobre el contenido.

- **Entregar**
  Pon tu artículo en limpio, incorporando las sugerencias de tu compañero/a. Después entrégaselo a tu profesor/a.

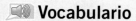 **Vocabulario**

Primera parte

Las partes del cuerpo humano Parts of the human body

la boca *mouth*
el brazo *arm*
la cabeza *head*
el corazón *heart*
el dedo (del pie) *finger (toe)*
la espalda *back*
el estómago *stomach*
la garganta *throat*
la lengua *tongue*
la muela *molar*
el oído *(inner) ear*
la oreja *(outer) ear*
el pecho *chest*
el pie *foot*
la pierna *leg*
el pulmón *lung*
la rodilla *knee*

Problemas de salud Health problems

doler (ue) *to hurt*
lastimarse *to hurt oneself*
romperse (un hueso) *to break (a bone)*
ser alérgico/a a *to be allergic to*
tener (ie) fiebre (f.) *to have a fever*
    dolor de cabeza (m.) *a headache*
    gripe (f.) *flu*
    infección (f.) *an infection*
    resfriado (m.) *a cold*
    tos (f.) *a cough*
    náuseas (f.) … *(to feel) nauseated*
torcerse (ue) *to twist*
toser *to cough*

Sugerencias y remedios médicos Medical advice and remedies

dejar de (fumar) *to quit (smoking)*
guardar cama *to stay in bed*
hacer una cita *to make an appointment*
mejorarse *to get better, to get well*
respirar *to breathe*
seguir (i, i) los consejos del médico *to follow the doctor's advice*
tomar la presión *to take blood pressure*
    la temperatura *temperature*

Medicinas comunes Common medicines

el antiácido *antacid*
el antibiótico *antibiotic*
la aspirina *aspirin*
el calmante *tranquilizer, painkiller*
el jarabe *cough syrup*
la pastilla *pill, lozenge*

En el consultorio del médico At the doctor's office

el diagnóstico *diagnosis*
el dolor *pain, ache*
la enfermedad *illness*
el examen físico *checkup*
la inyección *shot*
el/la paciente *patient*
la radiografía *X-ray*
la receta *prescription*
el síntoma *symptom*
la sala de urgencias *emergency room*

Segunda parte

Sigan una dieta rica en… Follow a diet rich in . . .

(los) antioxidantes *antioxidants*
(el) calcio *calcium*
(la) fibra *fiber*
(las) proteínas *proteins*
(los) carbohidratos complejos *complex carbohydrates*

En moderación coman In moderation, eat foods
alimentos con… with . . .

(los) carbohidratos sencillos *simple carbohydrates*
(el) colesterol *cholesterol*
(las) grasas monoinsaturadas (poliinsaturadas) *monounsaturated (polyunsaturated) fats*

Eviten… Avoid . . .

las bebidas alcohólicas *alcoholic beverages*
la comida chatarra *junk food*
los dulces *sweets*
las grasas saturadas (trans) *saturated (trans) fats*

Las enfermedades y el bienestar Illnesses and well-being

la diabetes *diabetes*
los ejercicios aeróbicos *aerobics*
el estrés *stress*
el (sobre)peso *(excess) weight*

Tu línea y tu salud Your weight and your health

adelgazar *to lose weight*
bajar de peso *to lose weight*
cuidar(se) *to take care (of oneself)*
engordar *to gain weight*
estar a dieta *to be on a diet*
guardar la línea *to stay trim, to watch one's figure*
mantenerse (ie) en forma *to stay in shape*
padecer (zc) (de) *to suffer (from)*
ponerse en forma *to get in shape*
subir de peso *to gain weight*

Verbs and expresssions of emotion *See page 327.*   **Verbs and expressions of doubt and denial** *See page 337.*

11

¿Para qué profesión te preparas?

OBJETIVOS COMUNICATIVOS

- Describing professions and occupations using work-related terms
- Talking about the advantages of different professions
- Giving and following instructions from a friend
- Talking about future plans

- Reading and responding to want ads
- Writing a brief business letter
- Interviewing for a job
- Describing existing and nonexistent people and things

Readiness Check

El virreinato de la Plata: Argentina y Uruguay

«El trabajo no deshonra, dignifica».

Refrán: Work doesn't bring you dishonor, but dignity.

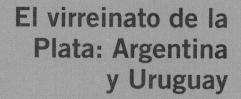

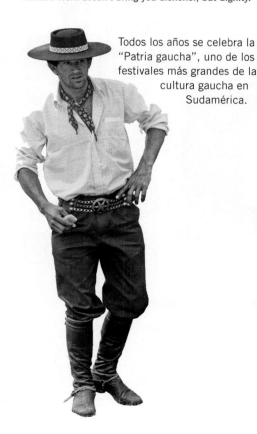

Todos los años se celebra la "Patria gaucha", uno de los festivales más grandes de la cultura gaucha en Sudamérica.

Las cataratas del Iguazú son cuatro veces más grandes que las del Niágara. Sus 275 cascadas son el resultado de una erupción volcánica. Ahora las cataratas son parte del Patrimonio de la Humanidad de la UNESCO.

¡Así lo decimos! VOCABULARIO

¡Así es la vida! El mundo del trabajo

Muchas personas esperan su turno en la Oficina de Empleo.

SR. FERNÁNDEZ: Dale tu currículum vítae al recepcionista.

DRA. MESSI: Ya se lo di. Ojalá que me llame pronto.

ANGÉLICA: Espero conseguir trabajo antes de que se me acaben los beneficios.

SERGIO: Pero no aceptes el sueldo mínimo sin antes negociar el contrato.

11-02
to 11-08

Vocabulario Los oficios y las profesiones

Variaciones

In Latin America you will hear **el/la contador/a**, but usually **el/la contable** in Spain. Likewise, **el/la plomero/a** in the Americas and **el/la fontanero/a** in Spain.

Los oficios y profesiones   Occupations and professions

el/la analista de sistemas   *systems analyst*
el/la arquitecto/a   *architect*
el/la bombero/a   *firefighter*
el/la carpintero/a   *carpenter*
el/la cartero/a   *mail carrier*
el/la cocinero/a   *cook, chef*
el/la contador/a   *accountant*
el/la dentista   *dentist*
el/la enfermero/a   *nurse*
el hombre / la mujer de negocios   *businessman/woman*
el/la ingeniero/a   *engineer*
el/la intérprete   *interpreter*
el/la mecánico/a   *mechanic*
el/la obrero/a de construcción   *construction worker*
el/la peluquero/a   *hairdresser*
el/la periodista   *journalist*
el/la plomero/a   *plumber*
el/la psicólogo/a   *psychologist*
el/la veterinario/a   *veterinarian*
el/la viajante   *traveling salesperson*

la arquitecta

Términos y expresiones de trabajo   Work-related terms and expressions

los beneficios   *benefits*
las cualificaciones   *qualifications*
el currículum vítae   *curriculum vitae (vita)*
el (des)empleo   *(un)employment*
la empresa   *company, firm*
el entrenamiento   *training*
la formación   *education*
la meta   *goal*
el puesto   *position (job)*
el sueldo (mínimo)   *(minimum) wage*
la (des)ventaja   *(dis)advantage*

Variaciones

El/la jefe/a ejecutivo/a has many variants: **jefe/a** may be **director/a**, **presidente/a**, or an adjective may be added, such as in **el/la principal oficial ejecutivo/a,** common in Puerto Rico.

Cargos   Positions

el/la director/a   *director*
el/la empleado/a   *employee*
el/la gerente   *manager*
el/la jefe/a   *boss*
el/la jefe/a ejecutivo/a   *CEO*

el peluquero

¡Manos a la obra!   Let's get to work!

apagar (fuegos/incendios)   *to put out, extinguish (fires)*
conseguir[1] (i, i)   *to get, to obtain*
diseñar   *to design*
estar en paro / sin trabajo   *to be out of work*
reparar   *to repair*
repartir   *to deliver, to distribute*
trabajar a tiempo completo / parcial   *to work full-time/part-time*

la contadora

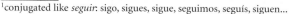
[1]conjugated like *seguir*: sigo, sigues, sigue, seguimos, seguís, siguen...

APLICACIÓN

11-1 ¿A quién llamas?   ¿A qué profesionales llamas en cada una de las siguientes situaciones? Empareja las descripciones con las profesiones u oficios. Luego, explica tus selecciones.

MODELO: Tienes el pelo muy largo y necesitas un corte nuevo.
Llamo a mi peluquera. Siempre voy a "Supercorte" donde no tengo que pagar mucho.

1. _____ No hay agua en el baño.
2. _____ Necesitas resolver algunos problemas emocionales.
3. _____ Tu perro está enfermo.
4. _____ Quieres reparar unas sillas de tu comedor.
5. _____ Necesitas ayuda para hacer los impuestos (*taxes*).
6. _____ Quieres un diseño original para tu casa nueva.

a. carpintero/a
b. plomero/a
c. psicólogo/a
d. contador/a
e. arquitecto/a
f. veterinario/a

11-2 ¿Qué es lo que hace?   Identifica la profesión u oficio que corresponde a cada persona a continuación. Luego explica algo más de su trabajo o describe alguna característica que se necesita para poder hacer este trabajo.

MODELO:

doña Maruja

Doña Maruja es enfermera. Les toma la temperatura y les pone inyecciones a sus pacientes. Tiene compasión.

1.

don Lucas

2.

el Sr. Castillo

3.

Pilar

11-3 Las profesiones y los oficios.   Escucha a las siguientes personas e indica la profesión u oficio que le interesa a cada una.

MODELO: Soy bilingüe. Me gusta trabajar en la computadora y contestar el teléfono.
secretario/a

a. analista de sistemas
b. arquitecto/a
c. cocinero/a
d. contador/a
e. dentista
f. mecánico/a
g. peluquero/a
h. periodista

1. _____   3. _____   5. _____   7. _____
2. _____   4. _____   6. _____   8. _____

11-4 ¿En qué orden?

Paso 1 Pon los siguientes aspectos de un trabajo en orden de importancia para ti personalmente. (1: más importante… 6: menos importante)

_____ la oportunidad de aprender más   _____ un buen horario de trabajo

_____ un sueldo o un salario adecuado   _____ el seguro médico

_____ un/a jefe/a paciente   _____ un trabajo a comisión

     _____ ¿otro? _____

Paso 2 Ahora, comparen sus listas. Cuando no estén de acuerdo, explíquense sus puntos de vista.

MODELO: E1: *Quiero un trabajo interesante porque no quiero estar aburrido/a.*
E2: *Bueno, para mí el horario de trabajo es lo más importante. Prefiero no tener que levantarme demasiado temprano. Después, para mí es…*

11-5 Avisos clasificados de *todo.com.uy.*   Este es un sitio en la Internet donde se puede poner y responder a avisos clasificados.

Paso 1 Lee los avisos y contesta las preguntas a continuación.

Pilotos de ambos sexos para nueva aerolínea uruguaya con sede en Montevideo. Se requiere un mínimo de seis años de experiencia con aviones en rutas regionales. Salario y beneficios. Llamar Oficina de Personal de AeroUR al 8989 3411.

1. ¿Cuál(es) de estos avisos tiene(n) puestos para hombres y mujeres?

2. ¿Qué empresa busca gente entrenada en aviación?

3. ¿Cuál(es) paga(n) salario y comisión?

4. ¿Cuál(es) paga(n) los gastos de viaje?

5. ¿Cuál de los puestos te atrae más y por qué?

Paso 2 Ahora eres jefe/a de personal. Escribe un aviso clasificado para *todo.com.uy* para anunciar un puesto en tu compañía.

Paso 3 Ahora túrnense para llamar a sus empresas con vacantes y hacerse más preguntas sobre la posición.

MODELO: E1: *Buenas tardes. AeroEur. ¿A quién le dirijo su llamada?*
E2: *Al jefe de personal, por favor…*

¡Hola!

Cultura en vivo

In contrast to the U.S. or Canada, it is acceptable in many Spanish-speaking countries to advertise for male or female applicants exclusively. Applicants also routinely include a photo with their application. What concerns might you have when responding to a gender-specific ad?

1. *Tú* commands

11-09
to 11-15

In **Capítulo 10** you learned that formal commands use the forms of the subjunctive. Here are the informal (**tú**) commands. Note how they compare with the subjunctive.

Toma estos formularios y rellénalos con tus datos personales. No te olvides de incluir una foto.

Infinitive	Affirmative	Negative	(Subjunctive)
comprar	**compra**	**no compres**	(compres)
comer	**come**	**no comas**	(comas)
escribir	**escribe**	**no escribas**	(escribas)
pensar	**piensa**	**no pienses**	(pienses)
dormir	**duerme**	**no duermas**	(duermas)
pedir	**pide**	**no pidas**	(pidas)
traer	**trae**	**no traigas**	(traigas)

- Regular affirmative **tú** commands have the same form as the third-person singular of the present indicative.

  Estudia para ser abogada.   *Study to be a lawyer.*
  Lee los avisos clasificados.   *Read the classified ads.*

- Negative **tú** commands use the subjunctive.

  No trabajes a comisión.   *Don't work on commission.*
  No estés sin trabajo.   *Don't be out of work.*

- Remember that irregularities in the subjunctive will also appear in the negative **tú** command.

  No apagues la computadora.   *Don't turn off the computer.*
  No te vayas.   *Don't leave.*

Mandatos afirmativos irregulares de la forma *tú*

Ten paciencia y vas a ver muchos pájaros exóticos.

- The following verbs have irregular **affirmative** command forms:

decir	**di**	**Di** por qué.	*Tell (Say) why.*
hacer	**haz**	**Haz** el informe.	*Do the report.*
ir	**ve**	**Ve** a la oficina de empleo.	*Go to the employment office.*
poner	**pon**	**Pon** tu solicitud aquí.	*Put your application here.*
salir	**sal**	**Sal** a tiempo.	*Leave on time.*
ser	**sé**	**Sé** amable con la jefa.	*Be nice to the boss.*
tener	**ten**	**Ten** paciencia.	*Be patient.*
venir	**ven**	**Ven** a mi oficina ahora.	*Come to my office now.*

- As with the formal commands, attach pronouns to the affirmative command and place them in front of the negative command. Remember to place an accent on the next-to-last syllable of the verb in the affirmative command form.

  Tenlo para esta tarde.   *Have it by this afternoon.*
  Háblale mañana.   *Talk to her tomorrow.*

APLICACIÓN

11-6 En la oficina de la presidenta Cristina Fernández. En 2007, Cristina Fernández se convirtió en primera mujer presidenta de Argentina, y con un formidable margen de votos. Su jefe de gabinete (*chief of staff*) está muy ocupado y cuando habla con su personal en la oficina, le da muchas órdenes. ¿Cuáles de estas órdenes son ilógicas, en tu opinión? Explica por qué.

MODELO: María, tráeme los periódicos de hoy, por favor.
Sí.
María, prepárame una empanada, por favor.
No, porque no se cocina en una oficina.

Cristina Fernández

1. Tomás, no trabajes más de cinco horas diarias.

2. Clarisa, escribe este informe en latín.

3. Ramón, ve a la piscina y nada por tres horas.

4. Josefina, búscame el informe del Secretario General de la Organización de Estados Americanos.

5. Raúl, llama al jefe de la oposición y dile que done mil dólares a nuestra campaña política.

6. Conchita, sé amable con los visitantes.

7. Eduardo, pon las sillas alrededor de la mesa para la reunión.

8. Julia, descansa. No hagas tu trabajo.

11-7 Tú, en la oficina de la presidenta. ¿Qué mandatos das tú en la oficina? Combina elementos de las dos columnas para formar mandatos lógicos.

MODELO: poner—los papeles en la mesa
Sandra, pon los papeles en la mesa, por favor.

(no) buscar	una cafetera para tu oficina
(no) comprar	copias de la agenda antes de la reunión
(no) repartir	a la cafetería por facturas (pan dulce argentino)
(no) salir	a trabajar el sábado
(no) decirle	la verdad al público
(no) hacer	información en la Internet
(no) ir	antes de las seis de la tarde
(no) venir	información sin antes consultar al director

Presencia hispana

The U.S. Hispanic Chamber of Commerce was founded in 1979 to increase business relationships and partnerships between the corporate sector and Hispanic-owned businesses; to promote international trade between Hispanic businesses in the U.S. and Latin America; to monitor legislation, policies, and programs that affect the Hispanic business community; and to provide technical assistance to Hispanic business associations and entre-preneurs. Why would a separate chamber of commerce for Hispanic businesses be important?

11-8 Un trabajo nuevo. Un/a buen/a amigo/a acaba de conseguir su primer trabajo y quieres darle buenos consejos. Complétalos con el mandato informal de un verbo lógico de la lista.

ponerse	hacer	llegar	ser
hablar	ir	pedir	tomar

MODELO: *Ten* paciencia con los clientes.

1. No _____ nervioso/a el primer día.
2. _____ a todas las reuniones obligatorias.
3. _____ en serio las sesiones de entrenamiento.
4. _____ bien tu trabajo.
5. _____ amable con los clientes.
6. ¡No _____ tarde!
7. ¡No _____ mal de tu jefe ni de tus colegas!
8. _____ un sueldo más alto después de seis meses.

 11-9A ¡Socorro! (*Help!*) En el trabajo surgen (*arise*) situaciones urgentes. Responde de una manera apropiada a las urgencias que te presenta tu compañero/a. **Estudiante B,** por favor ve al **Apéndice 1,** página A-20.

MODELO: ESTUDIANTE A: *La reunión es ahora, pero no hay café.*
ESTUDIANTE B: ¡(Llamar) al restaurante ahora mismo! *¡Llama al restaurante ahora mismo!*

Estudiante A:

Mis situaciones urgentes:	Posibles soluciones para mi compañero/a:
1. Hay un carpintero que necesita arreglar algo en tu oficina ahora.	• ¡(Dárselo) enseguida!
2. Hay un pequeño fuego en mi escritorio.	• ¡(Llamar) a la agencia de intérpretes!
3. Mi supervisora insiste en que lleve traje.	• ¡(Pedir) la opinión de otro contador!
4. No hay luz en todo el edificio.	• ¡(Llamar) al plomero ahora mismo!
5. Un periodista pide información confidencial.	• ¡(Explicarle) que es imposible irse de vacaciones ahora!

 11-10 Consejos. Túrnense para darse consejos sobre el trabajo. Respondan a cada consejo.

MODELO: E1: El jefe quiere que yo haga muchas cosas esta mañana.
E2: *Dile que no puedes hacerlas todas en una mañana.*
E1: *¡Tienes razón! ¡Buen consejo! / No me parece una buena idea porque...*

Algunos problemas

1. Gano muy poco por todo lo que tengo que hacer.
2. Necesito encontrar trabajo para pagar mis estudios.
3. Quiero estudiar para ser veterinario/a pero soy alérgico/a a ciertos animales.
4. Mi empresa va a despedir (*fire*) a cincuenta empleados.
5. La computadora de mi oficina es muy vieja y necesito una nueva.
6. Tengo buenas cualificaciones pero no hay muchas oportunidades de trabajo ahora.

2. The subjunctive and the indicative with adverbial conjunctions

11-16 to 11-21

Conjunciones que siempre requieren el subjuntivo

- Certain conjunctions are always followed by the subjunctive in the dependent clause because they express purpose, intent, condition, or anticipation. The use of these conjunctions presupposes that the action described in the dependent clause is uncertain or has not yet taken place. The following are some of these conjunctions.

a fin de que	*in order that*	**en caso de que**	*in case*
a menos (de) que	*unless*	**para que**	*in order that, so that*
antes (de) que	*before*	**sin que**	*without*
con tal (de) que	*provided (that)*		

Reparte los informes **para que** todos los **lean.**

Distribute the reports so that everyone reads them.

Carmen no va a aceptar el trabajo **a menos que** le **suban** el sueldo.

Carmen is not going to accept the job unless they raise the salary.

No me enojo **con tal que** el jefe me **dé** un buen horario.

I will not get angry provided that the boss gives me a good schedule.

Lleva la evaluación **en caso de que** la **necesitemos.**

Take the evaluation in case we need it.

Le recomiendo que visite la oficina de empleo **antes de que se cierre.**

I recommend that you visit the employment office before it closes.

PÓLIZA DE VIDA

Asegure su Crédito o Préstamo

Para que no pase nada

ASCAT seguros
Compañías del Grupo CAJA DE CATALUÑA

Conjunciones que se usan con el subjuntivo y el indicativo

- The subjunctive is used after some conjunctions that introduce dependent clauses referring to an action that has not yet taken place. Because the action has yet to take place, we cannot speak with certainty about it. The verb in the main clause may be in the future tense, the present indicative (with future meaning), or the imperative (direct command).

cuando	*when*	**hasta que**	*until*
después (de) que	*after*	**luego que**	*as soon as*
donde	*where*	**mientras que**	*as long as*
en cuanto	*as soon as*	**tan pronto como**	*as soon as*

José, habla con el gerente **cuando** él **llegue** a la oficina.

José, talk to the manager when he arrives at the office.

Le voy a explicar las responsabilidades **en cuanto llene** la solicitud de empleo.

I'm going to explain the responsibilities to you as soon as you fill out the job application.

No puedo hacer nada **mientras que** no me **den** la respuesta.

I can't do anything as long as they don't give me the answer.

No van a hablar con el empleado problemático **hasta que se vaya** su amigo.

They won't talk to the problematic employee until his friend leaves.

Cuando la supervisora **cambie** de posición, me voy a sentir mejor.

When the supervisor gets a job change, I'm going to feel better.

Vamos a entrevistarlos hasta que encontremos al mejor candidato.

- However, if the action referred to in the dependent clause is habitual or has already taken place, the present or past indicative is used after these conjunctions because we can speak with certainty about things that have already occurred or that occur regularly.

Ana pregunta por el sueldo **cuando tiene** una entrevista.	Ana asks about the salary whenever she has an interview. (habit)
Isabel preguntó por el sueldo **cuando se reunió** con el supervisor.	Isabel asked about the salary when she met with the supervisor. (past)
El veterinario nunca sale de la clínica **mientras que hay** animales que atender.	The veterinarian never leaves the clinic as long as there are animals to attend to. (habit)
Los Rosales salieron de la clínica **mientras que** el veterinario **atendía** a su mascota.	The Rosaleses left the clinic while the veterinarian attended to their pet. (past)

- When there is no change in subject, the following prepositions are used with the infinitive: **antes de, después de, para,** and **sin.**

Van a comprar un teléfono celular **después** de hablar con el dependiente.	They are going to buy a cellular phone after talking with the clerk.
No puedes preparar un contrato **sin usar** una computadora.	You can't prepare a contract without using a computer.
Trabajo mucho en la empresa **para aprender** sus normas.	I work a lot at the firm in order to learn the rules.

APLICACIÓN

11-11 Soy gaucha. El gaucho es una figura popular que se asocia con las pampas argentinas y uruguayas.

Paso 1 Lee la descripción de su vida diaria y subraya todas las conjunciones adverbiales. Identifica si se usa el subjuntivo, el indicativo o el infinitivo y explica por qué.

Soy Juana María Soldado y soy "gaucha" de profesión. Todos los días, antes de que salga el sol, me levanto, me visto y preparo mi yerba mate. Siempre pongo a calentar agua, y tan pronto como está caliente, la echo a una calabaza[1] que ya tiene yerba mate. Machaco[2] las hojas[3] para que se mezclen bien con el agua caliente. Es una bebida sabrosa y saludable. (Y además, ¡tiene la cafeína que necesito cuando me levanto tan temprano!) Después de tomar el mate, le doy agua y heno[4] a Diablo, mi caballo. En la estancia (el rancho) donde trabajo, tenemos cinco mil ovejas[5] y hoy es el día para llevarlas al mercado. Le pongo la silla a mi caballo y la ajusto para que esté segura. Lo monto[6] y me dirijo hacia las pampas donde encuentro las ovejas. A menos que sea un día extraordinario, es imposible atraparlas a todas, pero Diablo y yo lo intentamos. Al final del día, mis compañeros y yo preparamos una parrillada (una barbacoa) y nos acostamos temprano a fin de que al día siguiente podamos levantarnos bien temprano y continuar con nuestro trabajo.

—————
[1]gourd [2]I mash [3]leaves [4]hay [5]sheep [6]mount

Hoy en día no todos los gauchos son hombres.

Paso 2   Contesta las siguientes preguntas basándote en la lectura sobre Juana María.

1. ¿Cuándo se levanta Juana María?

2. ¿Cuándo va a preparar su mate mañana?

3. ¿Por qué le gusta tomar yerba mate?

4. ¿Qué hace después de tomarla?

5. ¿Por qué es imposible atrapar todas las ovejas?

6. ¿Por qué se acuestan temprano los gauchos?

11-12 En la oficina de Mundiplásticos.   El director de una compañía que fabrica artículos de plástico espera piratear a algunos ingenieros de una empresa rival. Escoge la conjunción más lógica entre paréntesis.

Hoy es 17 de mayo, y mi plan es piratear a cinco ingenieros de la empresa Plásticos, S.A., (1. para que / tan pronto como) pueda. He estudiado todos los documentos (2. para / sin) entender bien su organización. Quiero hablar con todos los empleados (3. en cuanto / a menos que) me lo impidan. Quiero invitarlos a mi fábrica (4. a fin de que / cuando) vean las máquinas modernas que tenemos aquí. ¡Estoy decidido! Voy a aumentar el número de empleados de mi empresa (5. antes de que / mientras que) sea demasiado tarde. El jefe de Plásticos, S.A., va a estar muy sorprendido (6. cuando / sin que) sus ingenieros renuncien a su posición.

Necesito ingenieros con experiencia para mi nueva empresa.

11-13 En la oficina de empleo.   Aquí tienes algunos consejos de la directora de empleos. Complétalos con la forma correcta del verbo entre paréntesis. Ten cuidado de usar el indicativo, el subjuntivo o el infinitivo según el contexto.

1. Le voy a enseñar los anuncios clasificados para que (Ud.: ver) _____ los nuevos empleos que publicamos hoy.

2. Ayer recibimos anuncios nuevos después de que (Ud.: salir) _____ de la oficina.

3. Voy a obtenerle una entrevista tan pronto como (yo: hablar) _____ con el jefe de personal.

4. Usted debe hacer copias de su currículum vítae antes de (Ud.: ir) _____ a la entrevista.

5. Vamos a ensayar (*rehearse*) su entrevista para que (Ud.: sentirse) _____ cómodo/a.

6. A menos que el taxi le (costar) _____ demasiado, debe ir a la entrevista en taxi en vez de ir en autobús.

7. Va a conocer a la supervisora cuando le (ellos: enseñar) _____ la línea de producción.

8. Va a tener éxito tan pronto como les (Ud.: decir) _____ que tiene buena preparación y mucha experiencia.

11-14 Estoy decidido/a. Escriban individualmente cinco resoluciones que tengan para el resto de este año. Luego, comparen sus oraciones para ver qué tienen en común. Empiecen la cláusula dependiente con **después de que**.

MODELO: Este año voy a... después de que...
Este año voy a buscar trabajo después de que termine mis clases.

11-15 Excusas en el trabajo. A veces es necesario dar excusas en el trabajo.

Paso 1 Primero escribe un mensaje por correo electrónico en el que le expliques a tu jefe cuándo vas a terminar el trabajo para hoy. Puedes completar las oraciones a continuación en tu mensaje.

MODELO: *Estimada Directora:*
Le prometo que voy a terminar el informe en cuanto tenga la información que necesito...

1. Le prometo que voy a terminar el informe en cuanto...
2. Mi colega promete ayudarme a menos que...
3. Quiero reunirme con el resto del equipo para que...
4. Pienso trabajar hasta que...
5. Voy a estar en la oficina mañana antes de que...
6. Siempre puedo terminar mi trabajo cuando...

Paso 2 Ahora, intercambien sus correos y contéstenlos de una manera lógica.

MODELO: *Estimado/a...*
Me alegro de que usted quiera trabajar en el proyecto hasta que...

🍦🍦 **11-16 ¿Cuándo vas a...?** Túrnense para entrevistarse sobre sus planes para el futuro.

MODELO: E1: ¿Cuándo vas a casarte? (cuando)
E2: *Voy a casarme cuando tenga un trabajo estable.*

1. ¿Cuándo vas a terminar tus estudios? (tan pronto como)
2. ¿Cuándo vas a buscar trabajo? (después de que)
3. ¿Hasta cuándo vas a estudiar español? (hasta que)
4. ¿Cuándo vas a escribir tu currículum vítae? (en cuanto)
5. ¿Cuándo vas a visitar Argentina y Uruguay? (luego que)
6. ¿Cuándo vas a tomar yerba mate? (con tal de que)

11-22
to 11-27

¿Cuánto saben?

Primero, pregúntate si puedes llevar a cabo las siguientes funciones comunicativas en español. Después, júntate con dos o tres compañeros/as de clase para presentar las situaciones. Hagan y respondan a por lo menos cuatro preguntas en cada situación.

✓ CAN YOU . . .	WITH YOUR CLASSMATE(S) . . .
☐ describe professions and occupations?	**Situación: En la oficina de empleo** En tu empresa, hay varias oportunidades de empleo. Explica los requisitos y las responsabilidades de cinco de los puestos vacantes. **Para empezar:** *Tenemos cinco vacantes: ingeniero, plomero, arquitecto, mecánico y...*
☐ talk about the advantages of different professions?	**Situación: Consejos** Explícale a un nuevo estudiante cuáles son las ventajas y desventajas de estudiar para ciertas profesiones u oficios. Usa el vocabulario de **¡Así lo decimos!** **Para empezar:** *Si te interesan los animales, debes estudiar para ser veterinario/a porque...*
☐ give and follow instructions from a friend?	**Situación: En la universidad** Usa mandatos de **tú** para decirle a un/a compañero/a lo que tiene que hacer para conseguir un buen trabajo. **Para empezar:** *Primero, conéctate a la Internet y busca una página web con anuncios clasificados para trabajo...*
☐ talk about future plans?	**Situación: En casa** Explícales a tus padres (o a tu pareja) cuándo vas a terminar los estudios. Usa una variedad de conjunciones (**antes de que, para que, cuando, tan pronto como,** etc.) con el infinitivo, el subjuntivo o el indicativo según el caso. **Para empezar:** *Voy a terminar mis estudios cuando... a menos que...*

📖 Perfiles

11-28 to 11-29

Mi experiencia

LOS EMPLEOS Y LAS RECOMENDACIONES

11-17 Para ti. ¿Tienes un trabajo en este momento? ¿Qué hiciste para conseguirlo? ¿Tuviste que conocer a alguien importante en la empresa para conseguir tu puesto? A la hora de conseguir trabajo, ¿qué crees que es más importante, tener buenos contactos dentro de la empresa o tener la experiencia necesaria para el puesto?

Hola, soy Cristina y estudio ciencias de comunicación social en la Universidad de Buenos Aires. Ahora estoy en mi último año y espero recibir mi título dentro de unos pocos meses. Este año tuve la oportunidad de hacer un internado[1] con el periódico *Clarín*, el más importante de Argentina. ¡Fue bárbaro y aprendí un montón! Espero que esta experiencia me ayude a conseguir un buen trabajo. ¡Pero es difícil en esta economía! Se dice que la tasa[2] de desempleo entre los jóvenes argentinos ha subido a más del 30%. Por eso, a la hora de buscar empleo es crucial conocer personalmente a una persona dentro de la organización que pueda ayudarle a uno. En Argentina, como en muchas partes del mundo hispano, "a quién se conoce" muchas veces es la clave[3] para obtener un puesto. Así pues, lo que voy a hacer primero es hablar con la esposa de mi primo, que es editora de un periódico regional. Ella sabe que soy seria y que merezco[4] una posición dentro de mi campo de estudios. Y si tan solo hay un trabajo a tiempo parcial, lo voy a aceptar porque es importante "tener el pie dentro" de la organización. Luego, en el futuro cuando consiga una posición de tiempo completo, seguramente voy a hacer algo similar por un/a amigo/a que también necesite ayuda.

Y así están las cosas por ahora. Por eso, cuando me llegan esos momentos de poca inspiración, me gusta escuchar la música de Fito Páez, uno de los cantautores más populares entre los jóvenes argentinos. Si no conocen su música, les recomiendo que escuchen "Yo vengo a ofrecer mi corazón". ¡Verán[5] cómo se animan!

[1]*internship* [2]*rate* [3]*key* [4]*deserve* [5]*You'll see*

11-18 En su opinión. Conversen en grupos de tres o más sobre las ventajas y desventajas de conseguir un puesto de trabajo a través de una recomendación familiar o de un/a amigo/a y preparen una lista.

Ventajas de entrar con recomendación	Desventajas de entrar con recomendación
Puede ayudarte cuando hay mucho desempleo.	*Los otros empleados pueden tener envidia de ti.*

Mi música

"YO VENGO A OFRECER MI CORAZÓN"
(FITO PÁEZ, ARGENTINA)

Fito Páez es uno de los cantautores más célebres del mundo latino. Su canción "Yo vengo a ofrecer mi corazón" ha sido interpretada por muchos cantantes internacionales, incluso por su compatriota, Mercedes Sosa, y por el cantautor cubano, Pablo Milanés. En la versión a continuación, Fito canta un dueto con la popularísima Ana Belén.

Antes de ver y escuchar

 11-19 ¿Por qué ofrecer su corazón? Haz una lista de las cosas que quieres cambiar en este mundo. Después intercambia tu lista con la de un/a compañero/a ¿Qué tienen en común? ¿Qué quieren hacer de manera diferente? ¿Qué cambios no quieren hacer nunca?

MODELO: *Quiero que se mejore la economía.*

Para ver y escuchar

11-20 La canción. Conéctate a la Internet para ver un video de la versión de "Yo vengo a ofrecer mi corazón" con Fito Páez y Ana Belén. Mientras la escuchas, rellena los espacios en blanco con las palabras o expresiones de la columna a la derecha.

> **Busca:** fito paez ana belen yo vengo a ofrecer; vengo ofrecer corazon letra
>
> **Si te interesa comprar la canción:** *Go to iTunes Store>Music>More to Explore>iMix>Arriba 6e.*

1. vengo a ofrecer _____
2. tanta _____ que se llevó el río
3. no será (*it won't be*) _____
4. abrir _____
5. me iré (*I will leave*) _____
6. te daré (*I will give you*) _____
7. hablo por _____
8. hablo de cambiar _____

a. todo
b. el pecho
c. nuestra casa
d. mi corazón
e. la vida
f. sangre
g. tranquilo
h. fácil

Después de ver y escuchar

11-21 ¿Qué quieren para el futuro? Cuando el cantautor dice que ofrece su corazón, es evidente que espera un futuro mejor para su país y su gente. Piensa en lo que esperas para el futuro de tus amigos, tu familia y tu propio futuro. Escribe un mínimo de cinco mandatos informales expresándoles tus esperanzas a diferentes personas.

MODELO: *Hermano, <u>busca</u> un trabajo cerca de nosotros. <u>No te vayas</u> lejos de aquí, por favor.*

11-22 Fito Páez. Busca más información sobre Fito Páez para escribir un párrafo en el que contestas estas preguntas: ¿Dónde nació? ¿Cuál es su nombre verdadero? ¿A qué edad empezó su carrera musical? ¿Qué tragedia personal sufrió en los años 80 durante la dictadura militar?

> **Busca:** fito paez biografia

Segunda parte

¡Así lo decimos! VOCABULARIO

¡Así es la vida! En busca de empleo

11-30

Un aspirante a una vacante da una buena impresión.

DRA. MENÉNDEZ: Buenas tardes, Sr. Torres. Siéntese, por favor.

SR. TORRES: Mucho gusto, Dra. Menéndez. Gracias por su interés en mi solicitud.

DRA. MENÉNDEZ: Pues, veo que usted tiene mucha experiencia y buenas cualidades.

DRA. MENÉNDEZ: ¿Cómo son las cartas de recomendación del Sr. Torres?

ALICIA: Son muy buenas. No hay ninguna que tenga comentarios negativos.

🔊 **Vocabulario** La búsqueda de empleo

La búsqueda de empleo The job search

el/la aspirante *applicant*
los avisos clasificados *classified ads*
la carta de presentación / recomendación *letter of introduction / recommendation*
el despacho *office*
la entrevista *interview*
el formulario *form*
la solicitud de empleo *employment application*
la vacante *vacancy*

Los beneficios Benefits

el aumento *raise*
la bonificación anual *yearly bonus*
la guardería *daycare center*
el plan de retiro *retirement plan*
la licencia por enfermedad / maternidad *sick/maternity leave*
el seguro médico *health insurance*

Verbos Verbs

ascender (ie) *to promote, to move up*
contratar *to hire*
dejar de *to stop doing something*
despedir (i, i) *to fire*
retirarse *to retire*
rellenar[1] *to fill completely, to fill out*

Adjetivos Adjectives

capaz *capable*
entusiasta *enthusiastic*
honrado/a, honesto/a *honest*
justo/a *just*

Una carta comercial A business letter

Saludos *Salutations, greetings*
Estimado/a señor/a: *Dear Sir/Madam:*

Despedidas *Closings*
Atentamente, *Sincerely yours,*
Cordialmente, *Cordially yours,*
Lo(s)/La(s) saluda atentamente, *Very truly yours,*

Variaciones
Retirarse is used frequently in Latin America, while **jubilarse** is the most common term in Spain.

Variaciones
In Mexico, a popular alternative to **despedir** is the verb **correr** as in **Lo corrieron del trabajo.** (*They fired him.*)

los avisos clasificados

los aspirantes al empleo

la entrevista en el despacho del director

---

[1]Also: completar, llenar (*to fill*)

Letras y sonidos

The consonants b and v

In Spanish, the letters **b** and **v** sound identical, with no distinction between them, as there is in English. While **b** and **v** are identical, two different sounds correspond to them, depending on the context. After a pause or the letters **m** or **n,** the sound for **b** and **v** is like the *b* in English *base.*

Hard bilabial:

bús-que-da   **ve-te-ri-na-rio**   **bom-be-ro**   **con-ven-to**

In all other positions, especially between vowels, the sound for **b** and **v** is softer. English has no sound similar, but this sound is approximated when one imitates the steady murmur of a motor boat in the distance.

Soft bilabial:

la-bús-que-da   **el-ve-te-ri-na-rio**   **con-ta-ble**   **a-vión**

APLICACIÓN

Cultura en vivo

¡Hola!

Cultura en vivo

In many Spanish-speaking countries, professions and trades are either typically male or typically female; however, women are making headway in areas such as the sciences and engineering. In the case of Spain, the European Union has established a set of guidelines that guarantees equal pay for equal work, regardless of sex. Do certain majors in your university seem to attract one sex over the other?

11-23 En busca de empleo. Empareja las siguientes definiciones con la expresión más lógica.

1. _____ Tu último jefe escribió excelentes comentarios.

2. _____ Te cuidan a tus hijos durante las horas de trabajo en este lugar.

3. _____ Firmas este documento. Los términos son por un año, pero el documento es renovable (*renewable*).

4. _____ Incluyes los nombres y números de teléfono de personas que te van a recomendar favorablemente.

5. _____ Este beneficio es esencial para cuidar la salud de los empleados.

6. _____ Esta persona necesita buenas cualificaciones; debe ser entusiasta y capaz.

7. _____ Después de trabajar bien por unos años en una empresa, tu sueldo sube.

8. _____ Este beneficio te permite dejar el trabajo temporalmente si sufres de problemas graves de salud.

a. las referencias

b. el seguro médico

c. el aumento

d. la guardería

e. la licencia por enfermedad

f. el contrato

g. la recomendación

h. el/la aspirante

11-24 ¿En qué orden? Indica el orden en que completas estos pasos para conseguir un puesto.

_____ llamar para hacer una cita con el/la jefe/a de personal

_____ volver a casa y esperar una llamada

_1_ leer los anuncios clasificados en el periódico

_____ rellenar la solicitud de empleo

_____ hacer preguntas sobre los beneficios del trabajo

_____ tener la entrevista

_____ contestar las preguntas sobre mi formación y experiencia

_____ preguntar sobre el sueldo

🔊 11-25 **La solicitud de empleo.** Trabajas en una agencia de empleo y Alejandra es una clienta. Escucha a Alejandra mientras explica su formación y su experiencia. Luego completa su solicitud de empleo.

AGENCIA LÓPEZ

Solicitud de Empleo

Nombre: _____ Apellidos: _____ _Ayala_

Edad: _____

Dirección: _Avenida_____ No._____

Teléfono: _____

Empleo deseado: _____

Sueldo mínimo: _____

Estudios universitarios: _____ años

Lugar: _____ ¿Título? **sí** **no**

Experiencia: _____ años Lugar: _Grimaldi_____

Idiomas: _____

Referencias: **sí** **no** Nombre(s) _____

🖱 11-26 **¿A qué empresa deseas solicitar?** El sitio web del periódico argentino *Clarín* tiene una amplia lista de oportunidades de empleo.

Paso 1 Conéctate a la Internet para ver los avisos clasificados del periódico *Clarín*. Escoge uno que te interese y contesta las preguntas que siguen.

> 🖱 **Busca:** empleos clarin

1. ¿Cómo se llama la empresa?
2. ¿Dónde tiene su sede (*head office*)?
3. ¿Qué vende o produce?
4. ¿Por qué te parece interesante?
5. ¿Hay información para solicitar un puesto?

Paso 2 Las cualificaciones para el trabajo. Escribe una lista de las cualificaciones que crees que se necesitan para el empleo que encontraste. Incluye el tipo de formación, de experiencia y de personalidad o de características físicas que requiere el puesto.

MODELO: Analista de sistemas
Formación: *título universitario...*
Experiencia: *2 años...*, etc.
Personalidad: *paciente, trabajador...*

👥 11-27 **Ensayar (*rehearse*) la entrevista.** Representen al/a la aspirante y al/a la jefe/a de personal para dramatizar una búsqueda de empleo.

MODELO: E1: *Buenas tardes. Soy... Quiero solicitar el puesto de...*
E2: *Sí, señor/ita. ¿Qué experiencia tiene usted?*

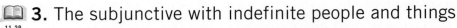

3. The subjunctive with indefinite people and things

11-38
to 11-43

Buscamos una persona que tenga experiencia con análisis de sistemas.

An adjective describes, limits, or modifies a noun. A clause that modifies a noun is an adjective clause.

Adjective

Tenemos aspirantes **cualificados.**	*We have qualified applicants.*

Adjective clauses

Gustavo Torres es un empleado **que tiene buenas cualificaciones.**	*Gustavo Torres is an employee who is qualified.*
Pero no hay ningún aspirante **que tenga experiencia en supervisión.**	*But there is no applicant who has experience in supervision.*

• The subjunctive is used in an adjective clause when it refers to a person, thing, or event that is indefinite or does not exist.

Buscamos una persona que **hable** español y portugués.	*We are looking for a person who speaks Spanish and Portuguese.*
Necesito un viajante que **trabaje** a comisión.	*I need a traveling salesperson who works on commission.*
No hay nadie que yo **conozca** en esta empresa.	*There is no one that I know at this company.*
No hay ninguna entrevista que **sea** fácil.	*There is no interview that is easy.*

• When the dependent clause refers to a person or thing that is certain or definite, the indicative is used; if it is indefinite or uncertain, the subjunctive is used.

Hay alguien aquí **que conozco.**	*There is someone here that I know.*
No hay nadie aquí **que conozca.**	*There is no one here that I know.*
Necesitamos a la recepcionista **que se expresa bien.**	*We need the receptionist who expresses herself well.* (We know her.)
Busco un secretario **que se exprese bien.**	*I am looking for a secretary who expresses himself well.* (I'm still looking.)

• The subjunctive is used when asking whether something or someone exists, or when saying that something or someone doesn't exist.

¿Conoce usted una empresa que **tenga** vacantes?	*Do you know any company that has vacancies?*
¿No hay ningún supervisor que **quiera** una oficina eficiente?	*Is there any supervisor who doesn't want an efficient office?*

APLICACIÓN

11-28 Las cataratas del Iguazú. Hay una leyenda que explica la creación de las cataratas.

Paso 1 Lee el párrafo sobre las cataratas y subraya las cláusulas adjetivales. Identifica cuáles usan el subjuntivo y cuáles el indicativo, y luego explica por qué.

¿Conoces la leyenda del origen de las cataratas del Iguazú?

Las cataratas del Iguazú captan la imaginación y fascinan a todos quienes las visitan. Están ubicadas en el río Iguazú en la frontera entre Brasil y Argentina. Su nombre, que viene del guaraní, significa "grandes aguas". Según la leyenda, un dios quería casarse con una hermosa indígena, pero ella estaba enamorada de otro y estos se escaparon juntos. En su furia, el dios partió las aguas y así condenó a los amantes a una caída[1] eterna. Por eso los indios de la región siempre las consideraron sagradas. El explorador español Cabeza de Vaca las encontró en 1541, pero ningún otro europeo las vio hasta el siglo XIX. Hoy en día las cataratas atraen a turistas de todo el mundo. Es cierto que no hay nadie que no se impresione de su grandeza y de su hermosura. Con un promedio[2] de 64 metros de altura, no hay ninguna cascada que no tenga una altura impactante.

---

[1]*fall* [2]*average*

Paso 2 Contesta las siguientes preguntas sobre las cataratas del Iguazú.

1. ¿Dónde están situadas?

2. ¿Cuál es el origen del nombre?

3. ¿Por qué crees que los indígenas las consideraron sagradas?

4. ¿Hay alguna cascada que sea pequeña?

5. ¿Conoces a alguien que las conozca?

6. ¿Quieres visitarlas algún día? Explica.

 Paso 3 Conéctate a la Internet para ver más imágenes de las cataratas. Elige una escena y escribe un párrafo describiéndola.

 Busca: iguazu foto

11-29 Cristina Fernández. El ayudante de la presidenta Fernández tiene que contratar a las mejores personas para su despacho. Haz el papel de ayudante y forma oraciones completas en español, usando **buscar** y **necesitar.** Incluye la información de lista en tus descripciones.

entender mi misión	traducir de/a varios idiomas
poder organizar la oficina	ser honrado/a y capaz
hablar tres idiomas	entender nuestra red de computadoras
conocer los planos de la casa presidencial	contestar todas las cartas
querer trabajar los fines de semana	tener experiencia diplomática
	¿…?

MODELO: *Busco una secretaria que… / Necesito un asistente que…*

1. intérprete
2. secretario/a
3. supervisor/a
4. contador/a
5. ayudante
6. chofer
7. arquitecto/a
8. analista de sistemas

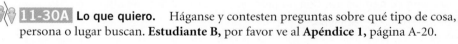

11-30A Lo que quiero. Háganse y contesten preguntas sobre qué tipo de cosa, persona o lugar buscan. **Estudiante B,** por favor ve al **Apéndice 1,** página A-20.

MODELO: carro
　　　　E1: *¿Qué tipo de carro buscas?*
　　　　E2: *Busco un carro que tenga cuatro puertas y que sea rojo.*

Estudiante A:

Mis preguntas	Mis respuestas
1. trabajo	• *tener* dos dormitorios y un baño
2. casa	• *tener* noticias internacionales
3. restaurante	• *estar* llena de acción y misterio
4. lugar para pasar las vacaciones	• *pagarme* bien al comenzar a trabajar
5. programa de televisión	• *tener* posibilidades de ascender rápido

11-31 Las profesiones y los oficios. Entrevístense en grupos de tres o cuatro para saber sus planes después de graduarse. Luego, hagan un resumen de sus planes. Usen las frases siguientes para hacer las preguntas.

MODELO: querer ser ingeniero/a
E1: *¿Hay alguien que quiera ser ingeniero o ingeniera?*
E2: *Sí, quiero ser ingeniero/a porque...*

1. querer ser periodista

2. pensar abrir una peluquería

3. desear ser contador/a

4. soñar con tener un restaurante

5. preferir ser dentista

6. creer que ciertos oficios son mejores que ciertas profesiones

7. pensar estudiar para veterinario/a

8. desear ser bombero/a

9. ¿...?

¿Hay alguien que quiera trabajar en televisión?

11-32 El mundo real y el mundo ideal. Hay grandes diferencias entre lo que existe y lo que deseamos que exista.

Paso 1 A continuación hay temas donde existen diferencias entre lo real y lo ideal. Escribe oraciones completas en cada categoría.

Lo real	Lo ideal
Tema: Las clases de la universidad	
• *Tengo muchas clases que se dan en línea.*	• *Quiero tener más clases que se den en persona.*
Tema: Los internados (*internships*) para estudiantes	
•	•
Tema: La búsqueda de trabajo	
•	•
Tema: Las residencias estudiantiles	
•	•
Tema: La ayuda financiera para estudiar	
•	•

Paso 2 En grupos de tres o cuatro estudiantes, compartan sus opiniones. Hagan una lista de algunas de sus ideas más interesantes para compartir después con el resto de la clase.

Ojalá que encuentre un buen trabajo.

11-44
to 11-47

11-33 En mi opinión. ¿Cúales son tus opiniones y deseos sobre el lugar donde vives?

Paso 1 Completa las oraciones para expresar tu opinión, tus deseos y tus experiencias de vivir en esta ciudad o en este pueblo. Usa el subjuntivo o el indicativo, según el caso. Tus respuestas pueden ser serias o cómicas.

MODELO: *En esta ciudad / este pueblo no hay nadie que quiera vivir en otro lugar.*

- tengo amigos que...
- me alegro de que mis amigos...
- no conozco a nadie que ...
- mis padres dudan que yo ...

- no quiero que mis amigos...
- busco un lugar que...
- ojalá que...
- conozco un café donde...

Paso 2 Ahora túrnense para expresar sus opiniones y comentarlas. Usen expresiones como: **Me alegro que..., Dudo que..., Es posible que..., Es increíble que...,** etc.

MODELO: E1: *En esta ciudad / este pueblo no hay nadie que quiera vivir en otro lugar.*
E2: *Dudo que tengas razón. Conozco a muchas personas que prefieren vivir en...*

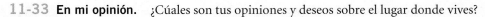

¿Cuánto saben?

Primero, pregúntate si puedes llevar a cabo las siguientes funciones comunicativas en español. Después, júntate con dos o tres compañeros/as de clase para presentar las situaciones. Hagan y respondan a por lo menos cuatro preguntas en cada situación.

✓ **CAN YOU . . .**

☐ read and respond to the want ads?

☐ write a brief business letter?

☐ interview for a job?

☐ describe existing and nonexistent people and things?

WITH YOUR CLASSMATE(S) . . .

Situación: En casa con amigos/as
Hagan los papeles de amigos/as que están buscando empleo en los avisos del periódico o de la Internet. Hablen sobre por qué les interesan o no las ofertas. Posibles puestos: **cocinero/a, camarero/a, dependiente/a, paseador/a de perros (*dog walker*), viajante, entrenador/a personal...**
Para empezar: *Aquí hay un aviso clasificado para... ¿Crees que es una buena opción para ti? ¿Por qué?*

Situación: Busco empleo
Escribe una carta en la que te presentas y expresas interés en una posición en la empresa. Pídele a un/a amigo/a que te dé sugerencias sobre el contenido de la carta.
Para empezar: *A quién le pueda interesar: Soy Pedro Gómez, un estudiante de...*

Situación: En una entrevista
Hagan los papeles de aspirante y director/a de una empresa. El/la aspirante escribe una carta de presentación. El/la directora/a le hace preguntas sobre sus cualificaciones.
Para empezar: *Buenas tardes. En su carta, usted dice que tiene experiencia en...*

Situación: En tu universidad
Conversen sobre las actividades y cosas que les interesan y las que no existen pero que les gustaría (*you would like*) tener.
Para empezar: *En esta universidad hay muchos deportes que me interesan, por ejemplo... pero no hay ningún deporte que...*

Observaciones

¡Pura vida! EPISODIO 11

En este episodio David le ofrece trabajo a Patricio.

Antes de ver el video

11-34 El pluriempleo. En Latinoamérica es común que la gente tenga más de un empleo. A continuación tienes un aviso que una persona puso en la Internet para buscar trabajo. Lee el aviso y escríbele una carta para recomendarle el tipo de trabajo que debe buscar. Explica tus razones para darle la recomendación.

> **Busco empleo**
>
> Tengo mucho tiempo libre durante la semana ya que solo trabajo dos días. Busco empleo en algo serio. Tengo experiencia como ayudante administrativo y ayudante clínico. Ahora, trabajo como operador de comunicaciones. Soy muy hábil con las manos. Tengo licencia de conducir y tengo un carro grande.

MODELO: *Le recomiendo que...*

A ver el video

 11-35 Las características del trabajo. Mira el episodio número once de **¡Pura vida!** para identificar las características del trabajo que David le ofrece a Patricio.

La oficina de CREFASI

David Ortiz-Smith

Patricio

Características	Sí	No
1. salario mínimo		
2. bonificación anual		
3. oficina con ventana		
4. plan de retiro		
5. seguro médico		
6. una beca universitaria		
7. un mes de vacaciones al año		
8. secretaria		
9. supervisión de cinco empleados		
10. camioneta		

Después de ver el video

 11-36 Busco empleo. Conéctate a la Internet para ver avisos clasificados. Escoge uno y escribe por lo menos cinco razones por las que te interesa o no el trabajo.

> **Busca:** computrabajo argentina; acciontrabajo argentina

Nuestro mundo

11-51
to 11-52

🌎 Panoramas

📖 El virreinato de la Plata: Argentina y Uruguay

Argentina y Uruguay tienen mucha variedad topográfica y climática: la Patagonia, los Andes, las pampas, los bosques, los ríos, las cataratas y las costas.

En 2010, se le nombró al argentino Leo Messi el "Mejor Jugador del Mundo de la FIFA".

Los glaciares de El Califate atraen a turistas de todo el mundo.

La bella ciudad de Colonia del Sacramento, Uruguay fue fundada en 1680 por los portugueses y perteneció a Brasil y a Uruguay en diferentes épocas. Ahora, su barrio histórico es un sitio del Patrimonio de la Humanidad de la UNESCO.

El tango, la música y el baile típico de Argentina y Uruguay, se originó en los barrios pobres de las afueras de las ciudades que bordeaban el río de la Plata a fines del siglo XIX.

Buenos Aires es una ciudad cosmopolita, con mucha vida cultural y social.

Argentina y Uruguay

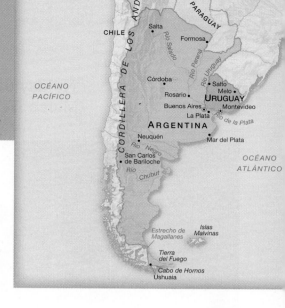

	Argentina	Uruguay
Población:	41 millones	3,5 millones
PIB per cápita:	$14.200	$12.200
Porcentaje de mujeres en la fuerza laboral:	60%	72%
Sueldos femeninos:	66% del sueldo mas.	100% del sueldo mas.
Número mínimo de días de vacaciones:	Depende del número de años en el trabajo: 0–5: 2 semanas 20+: 5 semanas	2 semanas
Días de licencia por paternidad:	2 días	3 días

11-37 Identifica. Identifica, describe y/o explica lo siguiente.

1. un sitio del Patrimonio de la Humanidad de Uruguay

2. un lugar donde hay glaciares

3. dónde se encuentra la Patagonia

4. el nombre de un futbolista famoso argentino

5. una ciudad argentina con mucha actividad cultural

11-38 Desafío. Consulta el mapa y la caja para contestar estas preguntas.

1. la capital de Argentina y la de Uruguay

2. la diferencia entre los sueldos para hombres y mujeres

3. el país donde los trabajadores tienen derecho a cinco semanas de vacaciones

4. las islas Falkland, según los argentinos

5. el río que forma la frontera entre Argentina y Uruguay

6. el país más poblado de los dos

11-39 Proyecto: La diversidad de Argentina y Uruguay. Conéctate a la Internet para ver más imágenes de Argentina y Uruguay. Escoge una región: la Patagonia, las pampas, los Andes o la costa. Después descríbela según los criterios que siguen.

> **Busca:** patagonia; pampas; andes; costa argentina; costa uruguay

- sitios de interés
- deportes
- gastronomía
- productos
- clima
- artes

MODELO: Uno de los productos agrícolas más importantes de Argentina es la carne. Según las estadísticas hay entre 50 y 55 millones de cabezas de ganado principalmente en las pampas...

"No hay que complicar la felicidad"
(Marco Denevi, Argentina)

Marco Denevi (1922–1998) es uno de los cuentistas latinoamericanos más conocidos. Escribió varias novelas, incluyendo *Rosaura a las diez* (1955) y *Ceremonia secreta* (1960). Esta última fue convertida en una película estadounidense con Mia Farrow de protagonista. Denevi es conocido por sus narrativas, minidramas y minicuentos, los cuales comentan verdades humanas y sociológicas.

En "No hay que complicar la felicidad", hay dos novios anónimos que no están satisfechos con su felicidad. La conclusión es, a la vez, sorprendente (*surprising*) y misteriosa.

ANTES DE LEER

11-40 El poder de la imaginación. En la literatura, puede haber varios niveles de interpretación. Esto ocurre especialmente cuando es necesario imaginarnos los motivos de un personaje o adivinar (*guess*) el final de una historia. Muchas veces el autor nos deja con la sensación de ambigüedad o de misterio. Lee las primeras diez líneas de este minidrama y escribe tres preguntas que se te ocurran. Al final, vuelve a tus preguntas para ver si las puedes contestar.

MODELO: *¿Quién es Él?*

11-41 A buscar. Busca esta información en la ilustración.

1. Aquí vemos a dos _____.

   a. amigos   b. enemigos   c. novios   d. hermanos

2. Están en _____.

   a. una iglesia   b. una clase   c. una casa   d. un parque

3. Según la ilustración, están muy _____.

   a. impacientes   b. enamorados   c. enojados   d. aburridos

11-42 Anticipación. En este drama los protagonistas realizan (*carry out*) acciones recíprocas. ¿Cuáles de estas acciones crees que se hacen?

_____ Se miran.	_____ Se gritan.
_____ Se besan.	_____ Se detestan.
_____ Se aman (quieren).	_____ Se matan (*kill each other*).

11-43 Una historia de... Lee ahora la siguiente historia de Marco Denevi.

"No hay que complicar la felicidad"

Un parque. Sentados bajo los árboles, Ella y Él se besan.

Él: Te amo.
Ella: Te amo.

Vuelven a besarse.

Él: Te amo.
Ella: Te amo.

Vuelven a besarse.

Él: Te amo.
Ella: Te amo.

Él se pone violentamente de pie.

Él: ¡Basta!° ¿Siempre lo mismo? ¿Por qué, cuando te digo que te amo no contestas que amas a otro?
Ella: ¿A qué otro?
Él: A nadie. Pero lo dices para que yo tenga celos°. Los celos alimentan° al amor. Despojado de este estímulo, el amor languidece°. Nuestra felicidad es demasiado simple, demasiado monótona. Hay que complicarla un poco. ¿Comprendes?
Ella: No quería confesártelo porque pensé que sufrirías°. Pero lo has adivinado°.
Él: ¿Qué es lo que adiviné?

Ella se levanta, se aleja (gets up, moves away) unos pasos.

Ella: Que amo a otro.
Él: Lo dices para complacerme°. Porque te lo pedí.
Ella: No. Amo a otro.
Él: ¿A qué otro?
Ella: No lo conoces.

Enough

jealousy / nourish; add spice
languishes

you would suffer / you've guessed it

please me

Un silencio. Él tiene una expresión sombría°.

Él: Entonces, ¿es verdad?
Ella: (*Dulcemente*) Sí, es verdad. Está allí.

somber

gestures   *Él se pasea haciendo ademanes° de furor.*

I'm not faking   **Él:**   Siento celos. No finjo°, créeme. Siento celos. Me gustaría matar a ese otro.

                Ella: (*Dulcemente*) Está allí.

                Él: ¿Dónde?

                Ella: Nos espía. También él es celoso.

I'll look for him **Él:**   Iré en su busca°.

                Ella: Cuidado. Quiere matarte.

                Él: No le tengo miedo.

Él desaparece entre los árboles. Al quedar sola ella se ríe.

Ella: ¡Qué niños son los hombres! Para ellos hasta el amor es un juego.

Se oye el disparo de un revólver. Ella deja de reír.

Ella: Juan.

Silencio.

Ella: (*Más alto*) Juan.

Silencio.

Ella: (*Grita.*) ¡Juan!

heartrending cry *Silencio. Ella corre y desaparece entre los árboles. Después de unos instantes se oye el grito desgarrador° de ella.*

Ella: ¡Juan!

curtain *Silencio. Después desciende el telón°.*

DESPUÉS DE LEER

11-44 La cronología.   Pon en orden las siguientes acciones de la historia.

_____ La novia no lo toma en serio (*doesn't take him seriously*).

_____ La novia dice que ama a otro.

_____ La novia grita.

_____ Los novios se besan.

_____ El novio quiere tener celos.

_____ El novio desaparece.

11-45 ¿Comprendiste?   Contesta brevemente en español las siguientes preguntas.

1. Según él, ¿por qué es importante tener celos?

2. ¿Tiene ella la misma opinión?

3. ¿Por qué dice ella que tiene otro novio?

4. ¿Qué busca él entre los árboles?

5. ¿Qué hace ella cuando él sale de la escena?

6. ¿Qué se oye desde los árboles?

7. ¿Qué se oye al final?

11-46 Imagínate.   Imagínate lo que pasa después. ¿Cuál de estos desenlaces (*conclusions*) te parece el más posible? ¿Por qué?

_____ Todo es una broma (*joke*) del novio.

_____ El segundo amante sale de los árboles. Besa a la novia.

_____ Un policía llega y detiene (*arrests*) a la novia.

_____ El novio mata al segundo amante por celos.

_____ ¿...?

11-47 Una carta para pedir consejos.   Asume el punto de vista de uno de los personajes (Él, Ella o el otro) y escribe una carta para pedirle consejos a doña Eulalia, una famosa consejera.

MODELO: *lunes, 4 de abril de 2011*
Estimada doña Eulalia:
¡Necesito sus consejos! Mi novio, Juan,...

11-48 ¿Cuál es su opinión?   Hablen en español de las siguientes cuestiones de amor. Usen las siguientes expresiones para dar su opinión: **Sí, estoy de acuerdo porque…, No estoy seguro/a. Depende de…, No estoy de acuerdo porque…**

MODELO: A los hombres les gusta tener celos.
E1: *Estoy de acuerdo. Los hombres son mucho más celosos que las mujeres.*
E2: *No estoy de acuerdo. Soy hombre y no tengo celos de mi novia…*
E3: *Bueno, depende de…*

1. Los celos alimentan el amor.

2. El amor lo vence (*conquers*) todo.

3. Es bueno confesárselo todo a tu novio/a o esposo/a.

4. Los novios deben siempre complacerse (*please each other*).

5. En el amor, todos somos niños.

6. Es imposible ser feliz en el amor.

 **Taller**

11-49 Un currículum vítae y una carta de presentación para solicitar trabajo.
En esta actividad, vas a escribir tu currículum vítae y una carta para solicitar un puesto.

ANTES DE ESCRIBIR

- **El puesto.** Primero, inventa el puesto que vas a solicitar. ¿Qué tipo de empresa es? ¿Qué tipo de trabajo?

- **Tus datos personales y tu experiencia.** Escribe una lista de tus experiencias académicas y laborales con la fecha de cada una.

A ESCRIBIR

Montevideo,
2 de abril de 2011

Estimados Señores:

Soy Alberto Gómez, un estudiante de Informática en la Universidad de la República. Me interesa el puesto de programador que ustedes anuncian en la página web de *Clarín*. Tengo experiencia trabajando…

- **El currículum vítae.** Escribe tu currículum vítae en una hoja de papel aparte. Usa la información a continuación como guía. La información que incluyas (especialmente las aficiones) debe reflejar de alguna manera el tipo de puesto que solicitas.

(Foto)	Correo electrónico
Nombre y apellidos	Datos académicos (fechas y títulos)
Fecha de nacimiento	Experiencia profesional (fechas y títulos)
Lugar de nacimiento	Publicaciones, colaboraciones, honores
Estado civil	Lenguas
Domicilio actual	Aficiones (viajar, jugar al tenis...)
Teléfonos	Referencias

- **La carta de presentación.** Incluye esta información:

Nombre	Saludo formal	Breve resumen de tus cualificaciones
Dirección	Presentación	
Fecha	Trabajo que solicitas	Despedida formal
Destinatario		Firma

DESPUÉS DE ESCRIBIR

- **Revisar.** Revisa tu currículum vítae y la carta para verificar los siguientes puntos.
  - ☐ las expresiones impersonales
  - ☐ la ortografía y la concordancia
  - ☐ el uso del subjuntivo y del indicativo

- **Intercambiar**
  Intercambia tu trabajo con el de un/a compañero/a para hacer correcciones y sugerencias, y para comentar sobre el contenido.

- **Entregar**
  Pon tu trabajo en limpio, incorporando los comentarios de tu compañero/a. Después, entrégaselo a tu profesor/a.

🔊 Vocabulario

Oficios y profesiones Occupations and professions

el/la analista de sistemas *systems analyst*
el/la arquitecto/a *arquitect*
el/la bombero/a *firefighter*
el/la carpintero/a *carpenter*
el/la cartero/a *mail carrier*
el/la cocinero/a *cook, chef*
el/la contador/a *accountant*
el/la dentista *dentist*
el/la enfermero/a *nurse*
el hombre / la mujer de negocios *businessman/woman*
el/la ingeniero/a *engineer*
el/la intérprete *interpreter*
el/la mecánico/a *mechanic*
el/la obrero/a de construcción *construction worker*
el/la peluquero/a *hairdresser*
el/la periodista *journalist*
el/la plomero/a *plumber*
el/la psicólogo/a *psychologist*
el/la veterinario/a *veterinarian*
el/la viajante *traveling salesperson*

Términos y expresiones de trabajo Work-related terms and expressions

los beneficios *benefits*
las cualificaciones *qualifications*
el currículum vítae *curriculum vitae (vita)*
el (des)empleo *(un)employment*
la empresa *company, firm*
el entrenamiento *training*
la formación *education*
la meta *goal*
el puesto *position (job)*
el sueldo (mínimo) *(minimum) wage*
la (des)ventaja *(dis)advantage*

Cargos Positions

el/la director/a *director*
el/la empleado/a *employee*
el/la gerente *manager*
el/la jefe/a *boss*
el/la jefe/a ejecutivo/a *CEO*

¡Manos a la obra! Let's get to work!

apagar (gu) (fuegos/incendios) *to put out, to extinguish (fires)*
conseguir (i, i) *to get, to obtain*
diseñar *to design*
estar en paro / sin trabajo *to be out of work*
reparar *to repair*
repartir *to deliver, to distribute*
trabajar a tiempo completo/parcial *to work full-time/part-time*

La búsqueda de empleo The job search

el/la aspirante *applicant*
los avisos clasificados *classified ads*
la carta de presentación / recomendación *letter of introduction / recommendation*
el despacho *office*
la entrevista *interview*
el formulario *form*
la solicitud de empleo *job application*
la vacante *vacancy*

Los beneficios Benefits

el aumento *raise*
la bonificación anual *yearly bonus*
la guardería *nursery, daycare center*
el plan de retiro *retirement plan*
la licencia por enfermedad/maternidad *sickness/maternity leave*
el seguro médico *health insurance*

Verbos Verbs

ascender (ie) *to promote, to move up*
contratar *to hire*
dejar de *to stop doing something*
despedir (i, i) *to fire*
retirarse *to retire*
rellenar *to fill completely, to fill out*

Adjetivos Adjectives

capaz *capable*
entusiasta *enthusiastic*
honrado/a, honesto/a *honest*
justo/a *just*

Una carta comercial A business letter

Saludos *Salutations, greetings*
Estimado/a señor/a: *Dear Sir/Madam:*
Despedidas *Closings*
Atentamente, *Sincerely yours,*
Cordialmente, *Cordially yours,*
Lo(s)/La(s) saluda atentamente, *Very truly yours,*

Adverbial conjunctions *See page 359.*

12
El futuro es tuyo

Readiness Check

Los hispanos en Estados Unidos

«Hay tres cosas que el ser humano necesita en su vida: alguien a quien amar, algo que hacer y una esperanza para el futuro».

Refrán: There are three things that human beings need in their lives: someone to love, something to do, and hope for the future.

Desde 2003, Soledad O'Brien es presentadora y corresponsal especial para CNN donde sus reportajes y documentales le han ganado numerosos premios. Es neoyorquina de ascendencia cubana y australiana.

El cuadro *Paisajes humanos No. 95* de Melesio Casas representa a trabajadores mexicoamericanos en un campo estadounidense con el logotipo del sindicato (el águila) del United Farm Workers en el fondo.

¡Así lo decimos! VOCABULARIO

¡Así es la vida! El impacto de la tecnología

 El Dr. Jorge Díaz, profesor de ingeniería en la Universidad de Chile en Santiago, enseña clases a distancia desde un salón de conferencia a los estudiantes de la Universidad de Valparaíso.

DR. DÍAZ: Bienvenidos a nuestro primer curso virtual. Es cierto que la tecnología ha revolucionado la educación, y como les han dicho todos sus profesores, es importante que hagan la tarea antes de venir a clase.

Dr. Jorge Díaz

Carmen Valdespino

 Carmen Valdespino, estudiante de ingeniería, Universidad de Valparaíso
Les aseguro que la tecnología ha revolucionado mi carrera. En la universidad hago todos mis diseños en computadora. Asisto a reuniones internacionales a distancia por videoconferencia. Escucho conferencias en mi iPod©. Bajo mis libros de texto a mi iPad©. Busco los recursos de la biblioteca en la Internet, y a veces asisto a clase desde mi casa y vestida en pijama. ¡No puedo imaginarme otra manera de hacerlo!

Vocabulario La computadora y otros aparatos electrónicos

12-02 to 12-06

Variaciones
Los auriculares are commonly called **los cascos** in Spain.

Variaciones
Variations on *the Internet* abound in Spanish and include **la red (informática), la red mundial,** and **el/la Internet.**

Los aparatos electrónicos — Electronic devices

la antena parabólica   *satellite dish*
los auriculares   *earbuds, headphones*
el cajero automático   *ATM*
el disco duro (externo)   *(external) hard drive*
el DVD   *DVD*
el escáner   *scanner*
la fotocopiadora   *photocopier*
la grabadora de DVD   *DVD recorder*
la impresora   *printer*
el lector de CD/DVD   *CD/DVD reader*
la marca   *brand*
la memoria USB   *memory stick*
la pantalla   *screen*
el ratón (inalámbrico)   *(wireless) mouse*
el reproductor de mp3   *mp3 player*
el teclado   *keyboard*

Recursos en la computadora — Computer resources

la hoja electrónica   *spreadsheet*
el hipervínculo   *hyperlink*
el juego electrónico   *computer (electronic) game*
la página web   *web page*
el sitio web   *web site*

Verbos — Verbs

apagar   *to turn off*
archivar   *to file, to save*
bajar   *download*
borrar   *to erase*
encender (ie)   *to turn on*
enviar   *to send, to post online*
fallar   *to fail (e.g., computer disk)*
fotocopiar   *to photocopy*
funcionar   *to function, to work*
grabar   *to record*
imprimir[1]   *to print*
instalar   *to install*
programar   *to program*
subir   *to upload*
tener éxito   *to be successful*

Adjetivos — Adjectives

digital   *digital*
electrónico/a   *electronic*
tecnológico/a   *technological*

Instala una antena parabólica en su casa.

Saca dinero del cajero automático.

Escucha música por auriculares en su reproductor mp3.

[1]The past participle is **imprimido. He imprimido el documento.** With the verb **estar** the past participle is **irregular: impreso. El documento está impreso,** but **está imprimido** is also acceptable.

APLICACIÓN

12-1 ¿Para qué se usa? Empareja los aparatos con sus usos.

1. _____ la grabadora de DVD
2. _____ el reproductor de mp3
3. _____ la antena parabólica
4. _____ el hipervínculo
5. _____ el cajero automático
6. _____ la pantalla
7. _____ la impresora
8. _____ la memoria USB

a. para recibir programas internacionales

b. para ver un documento en la computadora

c. para imprimir un documento

d. para escuchar música

e. para transferir documentos de una computadora a otra

f. para grabar un programa de televisión

g. para sacar dinero en efectivo

h. para hacer referencia a otra página web o recurso en la Internet

12-2 Otro avance tecnológico. Lee el artículo y contesta las preguntas a continuación.

Imagínate un mega televisor de alta definición que dé una imagen clara y conserve electricidad también. Esta es la meta de los fabricantes de la próxima generación de televisores. Este televisor "verde" responde a las peticiones tanto de los consumidores como de los legisladores y defensores del medio ambiente[1]. Y para los que bajan sus películas directamente de la Internet, todos los televisores tienen conexión directa por DSL. Pero, ¿es alcanzable el costo de tal aparato al consumidor mediano? ¿O va a tener que esperar algunos años hasta que bajen los precios? Ya veremos[2]...

[1] *environment* [2] *We'll see*

1. ¿De qué tipo de aparato se trata?

2. ¿Qué beneficios tiene?

3. ¿Por qué lo llaman "verde"?

4. ¿Qué tipo de persona busca un aparato como este?

5. ¿Crees que es un avance tecnológico importante? Explica tus razones.

6. ¿Te gustaría tener uno? ¿Por qué?

12-3 En la oficina. La Sra. Molina habla con Rafael, su ayudante, sobre problemas que tiene con su computadora. Completa su conversación con los verbos de la lista.

apagar	borrar	encender	instalar
archivar	falló	imprimir	programar

SRA. MOLINA: ¡Ay! Otro día más. Son las seis de la tarde. Voy a (1) _____ estos documentos en mi memoria USB antes de irme. No quiero (2) _____ ninguno porque todos son muy importantes. Ayer me (3) _____ el disco duro externo y perdí casi todo mi trabajo.

RAFAEL: ¿Necesita copias? Si usted quiere, las puedo (4) _____ en color con la nueva impresora. Si no, tengo que (5) _____ la fotocopiadora, pero no sé si va a funcionar.

SRA. MOLINA: Bueno, en color entonces. ¿Mañana vas a (6) _____ el nuevo software en mi computadora?

RAFAEL: Claro. Pero primero voy a (7) _____ la computadora para que se apague automáticamente. Así ahorramos energía.

SRA. MOLINA: Bueno, eso es para otro día. No te olvides de (8) _____ la computadora antes de irte esta noche.

RAFAEL: De acuerdo. ¡Buenas noches!

12-4 Compre.com. Se puede encontrar cualquier aparato electrónico en *Compre.com*. Escucha la descripción de uno de ellos y completa las siguientes oraciones.

1. El anuncio es para un sistema de…
   a. audio.
   b. computadora portátil.
   c. videocámara digital.

2. No incluye…
   a. lector de CD.
   b. receptor.
   c. televisor.

3. A la persona que compre este sistema, le gusta(n)…
   a. la fotografía.
   b. los juegos electrónicos.
   c. la música.

4. Puedes comprar este sistema en…
   a. seis meses.
   b. un año.
   c. un año y medio.

5. Se compra este sistema…
   a. directamente de la fábrica.
   b. en la Internet.
   c. en tiendas especializadas.

12-5 **Texting en español.** Aquí tienes un mensaje que le envió una estudiante a su amigo. ¿Lo puedes leer? Conéctate a la Internet para ayudarte a descifrarlo y a escribir uno tuyo.

> **Busca:** spanish about sms

> q pasa no te vi en kls
>
> vs fsta julia
>
> pf m1ml
>
> bss amr

12-6A **Un producto innovador.** Cada uno de ustedes tiene anuncios para dos aparatos nuevos, pero les falta alguna información. Háganse preguntas para completar la información y luego, decidan cuál desean comprar según sus características y su costo. **Estudiante B,** por favor ve al **Apéndice 1,** página A-20.

Posibles preguntas:

¿Cuántos/as...?   ¿Hay...?

¿Qué tipo de...?   ¿Cómo es/son...?

MODELO: ESTUDIANTE A: *El aparato "Mora" puede contener 7.000 canciones. ¿Cuántos gigabytes de memoria tiene?*

ESTUDIANTE B: ...

Estudiante A:

	Aparato "Mora"	Aparato "Fresa"
Memoria		160 gigabytes
Características	7.000 canciones	
		200 horas de video
	Auriculares con micrófono	
Velocidad		El más rápido de todos los modelos
Fecha de envío (*shipping*)	en 48 horas	
Costo de envío		gratuito
Regalo extra	Antes del 31 de diciembre bajar gratis 40 canciones	
Costo		200 €

¡Así lo hacemos! ESTRUCTURAS

1. The past participle

12-07 to 12-10

The past participle can be used as an adjective both in Spanish and in English.

Tenemos un programa antivirus **instalado** en la computadora.	*We have an antivirus program installed on the computer.*
Los documentos están **archivados** en la memoria USB.	*The documents are saved on the memory stick.*

- In English, the past participle is usually the *-ed* or *-en* form of the verb. In Spanish the regular participle is formed by adding **-ado** to the stems of **-ar** verbs and **-ido** to the stems of **-er** and **-ir** verbs.

grabar	grab**ado**	*recorded*
encender	encend**ido**	*turned on*
servir	serv**ido**	*served*

- An accent mark is used when a past participle has the combination of vowels **ai, ei,** or **oi.**

creer	**creído**	*believed*	oír	**oído**	*heard*
leer	**leído**	*read*	traer	**traído**	*brought*

- The following verbs have irregular past participles.

abrir	**abierto**	*opened*	ir	**ido**	*gone*
cubrir	**cubierto**	*covered*	morir	**muerto**	*dead*
decir	**dicho**	*said*	poner	**puesto**	*put, placed*
descubrir	**descubierto**	*discovered*	romper	**roto**	*broken*
escribir	**escrito**	*written*	ver	**visto**	*seen*
hacer	**hecho**	*done, made*	volver	**vuelto**	*returned*

El documento está **abierto.**	*The document is open.*
La pantalla de mi computadora está **rota.**	*My computer monitor is broken.*

- When the past participle is used as an adjective in Spanish, it agrees in gender and number with the noun it modifies.

Vimos las conferencias **grabadas** por nuestro supervisor.	*We saw the lectures recorded by our supervisor.*
¿Tienes programas **abiertos** en este momento?	*Do you have programs open now?*

- The verb **estar** may be used with the past participle to describe a state or condition that is the result of a previous action. As with any adjective, the past participle used this way agrees in gender and number with the noun it modifies.

La fotocopiadora **está encendida**; la secretaria la encendió.	*The photocopier is turned on; the secretary turned it on.*
Los documentos confidenciales **están borrados;** los borraron mis ayudantes.	*The confidential documents are erased; my assistants erased them.*

Los programas están instalados y los archivos copiados al disco duro externo.

APLICACIÓN

12-7 La Calle Ocho. La Calle Ocho está en el centro de la Pequeña Habana en Miami. Completa la conversación entre dos turistas cubanas que están visitando este barrio de Miami. Usa la forma correcta del participio pasado de los verbos en la lista.

abrir	dormir	perder	poner	vestir
morir	hacer	pintar	preparar	

La Calle Ocho en la Pequeña Habana, Miami

FLOR: Vamos, Rosa. Busca las llaves del carro y vamos a pasear por la Calle Ocho.

ROSA: ¿Y dónde están las llaves? ¡No me digas que están (1) _____ otra vez!

FLOR: No te preocupes. Creo que las tienes en tu bolso.

ROSA: Tienes razón. ¡Qué día más bonito! Deja la ventana (2) _____ en el carro. Me gusta el aire fresco.

FLOR: Cómo no, te la abro enseguida.

ROSA: ¿Qué te parece ese mural (3) _____ en la pared?

FLOR: Es lindo, pero no muy original. Prefiero los murales de Los Ángeles.

ROSA: Tu nieta Laura estaba muy bien (4) _____ ayer en la fiesta. Y su familia es preciosa.

FLOR: ¡Ay, gracias! Es verdad. Y el bebé de Laura es un encanto. No hay nada más tranquilo que un bebé (5) _____.

ROSA: Mira la guayabera[1] blanca que lleva ese señor. Esas camisas son típicas del trópico, pero las guayaberas (6) _____ en Panamá son más baratas.

FLOR: Es verdad, pero prefiero las de *La casa de las guayaberas* aquí en la Calle Ocho, porque son más elegantes.

ROSA: Mira, allí hay un restaurante cubano. ¿Entramos? Es la una y estoy (7) _____ de hambre.

FLOR: ¡Bueno! Las mesas ya están (8) _____ y la comida está (9) _____. Voy a aparcar aquí mismo.

_____
[1] Men's shirt typical of the Caribbean, usually long-sleeved and with four pockets in front.

12-8 La avenida Bergenline, Union City, NJ. Esta avenida comercial, la más larga del estado de Nueva Jersey, tiene más de 300 tiendas y restaurantes, y muchos de ellos son hispanos. ¿Cómo te sentías después de pasar varios días en esta zona? Usa participios pasados para expresar cómo te sentías.

(bien/mal) atender (*attended to*)	encantar	preparar
cansar	enojar	sorprender
decidir (ir a...)	interesar	(bien/mal) vestir
desilusionar	preocupar	¿...?

MODELO: ¿Cómo te sentías cuando llegaste a Union City?
Me sentía emocionado/a.

¿Cómo te sentías...

1. en el club bailando salsa?
2. cuando perdiste tu tarjeta de crédito?
3. después de ver un concierto de Marques Houston?
4. en la fiesta de unos amigos cubanos?
5. cuando perdiste (*missed*) el tren a Manhattan?
6. cuando cenaste en un restaurante argentino?

12-9 **¿Quién…?** Pregúntense si tienen algunos de estos artículos. Incluyan en sus respuestas descripciones de cómo son.

> **MODELO:** artículo / hacer en Nuevo México
> E1: *¿Tienes algún artículo hecho en Nuevo México?*
> E2: *Sí, tengo un collar de plata hecho en Nuevo México.*

Un collar hecho en Nuevo México

1. producto / importar de China
2. correo electrónico / enviar por una persona famosa
3. programa para editar música / instalar en tu computadora
4. fotografías / subir en Facebook
5. mensaje divertido / grabar en tu teléfono móvil
6. página web / escribir por ti
7. aparato electrónico / romper en casa en este momento
8. video cómico / bajar de la Internet

12-10 **¡Juego!** Formen dos equipos para desafiarse (*challenge each other*) a hacer frases usando participios como adjetivos. Luego díganse si la respuesta es lógica o no.

> **MODELO:** EQUIPO 1: la computadora
> EQUIPO 2: *La computadora está rota.*
> EQUIPO 1: *Es lógico.*

Posibles sustantivos	**Posibles participios**
los auriculares	instalar
la impresora	grabar
la memoria USB	cubrir
el escáner	abrir
el ratón	subir
el reproductor de mp3	preparar
los programas	bajar
la música	borrar
los videos	encender
las fotos	perder
el disco duro	apagar
el teléfono celular	archivar
los documentos	pedir
el televisor	hacer

2. The present perfect indicative

¿Has visto mi computadora nueva?

Sí, la he puesto en tu oficina.

The present perfect in English and Spanish is a compound tense because it requires two verbs. English uses the present tense of the auxiliary verb *to have* + past participle. Spanish uses the present tense of the auxiliary verb **haber** + past participle.

	haber	past participle	to have	past participle
yo	he		*I have*	
tú	has		*you have*	
Ud.	ha		*you* (for.) *have*	
él/ella	ha	**tomado**	*he/she has*	*taken*
		comido		*eaten*
		vivido		*lived*
nosotros/as	hemos		*we have*	
vosotros/as	habéis		*you* (pl.) *have*	
Uds.	han		*you* (for. pl.) *have*	
ellos/as	han		*they have*	

EXPANSIÓN
More on structure and usage

Some common expressions used with the present perfect include **alguna vez** (*ever, once*), **ya** (*already*), and **todavía no** (*not yet*).

¿Alguna vez has querido ser astronauta?
Have you ever wanted to be an astronaut?

¿Ya has escuchado toda la música en tu mp3?
Have you already listened to all the music on your mp3?

No, todavía no la he escuchado toda.
No, I haven't listened to all of it yet.

- In general, the present perfect is used to refer to a past action or event that is perceived as having some bearing on the present.

  ¿Ya **has usado** la impresora? — *Have you already used the printer?*

  No **he comprado** todavía un disco duro externo para archivar mis documentos importantes. — *I haven't bought an external hard drive to save my important documents yet.*

- The auxiliary verb **haber** agrees with the subject of the sentence. The past participle, however, is invariable when used in the perfect tense.

  Mi jefe me **ha dado** un ratón inalámbrico. — *My boss has given me a wireless mouse.*

  Los asistentes **han preparado** la hoja electrónica. — *The assistants have prepared the spreadsheet.*

- The auxiliary verb **haber** and the past participle cannot be separated by another word. Object pronouns and negative words are always placed before **haber.**

  No la he preparado. — *I haven't prepared it.*

  ¿La has grabado? — *Have you recorded it?*

- The verb **haber** is not interchangeable with **tener. Haber** means *to have* only when used as an auxiliary verb with the past participle. **Tener** means *to have* or *to own* in the sense of possession.

  Julia **tiene** muchos amigos en esa empresa. — *Julia has many friends in that company.*

  ¿Has tenido experiencia en hacer diseños? — *Have you had experience in doing designs?*

Acabar de + *infinitive*

You can use the present tense of **acabar**[1] **de** + infinitive in order to describe an event that has just happened.

Acabamos de ver la videoconferencia. — *We have just seen the videoconference.*

Acaban de borrar el archivo. — *They have just erased the file.*

———
[1]**Acabar** means to *finish*.

APLICACIÓN

12-11 Sandra Cisneros.   Esta escritora chicana (*House on Mango Street, Caramelo*) es una de las más importantes de su generación.

Paso 1   Lee el párrafo sobre Sandra Cisneros, subraya cada verbo en el presente perfecto e identifica su infinitivo.

MODELO: <u>Ha tenido</u> mucho éxito.
   Ha tenido: tener.

Sandra Cisneros, de padres mexicanos, nació en 1954 en Chicago, pero ahora vive en San Antonio donde dice que se siente "en casa". En su juventud, tuvo muchas experiencias que han influido en sus cuentos. Por ejemplo, ha tenido que cambiar muchas veces de casa. Ha vivido en apartamentos y casas pequeñas con pocas comodidades modernas. Ha ayudado a su mamá con sus hermanos más pequeños. Ha asistido a escuelas donde todos los muchachos eran de familias pobres y donde había pocos recursos educativos. Sin embargo, ha superado las dificultades de su juventud y ha ganado mucha fama por sus colecciones de cuentos cortos como *La casa en Mango Street* y *El Arroyo de La Llorona,* y por sus colecciones de poesía. Si has leído uno de sus cuentos, has visto su manera única de narrar. Además de recibir varios premios del *National Endowment for the Arts,* en 1996, fue honrada por *La Fundación MacArthur* con su *Genius Award*. En los últimos años, Sandra Cisneros ha recibido algunas críticas por su casa de San Antonio. Parece que a los vecinos no les gusta la manera en que Sandra la ha pintado.

La casa de Sandra Cisneros en San Antonio

Paso 2   Contesta ahora las preguntas sobre el texto que acabas de leer.

1. ¿Cuántos años tiene Sandra Cisneros y cuál es su nacionalidad?

2. ¿Dónde ha vivido?

3. ¿Qué dificultades ha tenido en la escuela?

4. ¿Cómo ha ganado fama?

5. ¿Por qué ha sido tan polémica (*controversial*) su casa de San Antonio?

6. ¿Has leído alguna obra suya? ¿Cuál? ¿Te ha gustado?

Paso 3   Escriban individualmente tres preguntas que les gustaría hacerle a Sandra Cisneros. Túrnense para hacer el papel de Cisneros y contestar las preguntas de su compañero/a. Usen el presente perfecto.

MODELO: E1: *Sra. Cisneros, ¿ha vivido en otras casas en San Antonio?*
   E2: *No. Esta es mi primera casa en San Antonio.*

12-12 José Hernández, astronauta chicano.
Completa la entrevista de un periodista con José Hernández. Usa el presente perfecto del verbo entre paréntesis en tu pregunta y añade más información lógica en tus preguntas.

MODELO: (viajar) *¿Ha viajado usted a la luna?*
No, no he estado todavía en la luna, pero algún día…

PERIODISTA: ¿…? (vivir)

HERNÁNDEZ: En varios lugares, pero he pasado más tiempo en Stockton, California.

PERIODISTA: ¿…? (estudiar)

HERNÁNDEZ: He estudiado mucha ingeniería eléctrica y computación.

PERIODISTA: ¿…? (tener)

HERNÁNDEZ: Hasta ahora he tenido la oportunidad de viajar en la nave Discovery.

PERIODISTA: ¿…? (impresionar)

HERNÁNDEZ: ¡Lo que más me ha impresionado es la vista de la tierra!

PERIODISTA: ¿…? (hablar)

HERNÁNDEZ: Sí, he pasado mucho tiempo en las escuelas hablando con los jóvenes sobre la importancia de completar su educación.

PERIODISTA: Gracias, señor… (ser) un placer.

HERNÁNDEZ: De nada. Y para mí también.

 12-13 ¿Alguna vez han…? Hazles preguntas a tus compañeros/as para saber qué experiencias han tenido con la tecnología. Pregúntales qué les ha pasado.

MODELO: perder un documento en la computadora
E1: *¿Alguna vez han perdido un documento en la computadora?*
E2: *No, todavía no he perdido ningún documento.*
E3: *¡Yo sí, he perdido muchos!*

- borrar un documento sin querer
- programar una computadora
- comprar algo por más de $500 en la Internet
- usar una hoja electrónica para organizar información
- calcular los impuestos (*taxes*) usando un programa en la computadora
- poner tu perfil en un sitio social como Facebook
- crear invitaciones o tarjetas usando la computadora
- poner un video en YouTube
- contribuir a un foro en línea
- participar en una videoconferencia
- tener problemas para comprar algo en la Internet
- ¿…?

12-14 Mis experiencias. Túrnense para hablar de experiencias que han tenido y también de experiencias que no han tenido, pero que desean tener.

comer...	escribir...	hacer...	leer...	trabajar...	visitar...
conocer...	estudiar...	ir...	salir...	ver...	volver...

MODELO: ver ...

E1: *¿Qué películas has visto este año?*
E2: *Acabo de ver la película de Almodóvar, Los abrazos rotos, en DVD.*
E1: *¿Has visto alguna de sus otras películas?*
E2: *Sí, ya he visto... / No, todavía no, pero...*

¿Has leído algún cuento de Sandra Cisneros?

¿Cuánto saben?

Primero, pregúntate si puedes llevar a cabo las siguientes funciones comunicativas en español. Después, júntate con dos o tres compañeros/as de clase para presentar las situaciones. Hagan y respondan a por lo menos cuatro preguntas en cada situación.

✓ CAN YOU ...

☐ discuss technology?

☐ describe people and things?

☐ talk about what has happened?

WITH YOUR CLASSMATE(S) ...

Situación: En casa
A ustedes les gusta tener los aparatos más novedosos. Hablen de los que han visto y los que quieren comprar.
Para empezar: *Hoy he visto en un sitio web...*

Situación: En una fiesta
Túrnense para describir a las personas y cosas que observen, usando participios pasados como adjetivos. Hablen también de cómo creen que se sienten las personas.
Para empezar. *Mira, la comida está servida... Los libros están... y los estudiantes están...*

Situación: En una cena entre amigos
A ustedes les gusta contar historias sobre sus experiencias. Hablen de las más interesantes que han tenido. Reaccionen con preguntas y comentarios a lo que les dice su compañero/a.
Para empezar: *He viajado varias veces a...*

📖 Perfiles

Mi experiencia

LA TECNOLOGÍA Y EL FUTURO

12-15 Para ti. ¿Has hecho una consulta alguna vez en algún foro? ¿Qué tipo de consulta has hecho? ¿Crees que se puede beneficiar de las respuestas en línea? Explica.

FORO: JUEGOS

Jugador Argentina	**¿Dónde estudiar gaming?**
	Bueno, gente, les digo que tengo 22 años y voy terminando una carrera corta en sistemas, realmente no quiero continuar con la rama[1], y mi sueño es meterme[2] en el mundo de los videojuegos como game developer. Estuve viendo las "carreras" en algunos sitios de educación a distancia y además de ser caras, realmente no me parecen nada serias. También estuve viendo la carrera de cine de animación y multimedia, que parece copada[3] y "en teoría" puede ayudar a meterte en el mundo del gaming, pero tampoco estoy seguro de cómo son los programas aquí en Argentina para este tipo de cosas. Si me pueden tirar[4] nombres u opiniones me hacen un gran favor.
Baco EE. UU.	**Re: ¿Dónde estudiar gaming?**
	¡Ja! mira, por lo que sé, hay cientos de carreras relacionadas con videojuegos en EE. UU., Japón, Nueva Zelanda y otros. Supongo que buscas una carrera en cine de animación y multimedia, y por ahora me estoy en esa[5]. Recuerda que para dedicarte a la parte artística no necesitas ser programador. En esa carrera lo más importante es tener título universitario… no es un curso. Estudias mil cosas además de animación que te preparan muy bien como literatura, guión[6], inglés, música, etc. Por ejemplo, aquí en Los Ángeles (el corazón del cine) hay un programa de diseño de videojuegos que es muy destacado[7], pero solo admiten 50 estudiantes al año. ¡'Ta bueno! Oye, ¿escuchas la música de Albita? Estoy preparando un proyecto de multimedia de su música. ¿Qué tal se recibe allá en Argentina?

[1]*branch*   [2]*to get involved in* or *to get into*   [3]*cool (Argentina)*   [4]*throw my way*   [5]*that's what I'm involved in*
[6]*script-writing*   [7]*outstanding*

12-16 En su opinión. ¿Creen que la respuesta de Baco fue acertada (*correct*)? ¿Cuáles son otras carreras que dependen de la tecnología? ¿Qué tipo de preparación requieren: carrera universitaria, cursos en una escuela técnica, experiencia dentro del campo, mucha imaginación, etc.? ¿Por cuántos años es necesario estudiar para recibir un título en esas carreras? ¿Hay algunas carreras más sexy que las demás?

MODELO: *La carrera de informática depende mucho de la tecnología. Es necesario estudiar…*

Mi música

"'TA BUENO YA" ALBITA (CUBANOAMERICANA)

La cubanoamericana Albita es una de las cantantes más versátiles de esta época. Ha cantado en cuatro inauguraciones presidenciales y ha sido Reina del Carnaval Calle Ocho en Miami. Su programa "La descarga con Albita" en MEGA TV ha ganado varios Emmy. Ella también ha recibido varios Grammy por su música.

Antes de ver y escuchar

 12-17 Lo que está pasando. En esta canción, Albita canta sobre lo que está pasando en las calles durante el Carnaval. Escribe cinco oraciones para describir cómo te imaginas la escena.

MODELO: *La gente ha llegado y está...*

Para ver y escuchar

 12-18 La canción. Ahora conéctate a la Internet para ver un video de "'Ta bueno ya" para verificar lo que está pasando. ¿Cómo caracterizas el tono de la canción? ¿Es triste, alegre, sentimental?

> **Busca:** albita ta bueno ya video; albita ta bueno ya letra
>
> **Si te interesa comprar la canción:** *Go to iTunes Store>Music>More to Explore>iMix>Arriba 6e*

Después de ver y escuchar

 12-19 El mensaje. En parejas, hablen de cuál es el mensaje (o los mensajes) de "'Ta bueno ya". Compartan sus opiniones y escriban una lista de posibles mensajes para esta canción.

12-20 ¡Carnaval! La palabra "carnaval" se deriva de "carne". Se refiere a la celebración de la semana antes del comienzo de la cuaresma (*Lent*), los 40 días cuando históricamente los creyentes cristianos no comían carne. ¿Has asistido alguna vez a un carnaval? ¿Has observado las costumbres de la cuaresma o conoces a alguien que las observe? Escribe un párrafo sobre cómo ha sido en tu experiencia.

MODELO: *Tengo un amigo que observa las costumbres de la cuaresma. Durante los 40 días, no...*

¡Así lo decimos! VOCABULARIO

📖 ¡Así es la vida! El medio ambiente: hablan los jóvenes

12-23

🔊 Entre los jóvenes hispanos de hoy hay una preocupación por la protección del medio ambiente. Ellos saben que, aunque sus países de origen tienen grandes riquezas naturales, el desarrollo industrial y la falta de preocupación de los gobiernos por proteger estos valiosos recursos naturales, hacen que el medio ambiente se deteriore.

🔊 Hablan los jóvenes...

SALVADOR: La energía nuclear destruirá el medio ambiente.

CRISTINA: ¡Estás equivocado! La energía nuclear es nuestro futuro.

PACO: Tendremos que desarrollar fuentes renovables de energía.

GONZALO: ¡Estás loco! La planta nuclear nos asegurará muchos años de energía económica.

Vocabulario El medio ambiente

12-24
to 12-29

Variaciones
The terms **la deforestación** and **la reforestación** are common in Latin America. In Spain, these same terms are **la despoblación** and **la repoblación forestal,** respectively.

Nuestro mundo y el medio ambiente	Our world and the environment

el bosque pluvial   *rain forest*
el calentamiento global   *global warming*
la deforestación   *deforestation*
el desarrollo   *development*
los desechos   *waste*
la energía (alternativa / solar)   *(alternative/solar) energy*
el envase (de aluminio)   *(aluminum) container*
las especies en peligro de extinción   *endangered species*
la escasez   *shortage*
la fábrica   *factory*
el humo   *smoke*
el medio ambiente   *environment*
la naturaleza   *nature*
los pesticidas   *pesticides*
la planta nuclear   *nuclear plant*
el pozo de petróleo   *oil well*
la radioactividad   *radioactivity*
el recurso natural   *natural resource*
el reciclaje   *recycling*
la reforestación   *reforestation*
la selva   *jungle*

Verbos	Verbs

ahorrar   *to save*
conservar   *to conserve, to preserve*
consumir   *to consume*
contaminar   *to contaminate, to pollute*
multar   *to fine*
proteger (j)   *to protect*
reciclar   *to recycle*
tirar   *to throw (away, out)*

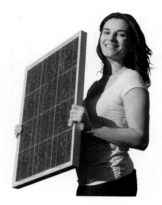

La energía alternativa es nuestro futuro.

El uso excesivo de pesticidas contamina el medio ambiente.

Es importante reciclar para proteger el medio ambiente.

Letras y sonidos

The Consonants t and d

In Spanish, the letter **t** sounds like the *t* in English *stop*.

Hard **t**: **te-lé-fo-no** **tra-í-do** **vuel-<u>t</u>o** **au-<u>t</u>o-má-<u>t</u>i-co**

The letter **d** in Spanish creates one of two sounds, depending on the context. After a pause or the letters **n** or **l,** the letter **d** sounds like the *d* in English *den*.

Hard **d**: **dis-co** **un-<u>d</u>i-se-ño** **<u>d</u>on-<u>d</u>e** **el-<u>d</u>i-se-ño** **suel-<u>d</u>o**

In all other contexts, especially between vowels, the sound is softer, like the *th* in English *then* or *father*.

Soft **d**: **los-<u>d</u>i-se-ños** **me-<u>d</u>i-da** **le-í-<u>d</u>o** **ver-<u>d</u>ad** **la re<u>d</u>**

In sum, Spanish has the same three sounds found at the beginning of the English words *ten* (but with less air expelled), *den* (hard **d**), and *then* (soft **d**). However, in Spanish, all three of these sounds are created with the tongue tip behind the upper front teeth only.

APLICACIÓN

12-21 ¿Qué solución hay? Empareja cada problema con la solución a la derecha.

1. _____ la contaminación del aire
2. _____ la deforestación
3. _____ tirar basura en el parque
4. _____ los desechos industriales
5. _____ la escasez de energía
6. _____ la escasez de agua
7. _____ tirar envases de plástico a la calle

a. poner más basureros en el parque
b. ahorrar agua
c. conservar electricidad
d. multar a las fábricas
e. establecer programas de reciclaje
f. plantar más árboles
g. usar un programa de inspección de las emisiones de automóviles

12-22 En las noticias. Completa cada titular con el verbo correspondiente.

consume	contamina	conservar	multa	protege

1. **Accidente en plataforma petrolífera _____ el Golfo de México**

2. **NIÑOS COSTARRICENSES APRENDEN A _____ ENERGÍA**

3. **El gobierno de la India _____ a la Dow Chemical por un accidente de pesticidas**

4. **La EPA regula y _____ el medio ambiente**

5. **EE. UU. _____ más energía por persona que cualquier otro país del mundo**

🔊 **12-23 Un anuncio público.** Escucha el anuncio de la radio y completa las afirmaciones que siguen.

1. El anuncio habla de un programa...
   a. del gobierno.
   b. de una organización no gubernamental.
   c. de la ONU.

2. Los participantes son...
   a. niños y jóvenes.
   b. ancianos.
   c. amas de casa.

3. Van a trabajar en la limpieza y...
   a. el control de los pesticidas.
   b. el reciclaje.
   c. la reforestación.

4. El trabajo será durante...
   a. las vacaciones.
   b. el año escolar.
   c. la Semana Santa.

👥 **12-24 Un plan de acción.** ¿Qué problemas y soluciones ven para el futuro?

Paso 1 Trabajen juntos para elegir cinco de los problemas más importantes para el futuro del mundo. Si hay uno que no está en la lista, añádanlo.

_____ la escasez de agua

_____ el sobreconsumo de los recursos naturales

_____ el sobreuso de pesticidas

_____ la contaminación del aire

_____ la contaminación nuclear

_____ la sobrepoblación

_____ las especies en peligro de extinción

_____ la deforestación

_____ el calentamiento global

_____ ¿...?

MODELO: E1: *En tu opinión, ¿cuáles son los problemas más importantes para el futuro del mundo?*
E2: *Creo que son...*

Paso 2 Propongan soluciones a los problemas que identificaron en **Paso 1.** A continuación hay algunas sugerencias.

aumentar el precio de la energía	limitar el número de autos por familia
combatir la sobrepoblación	limitar el consumo de energía por persona
desarrollar (*develop*) nuevos recursos de energía	mejorar la economía de la región
implementar un sistema de transporte público	montar una campaña publicitaria
	multar a...
	proponer leyes más fuertes

MODELO: *Para combatir la deforestación, los gobiernos del mundo deben...*

¡Hola!

Cultura en vivo ✳

Spain is the world's fourth largest producer of wind power and, with its ample sunshine, one of the most advanced countries in the development of solar energy. The Spanish government has committed to achieve a target of 23% of primary energy from renewable sources by 2020, the highest in the European Union. What are the goals in the U.S. and Canada?

3. The future tense

Las nuevas microcomputadoras serán aún más pequeñas.

The Spanish future tense is formed with only one set of endings for the **-ar, -er,** and **-ir** verbs. For regular verbs, the endings are attached to the infinitive (do not drop the **-ar, -er,** or **-ir**). Note that all endings, except for the **nosotros/as** forms, have written accent marks.

	tomar	comer	vivir
yo	tomar**é**	comer**é**	vivir**é**
tú	tomar**ás**	comer**ás**	vivir**ás**
Ud.	tomar**á**	comer**á**	vivir**á**
él/ella	tomar**á**	comer**á**	vivir**á**
nosotros/as	tomar**emos**	comer**emos**	vivir**emos**
vosotros/as	tomar**éis**	comer**éis**	vivir**éis**
Uds.	tomar**án**	comer**án**	vivir**án**
ellos/as	tomar**án**	comer**án**	vivir**án**

- As in English, the Spanish future tense expresses what will happen in the future. The English equivalent is *will* + verb.

  ¿Quién **protegerá** el medio ambiente? *Who will protect the environment?*
  Creo que los pesticidas **contaminarán** el río. *I think the pesticides will pollute the river.*

- The irregular verbs in the future are formed by adding the future endings to an irregular stem. The irregular stems can be grouped into three categories.

  1. Drop two letters to form the stem of the future.

     decir **dir-** diré, dirás,...   hacer **har-** haré, harás,...

  2. The **e** of the infinitive ending is dropped to form the stem of the future.

     haber **habr-** habrá   querer **querr-** querré, querrás,...
     poder **podr-** podré, podrás,... saber **sabr-** sabré, sabrás,...

  3. The **e** or the **i** of the infinitive ending is replaced by **d** to form the stem of the future.

     poner **pondr-** pondré, pondrás... tener **tendr-** tendré, tendrás...
     salir **saldr-** saldré, saldrás... venir **vendr-** vendré, vendrás...

     Haremos todos los cálculos en la hoja electrónica. *We will do all the calculations on a spreadsheet.*
     Habrá menos humo con la nueva fábrica. *There will be less smoke with the new factory.*
     Los técnicos **vendrán** a las ocho. *The technicians will come at eight.*

- Remember that the present tense is often used to express the immediate future in Spanish.

     Mañana **reclicamos** los envases. *Tomorrow we will recycle (are recycling) the cans.*
     Termino mi trabajo esta tarde. *I will finish my paper/work this afternoon.*

- The future may also be conveyed with the present tense of **ir a** + *infinitive.*

     Voy a consumir menos energía. *I am going to consume less energy.*
     ¿**Vas a tirar** los envases en el basurero? *Are you going to throw the containers in the trash can?*

- The idea of willingness, sometimes expressed with the English future, cannot be expressed with the Spanish future tense. Use verbs like **querer** or simple present tense to express willingness.

¿**Quieres** ayudarme con el reciclaje?	*Will you help me with the recycling?*
¿Me **traes** el informe sobre la planta nuclear?	*Will you bring me the report on the nuclear plant?*

- Probability or conjecture in the present may be expressed in Spanish with the future tense. This use of the future has many equivalents in English, for example, *probably, can, may, must, I wonder,* etc.

¿Dónde **estará** la memoria USB?	*I wonder where the memory stick might be?*
Estará en tu mochila.	*It's probably in your backpack.*
¿Qué hora **será**?	*What time can it be?*
Serán las seis.	*It must be six o'clock.*

La computadora estará pensando.

APLICACIÓN

12-25 Ralph Álvarez. El cubanoamericano Ralph Álvarez es presidente y jefe de operaciones (COO) de McDonald's Corporation. Para el año que viene, dice que iniciará aún más estrategias para mantener su liderazgo (*leadership*) en la industria de comida rápida.

Paso 1 Lee la entrevista con el portavoz (*spokesperson*) del Sr. Álvarez, subraya los verbos en el futuro y da el infinitivo. Luego expresa la misma acción, usando la expresión **ir a...**

MODELO: <u>sabrá</u>
saber; va a saber

PERIODISTA: ¿Cuándo se anunciarán las nuevas iniciativas del Sr. Álvarez para el próximo año?

PORTAVOZ: El Sr. Álvarez ya ha anunciado varias iniciativas. Primero, eliminará de la flota[1] los carros que usan mucha gasolina y comprará carros eléctricos o híbridos. Segundo, negociará precios más razonables de publicidad. Y tercero, promocionará los nuevos productos, como los cafés especiales que han tenido tanto éxito.

PERIODISTA: De acuerdo, pero ¿habrá discusiones internas para llegar a decisiones entre él y los directores de la empresa?

PORTAVOZ: Claro, el Sr. Álvarez siempre ha sido colaborador y continuará así. Creemos que las ventas del año que viene resultarán aún más positivas.

PERIODISTA: Y si bajan las ventas, ¿qué hará?

PORTAVOZ: Siempre se podrá mejorar algo. El Sr. Álvarez no dejará de buscar otras iniciativas para el futuro.

———
[1]*fleet*

Paso 2 Ahora resume lo que hará el Sr. Álvarez para mantener el liderazgo de su empresa. ¿Crees que tendrá éxito?

Presencia hispana

Ralph (Raúl) Álvarez, was born in Havana, Cuba, but left with his family after Fidel Castro gained power. He studied to be a teacher, but later earned a degree in accounting. He tried for many years to get hired by McDonald's, but once he was hired, it took him only twelve years to ascend to the number two spot in the company.

12-26 Una entrevista con la empresa Ecoverde. Isela tiene una entrevista con una empresa que se dedica a conservar el medio ambiente. Completa de una manera lógica la conversación entre ella y el director de personal, usando el futuro de los verbos a continuación.

decir	hacer	llamar	ser	trabajar
haber	informar	poder	tener	

ISELA: Si no le importa, tengo algunas preguntas sobre el puesto. ¿Me puede decir cuántas horas (1. yo) _____?

DIRECTOR: Sí, los nuevos investigadores trabajan ocho horas diarias.

ISELA: ¿(2. yo) _____ trabajar con alguno de los investigadores veteranos?

DIRECTOR: Sí, usted puede trabajar con varias personas con experiencia.

ISELA: ¿(3) _____ otras oportunidades para trabajar sola en proyectos?

DIRECTOR: Bueno, sí hay oportunidades pero los nuevos también (4) _____ que ayudar a los veteranos.

ISELA: ¿Cuándo (5) _____ usted su decisión?

DIRECTOR: La (6. yo) _____ por teléfono mañana por la mañana.

ISELA: ¿Usted me (7) _____ entonces cuánto me van a pagar?

DIRECTOR: Sí, (8. yo) le _____ sobre su sueldo cuando hagamos nuestra decisión.

ISELA: Gracias por responder a todas mis preguntas. (9) _____ una gran oportunidad para mí trabajar con ustedes en esta empresa.

12-27 ¿Por qué será? Usa las ideas de la columna a la derecha en el futuro para hacer una conjetura (*guess*) sobre cada situación a la izquierda.

MODELO: Recibes una llamada por teléfono a las siete de la mañana.
Será algo urgente.

1. Hay un paquete en tu escritorio.
2. La grabadora de DVD ha desaparecido.
3. No podemos ver la película.
4. La secretaria no ha hecho las fotocopias.
5. Un colega acaba de salir del edificio.
6. Ha fallado el disco duro de tu computadora.

- (haber) problemas con la antena parabólica
- (ser) una computadora portátil nueva
- la fotocopiadora (estar) rota
- alguien (estar) grabando un programa
- (tener) un virus
- (ir) al cajero automático a sacar dinero

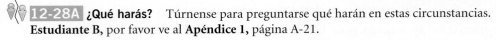 **12-28A ¿Qué harás?** Túrnense para preguntarse qué harán en estas circunstancias. **Estudiante B,** por favor ve al **Apéndice 1,** página A-21.

MODELO: ESTUDIANTE A: *Acabas de comprar un DVD nuevo.*
ESTUDIANTE B: (**ponerlo** en tu lector de DVD para verlo) *Lo pondré en mi lector de DVD para verlo.*

Estudiante A:

Las circunstancias de mi compañero/a	Lo que haré yo
1. Tu computadora funciona lentamente.	• **llamar** a la oficina que ofrece el puesto
2. Quieres un celular nuevo.	• **ir** a la Internet y **buscar** más información para comprarlo
3. Has terminado tus estudios en la universidad.	• no **descansar** hasta que la termine
4. Has conocido a tu pareja ideal.	• **llamar** a todos mis amigos para ver si quieren participar

4. The conditional tense

12-38
to 12-42

In Spanish, as in English, the conditional expresses an action that is conditional upon another action, or a future action in the past (*would/could/should* + action).

- In Spanish, the conditional is formed in a similar manner as the future; only the endings differ. Add the **-er/-ir** imperfect endings to the infinitive of regular verbs or the irregular stem.

	tomar	comer	vivir
yo	tomaría	comería	viviría
tú	tomarías	comerías	vivirías
Ud.	tomaría	comería	viviría
él/ella	tomaría	comería	viviría
nosotros/as	tomaríamos	comeríamos	viviríamos
vosotros/as	tomaríais	comeríais	viviríais
Uds.	tomarían	comerían	vivirían
ellos/as	tomarían	comerían	vivirían

- The conditional expresses what you would do under certain circumstances.

  ¿Qué **harías** para mejorar el medio ambiente?

  What would you do to improve the environment?

  Reciclaría envases de aluminio.

  I would recycle aluminum cans.

- The conditional is also used when the speaker is referring to an event that is future to another past event.

  Creíamos que **habría** más gente protestando enfrente de la planta nuclear.

  We thought (that) there would be more people protesting in front of the nuclear plant.

  Nos dijeron que no **contaminarían** el agua.

  They told us (that) they wouldn't pollute the water.

- The verb **deber,** when used in the conditional tense, is equivalent to the English *should* + infinitive.

  Deberías conservar recursos.

  You should conserve resources.

- The conditional has the same irregular stems as the future.

decir	**dir-**	diría, dirías,...	saber	**sabr-**	sabría, sabrías,...
hacer	**har-**	haría, harías,...	poner	**pondr-**	pondría, pondrías,...
haber	**habr-**	habría	salir	**saldr-**	saldría, saldrías,...
poder	**podr-**	podría, podrías,...	tener	**tendr-**	tendría, tendrías,...
querer	**querr-**	querría, querrías,...	venir	**vendr-**	vendría, vendrías,...

- Probability or conjecture in the past is often expressed in Spanish with the conditional.

  —¿A qué hora **sería** la conferencia de prensa?

  I wonder what time the press conference was?

  —**Sería** a las cuatro.

  It was probably at four.

APLICACIÓN

12-29 Marc Anthony. Marc Anthony es uno de los salseros neoyorquinos más admirados. Aquí tienes una narración sobre su juventud.

Paso 1 Léela y subraya los verbos en el condicional. ¿Cuáles expresan el futuro, con respecto a una acción en el pasado, y cuáles expresan el concepto de *should* en inglés?

Cuando tenía diez años, Marc Anthony ya sabía que sería cantante de salsa. Sus padres siempre le decían que tendría éxito porque le gustaba bailar y cantar los ritmos de las islas del Caribe. De niño, cantaba siempre con su padre mientras él tocaba la guitarra. Fue su padre quien le enseñó todo lo que sabía sobre la música puertorriqueña y quien le decía que algún día daría conciertos por todo el mundo. En 1990, conoció a Little Louis Vega, otro músico. Él le dijo que debería sacar un álbum de sus canciones. En ese álbum, también tocó Tito Puente, el gran percusionista puertorriqueño y otro modelo importante en la vida de Anthony. Tito y Celia Cruz lo animaron y lo guiaron mucho. De joven soñaba con crear música, pero nunca se imaginó que trabajaría al lado de esas dos leyendas del mundo hispano. Tampoco sabía que algún día estaría casado con otra caribeña famosa, Jennifer López.

Paso 2 Contesta las preguntas siguientes sobre el texto que acabas de leer.

1. ¿Quién es Marc Anthony?

2. ¿Qué hacía de joven?

3. ¿Quiénes le sirvieron de modelo?

4. ¿Quién le dijo que debería grabar un álbum de sus canciones?

5. ¿Qué sabía él de joven?

6. ¿Qué no sabía?

7. ¿Te gustaría asistir a uno de sus conciertos? Explica.

8. ¿Comprarías un álbum de Marc Anthony? ¿Por qué?

 Paso 3 Conéctate a la Internet para ver más imágenes de Marc Anthony y para escuchar su música. Escribe un párrafo en el que describas al artista o su música.

 Busca: marc anthony video; marc anthony foto

12-30 Lo que haría Mario López. El mexicoamericano Mario López es uno de los presentadores en el programa *Extra* en la cadena ABC. En 2008, ganó el segundo premio en *Dancing with the Stars,* y el mismo año, la revista *People* lo nombró "el soltero más sexy". Completa cada promesa que le hizo Mario a la revista con la forma correcta del verbo correspondiente en el condicional.

añadir	buscar	encontrar	poder
atraer	eliminar	haber	tener

MODELO: Dijo que _trabajaría_ para aumentar la presencia de hispanos en los medios de comunicación.

1. Prometió que _____ talento hispano para su programa.

2. Dijo que _____ más variedad de cantantes.

3. Nos aseguró que sus programas _____ a más televidentes.

4. Creía que _____ más éxito con los patrocinadores (*sponsors*).

5. Prometió que _____ los estereotipos.

6. Dijo que _____ diferentes maneras de atraer al público hispano.

7. Creía que _____ ayudar a la mujer latina.

8. Prometió que _____ otra hora a su programa.

12-31A Soledad O'Brien. Soledad O'Brien ha sido premiada por sus documentales en CNN. Ahora tú tienes la oportunidad de entrevistar al jefe/ a la jefa de una planta nuclear. Prepara las preguntas para entrevistarlo/la. Insiste siempre en que te dé respuestas directas. **Estudiante B,** por favor ve al **Apéndice 1,** página A-21.

MODELO: **reciclar** los desechos de su planta

ESTUDIANTE A: *Usted dijo que reciclaría los desechos de su planta...*

ESTUDIANTE A: *Tiene razón. Pero también dije que este proyecto tomaría su tiempo.*

ESTUDIANTE B: *Es verdad, pero dijo que...*

Estudiante A:

Preguntas del / de la entrevistador/a

Usted dijo que...

1. **ser** una planta nuclear ejemplar

2. **proteger** la naturaleza alrededor de la planta

3. **pagar** las multas de la EPA

4. no **contaminar** el agua del mar

5. **trabajar** en la reforestación de las montañas

6. **permitirnos** filmar dentro de su fábrica

12-32 En diferentes situaciones. Túrnense para contar lo que harían para proteger el medio ambiente de su país.

MODELO: *en la playa*
   E1: *¿Qué harías para proteger las playas?*
   E2: *Recogería la basura y los envases. ¿Y tú? ¿Qué harías?*
   E1: ...

1. con un millón de dólares
2. en tu universidad
3. en tu ciudad para hacerla más bella
4. en una carta al director del periódico
5. en un bosque
6. en tu carro para conservar gasolina
7. en tu casa para conservar agua
8. en tu casa para conservar energía

12-33 Adivinar. Tú y tu compañero/a están interesados en la vida de Marc Anthony y Jennifer López. Túrnense para hacerse preguntas sobre qué harían ellos en las siguientes situaciones.

MODELO: en el teatro
   E1: *¿Qué verían?*
   E2: *Pienso que verían* El rey león.

1. en un restaurante dominicano
2. en casa con sus hijos
3. en la playa Rincón, Puerto Rico
4. en el cine
5. en un concierto
6. en tu casa

12-43
to 12-47

¿Cuánto saben?

Primero, pregúntate si puedes llevar a cabo las siguientes funciones comunicativas en español. Después, júntate con dos o tres compañeros/as de clase para presentar las situaciones. Hagan y respondan a por lo menos cuatro preguntas en cada situación.

✓ CAN YOU . . .	WITH YOUR CLASSMATE(S) . . .
☐ talk about the environment?	**Situación: Una conversación** Túrnense para hablar de los problemas del medio ambiente que consideran los más importantes hoy en día. Usen vocabulario y expresiones de **¡Así lo decimos!** **Para empezar.** *Creo que el calentamiento global es uno de los problemas más grandes que tenemos que enfrentar porque...*
☐ talk about what will happen in the future?	**Situación: Un foro sobre el medio ambiente** Túrnense para contarse lo que pasará si no protegemos el medio ambiente. **Para empezar.** *En el futuro, tendremos que proteger los espacios verdes, los ríos y los lagos...*
☐ discuss what you and others would do?	**Situación: Una campaña** Túrnense para contarse lo que harían para mejorar el medio ambiente. Usen vocabulario y expresiones de **¡Así lo decimos!** y los verbos en el condicional. **Para empezar.** *Trabajaría para reducir las emisiones de las plantas de carbón...*
☐ speculate about the present and the past?	**Situación: Predicciones** Túrnense para contarse que dijo o prometió la gente que pasaría en el futuro. **Para empezar.** *Mis padres dijeron que yo estudiaría medicina. Mis profesores dijeron que estudiaría arte, pero yo dije que sería ingeniero...*

Observaciones

12-48
to 12-50

¡Pura vida! EPISODIO 12

En este episodio Felipe busca una camioneta.

Antes de ver el video

12-34 Vehículos usados en Costa Rica. Cuando Felipe va a la Internet encuentra una página web con camionetas a la venta. Lee sus características y explícale a Felipe por qué crees que la debería comprar o no.

MODELO: *En mi opinión...*

modelo	Chevrolet S10
año	1995
aire acondicionado	✗
vidrios eléctricos	✗
transmisión	Manual
motor	2500 cc diesel
dirección hidráulica	✓
cierre central	✗
kilometraje	224.000 km
color	blanco y azul
precio	US $8.000

Vehículos usados

A ver el video

 12-35 Felipe en la Internet. Mira el episodio número doce de **¡Pura vida!** para ver cómo Felipe busca otra camioneta. Luego, indica si las afirmaciones siguientes son ciertas (**C**) o falsas (**F**).

Felipe

Felipe en la Internet

Los amigos ayudan a Felipe

1. _____ Felipe se ha conectado a su correo electrónico.
2. _____ Recibe un mensaje que dice que ha ganado la lotería.
3. _____ El mecánico ha reparado su camioneta.
4. _____ Imprime la dirección de la agencia.

5. _____ Busca una camioneta en **Terra.es**.
6. _____ El teléfono de Marcela no manda mensajes instantáneos.
7. _____ A Marcela le interesan más los trajes de baño.
8. _____ Felipe le pide la moto a Patricio para ir a ver la camioneta.

Después de ver el video

 12-36 www.Terra.es. **Terra.es** es un buscador (*search engine*) muy popular en España. Conéctate a la Internet para ver qué se ofrece en **Terra.es** y anota qué hay en alguna de sus secciones.

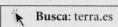 **Busca:** terra.es

Nuestro mundo

 Panoramas

 Los hispanos en Estados Unidos

12-51
to 12-52

Tradicionalmente los papeles para hispanos en la televisión y en el cine han sido de pandilleros (*gang members*) o ilegales, pero en años recientes son más evidentes en roles positivos. ¿Puedes identificar algún programa o película en que aparecen estas estrellas?

Benjamín Bratt

Eva Longoria Parker

Roselyn Sánchez

George López

América Ferrera

John Leguizamo

Los hispanos en Estados Unidos

Hispanos en EE. UU.[1]:	48,4 millones
Estado oficialmente bilingüe[2]:	Nuevo México
Familias hispanas en EE. UU. con computadora[2]:	7 millones
Los que usan la Internet[2]:	64%
Los que dicen que el medio ambiente es importante[2]:	92%
Los que creen que sus hijos tendrán un mejor futuro[2]:	73%

[1]Source: U.S. Census Bureau (2009)
[2]Source: Pew Hispanic Center

12-37 Identifica. Empareja las estrellas con su origen y algunos de sus papeles.

1. _____ Roselyn Sánchez
2. _____ Benjamín Bratt
3. _____ Eva Longoria Parker
4. _____ John Leguizamo
5. _____ América Ferrera
6. _____ George López

a. mexicoamericano/a – Películas: *The Sisterhood of the Traveling Pants; Real Women Have Curves;* Televisión: "Ugly Betty"

b. mexicoamericano/a – Películas: *Valentine's Day; The Spy Next Door;* Televisión: 118 episodios de una serie que lleva su nombre

c. puertorriqueño/a - Películas: *Act of Valor; Royal Pain* Televisión: "Without a Trace"

d. méxicoamericano/a – Películas: *Días de gracia;* Televisión: "Desperate Housewives"

e. colombiano/a – Películas: *Vanishing on 7th Street; Gamer; Love in the Time of Cholera;* Televisión: "ER"

f. peruanoamericano/a – Películas: *La Mission; Piñero; Miss Congeniality;* Televisión: "Law & Order"

12-38 Desafío. Consulta el mapa y la caja para identificar o explicar lo siguiente.

1. el número de hispanos en EE. UU.

2. la opinión que tienen los hispanoamericanos sobre el futuro

3. la ciudadanía (*citizenship*) de los puertorriqueños

4. el estado que es oficialmente bilingüe

5. la importancia de proteger el medio ambiente, según los hispanoamericanos

 12-39 Proyecto. Conéctate a la Internet para ver nombres de otras personalidades hispanas importantes. Elige una para investigar sus raíces (*roots*) y descubrir por qué es importante.

> ↗ **Busca:** contribuciones notables de hispanos

Cuando era puertorriqueña (fragmento), (Esmeralda Santiago, Puerto Rico/EE. UU.)

Esmeralda Santiago, la mayor de 11 hermanos, nació en Puerto Rico. Tenía trece años cuando su familia se mudó a Nueva York. Allí asistió a la Performing Arts School y después a Harvard y a Sarah Lawrence. Con su esposo, Frank Cantor, fundó CANTOMEDIA, una compañía que produce documentales. *Cuando era puertorriqueña* fue su primera obra, una memoria de su juventud en Puerto Rico y luego en Nueva York. Describe sus esfuerzos para primero aprender inglés y luego, para tener éxito en la escuela. A Esmeralda Santiago se le considera una de las escritoras hispanas más importantes de nuestra época.

ANTES DE LEER

12-40 Recuerdos de la escuela. En este fragmento, Santiago cuenta sobre su primer día en una escuela nueva y cómo quiso comunicarse en inglés. Piensa en tu primer día en una escuela nueva y escribe qué pasó y cómo te sentías.

A LEER

12-41 Cuando era puertorriqueña. Lee ahora el fragmento de esta conocida obra de Santiago.

El primer día de clases, Mami me llevó a un edificio de piedra que dominaba una cuadra de Graham Avenue, su patio de concreto encerrado° detrás de una verja de hierro° con púas° en las puntas. Los escalones del frente eran largos pero angostos°, y daban a dos puertas pesadas que se cerraron de golpe cuando entramos y bajamos por un corredor bien pulido°. Yo llevaba mi tarjeta de la escuela en Puerto Rico llena de *As* y *Bs*, y Mami tenía mi certificado de nacimiento. En la oficina, nos saludó un Mister Grant, un señor desanimado, con lentes bifocales y una sonrisa amable, que no hablaba español. Le dio a Mami un formulario a llenar. Yo entendía casi todas las palabras en los cuadritos que estábamos supuestas° a llenar: *Name, Address (City, State)* y *Occupation*. Se la devolvimos a Mister Grant, quien la revisó, miró mi certificado de nacimiento, estudió mis notas y escribió en una esquina "7–18."

Don Julio me había dicho° que si los estudiantes no hablaban inglés, las escuelas de Brooklyn los ponían un grado atrás hasta que lo aprendieran.

—¿Sében gré?° —le pregunté a Mister Grant, enseñándole los números que él había escrito. Señala con la cabeza que sí. —Ay no guan sében gré. Ay eyt gré. Ay tineyer.

—Tú no hablas inglés —me dijo, pronunciando las palabras inglesas poco a poco para que lo entendiera mejor—. Tienes que volver al séptimo grado hasta que lo aprendas.

—Ay jab *A* in scul Puerto Rico. Ay lern gud. Ay no sében gré gerl.

Mami se me quedó mirando, no entendiendo lo que yo estaba diciendo, pero sabiendo que [yo] le estaba faltando el respeto a un adulto.

—¿Qué es lo que está pasando? —me preguntó. Yo le dije que me querían poner en el séptimo grado, y que yo no quería. Este era el primer acto rebelde que me había visto fuera de mis malcrianzas° en casa.

—Negi, déjalo. Así se hacen las cosas aquí.

—A mí no me importa cómo se hagan las cosas aquí. Yo no voy a repetir el séptimo grado. Yo no soy bruta.

Mami miró al Mister Grant, quien parecía estar esperando que ella hiciera algo conmigo. Ella le sonrió y encogió° los hombros.

enclosed
iron grill / barbs / narrow

polished

supposed

had told me

Seventh grade?

rudeness

shrugged

—Mister Grant —le dije, aprovechando el momento–, ay go eyt gré six mons. Iv ay no lern inglis, ay go sében gré. ¿Okey?

—Así no es como se hacen las cosas aquí —me dijo, vacilante.

—Ay gud studen. Ay lern quik. Yu sí notas —le enseñé las *As* en mi tarjeta de la escuela—. Ay pas sében gré.

Así regateamos.

—Tienes hasta las Navidades —me dijo—. Yo estaré siguiendo tu progreso.

Tachó "7–18" y escribió "8–23" en el margen del papel. Escribió unas palabras en un papel, lo metió dentro de un sobre y me lo dio.

—Tu maestra es Miss Brown. Llévale esta notita. Tu mamá se puede volver a su casa.

Se despidió y desapareció en su oficina.

—¡Qué bien puedes hablar inglés! —exclamó Mami.

Yo estaba tan orgullosa de mí misma que por poco exploto. En Puerto Rico, si hubiera sido tan atrevida°, el equivalente del Mister Grant hubiera dicho que era una mal educada, y me hubiera mandado a casa con una nota para Mami. Pero aquí, era la maestra la que estaba recibiendo la nota, logré° lo que yo quería y mandaron a mi mamá a su casa.

—Ya yo sé llegar a casa después de la escuela –le dije–. No me tienes que venir a buscar.

—¿Estás segura?

—No te apures°.

Caminé por el corredor enlozado° en blanco y negro, pasando muchas puertas con ventanas, cada una con su número en tinta negra. Otros estudiantes se me quedaban mirando, trataban de llamarme la atención o no me hacían caso de tal manera que yo sabía que querían que yo supiera que no me estaban haciendo caso°. Les pasé como si supiera hacia donde iba, encabezándome° hacia un letrero que decía *STAIRS* con una flecha apuntando para arriba.

sassy

I got

Don't worry
tiled

querían… *they wanted me to think they didn't notice me.*
heading

DESPUÉS DE LEER

12-42 ¿Probable o improbable? Lee las siguientes oraciones e indica si cada una es probable (**P**) o improbable (**I**) según el fragmento que has leído. Corrige las oraciones improbables.

1. _____ La joven tenía doce años cuando empezó el octavo grado.

2. _____ El director de la escuela creía que hablaba bastante bien el inglés.

3. _____ La manera en que le habló al director no era respetuosa.

4. _____ Era evidente que su mamá no entendía mucho de la conversación con el director.

5. _____ Cuando caminaba por el pasillo, le parecía que nadie la veía.

12-43 Recuerdos del octavo grado. Escribe lo que recuerdas de tu escuela cuando estabas en el octavo grado. ¿Dónde estaba la escuela? ¿Quién era tu maestro/a? ¿Te gustaban las clases? Compara tu experiencia con la que tuvo la narradora durante su primer día en Brooklyn.

MODELO: *En el octavo grado asistí a la escuela… que estaba en …*

📖 Taller

12-54

12-44 Foro: El medio ambiente. Este es un foro para consultar dudas y participar en el debate sobre el medio ambiente. Aquí, expertos en el tema al igual que usuarios interesados se reúnen para compartir conocimientos e información. En este taller, vas a participar en la discusión.

ANTES DE ESCRIBIR

- **El problema.** Piensa en un problema ecológico que quieras debatir en el foro y los argumentos a favor y en contra.

MODELO:

Cristina (ayer) *Buenas tardes. En mi estado se ha montado una campaña para eliminar las bolsas de plástico para las compras. Yo las utilizo para tirar la basura. Entiendo que es por razones ecológicas, pero ¿van a sustituirlas por otras? ¿Hay bolsas que no perjudiquen el medio ambiente? Creo que hay que buscar alternativas a tirar la basura en bolsas de plástico.*

Ramón (hoy) *Hola, Cristina. ¡El gobierno de tu estado es muy progresista! Es verdad que las bolsas de plástico no se descomponen en la naturaleza, pero hay otras que son biodegradables y...*

A ESCRIBIR

- **Introducción.** Abre la discusión y haz una pregunta para animar a otros a responder.
- **Discusión.** Escribe por lo menos cuatro entradas sobre el tema de la discusión. Incluye voces a favor y otras en contra. Si es posible, pídeles a otros compañeros que también participen en la discusión.
- **Conclusión.** Resume o cierra tema.

DESPUÉS DE ESCRIBIR

- **Revisar.** Revisa tu discusión para verificar los siguientes puntos:
  - ☐ el uso del presente perfecto
  - ☐ el uso del futuro y del condicional
  - ☐ la concordancia y la ortografía
- **Intercambiar**
  Intercambia tu discusión con la de un/a compañero/a. Mientras leen los relatos, hagan comentarios y sugerencias sobre el contenido, la estructura y la gramática. Reaccionen también a los relatos.
- **Entregar**
  Pon tu foro en limpio, incorporando las sugerencias de tu compañero/a. Después, entrégaselo a tu profesor/a.

🔊 Vocabulario

La computadora y otros aparatos electrónicos *The computer and other electronics*

la antena parabólica *satellite dish*
los auriculares *earbuds, headphones*
el cajero automático *ATM*
el disco duro (externo) *(external) hard drive*
el DVD *DVD*
el escáner *scanner*
la fotocopiadora *photocopier*
la grabadora de DVD *DVD recorder*
la impresora *printer*
el lector de CD/DVD *CD/DVD player*
la marca *brand*
la memoria USB *memory stick*
la pantalla *screen*
el ratón (inalámbrico) *(wireless) mouse*
el reproductor de mp3 *MP3 player*
el teclado *keyboard*

Recursos en la computadora **Resources on the computer**

la hoja electrónica *spreadsheet*
el hipervínculo *hyperlink*
el juego electrónico *computer (electronic) game*
la página web *web page*
el sitio web *web site*

Verbos **Verbs**

apagar *to turn off*
archivar *to file, to save*
bajar *to download*
borrar *to erase*
encender (ie) *to turn on*
enviar *to send, to post online*
fallar *to fail (computer disk)*
fotocopiar *to photocopy*
funcionar *to function, to work*
grabar *to record*
imprimir *to print*
instalar *to install*
programar *to program*
subir *to upload*
tener éxito *to be successful*

Adjetivos **Adjectives**

digital *digital*
electrónico/a *electronic*
tecnológico/a *technological*

Nuestro mundo y el medio ambiente *Our world and the environment*

el bosque pluvial *rain forest*
el calentamiento global *global warming*
la deforestación *deforestation*
el desarrollo *development*
los desechos *waste*
la energía (alternativa/solar) *(alternative/solar) energy*
el envase (de aluminio) *(aluminum) container*
las especies en peligro de extinción *endangered species*
la escasez *shortage*
la fábrica *factory*
el humo *smoke*
el medio ambiente *environment*
la naturaleza *nature*
los pesticidas *pesticides*
la planta nuclear *nuclear plant*
el pozo de petróleo *oil well*
la radioactividad *radioactivity*
el recurso natural *natural resource*
el reciclaje *recycling*
la reforestación *reforestation*
la selva *jungle*

Verbos **Verbs**

ahorrar *to save*
conservar *to conserve, to preserve*
consumir *to consume*
contaminar *to contaminate, to pollute*
multar *to fine*
proteger (j) *to protect*
reciclar *to recycle*
tirar *to throw (away, out)*

Expressions used with the present perfect indicative *See page 394.*

B Activities

CAPÍTULO 1

1-5B **¿Cómo está usted?**   Your partner will assume the role of instructor; you are his/her student. Act out the following conversation using the information provided to complete your end of the conversation.

MODELO: ESTUDIANTE A: *Buenos días...*
           ESTUDIANTE B: *Hola...*

Estudiante B:

- Answer your instructor. Then ask him/her how he/she feels.
- Say that you are not feeling very well.
- Respond and then say good-bye to your instructor, that you'll see him/her later.

1-9B **Otra vez, por favor (*please*).**   Take turns spelling out your words in parentheses to your partner while he/she writes them down. Be sure to say in what category they belong. If you need to hear the spelling again, ask your partner to repeat by saying **Repite, por favor.**

MODELO: cosa (*thing*) (quesadilla)
           ESTUDIANTE A: *Es una cosa, cu – u – e – ese – a – de – i – ele – ele – a*
           ESTUDIANTE B: (After writing down the word) *¿Es una quesadilla?*
           ESTUDIANTE A: *¡Correcto!*

Estudiante B:

I say and spell ...	I write ...
1. persona famosa (Salma Hayek)	1. persona famosa: _____
2. ciudad (Tampa)	2. ciudad (*city*): _____
3. cosa (café)	3. cosa: _____
4. ciudad (San Francisco)	4. ciudad: _____

1-17B **Los días, los meses y las estaciones.** Take turns asking each other questions to fill in the missing days, dates and months on each of your grids.

MODELO: ESTUDIANTE A: (You need) *¿Un mes de otoño?*
ESTUDIANTE B: (You have) *octubre*

Estudiante B:

You need . . .	My partner gives me . . .	Your partner needs . . .
1. un mes de primavera		miércoles
2. el primer día de la semana		el 4 de julio·
3. un mes con veintiocho o veintinueve días		domingo
4. el Día de San Valentín		septiembre
5. un mes con cinco letras		agosto

1-29B **¡Escucha bien!** Take turns telling each other in Spanish what to do using the cues in English and acting out the commands.

MODELO: (Open your book)
ESTUDIANTE A: *Abre el libro.*
ESTUDIANTE B: (opens his/her book)
ESTUDIANTE A: *Correcto.*

Estudiante B:

You say in Spanish:
1. (Close your book)
2. (Take out your homework)
3. (Go to the chalkboard)

1-30B **Un pedido (*order*) por teléfono.** You are a student worker in the bookstore. A departmental worker calls you to give a supply order over the phone. Below is a list of items you have. Respond whether you have enough and mark the items the caller would be able to purchase. When you finish, compare your lists.

MODELO: ESTUDIANTE A: *Necesitamos cinco calculadoras. ¿Hay cinco calculadoras?*
ESTUDIANTE B: *Sí, tengo diez. / No, solo (only) hay cuatro.*

Estudiante B:

Hay...	Necesita...	Hay...	Necesita...	Hay...	Necesita...
79 bolígrafos	_____	30 lápices	_____	95 cajas de tiza	_____
22 libros	_____	96 mapas	_____	90 cajas de papel	_____
11 sillas	_____	1 mesa	_____	15 diccionarios	_____
14 cuadernos	_____			2 relojes	_____

CAPÍTULO 2

 2-9B **¿A qué hora?**   Complete your calendar by asking your partner when events with missing times take place. To ask your partner to repeat something, remember to say: **Repite, por favor.**

MODELO: la fiesta (20:30)

ESTUDIANTE A: *¿A qué hora es la fiesta?*

ESTUDIANTE B: *Es a las ocho y media de la noche.*

Hora	Actividad
_____	la clase de historia
10:30	la clase de arte
_____	la clase de español
13:30	la conferencia[1]
_____	la reunión
16:30	el examen
_____	el partido de fútbol
20:00	el programa "Ídolo americano" en la televisión
_____	la fiesta
24:00	el programa de noticias en la televisión

[1] *lecture*

2-16B **¿Quién eres? ¿Cómo eres?**   Ask questions to learn about your partner's new identity.

Paso 1   Assume the identity of one of the people outlined below and read through the information.

Estudiante B:

♂	♀
Juan López García	María Jiménez Cruz
Universidad Complutense de Madrid	Universidad Autónoma Nacional
España	México
arte	sociología
el profesor Sánchez	la profesora Alvarado
muy interesante	fantástica
25 estudiantes en la clase	15 estudiantes en la clase
alto y guapo	alta y simpática

1. ¿ _____ te llamas?
2. ¿ _____ estudias?
3. ¿ De _____ eres?
4. ¿ _____ eres?
5. ¿ _____ es tu clase de...?
6. ¿ _____ es el profesor de...?
7. ¿ _____ es tu clase favorita?
8. ¿ _____ estudiantes hay en la clase?

Paso 2   Ask each other about yourselves to find out what you have in common. Use interrogatives such as **qué, dónde, cómo, cuántos/as,** and **cuál** in the prompts above to help you form your questions.

MODELO: ESTUDIANTE A: *¿Dónde estudias?*

ESTUDIANTE B: *Estudio en la Universidad Nacional. ¿Y tú?*

ESTUDIANTE A: *Estudio...*

2-26B ¿De dónde eres? Take turns identifying the country your partner is from based on the language he/she tells you he/she speaks. Remember that in Spanish, the masculine form of the nationality corresponds to the language spoken there.

MODELO: ESTUDIANTE A: *Hablo italiano.*
ESTUDIANTE B: *¿Eres de Italia?*
ESTUDIANTE A: *Sí, es verdad.*

Estudiante B:

Hablo...	Mi compañero/a es de...
1. español	Corea
2. japonés	Inglaterra
3. chino	Portugal
4. alemán	Rusia

2-35B Entrevistas. Ask each other questions to share the information below. Be sure to respond using complete sentences and logical information.

MODELO: ESTUDIANTE A: *¿A qué hora llegas a clase?*
ESTUDIANTE B: (1:30 p.m.) *Llego a la una y media de la tarde.*

Estudiante B:

Mis preguntas	Mis respuestas
1. ¿Dónde estudias?	• todos los días
2. ¿Aprendes mucho en clase?	• tenis
3. ¿Qué música escuchas?	• solo los lunes, miércoles y viernes
4. ¿Qué comes en un restaurante?	• inglés, y un poquito de español
5. ¿Qué programa ves en la televisión?	• el *New York Times*

2-39B ¿Tienes? Take turns asking each other if you have the items on your list. If your partner has the item you want, you make a pair. The first person who has five pairs of items wins.

MODELO: ☐ un libro de historia
ESTUDIANTE A: *¿Tienes un libro de historia?*
ESTUDIANTE B: *Sí, tengo. (No, no tengo libro de historia, pero tengo un libro de física).*

Estudiante B:

☐ un cuaderno verde	☐ una novela de Hemingway	☐ un examen difícil
☐ una mochila negra	☐ un reloj grande	☐ un/a profesor/a inteligente
☐ un libro de francés	☐ un lápiz rojo	☐ un libro viejo
☐ una pintura de Dalí	☐ un cuaderno viejo	☐ un buen amigo

CAPÍTULO 3

 3-7B **Inventario en el almacén (*warehouse*).** You and your classmate are stock workers compiling end-of-year inventory figures. Each of you is missing data. Take turns asking each other questions to fill in the missing parts on each of your grids. **¡Ojo!** (*Watch out!*) Watch for agreement. Then check all your figures by calling out each item and quantity.

MODELO: ESTUDIANTE A: (You need) *¿Cuántas mesas tienes?*
ESTUDIANTE B: (You have) *Tengo setecientas cuarenta y siete mesas.*

Estudiante B:

600.450 CD	11.399 lápices
_____ diccionarios	2.700.000 bolígrafos
110 sillas	_____ cuadernos
5.002 escritorios	672 computadoras
2.400 libros de texto	_____ calculadoras
_____ pizarras	52 mapas

 3-27B **Las materias, la hora, el lugar.** Take turns asking and answering questions in order to complete the missing information on your class schedules.

MODELO: ESTUDIANTE A: *¿A qué hora es la clase de...?*
ESTUDIANTE B: *¿Qué clase es a la/s...?*
ESTUDIANTE A: *¿Dónde es la clase de...?*
ESTUDIANTE B: *¿Quién es el/la profesor/a de...?*

Estudiante B:

Hora	Clase	Lugar	Profesor/a
8:30	cálculo	Facultad de Informática	
9:00			Ramón Sánchez Guillón
10:00	biología	Facultad de Medicina	
	lingüística	Facultad de Letras	
1:55		Facultad de Ingeniería	Carlos Santos Pérez

3-36B **¿Dónde estoy?** Take turns acting out your situations while your partner tries to guess where you are. Then challenge other members of the class to guess where you are by acting out what you are doing.

MODELO: ESTUDIANTE A: (act out reading a book) *¿Dónde estoy?*
ESTUDIANTE B: *Estás en la biblioteca.*

Estudiante B:

1. (working out in gym)
2. (playing tennis on the tennis courts)
3. (painting a picture in art class)
4. (looking at the stars through a telescope in the observatory)
5. ¿...?

3-39B **¿Quién es?**   Take turns describing the following people using **ser, estar,** and **tener** and guessing who the person is.

> **MODELO:** ESTUDIANTE A: *Es una mujer. Tiene unos treinta años. Es muy inteligente. Está aquí en la clase con nosotros…*
> ESTUDIANTE B: *¡Es la profesora!*

Estudiante B:

1. Lil Wayne (rapper)	3. Lady Gaga (pop singer)
2. Miley Cyrus (actress, pop singer)	4. ¿…?

CAPÍTULO 4

 4-14B **Una entrevista para *Prensa Libre*.**   *Prensa Libre* is an independent newspaper in Guatemala. You are reporters who are preparing to interview the **Presidente de la República.** Ask and respond logically to each other's questions, being careful to use the correct object pronouns and verb forms.

> **MODELO:** ESTUDIANTE A: *¿Tienes tu cámara?*
> ESTUDIANTE B: *Sí, la tengo.*

Estudiante B:

Mis preguntas	Mis respuestas a las preguntas de mi compañero/a
1. ¿Vas a llamar al secretario antes de ir?	_____ La escucha cuando está cansado.
2. ¿El presidente quiere ver el artículo antes de publicarlo?	_____ No, lo van a visitar en junio.
3. ¿La esposa del presidente quiere leer la entrevista también?	_____ No, no las necesitamos.
4. El presidente juega fútbol, ¿verdad?	_____ Sí, la tiene.
5. ¿También toca el piano?	_____ Sí, la tengo.
6. ¿El presidente recibe al embajador norteamericano mañana?	_____ Sí, lo habla perfectamente bien.

4-25B **¡Estoy aburrido/a!**   Your partner is bored. Invite him/her to do something that he/she might enjoy. Continue offering suggestions until he/she accepts one.

> **MODELO:** ESTUDIANTE A: *Estoy aburrido/a.*
> ESTUDIANTE B: *¿Quieres ir a bailar? (¿Te gustaría…? ¿Prefieres…?)*
> ESTUDIANTE A: *Me encantaría. ¡Vamos! / Gracias, pero no puedo. No tengo dinero.*

Estudiante B:

Algunas actividades:	
almorzar conmigo	pasear por el centro
correr por el parque	tener una fiesta
ir al cine / al partido de…	tomar un café
ir al parque	venir a mi casa
jugar al…	ver una película de acción
llamar por teléfono a…	visitar a amigos / a la familia

4-37B Entrevista. First, interview your partner using the questions below to find out about him/her. Write down his/her answers. Then, read the profile about the person you will be role-playing. Answer your partner's questions based on the information you have.

MODELO: ESTUDIANTE A: *¿Conoces a alguna* (any) *persona famosa?*
ESTUDIANTE B: *Sí, conozco a Ricky Martin. Soy amigo/a de él.*

1. ¿Conoces a algún político importante?
2. ¿A qué artistas famosos conoces?
3. ¿Qué idiomas sabes hablar?
4. ¿Qué países conoces muy bien?
5. ¿Estudias biología?
6. ¿Juegas bien al fútbol?

Estudiante B:

> Soy amigo/a del presidente de Costa Rica.
>
> Toco muy bien el piano.
>
> No practico mucho los deportes.
>
> Vivo y trabajo en Ciudad de Guatemala.
>
> Hablo español y una lengua maya.
>
> Soy arqueólogo/a y estudio las pirámides mayas.

CAPÍTULO 5

5-6B Compras para su clóset del baño. Tienen que equipar el clóset de su baño. Tú tienes el volante (*flier*) del periódico con los productos en venta esta semana; tu compañero/a tiene una lista de posibles productos para comprar. Decidan qué productos van a comprar según los precios. ¿Cuánto gastan en total?

MODELO: ESTUDIANTE A: *Necesitamos … ¿Cuánto cuesta(n)?*
ESTUDIANTE B: *Está(n) en venta esta semana por … / Lo siento, no está(n) en venta esta semana.*
ESTUDIANTE A: *Bien, vamos a comprar … por … en total. / Entonces, necesitamos …*

Estudiante B:

Volante del periódico			
máquina de afeitar	$29	navajas desechables (*disposable*)	$3
desodorante superseco masculino	$3	loción perfume de rosa	$6
cepillos para el pelo	$5	loción sin perfume	$4
champú Todopelo	$3,50	crema Barbasol	$1,50
jabón desodorante	$0,50	cepillo de dientes	$1,50
secador ultrarrápido	$15	maquillaje "La Linda"	$10

5-27B En la agencia de bienes raíces (*real estate*). Eres un/a agente de bienes raíces en Panamá y tienes un cliente que busca una casa o apartamento. A continuación tienes varias posibilidades, pero tienes que hacerle preguntas a tu cliente para decidir cuál es la mejor opción para su situación.

Casa Linda

cuatro dormitorios, cocina grande,
dos baños; centro ciudad;
$1.200/mes,
luz y gas incluidos

Apartamento en la playa

tres dormitorios; un baño grande,
uno pequeño con ducha; cocina pequeña,
patio; se permiten perros. $1.300/mes,
luz y gas incluidos

Apartamento con vista al mar

cuatro dormitorios, dos baños con ducha, cocina,
patio pequeño; se permiten perros;
parking en la calle. $1.200/mes,
luz y gas incluidos

Casa cerca de la playa

tres dormitorios, cocina grande,
patio, tres baños; cerca de la línea de autobuses,
garaje para dos carros;
se permite un perro pequeño; $1.000/mes,
luz y gas extra

Apartamento en zona exclusiva

con gimnasio y acceso a la playa.
Seguridad las 24 horas; tres habitaciones grandes;
tres baños; garaje para un carro y espacio para bicicletas;
terraza; cerca de la línea de autobuses;
se permiten gatos; 1.200/mes,
luz y gas incluidos

MODELO: ESTUDIANTE A: *Busco una casa o un apartamento.*
ESTUDIANTE B: *¿Para cuántas personas?*
ESTUDIANTE A: *Para cinco. Queremos...*

Estudiante B:

- ¿Cuántos dormitorios necesitan?
- ¿Cuántos baños prefieren?
- ¿Cuánto quieren pagar al mes?
- ¿Necesitan estar cerca del transporte público?
- ¿Tienen mascotas (*pets*)?

- ¿Tienen carro?
- ¿Qué más necesitan?
- Entonces, creo que tengo una buena opción para ustedes. Es un apartamento/una casa....

5-35B **¿Qué estoy haciendo?**   Mientras (*While*) actúas una de las siguientes situaciones, tu compañero/a trata de adivinar (*guess*) lo que estás haciendo. Túrnense para actuar y adivinar.

MODELO: afeitarse

      ESTUDIANTE A: (act out shaving) *¿Qué estoy haciendo?*

      ESTUDIANTE B: *Estás afeitándote.*

Estudiante B:

1. secarse el pelo	4. lavarse las manos
2. ponerse el desodorante	5. dormirse
3. levantarse de la cama	6. ponerse impaciente

CAPÍTULO 6

6-12B **Las especialidades de la casa.**   Túrnense para hacer el papel (*play the role*) de mesero/a y cliente en los restaurantes de su lista. El/La mesero/a le tiene que recomendar a su cliente algunos platos que sirven en su restaurante. El/La cliente tiene que pedir una de las recomendaciones.

MODELO: ESTUDIANTE A: *Por favor, ¿qué me recomienda Ud. aquí en Casa Roma?*

      ESTUDIANTE B: *Nuestra especialidad es la comida italiana. Le recomiendo la pasta con marisco o la pizza Margarita.*

      ESTUDIANTE A: *¿Me trae por favor la pizza Margarita?*

      ESTUDIANTE B: *¡Enseguida!*

Estudiante B:

Restaurantes que visito:	Restaurantes donde trabajo y sus especialidades:
Casa Miguel	**Cocina Cándida:** Comida chilena. Pescado frito o a la parrilla. Sopa de mariscos.
Cafetería Universo	**El Unicornio:** Comida vegetariana. Tortilla de papa, arroz con frijoles, pastel de maíz, yogur de frutas.
El Rincón Argentino	**Café del Diablo:** Postres. Cafés de todo el mundo. Helado, pasteles, galletas, flanes. Jugos de frutas exóticas. Chocolate caliente.

6-26B El arroz con pollo. El arroz con pollo es un plato muy conocido en todo el mundo hispano. **Estudiante A** tiene la receta y tú tienes la lista de los ingredientes y utensilios que hay en tu cocina. Escriban una lista de los ingredientes que necesitan comprar y los utensilios que necesitan pedir prestados (*borrow*) para preparar este plato.

MODELO: ESTUDIANTE A: *Necesitamos una taza de arroz.*
ESTUDIANTE B: *No tenemos suficiente arroz. Tenemos que comprarlo.*

Estudiante B:

Ingredientes en tu cocina	Utensilios en tu cocina
aceite de maíz	un tazón de plástico
media taza de arroz	una cuchara
sal	un cuchillo pequeño
un pimiento rojo	una cazuela
un pollo pequeño	
una taza de jugo de tomate	
una cabeza de ajo	
una cebolla pequeña	
Para comprar: *arroz*	Para pedir prestado *(borrow)*:

6-32B Charadas. Túrnense para representar estas y otras acciones en el pasado para ver si su compañero/a puede adivinar la acción.

MODELO: ESTUDIANTE A: (Act out: *Corté el pan.*)
ESTUDIANTE B: *Cortaste el pan.*

Estudiante B:

Pelé una banana.	Freí un huevo en una sartén.
Mezclé dos huevos en un tazón.	Calenté la comida en el microondas.
Le eché azucar y leche al café.	¿...?

6-36B ¿Qué pasó?   Túrnense para preguntarse qué pasó en algunas situaciones. Contesta usando actividades lógicas de la lista.

MODELO: en la fiesta familiar

ESTUDIANTE A: *¿Qué pasó en la fiesta familiar?*

ESTUDIANTE B: *Mi mamá sirvió nuestra comida favorita.*

Estudiante B:

Algunas actividades:	Situaciones:
• no oír el diálogo	1. anoche
• dormirse	2. en el restaurante el sábado
• servir arroz con pollo	3. en el museo

CAPÍTULO 7

 7-6B Una invitación a un concierto de Jennifer López (J.Lo) y Marc Anthony.
Responde a la invitación de tu compañero/a. Usa las preguntas de la lista e incluye otras dos tuyas (*of your own*). Puedes preguntar cómo van a ir al concierto, si puedes invitar a otros amigos, si tu amigo/a quiere ir a cenar antes del concierto, etc.

MODELO: ESTUDIANTE A: *¿Quieres ir a un concierto de J.Lo y Marc Anthony?*

ESTUDIANTE B: *¡Estupendo! ¿A qué hora empieza?*

Estudiante B:

¿Qué día es?	¿Quiénes van?	¿A qué hora volvemos?
¿Dónde es?	¿Cuánto cuesta?	¿Vamos a cenar antes? etc.

 7-9B Una fiesta sorpresa.   En el foro de un amigo, hay entradas (*entries*) sobre una fiesta sorpresa que hubo. Cada uno/a de ustedes tiene parte de la información sobre la fiesta. Háganse preguntas para saber qué pasó en la fiesta.

Estudiante B:

La información que necesito:	La información que tengo:
1. ¿Quién dio la fiesta?	
2. ¿Quiénes estuvieron en la fiesta?	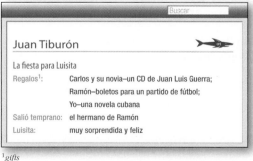
3. ¿Qué sirvieron?	
4. ¿Quiénes no fueron? ¿Por qué?	

Juan Tiburón

La fiesta para Luisita

Regalos[1]:   Carlos y su novia–un CD de Juan Luis Guerra;
            Ramón–boletos para un partido de fútbol;
            Yo–una novela cubana

Salió temprano: el hermano de Ramón

Luisita: muy sorprendida y feliz

[1]*gifts*

7-21B Consejos. Explíquense cómo se sienten y pidan consejos sobre lo que deben hacer. Pueden aceptar o rechazar los consejos, pero es necesario dar excusas si no los aceptan.

MODELO: ESTUDIANTE A: *Estoy aburrido/a. ¿Qué hago?*
ESTUDIANTE B: *¿Qué tal si das un paseo?*
ESTUDIANTE A: *No quiero. No me gusta salir de noche.*
ESTUDIANTE B: *Bueno, yo voy contigo. ¿Está bien?*
ESTUDIANTE B: *¡Perfecto!*

Estudiante B:

Situaciones	y mis reacciones	Sugerencias para mi compañero/a
Te sientes muy solo/a.	• ¡Fabuloso!	hacer un pícnic
Estás en la oficina todo el día sin salir.	• No me gusta(n)…	jugar al voleibol
Quieres conocer al golfista Phil Mickelson.	• ¡Ideal!	escuchar música
Tienes mucho calor.	• ¡Qué buena idea!	trabajar en la biblioteca
Compraste una raqueta nueva.	• Me da igual.	ver la televisión
	• ¡Qué mala idea!	volar un papalote
	• No quiero porque…	tomar un té verde

7-24B Una película excepcional. Ayer tu amigo salió con una amiga al cine y lo pasaron muy bien. Quieres saber los detalles de lo que hicieron esa noche.

Paso 1 Primero conjuga los verbos en cada pregunta en el pretérito.

MODELO: ¿A quién **invitar** (tú) al cine? *¿A quién invitaste al cine?*

Estudiante B:

- ¿Qué **ver** ayer en el cine?
- ¿Cómo **saber** (tú) de la película?
- ¿A qué hora **ir** ustedes al cine?
- ¿**Poder** ustedes llegar temprano a la película?
- ¿Qué **decir** tu amiga después de la película?
- ¿Adónde **ir** ustedes?
- ¿Cómo **ser**?
- ¿Qué **hacer** ustedes después?

Paso 2 Ahora hazle tus preguntas a tu compañero/a. Toma apuntes para poder informarle a la clase.

7-27B **¿Tienes?** Eres asistente deportivo. El/La entrenador/a te pide cosas para el partido. Si las tienes, dile que se las vas a traer. Si no las tienes, dile que se las vas a buscar.

MODELO: ESTUDIANTE A: *¿Tienes las botellas de agua para los jugadores?*
ESTUDIANTE B: *Sí, tengo botellas de agua. / No, no tengo botellas de agua.*
ESTUDIANTE A: *¿Me las traes? / ¿Me las buscas?*
ESTUDIANTE B: *Sí, te las traigo. / Sí, te las busco.*

Estudiante B:

Tengo...			
los boletos para el partido	el bate de aluminio	los uniformes del equipo	las botellas de agua
las pelotas	los guantes	el bolígrafo del/de la entrenador/a	la lista de los jugadores
las galletas	las naranjas	los lentes de sol del/de la entrenador/a	el cuaderno del/de la entrenador/a

CAPÍTULO 8

8-3B **¿Tienes?** ¿Qué compró Sara para su viaje a Machu Picchu? Túrnense para completar la informacion que falta en su recibo. Usen las siguientes preguntas para llenar su recibo: **¿Qué compró por…? ¿Qué compró de la talla…? ¿De qué talla es/son…?** Después confirmen las compras que hizo Sara y cuánto gastó.

MODELO: ESTUDIANTE A: *¿Qué compró por veinte nuevos soles?*
ESTUDIANTE B: *Compró una camiseta de algodón. ¿De qué talla es?*
ESTUDIANTE A: *Es de la talla cuarenta.*
ESTUDIANTE B: *Así que compró una camiseta de algodón de la talla cuarenta por veinte nuevos soles.*

falabella

DOCUMENTO DE VENTA

OUFDSYEVW9NGOLWI9TOD20J

Vendedor	T.T	EmpCent	Operac.	Fecha	Hora	EdPIZN T
51106219	9	001006	0367886	12/12/2010	19:16	0100000 00

Descripción	Talla	Importe (NUEVOS SOLES)
camiseta de algodón	40	NS 20
blusa de manga corta	36	_____
_____	40	NS 75
suéter de lana	_____	NS 80
_____	42	NS 200
zapatos de tacón alto	39	NS 39
_____	50	NS 100

TOTAL COMPRA NS _____

Gracias por su compra.
Visítenos en www.falabella.com

Estudiante B:

8-8B **¿Qué pasaba en el almacén ayer?** Cada uno/a de ustedes tiene una versión diferente de lo que pasaba ayer en el almacén. Describan lo que ven en su dibujo para encontrar seis diferencias.

> **MODELO:** ESTUDIANTE A: *Una mujer se probaba zapatos.*
> ESTUDIANTE B: *Es cierto. Una mujer se probaba zapatos.*

Estudiante B:

 8-11B **Atención al cliente (*Customer service*).** Cada uno/a de ustedes tiene información del directorio del almacén Saga Falabella. Túrnense para pedir información sobre dónde comprar los siguientes productos o cumplir (*carry out*) algún deber. Añadan más información cuando sea posible.

> **MODELO:** una blusa para tu mamá
> ESTUDIANTE A: *Quiero comprar una blusa para mi mamá porque es su cumpleaños.*
> ESTUDIANTE B: *La puede buscar en el segundo piso, en Ropa de mujer.*
> ESTUDIANTE A: *Muchas gracias.*

Estudiante B:

1. platos y vasos	4. una botella de aceite de oliva
2. una camisa barata	5. dónde pagar tu cuenta
3. un televisor grande de plasma	6. un suéter para tu sobrino que tiene dos años

saga falabella.

1.er piso	Ropa de hombre Calzado (zapatos, botas, sandalias)	6.° piso	
2.° piso	*Ropa de mujer (trajes, vestidos, ropa informal)*	7.° piso	Ropa formal (trajes de noche, vestidos de noche) Trajes de novia
3.er piso		8.° piso	Restaurante
4.° piso	Equipo deportivo (ropa, pelotas, bates)	9.° piso	
5.° piso		10.° piso	Oficinas de administración Cambio de moneda

 8-28B **Artículos encontrados.** Ustedes trabajan en la oficina de Artículos encontrados en un almacén. Comparen lo que encontraron con lo que la gente perdió. Cada uno/a tiene parte de la información.

> **MODELO:** un guante
> ESTUDIANTE A: *Encontré un guante.*
> ESTUDIANTE B: *¿Era pequeño?*
> ESTUDIANTE A: *Sí, era pequeño y de lana.*
> ESTUDIANTE B: *Ah, una señora perdió un guante pequeño de cuero. No es de ella.*

Estudiante B:

Encontré:	Alguien perdió:	¿Se encontró?
MODELO: un guante (pequeño; de lana)	• Una señora perdió un guante (pequeño; de cuero)	**NO**
1. una blusa (blanca; de seda; talla 10)	• Un chico perdió unos vaqueros (para hombre; talla mediana)	_____
2. un zapato (de cuero; número 9; de hombre)	• Una chica perdió unos calcetines (de algodón; de mujer)	_____
3. un bolso (rojo; con una billetera negra)	• Una mujer perdió unas sandalias (amarillas; de tacón alto)	_____
4. una camiseta (de algodón; que decía "Ecuador"; amarilla)	• Un hombre perdió una camisa (azul; talla 38)	_____
5. un collar (de plata; largo)	• Una chica perdió una sudadera (negra; sin capucha)	_____

8-31B Ofertas esta semana. Cada uno/a de ustedes tiene parte de un anuncio sobre las ofertas esta semana en el almacén. Usen una construcción impersonal con **se** en sus preguntas sobre los artículos, los descuentos y los precios para conseguir la información que falta.

MODELO: cadenas de plata

> ESTUDIANTE A: *¿Se venden cadenas de plata?*
> ESTUDIANTE B: *Sí, se venden cadenas de plata en el departamento de joyería.*
> ESTUDIANTE A: *¿Qué descuentos se dan?*
> ESTUDIANTE B: *Se dan descuentos del 25 al 50 por ciento.*

Estudiante B:

Saga Falabella Ofertas Fin de Temporada		
Ofertas por departamento	**Artículos que necesito**	**Descuentos que recibo**
Joyería: *Plata y oro: cadenas, aretes…* *Descuentos del 25% al 50%*	*cadenas de plata*	*del 25% al 50%*
Joyería:	relojes de pulsera	
Departamento juvenil: Ropa de niños para el verano, descuentos del 40%		
Departamento para mujeres chic:	faldas de diseñador	
Departamento para hombres: Camisas, trajes, corbatas, descuentos del 20% al 40%, tallas 36 a 42		
Departamento de calzado:	sandalias botas de invierno	
Departamento deportivo: Todo equipo deportivo (pelotas, raquetas, bates, trajes de baño), descuentos del 10% al 40%		

9-5B En el mostrador de AVIANCA. Eres un/a viajero/a en el mostrador (*counter*) de la aerolínea AVIANCA (aerolínea colombiana). Primero, responde a las preguntas del / de la agente y después, pregúntale la siguiente información.

MODELO: ESTUDIANTE A: *Buenas tardes. ¿Tiene su tarjeta de embarque?*
ESTUDIANTE B: *No, pero tengo el número de mi reservación.*

Estudiante B:

Información para el/la agente:	Preguntas para el/la agente:
destino = Caracas	1. la hora de salida (¿A qué hora...?)
equipaje = dos maletas	2. el número del vuelo (¿Cuál es ...?)
solo dos botellas de champú	3. el número de la puerta de embarque (¿Cuál es ...?)
el asiento = de ventanilla	4. la hora de abordar el avión (¿A qué hora debo ...?)
comprar un billete	5. si se sirve comida en el vuelo (¿Sirven...?)

 9-10B ¡Planes para las vacaciones de primavera! Hablen sobre los viajes que van a hacer en la primavera, usando las categorías del modelo. Luego, háganse las preguntas siguientes e intenten convencer (*convince*) al otro / a la otra para ir juntos/as.

Estudiante B:

	Mi viaje	El viaje de mi compañero/a
Transporte:	avión, taxi	
Destino:	Cancún	
Fecha de llegada:	el 2 de marzo	
Ruta:	Houston	
Propósito:	tomar el sol, divertirme, visitar Chichén Itzá	
Duración del viaje:	cinco días	

1. ¿Adónde vas?

2. ¿Por qué ruta vas a viajar?

3. ¿Cómo vas a viajar, por tren, por carro, por...?

4. ¿Cuándo es el viaje?

5. ¿Por cuánto tiempo vas?

6. ¿Para qué vas?

Al final, para convencer a tu compañero/a:

7. ¿Por qué no vienes conmigo? Creo que mi viaje va a ser...

9-12B **El robo en el museo.** Hubo un robo en un museo en Colombia y ustedes creen que encontraron algunos de los objetos robados. Túrnense para hacerse preguntas y descubrir (*discover*) qué objeto encontró cada uno. Contesten cada pregunta con un adverbio que termina en **-mente.**

MODELO: Encontré una pintura de Picasso (**enorme**) valiosa.

ESTUDIANTE A: *¿Qué encontraste?*

ESTUDIANTE B: *Encontré una pintura de Picasso enormemente valiosa.*

Estudiante B:

Preguntas para mi compañero/a	Respuestas para mi compañero/a
1. ¿Qué encontraste?	• Se escapó (**difícil**), por una ventana.
2. ¿Cómo lo encontraste?	• (**Seguro**) lo robó un empleado del museo.
3. ¿Qué valor crees que tiene?	• Es (**particular**) hermosa.
4. ¿Qué hiciste cuando encontraste el objeto?	• Encontré una figura (**exquisito**) hecha de oro.
5. ¿Qué hicieron los directores del museo?	• La puse (**tranquilo**) en mi mochila.

Figura de oro de los indios muiscas del Museo del Oro

9-25B **Desafío (*Challenge*).** Cada uno/a de ustedes tiene una lista de verbos diferentes en el indicativo y el subjuntivo. Dile a tu compañero/a el indicativo del verbo, y él/ella debe darte el presente de subjuntivo de ese verbo. Después, muéstrense su lista de respuestas y ayúdense a corregir las incorrectas.

MODELO: ESTUDIANTE A: *Indicativo: tomamos*

ESTUDIANTE B: *Subjuntivo: tomemos*

ESTUDIANTE A: *Correcto.*

Estudiante B:

Digo:	Mi compañero/a debe decir:	Yo marco:	
Indicativo	**Subjuntivo**	**Correcto**	**Incorrecto**
tomamos	*tomemos*	✓	
vemos	veamos		
voy	vaya		
lees	leas		
dormimos	durmamos		
ponen	pongan		
quiere	quiera		
siguen	sigan		

9-31B **¿Qué hacer?** Cuando tienen un problema, es normal pedirle consejos a un/a amigo/a. Túrnense para explicarle algún problema a su compañero/a. Él/Ella debe responder de una manera lógica con el subjuntivo. Luego, reaccionen a la recomendación.

MODELO: Te recomiendo que (**estudiar**) mucho.

ESTUDIANTE A: *Tengo un examen de química mañana.*

ESTUDIANTE B: *Te recomiendo que <u>estudies</u> mucho.*

ESTUDIANTE A: *Buena idea. / No tengo tiempo. / No puedo porque...*

Estudiante B:

Mis problemas:	Consejos para mi compañero:
1. Mi casa está en desorden y tengo invitados este fin de semana.	• Es difícil que (tú) (**encontrar**) un buen trabajo si no estudias más.
2. A mi mejor amigo no le gustan las películas que a mí me gustan.	• Te sugiero que (**buscar**) trabajo, o que les (**pedir**) dinero a tus padres.
3. Quiero estudiar en el extranjero, pero las clases son en español.	• Te aconsejo que (**buscar**) los libros en línea.
4. Mi trabajo no me da tiempo para estudiar.	• Me encanta México. Quiero que me (**invitar**) a mí al crucero.

CAPÍTULO 10

 10-5B **Consejos médicos.**   Habla con tu compañero/a para que te dé consejos sobre los siguientes síntomas.

MODELO: ESTUDIANTE A: *Me duelen los pulmones.*
ESTUDIANTE B: *Debes dejar de fumar.*

Estudiante B:

Mis síntomas:	Consejos para mi compañero/a:
1. Tengo gripe.	• tomar antiácidos
2. Tengo náuseas.	• tomarse la temperatura
3. Tengo un dolor de cabeza terrible.	• tomar más café
4. Toso mucho.	• ir de vacaciones
5. No tengo energía.	• no caminar tanto y usar más el carro
6. Tengo alergia a los mariscos.	• comprar *Kleenex*

 10-9B **En la sala de urgencias.**   Ustedes tienen que decidir qué deben hacer en situaciones urgentes. Un/a estudiante presenta unas situaciones. El/La otro/a responde con instrucciones lógicas de su lista, usando mandatos formales. Túrnense, cambiando de papel.

MODELO: ESTUDIANTE A: *El niño tiene gripe.*
ESTUDIANTE B: *Déle muchos liquídos como jugo o agua.*

Estudiante B:

Situaciones urgentes	Acciones
1. La paciente se rompió una pierna.	• buscar un tanque de oxígeno
2. El señor viejo está muy ansioso.	• darle un antiácido
3. La niña tiene resfriado.	• ponerle una inyección de penicilina
4. La señora tiene dolor de cabeza.	• tomarle la temperatura
5. Al joven le duele una muela.	• darle un jarabe para controlar la tos
6. ¿...?	• ¿...?

10-24B Te recomiendo que…   Un/a estudiante presenta los siguientes problemas y el/la otro/a ofrece recomendaciones. Túrnense, cambiando de papel. Pueden usar **te/le/les recomiendo que** más el subjuntivo.

MODELO: ESTUDIANTE A: *Estoy muy flaco/a.*
ESTUDIANTE B: *Te recomiendo que comas tres comidas completas todos los días.*

Estudiante B:

Mis problemas:	Recomendaciones para mi compañero/a:
1. Mi jefe/a padece de úlceras.	• tomar una aspirina
2. A mi abuelo/a le preocupa su alto nivel de colesterol.	• practicar juegos para la memoria
3. A mi amigo/a le falta energía.	• hacer jogging
4. No quiero engordar cuando voy de vacaciones.	• dejar de fumar
5. Creo que tengo una infección en la garganta.	• no comer postres

10-31B ¿Qué piensan?   Tienes una revista sobre la salud con información que puede ser cierta o no. Tu compañero/a te va a hacer preguntas que puedes contestar según las afirmaciones a continuación. Luego ustedes van a dar su opinión sobre las afirmaciones.

MODELO: ESTUDIANTE A: *¿Hay algún consejo para una persona que tiene problemas cardíacos?*
ESTUDIANTE B: *Según la revista, la aspirina es buena para el corazón.*
ESTUDIANTE A: *No creo que sea buena idea tomar mucha aspirina.*
ESTUDIANTE B: *Pues, es cierto que es bueno tomar una por día.*

Estudiante B:

La información que tengo:	Para reaccionar:
• Puedes hacer más ejercicio si tomas mucha agua.	• (no) creo
• Los bolivianos tienen una cura para el resfriado común.	• (no) dudo
• Hay una pastilla para mejorar la memoria.	• (no) es verdad
• Puedes bajar cinco kilos en ocho días comiendo solo pan y mantequilla.	• ojalá
• Un vaso de vino diario protege el corazón.	• (no) estoy seguro/a
• Hay una hierba paraguaya para mantenerte siempre joven.	• (no) niego
	• es lógico
	• es interesante
	• me alegro de
	• tal vez
	• es bueno (malo)

CAPÍTULO 11

 11-9B **¡Socorro! (*Help!*)**   En el trabajo surgen (*arise*) situaciones urgentes. Responde de una manera apropiada a las urgencias que te presenta tu compañero/a.

MODELO: ESTUDIANTE A: *La reunión es ahora, pero no hay café.*
ESTUDIANTE B: ¡(Llamar) al restaurante ahora mismo! *¡Llama al restaurante ahora mismo!*

Estudiante B:

Mis situaciones urgentes:	Posibles soluciones para mi compañero/a:
1. El gerente quiere el informe rápidamente.	• ¡(Apagarlo) ahora mismo!
2. El secretario pide seis semanas de vacaciones inmediatamente.	• ¡(Ponerte) traje mañana!
3. Hay agua por todas partes en el baño.	• ¡(No dársela) nunca!
4. La contadora dice que hay una gran discrepancia en nuestra cuenta.	• ¡(Decirle) que no puede trabajar en mi oficina ahora!
5. Necesitamos un intérprete para los invitados de China.	• ¡(Decirle) al electricista que venga enseguida!

 11-30B **Lo que quiero.**   Háganse y contesten preguntas sobre qué tipo de cosa, persona o lugar buscan.

MODELO: carro
ESTUDIANTE A: *¿Qué tipo de carro buscas?*
ESTUDIANTE B: *Busco un carro que tenga cuatro puertas y que sea rojo.*

Estudiante B:

Mis preguntas:	Mis respuestas:
1. puesto	• no *empezar* hasta las diez de la mañana
2. película	• *tener* un lago para pescar y una playa bonita
3. sueldo	• *tener* buenos actores y poca violencia
4. apartamento	• no *cerrarse* hasta la medianoche
5. periódico	• *tener* una bella vista de las montañas

CAPÍTULO 12

12-6B **Un producto innovador.**   Cada uno de ustedes tiene anuncios para dos aparatos nuevos, pero les falta alguna información. Háganse preguntas para completar la información y luego, decidan cuál desean comprar según sus características y su costo.

Posibles preguntas:

¿Cuántos/as...?   ¿Hay ....?
¿Qué tipo de ...?   ¿Cómo es/son ...?

MODELO: ESTUDIANTE A: *El aparato "Mora" puede contener 7.000 canciones. ¿Cuántos gigabytes de memoria tiene?*
ESTUDIANTE B: ...

Estudiante B:

	Aparato "Mora"	Aparato "Fresa"
Memoria	32 gigabytes	
Características		40.000 canciones
	40 horas de video	
		Auriculares con mando remoto y micrófono
Velocidad	Más rápido que el modelo original	
Fecha de envío (*shipping*)		en 24 horas
Costo de envío	$10	
Regalo extra		Antes del 31 de diciembre bajar gratis 100 canciones
Costo	$269	

12-28B ¿Qué harás? Túrnense para preguntarse qué harán en estas circunstancias.

MODELO: ESTUDIANTE A: *Acabas de comprar un DVD nuevo.*
ESTUDIANTE B: (**ponerlo** en tu lector de DVD para verlo) *Lo pondré en mi lector de DVD para verlo.*

Estudiante B:

Las circunstancias de mi compañero/a	Lo que haré yo
1. Hay un aparato nuevo e innovador que no tienes.	• **hacer** planes para el futuro con esa persona
2. Has organizado un grupo para reciclar envases y papel.	• **bajar** un programa antivirus de la Internet
3. Has encontrado un anuncio para un buen empleo.	• **buscar** uno por un precio razonable
4. Tienes que terminar una tarea importante para mañana.	• **volver** a casa hasta que encuentre trabajo

12-31B Soledad O'Brien. Soledad O'Brien ha sido premiada por sus documentales en CNN. Eres el/la jefe/a de una planta nuclear y la asistente de Soledad O'Brien te entrevista sobre algunos problemas en tu planta nuclear. Contesta sus preguntas con la información que tienes.

MODELO: **reciclar** los desechos de su planta
ESTUDIANTE A: *Usted dijo que reciclaría los desechos de su planta...*
ESTUDIANTE B: *Es verdad. Pero también dije que este proyecto tomaría su tiempo.*
ESTUDIANTE A: *Es verdad, pero...*

Estudiante B:

Respuestas del/de la jefe/a
Yo dije que...
1. **implementar** todos los cambios para el año 2015   4. **tener** que conseguir nueva maquinaria
2. **hacerlo** en colaboración con el estado   5. **necesitar** la ayuda de la comunidad
3. **ser** difícil hacerlo en menos de un año   6. **poder** filmar en cualquier momento

CAPÍTULO 13

 13-10B Cuando eran más jóvenes.   Túrnense para hacer y contestar las preguntas sobre lo que sus padres les permitían o les prohibían que hicieran cuando eran más jóvenes. Usen el imperfecto de subjuntivo en sus respuestas.

MODELO: ESTUDIANTE A: *¿Qué querían tus padres que hicieras los fines de semana?*
ESTUDIANTE B: *Querían que yo limpiara mi cuarto.*

Estudiante B:

Mis preguntas	Posibles respuestas a las preguntas de mi compañero/a
1. ¿Qué esperaban que leyeras en la Internet?	• mis tareas
2. ¿Qué sitios te prohibían que visitaras en la Internet?	• solo libros serios
3. ¿Qué carrera sugirieron que hicieras en la universidad?	• salir solo/a
4. ¿Qué deseaban que escucharas en la radio?	• solo los programas educativos

 13-34B ¿Qué harías si…?   Túrnense para reflexionar sobre lo que harían en estas situaciones hipotéticas.

MODELO: subir los precios de las entradas del cine
ESTUDIANTE A: *¿Qué harías si subieran los precios de las entradas del cine?*
ESTUDIANTE B: *Pues, iría menos…*

Estudiante B:

Mis preguntas	Posibles respuestas a las preguntas de mi compañero/a
¿Qué harías si…?	• **consultar** a un amigo que sabe mucho sobre aparatos electrónicos
1. (yo) no **tener** dinero para ir a un concierto	• **ir,** sin duda
2. (tú) **tener** dos entradas para el teatro	• **pedirle** su autógrafo
3. (tú) **tener** la oportunidad de participar como extra en una película	• **invitar** a todos mis amigos a cenar
4. **llamarte** una estrella de cine	• **visitar** el Teatro Chino *Grauman*
5. alguien **ofrecerte** un millón de dólares por una novela que escribiste	

CAPÍTULO 14

 14-8B ¿Cuánto tiempo hace que…?   A continuación tienen información sobre dos famosos artistas hispanos en el mundo del jazz.

Paso 1   Háganse y contesten preguntas sobre cuánto tiempo hace que participan en su arte o que hicieron algunas actividades en el pasado. Tomen apuntes de la información sobre los dos artistas.

MODELOS: Miguel Zenón estudia jazz desde 1995
ESTUDIANTE A: *¿Cuánto tiempo hace que Miguel Zenón estudia jazz?*
ESTUDIANTE B: *Hace … años que lo estudia. Empezó en 1995.*

Dafnis Prieto hizo su última gira por Europa en 1999

ESTUDIANTE B: *¿Cuánto tiempo hace que Dafnis Prieto hizo una gira por Europa?*

ESTUDIANTE A: *Hace… años que hizo una gira. Fue en 1999.*

Estudiante B:

Miguel Zenón

Dafnis Prieto

Perfil de Miguel Zenón:	Preguntas sobre Dafnis Prieto:
• Profesión: saxofonista y percusionista de jazz	¿Cuál es la profesión de Dafnis Prieto?
• Lugar/fecha de nacimiento: Puerto Rico/ 1976	¿Cuántos años hace que nació? ¿Dónde nació?
• recibió el premio Guggenheim en 2008; el MacArthur Genius Award en 2008	¿Cuántos años hace que decidió salir de Cuba?
• participa en el conjunto SF Jazz Collective desde 2004	¿Cuántos años hace que llegó a Nueva York?
• hizo una gira por África: 2003	¿Cuántos años hace que tocó en el MOMA?
• fue nombrado el mejor artista de jazz por la revista *Jazz Times* en 2006	¿Cuántos años hace que le gusta vivir en Nueva York?
• fue nominado al Grammy en 2009; 2010	¿Cuántos años hace que fue nominado al Grammy Latino?
• es profesor de música en el Conservatorio de New England desde 2009	¿Cuántos años hace que da clases? ¿Dónde?

CAPÍTULO 15

 15-20B **Una entrevista a un/a candidato/a.** Eres reportero/a y tu compañero/a es candidato/a en las próximas elecciones municipales. Trata de conseguir toda la información posible sobre su plataforma a la vez que contestas sus preguntas.

Estudiante B:

1. ¿Cómo piensa usted resolver el problema de la economía en su distrito?
2. ¿Nos puede explicar su posición sobre el seguro social?
3. ¿Quién será responsable de administrar las donaciones a su campaña?
4. ¿Cómo va a resolver el tráfico de drogas en esta ciudad?
5. ¿Por qué quiere usted ser candidato/a?

Appendix 2

EXPANSIÓN GRAMATICAL

The ***Expansión gramatical*** appendix includes grammar points that were included as part of the chapter content in the fifth edition of *¡Arriba!* By moving them to the newly created appendix, we lighten the grammar load in **Capítulos 10** through **15,** and are able to include more language input to reinforce and expand students' lexicon and cultural understanding. Furthermore, these grammar points are less frequent in everyday speech; therefore, we do not compromise students' communicative abilities by placing them in the appendix.

The explanation and activities in this section use the same format used throughout the text in **¡Así lo hacemos!** in order to facilitate their incorporation into the core lessons of the program. Additional practice activities are available in the Student Activities Manual in the Appendix.

These grammar points along with their corresponding communicative objectives include:

1. Indirect commands (Making suggestions indirectly)

2. The present perfect subjunctive (Expressing opinions about what **has** happened)

3. The future perfect and the conditional perfect (Talking about what **will** have happened in the future and what **would** have happened in the past)

4. The pluperfect subjunctive and the conditional perfect (Conjecturing about what **would have** been if something different **had happened**)

5. The passive voice (Relating what is or was caused by someone or something)

1. Indirect commands

Commands may be expressed indirectly, either to the person with whom you are speaking or to express what a third party should do.

- The basic format of an indirect command is as follows.

Que + *subjunctive verb* (+ *subject*)

¿Quién va a llamar al Dr. Estrada?	*Who is going to call Dr. Estrada?*
Que lo **llames** tú.	*You call him.*
Que lo **haga** Alicia.	*Let (Have) Alicia do it.*
Que no me **moleste** más el enfermero.	*Have the nurse not bother me anymore.*

Que le pongan una inyección.

Que le saquen una radiografía.

Que le receten antibióticos.

- This construction is also used to express your wishes for someone else.

¡Que no **te duela** la garganta mañana!	*I hope that your throat doesn't hurt you tomorrow!*

- Object and reflexive pronouns always precede the verb. In a negative statement, **no** also precedes the verb.

¡Que **se** vayan!	*Let them leave!*
¡Que papá **no se** tome la presión después de comer!	*Don't let Dad take his blood pressure after eating!*

- When a subject is expressed, it generally follows the verb.

¡Que lo hagas **tú!**	*You do it!*
¿La inyección? Que se la ponga **la enfermera.**	*The shot? Let the nurse give it to him.*

APLICACIÓN

EG-1 Viracocha, el dios creador. Según la mitología inca, Viracocha, el dios supremo, creó el mundo y a los seres humanos.

Paso 1 Lee el monólogo de Viracocha y subraya todos sus deseos expresados con mandatos indirectos. Luego escribe el infinitivo del verbo.

MODELO: ¡Que _haya_ luz!
        haber

Hoy voy a crear el mundo y a sus habitantes. Que se abran las aguas y que surjan[1] montañas además de los llanos[2]. Que aparezcan los pájaros en el aire, los animales en la tierra y toda clase de insectos. Que se creen el sol y la luna, el hombre y la mujer, y que ellos procreen hijos. Que salga el sol, que llueva mucho y que crezcan los alimentos en abundancia. Que no haya guerra y que reine la paz por todo el mundo.

---

[1]*rise* [2]*plains*

Paso 2 Ahora, escribe cuatro de los deseos de Viracocha.

MODELO: *Quiere que se abran las aguas.*

EG-2 ¿Y tú? Escribe cinco mandatos indirectos que representen tus deseos para el futuro.

MODELO: *Que tenga éxito en los exámenes.*

Espero que hayas buscado trabajo hoy.

2. The present perfect subjunctive

EG-05 to EG-09

- The present perfect subjunctive is formed with the present subjunctive of the auxiliary verb **haber** + the past participle.

	Present subjunctive of *haber*	Past participle
yo	**haya**	
tú	**hayas**	
Ud.	**haya**	
él/ella	**haya**	tomado
nosotros/as	**hayamos**	comido
vosotros/as	**hayáis**	vivido
Uds.	**hayan**	
ellos/as	**hayan**	

- The present perfect subjunctive, like the present subjunctive, is used when the main clause expresses a wish, emotion, doubt, denial, etc. pertaining to the subject of another clause. Generally, the verb in the main clause is in the present tense.

Dudamos que Antonio Villaraigosa **haya sido** nominado para gobernador.

We doubt that Antonio Villaraigosa has been nominated for governor.

Espero que el teléfono celular **haya funcionado** bien.

I hope that the cellular phone has worked well.

APLICACIÓN

EG-3 Un comité de búsqueda (*search*). La empresa Ecomundo fabrica productos para conservar el medio ambiente. Cuatro ejecutivos de la empresa conversan sobre los candidatos al puesto de ingeniero del medio ambiente que necesitan. Primero subraya los verbos en el presente perfecto y luego explica por qué se usa el indicativo o el subjuntivo.

MODELO: Espero que <u>hayamos recibido</u> suficientes solicitudes para el puesto.
Se usa el subjuntivo después de un verbo de emoción cuando hay un cambio de sujeto en los verbos.

RAMÓN: Aquí tienen todas las solicitudes que han llegado hasta hoy. Ojalá que hayan solicitado los mejores candidatos.

CARIDAD: Hemos recibido más de 20 solicitudes. ¿Quiénes han tenido tiempo para leerlas todas?

RAMÓN: Yo he leído 10, pero hay pocas que me han impresionado tanto como la que leí ayer por la tarde de Gabriela González.

CLEMENCIA: Yo creo que Gabriela González es un buen ejemplo. Es una ingeniera que ha sobresalido[1] en sus estudios y ha tenido mucho éxito en su carrera. Pero ya tiene un buen trabajo y realmente dudo que ella haya solicitado este puesto en serio.

URBANO: Bueno, vamos a entrevistar a los cinco mejores candidatos, a menos que ustedes hayan identificado a otros.

CARIDAD: De acuerdo. Creo que los mejores ya han presentado sus solicitudes. Vamos a cerrar la búsqueda para identificar a los finalistas. ¿Les parece bien?

---

[1]*excelled*

EG-4 Gabriela decide solicitar el puesto. Aunque Gabriela ya tiene un buen puesto con otra empresa, ha decidido solicitar el puesto de ingeniero del medio ambiente. Esa noche, Gabriela le cuenta a su amigo sobre la entrevista con Ecomundo. Empareja las frases para completarlas de una manera lógica.

MODELO: Gabriela: *Espero que les haya gustado mi currículum vítae.*

SAÚL:	No hay duda que...	• he aprendido mucho en esta entrevista.
GABRIELA:	Ojalá que...	• les has impresionado favorablemente.
SAÚL:	Es bueno que...	• hayan pasado varios días.
GABRIELA:	No los llamo hasta que...	• no te hayan avisado de inmediato.
SAÚL:	Es una lástima que...	• no hayan contratado a otro candidato.
GABRIELA:	Es cierto que...	• hayas tenido mucha experiencia.

EG-5 En su experiencia. Usen expresiones como: **es necesario, es bueno, es malo, es lógico** o **es excepcional,** para decir algo que hayan hecho antes de su primera entrevista para un trabajo.

MODELO: Es bueno que... (yo) *haya investigado sobre esa empresa.*

1. Es verdad que...
2. Es malo que...
3. Es cierto que...
4. Es necesario que...
5. Es verdad que...

3. The future perfect and the conditional perfect

El futuro perfecto

The future perfect is formed with the future of the auxiliary verb **haber** + *past participle*.

> Para el próximo año, habrán producido más películas con actores hispanos.

	Future	Past participle
yo	**habré**	
tú	**habrás**	
Ud.	**habrá**	
él/ella	**habrá**	tomado
		comido
nosotros/as	**habremos**	vivido
vosotros/as	**habréis**	
Uds.	**habrán**	
ellos/as	**habrán**	

- The future perfect is used to express an action which will have occurred by a certain point.

¿**Habrá hecho** Salma Hayek otra película para el año que viene?	*Will Salma Hayek have made another film by next year?*
Sí, **habrá hecho** dos.	*Yes, she will have made two.*
¿Cuándo **habrás terminado** el editorial?	*When will you have finished the editorial?*
Lo **habré terminado** en diez minutos.	*I will have finished it in ten minutes.*

El condicional perfecto

> Habría podido bailar toda la noche.

- The conditional perfect is formed with the conditional of the auxiliary verb **haber** + *past participle*.

	Conditional	Past participle
yo	**habría**	
tú	**habrías**	
Ud.	**habría**	
él/ella	**habría**	tomado
		comido
nosotros/as	**habríamos**	vivido
vosotros/as	**habríais**	
Uds.	**habrían**	
ellos/as	**habrían**	

- The conditional perfect is used to express an action that would or should have occurred but did not.

Habría visto el drama, pero preferí la comedia.	*I would have seen the drama, but I preferred the comedy.*
Habríamos grabado el programa, pero no teníamos cinta.	*We would have recorded the program, but we didn't have a tape.*

APLICACIÓN

EG-6 ¿Qué habrá pasado?   Expresa tus conjeturas sobre las situaciones siguientes.

MODELO: En el teatro todos están aplaudiendo.
> *Habrá terminado la obra.*

1. _____ El dramaturgo está muy frustrado.
2. _____ El director está enojado.
3. _____ El galán está muy triste.
4. _____ El actor no está en su camerino (*dressing room*).
5. _____ El protagonista está en el suelo.
6. _____ La televidente está muy contenta.

a. Habrá descubierto que tiene canas (*gray hair*).
b. Le habrá gustado el programa que veía.
c. Habrá terminado de vestirse.
d. Los actores no habrán memorizado el guión.
e. Habrá perdido el guión de la obra.
f. Alguien lo habrá asesinado.

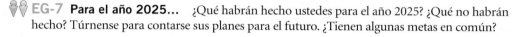

EG-7 Para el año 2025...   ¿Qué habrán hecho ustedes para el año 2025? ¿Qué no habrán hecho? Túrnense para contarse sus planes para el futuro. ¿Tienen algunas metas en común?

aprender	conseguir	escribir	terminar	visitar
conocer	empezar	ganar	trabajar	vivir

MODELO: terminar
> E1: *Para el año 2025 habré terminado mis estudios.*
> E2: *¿Sí? ¿En qué?*

EG-8 Habría hecho algo diferente.   Conversen entre ustedes para decidir cómo habría sido diferente sus vidas en las siguientes situaciones.

MODELO: tener mucho dinero
> E1: *Habría viajado por todo el mundo antes de empezar mis estudios.*
> E2: *Habría dejado mi puesto.*

1. vivir en España
2. ser actor/actriz
3. ser periodista
4. trabajar en un teatro
5. escribir drama
6. ser presentador/a
7. ser rico/a
8. ver a Jorge Ramos o a Soledad O'Brian en la calle

4. The pluperfect subjunctive and the conditional perfect

EG-15 to EG-21

El pluscuamperfecto del subjuntivo

* The pluperfect subjunctive is formed with the imperfect subjunctive of the auxiliary verb **haber** + *the past participle.*

	Imperfect subjunctive	Past participle
yo	**hubiera**	
tú	**hubieras**	
Ud.	**hubiera**	
él/ella	**hubiera**	tomado
		comido
nosotros/as	**hubiéramos**	vivido
vosotros/as	**hubierais**	
Uds.	**hubieran**	
ellos/as	**hubieran**	

* The pluperfect subjunctive is used in dependent clauses under the same conditions as the present perfect subjunctive. However, the pluperfect subjunctive is used to refer to an event prior to another past event. Compare the following sentences with the time line.

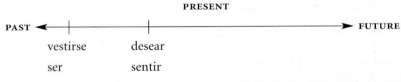

PRESENT

PAST ← | | → **FUTURE**

vestirse   desear

ser   sentir

Deseaba que su novio se **hubiera vestido** mejor para la fiesta.	*She wished that her boyfriend had dressed better for the party.*
Sentíamos que el desfile de moda **hubiera sido** tan malo.	*We were sorry that the fashion show had been so bad.*

Si me hubieras presentado antes a tu hermana, habría podido bailar con ella.

El condicional perfecto y el pluscuamperfecto de subjuntivo

The conditional perfect and pluperfect subjunctive are used in **si** clauses that express contrary-to-fact information that occurred before another point in the past. In the following example, the point in the past is probably the day of the concert or ticketed event. Before then, the problem was not explained, and the speaker did not look for other tickets.

Si me **hubieras explicado** el problema con las entradas, **habría buscado** otras.	*If you had explained to me the problem with the tickets, I would have looked for others.*

* The pluperfect subjunctive can also be used with **Ojalá** to express a contrary-to-fact situation that has already happened.

Ojalá hubieras conocido al cantante después del concierto.	*I wish you had met the singer after the concert.*
Ojalá no **hubieran cancelado** el baile.	*I wish they hadn't cancelled the dance.*

APLICACIÓN

EG-9 Si hubiera sabido...   Lee la conversación entre la directora y los miembros de la orquesta y subraya el pluscuamperfecto del subjuntivo y el condicional perfecto.

DIRECTORA: Vamos a empezar la pieza de Manuel de Falla, uno... dos... y...

VIOLINISTA: Disculpe, maestra. Si hubiera sabido que íbamos a ensayar esa pieza, habría traído la partitura[1].

CHELISTA: Sí, maestra. Yo también habría practicado más, si usted nos hubiera informado que íbamos a ensayar esa pieza hoy.

PERCUSIONISTA: Disculpe, maestra. Se me rompió un palillo[2]. Si no se me hubiera roto, habría estado mejor preparado para el ensayo.

CLARINETISTA: Maestra, si no hubiera perdido mi clarinete, habría llegado a tiempo para el ensayo.

DIRECTORA: Entonces, no vamos a ensayar. Si los organizadores me hubieran dicho que ustedes estaban tan mal preparados, nunca habría aceptado este puesto.

TROMPETISTA: Maestra, no importa. ¡Toquemos la pieza, por favor!

---

[1]*sheet music* [2]*stick*

EG-10 ¿Por qué le fue mal a la directora?   Vuelve a leer la conversación de la actividad EG-9 y explica por qué todo le salió mal a la directora.

MODELO: *La violinista... no sabía que debía traer la partitura.*

El chelista...

La clarinetista...

A la percusionista...

La directora...

EG-11 El desfile de modas en Caracas, Venezuela.   Explica qué habría sido diferente durante un desfile de modas que tuvo lugar en Caracas, según la información siguiente.

MODELO: Las modelos no llegaron a tiempo porque hubo un atasco (*traffic jam*) en la carretera.
Las modelos habrían llegado a tiempo si no hubiera habido un atasco.

1. No tuvimos asientos porque no planearon las cosas bien.
2. Muchas personas se enojaron porque no pudieron entrar a la casa de diseños.
3. El conjunto musical estaba tenso porque no había ensayado en ese lugar.
4. El público se quejó porque no había champán durante el desfile de modas.
5. No había suficientes programas para todos porque muchos se mojaron por la lluvia.
6. La casa de diseños perdió mucho dinero porque no pudieron vender todos los diseños.

EG-12 ¡Ojalá!   Túrnense para explicar momentos incómodos o vergonzosos (*embarrassing*) que tuvieron en el pasado. Su compañero/a debe hacer un comentario, usando **Ojalá** para expresar compasión por algo que les ocurrió en el pasado.

MODELO: E1: *Me puse el mismo vestido que otra estudiante para el baile formal de la universidad.*
E2: *¡Ojalá no te hubieras puesto ese vestido!*

📖 5. The passive voice

EG-22 to EG-26

La pirámide fue construida por los mayas en . . .

Spanish and English both have active and passive voices. In an active voice construction, the subject of the sentence is the doer of the action.

Óscar Arias fundó el Centro para la Paz.	*Óscar Arias founded the Center for Peace.*
Los dos bandos hicieron la guerra.	*The two sides waged war.*

- In the passive voice, the agent of the action can be expressed in a prepositional phrase most often introduced by **por.**

El Centro para la Paz fue fundado **por** Óscar Arias.	*The Center for Peace was founded by Óscar Arias.*
La guerra fue hecha **por** los dos bandos.	*The war was waged by the two sides.*

- The passive voice construction in Spanish is very similar to that in English. The direct object of the active sentence becomes the subject of the verb **ser. Ser** is followed by the *past participle* of the active verb. The past participle agrees in gender and number with the subject because it is used as an adjective.

ACTIVE VOICE

El congreso **aprobó la abolición** del ejército panameño en 1994.	*The congress approved the abolition of the Panamanian army in 1994.*

PASSIVE VOICE

La abolición del ejército panameño **fue aprobada** por el Congreso en 1994.	*The abolition of the Panamanian army was approved by Congress in 1994.*

ACTIVE VOICE

La sociedad civil **ha tratado** muy mal a **las mujeres** centroamericanas.	*Civil society has treated Central American women very poorly.*

PASSIVE VOICE

Las mujeres centroamericanas **han sido tratadas** muy mal por la sociedad civil.	*Central American women have been treated very poorly by civil society.*

- Generally the passive voice is used less frequently in spoken language in Spanish than in written narratives and documents.

APLICACIÓN

EG-13 **Botero lleva "la violencia" a Panamá.** Hubo una exposición importante del pintor colombiano Fernando Botero.

Paso 1 Lee el artículo y subraya las oraciones en voz pasiva y explica en cada caso quién hizo (**H**) la acción y quién(es) la recibieron (**R**).

MODELO: *La exposición fue organizada por la directora del museo.*

> *H: la directora; R: La exposición*

Una exposición del pintor colombiano se inauguró la semana pasada

PANAMÁ – Una exposicón de 50 pinturas y dibujos del pintor colombiano Fernando Botero fue inaugurada por el Museo de Arte Contemporáneo de Panamá, en la que el drama de la violencia en Colombia es expresado por hombres y mujeres gordos.

La colección *La violencia en Colombia* está compuesta por 23 óleos y 27 dibujos que Botero donó al Museo Nacional de Colombia. La colección fue traída al país por la galerista Carmen Alemán. Ella comentó que era la primera vez que se exhibían obras de Botero en Panamá.

El Museo de Arte Contemporáneo tuvo que hacer cambios relativos a la humedad, aire acondicionado, iluminación y reforzar el sistema de seguridad para albergar la obra de Botero, que se exhibirá hasta el 30 de abril.

La colección ya fue llevada por los organizadores a ciudades colombianas como Barranquilla, Manizales y Medellín, así como a Quito, Ecuador.

Paso 2 Ahora contesta las siguientes preguntas.

1. ¿Qué se organizó?
2. ¿Dónde tuvo lugar?
3. ¿Quién es Fernando Botero?
4. ¿Cuál es el tema de la exposición?
5. ¿Cómo son las personas representadas?
6. ¿Has visto otras piezas de Botero? ¿Cuál era el tema?

EG-14 **La guía del Palacio de la Moneda.** Completa las siguientes oraciones de la guía del Palacio de la Moneda (el palacio presidencial) de Chile con la construcción pasiva. Usa el pretérito del verbo **ser.**

MODELO: El Palacio de la Moneda (visitar) *fue visitado por* miles de turistas el año pasado.

1. Estos retratos (pintar) _____ grandes pintores.
2. Estos muebles (hacer) _____ un famoso diseñador del siglo XIX.
3. Estos libros (escribir) _____ escritores españoles.
4. Esta carta (firmar) _____ Sebastián Piñera.
5. Este discurso (escribir) _____ Salvador Allende.
6. Estos platos (regalar) _____ el rey de España.

EG-15 **En tu ciudad.** Escribe una guía de tu ciudad o de otra ciudad interesante en la que incluyas cinco lugares de interés. Usa la voz pasiva para contestar estas preguntas. Preséntale tu guía a la clase.

1. ¿Por quién fue diseñado/a (construido/a)?
2. ¿Para quién(es) fue construido/a?
3. ¿Por cuántas personas es visitado/a cada año?
4. ¿Es conocido/a en otras partes?

VERB CHARTS

Regular Verbs: Simple Tenses

Infinitive Present Participle Past Participle	Indicative					Subjunctive		Imperative
	Present	Imperfect	Preterit	Future	Conditional	Present	Imperfect	Commands
hablar hablando hablado	hablo hablas habla hablamos habláis hablan	hablaba hablabas hablaba hablábamos hablabais hablaban	hablé hablaste habló hablamos hablasteis hablaron	hablaré hablarás hablará hablaremos hablaréis hablarán	hablaría hablarías hablaría hablaríamos hablaríais hablarían	hable hables hable hablemos habléis hablen	hablara hablaras hablara habláramos hablarais hablaran	habla (tú), no hables hable (usted) hablemos hablad (vosotros), no habléis hablen (Uds.)
comer comiendo comido	como comes come comemos coméis comen	comía comías comía comíamos comíais comían	comí comiste comió comimos comisteis comieron	comeré comerás comerá comeremos comeréis comerán	comería comerías comería comeríamos comeríais comerían	coma comas coma comamos comáis coman	comiera comieras comiera comiéramos comierais comieran	come (tú), no comas coma (usted) comamos comed (vosotros), no comáis coman (Uds.)
vivir viviendo vivido	vivo vives vive vivimos vivís viven	vivía vivías vivía vivíamos vivíais vivían	viví viviste vivió vivimos vivisteis vivieron	viviré vivirás vivirá viviremos viviréis vivirán	viviría vivirías viviría viviríamos viviríais vivirían	viva vivas viva vivamos viváis vivan	viviera vivieras viviera viviéramos vivierais vivieran	vive (tú), no vivas viva (usted) vivamos vivid (vosotros), no viváis vivan (Uds.)

Regular Verbs: Perfect Tenses

	Indicative					Subjunctive	
	Present Perfect	Past Perfect	Preterit Perfect	Future Perfect	Conditional Perfect	Present Perfect	Past Perfect
he has ha hemos habéis han	hablado comido vivido	había habías había habíamos habíais habían hablado comido vivido	hube hubiste hubo hubimos hubisteis hubieron hablado comido vivido	habré habrás habrá habremos habréis habrán hablado comido vivido	habría habrías habría habríamos habríais habrían hablado comido vivido	haya hayas haya hayamos hayáis hayan hablado comido vivido	hubiera hubieras hubiera hubiéramos hubierais hubieran hablado comido vivido

Irregular Verbs

Infinitive Present Participle Past Participle	Indicative					Subjunctive		Imperative
	Present	Imperfect	Preterit	Future	Conditional	Present	Imperfect	Commands
andar andando andado	ando andas anda andamos andáis andan	andaba andabas andaba andábamos andabais andaban	anduve anduviste anduvo anduvimos anduvisteis anduvieron	andaré andarás andará andaremos andaréis andarán	andaría andarías andaría andaríamos andaríais andarían	ande andes ande andemos andéis anden	anduviera anduvieras anduviera anduviéramos anduvierais anduvieran	anda (tú), no andes ande (usted) andemos andad (vosotros), no andéis anden (Uds.)
caer cayendo caído	caigo caes cae caemos caéis caen	caía caías caía caíamos caíais caían	caí caíste cayó caímos caísteis cayeron	caeré caerás caerá caeremos caeréis caerán	caería caerías caería caeríamos caeríais caerían	caiga caigas caiga caigamos caigáis caigan	cayera cayeras cayera cayéramos cayerais cayeran	cae (tú), no caigas caiga (usted) caigamos caed (vosotros), no caigáis caigan (Uds.)
dar dando dado	doy das da damos dais dan	daba dabas daba dábamos dabais daban	di diste dio dimos disteis dieron	daré darás dará daremos daréis darán	daría darías daría daríamos daríais darían	dé des dé demos deis den	diera dieras diera diéramos dierais dieran	da (tú), no des dé (usted) demos dad (vosotros), no deis den (Uds.)
decir diciendo dicho	digo dices dice decimos decís dicen	decía decías decía decíamos decíais decían	dije dijiste dijo dijimos dijisteis dijeron	diré dirás dirá diremos diréis dirán	diría dirías diría diríamos diríais dirían	diga digas diga digamos digáis digan	dijera dijeras dijera dijéramos dijerais dijeran	di (tú), no digas diga (usted) digamos decid (vosotros), no digáis digan (Uds.)

Irregular Verbs (continued)

Infinitive / Present Participle / Past Participle	Indicative Present	Imperfect	Preterit	Future	Conditional	Subjunctive Present	Imperfect	Imperative Commands
estar estando estado	estoy estás está estamos estáis están	estaba estabas estaba estábamos estabais estaban	estuve estuviste estuvo estuvimos estuvisteis estuvieron	estaré estarás estará estaremos estaréis estarán	estaría estarías estaría estaríamos estaríais estarían	esté estés esté estemos estéis estén	estuviera estuvieras estuviera estuviéramos estuvierais estuvieran	está (tú), no estés esté (usted) estemos estad (vosotros), no estéis estén (Uds.)
haber habiendo habido	he has ha hemos habéis han	había habías había habíamos habíais habían	hube hubiste hubo hubimos hubisteis hubieron	habré habrás habrá habremos habréis habrán	habría habrías habría habríamos habríais habrían	haya hayas haya hayamos hayáis hayan	hubiera hubieras hubiera hubiéramos hubierais hubieran	
hacer haciendo hecho	hago haces hace hacemos hacéis hacen	hacía hacías hacía hacíamos hacíais hacían	hice hiciste hizo hicimos hicisteis hicieron	haré harás hará haremos haréis harán	haría harías haría haríamos haríais harían	haga hagas haga hagamos hagáis hagan	hiciera hicieras hiciera hiciéramos hicierais hicieran	haz (tú), no hagas haga (usted) hagamos haced (vosotros), no hagáis hagan (Uds.)
ir yendo ido	voy vas va vamos vais van	iba ibas iba íbamos ibais iban	fui fuiste fue fuimos fuisteis fueron	iré irás irá iremos iréis irán	iría irías iría iríamos iríais irían	vaya vayas vaya vayamos vayáis vayan	fuera fueras fuera fuéramos fuerais fueran	ve (tú), no vayas vaya (usted) vamos, no vayamos id (vosotros), no vayáis vayan (Uds.)
oír oyendo oído	oigo oyes oye oímos oís oyen	oía oías oía oíamos oíais oían	oí oíste oyó oímos oísteis oyeron	oiré oirás oirá oiremos oiréis oirán	oiría oirías oiría oiríamos oiríais oirían	oiga oigas oiga oigamos oigáis oigan	oyera oyeras oyera oyéramos oyerais oyeran	oye (tú), no oigas oiga (usted) oigamos oíd (vosotros), no oigáis oigan (Uds.)

Irregular Verbs (continued)

Infinitive Present Participle Past Participle	Indicative					Subjunctive		Imperative
	Present	Imperfect	Preterit	Future	Conditional	Present	Imperfect	Commands
poder pudiendo podido	puedo puedes puede podemos podéis pueden	podía podías podía podíamos podíais podían	pude pudiste pudo pudimos pudisteis pudieron	podré podrás podrá podremos podréis podrán	podría podrías podría podríamos podríais podrían	pueda puedas pueda podamos podáis puedan	pudiera pudieras pudiera pudiéramos pudierais pudieran	
poner poniendo puesto	pongo pones pone ponemos ponéis ponen	ponía ponías ponía poníamos poníais ponían	puse pusiste puso pusimos pusisteis pusieron	pondré pondrás pondrá pondremos pondréis pondrán	pondría pondrías pondría pondríamos pondríais pondrían	ponga pongas ponga pongamos pongáis pongan	pusiera pusieras pusiera pusiéramos pusierais pusieran	pon (tú), no pongas ponga (usted) pongamos poned (vosotros), no pongáis pongan (Uds.)
querer queriendo querido	quiero quieres quiere queremos queréis quieren	quería querías quería queríamos queríais querían	quise quisiste quiso quisimos quisisteis quisieron	querré querrás querrá querremos querréis querrán	querría querrías querría querríamos querríais querrían	quiera quieras quiera queramos queráis quieran	quisiera quisieras quisiera quisiéramos quisierais quisieran	quiere (tú), no quieras quiera (usted) queramos quered (vosotros), no queráis quieran (Uds.)
saber sabiendo sabido	sé sabes sabe sabemos sabéis saben	sabía sabías sabía sabíamos sabíais sabían	supe supiste supo supimos supisteis supieron	sabré sabrás sabrá sabremos sabréis sabrán	sabría sabrías sabría sabríamos sabríais sabrían	sepa sepas sepa sepamos sepáis sepan	supiera supieras supiera supiéramos supierais supieran	sabe (tú), no sepas sepa (usted) sepamos sabed (vosotros), no sepáis sepan (Uds.)
salir saliendo salido	salgo sales sale salimos salís salen	salía salías salía salíamos salíais salían	salí saliste salió salimos salisteis salieron	saldré saldrás saldrá saldremos saldréis saldrán	saldría saldrías saldría saldríamos saldríais saldrían	salga salgas salga salgamos salgáis salgan	saliera salieras saliera saliéramos salierais salieran	sal (tú), no salgas salga (usted) salgamos salid (vosotros), no salgáis salgan (Uds.)

Irregular Verbs (continued)

Infinitive / Present Participle / Past Participle	Indicative					Subjunctive		Imperative
	Present	Imperfect	Preterit	Future	Conditional	Present	Imperfect	Commands
ser siendo sido	soy eres es somos sois son	era eras era éramos erais eran	fui fuiste fue fuimos fuisteis fueron	seré serás será seremos seréis serán	sería serías sería seríamos seríais serían	sea seas sea seamos seáis sean	fuera fueras fuera fuéramos fuerais fueran	sé (tú), no seas sea (usted) seamos sed (vosotros), no seáis sean (Uds.)
tener teniendo tenido	tengo tienes tiene tenemos tenéis tienen	tenía tenías tenía teníamos teníais tenían	tuve tuviste tuvo tuvimos tuvisteis tuvieron	tendré tendrás tendrá tendremos tendréis tendrán	tendría tendrías tendría tendríamos tendríais tendrían	tenga tengas tenga tengamos tengáis tengan	tuviera tuvieras tuviera tuviéramos tuvierais tuvieran	ten (tú), no tengas tenga (usted) tengamos tened (vosotros), no tengáis tengan (Uds.)
traer trayendo traído	traigo traes trae traemos traéis traen	traía traías traía traíamos traíais traían	traje trajiste trajo trajimos trajisteis trajeron	traeré traerás traerá traeremos traeréis traerán	traería traerías traería traeríamos traeríais traerían	traiga traigas traiga traigamos traigáis traigan	trajera trajeras trajera trajéramos trajerais trajeran	trae (tú), no traigas traiga (usted) traigamos traed (vosotros), no traigáis traigan (Uds.)
venir viniendo venido	vengo vienes viene venimos venís vienen	venía venías venía veníamos veníais venían	vine viniste vino vinimos vinisteis vinieron	vendré vendrás vendrá vendremos vendréis vendrán	vendría vendrías vendría vendríamos vendríais vendrían	venga vengas venga vengamos vengáis vengan	viniera vinieras viniera viniéramos vinierais vinieran	ven (tú), no vengas venga (usted) vengamos venid (vosotros), no vengáis vengan (Uds.)
ver viendo visto	veo ves ve vemos veis ven	veía veías veía veíamos veíais veían	vi viste vio vimos visteis vieron	veré verás verá veremos veréis verán	vería verías vería veríamos veríais verían	vea veas vea veamos veáis vean	viera vieras viera viéramos vierais vieran	ve (tú), no veas vea (usted) veamos ved (vosotros), no veáis vean (Uds.)

Stem-Changing and Orthographic-Changing Verbs

Infinitive / Present Participle / Past Participle	Indicative					Subjunctive		Imperative
	Present	Imperfect	Preterit	Future	Conditional	Present	Imperfect	Commands
almorzar (ue) (c) almorzando almorzado	almuerzo almuerzas almuerza almorzamos almorzáis almuerzan	almorzaba almorzabas almorzaba almorzábamos almorzabais almorzaban	almorcé almorzaste almorzó almorzamos almorzasteis almorzaron	almorzaré almorzarás almorzará almorzaremos almorzaréis almorzarán	almorzaría almorzarías almorzaría almorzaríamos almorzaríais almorzarían	almuerce almuerces almuerce almorcemos almorcéis almuercen	almorzara almorzaras almorzara almorzáramos almorzarais almorzaran	almuerza (tú) no almuerces almuerce (usted) almorcemos almorzad (vosotros) no almorcéis almuercen (Uds.)
buscar (qu) buscando buscado	busco buscas busca buscamos buscáis buscan	buscaba buscabas buscaba buscábamos buscabais buscaban	busqué buscaste buscó buscamos buscasteis buscaron	buscaré buscarás buscará buscaremos buscaréis buscarán	buscaría buscarías buscaría buscaríamos buscaríais buscarían	busque busques busque busquemos busquéis busquen	buscara buscaras buscara buscáramos buscarais buscaran	busca (tú) no busques busque (usted) busquemos buscad (vosotros) no busquéis busquen (Uds.)
corregir (i, i) (j) corrigiendo corregido	corrijo corriges corrige corregimos corregís corrigen	corregía corregías corregía corregíamos corregíais corregían	corregí corregiste corrigió corregimos corregisteis corrigieron	corregiré corregirás corregirá corregiremos corregiréis corregirán	corregiría corregirías corregiría corregiríamos corregiríais corregirían	corrija corrijas corrija corrijamos corrijáis corrijan	corrigiera corrigieras corrigiera corrigiéramos corrigierais corrigieran	corrige (tú) no corrijas corrija (usted) corrijamos corregid (vosotros) no corrijáis corrijan (Uds.)
dormir (ue, u) durmiendo dormido	duermo duermes duerme dormimos dormís duermen	dormía dormías dormía dormíamos dormíais dormían	dormí dormiste durmió dormimos dormisteis durmieron	dormiré dormirás dormirá dormiremos dormiréis dormirán	dormiría dormirías dormiría dormiríamos dormiríais dormirían	duerma duermas duerma durmamos durmáis duerman	durmiera durmieras durmiera durmiéramos durmierais durmieran	duerme (tú), no duermas duerma (usted) durmamos dormid (vosotros), no durmáis duerman (Uds.)
incluir (y) incluyendo incluido	incluyo incluyes incluye incluimos incluís incluyen	incluía incluías incluía incluíamos incluíais incluían	incluí incluiste incluyó incluimos incluisteis incluyeron	incluiré incluirás incluirá incluiremos incluiréis incluirán	incluiría incluirías incluiría incluiríamos incluiríais incluirían	incluya incluyas incluya incluyamos incluyáis incluyan	incluyera incluyeras incluyera incluyéramos incluyerais incluyeran	incluye (tú), no incluyas incluya (usted) incluyamos incluid (vosotros), no incluyáis incluyan (Uds.)

Stem-Changing and Orthographic-Changing Verbs (continued)

Infinitive Present Participle Past Participle	Indicative					Subjunctive		Imperative
	Present	Imperfect	Preterit	Future	Conditional	Present	Imperfect	Commands
llegar (gu) llegando llegado	llego llegas llega llegamos llegáis llegan	llegaba llegabas llegaba llegábamos llegabais llegaban	llegué llegaste llegó llegamos llegasteis llegaron	llegaré llegarás llegará llegaremos llegaréis llegarán	llegaría llegarías llegaría llegaríamos llegaríais llegarían	llegue llegues llegue lleguemos lleguéis lleguen	llegara llegaras llegara llegáramos llegarais llegaran	llega (tú), no llegues llegue (usted) lleguemos llegad (vosotros), no lleguéis lleguen (Uds.)
pedir (i, i) pidiendo pedido	pido pides pide pedimos pedís piden	pedía pedías pedía pedíamos pedíais pedían	pedí pediste pidió pedimos pedisteis pidieron	pediré pedirás pedirá pediremos pediréis pedirán	pediría pedirías pediría pediríamos pediríais pedirían	pida pidas pida pidamos pidáis pidan	pidiera pidieras pidiera pidiéramos pidierais pidieran	pide (tú), no pidas pida (usted) pidamos pedid (vosotros), no pidáis pidan (Uds.)
pensar (ie) pensando pensado	pienso piensas piensa pensamos pensáis piensan	pensaba pensabas pensaba pensábamos pensabais pensaban	pensé pensaste pensó pensamos pensasteis pensaron	pensaré pensarás pensará pensaremos pensaréis pensarán	pensaría pensarías pensaría pensaríamos pensaríais pensarían	piense pienses piense pensemos penséis piensen	pensara pensaras pensara pensáramos pensarais pensaran	piensa (tú), no pienses piense (usted) pensemos pensad (vosotros), no penséis piensen (Uds.)
producir (zc) (j) produciendo producido	produzco produces produce producimos producís producen	producía producías producía producíamos producíais producían	produje produjiste produjo produjimos produjisteis produjeron	produciré producirás producirá produciremos produciréis producirán	produciría producirías produciría produciríamos produciríais producirían	produzca produzcas produzca produzcamos produzcáis produzcan	produjera produjeras produjera produjéramos produjerais produjeran	produce (tú), no produzcas produzca (usted) produzcamos producid (vosotros), no produzcáis produzcan (Uds.)
reír (i, i) riendo reído	río ríes ríe reímos reís ríen	reía reías reía reíamos reíais reían	reí reíste rio reímos reísteis rieron	reiré reirás reirá reiremos reiréis reirán	reiría reirías reiría reiríamos reiríais reirían	ría rías ría riamos riáis rían	riera rieras riera riéramos rierais rieran	ríe (tú), no rías ría (usted) riamos reíd (vosotros), no riáis rían (Uds.)

Stem-Changing and Orthographic-Changing Verbs (continued)

Infinitive Present Participle Past Participle	Indicative						Subjunctive		Imperative
	Present	Imperfect	Preterit	Future	Conditional		Present	Imperfect	Commands
seguir (i, i) (ga) siguiendo seguido	sigo sigues sigue seguimos seguís siguen	seguía seguías seguía seguíamos seguíais seguían	seguí seguiste siguió seguimos seguisteis siguieron	seguiré seguirás seguirá seguiremos seguiréis seguirán	seguiría seguirías seguiría seguiríamos seguiríais seguirían		siga sigas siga sigamos sigáis sigan	siguiera siguieras siguiera siguiéramos siguierais siguieran	sigue (tú), no sigas siga (usted) sigamos seguid (vosotros), no sigáis sigan (Uds.)
sentir (ie, i) sintiendo sentido	siento sientes siente sentimos sentís sienten	sentía sentías sentía sentíamos sentíais sentían	sentí sentiste sintió sentimos sentisteis sintieron	sentiré sentirás sentirá sentiremos sentiréis sentirán	sentiría sentirías sentiría sentiríamos sentiríais sentirían		sienta sientas sienta sintamos sintáis sientan	sintiera sintieras sintiera sintiéramos sintierais sintieran	siente (tú), no sientas sienta (usted) sintamos sentid (vosotros), no sintáis sientan (Uds.)
volver (ue) volviendo vuelto	vuelvo vuelves vuelve volvemos volvéis vuelven	volvía volvías volvía volvíamos volvíais volvían	volví volviste volvió volvimos volvisteis volvieron	volveré volverás volverá volveremos volveréis volverán	volvería volverías volvería volveríamos volveríais volverían		vuelva vuelvas vuelva volvamos volváis vuelvan	volviera volvieras volviera volviéramos volvierais volvieran	vuelve (tú), no vuelvas vuelva (usted) volvamos volved (vosotros), no volváis vuelvan (Uds.)

Appendix 4

SPANISH-ENGLISH VOCABULARY

A

abandonar to abandon 7
abarcar to extend to 14
abogar to advocate 7
abolir to abolish 15
abordar to board 9
abrazar to embrace 10
abrazo, el hug; embrace 2
abrigo, el coat 8
abril April 1
abrir to open 1, 2, 12
abstener to abstain 9
abuelita, la grandma (*diminutive*) 4
abuelo/a, el/la grandfather/grandmother 4
abundar to abound 6
aburrido/a boring 1
aburrir to bore; to tire 6
abuso, el abuse 15
acabar (de) (+ *inf.*) to finish; to have just (done something) 5, 11, 12
académico/a academic 3
acampar to camp 5
acceder to accede 15
accessorio, el accessory 8
accidente, el accident 10
acción, la action 15
aceite (de oliva), el (olive) oil 6
aceituna, la olive 6
acelerar to accelerate 15
aceptar to accept 4
acerca de with respect to 8
acertado/a correct 12
acomodar to accommodate 5
acompañante, el/la escort; companion 7
acompañar to accompany 6
aconsejar to advise 9
acontecimiento, el event 7
acordeón, el accordion 14
acostar (ue) to put in bed 5
acostarse (ue) to go to bed 5
acostumbrar to be accustomed to 13
acostumbrarse to become accustomed 8
actividad, la activity 8
activista, el/la activist 15
activo/a active 2
actor, el actor 5
actriz, la actress 1

actual current 10, **15**
actualidad, la current events 13
actuar to act 5, **13**
acuático/a aquatic 9
acudir to present oneself 11
acueducto, el aqueducto 2
acuerdo, el accord **15**
acupuntura, la acupuncture 10
adaptador eléctrico, el electrical adaptor 9
adecuado/a adequate 7
adelgazar to lose weight 10
ademán, el gesture 11
además in addition 4, 9
Adiós. Good-bye. **1**
adivinar to guess 5
administración, la administration 2
administración de empresas, la business administration 3
admiración, la admiration 9
admirador/a, el/la admirer 9
admitir to admit 7
¿Adónde…? To where…? 2
adoptivo/a adoptive 14
adorar to adore 14
adornado/a adorned 8
adornar to adorn 9
adquirir (ie, i) to acquire 13
aduana, la customs 9
advertir (ie, i) to warn 14
aeróbico/a aerobic 10
aerolínea, la airline 9
aeropuerto, el airport **9**
afectar to affect 9
afectuoso/a affectionate 4
afeitarse to shave 5
afianzar (c) to strengthen; to fortify 15
aficionado/a, el/la fan 7
a fin de que in order that **11**
afirmación, la statement 12
afirmar to affirm 6
afrodisíaco aphrodisiac 6
afrontar to face **15**
afueras, las outskirts 9
agarrar to grab 11
agencia de viajes, la travel agency 9
agente de viajes, el/la travel agent 9
agosto August **1**

agradable agreeable 5
agradecer to thank 13
agregar to add 10
agrícola agricultural 4
agua (mineral), el (*fem.*) (mineral) water **6**
aguacate, el avocado 6
águila, el (*fem.*) eagle 12
ahora (mismo) (right) now **2**
ahorrar to save 12
aire acondicionado, el air conditioning 5
aire libre, al outside 4
ajo, el garlic 6
ajustar to adjust 11
alabanza, la praise 12
albergar to house 3
álbum, el album 5
alcalde/sa, el/la mayor **15**
alcanzable reachable 12
alcanzar to reach 2
alegrarse (de) to become happy; to be glad 5
alegrarse de to become happy; to be glad 10
alegremente happily 9
alejarse to go away 11
alemán, el German 2
alergia, la allergy 10
alérgico/a allergic 10
álgebra, el (*fem.*) algebra 3
algo something; anything 3, 6, 7
algodón, el cotton 8
alguien someone 7
algún día someday 4
alguno/a/os/as some 5, 7
alimentación, la nutrition 6
alimentar to nourish 11
alimentos, los foods 10
aliviado/a alleviated 14
aliviar to alleviate 10
allá there 9
alma, el (*fem.*) soul 8
almacén, el department store 8
almorzar (ue) to eat lunch 8
almuerzo, el lunch 2, **6**
alpinismo, el mountain climbing 6, 7
alquilar to rent 5
alquiler, el rent 15
alrededor about; around 12

alta costura, la high fashion 14
altavoz, la speaker 7
alternarse to alternate 8
altiplano, el high plateau 10
alto/a tall 2
altura, la altitude 8
aluminio, el aluminum 7
amado/a beloved 13
amanecer, el dawn 11
amante, el/la lover 6
amar to love 6
amarillo/a yellow 1
amasar to mix 10
ambiental environmental 10
ambiente, el atmosphere 6
ambigüedad, la ambiguity 11
ambulancia, la ambulance 10
a menos (de) que unless 11
americana, la blazer (Spain) 8
amigo/a, el/la friend 1
amor, el love 6
amoroso/a amorous 6
ampliar to expand 6
amplio/a wide; ample 10
amueblado/a furnished 5
añadir to add 6
análisis, el analysis 3
analista (de sistemas), el/la (systems) analyst 11
anaranjado/a orange 1
ancho/a wide 5
anciano/a, el/la old person 12
andino/a Andean 8
anécdota, la anecdote 6
anfitrión/anfitriona, el/la host/hostess 7
angosto/a narrow 12
anillo de oro, el gold ring 8
animadamente enthusiastically 9
animado/a animated 9
animal, el animal 3
animar to encourage; to cheer 3
animarse to be game 5
aniversario, el anniversary 6
año, el year 1
anoche last night 6, **8**
años, tener… to be… years old 3
anotar to note; to write down 5

ansioso/a anxious 9
ante before 7
anteayer day before yesterday 6, 8
antena parabólica, la satellite dish 12
antepasado/a, el/la ancestor 4
antes (de) before 2
antes (de) que before 11
antiácido, el antacid 10
antibiótico, el antibiotic 10
anticipación, la anticipation 9
anticipar to anticipate 8
antiguo/a ancient 3, 5
antioxidantes, los antioxidants 10
antropología, la anthropology 3
anualmente yearly 7
anudado/a knotted 15
anunciar to announce 8
anuncios clasificados, los classified ads 13
apagar (fuegos/incendios) to turn off; to put out; to extinguish (fires) 11, 12
aparato, el appliance 6
aparatos electrónicos, los electronics 12
aparecer to appear 9
aparencia, la appearance 1
aparente apparent 15
aparentemente apparently 15
apartamento, el apartment 3
apasionar to impassion 6
apellido, el surname 2
apender to learn 7
aperitivo, el appetizer 2
apetecer to feel like; to appeal to 6
aplaudir to applaud 14
apoderarse to take hold 15
apodo, el nickname 2
aporte, el contribution 15
apoyar to support 8, 15
apoyo, el support 4
apreciado/a appreciated 11
apreciar to appreciate 4
aprender to learn 2
apropriado/a appropriate 10
aprovechar to take advantage of 12
aproximadamente approximately 3
apunte, el note 5

aquel/la that (over there) 4 that one (over there) 4
aquello that (neuter) (over there) 4
aquellos/as those (over there) 4
aquí here 1
aquietar to calm down 15
árabe, el Arab; Arabic 2
araña, la spider 8
árbitro, el referee 5
árbol, el tree 4
archipiélago, el archipelago 8
archivar to file; to save 12
arco, el bow 8
arder to burn 15
ardilla, la squirrel 8
área, el (fem.) 7
arenisca, la sandstone 9
aretes (de diamantes), los (diamond) earrings 8
argentino/a Argentine 2
argumento, el argument 4
aria, el (fem.) aria 14
arma, el (fem.) weapon 15
armado/a armed 15
armar to assemble; to furnish 8
arpa, el (fem.) harp 5, 14
arqueólogo, el archeologist 8
arquitecto/a, el/la architect 2, 11
arquitectura, la architecture 7
arrancar to yank 1
arreglo, el arrangement 5
arrepentido/a repentant 10
arribada, la arrival 5
arriba de above 5
arrojar to throw 10
arroz, el rice 6
arte, el art 3
artefacto, el artifact 5
artesanía, la handicraft 3
artesano/a, el/la artisan 3
artículo, el article 7, 13
artritis, la arthritis 10
arzobispo, el archbishop 4
ascendencia, la ancestry 10
ascendente ascending 6
ascender (ie) to promote; to move up 11
asco disgust 6
asegurar to assure 5
asesinato, el murderer 15
asesor/a, el/la consultant; advisor 15
asiento (de ventanilla /de pasillo), el (window/aisle) seat 9
asistente, el/la assistant 7

asistente de vuelo, el/la flight attendant 9
asistir (a) to attend 2
asma, el (fem.) asthma 10
asociación, la association 7
asociar to associate 2
aspecto, el aspect 8
aspiración, la aspiration 15
aspiradora, la vacuum cleaner 5
aspirante, el/la job candidate 11
aspirina, la aspirin 10
asunto, el matter 15
atacar to attack 10
ataque, el attack 4
atención al cliente, la customer service 8
atentamente sincerely yours 11
aterrizar to land 9
a tiempo on time 3
atletismo, el track and field 7
atmósfera, la atmosphere 3
atracción, la attraction 9
atractivo/a attractive 3
atraer to attract 6
atrapar to trap 4
atrás behind 7
a través along 8
atrevido/a sassy; daring 12
atribuir to attribute 14
audición, la audition 14
audio parlantes, los speakers 8
auditorio, el auditorium 3
aumentar to increase 6, 15
aumento, el raise; increase 4, 6, 11
aunque although 4; even though 7
auriculares, los earbuds 12
ausente absent 15
auténtico/a authentic 14
auto, el car 9
autobiográfico autobiographical 2
autobús, el bus 5, 9
autógrafo, el autograph 14
autónomo/a autonomous 2
autor/a, el/la author 2
autoridad, la authority 14
autorretrato, el self-portrait 3
avance, el advance 3
avanzado/a advanced; advancing 3 advancted 8
ave, la bird 3
avenida, la avenue 12
aventura, la adventure 4

avergonzado/a ashamed 10
avión, el plane 9
aviso, el notice; announcement 13
avisos clasificados, los classified ads 11
ayer yesterday 6
ayuda, la help 5
ayudante, el/la assistant 6
ayudar to help 2
azúcar, el sugar 3, 6
azucena, la lily 10
azul blue 1

B
bailable danceable 9
bailar to dance 2
bailarín/a, el/la dancer 14
baile, el dance 3, 14
baile de salón, el ballroom dancing 14
bajar to decrease; to download; to lower 4, 12
bajar de peso to lose weight 10
bajarse (de) to get off (of); to get down (from) 9
bajo, el bass 3
bajo/a short (in stature) 2
balada, la ballad 13
balboa, el monetary unit of Panama 5
ballet, el ballet 1, 14
balón, el (soccer, basket) ball 7
banana, la banana 6
bañarse to bathe 5
banco, el bank; bench 8
banda, la band 4, 14
baño, el bathroom 5
banquete, el banquet 7
bar, el bar 2
barato/a cheap; inexpensive 1
barbaridad, la outrage 5
barco, el boat 5, 9
barítono/a baritone 14
barrio, el neighborhood 3
basado/a based 6
básquetbol, el basketball 5, 7
bastante quite; fairly 3
bastar to be enough 8
basurero, el garbage can 5
batalla, la battle 1
bate, el bat 7
batería, la drums 8, 14
batir to beat 6
bebida, la beverage 6
bebidas alcohólicas, las alcoholic beverages 10
béisbol, el baseball 4

beisbolista, el baseball player 2
belleza, la beauty 9
bellísimo/a really beautiful 6
bello/a beautiful 2
beneficio/s, el/los benefit/s 11
benéfico/a charitable 14
beso, el kiss 4
biblioteca, la library 2
bibliotecario/a, el/la librarian 15
bicicleta, la bicycle 2
bien well 1
bien, el good 6
bienes, los goods 5
bienes raíces, los real estate 5
bienestar, el well-being 6
bien hecho/a well made 14
bienvenida, la welcome 2
bilingüe bilingual 12
billetera, la wallet 8
biografía, la biography 2
biología, la biology 3
biológico/a biological 10
biosfera, la biosphere 3
bistec, el steak 6
blanco/a white 1
bloque, el block 8
blusa, la blouse 8
boca, la mouth 10
bocadillo, el sandwich 6
boda, la wedding 3
boicot, el boycott 15
boleto (electrónico), el (e-)ticket 3, 4, 9
bolígrafo, el pen 1
bolívar, el Colombian currency 9
bolsa, la (big) bag 7
bolso, el bag; purse 7, 8
bomba (nuclear), la (nuclear) bomb 15
bomba, la firetruck fire station (Chile); gas station (Andes) 15
bomba, ser una to be gorgeous 15
bombero/a, el/la firefighter 10, 11
bondad, la goodness 7
bonificación anual, la yearly bonus 11
bonito/a pretty; cute 2
booby con patas azules, el blue-footed booby 8
bordar to embroider 4
bordo, a aboard 6
bosque, el forest 9, 10, 12
bosque pluvial, el rain forest 12

botas, las boots 8
botella, la bottle 7
brasileño/a Brazilian 2
brazo, el arm 10
breve brief 6
brillante brilliant 3
brillar to shine 8
brillo de labios, el lip gloss 5
broma, la joke 11
bucear to scuba dive; snorkel 9
buche, el belly 8
budista Buddhist 14
Buenas noches. Good evening. 1
Buenas tardes. Good afternoon. 1
¿Bueno? Hello? (on the phone) 4
bueno… well . . . 5
bueno/a good 1, 9, 10
Buenos días. Good morning. 1
¡Buen provecho! Enjoy your meal! 6
buscador, el search engine 12, 13
buscar to look for 1, 2
búsqueda, la search 11
búsqueda de empleo, la job search 11

C
cabecear to make a head shot 7
cabeza, la head 10
cacique, el chief 9
cada each 5
cadáver, el cadaver 14
cadena (de plata), la (silver) chain 8
caerse to fall down 15
café (al aire libre), el (outdoor) café 4
café, el coffee 6
cafeína, la caffeine 6
cafetera, la coffee maker 6
cafetería, la cafeteria 2
caída, la fall 11
caja, la box; cash register 8
cajero automático, el ATM (automatic teller machine) 4, 8, 12
calabaza, la gourd; squash 11
calamar, el squid 2, 6
calavera, la skull 3
calcetines, los socks 8
calcio, el calcium 10
calculadora, la calculator 1
calcular to calculate 7

cálculo, el calculus 3
calentamiento, el warm-up 10
calentamiento global, el global warming 12
calentar (ie) to heat 6
calidad, la quality 13
caliente hot 6
calle, la street 2
calmante, el tranquilizer 10
calor, hace it is hot 7
calor, tener to be hot 3
caloría, la calorie 6
calzado, el footwear 8
calzar to wear a shoe size 8
cama, la bed 5, 10
cámara, la camera 4
cámara de video, la video camera 9
cámara digital, la digital camera 9
camarero/a, el/la waiter/waitress 6
camarones, los shrimp 6, 10
cambiar to change 4
cambio, el change; exchange 4
caminar to walk 2
camino, el path; road 2
camión, el pickup truck; van 9 truck; bus (Mexico) 8
camioneta, la pickup truck van 1
camisa, la shirt 8
camiseta (sin mangas) t-shirt (tank top) 8
campamento, el camp 9
campaña, la campaign 12, 15
campeón/campeona, el/la champion 7
campesino, el peasant; farmer 5
campo, el country 5
caña, la small beer 2; reed/ Canadá Canada 6
canadiense Canadian 2
canal, el canal; channel 13
canas, tener to be grey-haired 4
cancelar to cancel 9
cáncer, el cancer 10
cancha (de tenis), la (tennis) court 2, 3
canción, la song 2
candidato/a, el/la candidate 6, 15
cansado/a tired 4
cansancio, el fatigue 10
cansar to tire 7
cantante, el/la singer 1
cantar to sing 5

cantautor/a, el/la songwriter 2
cantero de jardín, el flower bed 14
cantidad, la quantity 6
capacidad, la capacity 11
capaz capable 11
capilla, la chapel 8
capital, la capital city 1, 2
capucha, la hood 8
cara, la face 5
carácter, el character 13
característica, la characteristic 11
carbohidratos, los carbohydrates 10
cárcel, la jail 15
cardiólogo, el cardiologist 10
cardo, el thistle/nettle 1
cargador, el charger 9
cargo, el position 11
cargo político, el political post 15
caricatura política, la political cartoon 13
cariño, con with affection 4
caritativo/a charitable 9
carnaval, el Mardi Gras 9
carne, la meat 6
carnero, el mutton 6
caro/a expensive 1
carpintero/a, el/la carpenter 1
carrera, la career 3
carro, el car 3, 9
carta comercial, la business letter 11
carta de presentación, la cover letter 11
carta de recomendación, la letter of recommendation 11
cartel, el poster 7
cartelera, la entertainment section 13
cartero/a, el/la mail carrier 11
casa, la house 4, 5
casado/a married 4
casarse to marry 4
cascadas, las cascades 9, 11
casco, el helmet; earbud 12
casi almost 10
caso, hacer to pay attention 13
castaño/a brown; brunette 2
castigar to punish 10
castillo, el castle 13
cataratas, las falls 11 waterfall 9

catedral, la cathedral 9
católico/a Catholic 9
causa, la cause 7
causar to cause 5
cavar to dig 14
caza, la hunting 10
cazuela, la stewpot; casserole 6
cebolla, la onion 3, 6
cebolleta, la shallot 6
celebración, la celebration 7
celebrar to celebrate 5
celebridad, la celebrity 7
celofán, el cellophane 14
celos, los jealousy 11
celos, tener to be jealous 11
celoso/a jealous 11
celta Celtic 2
cementerio, el cemetery 14
cena, la dinner 2, 6
cenar to have dinner 6
cenizas, las ashes 9
censo, el census 13
censura, la censorship 13
censurar to censure 13
centenares, los hundreds 4
centenario, el centennial 5
centro, el downtown 3, 4
centro comercial, el shopping center; mall 8
centro estudiantil, el student union 3
centro histórico, el historical center 9
cepillarse to brush 5
cepillo de dientes, el toothbrush 8
cerámica, la ceramic 4
cerca (de) nearby; close (to) 2
cercano/a nearby 8
cerdo, el pork 10
ceremonia, la ceremony 4
cerrado/a closed 3
cerrar (ie) to close 1
cerveza, la beer 3, 6
cesta, la basket 3
chaito chao 14
champán, el champagne 8
champú, el shampoo 5
chancla, la flip-flop 8
chaqueta, la jacket 8
charada, la charade 6
charango, el guitar-like instrument 4
chelista, el/la chellist 14
chelo, el cello 14
chévere super 7
chicano/a Mexican-American 12

chico/a, el/la boy/girl 3
chileno/a Chilean 2
chimichurri, la sauce popular in Argentina 6
chinchilla, la chinchilla 14
chino, el Chinese 2
chismoso/a gossipy 5
chispa, la spark 10
chofer, el chauffeur 11
chorizo, el sausage 2
chubasco, el heavy rain; shower 7
ciclismo, el cycling 7
cielo, el heaven; sky 8
ciencia, la science 2
ciencia ficción, la science fiction 7
ciencias políticas, las political science 3
ciencias sociales, las social science 3
científico/a, el/la scientist 1, 8
cien(to) hundred 5
cierto/a certain 10 true; certain 2
cigarra, la cricket 8
cine, el film; movie theater 2, 13
cinematografía, la cinematography 13
cinematógrafo/a, el/la cinematographer 13
ciprés, el cypress 14
circulación, la circulation 13
cita, (hacer una) (to make an) appointment 10, 11
ciudad, la city 1, 2
ciudadanía, la citizenship 12
ciudadano/a, el/la citizen 15
civilización, la civilization 3
clarinete, el clarinet 14
claro of course 4
claro/a clear; light (color) 1, 6
clase, la class 1
clase turista, la coach class 9
clásico/a classic 14 classical 4
cláusula, la clause 10
clavar to drive; to thrust 15
clave, la key 11
claxon, el horn 15
cliente, el/la client; customer 2
clima, el climate 4, 5
clínica, la clinic 11
cobardía, la cowardice 1
cobrar to charge 4
cobre, el copper 6
coche, el car 9
cochinillo, el suckling pig 8

cocina, la cuisine; kitchen 3 kitchen 5
cocinar to cook 6
cocinero/a, el/la chef; cook 6, 11
coco, el coconut 6
cocodrilo, el crocodile 9
codazo, el elbow jabs 15
codicia, la greed 10
código, el code 15
coincidir to coincide 13
cola, hacer to stand in line 9
cola, la line 9
colaborar to collaborate 9
colección, la collection 3
colega, el/la colleague 11
cólera, el cholera 5
colesterol, el cholesterol 10
colgar (ue) to hang 3
collar, el necklace 8
colombiano/a Colombian 2
colonia, la colony; cologne 8
colonizador/a, el/la colonizer 9
color café, el brown 1
colorido/a brightly colored; coloring 9
combatiente, el/la combatant 4
combatir to combat 9, 15
combinación, la combination 10
comedia (musical), la (musical) comedy 4, 13, 14
comedor, el dining room 5
comentar to comment 5
comentario, el commentary 3
comentarista, el/la newscaster; commentator 7, 13
comentarista deportivo, el/la sportscaster 13
comenzar (ie) to begin 7
comer to eat 2, 6, 8, 9, 10, 11, 12
comerciar to trade 9
comercio, el commerce 3
comestibles, los provisions; groceries 9
cometer to commit 14
cómico/a comic 4
comida, la food; meal 2, 3, 4, 6
comida basura, la junk food 10
comida chatarra, la junk food 10
comienzo, el beginning 5
comisión, la fee; commission 8

comité, el committee 4
cómo how; what 1, 2
como since; as 5
¿Cómo...? How...? 2
cómoda, la dress 5 dresser 5
comodidad, la comfort 14
comodidades, las comforts 9
cómodo/a comfortable 9
¿Cómo estás? How are you? (inf.) 1
¿Cómo está usted? How are you? (for.) 1
¿Cómo se llama usted? What's your name? (for.) 1
¿Cómo se escribe...? How do you spell . . . ? 1
compañero/a de clase, el/la classmate 8
compañero/a de reparto, el/la co-star 13
compañia, la company; firm 13
comparación, la comparison 5
comparar to compare 5
compartir to share 2
compatriota, el/la compatriot 5
competir (i, i) to compete 10
complacer to please 11
complejo/a complex 10
complementar to complement 3
completo/a complete 6
complicado/a complicated 3
complicar to complicate 11
componer to compose 14
composición, la composition 2
compositor/a, el/la composer 7, 14
comprar to buy 2, 8, 9, 11
compras, ir de to go shopping 8
comprender to understand 2, 7
comprensión, la comprehension 13
comprobar (ue) to prove 15
compromiso, el commitment; obligation 7, 11
computación, la computer science 3
computadora, la computer 1, 3, 12
computadora portátil, la laptop computer 1
común common 1
comunicaciones, las communications 3
comunidad, la community 3
con with 1

con cariño with affection **4**
conceder to grant **2**
concepto, el concept **4**
concienciar al público to raise public consciousness **15**
concierto, el concert **2, 3, 4**
concordancia, la agreement **10**
concreto/a concrete **7**
concurso, el contest; game show; pageant **13**
condenado/a condemned **13**
condenar to condemn **11**
condición, la condition **5**
cóndor, el condor **8**
conducir to drive **2**
conductora, el/la conductor **15**
conectar to connect **5**
conexión, la connection **12**
confeccionar to make up **15**
conferencia, la lecture **2**
conferencia de prensa, la press conference **15**
confianza, la trust; confidence **10**
conflicto, el conflict **8, 15**
confundir to confuse **10**
congelador, el freezer **6**
congestionado/a congested **10**
congregar to gather **15**
congresista, el/la congressman/woman **15**
congreso, el congress **15**
conjetura, la conjecture **12**
conjunto, el outfit; group **4, 8, 14**
conmemorar to commemorate **3**
conmigo with me **4**
conocedor, el connoisseur **6**
conocer (zc) to know (someone); to be familiar with **4**
conocido/a known **6**
conocimiento, el knowledge **2**
conquista, la conquest **3**
consecuencias, las consequences **15**
conseguir (i, i) to get; to obtain **9, 11**
consejo, el advice **7, 10**
consenso, el consensus **14**
conservador/a conservative **13**
conservar to conserve; to preserve **7, 8, 12**
considerado/a considered; considerate **15**
considerar to consider **3**
construcción, la construction **2, 5**

construir to construct **2**
consultar to consult **9**
consultorio, el doctor's office **10**
consultorio sentimental, el advice column **13**
consumidor/a, el/la consumer **1**
consumir to consume **12**
consumo, el consumption **6**
contabilidad, la accounting **3**
contactar to contact **10**
contador/a, el/la accountant **11**
con tal (de) que provided (that) **11**
contaminación, hay there is pollution; there is smog **7**
contaminar to contaminate; to pollute **12**
contar (ue) to tell (a story) **4**
contemporáneo/a contemporaneous **6**
contenedor, el container **13**
contener (ie) to contain **3**
contenido, el content **10**
contento/a happy **5**
contestar to answer **1**
contigo with you **4**
continuación, a following **6**
continuar to continue **6**
contra, (en) against **5**
contrabajo, el bass **14**
contrario, por el on the contrary **8**
contraste, el contrast **6**
contratar to contract **13** to hire **11**
contrato, el contract **9, 11**
contribuir to contribute **9**
contrincante, el/la opponent **15**
controlar to control **13**
control de seguridad, el security checkpoint **9**
convencer to convince **2**
convencional conventional **13**
convenio, el agreement **13**
conversación, la conversation **7**
conversar to converse **3**
convertir (ie, i) to convert **9**
convicción, la conviction **15**
cooperar to cooperate **8**
coordinador/a, el/la coordinator **11**
copado/a cool **12**
copia, la copy **7**
corazón, el heart **1**
corbata, la tie **8**

cordialmente cordially yours **11**
coreano, el Korean **2**
coreografiar to choreograph **14**
coreógrafo/a, el/la choreographer **14**
corneta, la cornet **14**
corredor, el corridor **12**
correo, el mail **2**
correr to run; to fire someone (Mexico) **2**
corresponsal, el/la correspondent **12**
corriente, la electric current **9**
corrupción, la corruption **15**
cortar to cut **6**
cosa, la thing **1**
cosecha, la harvest **15**
cosmopolita cosmopolitan **11**
cosquillas, hacer a to tickle **7**
costa, la coast **2, 6**
costar (ue) to cost **2**
costarricense Costa Rican **3**
costo, el cost **13**
costoso/a costly; expensive **7**
costumbre, la custom **6**
costura, la fashion **14**
creador/a, el/la creator **8**
crear to create **6**
creatividad, la creativity **2**
creciente growing **15**
creencia, la belief **2**
creer to believe **2, 6, 10, 12**
crema (de afeitar), la (shaving) cream **7**
cría, la raising; chick **5**
criadero, el hatchery **5**
criar to raise **7**
criarse to grow up **4**
crimen, el crime **14**
criollo/a creole **6**
cristalino/a clear; crystalline **5**
cristianizar to christianize **10**
cristiano/a Christian **9**
crítico/a, el/la critic **13**
crónico/a chronic **10**
cronología, la chronology **11**
crucero, el cruise **9**
cruzar to cross **14**
cuaderno, el notebook **1**
cuadra, la block **3**
cuadrado/a square **5**
cuadro, el picture; painting **5**
cuadros, de plaid **8**
cual/es which (one/s) **2**
¿Cuál(es)...? Which (one/ones) . . . ? **2**
cualidad, la quality **14**

cualificaciones, las qualifications **11**
cualquier/a any/one **9**
cuando when **2, 11**
¿Cuándo...? When . . . ? **2**
cuanto/a how much/many **1**
Cuaresma, la Lent **9**
cuarteto, el quartet **14**
cuarto, el room **5**
cuarto/a fourth; quarter **2, 8**
cuarto doble, el double room **9**
cubano/a Cuban **2**
cubeta, la bucket **5**
cubierto/a covered; enclosed **8**
cubrir to cover **8, 12**
cuchara, la spoon **6**
cucharada, la tablespoon **6**
cucharadita, la teaspoon **6**
cuchillo, el knife **6**
cuello, el neck; collar **15**
cuenta, la bill; account; bead **6**
cuenta, por su on one's own **7**
cuentista, el/la storyteller **11**
cuento, el story **12**
cuerda, la cord **14**
cuero, el leather **2, 8**
cuerpo, el body **5, 10**
cuestas, a on the back **14**
cuestionario, el questionnaire **10**
cueva, la cave **9**
cuidado, tener to be careful **3**
cuidadoso/a careful **9**
cuidar(se) to take care (of oneself) **10**
culebra, la snake **8**
culinario/a culinary **6**
culto/a cultured **14**
cultura, la culture **4**
cumpleaños, el birthday **1**
cumplir to complete **1**
cumplir (con) to make good (on a promise); to fulfill (a promise) **15**
cuñado/a, el/la brother-in-law/sister-in-law **4**
curar to cure **10**
curioso/a curious **7**
curriculum vítae, el curriculum vitae (vita) **11**
curso, el course **3**
curvado/a curved **9**

D

dañarse to break down **15**
daño, el damage; harm **15**
danza (moderna), la (modern) dance **14**

dar to give 1, **6**
dar igual to be the same **7**
dar la vuelta to turn **6**
dar una mirada rápida to skim through **13**
dar un paseo to go out; to take a walk **7**
dato, el data; information **1**
de acuerdo fine with me; okay; in agreement; agreed **4**
debajo (de) under; below **5**
debate, el debate **15**
debatir to debate **14, 15**
deber (+ inf.) to owe (to ought to do something) **2**
deber, el duty **15**
débil weak **10**
debut, el debut **14**
debutar to debut **10**
década, la decade **14**
decidir to decide **2**
décimo tenth **8**
decir (i) to say **6, 7** to tell **9, 12**
declaración, la declaration **6**
decoración, la decoration **3**
dedicado/a dedicated **9**
dedicar to dedicate **7**
dedo (del pie), el finger (toe) **10**
¿De dónde...? From where . . . ? **2**
defecto, el defect **13**
defender (ie) to defend **7**
defensa propia, la self-defense **14**
definir to define **4**
deforestación, la deforestation **12**
defraudar to disillusion **15**
dejar (de) to leave (behind); to quit (doing something) **3, 6, 10, 11**
delante de in front of **2, 3**
delgado/a thin **2**
delicia, la delight **6**
delicioso/a delicious **2**
demás, los the rest **10**
demasiado too much **9**
democracia, la democracy **15**
democratización, la democratization **15**
demográfico/a demographic **13**
demora, la delay **9, 9**
De nada. You're welcome. **1**
dentista, el/la dentist **10**
dentro de within; inside of **5**
denunciar to denounce **4**
departamento, el department **8**

dependiente/a, el/la sales clerk **8**
deporte, el sport **1, 7**
deportiva, la sección sports section **13**
deportivo/a sporting **7**
depósito, el deposit **9**
¿De quién(es)...? Whose . . . ? **2**
derecha, a la to/on the right **3**
derecho, el law; right **3, 15**
derechos humanos, los human rights **4, 8, 15**
de repente suddenly **8**
derivar to derive **6**
derredor, en around **15**
desafío, el challenge **3**
desanimado/a discouraged; lifeless **12**
desaparecer to disappear **9**
desarmar to disarm **15**
desarme, el disarmament **15**
desarrollar to develop **3**
desarrollo, el development **6, 12**
desastre (natural), el natural disaster **13, 15**
desayunar to have breakfast **4, 6**
desayuno, el breakfast **2, 6**
descafeinado/a decaffeinated **2**
descansar to rest **10**
descanso, el rest **10**
descender (ie) to descend **11**
descendiente, el/la descendants **3**
describir to describe **1**
descripción, la description **5**
descubierto/a discovered **13**
descubrir to discover **6, 12**
descuento, el discount **8**
desde from; since **2**
desear to desire **3** to wish; to desire **9**
desechos, los waste **12**
desempleo, el unemployment **6, 11, 15**
desengaño, el disillusionment **10**
desenlace, el conclusion **11**
desenterrar to dig up **5**
deseo, el desire **13**
desfile, el parade **2**
desfile de moda, el fashion show **14**
desgarrador/a heartrending **11**
desgraciadamente unfortunately **5**
deshonesto/a dishonest **15**
deshonrar to dishonor **11**

desierto, el desert **4**
desierto/a deserted **5**
desilusionar to disillusion **15**
desodorante, el deodorant **8**
desorden, el disorder **8**
desordenado/a disorganized **5**
desorientado/a disoriented **10**
despacho, el office **11**
despacio slowly **5**
despedida, la closing; farewell **1, 4, 11**
despedir (i, i) to fire **11**
despedirse (i, i) to say good-bye **4**
despegar to take off **9**
despejado/a clear **8**
despertarse (ie) to wake up **5**
despoblación, la depopulation **12**
despojar to strip **11**
desprender to loosen; detach **10**
después (de) (que) after **3, 7, 11**
destacado/a outstanding **12**
destacar to stand out **4**
destinatario/a, el/la addressee **11**
destino, el destination **2**
destruir to destroy **12**
desventaja, la disadvantage **6, 11**
detalle, el detail **6**
detener (ie) to arrest; to detain **11**
deteriorar to deteriorate **12**
detestar to detest **11**
detrás (de) behind **3**
deuda pública, la public debt **15**
¿De verdad? Really? **1**
devolver (ue) to return (something) **8, 9**
día, el day **1**
diabetes, la diabetes **10**
diagnóstico, el diagnosis **10**
diamantes, de diamond **8**
diario/a daily **2**
dibujar to draw **5**
dibujo, el drawing **5**
diccionario, el dictionary **1**
diciembre December **1**
dictador/a, el/la dictator **15**
dictadura, la dictatorship **15**
dientes, los teeth; cloves of garlic **5, 6, 10**
diestro/a skilled **15**
dieta, estar a to be on a diet **10**

dieta, la diet **6, 10**
dieta, seguir una to follow a diet **10**
diferente different **8**
difícil difficult **2, 6, 10**
dificultar to make difficult **4**
¿Diga? Hello? (*on the phone*) **4**
¿Dígame? Hello? (*on the phone*) **4**
dignidad, la dignity **4**
dignificar to dignify **11**
dilema, el dilemma **10**
dinámico/a dynamic **4**
dinero, el money **4**
dios, el god **8, 9**
directamente directly **7**
director/a, el/la director; conductor **9, 11, 14** editor-in-chief **13**
director/a de escena, el/la stage manager **14**
dirigido/a directed **13**
dirigir to conduct; to direct **9, 14**
discapacitado/a, el/la disabled person **3**
disco compacto, el compact disc (CD) **8**
disco duro (externo), el (external) hard drive **12**
discoteca, ir a una to go to a nightclub **7**
discreto/a discrete **13**
disculparse to apologize **15**
discurso, el speech **6, 7, 15**
discusión, la argument; discussion **8**
diseñador/a, el/la designer **14**
diseñar to design **2**
diseño, el design **3**
disfraz, el disguise; costume **14**
disfrutar de to enjoy **6**
disminuir to diminish; to lessen **13**
disparar to shoot **11**
disponible available **5**
dispuesto/a willing; ready; disposed **13, 14**
disputar to dispute **7**
distancia, la distance **8**
distinto/a different **6**
diva, la diva **14**
diversidad, la diversity **2**
divertido/a fun **3**
divertirse (ie, i) to enjoy oneself; to have fun **5, 7**
divorciado/a divorced **4**
doble double **9**

docencia, la teaching 13
doctor/a, el/la doctor 10
doctorado, el doctorate 3
documental, el documentary 13
dólar, el dollar 6
doler (ue) to hurt 10
dolor, el pain; ache 10
dolor de cabeza, el headache 10
doméstico/a domestic 3
dominar to dominate 12
domingo, el Sunday 1
dominicano/a Dominican 2
donar to donate 7
donde where 2, 11
¿Dónde...? Where . . . ? 2
dormir (ue, u) to sleep 4
dormirse (ue, u) to fall asleep 5
dormitorio, el bedroom 5
dote, el/la dowry 15
drama, el drama 13
dramático/a dramatic 13
dramatizar to dramatize 11
droga, la drug 14
drogadicción, la drug addiction 15
ducha, la shower 5
ducharse to shower 5
duda, la doubt 2
dudar to doubt 10
dudoso/a doubtful 10
dueño/a, el/la owner 15
dulces, los sweets 10
durabilidad, la durability 14
duradero/a lasting 15
durante during 2
durar to last 7
DVD, el DVD 12

E
echar to add; to throw in 6, 12
ecológico/a ecological 8
economía, la economy 3
económico/a economic 6
ecoturismo, el ecotourism 4
eco voluntariado, el eco-volunteering 5
ecuatoriano/a Ecuadorian 2
edad, la age 4
edición, la edition 13
edificio, el building 8
editar to edit 12
editor, el editor 13
editorial, el editorial (page) 13
educación, la education 6

educar to educate 10
EE. UU. United States 6
efectivo, en in cash 8
efectivo/a effective 5
efectuar to bring into effect 10
eficiente efficient 11
ejecución, la execution 14
ejecutivo/a, el/la executive 3
ejemplo, el example 2
ejercer to exercise 15
ejercicio, hacer to exercise 7
ejercicios aeróbiocs aerobics 10
ejército, el army 15
él he 1
el the 1
elaboración, la elaboration 15
elaborado/a elaborated 4
elaborar to elaborate 15
elástico, el elastic 14
elección, la election 7
electo/a elected 6
electricidad, la electricity 10
electricista, el/la electrician 11
eléctrico/a electrical 3, 9
electrizante electrifying 14
electrónico/a electronic 2, 12
elegir (i, i) to elect; to choose 13, 15
eliminación, la elimination 15
eliminar to end 15
ella she 1
ellos/as they 1
emanar to emanate 15
embajada, la embassy 15
embajador/a, el/la embassador 7
embalse, el dam 10
emisora, la radio station (business entity) 7
emoción, la emotion 8
emocional emotional; exciting 11
emocionante exciting 2
empanada (empanadilla), la turnover 6
empaquetado/a packaged 10
emparejar to pair 5
empatar to tie (the score) 7
empezar (ie) to begin 1, 3, 4, 7, 9
empleado/a, el/la employee 11
empresa, la company; firm 2, 11
empresario, el impresario 10
enamorarse (de) to fall in love (with) 5
encabezar to head 12

encajar to fit 8
Encantado/a. Delighted.; Pleased to meet you. 1
encantador/a enchanting; delightful 2, 4, 14
encantar to delight; to be extremely pleasing 6
encanto, el charm; delight 7
encargar to take on 14
encargarse de to be responsible for 5
en caso de que in case 11
encender (ie) to turn on 12
encerrar to enclose 12
encoger draw up 8
encontrar (ue) to find 1, 3, 4
encontrarse (ue) con to meet up with someone 5
en cuanto as soon as 11
encuentro, el encounter 8
encuesta, la survey; poll 10
enemigo/a, el/la enemy 3
energía (alternativa/solar), la (alternative/solar) energy 7, 12
enero January 1
enfermar to make sick 5
enfermarse to become sick 5
enfermedad, la illness 5, 6, 10
enfermero/a, el/la nurse 11
enfrentar to confront 7
enfrente in front 12
enfrente de facing; across from 3, 14
engañar to deceive 13
engaño, el deceit 4
engordar to gain weight 10
enlace, el hyperlink 12
enlozado/a tiled 12
enojar to anger 10
enojarse (con) to get angry (with) 5, 14
enojo, el anger 15
enorme enormous 3
ensalada, la salad 6
ensayar to rehearse 11, 13
ensayo, el rehearsal 10, 13
enseguida right away 6
enseñar to teach 2, 7
entender (ie) to understand 4
enterarse to become aware 15
enterrar (ie) to bury 14
entonación, la intonation 14
entonces then 7
entrada, la appetizer 6 ticket 4
entre between 3
entregar to deliver; to turn in 1
entrenador/a, el/la trainer; coach 7

entrenamiento, el training 4, 11
entrenar to train 6
entre sí themselves 4
entretener (ie) to entertain 5
entretenimiento, el entertainment 7
entrevista, la interview 2, 11
entrevistador/a, el/la interviewer 11
entusiasta enthusiastic 2
envase (de aluminio), el (aluminum) container 12
enviar to send; to post online 12
en vías de desarrollo developing 4
envío, el shipment 4
época, la epoch 4
equidad, la equity 15
equipaje, el baggage 9
equipo, el team; equipment 5
equivocado/a mistaken 15
equivocarse to make a mistake 9
erradicar to eradicate 6
erupción, la eruption 5
escala, la stopover 9
escalar to climb 9
escalofrío, el chill 10
escalón, el step 12
escándalo, el scandal 13
escáner, el scanner 12
escaparse to escape 4
escasez, la shortage 12
escaso/a scarce 10
escena, la scene 8
escenario, el stage 8, 14
esclavo/a, el/la slave 9
escoger to choose 5
escolar scholastic 12
escribir to write 1, 2, 8, 10, 11, 12
escritor/a, el/la writer 6
escritorio, el desk 15
escuchar to listen 1, 2
escuela, la school 5
escultor/a, el/la sculptor 9
escultura, la sculpture 8
ese/a that; that one 4
esencial essential 13
esfuerzo, el effort 4, 15
esmeralda, la emerald 9
esmoquin, el tuxedo 14
esos/as those 4
espaguetis, los spaghetti 10
espalda, la back 10
España Spain 2

español, el Spanish 2
español/a Spanish 1, 2
español/a, el/la Spaniard 9
espátula, la spatula 6
especial special 5
especialidad de la casa, la house specialty **6**
especializar to specialize 6
especialmente especially 8
especie, la species 3, 5, **12**
especies en peligro de extinción, las endangered species **12**
espectacular spectacular 5
espectáculo, el show business 7
espectador/a, el/la spectator **13**
esperanza, la hope 8
esperar to hope; to wait for 7, **10** to wait for **9**
espiar to spy 11
espíritu, el spirit 11
esposo/a, el/la husband; wife 1, 3, **4**
esquí (acuático), el (water) skiing 7
esquiar to ski 7
esquina, la corner 3
establecer (zc) to establish 12
estación, la season; station 1, 8
estacionar to park 11
estación de radio, la radio station 13, **13**
estadía, la stay 9
estadio, el stadium 3
estadísticas, las statistics 3
estado, el state 7
estado libre asociado, el commonwealth 7
estancia, la ranch 11
estandarte, el standard 15
estante, el bookcase 5
estar to be 3, 5, 7, **9**
estar seguro/a (de) to be sure of **10**
estatua, la statue 9
estatura, la height 5
esta vez this time 4
este... uhh... 5
este/a this; this one **4**
estereotipo, el stereotype 12
estilo, el style 6, **14**
estimado/a esteemed **11**
estimularse to stimulate 9
estímulo, el stimulus 11
Estocolmo Stockholm 4
estómago, el stomach **10**

estornudar to sneeze 10
estos/as these; these ones **4**
estratégico/a strategic 7
estrechar (la mano) to extend one's hand) 15
estrecho/a narrow; tight (clothing) 5, **8**
estrella, la star 5
estrenar to debut 13
estrés, el stress **10**
estricto/a strict 6
estudiante, el/la student **1**
estudiantil student (*adj.*) 6
estudiar to study 1, 2
estudio, el studio; study 3, **13**
estufa, la stove 6
estupendo/a terrific 7
etapa, la stage 3
eterno/a eternal 8
ética, la ethics 11
etnia, la ethnicity 13
étnico/a ethnic 10
eusquera, el Basque language 2
evento, el event 7
evitar to avoid **10**
evolución, la evolution 8
exagerar to exaggerate 6
examen, el exam 3
examen físico, el medical checkup 10
excelente excellent 2
excepcional exceptional 7
excesivo/a excessive 12
excursión, ir de to go on an outing; to tour 9
excursión, la excursion 6, **9**
excusa, la excuse 5
exhausto/a exhausted 8
exhibir to exhibit 14
exigente challenging; demanding 3
existir to exist 8
éxito, el success 5
éxito, tener to be successful 12
exótico/a exotic 1, 5
expediente, el dossier 11
experiencia, la experience 5
experimentar to experience 2
explicar to explain 5
explícito/a explicit 13
explotación, la exploitation 7
explotar to exploit 15
exponer to explain 15
exportar to export 6
exposición, la exposition; show 3
expresar to express 15
expresarse to express oneself 11
extender (ie) to extend 3

extenso/a extensive 3
extinción, la extinction 5
extranjero, el abroad 4, **9**
extranjero/a foreign 7
extranjero/a, el/la foreigner 7
extraño/a strange 10
extraordinario/a extraordinary 11
extremo/a extreme 6
extrovertido/a outgoing 1

F

fábrica, la factory 12
fabricante, el manufacturer 12
fabricar to make; to fabricate 14 to manufacture 12
fábula, la fable 8
fabuloso/a fabulous; great 2, **7**
fácil easy 2, 6, 7, **10**
facilidad, la facility 11
facilitar to facilitate 5
fácilmente easily 9
factor, el factor 10
facturar el equipaje to check luggage 9
Facultad de Arte, la School of Art 3
Facultad de Ciencias, la School of Sciences 3
Facultad de Derecho, la School of Law 3
Facultad de Ingeniería, la School of Engineering 3
Facultad de Matemáticas, la School of Mathematics 3
Facultad de Medicina, la School of Medicine 3
falda, la skirt; slope 8
fallar to fail (computer disk) 12
falso/a false 2
falta, la lack 12
faltar to be missing; to be lacking 8
familia, la family 3, 4
familia política, la in-laws 4
familiarizarse to familiarize oneself 14
fanático/, el/la fanatic 2
fantasía, la fantasy 14
fantástico/a fantastic 7, **10**
farmacia, la pharmacy 8
fascinante fascinating 1
fascinar to be fascinating 6
fatiga, la fatigue 10
favor, a in favor of 15
febrero February **1**
fecha, la date 1, 5
fecha de vencimiento, la expiration date 10

felicidad, la happiness 4
feliz happy 1
femenino/a feminine 6
feminidad, la femininity 14
feo/a ugly 2
feria, la fair 9
feroz ferocious 10
fibra, la fiber 10
ficción, la fiction 4
fiebre, la fever 5, **10**
fiesta, la party; celebration 1, 3
figura, la figure 3, 9
figurar to represent 2
filarmónico/a philharmonic 14
filmación, la filming 13
filmar to film **13**
filme negro, el film noir 4
filosofía, la philosophy 15
fin, el end 7
final, al finally 5
final, el end **13**
financiera, la sección business section 13
financiero/a financial 3
finanzas, las finance 3
fingir to pretend 11
firma, la signature 11
firmar to sign 7, **15**
física, la physics 3
físico/a physical 5
flaco/a skinny 2
flamenco, el flamenco **14**
flamenco/a flamenco (dance) 2
flan, el custard dessert 6
flanquear to flank 15
flauta, la flute **14**
flecha, la arrow 8
flor, la flower 7, **9**
florecer to flourish 15
florería, la flower shop **8**
folleto, el brochure 9
fondo, el bottom; background 14
fondos, los funds 14
footing, hacer to go jogging 7
forma, en in shape 10
formación, la education **11**
formar to form 8
fórmula, la formula 5
formular to formulate 3
formulario, el form 11
foro, el forum 7, 14
fortalecer (zc) to strengthen; to fortify 6, **15**
fortaleza, la fortress 7
foto, la photograph 7

fotocopiadora, la photocopier **12**
fotocopiar to photocopy **12**
fotógrafo/a, el/la photographer **1**
fragmento, el fragment **12**
francés, el French **2**
francés/esa French **1**
Francia France **2**
frase, la phrase **5**
fraude (electoral), el (electoral) fraud **15**
frecuencia, con frequently **5, 8**
frecuente frequent **11**
frecuentemente frequently **8**
freír (i, i) to fry **6**
fresco, hace it is cool **7**
fresco/a fresh **6**
frigorífico, el refrigerator **6**
frijoles, los beans **6**
frío, hace it is cold **7**
frío, tener to be cold **3**
frío/a cold **6**
frito/a fried **6**
frontera, la frontier; border **3, 8**
frutas, las fruits **6**
fruto, el fruit; benefit; profit **10**
fuego, el fire **10**
fuegos artificiales, los fireworks **9**
fuente, la source **13**
fuera outside **5**
fuerte strong **6**
fuerza, la force **15**
fumar to smoke **8, 10**
función, la show; function; event **4**
funcionar to function; to work **10, 12**
fundación, la founding; foundation **7, 13**
fundado/a founded **9**
fundar to found **7**
furgoneta, la van **9**
furia, la fury **10**
furibundo/a raging **14**
furioso/a angry **5**
fusión, la fusion **14**
fusionar to fuse **3**
fútbol (americano), el soccer (football) **2, 5, 7**
futuro, el future **12**

G

gabardina, la gabardine (lightweight wool) **14**
gabinete, el cabinet **11**

gafas, las glasses **15**
galán, el leading man **13**
galápago, el tortoise **8**
galletas, las cookies **6, 10**
ganador/a, el/la winner **2**
ganar to earn; to win **2, 4, 7** to win **7**
ganas de, tener + inf. to be eager (to); feel like (doing something) **3**
ganga, la bargain; good deal **8, 9**
garaje, el garage **5**
garantizado/a guaranteed **5**
garantizar to guarantee **15**
garganta, la throat **10**
garza, la crane **8**
gasolina, la gasoline **12**
gastado/a worn out; spent **10**
gastar to spend **5, 8**
gasto, el expense **5**
gato/a, el/la cat **5, 8**
gaucho, el Argentine cowboy **11**
gemelo/a, el/la twin **10**
genealógico/a genealogical **4**
generación, la generation **7**
generalizar to generalize **4**
generalmente generally **9**
generar to generate **15**
género, el genre **4**
generoso/a generous **5**
genético/a genetic **10**
gente, la people **1, 8, 13**
geografía, la geography **3**
geología, la geology **3**
gerente, el/la manager **9, 11**
gesto, el gesture **14**
gimnasia, la gymnastics **7**
gimnasio, el gymnasium **3**
gira, la tour **9**
gitano/a, el/la gypsy **14**
globalización, la globalization **4**
gloria, la glory **7**
gobernador/a, el/la governor **15**
gobierno, el government **2, 6, 12, 15**
gol, el goal **7**
golf, el golf **2, 7**
golpe, de suddenly **12**
golpear to thump **14**
golpe de estado, el coup d'état **15**
gordo/a chubby; fat **2, 5**
gorra, la cap **8**
gorro, el stocking cap **8**
gozar de to enjoy **9**

grabación, la recording **9**
grabado/a recorded **13**
grabadora de DVD, la DVD recorder **12**
grabar to record **7, 13**
Gracias. Thank you. **1, 4**
gracioso/a funny **4**
gradas, las bleachers **15**
grado, el degree **10**
gramática, la grammar **13**
grande big **1, 2**
Gran Depresión, la Great Depression **3**
granja, la farm **15**
granjero, el farmer **15**
grasa, la fat **6, 10**
grasas monoinsaturadas (polliinsaturadas), las monounsaturated (polyunsaturated) fats **10**
grasas saturadas (trans), las saturated (trans) fats **10**
gratis free **10**
grave serious **7**
gripa, la flu (Mexico) **10**
gripe, la flu **10**
gripe porcina, la swine flu **10**
gris grey **1**
gritar to yell **11**
grito, el cry; shout **11**
grosero/a crude; rough **15**
grupo, el group **5, 14**
guacamayo, el macaw **5**
guante, el glove **7**
guapo/a good-looking **2**
guaraní, el Guarani **10**
guardar to save; to keep **6, 10**
guardar la cama to stay in bed **10**
guardar la línea, la to stay trim; to watch one's figure **10**
guardería, la nursery; daycare center **11**
guardia, el/la guard **9**
guay super **13**
guayabera, la men's shirt typical of the Caribbean **12**
gubernamental governmental **12**
guerra, la war **3, 5, 15**
Guerra Civil, la Civil War **3**
guerrero, el warrior **3**
guía, el/la tour guide **6, 7, 9**
guiar to guide **10**
guía turística, la guidebook **9**
guión, el script **12, 13**
guionista, el/la script writer **13**
guitarra, la guitar **3, 14**

gustar to like **2, 6**
gusto, el taste; pleasure **5**

H

haber (*auxiliary verb*) **12, 14**
habilidad, la ability **8**
habitación, la room **9**
habitante, el/la inhabitant **8**
habitar to inhabit; to live **6**
hábito, el habit **5**
hablar to speak **2, 7, 8, 10**
hace (in time expressions) ago; since **5, 14**
hacer to do; to make **2**
hacer (las maletas) to pack (the suitcases) **9**
hacer cola to stand in line **9**
hacer juego (con) to match; to go well with **8**
hacer la cama to make the bed **5**
hacerse daño to hurt oneself (*Spain*) **10**
hacer una cita to make an appointment **10**
hacer un crucero to take a cruise **9**
hacia toward **7**
hamaca, la hammock **8**
hambre, tener to be hungry **3**
hamburguesa, la hamburger **6**
harina, la flour **6**
hasta until **6**
Hasta luego. See you later. **1**
Hasta mañana. See you tomorrow. **1**
Hasta pronto. See you soon. **1**
hasta que until **11**
hay there is/are **1, 7**
hay que one must **8**
haz do; make (*inf. command*) **9**
heladera, la cooler **7**
heladería, la ice cream shop **8**
helado, el ice cream **6**
helicóptero, el helicopter **9**
heno, el hay **11**
herencia, la heritage **15**
hermanastro/a, el/la stepbrother/stepsister **4**
hermano/a, el/la brother/sister **3, 4**
hermoso/a beautiful **6**
híbrido/a hybrid **3**
hielo, el ice **7**
hierro, el iron **6**
hijo/a, el/la son/daughter **4, 6**
hipermercado, el hypermarket **6**

hipervínculo, el hyperlink 12
hipótesis, la hypothesis 3
hipotético/a hypothetical 13
hispano/a Hispanic 1
historia, la history 3
histórico/a historical 6
hockey, el hockey 7
hogar, el home 4
hoja, la leaf 5
hoja electrónica, la spreadsheet 12
hojear to leaf through 13
Hola. Hello; Hi. 1
holandés/esa Dutch 7
hombre, el man 1
hombre de negocios, el businessman 11
hombre/mujer del tiempo, el/la meteorologist 13
hombro, el shoulder 12
homeopatía, la homeopathy 10
honestidad, la honesty 15
honesto/a honest 11
honradez, la honesty 15
honrado/a honest; honored 11
horario, el schedule 2, 3
hornear to bake; to roast 6
horno, el oven 6
horóscopo, el horoscope 13
horrorizado/a horrified 14
hospital, el hospital 3
hostal, el inn 9
hotel (de lujo), el (luxury) hotel 9
hoy today 2
hoy en día nowadays 3
huelga, la strike 15
huelguista, el/la striker 15
huella, la trace 12
hueso, el bone 10
huésped, el guest 5
huevo, el egg 5, 6
huir to flee 14
humanidad, la humanity 11
humanista humanist 8
humano/a human 10
humedad, hace to be humid 7
humildad, la humility 15
humilde humble 6
humo, el smoke 12
humorístico/a humoristic 4
huracán, el hurricane 4

I

ibero/a Iberian 2
ida y vuelta roundtrip 9
ideal ideal 1
idealista idealistic 1

identidad, la identity 13
identificar to identify 7
ideología, la ideology 4
idioma, el language 7
iglesia, la church 7
igualdad, la equality 5
igual de equally 7
igualmente likewise 1
ilegalidad, la illegality 7
ilógico/a illogical 10
iluminar to illuminate 8
ilusión, la illusion 9
ilustrar to illustrate 10
imagen, la image 8
imaginar to imagine 10
imaginería, la statuary 4
impaciente impatient 1
impactante stunning 5
imperio, el empire 8
implementar to implement 12
importante importante 9
importar to import 12
imposible impossible 9, 10
impresionante impressive 14
impresionar to impress 6
impresora, la printer 12
imprimir to print 12
improvisar to improvise 14
impuestos, los taxes 11, 15
impulsar to push; to promote 15
inacabado/a unfinished 13
inaugurar to inaugurate 5
inca Inca 15
incendio, el fire 11
incentivo, el incentive 11
incluir to include 4
incluso even; including 9
incógnito/a unknown 7
incómodo/a uncomfortable 9
incorporar incorporate 6
incorporarse to join 7
increíble incredible 7, 10
indefinido/a indefinite 7
indicar to indicate 6
índice, el index; sign 13
índice de natalidad, el birthrate 4
indiferente indifferent 8
indígena indigenous 3
indispensable crucial 9
industria, la industry 6
inesperado/a unexpected 15
infantil childish 8
infección, la infection 10
inflación, la inflation 15
influencia, la influence 3
influido/a influenced 12

influir to influence 2
influyente influential 9, 13
informar to inform 7 to report 13
informática, la computer science 3
ingeniería (eléctrica), la (electrical) engineering 2, 3
ingeniero/a, el/la engineer 3, 5, 11
inglés, el English 2
ingrediente, el ingredient 6
iniciado/a initiated 9
iniciar to begin 9 to initiate 13
iniciativa, la initiative 11
inicio, el beginning; home (*website*) 4
injusticia, la injustice 15
inmediatamente immediately 9
inmediato/a immediate 9
inmenso/a immense 8
inmigración, la immigration 15
inmoralidad, la immorality 7
inmunología, la immunology 1
innecesario/a unnecessary 10
innovador/a innovative 14
inolvidable unforgettable 7
insertar to insert 8
insistir (en) to insist (on) 9
inspeccionar to inspect 14
inspector/a de aduanas, el/la customs inspector 9
inspiración, la inspiration 6
inspirador/a inspiring 14
instalar to install 12
instar to urge 15
instrumento, el instrument 2, 14
intacto/a intact 3
integración, la integration 11
inteligente intelligent 1
intendente, el/la mayor 15
intenso/a intense 8
intercambiar to exchange 1
intercambio, el exchange 2
interés, el interest 8
interesante interesting 1, 3
interesar to be interesting 6
internacional international 2
internado, el internship 10
interpretar to perform (*Spain*) 14
intérprete, el/la interpreter 4, 11
intervención, la intervention 15

íntimo/a intimate 10
intriga, la intrigue 10
introvertido/a introverted 1
invasión, la invasion 7
inventar to invent 5
invertir to invest 15
investigación, la research; investigation 3
investigador/a, el/la researcher 3
investigar to investigate 6 to research 8
invierno, el winter 1
invitación, la invitation 4
invitar to invite 3, 4
involucrar to be involved 13
inyección, la shot 10
ir to go 1, 3, 8, 10, 12
ir de excursión to go on an outing; to tour 9
irlandés/esa, el/la Irish 9
irónico/a ironic 14
irse to go away; to leave 5
isla, la island 2, 7, 9
italiano, el Italian 2
itinerario, el itinerary 4
izquierda (de), a la to/on the left of) 3

J

jabón, el soap 5
jaguar, el jaguar 9
jamás never 4
jamón, el ham 6
japonés, el Japanese 2
jarabe, el cough syrup 10
jardín, el garden 5
jeans, los jeans 8
jefe/a, el/la boss 9, 11
jefe/a ejecutivo/a, el/la CEO 11
jesuita, el Jesuit 10
jogging, hacer to go jogging 7
jornalero, el day laborer 15
joven young 2
joven, el/la youth 6
joya, la jewel 8
joyería, la jewelry store 8
jubilado/a, el/la retiree 3
jubilarse to retire 11
judías verdes, las green beans string beans 6
judío/a Jewish 14
judío/a, el/la Jew 2
juego electrónico, el computer (electronic) game 12
Juegos Olímpicos, los Olympic Games 3

jueves, el Thursday 1
juez/a, el/la judge 8, **15**
jugador/a, el/la player 2
jugar (ue) a to play 4
jugo, el juice 6
julio July 1
junio June 1
juntarse to get together 5
juntos/as together 4
jurado, el jury 14
justicia, la justice 7, **15**
justificar to justify 14
justo/a just **11**
juvenil juvenile 7
juventud, la youth 1

K
kilo, el kilogram 6

L
la the **1**
labio, el lip 5
laboral work (*adj.*) 7
laboratorio (de lenguas/de idiomas), el (language) laboratory 2, **3**
lácteo/a milky 10
lado (de), al next to 3
lado, el side 7
lago, el lake 8, **9**
lágrima, la tear 8
lamentable regrettable 10
lamentar to regret 10
lámpara, la lamp 5
lana, la wool 8
languidecer to languish 11
lanza, la lance 10
lanzar to launch 7
lápida, la tomb stone 14
lápiz, el pencil 1
largo long 5
las the **1**
lástima, la shame 10
lastimarse to hurt oneself 10
latir to beat 15
lavadora, la washing machine 5
lavaplatos, el dishwasher 5
lavar la ropa to wash clothes 5
lavar los platos to wash dishes 5
lavarse to wash 5
le him/her (*masc./fem.*); you (*for.*) (*masc./fem.*) 6
lección, la lesson; moral 1
leche, la milk 6
lechuga, la lettuce 6
lector/a, el/la reader 7, **13**

lector de CD/DVD, el CD/DVD player 12
leer to read 1, 2, 7, **12**
legumbre, la vegetable 3
lejano/a faraway 11
lejos (de) far 3
lema publicitario, el motto 13, **15**
lengua, la tongue; language 2, **10**
lentamente slowly 9
lentejuelas, las sequins 14
lentes, los glasses 12
lentes de natación, los swim goggles 7
lentes de sol, los sunglasses 7
lento/a slow 9
les them (*masc./fem.*); you (*for. pl.*) 6
lesión, la injury 10
letra, la letter; lyric 2, 3
letrero, el sign 9
levantar to lift 5
levantarse to get up; to stand up 5
léxico, el lexicon 15
ley, la law 6, **15**
leyenda, la legend 5
liberar to liberate 9
libra, la pound 10
libre free 4
librería, la bookstore 3
libro, el book 1
licencia por enfermedad/maternidad sickness/maternity leave 11
licenciatura, la degree 3
líder, el/la leader 15
liderazgo, el leadership 9
limitar to limit 10
límite, el limit 6
limón, el lemon 6
limonada, la lemonade 6
limosina, la limousine 14
limpiar (la casa) to clean (the house) 5
limpio/a clean 6
lindo/a pretty 12
línea, la line; figure 5, **10**
línea ecuatorial, la equator 8
lingüístico/a linguistic 13
liquidación, la clearance sale 8
listo/a clever; ready 9
literatura, la literature 3
llama, la flame 10
llamar to call 5
llamarse to be called 5
llave, la key 12

llegada, la arrival 2, 3, **9**
llegar to arrive 2
llenar el lavaplatos to fill the dishwasher 5
llevar to take; to wear; to spend time in 5, 6, **8**
llevar a cabo to carry out 5
llorar to cry 7
lloroso/a teary 10
llover (ue) to rain 7
lluvia, la rain 7
lobo, el wolf 8
lobo marino, el sea lion 6
loco/a crazy 7
locutor/a, el/la announcer 13
lógico/a logical 5, 7, **10**
logotipo, el emblem 12
lograr to achieve 12, **15**
logro, el achievement 4
lo/la him/her it (*masc./fem.*); them (*masc./fem.*) 4
lo que what; that which 5, **15**
loro, el parrot 9
Lo siento. I'm sorry. 4, 5
los/las you (*for.*) (*masc./fem.*) 1, **4**
Lo(s)/La(s) saluda atentamente,... Very truly yours, . . . 11
lucha, la struggle 15
lucir to shine 14
luego later 1
luego que as soon as 11
lugar, el place 7
lujo, el luxury 9
lujoso/a luxurious 5
luna, la moon 8
lunes, el Monday 1
luto, el mourning 6
luz, la light 5

M
machacar to crush 11 to mash 11
madera, la wood 3
madrastra, la stepmother 4
madre, la mother 4
madrugada, la dawn 4
maduro/a mature 6
maestro/a, el/la master/mistress; teacher 15
magia, la magic 14
magnífico/a great; wonderful 7
maíz, el corn 6
mal bad 1
malcrianza, la rudeness 12
maleta, la suitcase 4, **9**

maletas, (hacer) las (to pack) the suitcases 9
maletín, el briefcase 4
malo/a bad 1, **10**
mamá, la mom 4
mañana, la morning; tomorrow 1, 2, **8**
manantial, el spring 10
mandar to send 4, 6, **9**
mandato, el command 11
manera, la way 3, 6
manga, la sleeve 8
manga, sin sleeveless 8, **8**
manga corta/larga, de short-/long-sleeved 8
manifestación, la protest 15
mano, a by hand 4
mano, la hand 1, 5, **10**
¡Manos a la obra! Let's get to work! 11
mantener (ie) to maintain, to support (a family etc.) 4, 12, **15**
mantenerse (ie) en forma to stay in shape 10
mantequilla, la butter 6
manzana, la apple; block (*Spain*) 3, **6**
mapa, el map 1
Mapoma Marathon in Madrid 1
maquiladora, la assembly plant 15
maquillaje, el makeup 5
maquillarse to apply makeup 5
máquina, la machine 11
máquina de afeitar, la electric razor 5
mar, el sea; ocean 2, 6, **7**
maracas, las maracas 14
maratón, el marathon 6
maravillado/a surprised 4
maravillosamente marvelously 9
maravilloso/a marvelous 4
marca, la brand 12
marcador, el marker 1
marcar to mark 7
marcharse to go away 9
marco, el framework 4
margen, el margin 11
mariachi, el mariachi musician (*Mexico*) 3
marimba, la marimba 14
marino/a marine 6
mariscos, los seafood 2, **6**
martes, el Tuesday 1
marzo March 1

más... que more . . . than **5**
mascota, la pet **6**
masivo/a massive **5**
Más o menos. So-so; More or less. **1**
matar to kill **10**
matemáticas, las mathematics **2, 3**
materia, la academic subject; course **3**
matrimonio, el matrimony **4**
mayo May **1**
mayor older **4**
me me **4**
mecánico/a, el/la mechanic **11**
mecánicos, los jeans (Cuba) **8**
Me da igual. It's all the same to me. **7**
medianoche, la midnight **2**
mediante through; by way of **15**
medicina, la medicine **3, 10**
médico/a medical **10**
médico/a el/la doctor **10**
medida, la measurement; measure **12**
medio/a half **2**
medio ambiente, el environment **5, 12**
medio de transporte, el mode of transportation **5**
mediodía, el noon **2**
medios, los means; media **13, 14**
medir (i, i) to measure **6**
Me encantaría. I would love to. **4**
Me gusta... I like **2**
mejor better **3, 5, 9, 10**
mejorar to improve **6, 7, 15**
mejorarse to get better; to get well **10**
Me llamo... My name is . . . **1**
memoria, la memory **6**
memoria USB, la flash drive **12**
memorizar to memorize **10**
mencionar to mention **6**
menor younger **4, 5**
menos less **2**
menos, por lo at least **6**
menos... que less . . . than **5**
mensaje, el message **2**
mente, en in mind **15**
mentiroso/a lying **6**
menú, el menu **6**
menú de degustación, el tasting menu **6**
menudo, a often **8**

mercado (al aire libre) (open-air) market **8**
mercado, el market **5**
mercado callejero, el fleamarket **8**
mercado global, el global markets **15**
merecer (zc) to deserve **2**
merengue, el Caribbean dance **7**
merienda, la snack **6**
mérito, el merit **11**
mes, el month **1**
mesa, la table **1**
mesa de noche, la nightstand **5**
mesero/a, el/la waiter/waitress **3, 6**
mestizo/a of mixed race **4**
meta, la goal **7, 11**
meteorólogo/a, el/la weatherman/woman **13**
meterse to get involved in **12**
metro, el meter **8**
mexicano/a Mexican **2**
mezcla, la mixture **2**
mezclar to mix **5, 6**
mezclilla, de mixed fibers **8**
mí me **6**
micrófono, el microphone **15**
microondas, el microwave **6**
microscopio, el microscope **1**
miedo, tener (ie) to be afraid **3, 10**
miembro, el member **4**
mientras while **5**
mientras que as long as **11**
miércoles, el Wednesday **1**
migración, la migration **4**
migrante migrant **15**
milenio, el millennium **3**
militar military **4**
milla, la mile **15**
millón/millones, el/los million/s **2**
mi/mis my **1, 3**
(mini)falda, la (mini-) skirt **8**
mínimo, el minimum **5**
mínimo/a minimum **9**
ministro/a, el/la minister **4, 6, 15**
Mi nombre es... My name is . . . **1**
minoría, la minority **13**
minuto, el minute **6**
mío/a/os/as mine; my; (of) mine **13**
mirada, la glance **13**
mirar to look at; to watch **2**

misa, la Mass **7**
miseria, la misery **8**
mismo/a same **5**
misterio, el mystery **1**
misterioso/a mysterious **1**
mito, el myth **10**
mochila, la backpack **1**
moda, de in style **8**
moda, la fashion; style **14**
modelo, el/la model **14**
moderación, la moderation **10**
moderno/a modern **3**
modo (de, vestir), el way/manner (of dressing) **4, 14**
mola, la Panamanian embroidery **5**
moler (ue) to grind **4**
molestar to be a bother; to annoy **6, 10**
molesto/a annoyed **5**
monarquía, la monarchy **15**
moneda, la coin **8**
monjita, la little nun **14**
monótono/a monotonous **11**
montaña, la mountain **2, 9**
montañoso/a mountainous **4**
montar mount **11** to ride **11**
montar a caballo horseback riding **9**
montar en bicicleta to go bike riding **7, 9**
montón, el pile **11**
monumento, el monument **8, 9**
morado/a purple **1**
moraleja, la moral of the story **8**
moralidad, la morality **2**
moreno/a brunet/te **2**
morir (ue, u) to die **7, 8, 12**
moro/a, el/la Moor (Arab) **13**
mostrador, el counter **9**
mostrar (ue) to show **8**
motivar to motivate **13**
motivo, el motive **10**
movilidad, la mobility **6**
movimiento, el movement **8**
muchacho/a, el/la boy/girl **2**
Mucho gusto. Pleased to meet you. **1**
mudanza, la move **14**
muebles, los furniture **5**
muela, la molar **10**
muerte, la death **3**
muestra, la sample **15**
mujer, la woman **1**

mujer de negocios, la businesswoman **11**
multa, la fine **12**
multar to fine **12**
multinacional multinational **15**
mundial world (*adj.*) **15**
mundialmente world-wide **9**
mundo, el world **1**
muralista, el/la muralist **3**
muralla, la wall **9**
músculo, el muscle **10**
musculoso/a muscular **13**
museo, el museum **2, 3**
música, la music **1, 14**
músico/a, el/la musician **8, 14**
musulmán/ana, el/la Muslim **13**
mutuo/a mutual **6**
muy very **1**

N

nacer to be born **2**
nacimiento, el birth **1**
nación, la nation **1**
nacionalidad, la nationality **2**
Naciones Unidas, las United Nations **7**
nada nothing **6, 7**
nadar to swim **5, 7**
nadie no one; nobody **7**
naranja, la orange **6**
nariz, la nose **5**
narración, la narration **12**
narrador/a, el/la narrator **14**
naturaleza, la nature **5, 12**
naturaleza muerta, la still life **6**
náusea, la nausea **10**
navaja de afeitar, la razor blade **5**
navegable navigable **5**
navegante, el/la navigator **7**
navegar a vela to sail **9**
Navidad, la Christmas **4**
necesario/a necessary **7, 9**
necesitado/a in need **7**
necesitar to need **1, 9**
necio/a, el/la fool **10**
negar (ie) to deny **10**
negativo/a negative **7**
negocio, el business **3**
negro/a black **1**
neoyorquino/a New Yorker **12**
nervioso/a nervous **3, 5**
nevar (ie) to snow **7**
nevera, la refrigerator **6**
ni... ni neither . . . nor **7**

nido, el nest 11

niebla, la fog 9

nieto/a, el/la grandson/granddaughter 4

nilón, el nylon 14

ninguna vez never 7

ningún/ninguna none 7

ninguno/a no one; none 6, 7

niños/as, los/las children 1, 7

nivel, el level 10

nobleza, la nobility 15

noche, la night 2

Nochevieja, la New Year's Eve 9

noción, la notion 13

nocivo/a harmful 15

No comprendo. I don't understand. 1

no creer to not believe 10

no estar seguro/a (de) to not be sure of 10

nombrar to name 7

nombre, el name 1

nominación, la nomination 13

no pensar (ie) to not think 10

normalmente normally 9

norteamericano/a American (US) 2

nos us 4, 6

No sé. I don't know. 1

nosotros/as we 1, 14

nota, la grade 3

No te preocupes. Don't worry. 10

noticias, las news 13

noticias en línea, las news online 13

noticiero, el newscast 13

notificar to notify 14

novedad, la news 13

novedoso/a new 12

novela, la novel 2, 7

novelista, el/la novelist 2

noveno/a ninth 8

noviembre November 1

novio/a, el/la boyfriend/girlfriend; groom/bride 3, 4

nube, la cloud 8

nublado/a cloudy 7

núcleo, el nucleus 4

nudo, el knot 15

nuera, la daughter-in-law 4

nuestro/a/os/as our (of) ours 3, 13

nuevo/a new 2

número, el number; size 5, 8

nunca never 7

Ñ

ñandutí, el cloth woven with a spider web pattern 10

O

o or 1

o... o either . . . or 7

objeto, el object 9

obligación, la obligation 15

obligar to oblige 6

obra, la play (theater); work 2, 13

obra maestra, la masterpiece 4

obrero/a de construcción, el/la construction worker 11

observar to observe 5

observatorio, el observatory 3

obtener (ie) to obtain 11

océano, el ocean 5

ocio, el leisure 4

octavo/a eighth 8

octubre October 1

ocupado/a busy 4

ocupar to occupy 7

ocurrir to occur 5, 7

odio, el hatred 10

oferta, la offer 1

oficial official 12, 13

oficina, la office 2

oficio, el trade 11

ofrecer (zc) to offer 3

oído, el inner ear 10

oír to hear 6, 8, 12

Ojalá I hope; God willing 9, 10

ojo, el eye 5

ola, la wave 5

olor, el perfume; odor; smell 8

olvidar(se) (de) to forget 5, 7

ONU, la UN 12

ópera, la opera 1, 14

opinar to express an opinion 5

opinión, la opinion 2

oportunidad, la opportunity 4

oportuno/a opportune 13

opresión, la oppression 15

optimista optimistic 1

opulencia, la opulence 4

oración, la sentence 6, 7

orden, el order 4

ordenar la casa to clean the house 5

oreja, la outer ear 10

orgánico/a organic 6

organización, la organization 7

orgulloso/a proud 2

orientación, la orientation 10

origen, el origin 3

originalidad, la originality 13

orilla, la bank; shore 5

orinar to urinate 10

ornamento, el ornament 8

oro gold 1, 8

orquesta (sinfónica), la (symphony) orchestra 4, 14

ortiga, la a prickly plant 1

ortografía, la spelling 6

os you (*inf. fam. Spain*) 4, 6

oscuro/a dark 8

oso, el bear 3

otorgar to be granted 13

otra vez again 5

otro/a other; another 2

oveja, la sheep 11

oxígeno, el oxygen 10

Oye. Listen. (*command*) 7

oyente de podcast, el/la podcast listener 13

oyeres whatever you hear 13

P

paciente patient 1

paciente, el/la patient 10

pacifista, el/la pacifist 15

padecer (zc) (de) to suffer (from) 10

padrastro, el stepfather 4

padre awesome 4

padre, el father 4

padres, los parents 2

pagar (en efectivo) to pay (in cash) 8

página, la page 1

página web, la web page 6, 12

pago, el payment 3

país (en vías de desarrollo), el (developing) country 2, 15

país, el country 8

paisaje, el landscape 1

paisano, el countryman 15

paja, la straw 14

pájaro, el bird 5, 9

palabra, la word 2

palacio, el palace 3

palmada, la clap 14

pampas, las plains of Argentina 11

pan, el bread 6

pana, la corduroy 14

panameño/a Panamanian 2

pandereta, la tambourine 8

pandillero, el gang member 12

panqueques, los pancakes 10

pantalla, la screen 12

pantalones, los pants 8

pantalones de mezclilla, los jeans (*Mexico*) 8

papalote, el kite 7

papas, las potatoes 6

papas fritas, las potato chips; French fries 10

papel, el paper; role 1 role (play, movie, or television) 13

papelería, la stationery shop 8

papel maché, el papier mâché 3

para for; in order to 1, 9

para colmo to make matters worse 13

paraíso, el paradise 2

parapente, hacer to hang-glide 9

para que in order that; so that 11

pardo/a brown 8

parecer (zc) to appear; to seem 6

pareja, la couple; partner 4

pariente, el/la relative (family) 4

parlamento, el parliament 15

paro, el strike (*Latin America*); unemployment (*Spain*) 15

paro, estar en el to be out of work 11

parodia, la parody 13

parque, el park 1

párrafo, el paragraph 5

parrilla, la grill 6

parrillada, la grill 11

parte, la part 3

participante, el/la participant 1

participar to participate 5

particularmente particularly 9

partidario/a partisan 4

partidario/a, el/la supporter 13

partido, (ir a un) (to go to a) game 2

partido, el game; match 5

partir to split; to divide 11

pasa, la raisin

pasado, el past 15

pasado/a last 6

pasaje (de ida y vuelta), el (roundtrip) fare; ticket 9

pasajero/a, el/la passenger 9

pasaporte, el passport 9

pasar to pass (a test); to approve 5

pasar la aspiradora to vacuum 5

pasarlo bien/mal/de maravilla to have a good/bad/wonderful time 7, 9

pasarlo bomba to have a great time 15

pasar por (...) to pass through (. . .) **9**
pasatiempo, el pastime **7**
paseador/a de perros, el/la dog walker **11**
pasear to take a walk **4**
paseo, dar un to take a walk **7**
paseo, el stroll **1** walk **7**
pasillo, el hallway; aisle **5**
pasión, la passion **4, 13**
paso, el step **4**
Paso por ti. I'll come by for you. **4**
pasta de dientes, la toothpaste **8**
pastel, el cake; pie **6**
pastilla, la pill; lozenge **10**
patear to kick **7**
patinaje, el skating **7**
patinar to skate **7**
patio, el yard; patio **5**
pato, el duck **8**
patrimonio, el heritage **10**
patrocinador/a, el/la sponsor **12**
patrocinar to sponsor **13**
patronato, el board of trustees **1**
pavo, el turkey **6**
paz, la peace **1, 4, 10, 15**
pecho, el chest **10**
pedagogía, la teaching **3**
pedazo, el piece **6**
pedicura, la pedicure **10**
pedido, el request **9**
pedir (i, i) to ask **9** to ask for; to request **6, 9, 10, 11**
pedir prestado to borrow **6**
peinarse to comb one's hair **5**
peine, el comb **5**
pelar to peel **6**
peli, la movie; film **4**
película, la movie; film **4, 7**
película, poner una to show a movie **4**
peligro, el danger **5, 9, 12**
peligroso/a dangerous **2**
pelo, el hair **5**
pelota, la baseball **7**
peluquero/a, el/la hairstylist **11**
pena, la pity; sorrow **8**
penalización, la punishment **15**
pendón, el banner **15**
penicilina, la penicillin **10**
península, la peninsula **3**
pensamiento, el thought **3**
pensar (ie) to think **3, 4, 9, 10, 11**

peor worse **5**
pequeño/a small **1**
percusión, la percussion **14**
percusionista, el/la percussionist **14**
perder (ie) to lose; to miss (someone) **4**
pérdida, la loss **10**
perdido/a lost **4**
peregrino/a, el/la pilgrim **13**
perejil, el parsley **6**
perezoso, el sloth **5**
perezoso/a lazy **1**
perfeccionar to perfect **10**
perfecto/a perfect **2, 7**
perfil, el profile **1**
perfume, el perfume **8**
perfumería, la perfume shop **8**
periódico, el newspaper **2, 4, 7**
periódico digital, el online newspaper **13**
periodista, el/la journalist **10, 11, 13**
perjudicar to damage; to harm **12**
perlas, las pearls **8**
permancer to remain **2**
permanente permanent **3**
permiso, el permit **3**
permitir to permit **2, 7, 9**
pero but **2, 3, 15**
perro/a, el/la dog **4, 5, 8**
perseverancia, la perseverance **13**
persona, la person **1**
personaje, el character **1**
personal, el personnel **11**
personalidad, la personality **7**
pertenencias, las belongings **13**
peruano/a Peruvian **2**
perversidad, la perversity **7**
pesado/a heavy **12**
pesas, levantar to lift weights **7**
pescado, el fish **6**
pescar to fish **9**
pesimista pessimistic **1**
peso, el weight **10**
pesquero/a fishing **6**
pesticidas, los pesticides **12**
petróleo, el oil **9**
piano, el piano **14**
PIB, el GDP **9**
picante spicy **6**
picar to chop **6**
pícnic, hacer un to have a picnic **7**
pico, el beak **8, 9**

pie, el foot **10**
piedra, la stone **4, 9**
piel, la skin; leather; fur **10, 14**
pierna, la leg **10**
pieza (musical), la (musical) piece **3, 14**
pijama, el pajamas **12**
pila, la battery **9**
piloto, el/la pilot **9**
pimienta, la pepper **6**
pincho, el bar snack **2**
pingüino, el penguin **6**
pintado/a painted **3**
pintor/a, el/la painter **1**
pintura, la painting **2**
pirámide, la pyramid **3**
pirata, el pirate **7**
piratear to pirate **11**
piropo, el compliment **9**
pisar to step on **11**
piscina, la pool **7** swimming pool **5**
piso, el floor **5, 8**
pizarra, la blackboard **1**
pizca, la pinch **6**
placer, el pleasure **6**
plancha, la iron; metal sheet **5**
planchar to iron **5**
plan de retiro, el retirement plan **11**
planear to plan **14**
plano de la ciudad, el city map **9**
planta nuclear, la nuclear plant **12**
plantar to plant **12**
plástico, el plastic **3**
plata, la silver **1, 8**
plataforma, la platform **15**
plátano, el banana **6, 8**
platería, la silver **4**
plato, el plate **6**
playa, la beach **5**
pleno/a long-form **13**
plomero/a, el/la plumber **11**
plumaje, el plumage **9**
población, la population **2**
pobre poor **2**
pobreza, la poverty **6, 9, 15**
poder (ue) to be able; can **4, 7**
poder, el power **11, 15**
poeta, el/la poet **2**
polémica, la controversy **12**
policía, la police **9**
poliéster, el polyester **14**
política, la politics **15**
político, el politician **15**
político/a political **6, 15**
pollo, el chicken **6, 10**

poner to put **4, 7, 12**
poner la mesa to set the table **5**
poner los ojos en blanco to role one's eyes **15**
ponerse to become **5**
ponerse en forma to get in shape **5**
por for; through; during; by **9**
por ahora for now **9**
por aquí around here **9**
por casualidad coincidentally **10**
por Dios for heaven's (*lit.* God's) sake **9**
por ejemplo for example **6, 9**
por eso that's why; therefore **2, 7, 9**
por favor please **1, 7, 9**
por fin finally; at last **6, 9**
por lo general in general **9**
porque because **2**
¿Por qué...? Why . . . ? **2, 9**
porquerías, las junk food **10**
por supuesto of course **7, 9**
portada, la front page **13**
portar to carry **15**
portátil, la computadora laptop computer **1**
portugués, el Portuguese **2**
portugués/esa, el/la Portuguese person **9**
por último finally **9**
posar to perch **13**
posible possible **10**
pozo de petróleo, el oil well **12**
practicar (un deporte) to practice (a sport) **2**
precio, el price **2, 5, 8**
precioso/a precious **6**
preciso/a essential **9**
precolombino/a pre-Colombian **5**
predecesor/a, el/la predecessor **6**
predecible predictable **4**
predominante predominant **9**
predominar to predominate **8**
preferencia, la preference **5**
preferir (ie, i) to prefer **2, 4**
pregunta, la question **1**
preguntar to ask **6**
prehispánico/a prehispanic **3**
prehistórico/a prehistoric **3**
premiar to reward **11**
premio, el prize **4, 5, 8, 13**
prenda, la garment **9, 14**

prensa, la press 4, **13**
preocupación, la preoccupation **10**
preocuparse to worry **8**
preparación, la preparation **6**
preparar to prepare **2**
presenciar to present **14**
presentación introduction **1**
presentador/a, el/la moderator 12, **13**
presidencia, la presidency **15**
presidente/a, el/la president 5, **15**
presidir to preside **15**
presión, la blood pressure **10**
prestación, la service **2**
préstamo, el loan **11**
prestar to lend **15**
prevaleciente prevalent **15**
prevenible preventable **7**
previo/a previous **2**
primavera, la spring **1**
primera actriz, la leading lady **13**
primera plana, la front page **13**
primer/o/a first 2, **7, 8**
primo/a, el/la cousin **4**
princesa, la princess **7**
príncipe, el prince **2**
principio, al at first **5**
principio, el beginning 3, **13**
prioridad, la priority **13**
prisa, tener (ie) to be in a hurry **3**
prístino/a pristine **9**
privacidad, la privacy **5**
privado/a private **3**
probablemente probably **3**
probador, el fitting room **8**
probar (ue) to try **6**
probarse (ue) to try on **8**
problema, el problem **5**
procesión, la procession **1**
proceso, el process **15**
producir (zc) to produce **6**
producto, el product 2, **8**
productor/a, el/la producer **13**
productos lácteos dairy products **6**
profesión, la profession **11**
profesor/a, el/la professor **1**
profundamente profoundly **10**
profundo/a deep; profound **5**
programación, la programming **13**
programador/a programmer **12**

programar to program 4, **12**
programas sociales, los social welfare programs **15**
progreso, el progress **15**
prohibido/a prohibited **6**
prohibir to prohibit 8, **9**
prolífico/a prolific **2**
promedio, el average **11**
promesa, la promise **6**
prometer to promise **6**
prominente prominent **9**
promoción, la promotion **11**
promocionar to promote **10**
promover (ue) to promote **15**
pronóstico, el forecast **4**
pronto soon **1**
pronunciar to pronounce **6**
propiedad, la property **10**
propina, la tip (monetary) **6**
propio/a own **13**
proponer to propose **6**
proporcionar to proportion; to provide 1, **10**
propósito, el goal; objective **7**
protagonista, el/la protagonist; star **13**
protección, la protection **10**
proteger (j) to protect 5, 6, **8, 12**
protegido/a protected **6**
proteínas, las proteins 6, **10**
protestar to protest **15**
provenir to orginate; to arise from **9**
provocar to provoke **10**
próximo/a nearby; close; next 2, **7**
proyecto, el project 5, **9**
prueba, la test; trial; sample 4, **10**
psicología, la psychology **3**
psicólogo/a, el/la psychologist **11**
púas, las barbs **12**
publicar to publish **6**
publicidad, la publicity **6**
publicista, el/la publicist **7**
publicitario/a publicity (adj.) **13**
público, el public; audience 12, **13**
público/a public **3**
pueblo, el people 2 town; the people; the masses 4, 10, **15**
puerta, la door **1**
puerta de embarque, la boarding gate **9**
puertorriqueño/a Puerto Rican **2**

pues well; because **3**
puesto, el place; stall; position (job) **11** position 2 stall **8**
pulir to polish **12**
pulmones, los lungs **10**
pulsera, la bracelet **8**
puntiagudo/a sharp **9**
punto, el point of view **6**
punto, en on the dot **2**
puntualmente punctually **9**
pureza, la purity **1**
puro/a pure **7**

Q

que that; which; who; whom **15**
qué what 1, **2**
¿Qué, tal? What's up? (*inf.*) **1**
¿Qué...? What? **2**
¡Qué asco! How revolting! **6**
¡Qué barbaridad? What nonsense! **1**
¡Qué bárbaro! How terrific! **9**
quedar to be left; to be remaining; to fit 6, **8**
quedarse to stay (somewhere); to remain 7, **9**
¡Qué estudiantes! What students! **1**
quehaceres, los chores **5**
¿Qué hora es? What time is it? **2**
¿Qué húbole? What's up? (*Venezuela*) **9**
quejar to complain **14**
quena, la Andean flute **8**
¡Qué padre! How awesome! **4**
¿Qué pasa? What's happening?; What's up? (*inf.*) **1**
querer (ie) to want; to love 7, 8, **9**
querido/a dear **4**
queso, el cheese **6**
¡Qué suerte! What luck! **2**
¿Qué tal sí... ? How about . . . ? **4**
¿Qué te gusta hacer? What do you like to do? **2**
quien who; whom 2, **15**
¿Quién(es)...? Who . . . ? **2**
¿Quieres ir a...? Do you want to go to . . . ? **4**
química, la chemistry **3**
quinto/a fifth **8**
quipu, el knotted string (Inca) **15**
quiropráctico/a, el/la chiropractor **10**
quitar to remove **5**

quitar la mesa to clear the table **5**
quitarse to take off (clothing) **5**
quizás perhaps **10**

R

radioactividad, la radioactivity **12**
radiografía, la X-ray **10**
radio por satélite, la satellite radio **13**
radioyente, el/la radio listener **13**
raíz, la root **10**
rama, la branch **10**
ramo, el bouquet **7**
rápidamente rapidly **9**
rápido/a rapid **2**
raqueta, la racket **7**
raro/a strange; uncommon **7**
rato, el short time; while **13**
ratón (inalámbrico), el (wireless) mouse **12**
rayas, de striped **8**
rayo, el ray **10**
rayón, el rayon **14**
razón, la reason **4**
razón, tener to have a point; to be right **3**
razonable reasonable **12**
reacción, la reaction **7**
reaccionar to react **7**
real royal **15**
realista realistic **1**
realizar to achieve 8 to carry out **11**
realmente really **6**
rebaja, en on sale **8**
rebaja, la sale **8**
rebelión, la rebellion **15**
recargable rechargeable **12**
recepcionista, el/la receptionist **5**
receptor, el receiver **12**
receta, la prescription 9, **10** recipe **6**
rechazar to reject **4**
recibir to receive **2**
recibo, el receipt **8**
reciclaje, el recycling **12**
reciclar to recycle 7, 12, **12**
recién casados, los newlyweds **4**
recientemente recently **6**
recíproco/a reciprocal **11**
reclamo de equipaje, el baggage claim area **9**
recoger to pick up **5**
recolección, la gathering **10**

recomendar (ie) to recommend **9**

recompensa, la compensation 9

reconocido/a recognized 3

recordar (ue) to remember 7

recorrer to go round; to travel through/across **9**

recorrido, el trip 6

recortar to clip 13

rectificar to rectify 15

recto, todo straight ahead 3

rectoría, la president's office **3**

recuerdo, el souvenir; memory 6, **9**

recuperar to recuperate 2

recurso (natural), el (natural) resource **12**

recursos humanos, los human resources 3

red, la network 6

redacción, la editing 13

redondo/a round 9

reducir (zc) to reduce 15

reencarnar to reincarnate 13

referir (ie, i) to refer 14

reflejar to reflect 3

reforestación, la reforestation **12**

refresco, el refreshment; soft drink 3, **4**, **6**

refrigerador, el refrigerator 6

refugio, el refuge 3

regalar to give a gift 13

regalo, el gift 4

regatear to bargain; to haggle over **8**

regateo, el haggling 8

régimen, el diet 10

región, la region 6

regla, la rule 10

regresar to return 6

regreso, de on return 11

reina, la queen 15

reino, el kingdom 8

reírse (i, i) to laugh 13

relación, la relation 4 relationship 6

relajamiento, el relaxation 10

relatar to relate 7

relativo/a relative 15

religioso/a religious 15

rellenar to fill completely; to fill out 11

relleno, el filling **4**

relleno/a filled 6

reloj, el clock; watch **1**

reloj de pulsera, el wristwatch 8, **8**

remediar to remedy 13

remedio, el remedy **10**

remesa, la remittance; payment 4

remolino, el whirlwind 9

remoto/a remote 4

remover (ue) to remove 14

rendir (i, i) to defeat 13

renombre, el renown 14

renovable renewable 11

renunciar to renounce 11

reparar to repair **11**

repartir to deliver; to distribute **11**

repaso, el review 13

repente, de suddenly **8**

repertorio, el repertoire **14**

repetir (i, i) to repeat **1**

Repita, por favor. Repeat please. **1**

repoblación, la repopulation 12

reponer to restock 10

reportaje, el feature 13

reportar report 13

reportero/a, el/la (television) reporter 4, 7, 13

representante, el/la representative **15**

representar to perform; to represent 6, 8, **13**, **14**

representativo/a representative 3

reproducir (zc) to reproduce 5, **14**

reproductor de mp3, el mp3 player **12**

república, la republic **15**

requisito, el requirement 3, 5

resaltar to feature 7

rescate, el rescue el 9

reseña, la review 4, 6, **13**

reserva/reservación, la reservation **9**

resfriado, el cold **10**

residencia, la residence 2

resolver (ue) to solve **15**

respetar to respect 6

respeto, el respect 15

respetuoso/a respectful 12

respirar to breathe **10**

respiratorio/a respiratory 10

responder to respond 6

responsabilidades, las responsibilities 11

responsable responsible 3

respuesta, la answer; response 1 response **1**

restaurante, el restaurant 6

resto, el rest 2

restos, los remains; leftovers 10

resultado, el result 5, 6

resumen, el summary 5

resumir to summarize 7

retar to challenge 5

retirado/a distant 10

retirarse to excuse oneself; to retire **11**, 15

retrasar to detain; to be behind 4

reunión, la meeting; get-together 2

reunirse to meet with someone 11

revelar to reveal 6

revisar to check; to review 1, 2, **10**, **12**, **13**

revista (del corazón), la (celebrity) magazine **13**

revista, la magazine **7**

revolucionado/a revolutionized 12

revolucionar to revolutionize 12

revólver, el revolver 11

rey, el king 15

rico/a rich; delicious 2, 4, 6

ridículo/a ridiculous 5, **6**, **10**

riesgo, el risk 10

rígido/a rigid 10

río, el river 2

riqueza, la wealth; richness 9

risa, la laughter 13

ritmo, el rhythm 1

roca, la rock 9

rodaje, el filming 4

rodar to film 10

rodeado/a surrounded 12

rodear to surround 7

rodilla, la knee **10**

rojo/a red 1

romano/a Roman 2

romántico/a romantic 1

romper to break 12

romperse (un hueso) to break (a bone) 10

ropa, la clothing 5, **8**

roquero/a, el/la rocker 2

rosado/a pink 1

roto/a broken 2

rubio/a blond 2

ruina, la ruin 4

rumbo a towards 6

Rusia Russia 2

ruso, el Russian 2

rústico/a rustic 3

ruta, la route 6

rutina, la routine 5

S

sábado, el Saturday 1

sabelotodo, el/la know-it-all 4

saber to know (something or how to do something) 2, **4**, 6, 7, **9**, **10**

sabor, el flavor 1

sabroso/a delicious; tasty **6**

sacar to take (out) 1, **5**

sacar fotos to take pictures 9

saco, el blazer 8

sacudir to shake; to dust 15

sagrado/a sacred 11

sal, la salt 6

sala, la living room 3, **5**

sala de espera, la waiting area **9**

sala de reclamación, de equipaje baggage claim area 9

sala de urgencias, la emergency room 10

salario, el salary 11

salida, la departure 2, 6, **9**

salir to leave; to go out **4**

salir bien to end well 9

salón, el room 9

salsa, la sauce 6

salsero/a, el/la salsa performer 12

saltar to leap 8

salto, el waterfall 9

salto en bungee, hacer to bungee jump 9

salud, la health 4, 7, **10**

saludable healthy 10

saludo/s, el/los greeting/s; salutation/s 1, **11**

salvadoreño/a Salvadorian 2

salvar to save 4

sandalias, las sandals 8

sándwich, el sandwich 3, **6**

sanfermines, los Sanfermín festival 2

sangre, la blood 11

sanidad, la sanitation; public health 15

sapo, el toad 8

sartén, la skillet; frying pan **6**

satisfacción, la satisfaction 9

satisfactorio/a satisfactory 6

satisfecho/a satisfied 8

saturado/a saturated 10

saxofón, el saxophone 14

se himself; herself; yourself; itself; themselves 5

secador, el hair dryer **5**
secadora, la dryer **5**
sección, la section **6**
sección deportiva, la sports section **13**
sección financiera, la financial section **13**
seco/a dry **6**
secretario/a, el/la secretary **11**
secreto, el secret **4**
secuestrar to kidnap **4**
sed, la thirsty **10**
sed, tener (ie) to be thirsty **3**, **7**
seda, la silk **8**
sede, la head office; seat of government **8**, **11**
seguir (i, i) to follow **9**, **10**
según according to **5**
segunda mano, de secondhand **8**
segundo/a second **7**, **8**
seguramente surely **3**
seguridad, la security **9**
seguro/a sure; certain **4**, **5**, **10**
seguro médico, el health insurance **11**
selección, la selection **7**
seleccionar to select **10**, **15**
selva, la jungle **5**, **9**, **10**, **12**
semana, la week **1**
Semana Santa, la Holy Week **1**
semejante similar **8**
semestre, el semester **3**
senador/a, el/la senator **15**
sencillez, la simplicity **14**
sencillo/a simple **5**
sensación, la sensation **11**
sensacionalista sensationalist **13**
sentarse (ie) to sit **5**
sentimental sentimental **4**
sentir (ie, i) to regret **9**, **10**
sentirse (ie, i) to feel **5**, **8**
señal, la signal **15**
señalar to point out **12**
señor, el (Sr.) Mr. **1**
señora, la (Sra.) Mrs. **1**
señorita, la (Srta.) Miss **1**
septiembre September **1**
séptimo/a seventh **8**
sepulcro, el grave **14**
ser to be **1**, **2**, **3**, **7**, **8**, **9**
ser humano, el human being **6**
serie, la series **13**
serio/a serious **10**
serpiente, la snake **6**
servicio, el service **2**
servicio de limpieza, el cleaning service **5**

servilleta, la napkin **6**
servir (i, i) to serve **2**, **3**, **4**, **5**, **8**
severo/a severe **8**
sexto/a sixth **8**
siempre always **2**, **3**, **7**, **8**
siglas, las call letters **7**
siglo, el century **1**, **6**
significado, el meaning **2**
significante significant **13**
significar to mean **13**
significativo/a significant **7**
siguiente following **4**
silla, la chair **1**
sillón, el armchair; overstuffed chair **5**
simbolizar to symbolize **10**
simpático/a kind; nice; amusing **1**, **8**
simpatizante, el/la sympathizer **15**
simpatizar to sympathize **8**
sindicalizar to unionize **15**
sindicato, el union **12**
sin duda without a doubt **10**
sin embargo nevertheless **7**
sinfonía, la symphony **14**
sinfónica, la symphonic orchestra **14**
sino but; but rather **1**, **15**
sin que without **11**
síntesis, la synthesis **3**
sintético/a synthetic **14**
síntoma, el symptom **10**
sin trabajo, estar to be out of work **11**
sirviente/a, el/la servant **4**
sitio, el place **4**
sitio web, el website **7**, **12**
situación, la situation **5**, **6**
situado/a situated **8**
sobre on **5**
sobreconsumo, el overconsumption **12**
sobrenatural supernatural **10**
sobrepeso, el excess weight; obesity **10**
sobrepoblación, la overpopulation **13**
sobrevivencia, la survival **4**
sobrevivir to survive **5**
socialista, el/la socialist **8**
sociología, la sociology **3**
socorro, el help **11**
sofá, el sofa; couch **5**
sol, hace it is sunny **7**
sol, tomar el to sunbathe **7**
solamente only **3**
soldado, el soldier **15**

solemne solemn **4**
solicitar to apply for **3**, **11**
solicitud de empleo, la job application **11**
sólido/a solid **6**
solista, el/la soloist **7**, **14**
solitario/a solitary **11**
solo only **3**
soltar (ue) to let go **2**
soltero/a single; unmarried **4**
sombría somber **11**
sombrilla, la umbrella **7**
soñar (ue) (con) to dream about) **4**
sonreír (i, i) to smile **15**
sopa, la soup **6**
soplar to blow **8**
sorprendente surprising **10**
sorprender(se) to surprise **10**
sorpresa, la surprise **6**
sospecha, la suspicion **11**
Soy... I am . . . **1**
subir to raise; to go up; to climb **6** to upload **12**
subir de peso to gain weight **10**
subrayar to underscore **5**
sucio/a dirty **6**
sudadera (con capucha), la (hooded) sweatshirt **8**
suegro/a, el/la father-in-law/mother-in-law **4**
sueldo (mínimo), el minimum wage **11**
sueño, el dream **6**, **12**
sueño, tener to be sleepy **3**
suerte, la luck **7**
suéter, el sweater **8**
sufrimiento, el suffering **15**
sufrir (de) to suffer (from) **8**
sugerencia, la suggestion **6**
sugerir (ie, i) to suggest **9**
sumamente very **7**
sumario, el summary **2**
superación, la overcoming **11**
superar to overcome **12**
supervisión, la supervision **11**
supervisor/a, el/la supervisor **11**
supuesto/a supposed **9**
sur, el south **6**
surfear to surf **7**
surgir to emerge **15**
suspender to suspend **14**
suspensivo/a suspenseful **4**
sustancia, la substance **15**
sustantivo, el noun **1**
suyo/a/os/as your (*for. pl.*) (of) ours; his/her (of) his/hers (of) its; their (of) yours **13**

T

tabla, la board; table **10**, **12**
tacaño/a stingy **5**
tacógrafo, el tachograph **9**
tacón, el heel **8**
táctica, la tactic **10**
talco, el talcum powder **8**
talentoso/a talented **14**
talla, la clothing size **8** size **8**
tallado, el carving **3**
tallado/a carved **3**
taller, el workshop **3**
tal vez perhaps **10**
también also too **1**, **2**, **7**
tambor, el drum **14**
tampoco neither; not either **7**
tan... como as much as **5**
tan pronto como as soon as **11**
tanque, el tank **10**
tanto... como as much as **5**
tantos/as... como as many as **5**
tapado/a stuffy **10**
tapas, las appetizers **2**
taquilla, la box office **8**
tarde late **2**
tarde, la afternoon **1**, **2**
tarea, la homework; task **1**
tarifa, la fee; commission **10**
tarjeta de crédito, la credit card **8**
tarjeta de embarque, la boarding pass **9**
tarjeta de memoria, la memory card **9**
tarjeta postal, la postcard **9**
tasa (de desempleo), la rate (of unemployment) **15**
tasa, la rate **11**
taxista, el/la taxi driver **4**
taza, la coffee cup/mug **6**
tazón (de cristal), el (glass) bowl **6**
te you (*inf.*) **4**, **6**
té, el tea **6**
teatro, el theater **3**, **4**, **13**
techo, el roof **3**
teclado, el keyboard **12**
técnica, la technique **6**
tecnología, la technology **13**
tecnológico/a technological **12**
Te gusta... you like . . . **2**
¿Te gustaría (+ *inf.*)? Would you like (+ *inf.*)? **4**
tejanos, los jeans (*Spain*) **8**
tejer to weave **15**
tejido, el weaving **4**
tela, la cloth; fabric **8**, **14**
tele, la television **6**

teléfono celular/móvil, el cell phone **1**

telenovela, la soap opera **13**

televidente, el/la television viewer **12, 13**

televisión (en directo), la live television **13**

televisión (en vivo), la live television **13**

televisión (por cable), la cable television **13**

televisión (por satélite), la satellite television **13**

televisión, la television **7, 13**

televisor de alta definición, el high-definition television **12**

telón, el curtain **11**

tema, el theme **5**

temer to fear **10**

temor, el fear **15**

temperatura, la temperature **9, 10**

tempestad, la storm **8**

templado/a temperate **6**

templo, el temple **8**

temporada, la season **7**

temporal temporary **3**

temprano/a early **2**

tender a to tend to **6**

tenedor, el fork **6**

tener (ie) to have **1, 2, 2, 7**

tengo I have **1**

tenis, el tennis **2**

tenista, el/la tennis player **2**

tensión, la tension, pressure **13**

tenso/a tense **14**

tentación, la temptation **6**

teoría, la theory **8**

tercer/o/a third **8**

terciopelo, el velvet **14**

termal thermal **10**

terminar to end; to finish **6, 10**

término, el term **4**

términos, los terms **11**

terrateniente, el landowner **5**

terraza, la terrace **5**

terremoto, el earthquake **14**

terreno, el land; terrain **4**

terrestre terrestrial **8**

terrorismo, el terrorism **15**

tesoro, el treasure **2**

testigo/a, el/la witness **13**

ti you (*inf.*) **6**

tibio/a lukewarm **7**

tiempo, el time; weather **2, 6, 7**

tiempo completo, trabajar a to work full-time **11**

tiempo parcial, trabajar a to work part-time **11**

tienda, la store; shop **8**

tienda especializa, la speciality store **8**

tierra, la earth; land **10**

tímido/a shy; timid **1**

tinta, la ink **12**

tío/a, el/la uncle/aunt **4**

típico/a typical **3**

tipo, el type **15**

tira cómica, la comic strip **14**

tirar to throw (away out) **12**

titular to title **7**

titular, el headline **13**

título, el degree; title **2, 6, 12**

tiza, la chalk **1**

toalla, la towel **7**

tobillo, el ankle **10**

tocar (un instrumento) to play (an instrument) **3, 4**

todo/a/os/as all; every; everyone **2, 3**

tomar to drink; to take **2, 6** to take; to drink **12**

tomarse la presión to take blood pressure (*Latin America*) **10**

tomar la tensión to take blood pressure (*Spain*) **10**

tomate, el tomato **6**

tonto/a stupid **13**

topografía, la topography **4**

torcer (ue) to twist **10**

torneo, el tournament **2**

torno a, en pertaining to **3**

toro, el bull **2**

toronja, la grapefruit **6**

torta, la cake **5**

torta de chocolate, la chocolate cake **6**

tortilla, la omelet **2, 6**

tortuga, la turtle **5**

torturar to torture **4**

tos, la cough **10**

toser to cough **10**

tostadora, la toaster **6**

tostar (ue) to toast **6**

trabajador/a hard-working **1**

trabajador/a, el/la worker **1**

trabajar to work **6**

trabajar (a comisión) to work (on commission) **2**

trabajo, el work **6, 11**

trabajo, estar sin to be out of work **11**

tradición, la tradition **4**

traducir (zc) to translate **11**

traer to bring **4, 7, 9, 11, 12**

traficar to traffic **7**

tráfico, el traffic **13**

tragedia, la tragedy **7, 13**

traje, el suit **8**

traje de baño, el swimsuit **7**

traje de noche, el evening gown **14**

tranquilamente calmly **8**

transferir (ie, i) to transfer **12**

transformar to transform **10**

transición, la transition **7**

transmitir to transmit **10, 13**

transporte, el transportation **3**

tras behind **15**

tratado, el treaty **15**

tratamiento, el treatment **10**

trayectoria, la trajectory **15**

trazar to race **9**

trekking, el hike **9**

tremendo/a tremendous **7**

tren, el train **6, 9** tren **7**

tribu, la tribe **10**

tribunal, el court **15**

triste sad **4, 5**

triunfo, el triumph **5**

trombón, el trombone **2, 14**

trompeta, la trumpet **14**

tú you (*inf.*) **1**

tul, el tulle (silk or nylon net) **14**

tumba, la tomb **15**

turismo, el tourism **5**

turista, el/la tourist **2**

turístico/a touristy **9**

turnarse to take turns **5**

tu/tus your (*inf.*) **1**

tuyo/a/os/as your (*inf.*) (of) yours **7, 13**

U

ubicación, la location **5**

ubicado/a located **8**

ufano/a conceited **8**

úlcera, la ulcer **10**

últimamente lately **15**

último/a last; latest **2, 4, 7**

una vez one time; once **5**

único/a only; unique **5, 8, 10**

unidad, la unity **4**

unido/a close close-knit **4**

uniforme, el uniform **7**

unirse (a) to join together **4, 15**

universidad, la university **1**

un/o/a a; one **1**

urgente urgent **9**

usar to use **4**

usted/es you (*for.*) (*masc./fem.*) **1**

usualmente usually **9**

utensilio, el utensil **6**

útil useful **15**

utilizar to use **4**

uvas, las grapes **6**

V

vacaciones, las vacation **5**

vacante, la vacancy **11**

vaciar to empty **5**

vacuna, la vaccine **10**

valer to be worth; to cost **9**

valioso/a useful **12**

valor, el value **10**

vamos let's go **4**

¿Vamos a... ? Should we go . . . ? **4**

vaqueros, los jeans (*Spain*) **8**

variar to vary **6**

variedad, la variety **5**

varios/as several; various **7**

vaso, el glass **6**

veces, a sometimes; at times **5**

vecino/a, el/la neighbor **5**

vegetariano/a, el/la vegetarian **6**

velocidad, la speed **9**

vencer to conquer **11**

vendedor/a ambulante, el/la street vendor **8**

vender to sell **2**

venganza, la revenge **4**

venir (ie) to come **4, 7**

venta, en on sale **5**

venta, la sale **9**

ventaja, la advantage **6, 7, 10, 11**

ventana, la window **9**

ventanilla, la window **9**

ver (la televisión/una película) to see; to watch (television/a movie) **2, 7, 7, 8, 12**

verano, el summer **1**

verdad, la truth **6, 10**

verdaderamente truly **9**

verdadero/a true **4**

verde green **1**

verduras, las vegetables **6**

verificar to verify **6**

verja, la iron grill **12**

versátil versatile **13**

versión, la version **10**

vestido, el dress **7, 8**

vestimenta, la clothing **9**

vestir (i, i) to dress **5**

vestirse (i, i) to get dressed **5**

veterano/a veteran **12**

veterinaria, la veterinary science **3**

veterinario/a, el/la veterinarian **11**

vez, la time; instance **5**

vez en cuando, de once in a while **5**

vía, la lane; way **5**

viajante, el/la traveling salesperson **11**

viajar to travel **2, 9**

viaje, el trip **1, 7, 9**

viajero/a, el/la traveler **9**

vías de desarrollo, en developing **15**

víctima, la victim **3**

vida, la life **2**

videograbadora, la VCR **12**

viejo/a old **2**

viento, el wind **14**

viento, hace it is windy **7**

vieres whatever you see **9**

viernes, el Friday **1**

vigilar to watch **15**

vigoroso/a vigorous **15**

villa, la town **15**

vinagre, el vinegar **6**

vino, el (tinto, blanco) (red white) wine **6**

viola, la viola **14**

violar to violate **15**

violencia, la violence **4**

violento/a violent **14**

violín, el violin **14**

virreinato, el viceroyalty **11**

visado, el visa **7**

visita, la guests; visit **5**

visitante, el/la visitor **9**

visitar to visit **2**

vista, la view **2, 5, 9**

vistoso/a showy **9**

vitamina, la vitamin **10**

viudo/a, el/la widow/er **4**

vivienda, la housing **15**

vivir to live **1, 2, 5, 6, 12**

vivo/a alive **3**

volante, el flier **5**

volar (ue) to fly **7**

volcán, el volcano **4, 5, 9**

voleibol, el volleyball **7**

voluntad, la will **7**

voluntario/a voluntary **5**

voluntario/a, el/la volunteer **5**

voluptuoso/a voluptuous **9**

volver (ue) to return **4, 7, 12**

vosotros/as you (*inf. pl.*) (*Spain*) **1, 4**

votante, el/la voter **13**

votar (por) to vote (for) **7, 15**

voto, el vote **13**

voz, la voice **8, 14**

vuelo, el flight **4, 9**

vuestro/a/os/as your; yours (*inf. pl.*); (of) yours **3, 13**

Y

y and **1**

ya already **14**

yerno, el son-in-law **4**

yo I **1**

yogur, el yogurt **6**

Z

zampoña, la panpipe **8**

zanahoria, la carrot **6**

zapatería, la shoe store **8**

zapatos, los shoes **8**

zoológico, el zoo **3**

zorro, el fox **8**

zumo, el juice **6**

A

a un/o/a **1**
abandon abandonar 7
ability la habilidad 8
aboard bordo a 6
abolish abolir **15**
abound abundar 6
about alrededor 12
above arriba de **5**
abroad el extranjero 4, **9**
absent ausente 15
abstain abstener 9
abuse el abuso 15
academic académico/a 3
academic subject la
   materia **3**
accede acceder 15
accelerate acelerar 15
accept aceptar **4**
accessory el accessorio **8**; la
   prenda 9, **14**
accident el accidente **10**
accommodate acomodar 5
accompany acompañar 6
accord el acuerdo **15**
according to según 5
accordion el acordeón 14
account la cuenta **6**
accountant el/la contador/a **11**
accounting la contabilidad **3**
ache el dolor **10**
achieve lograr 12, **15**;
   realizar 8
achievement el logro 4
acquire adquirir (ie, i) 13
across from enfrente de **3**, 14
act actuar **5**, **13**
action la acción 15
active activo/a **2**
activist el/la activista **15**
activity la actividad 8
actor el actor 5
actress la actriz 1
acupuncture la acupuntura
   10
add añadir 6; (**in**) echar **6**, 12;
   agregar 10
addressee el/la destinatario/a
   11
adequate adecuado/a 7
adjust ajustar 11
administration la
   administración 2

admiration la admiración 9
admirer el/la admirador/a 9
admit admitir 7
adoptive adoptivo/a 14
adore adorar 14
adorn adornar 9
adorned adornado/a 8
advance el avance 3
advanced avanzado/a 3, 8
advancing avanzado/a 3, 8
advantage la ventaja 6, 7,
   10, **11**
adventure la aventura 4
advice el consejo 7, **10**
advice column el consultorio
   sentimental 13
advise aconsejar 9
advisor el/la asesor/a **15**
advocate abogar 7
aerobic aeróbico/a **10**
aerobics ejercicios
   aeróbicos **10**
affect afectar 9
affection cariño **4**
affectionate afectuoso/a **4**
affirm afirmar 6
after después (de) (que)
   3, 7, **11**
afternoon la tarde 1, **2**
again otra vez **5**
against en contra **5**
age la edad 4
ago hace 5, **14**
agreeable agradable 5
agreed de acuerdo 4
agreement el convenio 13; la
   concordancia 10
agricultural agrícola 4
air conditioning el aire
   acondicionado 5
airline la aerolínea 9
airport el aeropuerto **9**
aisle el pasillo **5**
album el álbum 5
alcoholic beverages la
   bebidas alcohólicas 10
algebra el álgebra (*fem.*) 3
alive vivo/a **3**
all todo/a/os/as 2, **3**
allergic alérgico/a **10**
allergy la alergia 10
alleviate aliviar 10
alleviated aliviado/a 14

almost casi 10
along a través 8
already ya 14
also también 1, **2**, **7**
alternate alternarse 8
although aunque 4, **7**
altitude la altura 8
aluminum el aluminio 7
always siempre 2, **3**, **7**, **8**
ambiguity la ambigüedad 11
ambulance la ambulancia 10
American (US)
   norteamericano/a **2**
amorous amoroso/a 6
ample amplio/a 10
amusing simpático/a **1**, 8
analysis el análisis 3
analyst el/la analista **11**
ancestor el/la antepasado/a 4
ancestry la ascendencia 10
ancient antiguo/a 3 **and** y 1
Andean andino/a 8
Andean flute la quena 8
anecdote la anécdota 6
anger el enojo 15; enojar **10**
angry furioso/a **5**
animal el animal 3
animated animado/a 9
ankle el tobillo 10
anniversary el aniversario 6
announce anunciar 8
announcement el aviso 13
announcer el/la locutor/a 13
annoy molestar **6**, **10**
annoyed molesto/a **5**
another otro/a 2
answer contestar **1**; la
   respuesta 1
antacid el antiácido **10**
anthropology la
   antropología 3
antibiotic el antibiótico **10**
anticipate anticipar 8
anticipation la anticipación 9
antioxidants los
   antioxidantes **10**
anxious ansioso/a 9
any/one cualquier/a 9
anything algo 3, **6**, **7**
apartment el apartamento 3
aphrodisiac el afrodisíaco 6
apologize disculparse 15
apparent aparente 15

apparently aparentemente 15
appeal to apetecer **6**
appear aparecer 9
appearance la aparencia 1
appetizer el aperitivo 2; la
   entrada 6; las tapas 2
applaud aplaudir 14
apple la manzana 3, **6**
appliance el aparato 6
apply for solicitar 3, 11
appointment la cita **10**, 11
appreciate apreciar 4
appreciated apreciado/a 11
appropriate apropiado/
   a 10
approve pasar 5
approximately
   aproximadamente 3
April abril 1
aquatic acuático/a 9
aqueduct el acueducto 2
Arab el árabe 2
Arabic el árabe 2
archbishop el arzobispo **4**
archeologist el arqueólogo 8
archipelago el archipiélago 8
architect el/la arquitecto/a
   2, **11**
architecture la arquitectura 7
area el área (*fem.*) 7
Argentine argentino/a **2**
Argentine cowboy el
   gaucho 11
argument el argumento 4; la
   discusión 8
aria el aria (*fem.*) 14
arise from provenir 9
arm el brazo **10**
armchair el sillón **5**
armed armado/a 15
army el ejército **15**
around alrededor 12
around here por aquí 9
arrangement el arreglo 5
arrest detener (ie) 11
arrival la arribada 5; la
   llegada 2, 3, **9**
arrive llegar **2**
arrow la flecha 8
art el arte (*fem.*) **3**
arthritis la artritis 10
article el artículo 7, **13**
artifact el artefacto 5

artisan el/la artesano/a 3
as como 5
ascending ascendente 6
ashamed avergonzado/a 10
ashes la cenizas 9
ask pedir (i, i) 9; preguntar 6
ask for pedir (i, i) 6, 9, 10, 11
aspect el aspecto 8
aspiration la aspiración 15
aspirin la aspirina 10
assemble armar 8
assembly plant la
    maquiladora 15
assistant el/la asistente 7; el/la
    ayudante 6
associate asociar 2
association la asociación 7
as soon as en cuanto 11; luego
    que 11; tan pronto como 11
assure asegurar 5
asthma el asma (*fem.*) 10
at first al principio 5
at last por fin 6, 9
at least por lo menos 6
ATM (automatic teller
    machine) el cajero
    automático 4, 8, 12
atmosphere el ambiente 6; la
    atmósfera 3
attack atacar 10; el ataque 4
attend asistir (a) 2
at times a veces 5
attract atraer 6
attraction la atracción 9
attractive atractivo/a 3
attribute atribuir 14
audience el público 12, 13
audition la audición 14
auditorium el auditorio 3
August agosto 1
authentic auténtico/a 14
author el/la autor/a 2
authority la autoridad 14
autobiographical
    autobiográfico/a 2
autograph el autógrafo 14
autonomous autónomo/a 2
available disponible 5
avenue la avenida 12
average el promedio 11
avocado el aguacate 6
avoid evitar 10
awesome padre (adj.) 4

B
back la espalda 10
background el fondo 14
backpack la mochila 1
bad mal 1; malo/a 1, 10

bag el bolso 7, 8; la bolsa 7
baggage el equipaje 9
baggage claim el reclamo de
    equipaje 9; la sala de
    reclamación de equipaje 9
bake hornear 6
ballad la balada 13
ballet el ballet 1, 14
ballroom dancing el baile de
    salón 14
banana el plátano 6, 8; la
    banana 6
band la banda 4, 14
bank el banco 8; la orilla 5
banner el pendón 15
banquet el banquete 7
bar el bar 2
barbs la púas 12
bargain la ganga 8, 9;
    regatear 8
baritone el barítono 14
baseball el béisbol 4; la
    pelota 7
baseball player el beisbolista
    2
based basado/a 6
basket la cesta 3
basketball el básquetbol
    5, 7
Basque el eusquera 2
bass el bajo 3; el contrabajo
    14
bat el bate 7
bathe bañarse 5
bathroom el baño 5
battery la pila 9
battle la batalla 1
be estar 3, 5, 7, 9; ser 1, 2, 3, 7,
    8, 9
be . . . years old tener...
    años 3
be able poder (ue) 4, 7
be a bother molestar 6, 10
be accustomed to
    acostumbrar 13
beach la playa 5
bead la cuenta 6
beak el pico 8, 9
beans los frijoles 6
bear el oso 3
beat batir 6; latir 15
beautiful bello/a 2;
    hermoso/a 6
beauty la belleza 9
be behind retrasar 4
be born nacer 2
be called llamarse 5
because porque 2; pues 3
become ponerse 5

become accustomed
    acostumbrarse 8
become aware enterarse 15
become happy alegrarse (de) 5
become sick enfermarse 5
bed la cama 5, 10
bedroom el dormitorio 5
be enough bastar 8
beer la cerveza 3, 6
be extremely pleasing
    encantar 6
be familiar with conocer 4
be fascinating fascinar 6
before antes (de) 2, 11
be game animarse 5
begin comenzar (ie) 7;
    empezar (ie) 1, 3, 4, 7, 9;
    iniciar 9
beginning el comienzo 5; el
    inicio 4; el principio 3, 13
be glad alegrarse (de) 5, 10
behind atrás 7; detrás (de) 3;
    tras 15
be interesting interesar 6
be involved involucrar 13
belief la creencia 2
believe creer 2, 6, 10, 12
belly el buche 8
belongings la pertenencias 13
beloved amado/a 13
below debajo (de) 5
be missing faltar 8
bench el banco 8
benefit el beneficio 11
beverage la bebida 6
be worth valer 9
bicycle la bicicleta 2
big grande 1, 2
bilingual bilingüe 12
bill la cuenta 6
biography la biografía 2
biological biológico/a 10
biology la biología 3
biosphere la biosfera 3
bird el pájaro 5, 9; el ave 3
birth el nacimiento 1
birthday el cumpleaños 1
birthrate el índice de
    natalidad 4
black negro/a 1
blackboard la pizarra 1
blazer el saco 8; la americana
    (*Spain*) 8
bleachers las gradas 15
block el bloque 8; la cuadra 3;
    la manzana (*Spain*) 3, 6
blond rubio/a 2

blood la sangre 11
blood pressure la presión
    arterial 10
blouse la blusa 8
blow soplar 8
blue azul 1
blue-footed booby el booby
    con patas azules 8
board abordar 9; la tabla
    10, 12
boarding gate la puerta de
    embarque 9
boarding pass la tarjeta de
    embarque 9
board of trustees el
    patronato 1
boat el barco 5, 9
body el cuerpo 5, 10
bomb la bomba 15
bone el hueso 10
book el libro 1
bookcase el estante 5
bookstore la librería 3
boots la botas 8
border la frontera 3, 8
bore aburrir 6
boring aburrido/a 1
borrow pedir prestado 6
boss el/la jefe/a 9, 11
bottle la botella 7
bottom el fondo 14
bow el arco 5
box la caja 8
box office la taquilla 8
boy el chico 3; el muchacho 2
boycott el boicot 15
boyfriend el novio 3, 4
bracelet la pulsera 8
branch el ramo 7; la rama 10
brand la marca 12
Brazilian brasileño/a 2
bread el pan 6
break romper 12
break (a bone) romperse (un
    hueso) 10
break down dañarse 15
breakfast el desayuno 2, 6
breathe respirar 10
brief breve 6
briefcase el maletín 4
brightly colored colorido/a 9
brillant brillante 3
bring traer 4, 7, 9, 11, 12
brochure el folleto 9
broken roto/a 2
brother-in-law/sister-in-law
    el/la cuñado/a 4
brother/sister el/la
    hermano/a 3, 4

brown castaño/a 2; color café 1; pardo/a 8

brunette castaño/a 2; moreno/a 2

brush cepillarse 5

bucket la cubeta 5

Buddhist budista 14

building el edificio 8

bull el toro 2

bungee jump hacer salto en bungee 9

burn arder 15

bury enterrar (ie) 14

bus el autobús 5, 9; el camión (*Mexico*) 8

business el negocio 3

business administration la administración de empresas 3

business letter la carta comercial 11

businessman el hombre de negocios 11

business section la sección financiera 13

businesswoman la mujer de negocios 11

busy ocupado/a 4

but pero 2, 3, 15; sino 1, 15

but rather sino 1, 15

butter la mantequilla 6

buy comprar 2, 8, 9, 11

by por 9

by way of mediante 15

C

cabinet el gabinete 11

cable television la televisión (por cable) 13

cadaver el cadáver 14

café el café 4

cafeteria la cafetería 2

caffeine la cafeína 6

cake el pastel 6; la torta 5

calcium el calcio 10

calculate calcular 7

calculator la calculadora 1

calculus el cálculo 3

call llamar 5

call letters la siglas 7

calm down aquietar 15

calmly tranquilamente 8

calorie la caloría 6

camera la cámara 4

camp acampar 5; el campamento 9

campaign la campaña 12, 15

can poder (ue) 4, 7

Canada Canadá 6

Canadian canadiense 2

canal el canal 13

cancel cancelar 9

cancer el cáncer 10

candidate el/la candidato/a 6, 15

cap la gorra 8

capable capaz 11

capacity la capacidad 11

capital city la capital 1, 2

car el auto 9; el carro 3, 9; el coche 9

carbohydrates los carbohidratos 10

cardiologist el cardiólogo 10

career la carrera 3

careful cuidadoso/a 9

careful, to be tener cuidado 3

Caribbean dance el merengue 7

carpenter el/la carpintero/a 11

carrot la zanahoria 6

carry portar 15

carry out llevar a cabo 5; realizar 11

carved tallado/a 3

carving el tallado 3

cascades la cascadas 9, 11

cash register la caja 8

casserole la cazuela 6

castle el castillo 13

cat el/la gato/a 5, 8

cathedral la catedral 9

Catholic católico/a 9

cause causar 5; la causa 7

cave la cueva 9

CD/DVD player el lector de CD/DVD 12

celebrate celebrar 5

celebration la celebración 7; la fiesta 1, 3

celebrity la celebridad 7

cello el chelo 14

cellophane el celofán 14

cell phone el teléfono celular/móvil 1

Celtic celta 2

cemetery el cementerio 14

censorship la censura 13

censure censurar 13

census el censo 13

centennial el centenario 5

century el siglo 1, 6

CEO el/la jefe/a ejecutivo/a 11

ceramic la cerámica 4

ceremony la ceremonia 4

certain cierto/a 2, 10; seguro/a 4, 5, 10

chain la cadena 8

chair la silla 1

chalk la tiza 1

challenge el desafío 3; retar 5

challenging exigente 3

champagne el champán 8

champion el/la campeón/campeona 7

change cambiar 4; el cambio 4

channel el canal 13

chao chaito 14

chapel la capilla 8

character el carácter 13; el personaje 1

characteristic la característica 11

charade la charada 6

charge cobrar 4

charger el cargador 9

charitable benéfico/a 14; caritativo/a 9

charm el encanto 7

chauffeur el chofer 11

cheap barato/a 1

check revisar 1, 2, 10, 12, 13

check luggage facturar el equipaje 9

cheer animar 3

cheese el queso 6

chef el/la cocinero/a 6, 11

chellist el/la chelista 14

chemistry la química 3

chest el pecho 10

chick la cría 5

chicken el pollo 6, 10

chief el cacique 9

childish infantil 8

children los/las niños/as 1, 7

Chilean chileno/a 2

chill el escalofrío 10

chinchilla la chinchilla 14

Chinese el chino 2

chiropractor el/la quiropráctico/a 10

chocolate cake la torta de chocolate 6

cholera el cólera 5

cholesterol el colesterol 10

choose elegir (i, i) 13, 15; escoger 5

chop picar 6

choreograph coreografiar 14

choreographer el/la coreógrafo/a 14

chores los quehaceres 5

Christian cristiano/a 9

christianize cristianizar 10

Christmas la Navidad 4

chronic crónico/a 10

chronology la cronología 11

chubby gordo/a 2, 5

church la iglesia 7

cinematographer el/la cinematógrafo 13

cinematography la cinematografía 13

circulation la circulación 13

citizen el/la ciudadano/a 15

citizenship la ciudadanía 12

city la ciudad 1, 2

city map el plano de la ciudad 9

civilization la civilización 3

Civil War la Guerra Civil 3

clap la palmada 14

clarinet el clarinete 14

class la clase 1

classic clásico/a 14

classical clásico/a 4

classified ads los anuncios clasificados 11, 13

classmate el/la compañero/a de clase 8

clause la cláusula 10

clean limpio/a 6

clean (the house) limpiar, ordenar (la casa) 5

cleaning service el servicio de limpieza 5

clear claro/a 1, 6; cristalino/a 5; despejado/a 8

clearance sale la liquidación 8

clear the table quitar la mesa 5

clever listo/a 9

client el/la cliente 2

climate el clima 4, 5

climb escalar 9; subir 6

clinic la clínica 11

clip recortar 13

clock el reloj 1

close cerrar (ie) 1; próximo/a 2, 7; unido/a 4

close (to) cerca (de) 2

closed cerrado/a 3

close-knit unido/a 4

closing la despedida 1, 4, 11

cloth la tela 8, 14

clothing la ropa 5, 8; la vestimenta 9

clothing size la talla 8

cloud la nube 8

cloudy nublado/a 7

coach el/la entrenador/a 7

coach class la clase turista **9**
coast la costa 2, 6
coat el abrigo **8**
coconut el coco 6
code el código 15
coffee el café 6
coffee maker la cafetera **6**
coin la moneda 8
coincide coincidir 13
coincidentally por
    casualidad 10
cold el resfriado **10**; frío **3**;
    frío/a 6
cold, it is hace frío 7
collaborate colaborar 9
collar el cuello 15
colleague el/la colega 11
collection la colección 3
cologne la colonia **8**
Colombian colombiano/a **2**
Colombian currency el
    bolívar 9
colonizer el/la
    colonizador/a 9
colony la colonia 8
coloring colorido/a 9
comb el peine 5
combat combatir 9, **15**
combatant el/la
    combatiente 4
combination la combinación
    10
comb one's hair peinarse 5
come venir (ie) **4, 7**
comedy la comedia **4, 13, 14**
comfort la comodidad 14
comfortable cómodo/a 9
comforts las comodidades 9
comic cómico/a 4
comic strip la tira cómica 14
command el mandato 11
commemorate conmemorar 3
comment comentar 5
commentary el comentario 3
commentator el/la
    comentarista 7, **13**
commerce el comercio 3
commission la comisión 8; la
    tarifa 10
commit cometer 14
commitment el compromiso
    7, 11
committee el comité 4
common común 1
commonwealth el estado
    libre asociado 7
communications las
    comunicaciones **3**
community la comunidad 3

compact disc (CD) el disco
    compacto 8
companion el/la
    acompañante 7
company la compañía 13; la
    empresa 2, **11**
compare comparar 5
comparison la comparación 5
compatriot el/la
    compatriota 5
compensation la
    recompensa 9
compete competir (i,i) 10
complain quejarse 14
complement complementar 3
complete completo/a 6;
    cumplir 1
complex complejo/a **10**
complicate complicar 11
complicated complicado/a **3**
compliment el piropo 9
compose componer **14**
composer el/la compositor/a
    7, **14**
composition la composición 2
comprehension la
    comprensión 13
computer la computadora **1,
    3, 12**
computer (electronic) game
    el juego electrónico 12
computer science la
    computación 3; la
    informática 3
conceited ufano/a 8
concept el concepto 4
concert el concierto 2, 3, **4**
conclusion el desenlace 11
concrete concreto/a 7
condemn condenar 11
condemned condenado/a 13
condition la condición 5
condor el cóndor 8
conduct dirigir 9, 14
conductor el/la conductora
    15; el/la director/a 9,
    11, 14
confidence la confianza 10
conflict el conflicto 8, **15**
confront enfrentar 7
confuse confundir 10
congested congestionado/a 10
congress el congreso 15
congressman/woman el/la
    congresista 15
conjecture la conjetura 12
connect conectar 5
connection la conexión 12
connoisseur el conocedor 6

conquer vencer 11
conquest la conquista 3
consensus el consenso 14
consequences las
    consecuencias 15
conservative conservador/a 13
conserve conservar 7, 8, **12**
consider considerar 3
considerate considerado/a 15
considered considerado/a 15
construct construir 2
construction la
    construcción 2, **5**
construction worker el/la
    obrero/a de construcción **11**
consult consultar 9
consultant el/la asesor/a **15**
consume consumir **12**
consumer el/la
    consumidor/a 1
consumption el consumo 6
contact contactar 10
contain contener (ie) 3
container el contenedor 13; el
    envase 12
contaminate contaminar **12**
contemporaneous
    contemporáneo/a 6
content el contenido 10
contest el concurso 13
continue continuar 6
contract contratar 13; el
    contrato 9, **11**
contrast el contraste 6
contribute contribuir 9
contribution el aporte 15
control controlar 13
controversy la polémica 12
conventional convencional 13
conversation la
    conversación 7
converse conversar 3
convert convertir (ie, i) 9
conviction la convicción 15
convince convencer 2
cook cocinar 6; el/la
    cocinero/a 6, **11**
cookies la galletas 6, **10**
cool copado/a 12
cool, it is hace fresco 7
cooler la heladera 7
cooperate cooperar 8
coordinator el/la
    coordinador/a 11
copper el cobre 6
copy la copia 7
cord la cuerda 14
cordially yours cordialmente **11**
corduroy la pana **14**

corn el maíz **6**
corner la esquina 3
cornet la corneta **14**
correct acertado/a 12
correspondent el/la
    corresponsal 12
corridor el corredor 12
corruption la corrupción **15**
cosmopolitan
    cosmopolito/a 11
cost costar (ue) 2; el costo 13;
    valer 9
co-star el/la compañero/a de
    reparto 13
Costa Rican costarricense 3
costly costoso/a 7
costume el disfraz 14
cotton el algodón **8**
couch el sofá 5
cough la tos **10**; toser **10**
cough syrup el jarabe **10**
counter el mostrador 9
country el campo 5; el país **2,
    8, 15**
countryman el paisano 15
coup d'état el golpe de
    estado **15**
couple la pareja 4
course el curso 3; la materia **3;
    of** claro **3**
court el tribunal 15; la
    cancha 2, **3**
cousin el/la primo/a 4
cover cubrir 8, 12
covered cubierto/a 8
cover letter la carta de
    presentación **11**
cowardice la cobardía 1
crane la garza 8
crazy loco/a 7
cream la crema **5**
create crear 6
creativity la creatividad 2
creator el/la creador/a 8
credit card la tarjeta de
    crédito **8**
creole criollo/a 6
cricket la cigarra 8
crime el crimen 14
critic el/la crítico/a **13**
crocodile el cocodrilo 9
cross cruzar 14
crucial indispensable **9**
crude grosero/a 15
cruise el crucero **9**
crush machacar 11
cry el grito 11; llorar 7
crystalline cristalino/a 5
Cuban cubano/a **2**

cuisine la cocina 3
culinary culinario/a 6
culture la cultura 4
cultured culto/a 14
cup/mug la taza 6
cure curar 10
curious curioso/a 7
current actual 10, **15**
current events la actualidad 13
curriculum vitae (vita) el curriculum vítae **11**
curtain el telón 11
curved curvado/a 9
custard dessert el flan **6**
custom la costumbre 6
customer el/la cliente 2
customer service la atención al cliente **8**
customs la aduana **9**
customs inspector el/la inspector/a de aduanas 9
cut cortar 6
cute bonito/a **2**
cycling el ciclismo **7**
cypress el ciprés 14

D

daily diario/a 2
dairy products los productos lácteos 6
dam el embalse 10
damage dañar 15; el daño 15; perjudicar 12
dance bailar **2**; el baile 3, **14**; la danza 14
danceable bailable 9
dancer el/la bailarín/a **14**
danger el peligro 5, 9, **12**
dangerous peligroso/a 2
daring atrevido/a 12
dark oscuro/a 8
data el dato 1
date la fecha **1**, 5
daughter la hija 4, 6
daughter-in-law la nuera 4
dawn el amanecer 11; la madrugada 4
day el día **1**
day before yesterday anteayer **6**, 8
daycare center la guardería **11**
day laborer el jornalero 15
dear querido/a **4**
death la muerte 3
debate debatir 14, **15**; el debate 15
debut debutar 10; el debut 14; estrenar 13
decade la década 14

decaffeinated descafeinado/a 2
deceit el engaño 4
deceive engañar 13
December diciembre **1**
decide decidir **2**
declaration la declaración 6
decoration la decoración 3
decrease bajar 4, **12**
dedicate dedicar 7
dedicated dedicado/a 9
deep profundo/a **5**
defeat rendir (i, i) 13
defect el defecto 13
defend defender (ie) 7
define definir 4
deforestation la deforestación **12**
degree el grado 10; el título 2, 6, 12; la licenciatura 3
delay la demora 9, **9**
delicious delicioso/a 2; rico/a 2, 4, **6**; sabroso/a **6**
delight el encanto 7; encantar **6**; la delicia 6
Delighted. Encantado/a. **1**
delightful encantador/a 2, 4, **14**
deliver entregar 1; repartir **11**
demanding exigente 3
democracy la democracia **15**
democratization la democratización 15
demographic demográfico/a 13
denounce denunciar 4
dentist el/la dentista 10
deny negar (ie) **10**
deodorant el desodorante 8
department el departamento 8
department store el almacén **8**
departure la salida 2, 6, **9**
depopulation la despoblación 12
deposit el depósito 9
derive derivar 6
descend descender (ie) 11
descendant el/la descendiente 3
describe describir 1
description la descripción 5
desert el desierto 4
deserted desierto/a 5
deserve merecer (zc) 2
design diseñar 2; el diseño 3
designer el/la diseñador/a **14**

desire desear 3, **9**; el deseo 13
desk el escritorio 15
destination el destino 2
destroy destruir 12
detach desprender 10
detail el detalle 6
detain detener (ie) 11; retrasar 4
deteriorate deteriorar 12
detest detestar 11
develop desarrollar 3
developing en vías de desarrollo 4, 15
development el desarrollo 6, **12**
diabetes la diabetes **10**
diagnosis el diagnóstico 10
diamond de diamantes 8
dictator el/la dictador/a **15**
dictatorship la dictadura **15**
dictionary el diccionario 1
die morir (ue, u) 7, 8, **12**
diet la dieta **10**; el régimen 10; la dieta 6, **10**
different diferente 8; distinto/a 6
difficult difícil 2, 6, **10**
dig cavar 14
dig up desenterrar 5
digital camera la cámara digital **9**
dignify dignificar 11
dignity la dignidad 4
dilemma el dilema 10
diminish disminuir 13
dining room el comedor **5**
dinner la cena 2, **6**
direct dirigir 9, 14
directed dirigido/a 13
directly directamente 7
director el/la director/a 9, 11, **14**
dirty sucio/a 6
disabled person el/la discapacitado/a 3
disadvantage la desventaja 6, **11**
disappear desaparecer 9
disarm desarmar 15
disarmament el desarme 15
discount el descuento 8
discouraged desanimado/a 12
discover descubrir 6, **12**
discovered descubierto/a 13
discrete discreto/a 13
discussion la discusión 8
disguise el disfraz 14
disgust asco 6

dishonest deshonesto/a 15
dishonor deshonrar 11
dishwasher el lavaplatos **5**
disillusion defraudar 15; desilusionar 15
disillusionment el desengaño 10
disorder el desorden 8
disorganized desordenado/a 5
disoriented desorientado/a 10
disposed dispuesto/a 13, **14**
dispute disputar 7
distance la distancia 8
distant retirado/a 10
distribute repartir 11
diva la diva **14**
diversity la diversidad 2
divide partir 11
divorced divorciado/a 4
do hacer 2, 3, 7, 9, 12
doctor el/la doctor/a 10; el/la médico/a **10**
doctorate el doctorado 3
doctor's office el consultorio 10
documentary el documental 13
dog el/la perro/a 4, 5, 8
dog walker el/la paseador/a de perros 11
dollar el dólar 6
domestic doméstico/a 3
dominate dominar 12
Dominican dominicano/a **2**
donate donar 7
Don't worry. No te preocupes. **10**
door la puerta 1
dossier el expediente 11
dot, on the en punto 2
double doble **9**
double room el cuarto doble **9**
doubt dudar 10; la duda 2
doubtful dudoso/a **10**
download bajar 4, **12**
downtown el centro 3, **4**
dowry el/la dote 15
Do you want go to...? ¿Quieres ir a...? **4**
drama el drama 13
dramatic dramático/a 13
dramatize dramatizar 11
draw dibujar 5
drawing el dibujo 5
draw up encoger 8
dream el sueño 6, 12
dream (about) soñar (ue) (con) **4**

dress el vestido 7, **8**; vestir (i, i) **5**
dresser la cómoda **5**
drink tomar 2, **6**, **12**
drive clavar 15; conducir 2
drug la droga 14
drug addiction la drogadicción **15**
drum el tambor 14
drums la batería 8, **14**
dry seco/a 6
dryer la secadora **5**
duck el pato **8**
durability la durabilidad 14
during durante 2; por **9**
dust sacudir 15
Dutch holandés/esa 7
duty el deber **15**
DVD el DVD 12
DVD recorder la grabadora de DVD **12**
dynamic dinámico/a 4

E

each cada 5
eager, to be tener ganas **3**
eagle el águila (*fem.*) 12
earbud el casco **12**
earbuds los auriculares **12**
early temprano/a 2
earn ganar 2, 4, **7**
earrings aretes **8**
earth la tierra 10
earthquake el terremoto 14
easily fácilmente 9
easy fácil 2, 6, 7, **10**
eat comer 2, **6**, **8**, 9, **10**, **11**, **12**
eat lunch almorzar (ue) 8
ecological ecológico/a 8
economic económico/a 6
economy la economía 3
ecotourism el ecoturismo 4
eco-volunteering el eco voluntariado 5
Ecuadorian ecuatoriano/a **2**
edit editar 12
editing la redacción 13
edition la edición 13
editor el editor 13
editorial (page) el editorial **13**
editor-in-chief el/la director/a **13**
educate educar 10
education la educación 6; la formación **11**
effective efectivo/a 5
efficient eficiente 11
effort el esfuerzo 4, **15**
egg el huevo 5, **6**

eighth octavo/a **8**
either . . . or o... o 7
elaborate elaborar 15
elaborated elaborado/a 4
elaboration la elaboración 15
elastic el elástico **14**
elbow el codazo 15
elect elegir (i, i) 13, **15**
elected electo/a 6
election la elección 7
electrical eléctrico/a 3, **9**
electrical adaptor el adaptador eléctrico **9**
electric current la corriente 9
electrician el/la electricista 11
electricity la electricidad 10
electric razor la máquina de afeitar 5
electrifying electrizante 14
electronic electrónico/a 2, **12**
electronics los aparatos electrónicos **12**
elimination la eliminación 15
emanate emanar 15
embassador el/la embajador/a 7
embassy la embajada 15
emblem el logotipo 12
embrace abrazar 10; el abrazo 2
embroider bordar 4
emerald la esmeralda 9
emerge surgir 15
emergency room la sala de urgencias 10
emotion la emoción 8
emotional emocional 11
empire el imperio 8
employee el/la empleado/a 11
empty vaciar **5**
enchanting encantador/a 2, 4, **14**
enclose encerrar 12
enclosed cubierto/a 8
encounter el encuentro 8
encourage animar 3
end el fin 7; el final **13**; eliminar **15**; terminar 6, 10
endangered species las especies en peligro de extinción **12**
end well salir bien 9
enemy el/la enemigo/a 3
energy la energía 7, **12**
engineer el/la ingeniero/a 3, 5, **11**
engineering la ingeniería 2, **3**
English el inglés **2**
enjoy disfrutar de 6; gozar de 9

enjoy oneself divertirse (ie, i) 5, 7
Enjoy your meal! ¡Buen provecho! 6
enormous enorme 3
entertain entretener (ie) 5
entertainment el entretenimiento 7
entertainment section la cartelera 13
enthusiastic entusiasta **2**
enthusiastically animadamente 9
environment el medio ambiente 5, **12**
environmental ambiental 10
epoch la época 4
equality la igualdad 5
equally igual de 7
equator la línea ecuatorial 8
equipment el equipo 5
equity la equidad 15
eradicate erradicar 6
eruption la erupción 5
escape escaparse 4
escort el/la acompañante 7
especially especialmente 8
essential esencial 13; preciso/a **9**
establish establecer (zc) 12
esteemed estimado/a **11**
eternal eterno/a 8
ethics la ética 11
ethnic étnico/a 10
ethnicity la etnia 13
even incluso 9
evening gown el traje de noche 14
event el acontecimiento 7; el evento 7; la función 4
even though aunque 7
every todo/a/os/as 2, **3**
everyone todo/a/os/as **3**
evolution la evolución 8
exaggerate exagerar 6
exam el examen **3**
example el ejemplo 2; **for** por ejemplo 6, **9**
excellent excelente 2
exceptional excepcional 7
excessive excesivo/a 12
excess weight el sobrepeso 10
exchange el cambio 4; el intercambio 2; intercambiar 1
exciting emocional 11; emocionante 2
excursion la excursión 6, **9**
excuse la excusa 5

excuse oneself retirarse **11**, 15
execution la ejecución 14
executive el/la ejecutivo/a 3
exercise ejercer 15; ejercicio; hacer ejercicios 7
exhausted exhausto/a 8
exhibit exhibir 14
exist existir 8
exotic exótico/a **1**, 5
expand ampliar 6
expense el gasto 5
expensive caro/a **1**; costoso/a 7
experience experimentar 2; la experiencia 5
expiration date la fecha de vencimiento 10
explain explicar 5; exponer 15
explicit explícito/a 13
exploit explotar 15
exploitation la explotación 7
export exportar 6
exposition la exposición 3
express expresar 15
express an opinion opinar 5
express oneself expresarse 11
extend to abarcar 14; extender (ie) 3
extensive extenso/a 3
extinction la extinción 5
extinguish (fires) apagar (fuegos/incendios) **11**
extraordinary extraordinario/a 11
extreme extremo/a 6
eye el ojo **5**

F

fable la fábula 8
fabric la tela 8, **14**
fabricate fabricar 14
fabulous fabuloso/a 2, **7**
face afrontar 15; la cara 5
facilitate facilitar 5
facility la facilidad 11
facing enfrente de 3, **14**
factor el factor 10
factory la fábrica 12
fail (computer disk) fallar 12
fair la feria 9
fairly bastante 3
fall la caída 11
fall down caerse 15
fall asleep dormirse (ue, u) 5
fall in love (with) enamorarse (de) 5
falls la cataratas 11
false falso/a 2
familiarize oneself familiarizarse 14

family la familia 3, **4**
fan el/la aficionado/a **7**
fanatic el/la fanático/a **2**
fantastic fantástico/a **7, 10**
fantasy la fantasía **14**
far lejos (de) **3**
faraway lejano/a **11**
farewell la despedida 1, 4, **11**
farm la granja **15**
farmer el campesino 5; el granjero **15**
fascinating fascinante **1**
fashion la costura **14**; la moda **14**
fashion show el desfile de moda **14**
fat (*adj.*) gordo/a 2, **5**
fat (*noun*) la grasa 6, **10**
father el padre **4**
father-in-law el suegro **4**
fatigue el cansancio 10; la fatiga **10**
favor of, in a favor **15**
fear el temor 15; temer 10; tener miedo 3, **10**
feature el reportaje **13**; resaltar **7**
February febrero **1**
fee la comisión 8; la tarifa **10**
feel sentirse (ie, i) 5, **8**
feel like tener ganas **3**
feminine femenino/a **6**
femininity la feminidad **14**
ferocious feroz **10**
fever la fiebre 5, **10**
fiber la fibra **10**
fiction la ficción **4**
fifth quinto/a **8**
figure la figura 3, 9; la línea 5, **10**
file archivar **12**
fill completely rellenar **11**
filled relleno/a **6**
filling el relleno **4**
fill out rellenar **11**
fill the dishwasher llenar el lavaplatos **5**
film el cine 2, 13; filmar 13; la peli 4; la película 4, 7; rodar **10**
filming el rodaje 4; la filmación **13**
film noir el filme negro **4**
finally al final 5; por fin 6, 9; por último **9**
finance las finanzas **3**
financial financiero/a **3**
financial section la sección financiera **13**

find encontrar (ue) 1, 3, **4**
fine la multa 12; multar **12**
fine with me de acuerdo **4**
finger (toe) el dedo (del pie) **10**
finish acabar (de) (+ *inf.*) 5, 11, 12; terminar 6, **10**
fire despedir (i, i) 11, **11**; el fuego 10; el incendio **11**
firefighter el/la bombero/a 10, **11**
firetruck la bomba **15**
fireworks los fuegos artificiales **9**
firm la compañia 13; la empresa 2, **11**
first primer/o/a 2, 7, **8**
fish el pescado 6; pescar **9**
fishing pesquero/a **6**
fit encajar 8; quedar 6, **8**
fitting room el probador **8**
flame la llama **10**
flamenco el flamenco **14**; flamenco/a **2**
flamingo el flamenco **3**
flank flanquear **15**
flash drive la memoria USB **12**
flavor el sabor **1**
fleamarket el mercado callejero **8**
flee huir **14**
flier el volante **5**
flight el vuelo 4, **9**
flight attendant el/la asistente de vuelo **9**
flip-flop la chancla **8**
floor el piso 5, **8**
flour la harina **6**
flourish florecer **15**
flower la flor 7, 9, **10**;
flower bed el cantero de jardín **14**
flower shop la florería **8**
flu la gripa (*Mexico*) 10; la gripe **10**
flute la flauta **14**
fly volar (ue) **7**
fog la niebla **9**
follow seguir (i, i) 9, **10**
following a continuación 6; siguiente **4**
food la comida 2, 3, 4, **6**
foods los alimentos **10**
fool el/la necio/a **10**
foot el pie **10**
footwear el calzado **8**
for para 1, 9; por **9**
force la fuerza **15**

forecast el pronóstico **4**
foreign extranjero/a **7**
foreigner el/la extranjero/a **7**
forest el bosque 9, 10, **12**
forget olvidar(se) (de) 5, **7**
fork el tenedor **6**
form el formulario **11**; formar **8**
formula la fórmula **5**
formulate formular **3**
fortify afianzar (c) 15; fortalecer (zc) 6, **15**
fortress la fortaleza **7**
forum el foro 7, **14**
found fundar **7**
foundation la fundación 7, **13**
founded fundado/a **9**
founding la fundación 7, **13**
fourth cuarto/a 2, **8**
fox el zorro **8**
fragment el fragmento **12**
framework el marco **4**
France Francia **2**
fraud el fraude **15**
free gratis 10; libre **4**
freezer el congelador **6**
French el francés **2**; francés/esa **2**
French fries la papas fritas **10**
frequent frecuente **11**
frequently con frecuencia 5, 8; frecuentemente **8**
fresh fresco/a **6**
Friday el viernes **1**
fried frito/a **6**
friend el/la amigo/a **1**
from desde **2**
front, in enfrente **12**
frontier la frontera 3, **8**
front of, in delante de 2, **3**
front page la portada 13; la primera plana **13**
fruit el fruto 10; la frutas **6**
fry freír (i, i) **6**
frying pan la sartén **6**
fulfill cumplir **15**
full-time a tiempo completo **11**
fun divertido/a **3**
function funcionar 10, 12; la función **4**
funds los fondos **14**
funny gracioso/a **4**
fur la piel 10, **14**
furnish armar **8**
furnished amueblado/a **5**
furniture los muebles **5**
fury la furia **10**

fuse fusionar **3**
fusion la fusión **14**
future el futuro **12**

G

gabardine (lightweight wool) la gabardina **14**
gain weight engordar 10; subir de peso **10**
game el partido **5**
game show el concurso **13**
gang member el pandillero **12**
garage el garaje **5**
garbage can el basurero **5**
garden el jardín **5**
garlic el ajo **6**
garment la prenda 9, **14**
gasoline la gasolina **12**
gather congregar **15**
gathering la recolección **10**
GDP el PIB **9**
genealogical genealógico/a **4**
general, in por lo general **9**
generalize generalizar **4**
generally generalmente **9**
generate generar **15**
generation la generación **7**
generous generoso/a **5**
genetic genético/a **10**
genre el género **4**
geography la geografía **3**
geology la geología **3**
German el alemán **2**
gesture el ademán 11; el gesto **14**
get conseguir (i, i) 9, **11**
get angry (with) enojarse (con) 5, **14**
get better mejorarse **10**
get down (from) bajarse (de) **9**
get dressed vestirse (i, i) **5**
get in shape ponerse en forma **10**
get involved in meterse **12**
get off (of) bajarse (de) **9**
get together juntarse **5**
get-together la reunión **2**
get up levantarse **5**
get well mejorarse **10**
gift el regalo **4**
girl la chica 3; la muchacha **2**
girlfriend la novia 3, **4**
give dar 1, **6**
give a gift regalar **13**
glance la mirada **13**
glass el vaso **6**
glass bowl el tazón de cristal **6**
glasses la gafas 15; los lentes **12**

globalization la globalización 4

global market el mercado global 15

global warming el calentamiento global 12

glory la gloria 7

glove el guante 7

go ir 1, 3, 8, 10, 12

goal el gol 7; el propósito 7; la meta 7, 11

go to a nightclub ir a una discoteca 7

go away alejarse 11; irse 5; marcharse 9

go to bed acostarse (ue) 5

go bike riding montar en bicicleta 7, 9

god el dios 8, 9

God willing Ojalá 9, 10

gold el oro 1, 8

gold ring el anillo de oro 8

golf el golf 2, 7

good bueno/a 1, 9, 10; el bien 6

Good afternoon. Buenas tardes. 1

Good-bye. Adiós. 1

good deal la ganga 8, 9

Good evening. Buenas noches. 1

good-looking guapo/a 2

Good morning. Buenos días. 1

goodness la bondad 7

goods los bienes 5

go on an outing ir de excursión 9, 9

go out dar un paseo 7; salir 4

go round recorrer 9

go shopping ir de compras 8

gossipy chismoso/a 5

go up subir 6

gourd la calabaza 11

government el gobierno 2, 6, 12, 15

governmental gubernamental 12

governor el/la gobernador/a 15

go well with hacer juego (con) 8

grab agarrar 11

grade la nota 3

grammar la gramática 13

granddaughter la nieta 4

grandfather/grandmother el/la abuelo/a 4

grandma la abuelita (*diminutive*) 4

grandmother la abuela 4

grandson/granddaughter el/la nieto/a 4

grant conceder 2; otorgar 13

grapefruit la toronja 6

grapes las uvas 6

grave el sepulcro 14

great fabuloso/a 2, 7; magnífico/a 7

Great Depression la Gran Depresión 3

greed la codicia 10

green verde 1

green beans la judías verdes 6

greeting/s el/los saludo/s 1, 11

grey gris 1

grey hair canas 4

grill la parrilla 6; la parrillada 11

grind moler (ue) 4

groceries los comestibles 9

groom/bride el/la novio/a 3, 4

group el conjunto 4, 8, 14; el grupo 5, 14

growing creciente 15

grow up criarse 4

Guarani language el guaraní 10

guarantee garantizar 15

guaranteed garantizado/a 5

guard el/la guardia 9

guess adivinar 5

guest el huésped 5

guests la visita 5

guide guiar 10

guidebook la guía turística 9

guitar la guitarra 3, 14

guitar-like instrument el charango 4

gymnasium el gimnasio 3

gymnastics la gimnasia 7

gypsy el/la gitano/a 14

H

habit el hábito 5

haggle over regatear 8

haggling el regateo 8

hair el pelo 5

hair dryer el secador 5

hairstylist el/la peluquero/a 11

half medio/a 2

hallway el pasillo 5

ham el jamón 6

hamburger la hamburguesa 6

hammock la hamaca 8

hand la mano 1, 5, 10; **by a** mano 4

handicraft la artesanía 3

hang colgar (ue) 3

hang-glide hacer parapente 9

happily alegremente 9

happiness la felicidad 4

happy contento/a 5; feliz 1

hard drive el disco duro 12

hard-working trabajador/a 1

harm el daño 15; perjudicar 12

harmful nocivo/a 15

harp el arpa (*fem.*) 5, 14

harvest la cosecha 15

hatchery el criadero 5

hatred el odio 10

have tener (ie) 1, 2, 2, 7

have a good/bad/wonderful time pasarlo bien/mal/de maravilla 7, 9

have a great time pasarlo bomba 15

have a picnic hacer un pícnic 7

have a point tener razon 3

have breakfast desayunar 4, 6

have dinner cenar 6

have fun divertirse (ie, i) 5, 7

have just (done something) acabar (de) (+ *inf.*) 5, 11, 12

hay el heno 11

he él 1

head encabezar 12; la cabeza 10

headache el dolor de cabeza 10

headline el titular 13

head office la sede 8, 11

health la salud 4, 7, 10

health insurance el seguro médico 11

healthy saludable 10

hear oír 6, 8, 12

heart el corazón 1

heartrending desgarrador/a 11

heat calentar (ie) 6

heaven el cielo 8

heaven's (*lit.* God's) sake, for por Dios 9

heavy pesado/a 12

heavy rain el chubasco 7

heel el tacón 8

height la estatura 5

helicopter el helicóptero 9

Hello Hola. 1

Hello? (*on the phone*) ¿Bueno? 4; ¿Diga? 4; ¿Dígame? 4

helmet el casco 12

help ayudar 2; el socorro 11; la ayuda 5

here aquí 1

heritage el patrimonio 10; la herencia 15

Hi. Hola. 1

high-definition television el televisor de alta definición 12

high fashion la alta costura 14

high plateau el altiplano 10

hike el trekking 9

hire contratar 11

Hispanic hispano/a 1

historical histórico/a 6

historical center el centro histórico 9

history la historia 3

hockey el hockey 7

Holy Week la Semana Santa 1

home el hogar 4

home (*website*) el inicio 4

homeopathy la homeopatía 10

homework la tarea 1

honest honesto/a 11; honrado/a 11

honesty la honestidad 15; la honradez 15

honored honrado/a 11

hood la capucha 8

hope la esperanza 8; **for** esperar 7, 10

horn el claxon, la coraneta 15

horoscope el horóscopo 13

horrified horrorizado/a 14

horseback riding montar a caballo 9

hospital el hospital 3

host/hostess el/la anfitrión/anfitriona 7

hot caliente 6

hot, it is hace calor 7

hot, to be tener calor 3

hotel el hotel 9

house albergar 3; la casa 4, 5

house specialty la especialidad de la casa 6

housing la vivienda 15

how cómo 1, 2

How . . . ? ¿Cómo...? 2

How about . . . ? ¿Qué tal sí... ? 4

How are you? (*for.*) ¿Cómo está usted? 1

How are you? (*inf.*) ¿Cómo estás? 1

How awesome! ¡Qué padre! 4

How do you spell . . . ? ¿Cómo se escribe...? **1**
how much/many cuanto/a **1**
How revolting! ¡Qué asco! **6**
How terrific! ¡Qué bárbaro! **9**
hug el abrazo **2**
human humano/a **10**
human being el ser humano **6**
humanist humanista **8**
humanity la humanidad **11**
human resources los recursos humanos **3**
human rights los derechos humanos **4, 8, 15**
humble humilde **6**
humidity la humedad **7**
humility la humildad **15**
humorous humorístico/a **4**
hundred cien(to) **5**
hundreds los centenares **4**
hunger el hambre **3**
hunting la caza **10**
hurricane el huracán **4**
hurry tener prisa **3**
hurt doler (ue) **10**
hurt oneself hacerse daño (*Spain*) **10**; lastimarse **10**
husband el esposo **1, 3, 4**
hybrid híbrido/a **3**
hyperlink el enlace **12**; el hipervínculo **12**
hypermarket el hipermercado **6**
hypothesis la hipótesis **3**
hypothetical hipotético/a **13**

I

I yo **1**
I am... Soy... **1**
Iberian ibero/a **2**
ice el hielo **7**
ice cream el helado **6**
ice cream shop la heladería **8**
ideal el ideal **1**
idealistic idealista **1**
identify identificar **7**
identity la identidad **13**
ideology la ideología **4**
I don't know. No sé. **1**
I don't understand. No comprendo. **1**
I have tengo **1**
I hope Ojalá **9, 10**
I like Me gusta... **2**
I'll come by for you. Paso por ti. **4**
illegality la ilegalidad **7**
illness la enfermedad **5, 6, 10**

illogical ilógico/a **10**
illuminate iluminar **8**
illusion la ilusión **9**
illustrate ilustrar **10**
image la imagen **8**
imagine imaginar **10**
immediate inmediato/a **9**
immediately inmediatamente **9**
immense inmenso/a **8**
immigration la inmigración **15**
immorality la inmoralidad **7**
immunology la inmunología **1**
impassion apasionar **6**
impatient impaciente **1**
implement implementar **12**
import importar **12**
important importante **9**
impossible imposible **9, 10**
impresario el empresario **10**
impress impresionar **6**
impressive impresionante **14**
improve mejorar **6, 7, 15**
improvise improvisar **14**
I'm sorry. Lo siento. **4, 5**
in addition además **4, 9**
in agreement de acuerdo **4**
inaugurate inaugurar **5**
Inca inca **15**
in case en caso de que **11**
in cash en efectivo **8**
incentive el incentivo **11**
include incluir **4**
including incluso **9**
incorporate incorporar **6**
increase aumentar **6, 15**; el aumento **4, 6, 11**
incredible increíble **7, 10**
indefinite indefinido/a **7**
index el índice **13**
indicate indicar **6**
indifferent indiferente **8**
indigenous indígena **3**
industry la industria **6**
inexpensive barato/a **1**
infection la infección **10**
inflation la inflación **15**
influence influir **2**; la influencia **3**
influenced influido/a **12**
influential influyente **9, 13**
inform informar **7**
information el dato **1**
ingredient el ingrediente **6**
inhabit habitar **6**
inhabitant el/la habitante **8**
iniciate iniciar **13**

initiated iniciado/a **9**
initiative la iniciativa **11**
injury la lesión **10**
injustice la injusticia **15**
ink la tinta **12**
in-laws la familia política **4**
inn el hostal **9**
in need necesitado/a **7**
inner ear el oído **10**
innovative innovador/a **14**
in order that a fin de que **11**; para que **11**
in order to para **1, 9**
insert insertar **8**
inside of dentro de **5**
insist (on) insistir (en) **9**
inspect inspeccionar **14**
inspiration la inspiración **6**
inspiring inspirador/a **14**
install instalar **12**
instance la vez **5**
instrument el instrumento **2, 14**
in style de moda **8**
intact intacto/a **3**
integration la integración **11**
intelligent inteligente **1**
intense intenso/a **8**
interest el interés **8**
interesting interesante **1, 3**
international internacional **2**
internship el internado **10**
interpreter el/la intérprete **4, 11**
intervention la intervención **15**
interview la entrevista **2, 11**
interviewer el/la entrevistador/a **7**
intimate íntimo/a **10**
intonation la entonación **14**
intrigue la intriga **10**
introduction la presentación **1**
introverted introvertido/a **1**
invasion la invasión **7**
invent inventar **5**
invest invertir **15**
investigate investigar **6**
investigation la investigación **3**
invitation la invitación **4**
invite invitar **3, 4**
Irish el/la irlandés/esa **9**
iron el hierro **6**; la plancha **5**; planchar **5**
iron grill la verja **12**
ironic irónico/a **14**
island la isla **2, 7, 9**
it lo/la **4**

Italian el italiano **2**
itinerary el itinerario **4**
It's all the same me. Me da igual. **7**
I would love to. Me encantaría. **4**

J

jacket la chaqueta **8**
jaguar el jaguar **9**
jail la cárcel **15**
January enero **1**
Japanese el japonés **2**
jealous celoso/a **11**
jealousy los celos **11**
jeans los jeans **8**; los mecánicos (*Cuba*) **8**; los pantalones de mezclilla (*Mexico*) **8**; los tejanos (*Spain*) **8**; los vaqueros (*Spain*) **8**
Jesuit el jesuita **10**
Jew el/la judío/a **2**
jewel la joya **8**
jewelry store la joyería **8**
Jewish judío/a **14**
job application la solicitud de empleo **11**
job candidate el/la aspirante **11**
job search la búsqueda de empleo **11**
jog hacer footing **7**; hacer jogging **7**
join incorporarse **7**
join together unirse (a) **4, 15**
joke la broma **11**
journalist el/la periodista **10, 11, 13**
judge el/la juez/a **8, 15**
juice el jugo **6**; el zumo **6**
July julio **1**
June junio **1**
jungle la selva **5, 9, 10, 12**
junk food la comida basura **10**; la comida chatarra **10**; la porquería **10**
jury el jurado **14**
just justo/a **11**
justice la justicia **7, 15**
justify justificar **14**
juvenile juvenil **7**

K

keep guardar **6, 10**
key la clave **11**; la llave **12**
keyboard el teclado **12**
kick patear **7**
kidnap secuestrar **4**

kill matar 10
kilogram el kilo 6
kind simpático/a **1**, 8
king el rey **15**
kingdom el reino 8
kiss el beso 4
kitchen la cocina 3, **5**
kite el papalote **7**
knee la rodilla **10**
knife el cuchillo **6**
knot el nudo 15
knotted anudado/a 15
know conocer (zc) **4**; saber 2, **4**, 6, **7**, **9**, **10**
know-it-all el/la sabelotodo 4
knowledge el conocimiento 2
known conocido/a 6
Korean el coreano 2

L

laboratory el laboratorio 2, **3**
lack faltar 8; la falta 12
lake el lago 8, **9**
lamp la lámpara **5**
lance la lanza 10
land aterrizar **9**; el terreno 4; la tierra 10
landowner el terrateniente 5
landscape el paisaje 1
lane la vía **5**
language el idioma 7; la lengua 2, **10**
languish languidecer 11
laptop computer la computadora portátil 1
last durar 7; pasado/a 6; último/a 2, 4, 7
lasting duradero/a 15
last night anoche 6, **8**
late tarde 2
lately últimamente 15
later luego 1
latest último/a 2, 4, 7
laugh reírse (i, i) 13
laughter la risa 13
launch lanzar 7
law el derecho 3, **15**; la ley 6, **15**
lazy perezoso/a 1
leader el/la líder 15
leadership el liderazgo 9
leading lady la primera actriz 13
leading man el galán 13
leaf la hoja 5
leaf through hojear 13
leap saltar 8
learn aprender 2, 7
leather el cuero 2, 8; la piel 10, **14**

leave dejar (de) 3, **6**, **10**, **11**; irse **5**; salir **4**
lecture la conferencia 2
leftovers los restos 10
leg la pierna **10**
legend la leyenda 5
leisure el ocio 4
lemon el limón 6
lemonade la limonada 6
lend prestar 15
Lent la Cuaresma 9
less menos 2
less . . . than menos... que **5**
lessen disminuir 13
lesson la lección 1
let go soltar (ue) 2
Let's get to work! ¡Manos a la obra! **11**
let's go vamos 4
letter la letra 2, 3
letter of recommendation la carta de recomendación **11**
lettuce la lechuga **6**
level el nivel 10
lexicon el léxico 15
liberate liberar 9
librarian el/la bibliotecario/a 15
library la biblioteca 2
life la vida 2
lifeless desanimado/a 12
lift levantar 5
lift weights levantar pesas **7**
light (color; adj.) claro/a 1, 6
light (noun) la luz 5
like gustar 2, **6**
likewise igualmente 1
lily la azucena 10
limit el límite 6; limitar 10
limousine la limosina 14
line la cola **9**; la línea 5, **10**
linguistic lingüístico/a 13
lip el labio 5
lip gloss el brillo de labios 5
listen escuchar 1, **2**
Listen. Oye. (command) **7**
literature la literatura 3
little nun la monjita 14
live habitar 6; vivir 1, **2**, 5, **6**, **12**
live television la televisión en vivo y en directo 13
living room la sala 3, **5**
loan el préstamo 11
located ubicado/a 8
location la ubicación 5
logical lógico/a 5, 7, **10**
long largo 5
long as, as mientras que **11**

long-form pleno/a 13
look for buscar 1, **2**
look at mirar 2
loosen desprender 10
lose perder (ie) 4
lose weight adelgazar 10; bajar de peso **10**
loss la pérdida 10
lost perdido/a 4
love amar 6; el amor 6; querer (ie) **7**, 8, **9**
lover el/la amante 6
lower bajar 4, **12**
lozenge la pastilla 10
luck la suerte 7
lukewarm tibio/a 7
lunch el almuerzo 2, **6**
lungs los pulmones 10
luxurious lujoso/a 5
luxury el lujo 9
lying mentiroso/a 6
lyric la letra 2, 3

M

macaw el guacamayo 5
machine la máquina 11
magazine la revista 7, 13
magic la magia 14
mail el correo 2
mail carrier el/la cartero/a 11
maintain mantener 4, 12
make fabricar 14; hacer **2**, 3, **7**, 12
make a mistake equivocarse 9
make an appointment hacer una cita 10
make difficult dificultar 4
make matters worse, to para colmo 13
make sick enfermar 5
make the bed hacer la cama 5
make up confeccionar 15
makeup el maquillaje 5
mall el centro comercial 8
mama la mamá 4
man el hombre 1
manager el/la gerente 9, 11
manufacture fabricar 12
manufacturer el fabricante 12
many as, as tantos/as... como 5
map el mapa 1
maracas las maracas 14
marathon el maratón 6
Marathon in Madrid Mapoma 1
March marzo 1
Mardi Gras el carnaval 9

margin el margen 11
marimba la marimba 14
marine marino/a 6
mark marcar 7
marker el marcador 1
market el mercado 5, 8
married casado/a 4
marry casarse 4
marvelous maravilloso/a 4
marvelously maravillosamente 9
mash machacar 11
Mass la misa 7
the masses el pueblo 4, 10, **15**
massive masivo/a 5
master/mistress el/la maestro/a 15
masterpiece la obra maestra 4
match el partido 5; **with** hacer juego (con) 8
mathematics las matemáticas 2, **3**
matrimony el matrimonio 4
matter el asunto 15
mature maduro/a 6
May mayo 1
mayor el/la alcalde/sa 15; el/la intendente 15
me me 4; mí 6; **with** conmigo 4
meal la comida 2, 3, 4, **6**
mean significar 13
meaning el significado 2
means los medios 13, 14
measure la medida 12; medir (i, i) 6
measurement la medida 12
meat la carne 6
mechanic el/la mecánico/a 11
media los medios 13, 14
medical médico/a 10
medical checkup el examen físico 10
medicine la medicina 3, **10**
meeting la reunión 2
meet up with someone encontrarse (ue) con 5
meet with someone reunirse 11
member el miembro 4
memorize memorizar 10
memory el recuerdo 6, **9**; la memoria 6
memory card la tarjeta de memoria 9
men's shirt typical of the Caribbean la guayabera 12
mention mencionar 6

menu el menú **6**
merit el mérito **11**
message el mensaje **2**
metal sheet la plancha **5**
meteorologist el/la hombre/mujer del tiempo **13**
meter el metro **8**
Mexican mexicano/a **2**
Mexican-American chicano/a **12**
microphone el micrófono **15**
microscope el microscopio **1**
microwave el microondas **6**
midnight la medianoche **2**
migrant migrante **15**
migration la migración **4**
mile la milla **15**
military militar **4**
milk la leche **6**
milky lácteo/a **10**
millennium el milenio **3**
million el millón **2**
mind, in en mente **15**
mine mío/a/os/as **13**
minimum (*adj.*) mínimo/a **9**
minimum (*noun*) el mínimo **5**
minimum wage el sueldo mínimo **11**
minister el/la ministro/a **4, 6, 15**
minority la minoría **13**
minute el minuto **6**
misery la miseria **8**
Miss la señorita (Srta.) **1**
miss (someone) extrañar **4**
mistaken equivocado/a **15**
mix amasar **10**; mezclar **5, 6**
mixed fibers de mezclilla **8**
mixed race mestizo/a of **4**
mixture la mezcla **2**
mobility la movilidad **6**
model el/la modelo **14**
mode of transportation el medio de transporte **5**
moderation la moderación **10**
moderator el/la presentador/a **12, 13**
modern moderno/a **3**
molar la muela **10**
monarchy la monarquía **15**
Monday el lunes **1**
monetary unit of Panama el balboa **5**
money el dinero **4**
monotonous monótono/a **11**

monounsaturated (polyunsaturated) fats las grasas monoinsaturadas (poliinsaturadas) **10**
month el mes **1**
monument el monumento **8, 9**
moon la luna **8**
Moor (Arab) el/la moro/a **13**
moral la lección **1**; la moraleja **8**
morality la moralidad **2**
more . . . than más... que **5**
More or less. Más o menos. **1**
morning la mañana **1, 2, 8**
mother la madre **4**
mother-in-law la suegra **4**
motivate motivar **13**
motive el motivo **10**
motto el lema publicitario **13, 15**
mount montar **11**
mountain la montaña **2, 9**
mountain climbing el alpinismo **6, 7**
mountainous montañoso/a **4**
mourning el luto **6**
mouse el ratón **12**
mouth la boca **10**
move la mudanza **14**
movement el movimiento **8**
move up ascender (ie) **11**
movie el papel **13**; la peli **4**; la película **4, 7**
movie theater el cine **2, 13**
mp3 player el reproductor de mp3 **12**
Mr. el señor (Sr.) **1**
Mrs. la señora (Sra.) **1**
much as, as tan... como **5**; tanto... como **5**
multinational multinacional **15**
muralist el/la muralista **3**
murderer el asesinato **15**
muscle el músculo **10**
muscular musculoso/a **13**
museum el museo **2, 3**
music la música **1, 14**
musician el/la músico/a **8, 14**
Muslim el/la musulmán/ana **13**
mutton el carnero **6**
mutual mutuo/a **6**
my mi/mis **1, 3**; mío/a/os/as **13**
My name is . . . Me llamo... **1**; Mi nombre es... **1**
mysterious misterioso/a **1**
mystery el misterio **1**
myth el mito **10**

N

name el nombre **1**; nombrar **7**
napkin la servilleta **6**
narration la narración **12**
narrator el/la narrador/a **14**
narrow angosto/a **12**; estrecho/a **5, 8**
nation la nación **1**
nationality la nacionalidad **2**
natural disaster el desastre (natural) **13, 15**
nature la naturaleza **5, 12**
nausea la náusea **10**
navigable navegable **5**
navigator el/la navegante **7**
nearby cerca (de) **2**; cercano/a **8**; próximo/a **2, 7**
necessary necesario/a **7, 9**
neck el cuello **15**
necklace el collar **8**
need necesitar **1, 9**
negative negativo/a **7**
neighbor el/la vecino/a **5**
neighborhood el barrio **3**
neither tampoco **7**
neither... nor ni... ni **7**
nervous nervioso/a **3, 5**
nest el nido **11**
network la red **6**
never jamás **4**; ninguna vez **7**; nunca **7**
nevertheless sin embargo **7**
new novedoso/a **12**; nuevo/a **2**
newlyweds los recién casados **4**
news las noticias **13**; la novedad **13**
newscast el noticiero **13**
newscaster el/la comentarista **7, 13**
news online las noticias en línea **13**
newspaper el periódico **2, 4, 7**
New Year's Eve la Nochevieja **9**
New Yorker neoyorquino/a **12**
next próximo/a **2, 7**
next to al lado (de) **3**
nice simpático/a **1, 8**
nickname el apodo **2**
night la noche **2**
nightstand la mesa de noche **5**
ninth noveno/a **8**
nobility la nobleza **15**
nobody nadie **7**
nomination la nominación **13**
none ningún/ninguna **7**; ninguno/a **6, 7**
noon el mediodía **2**
no one nadie **7**; ninguno/a **6, 7**

normally normalmente **9**
nose la nariz **5**
not believe no creer **10**
not be sure of no estar seguro/a (de) **10**
note anotar **5**; el apunte **5**
notebook el cuaderno **1**
not either tampoco **7**
nothing nada **6, 7**
notice el aviso **13**
notify notificar **14**
notion la noción **13**
not think no pensar (ie) **10**
noun el sustantivo **1**
nourish alimentar **11**
novel la novela **2, 7**
novelist el/la novelista **2**
November noviembre **1**
now ahora **2**; **for now** por ahora **9**
nowadays hoy en día **3**
nuclear plant la planta nuclear **12**
nucleus el núcleo **4**
number el número **5, 8**
nurse el/la enfermero/a **11**
nursery la guardería **11**
nutrition la alimentación **6**
nylon el nilón **14**

O

obesity el sobrepeso **10**
object el objeto **9**
objective el propósito **7**
obligation el compromiso **7, 11**; la obligación **15**
oblige obligar **6**
observatory el observatorio **3**
observe observar **5**
obtain conseguir (i, i) **9, 11**; obtener (ie) **11**
occupy ocupar **7**
occur ocurrir **5, 7**
ocean el mar **2, 6, 7**; el océano **5**
October octubre **1**
odor el olor **8**
of course por supuesto **7, 9**
offer la oferta **1**; ofrecer (zc) **3**
office el despacho **11**; la oficina **2**
official oficial **12, 13**
often menudo a **8**
oil el aceite **6**; el petróleo **9**
oil well el pozo de petróleo **12**
old antiguo/a **5**; viejo/a **2**
older mayor **4**
old person el/la anciano/a **12**

olive la aceituna 6
Olympic Games los Juegos
Olímpicos 3
omelet la tortilla 2, 6
on sobre 5
once una vez 5
once in a while de vez en
cuando 5
one un/o/a 1
one must hay que 8
one time una vez 5
onion la cebolla 3, **6**
online newspaper el
periódico digital **13**
only solamente 3; solo 3;
único/a 5, 8, 10
on one's own por su
cuenta 7
on sale en rebaja **8**; en
venta 5
on the contrary por el
contrario 8
on time a tiempo 3
open abrir 1, 2, **12**
opera la ópera 1, **14**
opinion la opinión 2
opponent el/la
contrincante **15**
opportune oportuno/a 13
opportunity la oportunidad 4
oppression la opresión 15
optimistic optimista 1
opulence la opulencia 4
or o 1
orange anaranjado/a **1**; la
naranja 6
orchestra la orquesta 4, **14**
order el orden 4
organic orgánico/a 6
organization la
organización 7
orginate from provenir 9
orientation la orientación 10
origin el origen 3
originality la originalidad 13
ornament el ornamento 8
other otro/a 2
our/s nuestro/a/os/as 3, 13
outer ear la oreja 10
outfit el conjunto 4, 8, **14**
outgoing extrovertido/a **1**
outrage la barbaridad 5
outside al aire libre **4**;
fuera 5
outskirts las afueras 9
outstanding destacado/a 12
oven el horno 6
overcome superar 12
overcoming la superación 11

overconsumption el
sobreconsumo 12
overpopulation la
sobrepoblación 13
overstuffed chair el sillón **5**
owe (ought do something)
deber (+ *inf.*) **2**
own propio/a 13
owner el/la dueño/a 15
oxygen el oxígeno **10**

P

pacifist el/la pacifista 15
pack (the suitcases) hacer
(las maletas) 9
packaged empaquetado/a 10
page la página 1
pageant el concurso 13
pain el dolor 10
painted pintado/a 3
painter el/la pintor/a 1
painting el cuadro **5**; la
pintura 2
pair emparejar 5
pajamas la pijama 12
palace el palacio 3
Panamanian panameño/a **2**
Panamanian embroidery la
mola 5
pancakes los panqueques 10
pan pipe la zampoña 8
pants los pantalones 8
paper el papel 1
papier mâché el papel
maché 2
parade el desfile 2
paradise el paraíso 2
paragraph el párrafo 5
parents los padres **2**
park el parque **1**; estacionar
11
parliament el parlamento 15
parody la parodia 13
parrot el loro 9
parsley el perejil 6
part la parte 3
participant el/la participante 1
participate participar 5
particularly particularmente 9
partisan partidario/a 4
partner la pareja 4
part-time tiempo parcial **11**
party la fiesta 1, 3
pass (a test) pasar 5
passenger el/la pasajero/a **9**
passion la pasión 4, 13
passport el pasaporte 9
pass through (. . .) pasar por
(. . .) **9**

past el pasado 15
pastime el pasatiempo **7**
path el camino 2
patient el/la paciente **10**;
paciente (adj.) **1**
patio el patio 5
pay (in cash) pagar (en
efectivo) 8
pay attention hacer caso 13
payment el pago **3**; la remesa
4
peace la paz 1, 4, 10, **15**
pearls las perlas 8
peasant el campesino 5
pedicure la pedicura 10
peel pelar 6
pen el bolígrafo 1
pencil el lápiz 1
penguin el pingüino 6
penicillin la penicilina 10
peninsula la península 3
people, the el pueblo 2, 4,
10, **15**; la gente 1, 8, **13**
pepper la pimienta 6
perch posar 13
percussion la percusión 14
percussionist el/la
percusionista 14
perfect perfeccionar **10**;
perfecto/a 2, **7**
perform interpretar (*Spain*)
14; representar 6, 8, **13, 14**
perfume el olor **8**; el
perfume 8
perfume shop la perfumería **8**
perhaps quizás **10**; tal
vez **10**
permanent permanente 3
permit el permiso **3**; permitir
2, 7, **9**
perseverance la
perseverancia 13
person la persona 1
personality la personalidad 7
personnel el personal 11
pertaining to en torno a 3
Peruvian peruano/a **2**
perversity la perversidad 7
pessimistic pesimista **1**
pesticides los pesticidas 12
pet la mascota 6
pharmacy la farmacia 8
philharmonic filarmónico/a
14
philosophy la filosofía 15
photocopier la fotocopiadora
12
photocopy fotocopiar **12**
photograph la foto 7

photographer el/la
fotógrafo/a 1
phrase la frase 5
physical físico/a 5
physics la física 3
piano el piano 14
pick up recoger 5
pickup truck el camión **9**; la
camioneta 1
picture el cuadro 5
pie el pastel 6
piece el pedazo **6**; la pieza
3, **14**
pile el montón 11
pilgrim el/la peregrino/a 13
pill la pastilla **10**
pilot el/la piloto **9**
pinch la pizca **6**
pink rosado/a 1
pirate el pirata **7**; piratear 11
pity la pena 8
place el lugar **7**; el sitio 4
plaid de cuadros 8
plains of Argentina las
pampas 11
plan planear 14
plane el avión 9
plant plantar 12
plastic el plástico 3
plate el plato 6
platform la plataforma 15
play jugar (ue) a 4
play (an instrument) tocar
(un instrumento) 3, **4**
play (theater) la obra 2, **13**
player el/la jugador/a 2
please complacer **11**; por
favor 1, 7, **9**
Pleased meet you.
Encantado/a. **1**; Mucho
gusto. **1**
pleasure el gusto **5**; el placer 6
plumage el plumaje 9
plumber el/la plomero/a **11**
podcast listener el/la oyente
de podcast **13**
poet el/la poeta 2
point of view el punto de
vista 6
point out señalar 12
police la policía 9
polish pulir 12
political político/a 6, **15**
political cartoon la caricatura
política 13
political post el cargo
político **15**
political science la ciencias
políticas 3

politician el político 15
politics la política **15**
poll la encuesta 10
pollute contaminar 12
pollution la contaminación **7**
polyester el poliéster **14**
pool la piscina 7
poor pobre 2
population la población 2
pork el cerdo 10
Portuguese el portugués **2**
Portuguese person el/la portugués/esa 9
position el cargo 11; el puesto 2, 11
position (job) el puesto **11**
possible posible **10**
postcard la tarjeta postal **9**
poster el cartel 7
post online enviar 12
potato chips la papas fritas 10
potatoes la papas **6**
pound la libra 10
poverty la pobreza 6, 9, **15**
power el poder 11, **15**
practice (a sport) practicar (un deporte) **2**
praise la alabanza 12
precious precioso/a 6
pre-Colombian precolombino/a 5
predecessor el/la predecesor/a 6
predictable predecible 4
predominant predominante 9
predominate predominar 8
prefer preferir (ie, i) 2, **4**
preference la preferencia 5
prehispanic prehispánico/a 3
prehistoric prehistórico/a 3
preoccupation la preocupación 10
preparation la preparación 6
prepare preparar **2**
prescription la receta 9, **10**
present presenciar 14
present oneself acudir, presentarse 11
preserve conservar 7, 8, **12**
preside presidir 15
presidency la presidencia 15
president el/la presidente/a 5, **15**
president's office (Univ.) la rectoría 3
press la prensa 4, **13**
press conference la conferencia de prensa 15
pretend fingir 11

pretty bonito/a **2**; lindo/a 12
prevalent prevaleciente 15
preventable prevenible 7
previous previo/a 2
price el precio 2, 5, **8**
prickly plant la ortiga 1
prince el príncipe 2
princess la princesa 7
print imprimir **12**
printer la impresora 12
priority la prioridad 13
pristine prístino/a 9
privacy la privacidad 5
private privado/a 3
prize el premio 4, 5, 8, **13**
probably probablemente 3
problem el problema 5
process el proceso 15
procession la procesión 1
produce producir (zc) 6
producer el/la productor/a **13**
product el producto 2, 8
profession la profesión **11**
professor el/la profesor/a **1**
profile el perfil 1
profit el fruto 10
profound profundo/a **5**
profoundly profundamente 10
program programar 4, **12**
programmer el/la programador/a 12
programming la programación 13
progress el progreso 15
prohibit prohibir 8, **9**
prohibited prohibido/a 6
project el proyecto 5, 9
prolific prolífico/a 2
prominent prominente 9
promise la promesa 6; prometer 6
promote ascender (ie) **11**; impulsar 15; promocionar 10; promover (ue) **15**
promotion la promoción 11
pronounce pronunciar 6
property la propiedad 10
proportion proporcionar 1, 10
propose proponer 6
protagonist el/la protagonista 13
protect proteger (j) 5, 6, 8, **12**
protected protegido/a 6
protection la protección 10
proteins la proteínas 6, **10**
protest la manifestación 15; protestar **15**
proud orgulloso/a 2
prove comprobar (ue) 15

provide proporcionar 1, 10
provided (that) con tal (de) que 11
provisions los comestibles 9
provoke provocar 10
psychologist el/la psicológico/a 11
psychology la psicología **3**
public el público 12, **13**; público/a 3
public debt la deuda pública 15
public health la sanidad 15
publicist el/la publicista 7
publicity (adj.) publicitario/a 13
publicity (noun) la publicidad 6
publish publicar 6
Puerto Rican puertorriqueño/a 2
punctually puntualmente 9
punish castigar 10
punishment la penalización 15
pure puro/a 7
purity la pureza 1
purple morado/a 1
purse el bolso 7, **8**
push impulsar 15
put poner 4, 7, **12**
put in bed acostar (ue) 5
put out apagar (fuegos/incendios) **11, 12**
pyramid la pirámide 3

Q

qualifications las calificaciones, caulificaciones **11**
quality la calidad 13; la cualidad 14
quantity la cantidad 6
quarter cuarto/a 2, **8**
quartet el cuarteto **14**
queen la reina 15
question la pregunta 1
questionnaire el cuestionario 10
quit (doing something) dejar (de) 3, **6, 10, 11**
quite bastante **3**

R

race trazar; la raza 9
racket la raqueta **7**
radioactivity la radioactividad 12
radio listener el/la radioyente **13**
radio station la estación de radio 13, **13**

radio station (business entity) la emisora **7**
raging furibundo/a 14
rain la lluvia 7; llover (ue) **7**
rain forest el bosque pluvial 12
raise criar 7; el aumento 4, 6, **11**; subir 6
raise public consciousness concienciar al público 15
raisin la pasa 6
raising la cría 5
ranch la estancia 11
rapid rápido/a 2
rapidly rápidamente 9
rate la tasa 11
rate (of unemployment) la tasa (de desempleo) **15**
rayon el rayón **14**
razor blade la navaja de afeitar **5**
reach alcanzar 2
reachable alcanzable 12
react reaccionar 7
reaction la reacción 7
read leer **1**, 2, 7, **12**
reader el/la lector/a 7, **13**
ready dispuesto/a 13, **14**; listo/a 9
real estate los bienes raíces 5
realistic realista 1
Really? ¿De verdad? 1
really realmente 6
really beautiful bellísimo/a 6
reason la razón 4
reasonable razonable 12
rebellion la rebelión 15
receipt el recibo 8
receive recibir 2
receiver el receptor 12
recently recientemente 6
receptionist el/la recepcionista 5
rechargeable recargable 12
recipe la receta 6
reciprocal recíproco/a 11
recognized reconocido/a 3
recommend recomendar (ie) **9**
record grabar 7, **13**
recorded grabado/a 13
recording la grabación 9
rectify rectificar 15
recuperate recuperar 2
recycle reciclar 7, 12, **12**
recycling el reciclaje **12**
red rojo/a 1
reduce reducir (zc) 15
refer referir (ie, i) 14
referee el árbitro 5
reflect reflejar 3

reforestation la reforestación **12**

refreshment el refresco 3, 4, **6**

refrigerator el frigorífico **6**; el refrigerador **6**; la nevera **6**

refuge el refugio 3

region la región 6

regret lamentar **10**; sentir (ie, i) **9, 10**

regrettable lamentable **10**

rehearsal el ensayo 10, **13**

rehearse ensayar 11, **13**

reincarnate reencarnar 13

reject rechazar 4

relate relatar 7

relation la relación 4

relationship la relación 6

relative relativo/a 15

relative (family) el/la pariente **4**

relaxation el relajamiento 10

religious religioso/a 15

remain permancer 2; quedar **6**, 8; quedarse 7, **9**

remains los restos 10

remedy el remedio **10**; remediar 13

remember recordar (ue) 7

remittance la remesa 4

remote remoto/a 4

remove quitar 5; remover (ue) 14

renewable renovable 11

renounce renunciar 11

renown el renombre 14

rent alquilar 5; el alquiler 15

repair reparar **11**

repeat repetir (i, i) **1**

Repeat, please. Repita por favor. **1**

repentant arrepentido/a 10

repertoire el repertorio 14

repopulation la repoblación 12

report informar **13**; reportar 13

reporter el/la reportero/a 4, 7, **13**

represent figurar 2; representar 6, 8, **13, 14**

representative el/la representante **15**; representativo/a 2, 3

reproduce reproducir (zc) 5, **14**

republic la república 15

request el pedido 9; pedir (i, i) **6, 9, 10, 11**

requirement el requisito 3, 5

rescue el rescate 9

research investigar 8; la investigación 3

researcher el/la investigador/a 3

reservation la reservación 6; la reserva/reservación **9**

residence la residencia 2

resource el recurso 12

respect el respeto **15**; respetar 6

respectful respetuoso/a 12

respect to, with acerca de 8

respiratory respiratorio/a 10

respond responder 6

response la respuesta 1, **1**

responsibilities las responsabilidades 11

responsible responsable 3

rest descansar 10; el descanso 10; **the rest** los demas 10; el resto 2

restaurant el restaurante 6

restock reponer 10

result el resultado 5, 6

retire jubilarse 11; retirarse **11**, 15

retiree el/la jubilado/a 3

retirement plan el plan de retiro 11

return regresar 6; regreso de 11; volver (ue) **4**, 7, **12**

return (something) devolver (ue) 8, **9**

reveal revelar 6

revenge la venganza 4

review el repaso 13; la reseña 4, 6, **13**; revisar 1, 2, **10**, 12, **13**

revolutionize revolucionar 12

revolutionized revolucionado/a 12

revolver el revólver 11

reward premiar 11

rhythm el ritmo 1

rice el arroz 6

rich rico/a 2, 4, **6**

richness la riqueza 9

ride montar 11

ridiculous ridículo/a 5, **6**, 10

right el derecho 3, **15**

right to be tener razón 3

right away enseguida **6**

rigid rígido/a 10

risk el riesgo 10

river el río 2

road el camino 2

roast hornear **6**

rock la roca 9

rocker el/la roquero/a 2

role el papel **1, 13**

roll one's eyes poner los ojos en blanco 15

Roman romano/a 2

romantic romántico/a **1**

roof el techo 3

room el cuarto 5; el salón 9; la habitación 9

root la raíz 10

rough grosero/a 15

round redondo/a 9

roundtrip el viaje de ida y vuelta 9

route la ruta 6

routine la rutina 5

royal real 15

rudeness la malcrianza 12

ruin la ruina 4

rule la regla 10

run correr 2

Russia Rusia 2

Russian el ruso 2

rustic rústico/a 3

S

sacred sagrado/a 11

sad triste 4, **5**

sail navegar a vela 9

salad la ensalada 6

salary el salario 11

sale la rebaja 8; la venta 9

sales clerk el/la dependiente/a 8

salsa performer el/la salsero/a 12

salt la sal **6**

salutation/s el/los saludo/s 1, 11

Salvadorian salvadoreño/a 2

same igual 7; mismo/a 5

sample la muestra 15; la prueba 4, 10

sandals las sandalias 8

sandstone la arenisca 9

sandwich el bocadillo **6**; el sándwich 3, **6**

Sanfermín festival los sanfermines 2

sanitation la sanidad 15

sassy atrevido/a 12

satellite dish la antena parabólica 12

satellite radio la radio por satélite **13**

satellite television la televisión (por satélite) **13**

satisfaction la satisfacción 9

satisfactory satisfactorio/a 6

satisfied satisfecho/a 8

saturated saturado/a **10**

saturated (trans) fats las grasas saturadas (trans) **10**

Saturday el sábado **1**

sauce la salsa 6

sausage el chorizo 2

save ahorrar **12**; archivar **12**; guardar **6**, **10**; salvar 4

saxophone el saxofón **14**

say decir (i) 6, **7**

say good-bye despedirse (i, i) 4

scandal el escándalo 13

scanner el escáner **12**

scarce escaso/a 10

scene la escena 8

schedule el horario 2, **3**

scholastic escolar 12

school la escuela 5

School of Art la Facultad de Arte 3

School of Engineering la Facultad de Ingeniería 3

School of Law la Facultad de Derecho 3

School of Mathematics la Facultad de Matemáticas 3

School of Medicine la Facultad de Medicina 3

School of Sciences la Facultad de Ciencias 3

science la ciencia 2

science fiction la ciencia ficción 7

scientist el/la científico/a 1, 8

screen la pantalla 12

script el guión 12, **13**

script writer el/la guionista 13

scuba dive bucear 9

sculptor el/la escultor/a 9

sculpture la escultura 8

sea el mar 2, 6, **7**

seafood los mariscos 2, **6**

sea lion el lobo marino 6

search la búsqueda 11

search engine el buscador 12, **13**

season la estación 1, 8; la temporada 7

seat el asiento **9**

seat of government la sede 8, 11

second segundo/a 7, **8**

secondhand de segunda mano 8

secret el secreto 4

secretary el/la secretario/a 11

section la sección 6

security la seguridad 9
security checkpoint el control de seguridad 9
see ver 2, 7, 7, 8, 12
seem parecer (zc) 6
See you later. Hasta luego. 1
See you soon. Hasta pronto. 1
See you tomorrow. Hasta mañana. 1
select seleccionar 10, 15
selection la selección 7
self-defense la defensa propia 14
self-portrait el autorretrato 3
sell vender 2
semester el semestre 3
senator el/la senador/a 15
send enviar 12; mandar 4, 6, 9
sensation la sensación 11
sensationalist sensacionalista 13
sentence la oración 6, 7
sentimental sentimental 4
September septiembre 1
sequins las lentejuelas 14
series la serie 13
serious grave 7; serio/a 10
servant el/la sirviente/a 4
serve servir (i, i) 2, 3, 4, 5, 8
service el servicio 2; la prestación 2
set the table poner la mesa 5
seventh séptimo/a 8
several varios/as 7
severe severo/a 8
shake sacudir 15
shallot la cebolleta 6
shame la lástima 10
shampoo el champú 5
shape, in en informa en 10
share compartir 2
sharp puntiagudo/a 9
shave afeitarse 5
she ella 1
sheep la oveja 11
shine brillar 8; lucir 14
shipment el envío 4
shirt la camisa 8
shoes los zapatos 8
shoe store la zapatería 8
shoot disparar 11
shop la tienda 8
shopping center el centro comercial 8
shore la orilla 5
short (in stature) bajo/a 2
shortage la escasez 12
short-/long-sleeved de manga corta/larga 8

short time el rato 13
shot la inyección 10
shoulder el hombro 12
Should we go...? ¿Vamos a...? 4
shout el grito 11
show la exposición 3; la función 4; mostrar (ue) 8
show a movie poner una película 4
show business el espectáculo 7
shower ducharse 5; el chubasco 7; la ducha 5
showy vistoso/a 9
shrimp los camarones 6, 10
shy tímido/a 1
sickness/maternity leave licencia por enfermedad/maternidad 11
side el lado 7
sign el índice 13; el letrero 9; firmar 7, 15
signal la señal 15
signature la firma 11
significant significante 13; significativo/a 7
silk la seda 8
silver la plata 1, 8; la platería 4
similar semejante 8
simple sencillo/a 5
simplicity la sencillez 14
since desde 2; hace 5, 14
sincerely yours atentamente 11
sing cantar 5
singer el/la cantante 1
single soltero/a 4
sister la hermana 3, 4
sister-in-law la cuñada 4
sit sentarse (ie) 5
situated situado/a 8
situation la situación 5, 6
sixth sexto/a 8
size el número 5, 8; la talla 8
skate patinar 7
skating el patinaje 7
ski esquiar 7
skiing el esquí 7
skilled diestro/a 15
skillet la sartén 6
skim through dar una mirada rápida 13
skin la piel 10, 14
skinny flaco/a 2
skirt la falda 8
skull la calavera 3
sky el cielo 8
slave el/la esclavo/a 9
sleep dormir (ue, u) 4, 6, 9, 11; sueño 3

sleeve la manga 8
sleeveless sin manga 8, 8
slope la falda 8
sloth el perezoso 5
slow lento/a 9
slowly despacio 5; lentamente 9
small pequeño/a 1
small beer la caña 2
smell el olor 8
smile sonreír (i, i) 15
smog contaminación 7
smoke el humo 12; fumar 8, 10
snack la merienda 6
snake la culebra 8; la serpiente 6
sneeze estornudar 10
snorkel bucear 9
snow nevar (ie) 7
soap el jabón 5
soap opera la telenovela 13
soccer (football) el fútbol (americano) 2, 5, 7
social science las ciencias sociales 3
social welfare programs los programas sociales 15
sociology la sociología 3
socks los calcetines 8
sofa el sofá 5
soft drink el refresco 3, 4, 6
soldier el soldado 15
solemn solemne 4
solid sólido/a 6
solitary solitario/a 11
soloist el/la solista 7, 14
solve resolver (ue) 15
somber sombría 11
some alguno/a/os/as 5, 7
someday algún día 4
someone alguien 7
something algo 3, 6, 7
sometimes a veces 5
son/daughter el/la hijo/a 4, 6
song la canción 2
songwriter el/la cantautor/a 2
son-in-law el yerno 4
soon pronto 1
sorrow la pena 8
So-so Más o menos. 1
so that para que 11
soul el alma (fem.) 8
soup la sopa 6
source la fuente 13
south el sur 6
souvenir el recuerdo 6, 9

spaghetti los espaguetis 10
Spain España 2
Spaniard el/la español/a 9
Spanish (adj.) español/a 1, 2
Spanish (noun) el español 2
spark la chispa 10
spatula la espátula 6
speak hablar 2, 7, 8, 10
speaker el altavoz 7
speakers los audio parlantes 8
special especial 5
speciality store la tienda especializa 8
specialize especializarse 6
species la especie 3, 5, 12
spectacular espectacular 5
spectator el/la espectador/a 13
speech el discurso 6, 7, 15
speed la velocidad 9
spelling la ortografía 6
spend gastar 5, 8
spend time in llevar 5, 6, 8
spent gastado/a 10
spicy picante 6
spider la araña 8
spirit el espíritu 11
split partir 11
sponsor el/la patrocinador/a 12; patrocinar 13
spoon la cuchara 6
sport el deporte 1, 7
sporting deportivo/a 7
sportscaster el/la comentarista deportivo 13
sports section el sección deportivo 13
spreadsheet la hoja electrónica 12
spring el manantial 10; la primavera 2
spy espiar 11
square cuadrado/a 5
squash la calabaza 11
squid el calamar 2, 6
squirrel la ardilla 8
stadium el estadio 3
stage el escenario 8, 14; la etapa 3
stage manager el/la director/a de escena 14
stall el puesto 8, 11
standard el estandarte 15
stand in line hacer cola 9
stand out destacar 4
stand up levantarse 5
star el/la protagonista 13; la estrella 5
state el estado 7

statement la afirmación 12
station la estación 1, 8
stationery shop la papelería 8
statistics las estadísticas 3
statuary la imaginería 4
statue la estatua 9
stay (*noun*) la estadía 9
stay (*verb*) quedarse 7, 9
stay in bed guardar la cama 10
stay in shape guardar la línea 10; mantenerse (ie) en forma 10
steak el bistec 6
step el escalón 12; el paso 4; **on** pisar 11
stepbrother/stepsister el/la hermanastro/a 4
stepfather el padrastro 4
stepmother la madrastra 4
stereotype el estereotipo 12
stewpot la cazuela 6
still life la naturaleza muerta 6
stimulate estimular 9
stimulus el estímulo 11
stingy tacaño/a 5
Stockholm Estocolmo 4
stocking cap el gorro 8
stomach el estómago 10
stone la piedra 4, 9
stopover la escala 9
store la tienda 8
storm la tempestad 8
story el cuento 12
storyteller el/la cuentista 11
stove la estufa 6
straight ahead recto todo 3
strange extraño/a 10; raro/a 7
strategic estratégico/a 7
straw la paja 14
street la calle 2
street vendor el/la vendedor/a ambulante 8
strengthen afianzar (c) 15; fortalecer (zc) 6, 15
stress el estrés 10
strict estricto/a 6
strike el paro (*Latin America*) 15; la huelga 15
striker el/la huelguista 15
string beans las judías verdes 6
strip despojar 11
striped de rayas 8
stroll el paseo 1
strong fuerte 6
struggle la lucha 15
student el/la estudiante 1

student (*adj.*) estudiantil 6
student union el centro estudiantil 3
student teacher el/la pasante 3
studio el estudio 3, 13
study el estudio 3, 13; estudiar 1, 2
stuffy tapado/a 10
stunning impactante 5
stupid tonto/a 13
style el estilo 6, 14; la moda 14
substance la sustancia 15
success el éxito 5, 12
suckling pig el cochinillo 8
suddenly de golpe 12; de repente 8
suffer (from) padecer (zc) (de) 10; sufrir (de) 8
suffering el sufrimiento 15
sugar el azúcar 3, 6
suggest sugerir (ie, i) 9
suggestion la sugerencia 6
suit el traje 8
suitcase la maleta 4, 9
summarize resumir 7
summary el resumen 5; el sumario 2
summer el verano 1
sunbathe tomar el sol 7
Sunday el domingo 1
sunglasses los lentes de sol 7
sunny, it is hace sol 7
super chévere 7; guay 13
supernatural sobrenatural 10
supervision la supervisión 11
supervisor el/la supervisor/a 11
support apoyar 8, 15; el apoyo 4; mantener (ie) 15
supporter el/la partidario/a 13
supposed supuesto/a 9
sure seguro/a 4, 5, 10
surely seguramente 3
surf surfear 7
surname el apellido 2
surprise la sorpresa 6; sorprender(se) 10
surprised maravillado/a 4
surprising sorprendente 10
surround rodear 7
surrounded rodeado/a 12
survey la encuesta 10
survival la sobrevivencia 4
survive sobrevivir 5
suspend suspender 14
suspenseful suspensivo/a 4

suspicion la sospecha 11
sweater el suéter 8
sweatshirt la sudadera 8
sweets los dulces 10
swim nadar 5, 7
swim goggles los lentes de natación 7
swimming pool la piscina 5
swimsuit el traje de baño 7
swine flu la gripe porcina 10
symbolize simbolizar 10
sympathize simpatizar 8
sympathizer el/la simpatizante 15
symphony la sinfonía 14
symphony orchestra la sinfónica 14
symptom el síntoma 10
synthesis la síntesis 3
synthetic sintético/a 14

T
table la mesa 1; la tabla 10, 12
tablespoon la cucharada 6
tachograph el tacógrafo 9
tactic la táctica 10
take llevar 5, 6, 8; sacar 1, 5; tomar 2, 6, 12
take a cruise hacer un crucero 9
take advantage of aprovechar 12
take a walk dar un paseo 7; pasear 4
take blood pressure tomar la tensión 10; tomar la presión (*Latin America*) 10
take care (of oneself) cuidar(se) 6, 10
take hold apoderarse 15
take off despegar 9
take off (clothing) quitarse 5
take on encargar 14
take pictures sacar fotos 9
take turns turnarse 5
talcum powder el talco 8
talented talentoso/a 14
tall alto/a 2
tambourine la pandereta 8
tank el tanque 10
task la tarea 1
taste el gusto 5
tasting menu el menú de degustación 6
tasty sabroso/a 6
taxes los impuestos 11, 15
taxi driver el/la taxista 4

tea el té 6
teach enseñar 2, 7
teacher el/la maestro/a 15
teaching la docencia 13; la pedagogía 3
team el equipo 5
tear la lágrima 8
teary lloroso/a 10
teaspoon la cucharadita 6
technique la técnica 6
technological tecnológico/a 12
technology la tecnología 13
teeth los dientes 5, 6, 10
television la tele 6; la televisión 7, 13
television viewer el/la televidente 12, 13
tell decir (i) 9, 12
tell (a story) contar (ue) 4
temperate templado/a 6
temperature la temperatura 9, 10
temple el templo 8
temporary temporal 3
temptation la tentación 6
tend to tender a 6
tennis el tenis 2
tennis player el/la tenista 2
tense tenso/a 14
tension la tensión 13
tenth décimo 8
term el término 4
terms los términos 11
terrace la terraza 5
terrain el terreno 4
terrestrial terrestre 8
terrific estupendo/a 7
terrorism el terrorismo 15
test la prueba 4, 10
thank agradecer 13
Thank you. Gracias. 1, 4
that ese/a 4; que 15
that (over there) aquel/la 4; aquello 4
that one ese/a 4
that one (over there) aquel/la 4
that's why por eso 2, 7, 9
that which lo que 5, 15
the el; la; los; las 1
theater el teatro 3, 4, 13
their suyo/a/os/as 13
theme el tema 5
themselves entre sí 4
then entonces 7
theory la teoría 8
there allá 9
therefore por eso 2, 7, 9

there is/are hay **1**, **7**
thermal termal **10**
these estos/as **4**
these ones estos/as **4**
they ellos/as **1**
thin delgado/a **2**
thing la cosa **1**
think pensar (ie) **3**, **4**, **9**, **10**, **11**
third tercer/o/a **8**
thirst la sed **10**
thirsty, to be tener sed **3**, **7**
this este/a **4**
this one este/a **4**
this time esta vez **4**
thistle el cardo **1**
those esos/as **4**
those (over there) aquellos/as **4**
thought el pensamiento **3**
throat la garganta **10**
through mediante **15**; por **9**
throw arrojar **10**; echar **6**, **12**; tirar **12**
thrust clavar **15**
thump golpear **14**
Thursday el jueves **1**
ticket el boleto **3**, **4**, **9**; la entrada **4**
tickle hacer cosquillas **7**
tie la corbata **8**
tie (the score) empatar **7**
tight (clothing) estrecho/a **5**, **8**
tiled enlozado/a **12**
time el tiempo **2**, **6**, **7**; la vez **5**
timid tímido/a **1**
tip (monetary) la propina **6**
tire aburrir **6**; cansar **7**
tired cansado/a **4**
title el título **2**, **6**, **12**; titular **7**
toad el sapo **8**
toast tostar (ue) **6**
toaster la tostadora **6**
today hoy **2**
together juntos/as **4**
tomato el tomate **6**
tomb la tumba **15**
tomb stone la lápida **14**
tomorrow la mañana **1**, **2**, **8**
tongue la lengua **2**, **10**
too también **1**, **2**, **7**
too much demasiado **9**
to/on the left a la izquierda **3**
to/on the right a la derecha **3**
toothbrush el cepillo de dientes **8**
toothpaste la pasta de dientes **8**
topography la topografía **4**

tortoise el galápago **8**
torture torturar **4**
tour ir de excursión **9**; la gira **9**
tour guide el/la guía **6**, **7**, **9**
tourism el turismo **5**
tourist el/la turista **2**
touristy turístico/a **9**
tournament el torneo **2**
toward hacia **7**
towards rumbo a **6**
towel la toalla **5**
town el pueblo **4**, **10**, **15**; la villa **15**
trace la huella **12**
track and field el atletismo **7**
trade comerciar **9**; el oficio **11**
tradition la tradición **4**
traffic el tráfico **13**; traficar **7**
tragedy la tragedia **7**, **13**
train el tren **6**, **9**; entrenar **6**
trainer el/la entrenador/a **7**
training el entrenamiento **4**, **11**
trajectory la trayectoria **15**
tranquilizer el calmante **10**
transfer transferir (ie, i) **12**
transform transformar **10**
transition la transición **7**
translate traducir **11**
transmit transmitir **10**, **13**
transportation el transporte **3**
trap atrapar **4**
travel viajar **2**, **9**
travel agency la agencia de viajes **9**
travel agent el/la agente de viajes **9**
traveler el/la viajero/a **9**
traveling salesperson el/la viajante **11**
travel through/across recorrer **9**
treasure el tesoro **2**
treatment el tratamiento **10**
treaty el tratado **15**
tree el árbol **4**
tremendous tremendo/a **7**
trial la prueba **4**, **10**
tribe la tribu **10**
trip el recorrido **6**; el viaje **1**, **7**, **9**
triumph el triunfo **5**
trombone el trombón **2**, **14**
truck el camión **8**
true cierto/a **2**; verdadero/a **4**
truly verdaderamente **9**

trumpet la trompeta **14**
trust la confianza **10**
truth la verdad **6**, **10**
try on probar (ue) **6**, **8**
t-shirt (tank top) la camiseta (sin mangas) **8**
Tuesday el martes **1**
tulle el tul **14**
turkey el pavo **6**
turn dar la vuelta **6**
turn in entregar **1**
turn off apagar **12**
turn on encender (ie) **12**
turnover la empanada (empanadilla) **6**
turtle la tortuga **5**
tuxedo el esmoquin **14**
twin el/la gemelo/a **10**
twist torcer (ue) **10**
type el tipo **15**
typical típico/a **3**

U
ugly feo/a **2**
uhh . . . este... **5**
ulcer la úlcera **10**
umbrella la sombrilla **7**
UN la ONU **12**
uncle/aunt el/la tío/a **4**
uncomfortable incómodo/a **9**
uncommon raro/a **7**
under debajo (de) **5**
underscore subrayar **5**
understand comprender **2**, **7**; entender (ie) **4**
unemployment el desempleo **6**, **11**, **15**; el paro (*Spain*) **15**
unexpected inesperado/a **15**
unfinished inacabado/a **13**
unforgettable inolvidable **7**
unfortunately desgraciadamente **5**
uniform el uniforme **7**
union el sindicato **12**
unionize sindicalizar **15**
unique único/a **5**, **8**, **10**
United Nations Las Naciones Unidas **7**
United States EE. UU. **6**
unity la unidad **4**
university la universidad **1**
unknown incógnito/a **7**
unless a menos (de) que **11**
unmarried soltero/a **4**
unnecessary innecesario/a **10**
until hasta **6**; hasta que **11**
upload subir **12**
urge instar **15**

urgent urgente **9**
urinate orinar **10**
us nos **4**, **6**
use usar **4**; utilizar **4**
useful útil **15**; valioso/a **12**
usually usualmente **9**
utensil el utensilio **6**

V
vacancy la vacante **11**
vacation las vacaciones **5**
vaccine la vacuna **10**
vacuum pasar la aspiradora **5**
vacuum cleaner la aspiradora **5**
value el valor **10**
van el camión **9**; la camioneta **1**; la furgoneta **9**
variety la variedad **5**
various varios/as **7**
vary variar **6**
VCR la videograbadora **12**
vegetable la legumbre **3**
vegetables las verduras **6**
vegetarian el/la vegetariano/a **6**
velvet el terciopelo **14**
verify verificar **6**
versatile versátil **13**
version la versión **10**
very muy **1**; sumamente **7**
Very truly yours... Lo(s)/La(s) saluda atentamente... **11**
veteran el/la veterano/a **12**
veterinarian el/la veterinario/a **11**
veterinary science la veterinaria **3**
viceroyalty el virreinato **11**
victim la víctima **3**
video camera la cámara de video **9**
view la vista **2**, **5**, **9**
vigorous vigoroso/a **15**
vinegar el vinagre **6**
viola la viola **14**
violate violar **15**
violence la violencia **4**
violent violento/a **14**
violin el violín **14**
visa el visado **7**
visit la visita **5**; visitar **2**
visitor el/la visitante **9**
vitamin la vitamina **10**
voice la voz **8**, **14**
volcano el volcán **4**, **5**, **9**
volleyball el voleibol **7**
voluntary voluntario/a **5**

volunteer el/la voluntario/a 5
voluptuous voluptuoso/a 9
vote el voto 13
vote (for) votar (por) 7, **15**
voter el/la votante 13

W

wait for esperar 7, **9**, **10**
waiter/waitress el/la camarero/a **6**; el/la mesero/a 3, **6**
waiting area la sala de espera **9**
wake up despertarse (ie) **5**
walk caminar 2; el paseo **7**
wall la muralla 9
wallet la billetera 8
want querer (ie) 7, 8, **9**; **want to** tener ganas de 3
war la guerra 3, 5, **15**
warm-up el calentamiento 10
warn advertir (ie, i) 14
warrior el guerrero 3
wash lavarse **5**
wash clothes lavar la ropa **5**
wash dishes lavar los platos **5**
washing machine la lavadora **5**
waste los desechos 12
watch el reloj 1; mirar 2; vigilar 15
watch (television/a movie) ver (la televisión/una película) 2, 7, 7, 8, 12
watch one's figure guardar la línea **10**
water el agua (*fem.*) 6
waterfall el salto 9; las cataratas 9
wave la ola 5
way la manera 3, 6; la vía **5**
we nosotros/as 1, **14**
weak débil 10
wealth la riqueza 9
weapon el arma (*fem.*) 15
wear llevar 5, 6, 8

wear a shoe size calzar **8**
weather el tiempo 2, 6, **7**
weatherman/woman el/la meteorólogo/a 13
weave tejer 15
weaving el tejido 4
web page la página web 6, **12**
website el sitio web 7, 12
wedding la boda 3
Wednesday el miércoles 1
week la semana 1
weight el peso 10
welcome la bienvenida 2
well bien 1; pues 3
well . . . bueno... 5
well-being el bienestar 6
well made bien hecho/a 14
what cómo 1, 2; lo que 5, **15**; qué 1, 2
What? ¿Qué...? 2
What do you like do? ¿Qué te gusta hacer? 2
whatever you hear oyeres 13
whatever you see vieres 9
What luck! ¡Qué suerte! 2
What nonsense! ¡Qué barbaridad! 1
What's happening? ¿Qué pasa? 1
What students! ¡Qué estudiantes! 1
What's up? ¿Qué pasa? 1
What's up? (*inf.*) ¿Qué tal? 1
What's up? (*Venezuela*) ¿Qué húbole? 9
What's your name? (*for.*) ¿Cómo se llama usted? 1; (*inf.*) ¿Cómo te llamas? 1
What time is it? ¿Qué hora es? 2
when cuando 2, 11
When . . . ? ¿Cuándo...? 2
Where . . . ? ¿Dónde...? 2; **From where . . . ?** ¿De dónde...? 2; **To where . . . ?** ¿Adónde...? 2

which (one/s) cual/es 2
while el rato 13; mientras 5
whirlwind el remolino 9
white blanco/a 1
who que 15; quien 2, 15
Who . . . ? ¿Quién(es)...? 2
whom que 15; quien 2, 15
Whose . . . ? ¿De quién(es)...? 2
Why . . . ? ¿Por qué...? 2, 9
wide amplio/a 10; ancho/a 5
widow/er el/la viudo/a 4
wife la esposa 1, 3, 4
will la voluntad 7
willing dispuesto/a 13, **14**
win ganar 2, 4, **7**
wind el viento 14
window la ventana 9; la ventanilla **9**
windy, it is hace viento 7
wine (red, white) el vino (tinto, blanco) 6
winner el/la ganador/a 2
winter el invierno 1
wish desear 9
with con 1
within dentro de 5
without sin que 11
without a doubt sin duda 10
with you contigo 4
witness el/la testigo/a 13
wolf el lobo 8
woman la mujer 1
wonderful magnífico/a 7
wood la madera 3
wool la lana 8
word la palabra 2
work el trabajo 6, **11**; funcionar 10, **12**; la obra 2, **13**; trabajar 6
work (*adj.*) laboral 7
work (on commission) trabajar (a comisión) 2
worker el/la trabajador/a 1
workshop el taller 3

world el mundo 1
world (*adj.*) mundial 15
world-wide mundialmente 9
worn out gastado/a 10
worry preocuparse 8
worse peor 5
Would you like (+ *inf.*) . . . ? ¿Te gustaría (+ *inf.*)? 4
wristwatch el reloj de pulsera 8, 8
write escribir 1, 2, 8, 10, 11, 12
write down anotar 5
writer el/la escritor/a 6

X

X-ray la radiografía 10

Y

yank arrancar 1
yard el patio 5
year el año 1
yearly anualmente 7
yearly bonus la bonificación anual 11
yell gritar 11
yellow amarillo/a 1
yesterday ayer 6
yogurt el yogur 6
you tú (*inf.*) 1; usted/es (*for.*) 1; vosotros/as (*inf. pl. Spain*) 1, 4
you like Te gusta... 2
young joven 2
younger menor 4, 5
You're welcome. De nada. 1
your/s suyo/a/os/as (*for.*) 13; tu/tus (*inf.*) 1; tuyo/a/os/as (*inf.*) 7, 13; vuestro/a/os/as (*inf. pl. Spain*) 3, 13
youth el/la joven 6; la juventud 1

Z

zoo el zoológico 3

TEXT CREDITS

p. 279: "Los rivales y el juez," Ciro Alegría. Used by permission of Los Morochucos.

p. 379: "No hay que complicar la felicidad" by Marco Denevi. © Denevi, Marco, Falsificaciones, Buenos Aires, Corregidor, 1984, págs. 159–160. Used by permission.

p. 414: Cuando era puertorriqueña. New York: Vintage Español (Random House). 1994.

p. 478: © Anderson Imbert, Enrique, "El crimen perfecto," en *El gato de Chesire, Cuentos 2, Obras Completas*, Buenos Aires, Corregidor, 1999, pp. 101–102.

p. 508: "En solidaridad" (Fragment, edited by Eduardo Zayas-Bazán), *Más allá de mí* by Francisco Jiménez. © by Francisco Jiménez. Reprinted with author's permission.

PHOTO CREDITS

Photos in the Observaciones sections are stills from *¡Pura vida!* video to accompany *¡Arriba!, Comunicación y cultura*, 6th edition, ©2012.

COVER: © First Light / Alamy **p. 3 (left):** Salvador Dali (1904–1989), "The Discovery of America by Christopher Columbus, 1958-1959, oil on canvas, 410.2 × 310 cm. Salvador Dali Museum, St. Petersburg, Florida, USA. The Bridgeman Art Library International Ltd. © 2004 Salvador Dali, Gala-Salvador Dali Foundation/Artists Rights Society (ARS), NY.; **(right):** Diego Rivera, " Mexico from the Conquest to 1930". Mural.(Detail) Location: National Palace, Mexico City, Mexico. Photo: Leslye Borden/Photoedit. © Banco de México Diego Rivera & Frida Kahlo Museums Trust. Av. Cinco de Mayo No. 2, Col. Centro, Del. Cuauhtemoc 06059, Mexico, D.F. Reproduction authorized by the Instituto Nacional de Bellas Artes y Literatura.; **p. 5 (top):** Yuriy Chertok / Shutterstock; **(bottom):** © Jacom Stephens/istockphoto; **p. 9:** Susan M. Bacon; **p. 10:** Susan M. Bacon; **p. 11:** Susan M. Bacon; **p. 12:** Kim Sayer ©Dorling Kindersley; **p. 15:** Joanna B. Pinneo/Aurora Photos; **p. 16:** Jupiterimages/Thinkstock; **p. 18:** Copyright 2008 Getty Images; **p. 19:** © RD/Leon / Retna Digital/Retna Ltd./Corbis; **p. 21 (top):** © 2010 Photos.com, a division of Getty Images. All rights reserved.; **(bottom):** © 2010 Photos.com, a division of Getty Images. All rights reserved.; **p. 25 (left):** © Bettmann/CORBIS; **(right):** © Bettmann/CORBIS; **p. 33 (top, right):** Copyright © Siegfried Stolzfuss / eStock Photo; **p. 34 (top, left):** Susan M. Bacon; **(top, right):** © 2010 Photos.com, a division of Getty Images. All rights reserved.; **(bottom, left):** © 2010 Photos.com, a division of Getty Images. All rights reserved.; **p. 35 (top):** Steffen Foerster Photography / Shutterstock; **p. 36 (top):** The Granger Collection, NYC; **(bottom):** Tania Zbrodko/Shutterstock; **p. 38:** Getty Images Inc. — PhotoDisc; **p. 41 (left):** © imageZebra / fotolia; **(right):** Lev Radin / Shutterstock; **p. 43 (top, right):** © Photos.com/ Thinkstock; **(center, right):** Hemera/Thinkstock; **(bottom, left):** Thinkstock; **p. 44:** SIME/eStock Photography; **p. 45 (left):** © Rune Hellestad/Corbis; **(center):** AP Images/Peter Kramer; **(right):** AP Images/Kathy Willens; **p. 49:** jorgedasi /Shutterstock; **p. 51:** © PCN Photography / Alamy; **p. 53:** sedat saatcioglu / fotolia; **p. 54:** Daniel BerehulakAllsport Concepts/Getty Images; **p. 56:** © Getty Images; **p. 57 (top):** William Fernando Martinez/PictureGroup/AP Images; **(bottom):** Ethan Miller/Getty Images Inc. RF; **p. 59 (top):** All contents © 2010 Thinkstock. All rights reserved.; **(center, right):** Artpose Adam Borkowski / Shutterstock; **(bottom, right):** Jupiter Images; **(bottom, left):** Jeanne Hatch/ Shutterstock; **p. 61:** Ir?ne Alastruey/Jupiter Images; **p. 64 (bottom):** Susan M. Bacon; **p. 66:** Susan M. Bacon; **p. 69 (top):** Susan M. Bacon; **p. 70 (top, left):** Luna Vandoorne / Shutterstock; **(top, right):** SIME/eStock Photography; **(center, left):** © Martyn Unsworth / istockphoto; **(center, right):** Susan M. Bacon; **(bottom, left):** Elena Aliaga / Shutterstock; **(bottom, right):** Rob Wilson/Shutterstock; **p. 72:** © Victor Lerena/epa /CORBIS. All Rights Reserved; **p. 73:** © Sony Pictures Classics/ Courtesy Everett Collection; **p. 74:** Carlos Alvarez/Getty Images Inc. RF; **p. 77 (left):** © ranplett / Shutterstock; **p. 77 (right):** Viva la Vida, 1954 (print), Kahlo, Frida (1910–54) / Private Collection / © DACS / The Bridgeman Art Library; **p. 79 (top):** Andresr / Shutterstock; **(bottom):** Helder Almeida / Shutterstock; **p. 83:** Images.com; **p. 85:** © Lisa F. Young / istockphoto; **p. 88:** AP Images/Jorge Saenz; **p. 89:** Reuters / B Mathur / Landov; **p. 90:** © Stephen Coburn / Fotolia; **p. 91:** © CUARTOSCURO / ISAAC ESQUIVEL /epa / CORBIS All Rights Reserved; **p. 93 (top):** Brand X Pictures/Getty Images; **(top, center):** Goodshoot/Thinkstock; **(bottom, center):** Pixland / Thinkstock; **(bottom):** VisionsofAmerica/Joe Sohm/Getty Images; **p. 97:** AP Images; **p. 99:** Colman Lerner Gerardo / Shutterstock; **p. 102:** Howard Millard/Omni-Photo Communications, Inc.; **p. 103:** Courtesy of Nick Warren; **p. 104:** George Koroneos /Shutterstock; **p. 105 (top):** Courtesy of Marcie A. Bahn and Elizabethtown College; **p. 106 (top, left):** Susan M. Bacon; **(top, right):** Susan M. Bacon; **(center):** Susan M. Bacon; **(bottom, left):** © Charles & Josette Lenars/CORBIS; **(bottom, right):** Courtesy Metro de la Ciudad de México; **p. 108 (left):** David R. Frazier; **(center):** Ceremonial procession—detail of musicians. From Mayan fresco series found at Bonampak. (East wall, room 1). Museo Nacional de Antropología, Mexico City, D.F., Mexico. © SEF/Art Resource, NY; **(right):** ©Erich Lessing/Art Resource, NY; **p. 109:** Susan M. Bacon; **p. 113 (left):** AP/Wide World Photos; **(right):** Susan M. Bacon; **p. 115 (1st row):** Dick Luria / Thinkstock; **(2nd row, left):** Andresr / Shutterstock; **(2nd row, left center):** Phase4Photography / Shutterstock; **(2nd row, right center):** Chiyacat / Shutterstock; **(2nd row, right):** Tracy Whiteside / Shutterstock; **(3rd row, left):** Jacek Chabraszewski / Shutterstock; **(3rd row, center):** Phase4Photography/Shutterstock; **(3rd row, right):** Stuart Monk / Shutterstock; **p. 116:** Maria Teijeiro/Getty Images Inc. RF; **p. 120:** AP Images; **p. 122:** KennStilger47/Shutterstock; **p. 125:** Susan M. Bacon; **p. 126:** Susan M. Bacon; **p. 128:** Jack Hollingsworth / Thinkstock; **p. 129:** Courtesy of Guillermo Anderson, www.guillermoanderson.com; **p. 131 (top):** Susan M. Bacon; **(center):** Susan M. Bacon; **(bottom):** Susan M. Bacon; **p. 137:** Susan M. Bacon; **p. 140:** Honduras This Week; **p. 141 (left):** Comstock/Thinkstock; **(right):** BananaStock/Thinkstock; **p. 143 (top):** © Gisela Damm / eStock Photo; **p. 144 (top, left):** Susan M. Bacon; **(top, right):** Susan M. Bacon; **(center):** Susan M. Bacon; **(bottom, left):** Susan M. Bacon; **(bottom, right):** Susan M. Bacon; **p. 147:** © John Mitchell / Alamy; **p. 148:** JR Carvey/Streetly Studio/Getty Images Inc.; **p. 151 (left):** Philippe Colombi; **(right):** Susan M. Bacon; **p. 153 (top):** Comstock Images / Thinkstock; **(top, center):** Alon Brik / Shutterstock; **(bottom, center):** prodakszyn/Shutterstock; **(bottom):** bart78 / Shutterstock; **p. 155:** Zedcor Wholly Owned / Jupiter Images; **p. 158:** Otto Greule Jr/Getty Images; **p. 159 (top):** beltsazar / Shutterstock; **(bottom):** © 2010 Photos.com, a division of Getty Images. All rights reserved.; **p. 163:** IT Stock Free/Thinkstock; **p. 164 (top to bottom):** ARMANDO ARORIZO/Landov; AP Images/Evan Agostini; © FEDERICO RIOS/epa/Corbis; AP Images; © KENA BETANCUR/Reuters/Corbis; Ben Hider/Getty Images; **p. 166:** Jupiterimages/Thinkstock; **p. 167:** Arnold Turner/WireImage/Getty Images; **p. 169 (top):** All contents © 2010 Thinkstock. All rights reserved.; **(center):** Mehmet Dilsiz / Shutterstock; **(bottom):** Jupiterimages / Thinkstock; **p. 172:** Susan M. Bacon; **p. 176:** Brand X Pictures / Thinkstock; **p. 177 (top):** Peter Wilson © Dorling Kindersley; **p. 178 (top, left):** Susan M. Bacon; **(top, right):** Jack Parsons/Omni Photo Communications, Inc.; **(bottom, left):** Sascha Burkard / Shutterstock; **(bottom, right):** D. Donne Bryant; **p. 180 (top, left):** Tom Brakefield / Thinkstock; **(top, right):** Poznyakov / Shutterstock; **(bottom, left):** Susan M. Bacon; **p. 181:** Susan M. Bacon; **p. 185 (left):** Andrew Gunners/Jupiterimages; **(right):** JUAN J. REAL/Newscom; **p. 187:** Jose Luis Pelaez Inc / Jupiterimages; **p. 189:** Fuse/Jupiterimages; **p. 191 (bottom):** AP Images/Santiago Llanquin; **p. 194:** Susan M. Bacon; **p. 195:** Susan M. Bacon; **p. 196 (top):** Mark Stout Photography / Shutterstock; **(bottom):** Susan M. Bacon; **p. 197:** El Comercio de Ecuador/Newscom; **p. 199 (top):** © Image Source / SuperStock; **(top, center):** Alain Schroeder/Jupiterimages; **(bottom, center):** Jupiterimages; **(bottom):** Denkou Images/Jupiterimages; **p. 201 (top):** © Sebastian Vera; **(bottom):** Jupiterimages; **p. 203:** Patty Orly/Shutterstock; **p. 204:** Eric Risberg/ASSOCIATED PRESS; **p. 207:** Susan M. Bacon; **p. 208:** Philip Lee Harvey/Jupiterimages;

América del Sur

Mar Caribe

OCÉANO ATLÁNTICO

Barranquilla
Cartagena
Maracaibo Caracas
Barquisimeto
VENEZUELA
Río Orinoco
Medellín
Manizales
Bogotá
Cali
COLOMBIA
CORDILLERA DE LOS ANDES
Salto Ángel
GUYANA
Georgetown
Paramaribo
SURINAM
Cayenne
GUAYANA FRANCESA (Francia)

Quito
ECUADOR
Ecuador

Guayaquil
Cuenca
Islas Galápagos (Ec.)
Iquitos
Manaus
Río Amazonas
Belém
Fortaleza

Cajamarca
Trujillo
Río Madeira
PERÚ
Río Branco
B R A S I L
Recife

Lima
Machu Picchu
Cuzco
Ayacucho
BOLIVIA
Lago Titicaca
La Paz
Arequipa
Santa Cruz
Salvador
Brasilia

Arica
Cochabamba
Iquique
Sucre
Potosí
Belo Horizonte

OCÉANO PACÍFICO
I. Pinta
I. Fernandina I. Marchena
I. San Salvador
Santa Cruz
I. Santa Cruz
I. Isabela
Puerto Ayora
I. San Cristóbal
Puerto Villamil
Puerto Baquerizo Moreno
ISLAS GALÁPAGOS (ECUADOR)

Antofagasta
PARAGUAY
Asunción
Salto Iguazú
São Paulo
Santos
Río de Janeiro
Trópico de Capricornio

Salta
CHILE
San Miguel de Tucumán
ARGENTINA
Río Paraná
Río Uruguay
Pôrto Alegre
URUGUAY
Rivera

OCÉANO PACÍFICO
Cabo Norte
Volcán Katiki
Hanga Roa
Cabo Cumming
Mataveri
ISLA DE PASCUA (CHILE)

Coquimbo
Córdoba
Rosario
Valparaíso
Mendoza
Santiago
Buenos Aires
Montevideo
La Plata
Río de la Plata
OCÉANO ATLÁNTICO

Concepción
Bahía Blanca

Puerto Montt

OCÉANO PACÍFICO

Estrecho de Magallanes
Islas Malvinas (Br.)
Punta Arenas
TIERRA DEL FUEGO
Cabo de Hornos

✪ Capital
• Otras ciudades
▲ Volcán
∴ Ruinas